Global Business Ethics

Drawing on contributions from nineteen prominent scholars, this book reflects on the *quest for sustainable development* as a source of competitive advantage for organizations and as a global imperative for society. It highlights how organizations' decision-making processes and bundled capabilities can promote innovative approaches to address current ethical dilemmas, setting forth business ethics, corporate social responsibility, and sustainability as required tenets for participating in a global economy.

As societal and business stakeholders race toward the 2030 deadline to meet the United Nations' 17 Sustainable Development Goals, business plays a critical role in achieving global goals. It is thus increasingly crucial that organizational practices and policies incorporate a socially responsible agenda based on ethical decision-making to achieve a more just society. Incorporating people, technology, the natural environment, and economics in a way that is inclusive, honest, just, and sustainable becomes a management imperative challenge. Given the rapid pace of changes taking place in the global economy, the time for action is now, if we are to preserve our planet and ensure progress and prosperity.

This book will appeal to scholars in business ethics, management, international business, and sustainability, as well as to business executives. The chapters in this book were originally published in *International Studies of Management & Organization*.

Abraham Stefanidis is Professor and Director of Faculty Research at The Peter J. Tobin College of Business at St John's University, USA. He has studied, taught, and conducted research in Greece, Spain, Turkey, Germany, and the USA. Abraham Stefanidis' research focuses on International Human Resource Management, Global Business Ethics, and Disability.

Linda M. Sama is Retired Professor at The Peter J. Tobin College of Business at St John's University, USA, and the founder of a micro-lending organization. She serves as NGO representative to the U.N. for the International Association of Charities. Her research focuses on issues of Corporate Social Responsibility, Environmental Ethics, and Microfinance.

Global Business Ethics

The Quest for Sustainable Development

Edited by
Abraham Stefanidis and Linda M. Sama

Routledge
Taylor & Francis Group
LONDON AND NEW YORK

First published 2025
by Routledge
4 Park Square, Milton Park, Abingdon, Oxon, OX14 4RN

and by Routledge
605 Third Avenue, New York, NY 10158

Routledge is an imprint of the Taylor & Francis Group, an informa business

British Library Cataloguing in Publication Data
A catalogue record for this book is available from the British Library

ISBN13: 978-1-032-73634-1 (hbk)
ISBN13: 978-1-032-73639-6 (pbk)
ISBN13: 978-1-003-46520-1 (ebk)

DOI: 10.4324/9781003465201

Typeset in Minion Pro
by codeMantra

Publisher's Note
The publisher accepts responsibility for any inconsistencies that may have arisen during the conversion of this book from journal articles to book chapters, namely the inclusion of journal terminology.

Contents

Citation Information

The following chapters in this book were originally published in *International Studies of Management & Organization*, volume 50, issue 3 (2020), except Chapter 5, which was published in volume 50, issue 1 (2020). When citing this material, please use the original page numbering for each article, as follows:

Chapter 1

Why do U.S. public companies continue to join the UN global compact: Ethics or economics?
James Barrese, Cynthia Phillips and Victoria Shoaf
International Studies of Management & Organization, volume 50, issue 3 (2020), pp. 209–231

Chapter 2

Calculation, principle or bias? Information preference and ethical decision-making
Regina Bento, Lasse Mertins and Lourdes F. White
International Studies of Management & Organization, volume 50, issue 3 (2020), pp. 232–252

Chapter 3

Decoupling in CSR reports: A Linguistic Content Analysis of the Volkswagen Dieselgate scandal
Dirk Holtbrügge and Marcus Conrad
International Studies of Management & Organization, volume 50, issue 3 (2020), pp. 253–270

Chapter 4

The ethical challenge of Big Tech's "disruptive philanthropy"
Paul Manning, Nigel Baker and Peter Stokes
International Studies of Management & Organization, volume 50, issue 3 (2020), pp. 271–290

Chapter 5

Dynamic capabilities and environmental sustainability for emerging economies' multinational enterprises
Pervaiz Akhtar, Subhan Ullah, Saman Hassanzadeh Amin, Gaurav Kabra and Sarah Shaw
International Studies of Management & Organization, volume 50, issue 1 (2020), pp. 27–42

Notes on Contributors

Pervaiz Akhtar is Director of the MBA suite of programmes and Chair (Full Professor) in Business Analytics, Big Data, and Supply Chains at the University of Aberdeen, UK. Capitalizing on over 15 years of academic and industrial experiences in public, private, and non-profit-making organizations (UNICEF, JCCP, Oxfam, MSF, Islamic Relief, Red Cross, dairy industry, and FMCG companies such as Unilever and Reckitt Benckiser), he has published his research in top-ranked journals such as *International Journal of Operations & Production Management*, *British Journal of Management*, and *Business Ethics*, among others.

Saman Hassanzadeh Amin is Associate Professor at the Department of Mechanical and Industrial Engineering at Toronto Metropolitan University, Canada. He received his PhD from the University of Windsor in 2012. Dr. Amin's research interests include Supply Chain Management, Operations Management, Operations Research, Optimization, Information Technology, and Decision Support Systems.

Nigel Baker is a business consultant and media executive. He has served as Chief Executive of the Thomson Foundation, UK, and as a researcher at the University of Chester Business School, UK.

James Barrese is Retired Professor of Risk Management and Insurance from the Maurice R. Greenburg School of Risk Management, Insurance and Actuarial Science at The Peter J. Tobin College of Business at St. John's University, USA. His research interests include risk mitigation, the legal and ethical consequences of risk-based decisions, and the impact of risk in a global context.

Regina Bento is Professor of Management at the University of Baltimore, USA, where she holds BGE Distinguished Chair of Business. Born and raised in Brazil, Regina started her career as a psychiatrist (MD, Federal University of Rio de Janeiro-UFRJ, Brazil), studying the relationship between work and mental health. Interested in learning more about the nature of work and organizations, she earned an MS in Management (COPPEAD, UFRJ) and pursued doctoral studies at Harvard and MIT (PhD MIT, 1990). She has served in multiple leadership roles at the Academy of Management and has received numerous teaching and research awards.

Marcus Conrad received his PhD from the School of Business, Economics and Society at Friedrich-Alexander-University Erlangen-Nürnberg, Germany. He published several articles in peer-reviewed journals and edited volumes. He now works in the area of data science at a large German automotive supplier.

Dirk Holtbrügge is Professor of International Management at the School of Business, Economics and Society at Friedrich-Alexander-University Erlangen-Nürnberg, Germany. He has spent numerous teaching and research stays abroad in countries including China, France, India, Japan, Russia, South Africa, the United Kingdom, and the USA. His main research interests are intercultural management, management in emerging markets (China, India, and Russia), international human resources management, and corporate social and environmental responsibility. He has published 10 books and more than 100 articles in peer-reviewed journals.

Sven Horak is Zizza Tobin Professor of Management at The Peter J. Tobin College of Business at St. John's University, USA, specializing in Global Management, International HR, and Leadership. His research focuses on networking and relationship-building in a global context.

Gaurav Kabra is Associate Professor in the area of Operations and Supply Chain Management at Jindal Global Business School. He completed his doctoral research in the area of humanitarian supply chain management from Indian Institute of Technology Roorkee, India. His areas of interest include supply chain management, humanitarian logistics, social media analytics, and application of IT in business. He is the recipient of Emerald Literati Network Awards for Excellence – 2016.

Paul Manning is Professor of Business Ethics at the University of Chester Business School, UK. Paul's research focusses on business ethics, social capital, behavioral ethics, financial crime, HE pedagogy, and entrepreneurship.

Lasse Mertins is Professor of Practice and Vice Dean for Education and Partnerships at the Johns Hopkins Carey Business School, Baltimore, USA. He is Certified Management Accountant (CMA) with expertise in the areas of financial statement analysis, managerial accounting, and performance assessments. Before his academic career, Mertins worked as a management accountant in the food industry. He received his PhD from Virginia Tech, USA.

Cynthia Phillips is Associate Professor of Accounting at The Peter J. Tobin College of Business at St. John's University, USA. Her research interests include not-for-profit accounting, governance, corporate social responsibility, cost of higher education, and accounting pedagogy.

Linda M. Sama is Retired Professor from The Peter J. Tobin College of Business, USA, where she founded GLOBE, a microfinance learning initiative, and she served as Director of the Center for Global Business Stewardship and UN PRME liaison. Her research focuses on CSR and global business ethics.

Sarah Shaw is Reader in Logistics and Supply Chain Management at Hull University Business School, UK. Her PhD thesis investigated environmental supply chain performance measures. Her research interests include green/sustainable logistics, closed-loop supply chains, and performance measurement & reporting. She has recently won the "Leader of the Year" in the Women in Logistics Awards, 2017, UK. One of her publications was selected by Emerald Group Publishing to appear in *A Focus on Sustainable Supply Chains and Green Logistics*, part of *Emerald Gems* which brings together some of the most highly cited, read, and innovative research in its field.

Victoria Shoaf is Professor of accounting at The Peter J. Tobin College of Business at St. John's University, USA. Her research focuses on US and international accounting standards, corporate social responsibility and business ethics, and accounting pedagogy.

Abraham Stefanidis is Professor and Director of Faculty Research at The Peter J. Tobin College of Business at St John's University, USA. He has studied, taught, and conducted research internationally. He has served as Editor-in-Chief of *International Studies of Management & Organization*. Abraham Stefanidis' research focuses on International Human Resource Management, Global Business Ethics, and Disability.

Peter Stokes is Professor of Leadership and Professional Development at Leicester Castle Business School at De Montfort University, Leicester, UK. He has published a rich and varied body of work in world-class journals in the areas of Human Resource Management, Leadership Values and Behaviors, Business Ethics, Management Philosophy, Organizational Design, Strategy, Critical Management Studies, and Research Methodology, among others.

Subhan Ullah is Associate Professor in Accounting at the University of Nottingham, UK. He has taught courses in accounting as well as finance at the University of Hull, UK; Nottingham Trent University, UK; the University of Buckingham, UK; COMSATS University, Pakistan; and the University of Peshawar, Pakistan. His main research interests are in the areas of corporate governance, corporate social responsibility, sustainability, accounting information quality, and corporate finance. His research appears in leading international journals.

Lourdes F. White is Professor of Accounting at the University of Baltimore, USA. Her research and teaching focus on performance measurement, incentives, budgeting, and ethics. She earned a doctorate in Business from Harvard, and, prior to her academic career, she worked as a tax analyst in Rio de Janeiro, Brazil.

Preface – Global business ethics and sustainability

Abraham Stefanidis and Linda M. Sama

The quest for sustainable development as a source of competitive advantage for organizations and a global imperative for society was prioritized by all member states of the U.N. in 2015 when they crafted the 17 Sustainable Development Goals (SDGs). Seeking an end to poverty and attendant societal shortfalls, the SDGs serve as a clarion call for business organizations to join in the fight to ease hunger, reduce inequalities, advance social justice norms, and promote health and well-being and to be inclusive of all citizens, especially those living on the margins of society – all while thriving in an environmentally sustainable world. This book responds to that call with a resounding affirmation of these goals, respecting the inexorable bond between business and its societal stakeholders, and reflecting the ethical posture that business must assume in order to earn a sustainable competitive advantage in the marketplace.

The articles in this book explore ethical issues faced by the modern corporation, both in the U.S. and in the developing world, with research focused on how organizations' decision-making processes and bundled capabilities can promote innovative approaches to address current ethical dilemmas. Arguments forwarded in these pages support business ethics and corporate social responsibility (CSR), and sustainability as required tenets of organizations participating in a global economy. Macro-level (government and civil society) and micro-level (workers and organizations) analyses intersect across these chapters to paint a picture of the challenges, opportunities, and threats posed for the achievement of the United Nations' 17 Sustainable Development Goals (SDGs). Methods of analysis that include empirical testing, theoretical modeling, case studies, and content analysis converge on results which clarify the importance of moving organizations towards transparency in their operations while adopting a fundamental ethos that embraces ethics, good governance, and sustainability as key management priorities. As essentially a global business ethics book for today's business manager, the content is equally applicable to practitioners in the legal, scientific, medical, and journalistic fields who seek to advocate for sustainable development.

Contributions to this book's collection of articles, which originally appeared in recent issues of the *International Studies of Management & Organization* journal, cover the pressing issue of sustainability and guide future research relevant to several SDGs. The included articles offer theoretical and empirical insights into a broad spectrum of timely matters, such as an assessment of motivations for U.S. companies to join the UN Global compact, the micro-foundations of ethical decision-making under risk, the social responsibility of a highly visible corporation in the throes of an ethical dilemma and public scandal, the growing influence of large corporate foundations in global philanthropy, and the role of country- and firm-level dynamic capabilities in promoting environmentally sustainable practices and policies.

In the first article titled: "Business Ethics for a Global Society: Howard Bowen's Legacy and the Foundations of United Nations' Sustainable Development Goals," Sama, Stefanidis, and

Horak (2020) build on Howard R. Bowen's (1953) seminal treatise 'Social Responsibilities of the Businessman' to portray how Bowen's 11 Economic Goals for responsible business practice were visionary and remarkably evocative of the United Nations' 17 Sustainable Development Goals (SDGs). Recognizing businesses' moral imperative to institutionalize sustainable, responsible, and ethical practices, the authors introduce an insightful goal mapping between Bowen's (1953) 11 economic goals and the SDGs that provides the contextual preamble for the articles that follow.

In the second article titled: "Why Do U.S. Public Companies Continue to Join the UN Global Compact, Ethics or Economics?", Barrese, Phillips, and Shoaf (2020) present two opposing theories regarding the motivation of organizations to join UNGC. During the past two decades, more than twenty thousand organizations have become signatories to the United Nations Global Compact, taking on the commitment to evolve their business practices to achieve objectives related to at least one of the ten UNGC principles. Yet, since its inception in 2000, there has been an ongoing debate regarding the efficacy of UNGC in promoting the adoption of CSR practices in organizations. Employing Haack, Martignoni, and Schoeneborn's (2021) conceptual framework, the authors explore empirically whether contextual opacity and transparency can explain businesses' adoption of UNGC principles. Recognizing the importance of organizational learning, Barrese, Phillips, and Shoaf's empirical findings corroborate Haack et al.'s framework concluding that, under conditions of opacity, U.S. organizations adopt CSR practices ceremonially, whereas the adoption of such principles becomes more substantive under conditions of increasing transparency. The authors find that, after joining UNGC, U.S. firms improve in terms of CSR performance, highlighting that newly appointed CEOs are more likely to join the UNGC. Interestingly, the researchers emphasize that U.S. public companies that rely more on international sales, where UNGC is more highly valued, tend to sign the UNGC more than their counterparts – other non-signatory S&P 500 firms – a research finding which implies that UNGC membership may be associated with specific economic benefits.

In the third article by Bento, Mertins, and White (2020), titled "Calculation, Principle or Bias? Information Preference and Ethical Decision-Making," the authors highlight the findings of an exploratory study that examines how participants filter information related to complex decisions under conditions of risk and do so through different ethical lenses. Employing factor analysis on the study's outcomes, they determine three specific *Patterns in Information Preference* (PIPs): "Expected Value," "Responsibility," and "Autopilot," and they further discover that these *information preferences* reflected three different ethical decision-making modes, characterized as utilitarian, deontological, and psychological – the first two representing normative ethical lenses and the latter a behavioral or descriptive ethical approach. Moreover, the authors show that the ultimate decisions that emerge from the process are influenced by the participant's individual PIP. With modern businesses facing ethical dilemmas signifying substantial risk and generating decisions that impact various stakeholder groups, the interests and preferences of which may not be fully aligned, the article makes an important contribution in shedding light on the various approaches to ethical decision-making. Theoretically, it builds on ethical decision-making theory with a particular focus on decision-making under conditions of risk. It also draws from the *information preference* perspective to add to our understanding of how decision-makers filter and assign relative importance to different information flows. In terms of practice, the study offers recommendations for implementing similar experiments in business training settings and decision de-briefs that examine the ethics of risk. While contingent on the particular situation, time, and industry context that define a business's operations, these findings can be applied generally to inform decision-makers about the ethical consequences of risk-based decisions under varying conditions and heighten overall ethical awareness, resulting in more sustainable business models.

In the fourth article of this book, titled "Decoupling in CSR Reports A linguistic Content Analysis of the Volkswagen Dieselgate Scandal," Holtbrügge and Conrad (2020) focus on the automobile industry and compare Volkswagen's CSR reports with those of its biggest competitors to analyze the Volkswagen emission scandal 'Dieselgate' adopting linguistic content analysis. Focusing on 'decoupling,' which, in the CSR literature, refers to the gap between communication and realized actions, the authors employ Basu and Palazzo's (2008) process model to explain why certain companies display increased congruence between CSR reports' communication and actions, whereas others decouple CSR actions and communications. To this end, Holtbrügge and Conrad employ the case of Volkswagen, which intentionally deceived its stakeholders and society by installing a defeat device in more than eleven million diesel vehicles, resulting in increased levels of toxic emissions and pollutants. Linguistic content analysis on the CSR reports of the 15 largest car manufacturers worldwide reveals that CSR reports of de-couplers use more words with an individual or I-focus than those of 'implementors' (companies that consistently realize their CSR policies). Furthermore, the analysis corroborates that CSR reports of de-couplers contain more articles, fewer words per sentence, and fewer positive emotion words than those of implementors. In addition, de-couplers' reports display a more negative, downbeat emotional tone, use fewer words connected to risks and anxiety, and include more quotes than those of implementors. Theoretically, Holtbrügge and Conrad indicate that their study identifies specific linguistic categories that specify Basu and Palazzo's model in a concrete context. From a practical standpoint, the authors state that their linguistic analysis framework may help stakeholders to detect CSR decoupling before it becomes obvious in the form of public scandals.

In their conceptual article titled "The Ethical Challenge of Big Tech's Disruptive Philanthropy," Manning, Baker, and Stokes (2020) critically discuss the role of new technology companies ("big tech") and their connection to global philanthropy. The study focuses on new types of philanthropy that the authors call 'disruptive philanthropy,' which is understood as philanthropic activities of large technology firms such as Microsoft or Facebook. Many large firms, including the two referred here, set up philanthropic foundations. What makes them special is that the large scale of their giving caused critical voices to call them anti-democratic as their actions penetrate the public sphere, a domain many believe the government should closely manage, instead of allowing wealthy individuals, who use their resources and power to support free markets, untowardly influence according to their ideals. The study explores two research questions with one being focused on developing a better understanding of the new form of philanthropy and the second one exploring the implications for practitioners. As for the first goal of the study, the authors present new forms of philanthropy, including venture philanthropy that encourages foundations to use venture capital practices; impact investing, which uses investment strategies to support social and environmental aims; and data philanthropy where private firms make 'big data' available for the public or hybrid organizations manage activities under the tension of financial sustainability and social purpose. With reference to the study's practitioner focus, a conceptual framework is developed to help managers in non-profit organizations to better understand the risks involved when engaging with the new types of philanthropy.

Lastly, in their article regarding environmental sustainability, Akhtar, Ullah, Amin, Kabra, and Shaw (2020) enhance our understanding of how country-level capabilities, including government environmental policies, legal and market requirements, and technological advancements, as well as firm-level capabilities, such as organizational size, culture, and managerial characteristics, influence emerging economies multinational enterprises' sustainability policies and practices. Building on a theoretical framework that links capabilities with sustainability, the authors offer several novel propositions that have received limited attention in the extant literature. This conceptual article recommends the empirical testing of such relationships from future researchers who would integrate both country-level and firm-level data to investigate the sustainable policies and procedures of multinational enterprises in emerging economies.

Contribution of the book

We identify six avenues of future research suggested by the articles included in this book. The first avenue derives from the article about Howard Bowen's 11 Economic Goals for responsible business and points to research that should be undertaken to assess progress in achieving the SDGs, mapping that progress both backward and forward in time through comprehensive literature reviews and meta-analyses, and extrapolating results to foretell future directions for firms. A deeper understanding of the SDGs and how these goals require adjustment or enhancement under conditions of enormous stress or macro-environmental shocks, such as the recent pandemic, would benefit the private, public, and civil society sectors going forward, all of which are participants in framing the SDGs.

Another avenue of research extends from the work regarding the UNGC and the challenges inherent in measuring corporate motivation for engaging in its mandated ethical reporting. Do firms become signatories to increase reputation effects or in an earnest attempt to improve their CSR and sustainability practices? Self-reports of motivation are largely suspect, leading the researcher to look at behavior as an indicator of motivation. While the UNGC is light on enforcement, it would be interesting to see, over time, if a signatory firm would enhance its CSR profile, which would require longitudinal analysis.

A third avenue of research would build upon ethical decision-making under conditions of risk, given the growing need for effective risk management strategies in the modern business domain. Research could include how we define and measure risk as well as what ethical approaches and preferences we adopt in assessing its consequences. Longitudinal studies could benefit the field to gauge how the outcomes of risk-based decisions impact not only the firm but also the various stakeholder groups – both those for whom interests are aligned with the firm and those who challenge the firm's interests.

A fourth avenue of research is suggested by the linguistic content analysis of CSR reporting in the Volkswagen case presented here and involves replication studies that would strengthen the validity of claims emanating from this case study as well as non-linguistic analysis of CSR reports. Examining CSR reports from different countries, including emerging economies, would be a further direction for researchers to explore.

Adding to the work presented on 'disruptive philanthropy,' we join the authors in suggesting that a fifth avenue might look at governance mechanisms which are most effective in ensuring transparency around the business benefits that accompany philanthropic contributions to society. Visiting work that explores the concept of "greenwashing" and safeguards against it can be elucidating (see, for example, Stecker (2016)). Parquel, Benoît-Moreau, and Larceneux (2011) also explore the "greenwashing" concept from a marketing viewpoint and argue for the importance of understanding a firm's intrinsic motivations. Further, future research, as well as mainstream public debate, may devote more attention to the critical question of ownership of public spheres – should and to what degree wealthy individuals play a role in policy making and agenda setting at the national and global levels?

In addition, it is important that environmentally sustainable practices and policies, especially regarding emerging markets' multinational enterprises, be investigated further. A sixth avenue of research therefore asks two key questions: What macro-environmental factors, such as government policies, legal or market requirements, technological advances, and economic capacities, directly and indirectly affect environmental sustainability? How do those factors interact with multinational enterprises' micro-level capabilities, such as management characteristics, business operations, and environmental strategies, to influence environmentally sustainable outcomes? Future research may employ diverse methodologies, including case studies, surveys, and longitudinal secondary data research to illuminate how, and to what extent, formal and informal institutions coupled with organizational-level practices can enhance environmentally sustainable initiatives on behalf of organizations operating in an increasingly digitalizing economy (Sama, Stefanidis, and Casselman, 2022).

Finally, the collection of research included in this book seeks to contribute to the realization of the urgency and the need for prioritization of novel solutions in global organizations' and stakeholders' quest for a sustainable development advantage.

References

Akhtar, P., S. Ullah, S. H. Amin, G. Kabra, and S. Shaw (2020). "Dynamic capabilities and environmental sustainability for emerging economies' multinational enterprises." *International Studies of Management & Organization*, 50 (1): 27–42. DOI: 10.1080/00208825.2019.1703376

Barrese, J., C. Phillips, and V. Shoaf (2020). "Why do U.S. public companies continue to join the UN global compact: Ethics or economics?" *International Studies of Management & Organization*, 50 (3): 209–231. DOI: 10.1080/00208825.2020.1811525

Basu, K., and G. Palazzo (2008). "Corporate social responsibility: A process model of sensemaking." *Academy of Management Review*, 33 (1): 122–136. DOI: 10.5465/amr.2008.27745504

Bento, R., L. Mertins, and L.F. White (2020). "Calculation, principle or bias? Information preference and ethical decision-making." *International Studies of Management & Organization*, 50 (3): 232–252. DOI: 10.1080/00208825.2020.1811524

Bowen, H. R. (1953). *Social Responsibilities of the Businessman*. Iowa City: University of Iowa Press.

Haack, P., D. Martignoni, and D. Schoeneborn (2021). "A bait-and-switch model of corporate social responsibility." *Academy of Management Review*, 46 (3): 440–464. DOI: 10.5465/amr.2018.0139

Holtbrügge, D., and M. Conrad (2020). "Decoupling in CSR reports: A linguistic content analysis of the Volkswagen Dieselgate scandal." *International Studies of Management & Organization*, 50 (3): 253–270. DOI: 10.1080/00208825.2020.1811523

Manning, P., N. Baker, and P. Stokes (2020). "The ethical challenge of Big Tech's 'disruptive philanthropy'." *International Studies of Management & Organization*, 50 (3): 271–290. DOI: 10.1080/00208825.2020.1811522

Parquel, B., F. Benoît-Moreau, and F. Larceneux (2011). "How sustainability ratings might deter 'Greenwashing': A closer look at ethical corporate communication." *Journal of Business Ethics*, 102 (1): 15–28. DOI: 10.1007/s10551-011-0901-2

Sama, L. M., A. Stefanidis, and R. M. Casselman (2022). "Rethinking corporate governance in the digital economy: The role of stewardship." *Business Horizons*, 65 (5): 535–546. DOI: 10.1016/j.bushor.2021.08.001

Sama, L. M., A. Stefanidis, and S. Horak (2020). "Business ethics for a global society: Howard Bowen's legacy and the foundations of United Nations' sustainable development goals." *International Studies of Management & Organization*, 50 (3): 201–208. DOI: 10.1080/00208825.2020.1811526

Stecker, M. (2016). "Awash in a sea of confusion: Benefit corporations, social enterprise, and the fear of 'Greenwashing'." *Journal of Economic Issues*, 50 (2): 373–381. DOI: 10.1080/00213624.2016.1176481

Introduction: Howard Bowen and the United Nations' sustainable development goals

Linda M. Sama, Abraham Stefanidis and Sven Horak

ABSTRACT
This article builds on Howard R. Bowen's (1953) seminal treatise 'Social Responsibilities of the Businessman' to portray how Bowen's 11 Economic Goals for responsible business practice are visionary and remarkably evocative of the United Nations' 17 Sustainable Development Goals (SDGs). We reflectively discuss recent developments of corporate social responsibility and business ethics research and identify corresponding elements that can benefit both future research and practice. We maintain that the institutionalization of sustainable, responsible, and ethical business practices in any organization is not only achievable but morally imperative if the subsumed contract between business and society for the effective functioning of both is to be upheld.

In 2015, former Secretary-General of the U.N., Ban Ki-Moon called on world leaders from public, private, and civil society sectors to ratify 17 Sustainable Development Goals (SDGs) that represented a "call to action" by all member states to demonstrate targeted progress across a wide spectrum of pressing global issues threatening sustainability, peace, equity, and prosperity for all (Scheyvens, Banks, and Hughes 2016; U.N. 2014). Building on the work of the previous 15 years to meet the targets of the 8 Millennium Development Goals (MDGs), the SDGs were developed to overcome some of the limitations of the MDGs that, although successful by some measures, were shown to exhibit limited success in individual goal areas and uneven success across countries in most goal areas (Fehling, Nelson, and Venkatapuram 2013). As we race toward a 2030 deadline to meet the SDGs, we acknowledge the critical role that business plays in achieving global goals and a just society and how increasingly crucial it is that practices and policies of business organizations incorporate a social responsibility agenda, with decision-making reflecting ethical considerations. We focus on how progress and prosperity in business are achieved in the context of a sustainable future for the planet and all who inhabit it. In this article, we explore how business educators and researchers attend to the responsible management of business and feature work that highlights the progress made in addressing global goals and the challenges that remain in institutionalizing them.

At this juncture in the history of corporate social responsibility (CSR) and business ethics research, which spans over 67 years of investigative study since the publication of *Social Responsibilities of the Businessman* (Bowen 1953), we find ourselves at a critical crossroads that affords us an opportunity to take stock of our progress for guidance and to look to the future for innovative solutions to business's and society's most pressing ethical dilemmas. We argue that the role that ethical business plays in the implementation and integration of several of the SDG targets in the organizational *ethos* can move us toward a better understanding of measurement and ethical adjustment in our policies and processes.

In the introduction of a new, re-published edition of Bowen's seminal treatise on social responsibility, Jean-Pascal Gond notes that Howard R. Bowen's work is "more often ritually quoted than actually opened and read," rendering Bowen perhaps "the most famous unknown of the CSR field" (Bowen 2013, ix). Yet, delving into his original manuscript, the freshness of this economist's perspective on the role of business in society – an unapologetically normative perspective – clearly laid a foundation for much of the work that followed, including stakeholder theory (Freeman 1984) and the CSR pyramid (Carroll 1991), and prodded critique in the tradition of Friedman's shareholder theory (1970). It is interesting to note that the Economic Goals[1], forwarded by Bowen (2013, 8–12) as goals that responsible businesses should adopt, are visionary and remarkably evocative of the current SDGs.[2] While Bowen acknowledges that these are not a comprehensive list of goals and values, he does characterize these as illustrating "the kinds of goals in terms of which the social responsibilities of business must be defined" (p. 8). Bowen cites 11 such goals, which can be mapped to several of the SDGs when drilling down to their measurement targets, as displayed in Table 1. The degree to which there is goal correspondence from discourse dating back to 1953 with the efforts being made today by companies and countries to achieve the SDGs is remarkable and serves as an encouraging testament to the abiding value that industry and government attach to social goals working in concert with economic goals.

A trained Keynesian, Bowen's work accommodates the economic, philosophical, political, and historical views of luminaries as disparate as Veblen, an economist and social scientist who coined the term "conspicuous consumption"; Commons, a pro-labor, progressive economist; and Foucault, a postmodern historian/philosopher whose discourses on power and knowledge influenced academics in the social sciences. To be sure, a comprehensive CSR schema must perforce contemplate a wide spectrum of dimensions, including the historical, institutional, societal, and philosophical aspects and should imagine consequences of decisions that measure risk, reward, and salience of outcomes for diverse stakeholder groups.

The concept of CSR, and relatedly that of business ethics, is one that resonates with the purposes delineated in the 17 SDGs and their 169 targets, as explored in recent research (Buhmann, Jonsson, and Fisker 2019; Schönherr, Findler, and Martinuzzi 2017). Moreover, as business school educators, we are interested in the importance that students place on business ethics, sustainable practices, and the degree to which they may carry these concepts forward into their management careers. In a recent editorial for a special issue of Sustainability, Setó-Pamies and Papaoikonomou (2020) suggest that there is not only a moral imperative to "influence students' worldviews and attitudes towards sustainability" (p. 3) through training on CSR and the SDGs but that understanding the SDG agenda is also an increasingly valuable skill for organizations employing business graduates as their emerging strategies increasingly focus on the principles embedded in the SDGs. One result of this trend is that many business schools worldwide have committed resources to integrating CSR and the SDGs into their curricula as signatories of PRME (Principles for Responsible Management Education), which was founded in 2007 as an initiative of the United Nations Global Compact (UNGC). PRME brings together the UNGC and business schools around the world to engage in, support, and advocate for responsible management education, research, and thought leadership globally through the application of six principles: purpose, values, method, research, partnership, and dialogue. Meanwhile, over 11,000 business organizations worldwide are signatories to the UNGC, now celebrating 20 years. These UNGC signatories are called upon to demonstrate their commitment to implementing sustainable and ethical business practices related to ten guiding principles, also closely aligned with the SDGs. The convergence of an emphasis on CSR and the SDGs in both the business sector and in schools of business has opened up the prospect of making significant advances in promoting ethical and responsible business behavior and elevating the profile of the business enterprise as a vehicle for positive social change.

Table 1 Goal mapping between Bowen's (1953) 11 economic goals and the SDGs

Bowen's 11 Economic Goals	Description of Bowen's Goals	Corresponding SDGs	Corresponding Elements of SDGs
Goal 1: High Standard of Living	• High Productivity • Abundance	**SDG 1**: No Poverty **SDG 2**: Zero Hunger	• Sustainable jobs; Ensure protection for children and vulnerable groups • Promote Equality • Food security for all; support agriculture/small hold farmers
Goal 2: Economic Progress	• Technological Progress/efficiencies • Increase in scope and size of production, while considering prudent use of natural resources to sustain growth[3] • Increase non-material capital, e.g. education/training of workers	**SDG 8**: Decent Work and Economic Growth **SDG 12**: Responsible Consumption/Production **SDG 7**: Affordable and clean energy	• Inclusive, sustainable economic growth to drive progress; decent jobs for all • Decouple economic growth from environmental degradation • Increase resource efficiency • Promote sustainable lifestyles (education)
Goal 3: Economic Stability	• Mitigate fluctuations in economic activity	**SDG 8**: Decent Work and Economic Growth	• Lessen economic and financial shocks from macro disruptions • Smooth financial market volatility
Goal 4: Personal Security	• Collective responsibility for food, employment and health security	**SDG 2**: Zero Hunger **SDG 3**: Good Health and Well-being **SDG 9**: Industry, Innovation and Infrastructure	• Provide food and humanitarian relief to at-risk populations • Ensure healthy lives and improved well-being for all • Invest in infrastructure to help generate employment and income, and provide all with access to markets
Goal 5: Order	• Regular flow of goods • Equalization of supply and demand • Absence of violent strife in economic relationships	**SDG 10**: Reduced Inequality	• Reduce preferential trade status
Goal 6: Justice	• Equitable income distribution • Equal opportunity • Access to education and healthcare	**SDG 10**: Reduced Inequality **SDG 16**: Peace, Justice and Strong Institutions	• Reduce income inequality • Make progress on gender equality • Access to justice for all • Accountable, inclusive institutions at all levels • Protect human rights including access to water, health care and education for marginalized groups
Goal 7: Freedom	• Freedom of enterprise, consumer choice, occupational choice • Freedom to organize (labor unions, trade associations, etc.)	**SDG 8**: Decent Work and Economic Growth **SDG 16**: Peace, Justice and Strong Institutions	• Equal access to employment; lessen occupational segregation on basis of sex • Improved working conditions • Dispute resolution through functioning systems • Freedom of information
Goal 8: Development of Individual Person	• Safe, healthful and pleasant workplaces	**SDG 8**: Decent Work and Economic Growth	• Safe working conditions • Security in the workplace
Goal 9: Community Improvement	• Healthful, aesthetic environment, proper waste disposal • Community organization, services and facilities	**SDG 6**: Clean Water and Sanitation **SDG 11**: Sustainable Cities/ Communities	• Clean water, sanitation and hygiene access for all • Proper disposal of waste • Energy, housing, transportation services • Improve air quality
Goal 10: National Security	• Defense of liberal institutions	**SDG 16**: Peace, Justice and Strong Institutions	• Strengthen institutions to ease conflict, insecurity
Goal 11: Personal Integrity	• Truthful, honorable business practices • Adherence to "Rules of the Game"	**SDG 16**: Peace, Justice and Strong Institutions	• Shun corruption, bribery, theft, tax evasion, and fraud • Abide by the Rule of Law

Concluding remarks

Incorporating people, the planet, economic progress, and prosperity in a way that is inclusive, honest, just, and sustainable (United Nations 2014) is a management conundrum. However, we posit that it is not an intractable one. Current research points the way for corporations to achieve the goals of adopting substantive CSR practices with increased transparency and authenticity; assessing risk through a normative ethical lens; avoiding deception in CSR reporting; and investing in responsible social impact with scale and intentionality. Future studies should advance theory and, importantly, inform practice. Employing diverse research methods and both quantitative and qualitative designs, these narratives can serve to establish bridges between intention and action and between the demands of the market and those of society. Traversing these bridges requires agility, flexibility, and vigilance, so that avoidable pitfalls are averted and unavoidable events are navigated with adeptness and a strong moral compass. Modern global business enters a new era of pressing change and imminent threats, significantly demonstrated by the Covid-19 pandemic, that accrue to both society and business simultaneously. Hence, it is incumbent on organizations to pay closer attention to the warning signs and to be guided not only by precedent but also by vision and ingenuity to conceive of what is possible and then to make it happen. Harking back to Howard Bowen's 11 Economic Goals and mapping them to the SDGs, we reflectively evoke more recent developments in the field of CSRand business ethics research and identify corresponding elements that can benefit both future research and practice. In doing so, we maintain that the institutionalization of sustainable, responsible, and ethical business practices in any organization is not only achievable but morally imperative if the subsumed contract between business and society for the effective functioning of both is to be upheld.

Notes

1. Bowen did not speak of "global goals" but rather focused his work on American business.
2. Interpretation of the SDGs as they relate to Bowen's Economic Goals is an ad hoc analysis with reference to the SDG descriptions found on https://sustainabledevelopment.un.org/?menu=1300, and https://www.un.org/sustainabledevelopment/sustainable-development-goals/, Accessed 7/7/20
3. Bowen's (1953) language here is redolent of that associated with the U.N. definition of Sustainable Development. He writes (p.8): "It is important to utilize our natural resources prudently so that progress will not be slowed down by lack of land and natural materials." Thirty-four years later, the Brundtland Commission Report (World Commission on Economic Development, 1987) defined Sustainable Development as "development that meets the needs of the present without compromising the ability of future generations to meet their own needs."

References

Bowen, H. R. 1953. *Social Responsibilities of the Businessman.* Iowa City: University of Iowa Press.

Bowen, H. R. 2013. *Social Responsibilities of the Businessman.* Iowa City: University of Iowa Press (new, re-published edition).

Buhmann, K., J. Jonsson, and M. Fisker. 2019. "Do No Harm and Do More Good Too: Connecting the SDGs with Business and Human Rights and Political CSR Theory." *Corporate Governance* 19 (3): 369–403.

Carroll, A. B. 1991. "The Pyramid of Corporate Social responsibility: Toward the Moral Management of Organizational Stakeholders." *Business Horizons* 34 (4): 39–48.

Fehling, M., B. D. Nelson, and S. Venkatapuram. 2013. "Limitations of the Millennium Development Goals: A Literature Review." *Global Public Health* 8 (10): 1109–1122.

Freeman, R. E. 1984. *Strategic Management: A Stakeholder Approach.* Boston: Pitman Publishing, Inc.

Friedman, M. 1970. "The Social Responsibility of Business is to Increase Its Profits." The New York Times Magazine (September 13).

Scheyvens, R., G. Banks, and E. Hughes. 2016. "The Private Sector and the SDGs: The Need to Move beyond 'Business as Usual'." *Sustainable Development* 24 (6): 371–382.

Schönherr, N., F. Findler, and A. Martinuzzi. 2017. "Exploring the Interface of CSR and the Sustainable Development Goals." *Transnational Corporations* 24 (3): 33–47.

Setó-Pamies, D. and E. Papaoikonomou. 2020. "Sustainable Development Goals: A Powerful Framework for Embedding Ethics, CSR and Sustainability in Management Education." *Sustainability* 12 (5): 1–8.

United Nations (U.N.) 2014. *The Road to Dignity by 2030: Ending Poverty, Transforming All Lives and Protecting the Planet.* Synthesis Report of the Secretary-General on the Post-2015 Agenda. New York. http://www.un.org/ga/search/view_doc.asp?symbol=A/69/700andLang=E Accessed July 6, 2020.

World Commission on Economic Development (WCED). 1987. *Our Common Future (the Brundtland Report).* New York: Oxford University Press.

Why do U.S. public companies continue to join the UN global compact: ethics or economics?

James Barrese, Cynthia Phillips and Victoria Shoaf

ABSTRACT

Not long after the formation of the United Nations Global Compact (UNGC) in 2000, two opposing theories emerged regarding its efficacy and why organizations continue to join UNGC. The critics take the position that because it has low barriers to entry and no enforcement of compliance, it attracts organizations with low CSR performance who merely want to enhance their reputations. The advocates reject these arguments because of their belief in the purpose of the UNGC, to offer a platform for learning and improvement, especially for under-resourced organizations. Haack, Martignoni, and Schoeneborn have offered a conceptual framework that has the potential to bridge the differences between these two opposing theoretical positions by suggesting that CSR can be adopted ceremonially under conditions of opacity and evolve to substantive adoption over time as transparency increases. In this study, we use the Haack et al. conceptual framework to empirically test this proposition by investigating U.S. corporations that have joined UNGC. We expand the analysis to examine the motivations for ceremonially adopting CSR. Our results support the conditions proposed by Haack et al., and we emphasize the importance of organizational learning to achieve substantive adoption of CSR practices over time.

Introduction

Since its launch in July 2000, over twenty thousand organizations have signed on to the United Nations Global Compact (United Nations Global Compact Headquarters (UNGC) 2015), a voluntary public-private partnership with the objective of creating an "inclusive and sustainable global economy" (Kell 2012, 32). Signatories agree to evolve corporate practices to achieve objectives related to at least one of the ten UNGC principles in the areas of human rights, labor rights, protection of the environment, and anticorruption, and to demonstrate in a biannual report the progress made and actions taken in their implementation efforts (Rasche 2009, 514).

Approximately half of the signatories of the UNGC are from European countries, while only slightly over 5 percent are from North America. It has been noted that since European companies have been required by law to report performance in the areas covered by the ten principles, reporting for the UNGC is less burdensome for them (Bremmer 2008). Moreover, Janney, Dess, and Forlani (2009) find that when European firms join the UNGC, it is viewed favorably by investors, but when U.S. firms announce their participation, the market responds with negative abnormal returns.

Almost from its inception, there has been an ongoing debate about the effectiveness of the UNGC in promoting Corporate Social Responsibility (CSR) through its ten principles. On the one hand are those who believe that organizations join the UNGC ceremoniously merely to enhance their reputations, with no intention of improving their CSR practices and no need to, since the UNGC has no enforcement mechanism (Rizvi 2004; Sethi and Schepers 2014; Utting 2007; Williams 2004). In a scathing article on the ineffectiveness of the UNGC, Sethi and Schepers (2014) suggest that these organizations may join the UNGC merely to obscure their poor CSR performance. On the other hand are those who praise the UNGC in fulfilling its intention to offer an affiliation and opportunity for learning to improve CSR to those who might most need it (Kell and Levin 2003; Palazzo and Scherer 2010; Rasche 2009; Rasche and Waddock 2014). In a recent article, Haack, Martignoni, and Schoeneborn (2020) present a conceptual framework in which both sides of this debate might be validated, depending on conditions of transparency and opacity.

This study investigates the framework presented by Haack, Martignoni, and Schoeneborn (2020) empirically, using data from U.S. publicly-held companies who sign on to the UNGC to see if their joining UNGC is hypocritical, a ceremonial act to enhance reputation without the intention of making CSR improvements, or if it is opportunistic, taking advantage of conditions of opacity to initiate or promote CSR substantively. We focus on U.S. publicly-held companies because of the availability of data needed for the analysis.

Despite the small number of participants, the stream of new U.S. companies joining UNGC remains steady, even increasing slightly over the years. After verifying that the immediate economic payback of market reaction is still not an inducement, we expand the analysis to explore other potential explanations for U.S. companies joining the UNGC. Given the role of the chief executive officer (CEO) as the actual signatory, we examine governance characteristics to see if a new CEO or aspects of the CEO's background might motivate the signing. We study the possible economic incentive of strong business relationships in other countries, where UNGC participation is more widespread and affiliation with the United Nations (UN) is more highly valued. Then we investigate whether the ceremonial adoption is merely an opaque veil intended to disguise poor CSR performance or whether it provides an opportunity to improve CSR performance. Using the Kinder, Lydenberg, Domini Research and Analytics (KLD) database (now owned by MSCI), we look at the CSR ratings to gauge whether poor CSR performance might precede joining the UNGC, as suggested by the critics of UNGC and, if so, whether continued poor CSR performance supports their position that signing UNGC is an unethical subterfuge for these organizations.

Our study makes several contributions. First, it provides empirical evidence for the model proposed by Haack, Martignoni, and Schoeneborn (2020). In part, their model suggests that CSR can be adopted ceremonially under conditions of opacity and evolve to substantive adoption over time as transparency increases. We find that firms that join UNGC are poorer CSR performers than their counterparts, but that those firms improve their CSR performance after joining UNGC. We emphasize the importance of organizational learning for these firms to evolve to more substantive adoption of CSR, although we have only the circumstantial evidence of the results of organizational learning. Secondly, in investigating leadership characteristics that might motivate UNGC participation, we find evidence that newly-appointed CEOs are more likely to join the UNGC. This finding empirically validates the survey of Cetindamar and Husoy (2007), suggesting that a new CEO may strive to improve corporate image, to promote or initiate a program of CSR, or to increase employee satisfaction. We also find that U.S. public companies' signing on to the UNGC is positively associated with the level of their reliance on sales outside of North America, suggesting that UNGC membership might have some economic benefit where the association is more highly valued, namely, in Europe.

The remainder of the article includes sections that give an overview of the UNGC, briefly summarize the related literature, develop the hypotheses, describe the methodology employed in the study, and present results, followed by discussion and directions for future research.

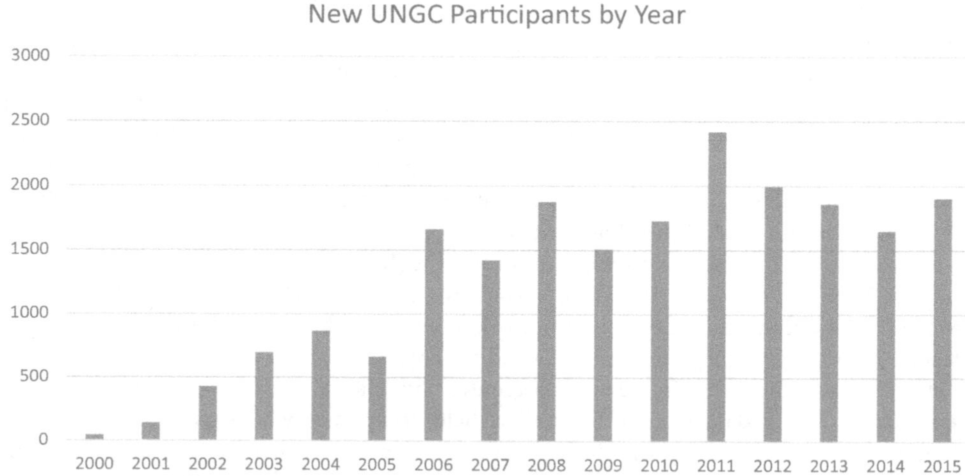

Figure 1. Total new UNGC participants by year. Data is compiled from the UNGC website: https://www.unglobalcompact.org/what-is-gc/participants.

Overview of the UN global compact and U.S. participation

In July 2000, the United Nations (UN) Secretary-General Kofi Annan launched the Global Compact as a voluntary public-private partnership with the objective of engaging the business community in the active pursuit of creating a global economy that is both just and sustainable (Kell 2012, 32). The UNGC now consists of ten principles in the areas of human rights, labor rights, protection of the environment, and anticorruption (added in 2004), all of which are rooted in existing international treaties. A list of the UNGC principles can be found in Appendix A. The UNGC's mission is to support companies to align their strategies and operations with ten ethical principles and to advance broader societal goals, with an emphasis on collaboration and innovation. Through UNGC's local networks, organizations can connect with other organizations and share best practices to improve their performance. Signatories file an annual Communication on Progress (COP), stating their continued support of the Compact and describing their progress and actions taken in their implementation efforts in each of the four issue areas (Rasche 2009, 514); these COPs are available on the UNGC's website: https://www.unglobalcompact.org/what-is-gc/participants. In 2011, the UNGC initiated a "Differentiation Program" for reporting, wherein participants select their level of implementation of the UNGC's ten principles (Learner, Active, or Advanced).

In its *Activity Report* (2015, 2) marking its fifteenth anniversary, UNGC declares that it is "the world's largest corporate sustainability initiative with over 8,000 companies and almost 5,000 non-business participants in over 160 countries that have committed to embed corporate sustainability–defined as long-term value creation by business in financial, social, environmental and ethical terms–in their strategies, operations and investments, and to report on progress." Indeed, UNGC membership has continued to grow, and many new signatories are added each year (Figure 1).

Although there have been over twenty thousand signatories of the UN Global Compact, eight thousands of these (40 percent) were subsequently delisted by the UNGC. If the signatory fails to submit a COP to the public Global Compact database within one year of joining the Global Compact, its status is changed from "Active" to "Non-communicating." Consecutive failure to submit a COP leads to removal (delisting) of the entity. Failure to submit the COP is the only cause for delisting; there is no other performance requirement for continued membership.

Signatories include small to large public and private companies, NGOs, and various other associations, and the UNGC distinguishes them by type. As indicated in Table 1, the *small to*

Table 1. Total UNGC signatories by type at the end of December 2015.

	Company	Small/Med enterprise	Business Assoc.	Labor Assoc.	Foundatn	City/Public Org.	NGO	Academic	Total
Total	5,968	9,891	937	55	478	344	2,356	828	20,857
Delisted	2,222	5,785	12	0	13	6	53	27	8,118
Total active	3,746	4,106	925	55	465	338	2,303	801	12,739
%	29.4	32.2	7.3	0.4	3.7	2.7	18.1	6.3	100.0

Data is compiled from the UNGC website: https://www.unglobalcompact.org/what-is-gc/participants. From the UNGC-defined types, Global and Local types are combined for Business Associations, Labor Associations, and NGOs. Public Sector Organizations are combined with Cities Company is defined by UNGC as having more than 250 employees and includes publicly-held and private companies.

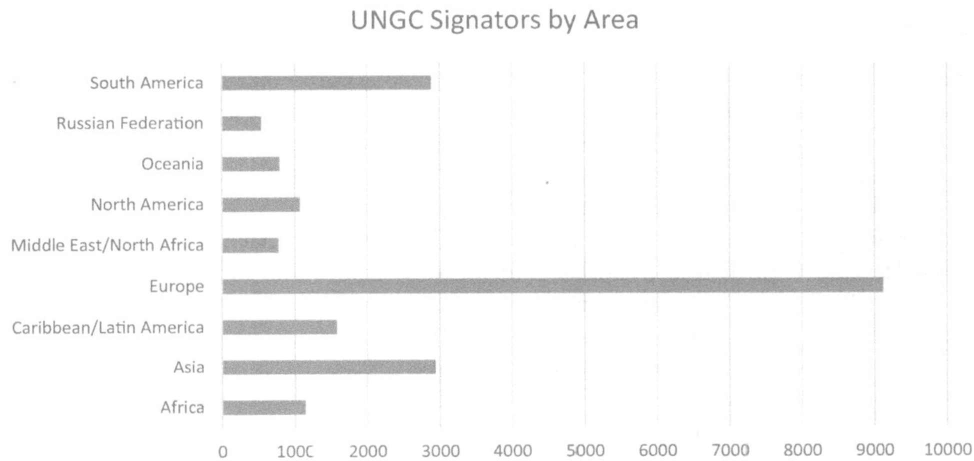

Figure 2. UNGC signatories at December 2015 by geographic region. Data is compiled from the UNGC website: https://www.unglobalcompact.org/what-is-gc/participants.

medium-sized enterprises form the largest group worldwide, followed by *companies*, which includes both privately-held and publicly-traded businesses having more than 250 employees.

Also shown in Table 1, small to medium-sized enterprises have the highest rate of delisting (58 percent of signatories), which has been attributed to lack of resources to devote to initiatives supporting the principles and to reporting (Garza 2013; Rasche, Waddock, and McIntosh 2013). However, companies also have a relatively high rate of delisting (37.2 percent of signatories).

At the end of 2015, signatories to the UNGC came from 165 out of 193 UN member countries. Figure 2 shows the relative numbers of signatories from each area of the world. The region of the world with the most UNGC signatories is Europe, which includes 9,116 signatories from 43 countries in the western and eastern areas of Europe. North America is one of the smaller regions; only 917 of UNGC signatories are from the United States.

The composition of signatories from the United States is different from that of the rest of the world. As shown in Table 2, fewer of the active UNGC signatories are companies and small to medium-sized enterprises in the U.S. than worldwide: 24.1 and 28.9 percent respectively in the U.S. compared to 29.4 and 32.2 percent respectively worldwide. This composition is perhaps reflective of the negative attitude in the U.S. toward the UN.

Local networks of UNGC signatories began to evolve as early as 2001 (Kell and Levin 2003, 158). The Global Compact Network USA, launched in 2007, has had some success in stimulating U.S. participation, through hosting events and promoting collaboration around best practices, but some of the more thriving European networks directly receive governmental backing (Kell 2012, 39), while the U.S. government is more "reserved" (Ziegler 2007, 65).

Table 2. U.S. UNGC signatories by type at the end of December 2015.

	Company	Small/Med enterprise	Business Assoc.	Labor Assoc.	Foundatn	City/Public Org.	NGO	Academic	Total
Total US	204	455	32	0	9	9	155	53	917
Delisted	75	300		0	0	0	6	0	381
Total US Active	129	155	32	0	9	9	149	53	536
%	24.1	28.9	6.0	0	1.7	1.7	27.8	9.9	100.0

Data is compiled from the UNGC website: https://www.unglobalcompact.org/what-is-gc/participants. From the UNGC-defined types, Global and Local types are combined for Business Associations, Labor Associations, and NGOs. Public Sector Organizations are combined with Cities. Company is defined by UNGC as having more than 250 employees and includes publicly-held and private companies.

Literature review

Foundational economic theory (Friedman 1970; Jensen 2001) posits that the purpose of all strategies of a firm should be to maximize profits and shareholder wealth. Proponents of economic theory argue that the adoption of CSR enhances a firm's financial performance (Arya and Zhang 2009; Mishra and Suar 2010; Orlitzky, Schmidt and Rynes 2003; Porter and Kramer 1999, 2002; Smith 2003). This position has engendered considerable debate in the CSR literature, with some researchers finding little or no correlation between CSR and financial performance (Aupperle, Carroll, and Hatfield 1985; Hillman and Keim 2001; McWilliams and Siegel 2000; Waddock and Graves 1997). Still, in two extensive reviews of articles on this topic (Malik 2015; Margolis, Elfenbein, and Walsh 2009), both authors find that, overall, the literature indicates that there is a positive association between CSR and firm performance.

Improving the firm's reputation is one theoretical mechanism that is found to drive the relationship between CSR adoption and firm performance (Brammer and Pavelin 2004; Bayoud and Kavanagh 2012). Fombrun, Gardberg, and Barnett (2000) show that CSR ("citizenship programs") can generate reputational gains, building competitive advantage, as well as mitigate the risk of reputational losses from alienating key stakeholders. Reputation relies on signals about unobservable intentions and future behaviors (Rao 1994), and the public adoption of CSR is viewed as providing a reputation-enhancing signal to stakeholders (Robinson, Kleffner, and Bertels 2011; Zerbini 2017). Particularly, the announcement of joining UNGC aligns the firm with a formal and well-known CSR initiative. Janney, Dess, and Forlani (2009) empirically test the effects of reputation and UN alignment in a market study of stockholder reactions to the announcement of firms' joining UNGC. They find that investors react favorably (positive abnormal returns) in European countries, where the UN is held in higher value, but react negatively in the U.S. market. Other researchers have noted the low participation of U.S. companies in the UNGC (Bremmer 2008), some suggesting that the litigious culture of the U.S. (Williams 2004; Ziegler 2007; Janney, Dess, and Forlani 2009) and the low value that the U.S. places on association with the UN (Hoessle 2015; Rasche, Waddock and McIntosh 2013) deter participation.

The main group of critics in the debate about the value of the UNGC pursue the reputation argument, proposing that participants ceremoniously join the UNGC to improve their reputation, without any intention of improving their implementation of the principles (Deva 2006; Williams 2004). The term "bluewashing" was coined by the Alliance for Corporate-free U.N. to describe this phenomenon (Rizvi 2004). Indeed, Sethi and Schepers (2014) suggest that the open admission policy of UNGC is "an open invitation to entice the worst performing companies to become signatories in good standing" and that the UNCG may just provide "a thin patina of respectability" without measureable impact. This group questions the legitimacy of UNGC membership as a good signal of CSR, not necessarily doubting the legitimacy of the UN, but because of the opacity of the conditions of membership in UNGC. They argue that its principles are too vague and are therefore hard to implement (Nolan 2005; Deva 2006) and that the Compact lacks accountability because it does not provide any verification of compliance to the principles or audit of the organization's reported progress (Rizvi 2004; Sethi and Schepers 2014; Utting 2007; Williams 2004).

At the same time, the group of supporters of the value of UNGC adoption view it from a different perspective, that of organizational learning. Theories of organizational learning, as synthesized by Crossan and Berdrow (2003) suggest that organizational learning creates a culture of knowledge sharing and/or knowledge transfer within an organization and is therefore a means for promoting and sustaining corporate organizational competitiveness. Rasche (2009) argues, along with others (Kell and Levin 2003; Palazzo and Scherer 2010), that criticizing UNGC for its opacity is based on a misunderstanding of the UNGC's intention to be an evolving platform for learning and collaboration and to stimulate progress, especially among poor performers that might need it most. Rasche and Waddock (2014) emphasize that UNGC has succeeded in its intended purpose of creating "a space for dialog, learning, and partnership" (212).

In his article on stakeholder theory, Jones (1995) supports institutional learning theory, or what he refers to as "social learning theory" (419), as having an important role in stakeholder management. He shows that a firm's policies are determined by its top leadership, in ways that are visible to stakeholders, and then they are developed in the firm through the process of social learning (418–419). Hemingway and Maclagan (2004) argue that the perspectives of individuals as key decision makers play a critical role in the formulation and implementation of CSR policy in organizations. The formulation of their argument is at its core based on Mosley, Pietri, and Megginson's (1996, 141) definition of CSR as "… managements' obligation to set policies, make decisions and follow courses of action beyond the requirements of the law that are desirable in terms of the values and objectives of society." To further support the development of their framework, Hemingway and Maclagan (2004) draw on the extant literature (Drumwright 1994; Fineman and Clarke 1996; Menon and Menon 1997; Swanson 1995; Wood 1991) and propose that while the consideration of economic motivations related to firm performance is important when evaluating CSR decisions in organizations, such decisions are also motivated by the personal values and interests of well-intentioned and ethical individual managers. Taking the issue a step further, Hemingway and Maclagan (2004) consider Wilson's (2002) speculation that the emerging generation of leaders have been educated to consider the greater good of society and the environment when making decisions, along with Wood's (1991) suggestion that ethical training, cultural background, and life experiences motivate human behavior. Thus, we suggest that the chief executive officer (CEO) plays a key role in making a public adoption of UNGC, whether hypocritically or to move the firm toward a substantive development of CSR practices.

Recently, Haack, Martignoni, and Schoeneborn (2020) have offered a conceptual framework that has the potential to bridge the differences between these two schools of thought on why firms adopt UNGC. Through modeling, Haack, Martignoni, and Schoeneborn (2020) demonstrate that, despite the commonly held position in CSR literature that transparency is needed for organizations to institutionalize CSR practices, it may sometimes be ideal for organizations to adopt CSR ceremonially under conditions of opacity.

> In such circumstances, opacity allows organizations to adopt the practice ceremonially in a first step ("bait") and then a switch to a regime of transparency prompts ceremonial adopters to become substantive adopters in a second step ("switch") (4–5).

As Haack and Scherer (2014) argued previously, low entry barriers allow firms to adopt a practice only ceremonially, but "differentiation, combined with increasing transparency, has the potential to fuel the self-reinforcing dynamics of *moral entrapment* and *creeping commitment* (20)." Haack, Martignoni, and Schoeneborn (2020) assert that firms adopting CSR ceremoniously are "more likely to subsequently adopt it substantively than to abandon it" (17). This framework suggests that poor CSR performers who are able to join UNGC because of its low barrier to admission may take advantage of its opacity to employ organizational learning to improve their CSR performance, uniting the two opposing camps on the usefulness of UNGC. In this study, we use the Haack, Martignoni, and Schoeneborn (2020) conceptual framework to empirically test this proposition by investigating U.S. corporations that have joined UNGC.

Hypotheses development

Joining UNGC is ceremonial, a public declaration of the organization's alignment to CSR principles, whether it is done opportunistically to enhance reputation, or as a prelude to formulating substantive CSR practices, or as a reflection of the organization's established CSR policies. Prior researchers have shown that firms pursue CSR initiatives for a multitude of reasons, including altruistic (for example, Mele 2002), or economic (Friedman 1970; Porter and Kramer 2002), or both (for example, Carroll 1999; Jones 1995). Likewise, a company's leadership may join the UNGC for ethical reasons, such as promoting or advancing the company's CSR agenda (Perez-Batres, Miller, and Pisani 2011; Hoessle 2015) or for purely economic benefits (Deva 2006; Rizvi 2004; Sethi and Schepers 2014), or both (Cetindamar and Husoy 2007). The locus of responsibility construct of Hemingway and Maclagan (2004) suggests that the motivation of managers, whether somewhere on the continuum of ethical reasoning, or somewhere in the spectrum of gain-seeking economic benefit, or both, will guide their decisions. As UNGC membership is requested by the CEO, who may or may not already have a CSR officer in place at the time, we first focus on the motivation of the CEO in signing on to the UNGC.

Janney, Dess, and Forlani (2009) suggest that the cost of compliance with UNGC principles in Europe is lower than in the U.S. because European firms are already mandated to comply by local law in many cases (419). It is also widely suggested in the early literature (Bremer 2008) that the cost of the required UNGC reporting is lower in Europe than the U.S. because similar reports are already required in Europe. It is true that many of the smaller organizations have been delisted or have withdrawn from UNGC because they cannot support the cost of reporting (Rasche et al. 2013). Given recent changes, however, we find that for larger U.S. companies, reporting costs should no longer be an issue. Sustainability reporting of some sort has become an increasingly common practice among large U.S. corporations. The Governance and Accountability Institute (GAI) reported that 85 percent (425) of the companies in the S&P 500 Index prepared sustainability reports in 2017, up significantly from 2011, when 20 percent (100) of those companies prepared such reports (GAI 2018). The fact that firms are already preparing and sharing sustainability reports also mitigates consideration of the theory that joining the UNGC is needed to respond to demands from various stakeholder groups.

There is a burgeoning literature which suggests that certain leadership characteristics may drive incentives for becoming a UNGC signatory. For instance, building on the upper echelons theory, Bamber, Jiang, and Wang (2010) show that observable demographic characteristics of managers' backgrounds can affect their managerial styles and decisions regarding voluntary disclosures. They find that the functional career track, age cohort, military experience, and M.B.A. education of the CEO, CFO and General Counsel are associated with transparent or opaque disclosure styles. We offer two hypotheses on CEO characteristics motivating the public adoption of CSR by joining UNGC. We posit that a relevant characteristic will be whether the CEO is new to the position. For a new CEO, signing UNGC could provide an internal signaling mechanism, to alert employees and the board to a new CSR focus for the firm. Additionally, it might be an external signal that will improve global reputation and interest investors who pursue ethical companies, or a signal intended for economic purposes, to foster sales and other economic alignments of like-minded organizations. In addition to whether the CEO is relatively new to the firm, we test whether having a non-U.S. background might affect the manager's decision to join the UNGC, given the higher level of acceptance of UNGC in other countries.

Hypothesis 1: The shorter the period of time the CEO is with the organization, the more likely the organization is to join the UNGC.

Hypothesis 2: U.S. organizations headed by non-U.S. CEOs are more likely to join the UNGC than U.S. firms headed by U.S. CEOs.

Association with the UNGC is clearly valued more highly in other parts of the world than the United States, especially in the European countries. Among internationally dispersed organizations, Cetindamar and Hussoy (2007) find that a major economic reason for firms joining UNGC is to improve their image and compete with firms in the global market. It may be that U.S. firms that do considerable business overseas consider it culturally beneficial to be associated with the UNGC. For instance, Ziegler (2007) recounts that Johnson Controls' CEO sent a letter requesting UNGC membership because of an invitation to do so by the CEO of French automobile manufacturer, Renault, a significant customer. Accordingly, we investigate whether the degree of international involvement is associated with U.S. firms joining the UNGC.

Hypothesis 3: U.S. firms that rely on international business are more likely to join the UNGC than U.S. firms that do not rely on international business.

It is still possible that the U.S. companies that are weaker-performing in CSR join the UNGC to give the impression that they are good global citizens, while maintaining low performance standards (*i.e.*, bluewashing). To investigate this possibility, rather than looking at what the companies themselves say they do through their own reporting, we examine their social responsibility indices provided by MSCI (formerly KLD). Chatterji, Levine, and Toffel (2009) and Kang (2015) compare KLD ratings for the environment category and the diversity and governance categories, respectively, against alternative well-recognized, independent, and credible publicly-available data sources to evaluate the accuracy of the ratings with respect to actual practice. They find the KLD ratings to have backward-looking (past performance) and forward-looking (predictive) ability in these categories. Accordingly, we use these indices to investigate whether U.S. firms that join the UNGC are lower performing on CSR issues, as suggested by Sethi and Schepers (2014).

Hypothesis 4: U.S. firms that join the UNGC are weak performers on CSR issues.

Finally, we examine whether poor CSR performers who are able to join UNGC because of its low barrier to admission may take advantage of its opacity to employ organizational learning to improve their CSR performance, bridging the two opposing camps on the usefulness of UNGC and empirically supporting the theory espoused by Haack, Martignoni, and Schoeneborn (2020). Sethi and Schepers (2014) suggest that there is little incentive for poorly performing firms to improve their behavior on CSR issues after joining UNGC because of the lack of accountability and simplistic reporting. However, if firms are able to ceremonially state their commitment to CSR by joining UNGC and then use their opacity to advance their CSR practices over time, it would support the opposing view that the UNGC offers an opportunity for organizational learning. Hence, we investigate whether the firms' measured behavior on CSR issues changes after associating with UNGC.

Hypothesis 5: U.S. firms improve their performance on CSR issues after joining the UNGC.

Other researchers have found results that may support this proposal. Berliner and Prakash (2015), focusing on the implementation of environmental and human rights initiatives by U.S. UNGC firms, find that U.S. firms that join the UNGC do not improve issues of concern in these areas, but that they do increase areas of strength, presumably because they are able to make low-cost improvements. They interpret these results to suggest that U.S. firms may join only to gain reputation effects while avoiding costly remediation of problems. However, it could as well be that these firms were on a learning curve and first were implementing those things that could be accomplished expediently and with low cost. Schembera (2018) finds that firms joining UNGC improve CSR performance over time, and the length of their membership affects their implementation of the UNGC principles. Hoessle (2015) surveys a small number of U.S. participants and finds that joining the UNGC is not the beginning, but a continuation of their implementation of CSR initiatives, although joining might have initiated their reporting these activities.

Table 3. Sample selection from active U.S. participants in UNGC-listed "Companies".

Number of U.S. "Companies" at 12/31/15	129
Less: nonpublic firms	(53)
Publicly-held US "Companies" at 12/31/15	76
Less: firms with insufficient Compustat data	(3)
Less: firms with insufficient KLD data	(11)
Sample U.S. "Companies" used in testing	62

Initial data is compiled from the UNGC website: https://www.unglobalcompact.org/what-is-gc/participants. It is then screened through Compustat and the MSCI-KLD databases for sufficient data for testing. Indicates that numbers preceding the underline are to be totaled.

Methods

Sampling

To establish whether the economic deterrent found by Janney, Dess, and Forlani (2009) still exists for U.S. firms—that is, whether U.S. publicly-traded companies signing on to the UNGC still face negative abnormal returns—we perform an event study similar to that done by Janney, Dess, and Forlani (2009), using only U.S. firms and extending the timeframe to those who joined UNGC through the end of 2015. The U.S. focus of this study precludes consideration of their dichotomous variable of interest (U.S./Europe). Janney, Dess, and Forlani (2009) observe that none of their control variables, AGE, LOGEMP, and DSALES[1] were significant. Like Janney, Dess, and Forlani (2009), we find no effect associated with the employment or total sales size controls.[2] Our models go beyond the specifications considered by Janney, Dess, and Forlani (2009), and we find that a different measure of firm size is significant, the log of assets. Interestingly, while the Janney, Dess, and Forlani (2009) model uses the announcement date for the event study, after a significant research effort, we were only able to identify thirty-nine of the seventy-three publicly-held U.S. firms in our initial group that even made a retrievable announcement of their signing on to UNGC. In itself, not widely announcing the signing indicates that firms do not anticipate a positive market reaction.

Of the 129 active U.S. companies active at the end of 2015, seventy-six are publicly-held U.S. firms that signed on to the UNGC from the time of its inception in 2000 to the end of 2015. Of the seventy-six public firms, three firms are dropped from the sample because they have insufficient data in Compustat for the relevant years. Of the remaining seventy-three firms, fifty-four are larger firms that are part of the S&P 500 and the other nineteen firms are included in the S&P 600. Eleven of these firms do not have sufficient KLD data or are not included in the KLD database at all, so are excluded, leaving sixty-two firms in the UNGC sample for testing. The winnowing of the sample is shown in Table 3.

Analysis

In order to test the likelihood of our hypothesized reasons for U. S. companies signing on to UNGC, we construct a matched sample comprised of publicly-held firms that did not sign on. The signatories that are included in our set are ordered by year of signing, as:

To create the match, each of the non-signatory S&P 500 firms with data for the relevant year is identified, and the firms are randomly ranked. The first non-UNGC firm is selected if its sales are similar to those of the first UNGC firm for that year; if not, the second non-UNGC firm is compared, and so on. This selection is repeated for each firm for each year. As a result, the samples are similar in terms of revenues for the year of signing. We find no statistically significant

'00	'01	'02	'03	'04	'05	'06	'07	'08	'09	'10	'11	'12	'13	'14	'15
1	2	2	1	4	0	5	2	6	9	5	5	6	4	3	7

differences between the UNGC and non-UNGC groups, based on t-tests for mean sales or asset differences. Hence, our full sample begins with one hundred twenty-four firms, half of which signed on to UNGC before the end of 2015 and half of which are not signatories to the UNGC by the end of 2015.

To ensure comparability of groups, we test the relative distribution of UNGC and non-UNGC firms by industry, based on North American Industry Classification System (NAICS) codes. We exclude firms from the utilities sector from the matched set because it violates the comparability of groups in the tests. Hence, when we compare the two groups using a chi-square test (not tabulated), the difference in industry composition between groups is not significant.

The names of the firms in both groups, the year of signing/matching, revenues for that year, and NAICS industry sectors are listed in Appendix B.

The model

We construct the following model and employ a Probit[3] regression procedure to predict the likelihood of a firm signing on to the UNGC according to the reasons posited in our hypotheses:

$$\text{UNGC Membership} = \begin{array}{l}\text{leadership characteristics} + \text{international business} + \\ \text{environmental and social performance} + \text{control variables} + e\end{array} \quad [1]$$

We identify variables to represent the factors of interest, as follows.

Leadership characteristics

To test the effect of specific leadership characteristics that might impact a firm's joining the UNGC, we create two variables. First, we determine whether the CEO in the signing year is relatively new to the firm (within two years of the signing year) by drawing information from ExecuComp on the CEO's name and start date. We create the variable NewCEO, whose value is 1 if the CEO is relatively new to the firm, and 0 otherwise. Then we search the Bloomberg Executive Profile website to assess whether the CEO is a native of the U.S. Where nationality is not specified, we use the nationality of the undergraduate institution attended as a proxy for the birth country. The variable NonNative has a value of 1 if the CEO is not native to the U.S., and 0 otherwise. The same procedures are followed for these two variables for firms in the matched group, based on the tenure and nationality of the CEO in the year in which the firm was selected for the matching.

International business

To determine whether reliance on international business influences signing on to the UNGC, we use the segment reporting sections of the relevant10-K reports at the year of signing or matching to compute the percentage of sales made outside of North America to total revenues. The variable NonNASales is the percentage of the firm's sales made outside of North America.

Environmental and social performance

In determining the possible influence of CSR performance on signing on to UNGC, we focus on the environmental and social categories, as they are directly analogous to the ten UNGC principles. We incorporate into these two categories the variables that the MSCI KLD database studied consistently over the period that includes the three years before our sample companies joined the UNGC to the latest data available (1997–2015). For the non-UNGC group, we use data from the three years prior to the matching year. We use the names for categories as they

Table 4. MSCI KLD categories used to construct variables for testing.

Environmental strengths (STR-ENV)	Environmental concerns (CON-ENV)
Beneficial products and services	Toxic spills & releases
Pollution prevention	Substantial emissions
Recycling	Climate change
Clean energy	Products safety
Other strengths	Other concerns
Social strengths (STR-SOC)	**Social concerns (CON-SOC)**
Indigenous peoples relations	Indigenous peoples concerns
Human rights other strengths	Human rights other concerns
Board of directors diversity	Negative economic community impact
Union relations	Union relations
Cash profit sharing	Employee health & safety
Employee involvement	Employee relations other concerns
Employee relations other strengths	Diversity controversies
Product quality	Marketing-contracting concerns
Benefits to economically disadvantaged	Anticompetitive practices
	Other product concerns

The names of these categories correspond to the names on the KLD output, for the most part. There are some differences between the KLD output and the selections offered on WRDS for the MSCI/KLD database. For instance, Clean Energy (in Environmental Strengths) appears in the WRDS selections as Climate Change (from 1991), but the output file reads Clean Energy. An exception is Toxic Spills & Releases (in Environmental Concerns), which includes Hazardous Waste (from 1991 to 2009) and Operational Waste (from 2010), which is called Non-Carbon Releases on the output file.

appear in the output of the KLD files as of fall 2017 (which does not always agree with the WRDS options for the MSCI KLD database). We include older scores on categories that were subsumed into a new category. The categories used to construct the variables appear in Table 4.

For each firm, we count the number of environmental strengths, environmental concerns, social strengths, and social concerns for the three-year period prior to signing on to UNGC (or the year of matching). These totals become the STR-ENV, CON-ENV, STR-SOC, and CON-SOC variables.

Controls

Following other researchers (e.g. Janney, Dess, and Forlani 2009; Berliner and Prakash 2015), we control for firm size. Janney, Dess, and Forlani (2009) use sales and employee variables as controls. We consider these variables as well, but also follow the more traditional path and consider the value of assets (ASSETS) as a size proxy because we use sales to construct the matched sample. We use the log-10 of SALES, #EMP, and ASSETS in our tests to normalize the data distribution to meet regression assumptions. Earlier studies control for industry as well, using the operating sector as a proxy for industry differences. Given the comparatively small size of our sample, we do not attempt to control for industry; instead, we use a binary indicator to identify firms whose primary business is to provide services, based on the firm's NAISC code (the SERVICES variable), whose value is 1 if the firm is service provider and 0 otherwise.

The detailed specification of our model to predict the likelihood of a firm signing on to UNGC, is:

$$\text{UNGC Membership} = \begin{array}{l} \text{NewCEO} + \text{NonNative} + \text{NonNASales} + \text{STR}-\text{ENV} + \\ \text{CON}-\text{ENV} + \text{STR}-\text{SOC} + \text{CON}-\text{SOC} + \text{SALES} \\ + \text{EMP} + \text{ASSETS} + \text{SERVICES} + e \end{array} \quad [2]$$

Predicted relationships for variables in the Probit model described above for predicting a U.S. firm's joining the UNGC (0 = N, 1 = Y) are:

NewCEO + (Hypothesis 1)

NonNative + (Hypothesis 1)

NonNASales + (Hypothesis 2)

STR-ENV − (Hypothesis 3)

CON-ENV + (Hypothesis 3)

STR-SOC − (Hypothesis 3)

CON-SOC + (Hypothesis 3)

SALES (Control variable)

ASSETS (Control variable)

#EMP (Control variable))

SERVICES (Control variable)

Sample descriptive statistics are provided in Table 5. Results of *t*-tests, presented in Table 6 show that there is no significant difference between UNGC and non-UNGC sample mean values for the number of new CEOs, non-native CEOs, the number of environmental and social concerns, or any of the size measures used as controls (assets, sales, or employees). We use a Probit regression procedure to estimate the relationship between the likelihood of U.S. firms joining the UNGC and the proposed related variables.

Results

Table 7 reports the regression results for three model specifications. Statistically significant factors are identified by p-values below 0.05 (noted by an asterisk). The first model includes all variables considered in the hypotheses. High VIF indicators in Model I led us to remove the LgSALES variable, the primary cause of the multicollinearity[4], and create Model II, our preferred model.

For completeness, Model III substituted the prior year return on equity (ROEm1) for sales under a preliminary hypothesis that bad prior financial performance drives membership. The results for ROEm1 are not consistent with that hypothesis.

Results from all three models show that five of the independent variables considered are statistically significant, and the results are consistent with expectations. The predictive power of the models is good; the 82 percent concordant percentage of model II indicates the percent of observations for which the model prediction equals the observed occurrence and the probability prediction for a firm with characteristics equal to the mean of the sample is 45.6 percent. Still, McFadden's Pseudo R^2 estimates are in the 26 percent range for the three models presented, suggesting that the models have only partially explained the reasons that U.S. companies join UNGC.

We find partial support for our first two hypothesis. Joining the UNGC is positively associated with a firm having a recently appointed CEO as posed in Hypothesis 1, but the CEO's country of origin construct in Hypothesis 2 did not prove statistically significant. Positive and significant coefficients suggest that the likelihood a firm became a member of the UNGC was higher when the firm operated in one of the service industries, and increased when the firm had a new CEO within the past two years.

The results most strongly support our third hypothesis, that firms with extensive international business are more likely than other U.S. firms to join the UNGC, as indicated by the relatively

Table 5. Descriptive statistics.

Panel A: Sample group of U.S. companies that joined UNGC 2000–2015

UNGC = 1, N=62

	Minimum	Maximum	Mean	Std Dev
NewCEO	0	1	0.26	0.44
NonNative	0	1	0.22	0.42
NonNASales	0	0.96	0.50	0.24
CON-ENV	0	12	2.24	3.32
STR-ENV	0	9	2.50	2.803
CON-SOC	0	16	3.58	4.09
STR-SOC	0	12	3.34	3.02
Sales	137.44	180,929.00	23,305.46	38,625.75
LgSALES	2.14	5.26	3.99	0.60
Assets	78.33	2,187,631.00	76,821.44	294,015.68
LgASSETS	1.89	6.34	4.11	0.73
#EMP	0.61	387.00	55.25	75.38
Lg#Emp	−0.22	2.59	1.42	0.56
Services	0	1	0.34	0.48

Panel B: Sample group of U.S. companies that have not joined UNGC

UNGC = 0, N=62

	Minimum	Maximum	Mean	Std Dev
NewCEO	0	1	0.0645	0.2477
NonNative	0	1	0.0968	0.2981
NonNASales	0	1	0.2719	0.2580
CON-ENV	0	6	0.8871	1.6206
STR-ENV	0	9	1.4839	2.3028
CON-SOC	0	19	2.9032	4.0396
STR-SOC	0	12	2.1129	2.9371
Sales	294.00	233,715.00	22,626.49	37,685.63
LgSALES	2.4683	5.3687	3.8911	0.6730
Assets	1,198.66	2,175,052.000	92,225.52	312,749.81
LgASSETS	3.0787	6.3375	4.1918	0.6890
#EMP	0.5460	326.0000	59.4347	83.5627
Lg#Emp	−0.2628	2.5132	1.2913	0.7139
Services	0	1	0.5161	0.5038

Panel C: Total sample of U.S. companies

Total, N= 124

	Minimum	Maximum	Mean	Std Dev
NewCEO	0	1	0.1613	0.3693
NonNative	0	1	0.1613	0.3693
NonNASales	0	1	0.3838	0.2710
CON-ENV	0	12	1.5645	2.6876
STR-ENV	0	9	1.9919	2.6055
CON-SOC	0	19	3.2419	4.0633
STR-SOC	0	12	2.7258	3.0292
Sales	137.44	233,715.00	22,965.98	38,004.68
LgSALES	2.1381	5.3687	3.9393	0.6361
assets	78.33	2,187,631.00	84,523.48	302,389.85
LgASSETS	1.8939	6.3400	4.1522	0.7093
#EMP	0.5460	387.0000	57.3445	79.2786
Lg#Emp	−0.2628	2.5877	1.3559	0.6438
Services	0	1	0.4274	0.4967

NewCEO=Binary with value set to 1 if the CEO is new (within 2 years of the filing date); 0 otherwise.
NonNative=Binary with value set to 1 if the CEO is not native to the U.S.; 0 otherwise.
NonNASales=Percentage of sales made by the firm outside of North America.
CON-ENV=Sum of environmental concerns reported by KLD for the 3 years prior to the joining/matching year.
STR-ENV=Sum of environmental strengths reported by KLD for the 3 years prior to the joining/matching year.
CON-SOC=Sum of social concerns reported by KLD for the 3 years prior to the joining/matching year.
STR-SOC=Sum of social strengths reported by KLD for the 3 years prior the joining/matching year.
SALES=Total revenues for the fiscal year of joining/matching.
LgSALES=Log-10 of the total revenues for the fiscal year of joining/matching.
ASSETS=Total assets at the end of the fiscal year of joining/matching.
LgASSETS=Log-10 of the total assets at the end of the fiscal year of joining/matching.
#EMP=Number of firm employees at the end of the fiscal year of joining/matching.
Lg#Emp=Log-10 of the number of firm employees at the end of the fiscal year of joining/matching.
SERVICES=Binary with value set to 1 if the two-digit NAICS code <22 or >41.

Table 6. *T*-tests of mean differences in variables between sample groups.

Mean difference *t*-tests						
	Non-UNGC	UNGC	Difference	Standard error	*t*-stat	*p* Value
NewCEO	0.064	0.258	0.193	0.064	3.01	0.3200
NonNative	0.097	0.225	0.129	0.065	1.96	0.0512
NonNASales	0.272	0.495	0.223	0.044	5.03	0.0001
CON-ENV	0.887	2.241	1.354	0.468	2.88	0.4600
STR-ENV	1.484	2.500	1.016	0.460	2.20	0.0292
CON-SOC	2.903	3.580	0.677	0.730	0.92	0.3554
STR-SOC	2.113	3.338	1.225	0.534	2.29	0.0224
SALES	22,626.490	23,305.460	678.970	6853.484	0.09	0.9212
LgSALES	3.891	3.987	0.096	0.114	0.84	0.4014
ASSETS	92,225.520	76,821.440	−15,404.080	54,515.120	−0.28	0.7780
LgASSETS	4.192	4.112	−0.079	0.127	−0.62	0.5357
#EMP	59.435	55.254	−4.18	14.292	−0.29	0.7704
Lg#Emp	1.291	1.420	0.129	0.115	1.11	0.2654
SERVICES	0.516	0.338	−0.177	0.088	−2.01	0.0462

NewCEO=Binary with value set to 1 if the CEO is new (within 2 years of the filing date); 0 otherwise.
NonNative=Binary with value set to 1 if the CEO is not native to the U.S.; 0 otherwise.
NonNASales=Percentage of sales made by the firm outside of North America.
CON-ENV=Sum of environmental concerns reported by KLD for the 3 years prior to the joining/matching year.
STR-ENV=Sum of environmental strengths reported by KLD for the 3 years prior to the joining/matching year.
CON-SOC=Sum of social concerns reported by KLD for the 3 years prior to the joining/matching year.
STR-SOC=Sum of social strengths reported by KLD for the 3 years prior the joining/matching year.
SALES=Total revenues for the fiscal year of joining/matching.
LgSALES=Log-10 of the total revenues for the fiscal year of joining/matching.
ASSETS=Total assets at the end of the fiscal year of joining/matching.
LgASSETS=Log-10 of the total assets at the end of the fiscal year of joining/matching.
#EMP=Number of firm employees at the end of the fiscal year of joining/matching.
Lg#Emp=Log-10 of the number of firm employees at the end of the fiscal year of joining/matching.
SERVICES=Binary with value set to 1 if the two-digit NAICS code <22 or >41.

Table 7. Tests of the likelihood of a firm joining UNGC.

	Model I			Model II			Model III		
Parameter	Estimate	Std.Error	$p>\chi^2$	Estimate	Std.Error	$p>\chi^2$	Estimate	Std.Error	$p>\chi^2$
Intercept	0.1792	1.2465	0.8857	0.7940	0.9509	0.4037	0.7603	0.9537	0.4253
NewCEO	0.9182	0.3865	0.0175*	0.9577	0.3859	0.0131*	0.9305	0.3883	0.0166*
NonNative	0.3862	0.3822	0.3122	0.3467	0.3788	0.3600	0.3368	0.3813	0.3771
NonNASales	2.1254	0.5771	0.0002*	2.1455	0.5737	0.0002*	2.1584	0.5756	0.0002*
SERVICES	0.7414	0.3556	0.0371*	0.6748	0.3428	0.0490*	0.7096	0.3493	0.0422*
CON-ENV	0.1505	0.0679	0.0267*	0.1500	0.0679	0.0272*	0.1556	0.0681	0.0223*
STR-ENV	0.0644	0.0596	0.2793	0.0581	0.0590	0.3248	0.0586	0.0592	0.3225
CON-SOC	0.0474	0.0454	0.2969	0.0520	0.0452	0.2492	0.0534	0.0453	0.2385
STR-SOC	0.0752	0.0504	0.1352	0.0767	0.0503	0.1271	0.0793	0.0505	0.1166
LgASSETS	−0.9034	0.3898	0.0205*	−0.7119	0.2765	0.0100*	−0.7175	0.2774	0.0097*
LgSALES	0.4200	0.5689	0.4604						
Lg#EMP	−0.0954	0.3782	0.8009	0.0982	0.2666	0.7125	0.0872	0.2678	0.7446
ROEm1							0.1701	0.3107	0.5840
Concordant%		81.9			82			81.9	
Discordant%		17.9			17.9			18	
McFadden's Pseudo R^2 (%)		26.67			26.36			26.53	

*indicates significance at >.05.

high positive coefficient and strong statistical significance of the non-North American sales variable. It is consistent with the findings of Cetindamar and Husoy (2007) that firms join UNGC for the economic benefits of competing in global markets, as well as the notion that the UNGC is more highly valued outside the U.S., a pattern mentioned by Janney, Dess, and Forlani (2009, 412): "Many firms (especially those with US-based headquarters) saw the UNGC as more of a burden than a benefit." This outcome is both consistent with the findings of Janney, Dess, and

Forlani (2009), and extends their study. They found that North American firms were less likely than European firms to become UNGC members; we demonstrate that membership likelihood increases with the percent of sales located outside of North America.

Our fourth hypothesis is also supported. Membership likelihood increases with the prevalence of environmental concerns. The Environmental Concern measure (CON-ENV) is positive and significant; that is, higher values of environmental concerns make taking the action to become a member more likely. Some have speculated that this is not based on altruism but on a desire to present a positive image to combat the perception that a firm is a bad actor based on its environmental record. Below we test whether joining UNGC reflects a change in CSR performance or is indeed merely an unethical attempt to influence perception.

The size control variable (LgASSETS), the log of assets, is negative and significant, a finding consistent with a theory that larger firms are less likely to perceive a benefit from membership. Because the sample for this study was created using a method where the size of sales for UNGC signatories was approximately equal to that of non-signatory firms, the finding that size matters seems a contradiction. The cause of this statistical outcome is seen in the difference between the sales-to-asset ratio for the two subsets of the sample. The average sales-to-asset ratio of UNGC firms is 94 percent; the average for non-UNGC firms sampled is 77 percent. To determine whether this finding is a sampling anomaly requires a larger sample, something not possible with the current UNGC members as defined by our sample. No other control or concern variables considered helped predict the likelihood of UNGC membership.

Having found that UNGC signatories have a history of poor CSR performance, we next test Hypothesis 5 to see whether their performance improves after joining UNGC. Using the same methodology described above, we analyze the number of environmental strengths, environmental concerns, social strengths, and social concerns. Our findings are consistent with Berliner and Prakash (2015), as we find that UNGC signatories improve their strengths in the period after signing but show less improvement in alleviating concerns. Table 8 shows the results of testing for significance of the changes prior to and after signing. The cumulative mean of environmental strengths increased significantly after signing (p=.014) as did the cumulative mean of social strengths, but only at a 90 percent confidence level (p=.080). Mean values associated with environmental concerns decreased and social concerns increased, but the differences are not statistically different from zero.

Similarly, we analyze the number of environmental strengths, environmental concerns, social strengths, and social concerns for the six years after signing on to UNGC (or the year of matching). Figure 3 graphs the mean changes in environmental and social strengths over the six years following joining UNGC, along with the net average changes in these categories (i.e., netting changes in strengths and concerns).

We find these results supportive of Hypothesis 5, that companies improve their CSR performance after joining the UNGC. These findings are also consistent with Berliner and Prakash (2015), who find that U.S. firms increase CSR performance in areas of strength after signing.

Discussion

Summary of the findings

Our most significant finding is the association between firms' joining the UNGC and the percentage of their sales outside of North America. We interpret this result as an indication that joining UNGC may result from a desire to impress customers in countries that do value membership, as suggested anecdotally by Ziegler (2007), and may accordingly yield economic benefits. This finding warrants further research as to whether it is region-specific, resulting from concentration of sales in countries with very strong investment in UNGC membership, such as Europe. There may

Table 8. Test of changes in firm performance after signing the UNGC.

	Environmental		Social	
	Strengths	Concerns	Strengths	Concerns
t−3 Average	2.500	2.242	3.339	3.581
t−3 Std.Dev	2.804	3.318	3.019	4.091
t−3 Count	62	62	62	62
t+3 Average	3.811	2.075	4.415	4.547
t+3 Std.Dev	3.181	3.368	3.875	4.762
t+3 Count	67	67	67	67
Mean difference	1.3113	−0.1665	1.0764	0.9665
SD of mean diff	0.5271	0.5889	0.6092	0.7800
T-statistic	2.4880	−0.2827	1.7669	1.2391
p Value	0.014**	0.778	0.080*	0.218

t−3 represents the totals for KLD variables for the three years prior to signing on to UNGC.
t+3 represents the totals for KLD variables for the three years after signing on to UNGC.
62 firms have three years of data prior to signing; 67 firms have 3 years of data after signing.

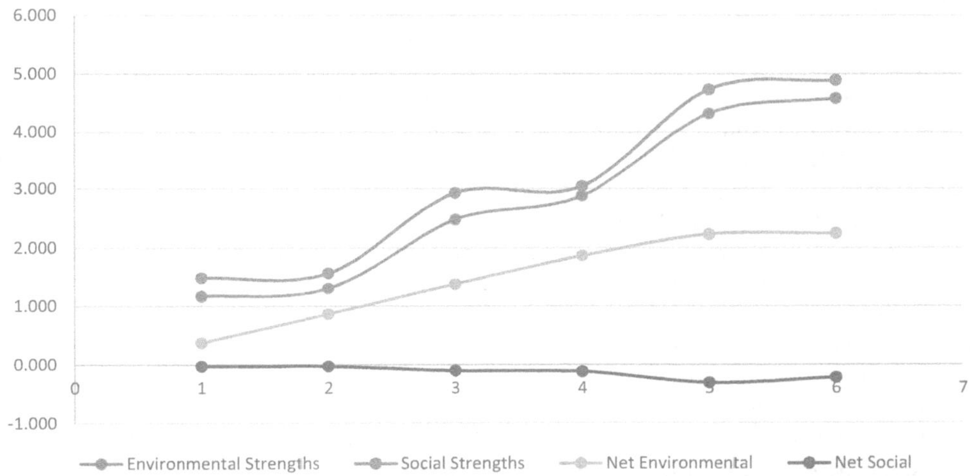

Figure 3. Average strengths and net strengths, by year after becoming a UNGC signatory. Data points represent the mean of each KLD variable for the years (horizontal axis) following signing on to UNGC. Net values are mean Strengths less mean Concerns for each year.

be other significant related factors, like the location of subsidiaries or concentration of customers, which might be important to the decision to join UNGC.

Our finding that a new CEO is more likely to sign onto the UNGC empirically validates the survey of Cetindamar and Husoy (2007), suggesting that a new CEO may strive to improve corporate image, to promote or initiate a program of CSR, or to increase employee satisfaction. Further research is needed into other possible leadership characteristics that might influence UNGC participation. Characteristics suggested by Bamber, Jiang, and Wang (2010), such as MBA training or the functional track of the CEO, might have a positive impact. Whether the motivation is solely ethical (to be a good corporate citizen, to promote or initiate a program of CSR), or whether it is primarily economic (to improve global business), or both, is unclear.

Our findings also support the suggestion made by previous researchers (Berliner and Prakash, 2015; Sethi and Schepers, 2014) that poorer performing firms on CSR matters, at least regarding environmental issues, may join the UNGC to gain reputation effects. However, we find that the U.S. UNGC signatories did not, as Sethi and Schepers (2014) suggest, merely join UNGC for the reputational effects and then ignore the CSR issues, in that they have shown some improvement, especially in environmental matters, over the subsequent years. However, like Berliner and Prakash (2015), we find demonstrated growth in environmental and social strengths but slower movement in alleviating concerns. We must concur with their conclusion that U.S. firms are slow to address the costly remediation in areas of concern.

Implications for research and practice

This study provides empirical evidence for the model proposed by Haack, Martignoni, and Schoeneborn (2020). In part, their model suggests that CSR can be adopted ceremonially under conditions of opacity and evolve to substantive adoption over time as transparency increases. The UNGC provides an ideal setting for testing this proposition. It is a globally well-known CSR initiative, and organizations must announce joining. Regardless of the motivations, it is therefore a ceremonial CSR adoption. There are low barriers to entry and little monitoring, providing opacity. Since its inception, there has been an ongoing debate among researchers regarding its efficacy. One school (Rizvi 2004; Sethi and Schepers 2014; Utting 2007; Williams 2004) holds that the motivation for joining UNGC is merely to improve the organization's reputation, and the easy entry and opacity provide no reason for growth and substantive (possibly costly) implementation of CSR policies. The opposing school (Kell and Levin 2003; Palazzo and Scherer 2010; Rasche 2009) believes that the low barriers to entry make it possible for organizations, some with lower CSR performance and fewer resources, to affiliate themselves with a well-organized vehicle for organizational learning, so that they will be able to improve CSR performance. This study, which finds that firms that join UNGC are poorer CSR performers than their counterparts, also shows that those firms improve their CSR performance after joining UNGC. Schembera (2018) shows that improved performance on CSR issues is positively associated with duration of UNGC participation. Further study is needed to demonstrate whether the CSR performance of U.S. firms continues to improve over longer periods of time after joining UNGC.

Haack, Martignoni, and Schoeneborn (2020) point out that it may take time for a ceremonial adoption of CSR to develop into a substantive adoption, and they suggest allowing for continued opacity during "a stage of transformation" so that organizations do not abandon CSR practices (32). Besides mustering resources, organizational learning during this duration would be essential, especially since there is an indication that firms that are lower performers in CSR join. The UNGC is organized to foster local networks, where organizations can connect with other organizations and share best practices to improve their performance. However, an internal organizational learning process, clearly linked to this strategic priority, would be essential. It is possible that organizations, especially under-resourced ones, may not have mechanisms in place to channel organizational learning.

Crossan, Lane, and White (1999) noted the importance of managerial capability to balance internal processes of the organization to promote organizational learning. When a newly-appointed CEO aligns with UNGC, as our study finds, and has the purpose of joining ceremoniously to initiate or promote a CSR agenda at the firm, that CEO would need to ensure that the management team is on board with the initiative and is proficient in rolling out the organizational learning process. While Crossan and Berdrow (2003) study the change at an organization where "one individual was able to move intuitive insights through interpretation, integration, and institutionalization without much assistance from others" (1102), partly because of his senior position, they find it unusual, sometimes resulting in changes in behavior but not changes in thinking, suggesting a "fragile" state of organizational learning (1098). Moving to a substantive adoption of CSR practices requires a change in behavior certainly, but would also require a change in interpretation and integration into the firm's culture. Importantly, CSR practices would have to be institutionalized to ensure their continuity.

While this study supports the group of researchers who endorse UNGC's efficacy because they view it as an opportunity for organizational learning and, Ultimately, for substantive adoption of CSR practices in the model of transitory opacity presented by Haack, Martignoni, and Schoeneborn (2020), we echo their concern that organizations may not be afforded the time needed to fully develop substantive CSR practices. In this digital age, transparency seems to be the new norm, and the time allowed for organizational learning may be very short. As Cousins (2018) points out, "volatility, uncertainty, complexity and ambiguity, the acronym VUCA, has come to define the digital economy as highly disruptive environment and potentially punitive to incrementally focused organizations" (1). Strong leadership and a unified management team will probably be essential to move their organizations beyond slow, incremental progress.

Limitations of the study and proposals for future research

This study is limited by the narrow scope of its focus. For operational reasons, our empirical tests were based on publicly-held U.S. companies because of the availability of information about their leadership and CSR performance through KLD. The UNGC has a range of other participants: privately-held companies, small to medium size companies, not-for-profit organizations, NGOs, governmental agencies, even universities. Their motivations for joining the UNGC would differ, although reputation, if not economics, might still apply.

Haack, Martignoni, and Schoeneborn (2020) suggest that the motives for ceremonial adoption might profoundly affect the substantive adoption. While we find that U.S. firms with significant non-U.S. business are more likely to join UNGC, we cannot disentangle whether their motives are hypocritical or opportunistic. Likewise, it is unclear from our findings whether new CEOs adopt UNGC for reputational effects to improve business or to drive a CSR initiative, or both. We agree that future research examining motivations for ceremonial adoption of CSR, like joining UNGC, would shed light on the potential for substantive adoption.

Although researchers have explored organizational learning for over fifty years (Fiol and Lyles 1985), there still seems to be considerable variation in how it manifests itself in organizations and how it can be used purposefully to promote change. The framework presented by Crossan, Lane, and White (1999) and the investigation of its application to a particular organization (Crossan and Berdrow 2003), are advantageous in offering some applications for practice. Further directed studies might be useful to practitioners, especially those like new UNGC signatories, who need to implement organizational change quickly and may have limited resources.

Notes

1. AGE represents the age of the firm from its Initial Public Offering; LOGEMP is a size measure based on the log of the number of employees at the time the firm joined the global compact; and DSALES is also a size measure operationalized as a dichotomous variable split at the median sales volume for firms in the sample.
2. We were unable to find useful firm age data – for example, the firms considered include Ford, incorporated in 1903, but along with other auto companies it instituted large structural changes in 2008; one could reasonably argue that it is faulty to characterize Ford as a 115-year-old firm.
3. The choice of Logit or Probit for estimating a dichotomous dependent variable model is largely one of preference; the results rarely differ. The Logit model assumes the random error of the model is distributed following a logistic probability distribution; Probit assumes the error is normally distributed, while the logistic is somewhat thicker in the tails (see, for instance, http://visionlab.harvard.edu/Members/Anne/Math/Logistic_vs_Gaussian.html).
4. A variance inflation factor analysis was performed and, while none were very high, the VIF for sales, 7.8, was of sufficient concern that we produced Model II.

ORCID

Cynthia Phillips http://orcid.org/0000-0002-5201-6245

References

Arya, B., and G. Zhang. 2009. "Institutional Reforms and Investor Reactions to CSR Announcements: Evidence from an Emerging Economy." *Journal of Management Studies* 46 (7):1089–1112. doi: 10.1111/j.1467-6486.2009.00836.x.

Aupperle, K., A. Carroll, and J. Hatfield. 1985. "An Empirical Examination of the Relationship between Corporate Social Responsibility and Profitability." *Academy of Management Journal* 28 (2):446–463.

Bamber, L., J. Jiang, and I. Wang. 2010. "What's My Style? The Influence of Top Managers on Voluntary Corporate Financial Disclosure." *The Accounting Review* 85 (4):1131–1162. doi: 10.2308/accr.2010.85.4.1131.

Bayoud, N. S., and M. Kavanagh. 2012. "Corporate Social Responsibility Disclosure: Evidence from Lyban Managers." *Global Journal of Business Research* 6 (5):73–83.

Berliner, D., and A. Prakash. 2015. "Blue Washing the Firm? Voluntary Regulations, Program Design and Member Compliance with the United Nations Global Compact." *Policy Studies Journal* 43 (1):115–38. doi: 10.1111/psj.12085.

Brammer, S. J., and S. Pavelin. 2004. "Building a Good Reputation." *European Management Journal* 22 (6): 704–713. doi: 10.1016/j.emj.2004.09.033.

Bremmer, J. 2008. "How Global is the Global Compact?" *Business Ethics: A European Review* 17 (3):227–244.

Carroll, A. B. 1999. "Corporate Social Responsibility: Evolution of a Definitional Construct." *Business & Society* 38 (3):268–295. doi: 10.1177/000765039903800303.

Cetindamar, D., and K. Husoy. 2007. "Corporate Social Responsibility Practices and Environmentally Responsible Behavior: The Case of the United Nations Global Compact." *Journal of Business Ethics* 76 (2):163–176. doi: 10.1007/s10551-006-9265-4.

Chatterji, A., D. Levine, and M. Toffel. 2009. "How Well Do Social Ratings Actually Measure Corporate Social Responsibility?" *Journal of Economics & Management Strategy* 18 (1):125–169. doi: 10.1111/j.1530-9134.2009.00210.x.

Cousins, B. 2018. "Design Thinking: Organizational Learning in VUCA Environments." *Academy of Strategic Management Journal* 17 (2) Online ISSN: 1939–6104.

Crossan, M., and I. Berdrow. 2003. "Organizational Learning and Strategic Renewal." *Strategic Management Journal* 24 (11):1087–1105. doi: 10.1002/smj.342.

Crossan, M., H. Lane, and R. White. 1999. "An Organizational Learning Framework: From Intuition to Institution." *Academy of Management Review* 24 (3):522–537. doi: 10.5465/amr.1999.2202135.

Deva, S. 2006. "Global Compact: A Critique of the U.N.'S 'Public-Private' Partnership for Promoting Corporate Citizenship." *Syracuse Journal of International Law and Commerce* 34 (1):107–151.

Drumwright, M. E. 1994. "Socially Responsible Organizational Buying: Environmental Concern as a Noneconomic Buying Criterion." *Journal of Marketing* 58 (3):1–19. doi: 10.2307/1252307.

Fineman, S., and K. Clarke. 1996. "Green Stakeholders: Industry Interpretations and Response." *Journal of Management Studies* 33 (6):715–731. doi: 10.1111/j.1467-6486.1996.tb00169.x.

Fiol, C. M., and M. Lyles. 1985. "Organizational Learning." *Academy of Management Review* 10 (4):803–813. doi: 10.5465/amr.1985.4279103.

Fombrun, C., N. Gardberg, and M. Barnett. 2000. “Opportunity Platforms and Safety Nets: Corporate Citizenship and Reputational Risk.” *Business and Society Review* 105 (1):85–106. doi: 10.1111/0045-3609.00066.

Garza, C. 2013. “U.S. Companies Drag Their Feet on UN Global Compact. ISOS Group.” http://www.triplepundit.com/2013/05/companies-dragging-feet-sign-global-compact/.

Governance and Accountability Institute (GAI). 2018. *Companies publish sustainability reports in 2017.* https://www.ga-institute.com/press-releases/article/flash-report-85-of-sp-500-indexR-companies-publish-sustainability-reports-in-2017.html.

Haack, P., D. Martignoni, and D Schoeneborn. 2020. “A Bait-And-Switch Model of Corporate Social Responsibility.” *The Academy of Management Review* doi: 10.5465/amr.2018.0139.

Haack, P., and A. G. Scherer. 2014. “Why Sparing the Rod Does Not Spoil the Child: A Critique of the ‘Strict Father’ Model in Transnational Governance.” *Journal of Business Ethics* 122 (2):225–240. doi: 10.1007/s10551-014-2218-4.

Hemingway, C. A., and P. W. Maclagan. 2004. “Managers’ Personal Values as Drivers of Corporate Social Responsibility.” *Journal of Business Ethics* 50 (1):33–44. doi: 10.1023/B:BUSI.0000020964.80208.c9.

Hillman, A., and G. Keim. 2001. “Shareholder Value, Stakeholder Management, and Social Issues: What’s the Bottom Line?” *Strategic Management Journal* 22 (2):125–139. doi: 10.1002/1097-0266(200101)22:2<125::AID-SMJ150>3.0.CO;2-H.

Hoessle, U. 2015. “US Companies and the Implementation of the UN Global Compact’s Principles.” Journal of Corporate Citizenship 2015 (59):9–36.

Janney, J., G. Dess, and V. Forlani. 2009. “Glass Houses? Market Reactions to Firms Joining the UN Global Compact.” *Journal of Business Ethics* 90 (3):407–423. doi: 10.1007/s10551-009-0052-x.

Jensen, M. 2001. “Value Maximization, Stakeholder Theory, and the Corporate Objective Function.” *Journal of Applied Corporate Finance* 14 (3):8–21. doi: 10.1111/j.1745-6622.2001.tb00434.x.

Jones, T. M. 1995. “Instrumental Stakeholder Theory: A Synthesis of Ethics and Economics.” *Academy of Management Review* 20 (2):404–437. doi: 10.5465/amr.1995.9507312924.

Kang, J. 2015. “Effectiveness of the KLD Social Ratings as a Measure of Workforce Diversity and Corporate Governance.” *Business & Society* 54 (5):599–631. doi: 10.1177/0007650312461602.

Kell, G. 2012. “12 Years Later: Reflections on the Growth of the UN Global Compact.” *Business & Society* 52 (1):31–52.

Kell, G., and D. Levin. 2003. “The Global Compact Network: An Historic Experiment in Learning and Action.” *Business and Society Review* 108 (2):151–181. doi: 10.1111/1467-8594.00159.

Malik, M. 2015. “Value-Enhancing Capabilities of CSR: A Brief Review of Contemporary Literature.” *Journal of Business Ethics* 127 (2):419–438. doi: 10.1007/s10551-014-2051-9.

Margolis, J. D., H. A. Elfenbein, J. P. Walsh. 2009. “Does it Pay to Be Good ... And Does it Matter? A Meta-Analysis of the Relationship Between Corporate Social and Financial Performance.” SSRN: https://ssrn.com/abstract=1866371.

McWilliams, A., and D. Siegel. 2000. “Corporate Social Responsibility and Financial Performance: Correlation or Misspecification?” *Strategic Management Journal* 21 (5):603–609. doi: 10.1002/(SICI)1097-0266(200005)21:5<603::AID-SMJ101>3.0.CO;2-3.

Mele, D. 2002. *Not Only Stakeholder Interests. The Firm Oriented toward the Common Good.* Notre Dame, IL: University of Notre Dame Press.

Menon, A., and A. Menon. 1997. “Enviropreneurial Marketing Strategy: The Emergence of Corporate Environmentalism as Market Strategy.” *Journal of Marketing* 61 (1):51–67. doi: 10.2307/1252189.

Mishra, S., and D. Suar. 2010. “Does Corporate Social Responsibility Influence Firm Performance of Indian Companies?” *Journal of Business Ethics* 95 (4):571–601. doi: 10.1007/s10551-010-0441-1.

Mosley, D., P. H. Pietri, and L. C. Megginson. 1996. *Management: Leadership in Action.* New York, NY: Harper Collins.

Nolan, J. 2005. “The United Nations’ Compact with Business: Hindering or Helping the Protection of Human Rights?” *University of Queensland Law Journal* 24 (2):445–466.

Orlitzky, M., F. Schmidt, and S. Rynes. 2003. “Corporate Social and Financial Performance: A Meta-Analysis.” *Organization Studies* 24 (3):403–41. doi: 10.1177/0170840603024003910.

Palazzo, G., and A. G. Scherer. 2010. “The United Nations Global Compact as a Learning Approach.” In *The United Nations Global Compact: Achievements, Trends and Challenges*, edited by A. Rasche and G. Kell, 234–247. Cambridge: Cambridge University Press.

Perez-Batres, L., V. Miller, and M. Pisani. 2011. “Institutionalizing Sustainability: An Empirical Study of Corporate Registration and Commitment to the United Nations Global Compact Guidelines.” *Journal of Cleaner Production* 19 (8):843–851. doi: 10.1016/j.jclepro.2010.06.003.

Porter, M. E., and M. R. Kramer. 1999. “Philanthropy’s New Agenda: Creating Value.” *Harvard Business Review* 77 (6):121–131.

Porter, M. E., and M. R. Kramer. 2002. "The Competitive Advantage of Corporate Philanthropy." *Harvard Business Review* 80 (12):56–69.

Rao, H. 1994. "The Social Construction of Reputation: Certification Contests, Legitimation, and the Survival of Organizations in the American Automobile Industry: 1895–1912." *Strategic Management Journal* 15 (S1):29–44. doi: 10.1002/smj.4250150904.

Rasche, A. 2009. "A Necessary Supplement: What the United Nations Global Compact is and is Not." *Business & Society* 48 (4):511–537. doi: 10.1177/0007650309332378.

Rasche, A., S. Waddock, and M. McIntosh. 2013. "The United Nations Global Compact: Retrospect and Prospect." *Business & Society* 52 (1):6–30. doi: 10.1177/0007650312459999.

Rasche, A., and S. Waddock. 2014. "Global Sustainability Governance and the UN Global Compact: A Rejoinder to Critics." *Journal of Business Ethics* 122 (2):209–216. doi: 10.1007/s10551-014-2216-6.

Rizvi, H. 2004. "UN Pact With Business Lacks Accountability." Global Policy Forum. https://www.globalpolicy.org/component/content/article/225/32254.html.

Robinson, M., A. Kleffner, and S. Bertels. 2011. "Signaling Sustainability Leadership: Empirical Evidence of the Value of DJSI Membership." *Journal of Business Ethics* 101 (3):493–505. doi: 10.1007/s10551-011-0735-y.

Schembera, S. 2018. "Implementing Corporate Social Responsibility: Empirical Insights on the Impact of the UN Global Compact on Its Business Participants." *Business & Society* 57 (5):783–743. doi: 10.1177/0007650316635579.

Sethi, S. P., and D. H. Schepers. 2014. "United Nations Global Compact: The Promise-Performance Gap." *Journal of Business Ethics* 122 (2):193–208. doi: 10.1007/s10551-013-1629-y.

Smith, N.C. 2003. "Corporate Social Responsibility: Whether or How?" *California Management Review* 45 (4): 52–76. doi: 10.2307/41166188.

Swanson, D. L. 1995. "Addressing a Theoretical Problem by Reorienting the Corporate Social Performance Model." *Academy of Management Review* 20 (1):43–64. doi: 10.5465/amr.1995.9503271990.]

United Nations Global Compact Headquarters. 2015. Activity Report. https://www.unglobalcompact.org/docs/publications/UNGC_2015_Activity_Report.pdf.

Utting, P. 2007. "CSR and Equality." *Third World Quarterly* 28 (4):697–712. doi: 10.1080/01436590701336572.

Waddock, S., and S. Graves. 1997. "The Corporate Social Performance-Financial Performance Link." *Strategic Management Journal* 18 (4):303–319. doi: 10.1002/(SICI)1097-0266(199704)18:4<303::AID-SMJ869>3.0.CO;2-G.

Williams, O. 2004. "The UN Global Compact: The Challenge and the Promise." *Business Ethics Quarterly* 14 (4): 755–774. doi: 10.5840/beq200414432.

Wilson, D. 2002, January 16. "This Juvenile Posturing Is For Punks." *The Guardian*, 8.

Wood, D. L. 1991. "Corporate Social Performance Revisited." *Academy of Management Review* 16 (4):691–718. doi: 10.5465/amr.1991.4279616.

Zerbini, F. 2017. "CSR Initiatives as Market Signals: A Review and Research Agenda." *Journal of Business Ethics* 146 (1):1–23. doi: 10.1007/s10551-015-2922-8.

Ziegler, O. 2007. "Global Compact Membership in Europe and the US, a Case Study of the Automobile Industry." *Journal of Corporate Citizenship* 2007 (26):53–68.

Appendix A

The ten principles of the UN Global Compact

Human rights

- Principle 1: Businesses should support and respect the protection of internationally proclaimed human rights
- Principle 2: Make sure that they are not complicit in human rights abuses

Labor

- Principle 3: Businesses should uphold the freedom of association and the effective recognition of the right to collective bargaining
- Principle 4: The elimination of all forms of forced and compulsory labor
- Principle 5: The effective abolition of child labor
- Principle 6: The elimination of discrimination in respect of employment and occupation

Environment

- Principle 7: Businesses should support a precautionary approach to environmental challenges
- Principle 8: Undertake initiatives to promote greater environmental responsibility
- Principle 9: Encourage the development and diffusion of environmentally friendly technologies

Anti-corruption

- Principle 10: Businesses should work against corruption in all its forms, including extortion and bribery

Appendix B

Panel A: U.S. Companies in the sample that joined UNGC 2000–2015.

Firm	Ticker	Year joined	Revenues (in $ millions)	NAICS sector code	Sector/Industry
ABM Industries Inc.	ABM	2011	4,246.8	56	Waste Mgmt, Remediation
AECOM Technology Corp.	ACM	2012	8,218.2	54	Prof., Scientific, Tech. Svcs.
Autodesk, Inc.	ADSK	2009	1,713.7	51	Information
Allergan	AGN	2002	1,223.2	31-33	Manufacturing
Hess Corp.	AHC	2013	366.3	51	Information
Arthur J. Gallagher & Co.	AJG	2011	2,134.2	52	Finance and Insurance
Arrow Electronics, Inc.	ARW	2012	20,405.1	42	Wholesale Trade
Anixter Intl.	AXE	2015	6,190.5	42	Wholesale Trade
Bunge Limited	BG	2010	45,707.0	31-33	Manufacturing
Bristol-Myers Squibb	BMY	2010	19,484.0	31-33	Manufacturing
Citi	C	2007	157,333.0	52	Finance and Insurance
CA Technologies	CA	2008	4,271.0	51	Information
CBRE Group, Inc.	CBG	2007	6,034.2	53	Real Estate, Rental, Leasing
Cabot Corp.	CBT	2015	2,871.0	31-33	Manufacturing
Cigna Corp.	CI	2006	16,547.0	52	Finance and Insurance
The Clorox Company	CLX	2015	5,655.0	31-33	Manufacturing
Campbell Soup Company	CPB	2009	7,586.0	31-33	Manufacturing
Cisco Systems	CSCO	2001	22,293.0	31-33	Manufacturing
DuPont	DD	2001	25,106.0	31-33	Manufacturing
Ecolab Inc.	ECL	2012	11,838.7	31-33	Manufacturing
Eastman Chemical Company	EMN	2014	9,527.0	31-33	Manufacturing
Ford Motor Company	F	2008	146,277.0	31-33	Manufacturing
Fluor Corp.	FLR	2010	20,849.3	23	Construction
FMC Corp.	FMC	2015	3,276.5	31-33	Manufacturing
General Electric Company	GE	2008	180,929.0	31-33	Manufacturing
General Mills	GIS	2008	14,691.3	31-33	Manufacturing
General Motors Company	GM	2015	152,356.0	31-33	Manufacturing
Keurig Green Mountain, Inc.	GMCR	2004	137.4	31-33	Manufacturing
Gap Inc.	GPS	2003	15,854.0	44-45	Retail Trade
Harman Intl. Industries, Inc.	HAR	2012	4,364.1	31-33	Manufacturing
Huntsman Corp.	HUN	2011	11,221.0	31-33	Manufacturing
Intl. Flavors & Fragrances Inc.	IFF	2015	3,023.2	31-33	Manufacturing
Intel Corp.	INTC	2009	35,127.0	31-33	Manufacturing
Interpublic Group	IPG	2015	7,613.8	54	Prof., Scientific, Tech. Svcs.
Johnson Controls Inc.	JCI	2004	26,553.4	31-33	Manufacturing
JLL	JLL	2009	2,480.7	53	Real Estate, Rental, Leasing
Johnson & Johnson	JNJ	2013	71,312.0	31-33	Manufacturing
Kimberly - Clark Corp.	KMB	2010	19,746.0	31-33	Manufacturing
The Coca-Cola Company	KO	2006	24,088.0	31-33	Manufacturing
Eli Lilly and Company	LLY	2009	21,836.0	31-33	Manufacturing
Lexmark Intl. Inc.	LXK	2008	4,528.4	31-33	Manufacturing
ManpowerGroup	MAN	2006	17,562.5	56	Waste Mgmt, Remediation
Microchip Technology Inc.	MCHP	2013	1,931.2	31-33	Manufacturing
3M	MMM	2014	31,821.0	31-33	Manufacturing
Monsanto Company	MON	2009	11,724.0	31-33	Manufacturing
Mosaic	MOS	2012	9,974.1	31-33	Manufacturing
Merck & Co., Inc.	MRK	2009	27,428.3	31-33	Manufacturing
Microsoft Corp.	MSFT	2006	44,282.0	51	Information
The NASDAQ OMX Group	NDAQ	2012	3,108.0	52	Finance and Insurance
Newmont Mining Corp.	NEM	2004	4,590.0	21	Mining, Oil & Gas Extract.
NIKE Inc.	NKE	2000	9,488.8	31-33	Manufacturing
Owens Corning	OC	2010	4,997.0	31-33	Manufacturing
PepsiCo Inc.	PEP	2008	43,251.0	31-33	Manufacturing
Pfizer Inc.	PFE	2002	32,373.0	31-33	Manufacturing
Qualcomm Inc.	QCOM	2013	24,866.0	31-33	Manufacturing
Starbucks Corp.	SBUX	2004	5,294.2	72	Accom. & Food Services
Steelcase	SCS	2009	2,291.7	31-33	Manufacturing
State Street Corp.	STT	2014	10,687.0	52	Finance and Insurance
Symantec Corp.	SYMC	2006	5,199.4	51	Information
Molson Coors Brewing Co.	TAP	2009	3,032.4	31-33	Manufacturing
Teradata Corp.	TDC	2011	2,379.0	31-33	Manufacturing
Tiffany & Co.	TIF	2011	3,642.9	44-45	Retail Trade

Revenues are total revenues for the year of signing on to UNGC as reported on COMPUSTAT. NAICS codes for each firm are taken from COMPUSTAT and replaced by NAICS Sectors, available at www.naics.com.

Panel B: U.S. Companies in the matched sample that did not join UNGC 2000–2015.

Firm	Ticker	Year Joined	Revenues (in $ millions)	NAICS sector code	Sector/Industry
Apple Inc.	AAPL	2015	233,715.0	31-33	Manufacturing
Analog Devices	ADI	2006	2,573.2	31-33	Manufacturing
Archer-Daniels-Midland Co	ADM	2009	69,198.0	31-33	Manufacturing
Aetna Inc.	AET	2014	58,003.2	52	Finance and Insurance
Apartment Invst. & Mgmt. Co	AIV	2008	1,470.4	53	Real Estate, Rental, Leasing
Akamai Technologies Inc.	AKAM	2007	636.4	31-33	Manufacturing
Amgen Inc.	AMGN	2009	14,642.0	31-33	Manufacturing
Anadarko Petroleum Corp.	APC	2001	8,369.0	21	Mining, Oil & Gas Extract.
Avalonbay Communities Inc.	AVB	2011	973.8	53	Real Estate, Rental, Leasing
Crown Castle Intl. Corp.	CCI	2015	3,663.9	23	Construction
Colgate-Palmolive Co	CL	2004	10,584.2	31-33	Manufacturing
Comcast Corp.	CMCSA	2015	74,510.0	51	Information
CME Group Inc.	CME	2011	3,270.8	52	Finance and Insurance
Capital One Financial Corp.	COF	2015	25,038.0	52	Finance and Insurance
Cognizant Tech Solutions	CTSH	2015	12,416.0	31-33	Manufacturing
CVS Health Corp.	CVS	2009	98,729.0	44-45	Retail Trade
Dover Corp.	DOV	2015	6,956.3	31-33	Manufacturing
Devon Energy Corp.	DVN	2013	10,397.0	21	Mining, Oil & Gas Extract.
Equifax Inc.	EFX	2008	1,935.7	56	Waste Mgmt, Remediation
Equinix Inc.	EQIX	2010	1,220.3	48-49	Transp. & Warehousing
Express Scripts Holding Co	ESRX	2009	24,758.4	44-45	Retail Trade
Essex Property Trust	ESS	2007	402.0	53	Real Estate, Rental, Leasing
Extra Space Storage Inc.	EXR	2010	294.0	52	Finance and Insurance
FEDX Corp.	FDX	2000	19,629.0	48-49	Transp. & Warehousing
First Solar Inc.	FSLR	2012	3,368.5	31-33	Manufacturing
TechnipFMC Plc.	FTI	2006	9,250.7	21	Mining, Oil & Gas Extract.
Garmin Ltd.	GRMN	2013	2,631.9	31-33	Manufacturing
Goldman Sachs	GS	2011	36,793.0	52	Finance and Insurance
Halliburton Co.	HAL	2006	22,504.0	21	Mining, Oil & Gas Extract.
Home Depot Inc.	HD	2004	73,094.0	44-45	Retail Trade
Hologic Inc.	HOLX	2009	1,637.1	31-33	Manufacturing
Helmerich & Payne	HP	2001	815.2	21	Mining, Oil & Gas Extract.
Block H & R Inc.	HRB	2014	3,078.7	52	Finance and Insurance
Humana Inc.	HUM	2002	11,280.8	62	Health Care, Social Asst.
JPMorgan Chase & Co.	JPM	2008	101,491.0	52	Finance and Insurance
Kimco Realty Corp.	KIM	2015	1,725.3	53	Real Estate, Rental, Leasing
Kroger Co	KR	2008	76,000.0	44-45	Retail Trade
Kohl's Corp.	KSS	2010	18,391.0	44-45	Retail Trade
Lowe's Companies Inc.	LOW	2009	48,230.0	44-45	Retail Trade
Medtronic Plc.	MDT	2009	15,835.0	31-33	Manufacturing
McCormick & Co., Inc.	MKC	2010	3,336.8	31-33	Manufacturing
Morgan Stanley	MS	2014	37,661.0	55	Mgmt. of Co./Enterprise
Northrop Grumman Corp.	NOC	2013	24,661.0	31-33	Manufacturing
Netapp Inc.	NTAP	2009	3,931.4	31-33	Manufacturing
Procter & Gamble Co.	PG	2012	83,680.0	31-33	Manufacturing
Public Storage	PSA	2008	1,766.0	52	Finance and Insurance
Robert Half Intl. Inc.	RHI	2004	2,675.7	56	Waste Mgmt, Remediation
Red Hat Inc.	RHT	2011	1,133.8	51	Information
Rockwell Automation	ROK	2006	5,561.4	31-33	Manufacturing
Raytheon Co	RTN	2012	24,414.0	31-33	Manufacturing
Constellation Brands	STZ	2004	4,087.6	31-33	Manufacturing
Stryker Corp.	SYK	2002	3,011.6	31-33	Manufacturing
Torchmark Corp.	TMK	2009	3,222.4	52	Finance and Insurance
Price (T. Rowe) Group	TROW	2011	2,750.2	52	Finance and Insurance
Total System Services Inc.	TSS	2012	1,871.0	52	Finance and Insurance
Texas Instruments Inc.	TXN	2012	12,690.0	31-33	Manufacturing
Textron Inc.	TXT	2010	10,525.0	31-33	Manufacturing
United Technologies Corp.	UTX	2003	31,059.0	31-33	Manufacturing
Viacom Inc.	VIAB	2013	13,794.0	51	Information
Wynn Resorts Ltd.	WYNN	2006	1,432.3	71	Arts, Entertainmt, Recreat.
Xerox Corp.	XRX	2008	17,608.0	31-33	Manufacturing
Zions Bancorporation	ZION	2012	2,458.6	52	Finance and Insurance

Revenues are total revenues for the year of signing on to UNGC as reported on COMPUSTAT. NAICS codes for each firm are taken from COMPUSTAT and replaced by NAICS Sectors, available at www.naics.com.

Calculation, principle or bias? Information preference and ethical decision-making

Regina Bento, Lasse Mertins and Lourdes F. White

ABSTRACT
This study proposes a novel information preference perspective to integrate ethics, managerial decision-making and risk. It argues that individuals confronting complex decisions, which involve risk, tend to process the available information through filters that reflect different ethical frames. We used an experiment where participants were asked to play the role of the co-owner of a car racing company who had to decide whether to run a crucial race, under various kinds of potential risk. The results revealed three key findings. First, participants had indeed filtered the information they received, with significant differences not only in what they considered most important, but also what they saw as least important. Moreover, factor analysis revealed that such individual filtering had configured three distinct patterns of preferences and that there was an internal logic to these patterns, characterizing what we called "Patterns in Information Preference (PIPs): "Expected Value", "Responsibility" and "Autopilot." Second, the PIPs that emerged from participants' filtering processes reflected different ethical approaches to decision-making under conditions of risk (utilitarian, deontological and psychological), as the filtering favored information that supported an ethical approach over the others and discounted information not aligned with that particular approach. Third, participants' PIPs influenced the decisions they made (and thus their respective potential ethical implications): we found that the "Responsibility" PIP had a significant association with the decision to forfeit the car race, whereas the "Autopilot" PIP was significantly associated with the decision to run. We discuss these findings from the perspective of descriptive and normative ethics, examine the limitations of the study, and explore implications and directions for future research.

Introduction

In the last ten years there has been an increasing realization of the importance of studying ethical issues in decision-making under conditions of risk (Campbell 2015; Lewens 2007; Petrick 2011; Scharding 2015; Scordis 2011; Wehinger 2013; Young and Hasler 2010). This realization reflects the ongoing turbulence associated with the "Volatility, Uncertainty, Complexity and Ambiguity" (VUCA) characteristic of the managerial environment (Bennett and Lemoine 2014), and it has been strengthened by events such as the 2007–2009 U.S. financial crisis and its aftermath

Submitted to *International Studies of Management and Organization* Special Business Ethics issue: "People, Planet, Progress: Business Ethics for a Global Society"
Note: An earlier version of this paper was presented at IVBEC.

(Donaldson 2012; Melé, Argandoña, and Sanchez-Runde 2011; Schoen 2017), and the global crisis of the 2020 coronavirus pandemic (Harford 2020).

Our study contributes to the exploration of the intersection of ethics and risk by proposing a novel "information preference" perspective to address this intersection in a way that builds on insights from utilitarian, deontological and psychological approaches to ethics in decision-making. The information preference perspective proposed here represents a creative effort to integrate, combine and contrast these three different approaches to the study of the ethics of managerial decision-making and risk. This is particularly relevant since business practice and education still treat risk and decision-making in ways that overemphasize narrowly utilitarian forms of reasoning.

According to behavioral psychology, in complex risk situations the multiple types of information potentially available to decision-makers are not all processed equally, but go through filters of accessibility and framing (Kahneman 2002). This study offers key propositions that inspired three research questions which were investigated empirically. First, it proposes that the information filtering process leads to the emergence of identifiable "Patterns of Information Preference" (PIPs) which differ across decision-makers. Second, it proposes that the emergent PIPs have an internal logic that reflects different approaches to the ethics of decision-making (utilitarian, deontological and psychological). Third, it proposes that PIPs influence the decisions that are ultimately made, and thus their potential ethical implications.

We investigated these propositions empirically by designing an experiment based on the classic "Carter Racing Case." Participants were asked to take on the role of Terry Carter, the co-founder and owner of Carter Racing, a small but growing car racing organization at a defining moment in its struggle to achieve targets to ensure its sustainable future. Carter has to make a decision about participating in the Pocono race, with high stakes for current and future sponsorships and advertising revenue. The company has had a successful racing season, but Carter has just received conflicting advice about today's race. There is the possibility of an engine blowout which might endanger the driver (Brittain and Sitkin 1986, 1990; Erez and Grant 2014; Sinclair, Ashkanasy, and Chattopadhyay 2010; Sitkin and Weingart 1995).

The decision context of the case involves risk and uncertainty in a complex web of potentially relevant financial and ethical considerations. The case provides information about multiple aspects of the situation, including qualitative and quantitative information about risk for the firm and its stakeholders. After indicating their decision, the 174 participants in this study were asked to rate the relevance of the various types of information for their decision-making process, and to provide information about themselves.

A broad array of information about the potential risks in the situation was dispersed throughout the instrument and attributed to different sources. This information could be potentially relevant for decision-making to be approached from different normative ethics perspectives, such as: a) an utilitarian approach that draws from Expected Value Theory (EVT) to emphasize the expected value of the possible consequences of different alternatives; and b) a deontological approach that emphasizes issues such as moral duty, responsibility toward the driver and the integrity of the firm. Moreover, the case information could also bring into play cognitive biases and other phenomena which, according to the psychological approach, may lead the actual decision-making about risk to depart from the purely 'rational' normative prescriptions of utilitarian and deontological approaches.

The empirical investigation yielded three key findings. First, participants had indeed filtered the information they received, with significant differences not only in what they considered most important, but also what they saw as least important. Moreover factor analysis revealed that such individual filtering had configured three distinct patterns of preferences and that there was an internal logic to these patterns, characterizing what we called "Patterns in Information Preference (PIPs): "Expected Value", "Responsibility" and "Autopilot." Second, the PIPs that emerged from participants' filtering processes reflected different ethical approaches to decision-making under conditions of risk (utilitarian, deontological and psychological), with the filtering processes favoring information that supported an ethical approach over the others and discounting information not aligned with that particular approach. Third, participants' PIPs influenced the decisions they made (and their respective potential ethical implications): we found that the "Responsibility" PIP had a significant association with the decision not to run to forfeit the car race, whereas the "Autopilot" PIP was significantly associated with the decision to run.

The next sections review the literature and articulate the study's conceptual background, propositions and research questions. This is followed by a description of the methodology and the presentation of results. We then discuss the study's findings, limitations, and implications for research and practice in the intersection of ethics and decision-making under conditions of risk.

Literature review and conceptual background

The novel "information preference" perspective proposed in this study builds on a conceptual foundation that integrates the scholarly literature from normative and descriptive ethics. Drawing from moral philosophy, we apply normative ethics (including utilitarian and deontological approaches) to focus on what decision-makers *ought* to do when confronting risk, and contrast the prescriptions offered by the different ideologies underlying these two normative approaches. Drawing from descriptive ethics, we explore psychological approaches to understand the *behavior* of decision-makers when confronting risk.

In the subsections that follow we offer a summary exploration of how these ethical approaches to decision-making may conflict with or complement each other when studying risk, establishing the theoretical groundwork for the propositions and research questions presented in the next section. While so many ethical decision frameworks assume certainty (e.g., choosing between alternative A that "certainly" benefits one group of stakeholders vs. alternative B that "certainly" benefits another group) here we examine how these frameworks apply to situations where the decision-maker is choosing among alternative decisions that lead to outcomes that are far from certain, involving subjective probability estimates.

Normative ethics and risk: utilitarian and deontological approaches

Utilitarian approach

Management scholarship, education and practice tend to approach decision-making under risk from a perspective informed by an "ideology of numbers" (Chelli and Gendron 2013). This ideology underlies prominent management belief systems and theories (Ghoshal 2005) and leads decision-makers to focus on quantitative analyses such as Expected Value Theory (EVT), relying on cost-benefit analyses and calculations of expected value (EV) to seek value maximization. When confronted with ethical dilemmas in situations that involve risk, those decision-makers are likely to use consequentialist approaches where they adopt a narrow form of utilitarianism that compares possible "consequences" of different alternatives, stressing quantitative methods and financial considerations to decide the "right" thing to do. This may be particularly in risk situations, where the "right" thing to do is unclear given the range of possible outcomes.

A possible advantage of an EVT-based utilitarian approach is that it explicitly recognizes that in risk situations ethical decision-making is *not* about choosing the best consequence among a set of deterministic consequences, because the decision-maker does not know, with certainty, the consequences of each choice. Rather, in situations that involve risk, this utilitarian approach helps the decision-maker choose one course of action over others based on the expected consequences of those actions – which, ultimately, are not really under control of the decision-maker.

Consequentialist approaches to risk (and classical forms of utilitarianism in particular) have been criticized, among other reasons, for assuming that actors fully know the consequences and likelihood of the various alternatives (Hansson 2010), and for leaving out other aspects that are morally relevant, such as the distribution and comparability of different types of risk across diverse stakeholders. For example, those criticisms point out that an utilitarian approach to risk may not adequately address ethical issues related to the rights of the decision-maker versus the rights of those affected by the risk, such as the decision-makers' intent and right to impose risk on others, the degrees of consent of those affected by the risk, the power relationships involved, the nature and gravity of impact for the various parties, and the appropriateness of technocratic, authoritarian and participative models for making decisions about risks (Cranor 2007; Hansson 2007; 2010; Hayenhjelm and Wolff 2012; Peterson 2007; Wolff 2007).

Even though the overreliance on utilitarian approaches has been widely criticized, it is still quite prevalent in the day-to-day of business education and practice (Brittain and Sitkin 1990; Ghoshal 2005; Scharding 2015). The over-emphasis on narrowly utilitarian approaches often involves downplaying or ignoring issues that are the focus of other ethics approaches, such as deontological concerns about moral duty and responsibility, and the warnings offered by descriptive ethics about the biases and other psychological phenomena that may create blind spots for decision-makers.

The quantitative nature of utilitarian types of analyses, with their ostensible precision and sophistication, may offer a sense of objectivity and control, but this might prove to be illusory. Over-reliance on these forms of thinking is believed to have contributed to the flawed decision-making underlying disasters such as NASA's Challenger Shuttle (Brittain and Sitkin 1990), as well as to the 2008 financial crisis and its repercussions (Donaldson 2012; Melé, Argandoña, and Sanchez-Runde 2011; Scharding 2015; Schoen 2017).

Deontological approach

Given the criticisms and limitations of the utilitarian approach, there has been a growing interest in a deontological approach to ethical decision-making under risk, especially in the practice of risk assessment. Instead of simply *assessing* risks, one must recognize that the probabilities themselves are uncertain (Cranor 2007); that various stakeholders may be differently affected by the distribution of risks of harm (Hayenhjelm and Wolff 2012; Hill 2012; Scanlon 1998); and that when an environment becomes perceived as risky, the resulting "free floating fear" may traumatize even those not directly harmed by the risk itself (Nozick 1974).

For example, when analyzing the ethics of risk evaluation in the 2008 US financial crisis, Scharding (2015) acknowledges that EVT, the dominant form of utilitarianism, can be "very helpful in examining questions about risk" (2015, 250). But after pointing out the weaknesses of EVT, Scharding then calls for a deontological approach, based on Kantian ethics (Kant 2002), "one of the dominant forms of non-consequentialist reasoning" (Scharding 2015, 250).

Scharding (2015) contrasts decisions guided by EVT with decisions that follow two other distinct types of deontological reasoning: Kant's prudent and moral reasoning. In decisions that follow Kant's "prudential reasoning," decision-makers may still incorporate EVT considerations; however, the focus of the prudent approach to risk will be on preserving and promoting the viability of long-term interests, not on short-term value maximization.

In decisions that follow Kant's "moral reasoning," decision-makers may also use EVT considerations to develop a sense of how risky a course of action could be; however, the determinant factor in deciding about the permissibility of an action is the morality of the "rule" that could be neutrally formulated to support that action – in other words, the result of the EVT calculations will not be as determinative of the decision as it would have been within the consequentialist frame of a narrowly utilitarian approach.

Contrasting the consequentialist and non-consequentialist perspectives of utilitarian and deontological approaches, Scharding (2015) suggests that, given the different requirements they pose for decision-makers, risk aversion is likely to be lower in EVT than in prudential decision-making, and lower in prudential than in moral decision-making.

Descriptive ethics and risk: psychological approaches

Descriptive ethics can help explain how individual characteristics and cognitive limitations may limit a decision-maker's ability to think through and make decisions that involve risks for oneself and others. The prescriptions offered by the normative approaches summarized above, whether guided by utilitarian or deontological norms, do not fully address the ethics of risk. Lewens reminds us that people can be "very bad at reasoning about risk" (2007, 15). The conceptual foundation for this study goes beyond the prescriptive focus on how people *should* make decisions about risk, and combines it with a descriptive ethics perspective that draws from behavioral psychology to study how they *actually* do it.

Psychological phenomena may affect both ethical awareness and ethical judgment. Descriptive ethics offers a sobering picture of the limits of ethical awareness. When dealing with risk, a decision-maker may not even recognize the ethical nature of the issues possibly involved in the alternative courses of action, and may also fail to consider the ethicality of his/her right to be making the decision in the first place. If those issues are not even identified, or are dismissed, ethical judgment processes are not engaged, and therefore normative considerations (such as those suggested by utilitarian and deontological approaches) will not come to the foreground.

For example, ethical awareness in a risk situation is likely to be lower if: decision-makers believe that the situation would not be perceived as ethically problematic by their peers or reference group (Fiske and Taylor 1991); the situation is framed in economic terms, using business or economic language that emphasizes the bottom-line, and excluding terms that might trigger ethical thinking (Kouchaki et al. 2013); or the situation is not perceived as posing a serious threat of harm to others (Butterfield, Treviño, and Weaver 2000; Jones 1991). This is why the moral intensity of an issue or situation may be perceived differently, depending on someone's ethical awareness (Jones 1991; Shawver and Miller 2017).

Descriptive ethics also reminds us that cognitive weaknesses and biases may taint ethical judgment in decisions about risk. Even if the hurdle of ethical awareness is somehow overcome – i.e., if the decision-maker is able to perceive ethical issues in the decision – the process of ethical judgment which then unfolds might, in turn, be constrained by other psychological phenomena.

Some of those phenomena may be triggered by idiosyncratic factors related to individual characteristics of the decision-maker (Kish-Gephart, Harrison, and Treviño 2010; Tenbrunsel and Smith-Crowe 2008). Other phenomena may be more general, reflecting cognitive limitations and biases that are widely shared (Bazerman and Tenbrunsel 2011). Those cognitive weaknesses and biases can be largely attributed to the human need to reduce uncertainty and increase control, even if such control is illusory (Treviño and Nelson 2017).

The processes of gathering and evaluating information can offer a gateway for biases to intrude into decisions about risk. For example, gathering information may be compromised by a tendency to stop too soon (due to overconfidence) or to look for evidence that supports one's assumptions and preferences, disregarding clues that might throw them into question (i.e., a confirmation bias). Those biases may unfold consciously or unconsciously (Bazerman and Tenbrunsel 2011), and their impact on the ethics of risk can be quite material and concrete.

By the same token, weaknesses and biases in the process of evaluating information may lead even the most well-intentioned decision-maker to misread situations of risk, misjudge possible consequences, and misapprehend their ethical implications. People would not be able to function in the world if every piece of information and stimuli were granted the same attention; instead, the information is filtered through perceptual, interpretive and evaluative processes, where some receive more priority than others. These filtering processes are largely unconscious, and their efficiency enables decision-makers to deal, more or less successfully, with their complex environments. However, the filtering processes are also fallible, and this can have a direct impact on one's ability to address risk in ethically responsible ways.

On the one hand, the cognitive efficiency of script schemas allows people to identify patterns in common or repetitive situations and then apply routines to respond to recognizable patterns in familiar ways, without having to analyze each one in thorough, time-consuming, cumbersome detail (Gioia 1992; 2017). On the other hand, schemas can lead decision-makers to disregard red flags that might signal the need to switch from automatic pilot and engage in a more thoughtful and analytic process – i.e., to switch from a fast thinking, intuitive System I to a more deliberative and reasoned System II (Kahneman 2002; Kahneman and Tversky 1979).

When this happens, the information about risk is available, but it is not processed adequately. Decision-makers then stick to the current course of action and continue to follow their script schemas unquestioningly (Gioia 2017), either because they discount the information about the risk that threatens to destabilize the status quo, or because they are not even able to see the need for a new decision. In either case, there are ethical implications to disregarding information and not addressing the risk. The risk may not go away – and being cloaked in invisibility will not make its potential for harm any less material. In this circumstance, staying the course without further consideration of the information about the risk may be compared to a ship that keeps running in the direction of an unseen and unacknowledged iceberg, on the assumption that it is not there. The lack of intent may attenuate, but does not nullify the ethical implications of decision-making under risk and the abrogation of responsibility for possible outcomes.

Recognizing that there is a risk and that it requires careful deliberation does not exempt decision-makers from other kinds of shortcomings in ethical judgment. According to descriptive ethics, even when decision-makers realize the need to address a risk that raises ethical issues, cognitive biases may still limit their consideration of the relative "rightness" or "wrongness" of various alternatives. Those biases can lead decision-makers (consciously or not) to emphasize or deemphasize different types of information that would be relevant to the ethical considerations proposed by normative approaches to risk (whether utilitarian or deontological).

For example, cognitive limitations might lead decision-makers to exaggerate, misinterpret or leave out information that would be ethically relevant for articulating and judging consequences or moral principles. Therefore, they might affect in various ways a decision-makers' ability to accurately estimate probabilities for EVT calculations, or to apply deontological reasoning to discern Kantian prudential and moral actions, and thus fall short of either utilitarian or deontological prescriptions.

As will be discussed in the next section, some cognitive biases may be particularly relevant for the ethics of risk. For example: availability heuristics (Slovic et al. 2002) may lead decision-makers to pay more attention to information readily available about past performance; optimism bias (Sharot 2011a; 2011b) may lead them to pay more attention to information that reassures them about the likelihood of positive outcomes; and confirmation bias (Charness and Dave 2017; Klayman 1995), may lead them to pay more attention to information that is compatible with their assumptions, beliefs and desires.

Research questions

Based on the ethical approaches examined above, the empirical part of this study explored ethical issues in decision-making involving risk situations where the available information suggests that a sustainable future for the organization is in question, and outcomes may bring different types of potential harm or benefit for different stakeholders.

According to the utilitarian approach, some individuals may recognize one or more types of risk and attempt to figure out "the right thing to do" by seeking a solution that brings the highest overall utility. In business contexts, this often translates into quantitative analyses that focus on the EV of the various alternatives, combining calculations involving the probabilities and the associated consequences of different scenarios, typically relying on financial information.

Alternatively, according to the deontological decision-making approach, other individuals prioritize information relevant for considering aspects of the situation related to moral law, duty and responsibility, regardless of the immediate consequences for the various stakeholders. Those decision-makers would thus give preferential consideration to information that is pertinent to universalized moral principles such as respect for human life and the rights of the 'whole person,' contributing to assessments that follow Kant's prudential and moral reasoning.

Furthermore, according to the psychological approach to the ethics of risk, in complex situations decision-makers will experience cognitive limitations that constrain their ability to process, equally thoroughly, all the various types of information potentially available. Therefore, decision-makers may disregard or downplay information which might otherwise signal the need for reevaluating previous or current ways of doing business. When that happens, decision-makers may (consciously or unconsciously) ignore informational red flags about possible threats. They will then, by default, stay on the course set up by previous decisions, sticking to the status quo without further engaging in active consideration of the various types of risk potentially involved in the situation.

This can be explained by various kinds of cognitive biases, such as: rationalization (e.g., using logical arguments to justify tacitly accepted assumptions that there is no need to reevaluate the status quo to take new elements of risk into consideration); optimism bias (e.g., an unquestioned faith in indicators about the stability of the status quo, and an unquestioned disbelief in information about possible threats to it); confirmation bias (e.g., perceiving as highly relevant the pieces of information that are compatible with the decision-makers' current assumptions and beliefs, while downplaying the relevance of information that contradicts them); and availability heuristics (e.g., increasing the relevance of easily recalled information – i.e., what has already happened—and devaluing the significance of something that has not happened yet – i.e., the potential risks in the situation). Combined or in isolation, these cognitive biases would lead a decision-maker to prioritize types of information that stress the stability of the current situation and downplay risk.

Therefore, drawing from the ethical approaches above, we offer the following propositional statement:

> In risk situations where the available information suggests that a sustainable future for the organization is in question, and outcomes may bring different types of potential harm or benefit for different stakeholders, decision-makers will filter the available information in different ways. Those perceptions of information relevance will not be random, reflecting instead patterns that can be explained by internally consistent preferences for certain types of information which they consider to be more relevant, or less, in responding to these situations.

This proposition inspired the first research question investigated in this study:

> RQ1: Will distinct patterns of information preference (**PIPs**) emerge from the decision-makers' perceptions about the relevance of different types of information for their decision-making process?

Furthermore, we propose that the decision-makers' information filtering will be influenced by different ethical perspectives. The internal logic of the PIPs that emerge from the filtering process will reflect different approaches to the ethics of decision-making under conditions of risk: utilitarian, deontological and psychological. Therefore:

a. Some decision-makers will prioritize information that reflects the **utilitarian** ethical approach. They will prefer information relevant to EVT-based utilitarian evaluations, so that their PIP will emphasize items related to the likelihood and magnitude of the costs and benefits of different alternatives.

b. Some decision-makers will prioritize information that reflects the **deontological** ethical approach. They will prefer information that is pertinent to the evaluation of issues of moral law, duty and responsibility involved in the situation, so that their PIP will emphasize items of long-term concern and timeless importance (such as life and death, and a sustainable future) over short-term issues of financial gains or losses.
c. Some decision-makers will take cognitive shortcuts that reflect the **psychological** ethical approach. They will prefer to use information readily available about past performance (availability heuristics), information that is compatible with the decision-makers' assumptions, beliefs and desires (confirmation bias), and reassuring information about the likelihood of positive outcomes (optimism bias).

We therefore offer the following propositional statement:

> The emerging "patterns of information preference" (PIPs) will reflect preferences for the types of information that support an ethical perspective and disregard for other types of information not aligned with that particular perspective.

This proposition inspired the second research question investigated this study, and its corresponding subsets of questions:

> RQ2: Do the types of information prioritized in different PIPs reflect different ethical approaches to decision-making under risk?
>
> RQ2a: Will some decision-makers prioritize information that reflects the utilitarian ethical approach?
>
> RQ2b: Will some decision-makers prioritize information that reflects the deontological ethical approach?
>
> RQ2c: Will some decision-makers take cognitive shortcuts that reflect the psychological ethical approach?

Finally, we expect that the distinct patterns of information preference (PIPS) that emerge in the decision-making process will be associated with reaching different decisions. Building on the previous proposition, stating that different PIPs reflect different ethical approaches, we thus propose that different PIPs will ultimately lead decision-makers to different decisions about the risk situation. Therefore:

a. The utilitarian ethical approach can be expected to lead to decisions where the underlying calculative reasoning is to maximize Expected Value (EV), based on the likelihood and magnitude of the material costs and benefits of various alternatives, and taking material risk into account.
b. The deontological ethical approach can be expected to lead to decisions that follow Kant's "prudential reasoning" (where the desirability of an action depends on its contribution to long-term goals, rather than short-term value maximization) or Kant's "moral reasoning" (where the permissibility of an action depends on the morality of the rule that would support it), avoiding the kinds of risk that threaten human life and the rights of the 'whole person.'
c. The psychological ethical approach will characterize decision-making processes where phenomena such as availability heuristics, confirmation bias, and optimism bias may interfere with the types of reasoning underlying the other two approaches (e.g., the calculative reasoning of EV maximization, as well as Kant's prudential and moral reasoning), distorting the perception of risk that would be most relevant to each.

This proposition inspired the third research question investigated this study, and its corresponding subsets of questions:

> RQ3: Will different PIPs lead to different decisions, according to the ethical approaches reflected in the types of information they prioritize or deemphasize?
>
> RQ3a: Will PIPs that reflect the utilitarian ethical approach lead to decisions that maximize expected value (EV) and are characterized by low risk aversion?
>
> RQ3b: Will PIPs that reflect the deontological ethical approach lead to more risk-averse decisions, which will protect human life and rights, prioritizing long-term goals rather than short-term value maximization?
>
> RQ3c: Will PIPs that reflect the psychological ethical approach lead to decisions to maintain the status quo, downplaying the potential risk of harm associated with staying the course?

Methodology

This study used an experimental methodology to address issues at the intersection of ethics and decision-making about risk. We conducted an experiment based on the "Carter Racing Case," where participants play the role of Terry Carter, who has to decide whether the car racing company should run in today's race, amidst conflicting advice about the possibility of an engine blowout which might endanger the driver.

Instrument

The Carter Racing case was originally developed by Brittain and Sitkin (1986; 1990) as a disguised version of the circumstances surrounding NASA's decision to launch the Challenger Space Shuttle, which led to the tragic death of seven astronauts. Engineers had discovered a fatal flaw in small parts that could trigger mechanical failure under certain atmospheric conditions, but administrators decided at the last minute to go ahead with the scheduled Challenger launch, under intense pressure from media, government and the public to produce results, going against the warnings from expert engineers (Treviño and Nelson 2017). The Carter Racing case has been widely used in management research and education (Brittain and Sitkin 1986; 1990; Erez and Grant 2014; Sinclair, Ashkanasy, and Chattopadhyay 2010; Sitkin and Weingart 1995).

The case provides qualitative and quantitative information about multiple aspects of the situation, potentially relevant for different ethical approaches to decision-making about risk. The case portrays a critical time for the long-term future of Carter Racing, a family-owned and operated car racing company. Terry Carter must decide whether or not to run today's race (the Pocono), the biggest car race of the season. The case contains information about the company's successful track record of finishing among the top five winners in past races. It also contains information about the immediate financial pressures surrounding the decision: running this high-profile race will help secure advertising revenues and sponsorships; forfeiting the race will bring financial penalties. Despite past successes, the racing team has had engine blowouts earlier in the season. An engine blowout in this major race would bring financial losses that might threaten the firm's survival. Although previous blowouts have not injured the driver, there is a possibility of physical harm and even death if an engine blowout leads to an accident in the Pocono race.

The case contains quotes from the company's mechanics, with one contending that cold temperatures could explain their past engine failures, while another argues that car racing is risky anyway and "nobody ever won a race sitting in the pits." The engine mechanic (Paul Smith) is against running the race: he believes that the engine problems may be related to cold air temperatures, and last night was below freezing; today's temperature is 40 degrees Fahrenheit, the coldest for all races in the whole season. However, the chief mechanic (Tom Burns) is firmly in favor of running the race. Based on 20 years of experience, Burns does not believe that temperature is an issue; moreover, he argues that car racing is inherently dangerous, that the drivers accept having their lives on the line, and that his own career and the firm's future are at risk in every race.

We obtained authorization to modify the case so that it fit the experimental design. In our version, shortly before the race the company's accountant (Alex Edwards) provides Terry Carter with a summary, gathered from various sources, of detailed estimates of the probability that the car engine may fail, and the lost revenues and penalties the company will incur if it forfeits the race. Four versions of the case were created by including information about high/low levels of risk likelihood and impact. The information about risk impact and likelihood was inspired by the risk assessment dimensions of the COSO framework (COSO 2017). The role played by the accountant in our version of the case is consistent with recent research on Enterprise Risk Management (ERM), whereby accountants are increasingly expected to become directly involved in providing qualitative and quantitative information (both operational and financial) to support decisions about risk (Bento, Mertins, and White 2018).

The experiment

The experiment involved 174 participants (103 students from a German university and 71 students from an American university) and 69% were undergraduates. They were recruited via web-based tools for managing participants of experiments – hroot (Bock, Baetge, and Nicklisch 2014) and Sona Systems – and received €10/$10 for their participation in this study.

Participants were asked to face the same decision as in the original case, about whether or not to run. In addition, the case also explicitly mentioned the risk to the driver, who can potentially die from the accident, should an engine blowout occur. In our instrument, after making their decision, participants were then asked to rate the relevance of the various types of information in the case; and finally they provided information about themselves.

Participants were randomly assigned to scenarios based on four combinations of high/low likelihood and impact. In the four scenarios, 'Impact' refers to the financial impact calculations contained in the estimates compiled by Alex Edwards, the accountant. 'Likelihood' refers to the experts' estimated probability that a risk event (engine blowout) will occur. Across the four scenarios, strictly financial EV calculations based on risk impact and likelihood would all lead to a financial conclusion favoring the decision to run the race (i.e., the EV of the decision to run was higher than the EV of the decision to forfeit the race, and the only aspect that differed across the four conditions was the magnitude of the difference between the two EVs). This design simulated an ethical dilemma, where deontological concerns such as the intention to protect the life of the driver by *not* running the race conflicted with narrow utilitarian concerns of maximizing short-term financial results by running the race to benefit the owners of the company. These scenarios were not designed to test predicted effects of impact and likelihood on the decision to run. Rather, the scenarios helped us compare the potential influence of the Expected-Value criteria overall with other PIPs on the decision to run while controlling for the participants' perceptions of different magnitudes of likelihood and impact.

The question about the decision to run used a 10-point Likert scale (1 – definitely withdraw; 10 – definitely race). After participants had made the decision, they were asked to rate, on a scale ranging from 1 (not relevant at all) to 5 (extremely relevant), how relevant eight information items had been in their decision-making: a) the estimate of the financial impact in case of engine failure; b) the estimate of the loss if the company pulled out of the race; c) the estimate of the likelihood of engine failure; d) the risk for the driver in case of engine failure; e) the long-term future of Carter Racing Co.; f) the concern about the increased risk of engine failure at lower

Table 1. Factor analysis of PIPs.

	Patterns of Information Preferences (PIPs)		
Information Items	*Expected-Value*	*Responsibility*	*Autopilot*
Estimated financial impact in case of engine failure	0.829	−0.182	−0.235
Estimated loss if the company pulls out of the race	0.826	−0.182	0.057
Estimated likelihood of engine failure	0.533	0.261	−0.232
Risk for the driver in case of engine failure	−0.069	0.717	−0.170
The company's long-term future	0.125	0.703	0.477
Concern about increased risk of engine failure at lower temperatures	0.197	0.560	−0.510
The team's track record of finishing as one of the top five winners	−0.055	0.026	0.809
Car racing is an inherently risky business	−0.301	−0.147	0.567
% of Variance Explained:	22.58%	18.18%	20.08%

temperatures; g) the team's recent track record of finishing as one of the top five winners in previous races of the season; and h) car racing is inherently risky.

The questionnaire concluded with a question about the participants' knowledge of car racing, followed by questions about individual characteristics of the respondents (e.g., gender, age, college major, educational level). Overall, it took the participants about 20 min to complete the questionnaire.

Results

Patterns of information preference (PIPs)

The results shown on Table 1 indicate that, in regard to RQ1, there were different perceptions about the relevance of various information items for the participants' decision-making process, and these differences emerged as distinct patterns as evidenced by the three factors resulting from the factor analysis.

Taken together, these three factors explained over 60% of the total variance in the extent to which the participants considered each of the eight information items as having been relevant for their decisions. In regard to RQ2, the three factors can be explained by utilitarian, deontological and psychological approaches to the ethics of risk, as elaborated later in the "Discussion" section.

We labeled one factor the "Expected-Value" PIP, as it involved quantifiable information that a decision-maker could include in calculations to compare possible outcomes (e.g., the expected value of running the race, including a possibility of engine blowout, compared to the financial loss resulting from forfeiting the race). This factor emphasized the three variables related to the quantitative information on estimates about the loss if the company pulled out of the race, and estimates about the impact and likelihood of an engine blowout if it stayed in the race. Among the three factors, the Expected-Value PIP explained the most (about 23%) about the variances in the relevance ratings participants assigned to the information items.

We labeled the next factor emerging from the factor analysis as the "Responsibility" PIP which emphasized three main variables: the risk for the driver, the company's long-term future, and the concern about increased risk of engine failure at lower temperatures (which would threaten both the life of the driver and the long term future of the company). This factor assigned low relevance ratings to the aspects of the decision that involved financial calculations such as the likelihood and impact of engine failure, and the loss associated with forfeiting the race.

Four other variables loaded on the third factor, which we labeled the "Autopilot" PIP, as it assigned high relevance to aspects of the decision related to the continuation of the current state of affairs, while discarding the relevance of another variable that could change the course of the company. Participants who scored high on Autopilot tended to assign a high relevance to track record, the inherent risk of car racing, and the company's long-term future (positive factor

Table 2. Descriptive statistics of group PIP mean scores.

PIP scores	Expected-value PIP Group	Responsibility PIP Group	Autopilot PIP Group
Expected-value mean	0.80*	−0.47	−0.46
(standard deviation)	(0.55)	(0.85)	(0.98)
Responsibility mean	−0.35	0.86*	−0.53
(standard deviation)	(0.82)	(0.59)	(0.94)
Autopilot mean	−0.50	−0.30	0.96*
(standard deviation)	(0.80)	(0.80)	(−0.73)
N	64	58	52

* The mean score for this PIP in this group is significantly different from mean scores of the same PIP in the other two groups, all p values <0.001

loadings), while assigning a low relevance to the concern about increased engine failure risk at lower temperatures (negative factor loading).

Subsequent analyses used the factor scores computed for each of the three PIPs first to investigate between-subject differences in PIPs, and then to explore possible associations between PIPs and the decisions the participants reached in their decision-making process. Individual scores for each PIP were computed based on the weights from the factor analysis and the relevance ratings participants assigned to each of the eight information items so that three PIP factor scores were obtained for each individual participant.

PIP differences across decision-makers

Participants were grouped according to which PIP factor score was their highest, yielding three groups: Expected-Value PIP group (64 participants), Responsibility PIP group (58 participants) and Autopilot PIP group (52 participants). The Expected-Value group had the largest number of participants (64 out of 174 or 37%), as would be expected given the predominance of the ideology of numbers we discussed earlier. Next, we compared the mean PIP scores among the groups, to examine significant differences in the participants' perceptions of the relevance of different types of information for their decisions.

As shown in Table 2, in regard to RQ1, participants in the Expected-Value group had a significantly higher mean Expected-Value score than the Expected-Value scores in the other two groups (p values < 0.001). There were no significant differences between Expected-Value scores of participants in the Responsibility and Autopilot groups. Similar relationships were found for the Responsibility scores (significantly higher for the Responsibility group compared to the other two groups) and for the Autopilot scores (significantly higher for the Autopilot group compared to the other two groups).

PIPs and the decision to run

Regression analysis

In regard to RQ3, the different PIPs that emerged in the decision-making process are associated with reaching different decisions. We used regression analysis to examine the magnitude of the effect of each of the three PIPs on the decision to run the race. The results of this regression analysis (Panel A of Table 3) reveal that, combined, these three PIPs explain more than one-third of the variance in the decision to run (adjusted $R^2 = 0.35$, $p < 0.001$). The Responsibility and Autopilot PIPs are both significant in explaining the decision to run. Participants with higher Responsibility PIP scores were less willing to run (negative β weight), than those with lower Responsibility PIP scores. Participants who rated higher in the Autopilot PIP showed a greater

Table 3. Regression analyses of the decision to run.

	Unstandardized coefficients		95% confidence interval for B				
Variables	B	Std error	Lower	Upper	Standardized β	t	Significance
Panel A: Regression analysis of the decision about running the race using PIPs							
Expected-Value	0.04	0.15	−0.25	0.34	0.02	0.29	0.769
Responsibility	−0.52	0.15	−0.81	−0.23	−0.21	−3.48	0.001
Autopilot	1.36	0.15	1.06	1.65	0.56	9.09	0.001
$N = 174$, $R^2 = 0.36$, adjusted $R^2 = .0.35$, $F = 31.63$, significance of $F < 0.001$.							
Panel B: Regression analysis of the decision about running the race using PIPs and other variables							
Expected-Value	0.03	0.15	−0.27	0.33	0.01	0.18	0.854
Responsibility	−0.46	0.16	−0.77	−0.15	−0.19	−2.90	0.004
Autopilot	1.32	0.15	1.00	1.63	0.54	8.29	0.001
Gender	−0.36	0.35	−1.06	0.34	−0.07	−1.03	0.307
Knowledge	0.08	0.18	−0.27	0.42	0.03	0.45	0.657
Age	−0.01	0.03	−0.06	0.05	−0.01	−0.23	0.822
Condition	−0.02	0.14	−0.29	0.25	−0.01	−0.14	0.886

$N = 174$, $R^2 = 0.37$, adjusted $R^2 = 0.34$, $F = 13.62$, significance of $F < 0.001$.

willingness to run (positive β weight) than those with lower Autopilot PIP scores. These findings address RQ3b and RQ3c, respectively. The Expected-Value PIP scores had no discernible direct effect on the decision to run, unlike what was anticipated under RQ3a.

Based on the results from Panel A, among the three PIPs, the Autopilot PIP scores had the greatest influence on the decision to run, as evidenced by the highest standardized beta coefficient (0.56) compared to the standardized beta coefficients of the Responsibility (−0.21) and Expected-Value (0.02) PIP scores. Similar conclusions are obtained by comparing the 95% confidence intervals for the unstandardized coefficients: the confidence interval for the Autopilot unstandardized coefficient contains greater coefficients than the ones included in the other confidence intervals obtained for the other PIPs.

We were also interested in examining if the association between PIPs and the decision to run would change after controlling for other individual and task-level variables. Panel B of Table 3 suggests that the influence of PIPs on the decision outcomes remained significant for the Responsibility and Autopilot PIPs (RQ3b and RQ3c), while gender, prior knowledge about car racing, age and experimental condition (high/low likelihood and impact) were not significant. The Expected Value-PIP remained unrelated to the decision to run the race, in contrast with RQ3a. Similarly to the results in Panel A, the standardized coefficient for the Autopilot PIP (0.54) indicates the highest magnitude of PIP effects on the decision to run, and the 95% confidence intervals for the unstandardized coefficients confirmed that the Autopilot PIP had the highest coefficients compared to the confidence intervals for the other PIPs.

Discussion

This study explored risk decision-making through the perspective of information preference, drawing from both normative (utilitarian, deontological) and descriptive (psychological) approaches to the ethics of risk. We conducted an experiment based on the "Carter Racing Case," where Terry Carter, the co-owner of the car racing company, has to decide whether to run in the next morning's race. On the one hand, the race is critical for the company, and forfeiting it would bring short-term financial and reputational costs. On the other hand, there is the risk of an engine blowout if temperatures dip below a certain threshold, as the forecast indicates they might, which would threaten the life of the driver and the long-term survival of the company.

The 174 participants in the experiment were asked to take on the role of Terry Carter in an adapted version of the Carter Racing Case, where they were presented with qualitative and quantitative information potentially relevant not only for risk assessment, but also for considering the decision from different ethical approaches to risk. Analysis of the empirical results from the experiment revealed two particularly interesting sets of findings.

First, the findings indicated that, as predicted, distinct "patterns of information preference" (PIPs) emerged from the decision-makers' perceptions about the relevance of different types of information for their decision-making process. Furthermore, these three emergent patterns – Expected Value, Responsibility and Autopilot PIPs – could be interpreted, respectively, from the perspective of utilitarian, deontological and psychological approaches to ethics.

Second, two of those PIPs (Responsibility and Autopilot) were found to be significantly associated with the decision reached by the participants, in terms of whether to run the race (a negative association with the Responsibility PIP, and a positive one with the Autopilot PIP). Moreover, the link between these two PIPs and the decisions associated with each could be interpreted, respectively, from the perspectives of both normative and descriptive approaches to ethics.

In the subsections that follow, we draw from normative ethics (utilitarian and deontological approaches) and descriptive ethics (psychological approach) to discuss these two sets of findings, and then go on to examine the limitations of the study and its implications for future research.

First set of findings: the three PIPs

This first set of empirical findings offers two particularly interesting insights. The patterns of information preference that emerged from the factor analysis indicated that, as anticipated by our review of the literature on the various approaches to the ethics of risk, participants did value different pieces of information in diverse ways. Moreover, those preferences were not random, but resulted in emergent patterns that could be interpreted from different ethical approaches, including both normative ethics (utilitarian and deontological approaches) and descriptive ethics (psychological approach).

Expected value PIP

The information preferences that loaded on the "Expected Value" PIP can be interpreted through the utilitarian approach to ethics. All three information items that loaded on this factor referred to quantitative information: estimates about the likelihood of engine failure, the financial impact in case of engine failure (costs directly associated with immediate consequences of a blowout, such as engine replacement, loss of future advertising revenue, etc.), and the loss if the company forfeited the race (fines, loss of current advertising revenue that would have to be reimbursed to the sponsors, etc.).

Those estimates would be relevant for EV calculations about the "right" decision from a narrowly utilitarian perspective. Participants with high Expected Value PIP scores emphasized data about immediate financial risks. They focused on estimates that would be relevant for EV calculations, in detriment of other considerations that might otherwise put in doubt the reliability of the underlying estimates, or that might indicate the need to consider other ethical aspects that might be at stake, such as the possible threat of harm to the driver.

Responsibility PIP

The information preferences that loaded on the "Responsibility" PIP can be interpreted through the deontological approach to ethics. The three information items that loaded on this factor placed a high relevance on concerns for the life of the driver and also on concerns about the long term implications of the decision for the future of the company, together with a high preoccupation about the possibility of engine failure.

These pieces of information are congruent, for example, with the deontological concerns of Kantian prudential reasoning about preserving and promoting the viability of long-term collective interests (such as the future of the company), combined with Kantian moral reasoning about universal principles (such as respect for life). The information preferences in the Responsibility PIP are also congruent with the emphasis on responsibility that characterizes the Responsibility Management paradigm (Pirson 2017, 2019, 2020; Pirson and Lawrence 2010), where leaders are seen as stewards who place the long-term dignity and well-being of members of their community above the economistic pursuit of maximizing short-term profit.

Autopilot PIP

The information preferences that loaded on the "Autopilot" PIP indicate that decision-makers who scored high on this PIP tended to consider two pieces of information as highly relevant (positive factor loadings): the company's successful track record and the inherent risk of car racing. Moreover, they assigned low relevance (negative factor loading) to the information about the chief mechanic's worries about possible engine failure in cold weather. While the engine mechanic's worries about a potentially catastrophic engine blowout in cold weather (and the threat it would involve for the driver) were ascribed low relevance in the Autopilot PIP, the exact opposite happened in the Responsibility PIP, where the perception of the engine mechanic's worry as highly relevant for the decision was associated with a high Responsibility PIP.

This Autopilot PIP can be interpreted through the lenses of descriptive ethics, where psychological phenomena may lead the decision-maker to simply "stay the course" without actually engaging in ethical judgment of the risks associated with trying to preserve the status quo. This often involves cognitive schemas that prioritize the status quo (e.g., by emphasizing the company's track record) and that downplay or ignore red flags signaling vulnerability to changing circumstances (e.g., by attributing low relevance to the information about the risk of engine blowout under cold temperature conditions).

Some of the psychological phenomena that might contribute to explaining this Autopilot PIP include: rationalization ("car racing is risky anyway"); optimism bias (e.g., exaggerating the relevance of a good track record as a reliable predictor of a successful race, and undervaluing the likelihood of a bad outcome such as an engine blowout); confirmation bias (e.g., perceiving as highly relevant the pieces of information that were compatible with the racing company's assumptions and beliefs about the safety record of the company, while downplaying the relevance of information about current low temperatures); and availability heuristics (e.g., increasing the relevance of easily recalled information – i.e., track record – and devaluing something that has not happened yet – i.e., a fatal accident from an engine blowout).

Of course, this list of biases and cognitive limitations does not mean to be exhaustive, and we did not test each of its elements separately. These are simply examples of psychological phenomena that are in line with research in this field, and they constitute a plausible explanation for why these specific three pieces of information loaded on this particular factor of the "Autopilot" PIP.

Second set of findings: PIPs and the decision to run

Our empirical results suggest that PIPs do matter, not only in terms of their possible ethical interpretations, but also because they are associated with the decisions ultimately reached. The results from the regression analysis indicated the Responsibility PIP to be significantly associated with a **lower** level of willingness to run, and the Autopilot PIP to be significantly associated with a **higher** level of willingness to run. The associations between each of those two PIPs and the decision about the race are congruent with deontological and psychological ethics. The Responsibility PIP emphasizes concerns about the life of the driver and the long-term future of the firm, therefore explaining its association with a lower willingness to risk it all by running the race. By the same token, the Autopilot PIP focuses on the status quo, rather than on what might threaten it; therefore, it is logical that it would be associated with the decision to run – i.e., the decision to "stay the course" and stick to what had been done in all the previous races of the season.

The regression analysis, however, found no significant association between the Expected Value PIP and the decisions reached by the decision-makers. This finding is consistent with our results that the Autopilot PIP was the most influential in the decision to run, leading participants to prioritize "staying the course" and to filter out considerations of future gains and losses.

Limitations, implications and directions for future research

This study involved the limitations discussed below, which also suggest intriguing implications and directions for future research. For example, individual characteristics of decision-makers were used here as control variables. However, meta-analytic research on ethics and decision-making (Kish-Gephart, Harrison, and Treviño 2010) suggests the importance of going beyond demographic characteristics such as those used in this study (e.g., gender, age) to consider psychological aspects – for instance, cognitive moral development (Kohlberg 1969; 1981; Rest 1986), moral philosophies of idealism versus relativism (Forsyth 1992), Machiavellianism (Christie and Geis 1970; Nelson and Gilbertson 1991), and locus of control (O'Fallon and Butterfield 2005; Rotter 1966). Participants in this study were university students, which potentially limits the generalizability of the findings; differences in age and program status (e.g., undergraduate vs. graduate) did not influence the results.

It should also be noted that this study did not attempt to investigate multiple types of consequentialist and non-consequentialist approaches to the ethics of risk; rather, it focused on utilitarian aspects of the former and deontological aspects of the latter. Following Scharding (2015), this study did not venture into value ethics, and the quantitative information provided in the case did not go beyond the scope of what would be minimally necessary to support EV calculations in a relatively narrow utilitarian approach. While EVT-based utilitarian considerations are the most common of the consequentialist approaches in management theory and practice, future studies should seek to broaden this scope.

Moreover, our experiment focused on relatively fast decision-making about the situation in the case, without requiring participants to engage into specific forms of elaborate and sophisticated ethical analysis. While this can be seen as a limitation, the literature has actually pointed out the value of efforts to study fast decision-making and intuitive ethics (Kahneman 2011; Kahneman and Tversky 1979). As Haidt (2001) observes, much moral judgment happens "quickly, effortlessly and automatically," and often at an unconscious level. Neuroscience studies in moral psychology have offered empirical evidence that "ethical judgments are often more intuitive, impulsive and automatic than deliberative" (Treviño and Nelson 2017, 95).

In our study we relied on participants' self- reports to assess the perceived relevance of different types of information. This limitation could be lessened, for example, by using eye-tracking technologies (Meißner and Oll 2019; Sirois, Bédard, and Bera 2018), and functional magnetic resonance imaging (fMRI) (Robertson et al. 2007; Rommel and Folger 2009). However, by approaching the ethics of risk through the perspective of information preference, this study mitigated the social desirability issues that may arise when participants are directly asked about the "right" thing to do. Instead, our experiment used information as if it were the "dye" injected into the bloodstream during a magnetic resonance imaging test. The flow of the dye in a diagnostic MRI generates images that can provide clues about the organ(s) being targeted. By the same token, this study used the Carter Racing case to "inject" in an experiment the "dye" of information about a risk situation. It then observed the "images" (i.e., the PIPs, or patterns of information preference) that emerged when the "dye" was processed through the participants' decision-making process. And finally it analyzed, across the results from all participants, whether the emergence of different "images" (i.e., PIPs) were associated with different "diagnostic" implications (i.e., the ethical implications of the decisions that were reached).

This study illustrates the fruitfulness of exploring risk decision-making by combining normative ethics (including the contrasting prescriptions of utilitarian and deontological approaches) and descriptive ethics (including the behavioral explanations and motivational insights provided by psychological approaches). The information this experiment provided to participants could be potentially relevant for various ethical approaches to decision-making about risk: for example, some of it would be particularly relevant for EV calculations; some of it would be relevant to deontological concerns about moral principles, such as those related to respect for human life, and the rights and responsibilities of the decision-maker in the case; and some of it would be relevant to psychological processes that affect how decision-makers think about consequences, what helps them value or trust different types of information, and how they prioritize possibly conflicting values.

The study did not guide participants to use any of that information one way or another, and it did not intentionally direct their attention to different types of information before reaching a decision. We designed the experiment so that participants filtered the information provided in the case and then made their decision. It was only after they had made their decisions that they were asked to indicate how relevant each piece of information had been for their decision-making process. And even then we did not link together the perceived relevance of various types of information in a way that would make them fit into predetermined categories. Rather, the patterns emerged from the data. The labeling of the three PIPs came from the types of information preference that loaded on each of them, which then led us to draw from ethical approaches to explain the PIPs.

This study made strides toward its goal of exploring the potential of an information preference perspective as a creative way to approach the ethics of risk. Future studies intending to further develop a measurement theory of PIPs should consider using large samples which could then be broken down into the multiple samples necessary for conducting a combination of exploratory and confirmatory factor analysis. For example, future research may develop scales to measure PIPs under different decision contexts, and evaluate their reliability.

Furthermore, this study was not meant to investigate possible alternative directions of influence or causality, which are relevant topics to be addressed in future research. On the one hand, it can be argued that the personal ethics of decision-makers will drive their information preferences (i.e., the types of information they consider most relevant when addressing the ethical issues involved in a risk situation); the preferential use of certain types of information in the decision-making process will then, in turn, influence the content of the resulting decision. On the other hand, an argument can also be made for the opposite direction of influence: the information choices of decision-makers may trigger different levels or types of ethical awareness; these distinctions in ethical awareness will then influence the ethical approaches they will take toward risk and the ethical considerations that will actively come into play; this will then drive the decisions they ultimately reach. It is also possible, of course, that both arguments are valid, and that the influence might be reciprocal, going in both directions.

The information preference perspective we used in this study holds promise for addressing the ethics of risk through management learning and education. For example, participants in our study, after reading the case and making their decisions, were asked to rate the relevance of different pieces of information for their decision-making. A similar procedure could be used in the context of corporate training, graduate or undergraduate courses, where it would be a provocative springboard for a debriefing that would discuss the various approaches to the ethics of risk. This sort of discussion would be probably more vivid and engaging for these audiences than a traditional lecture about ethics, since it would explore those issues by drawing from the participants' own immediate experience. This experiential approach would contribute to develop both their ethical awareness and their ethical judgment.

Strictly utilitarian approaches, such as EV calculations (Hansson 2007; Scharding 2015), are still omnipresent in business research and education. Their prevalence is understandable in light of the ideology of numbers that pervades Western capitalist societies (Chelli and Gendron 2013), and the influential management theories and practices that promote ideas of shareholder primacy and value maximization (Friedman 2001; Smith and Rönnegard 2016; Vermaelen 2009).

In contrast, this study was inspired by the field's growing realization that the consequentialist blind spots of those kinds of narrowly utilitarian approaches need to be mitigated by expanding the conversation to include deontological considerations in non-consequentialist approaches (Cranor 2007; Hansson 2007; Hill 2012; Rawls 1971; Scharding 2015). Moreover, it explicitly acknowledges that even the combination of utilitarian and deontological approaches is not comprehensive enough to fully address the ethical issues in decision-making about risk.

The utilitarian and deontological approaches of normative ethics can offer valuable ethical guidance about what decision-makers "should do" when addressing risk, but this guidance must be combined with a clear-eyed understanding of the murkiness of actual decision-making processes. Pursuing this clear view of a murky process is where the insights that descriptive ethics derives from behavioral psychology can be particularly helpful: psychological approaches offer critical realizations about what decision-makers actually do when dealing with risk, as Harding (2020) observed regarding the COVID-19 pandemic.

In other words: normative approaches can help decision-makers discern the "right" thing to do in a decision that involves risk, even if they might offer conflicting guidance about what is "right," given the differences in the norms that guide their prescriptions (e.g., utilitarian vs. deontological rules). In addition to the challenge of "knowing" what is right, there is still the matter of then "doing" what is right. Descriptive ethics, given its grounding in behavioral psychology, can play a significant role in both areas.

Conclusion

This study explored the intersection of ethics and risk using an information preference perspective that draws from normative and descriptive ethics to combine utilitarian, deontological and psychological approaches to decision-making about risk. The information preference perspective inspired an experiment that offered empirical support for the potential of such a combined approach to the ethics of risk.

We hope that the information preference perspective that is offered here will help promote Lewens's (2007) vision for the mutual contributions that the study of the ethics of risk can make to both risk and philosophy:

> [...] Philosophy may be used to clarify important practical questions about risk and to improve our responses to those questions. But we should not expect the lines of communication to work in one direction only. There are also important questions to be asked about how philosophy itself – most obviously ethics – can learn from the practical study of risk (Lewens 2007, 17).

The enduring supremacy of utilitarian approaches to ethics in business practice and education needs to be studied and challenged for society to make real progress toward a broader conceptualization of business ethics in decisions that involve risk.

Acknowledgements

The authors gratefully acknowledge partial funding for this study from the Johns Hopkins University's Carey Business School (Black and Decker Grant) and from the University of Baltimore's Merrick School of Business (Summer Research Grant).

ORCID

Regina Bento http://orcid.org/0000-0002-9481-6881

References

Bazerman, M., and A. Tenbrunsel. 2011. *Blind Spots: Why We Fail to Do What's Right and What to Do about It.* Princeton, NJ: Princeton University Press.

Bennett, N., and G. J. Lemoine. 2014. "What a Difference a Word Makes: Understanding Threats to Performance in a VUCA World." *Business Horizons* 57 (3):311–317. doi:10.1016/j.bushor.2014.01.001.

Bento, R., L. Mertins, and L. White. 2018. "Risk Management and Internal Control: A Study of Management Accounting Practice." *Advances in Management Accounting* 30:1–25.

Bock, O., I. Baetge, and A. Nicklisch. 2014. "Hroot: Hamburg Registration and Organization Online Tool." *European Economic Review* 71:117–120. (October): doi:10.1016/j.euroecorev.2014.07.003.

Brittain, J., and S. Sitkin. 1986. *Carter Racing Case Study.* Chapel Hill, NC: Delta Leadership, Inc. http://deltaleadership.com/product/carter-racing-case-study/.

Brittain, J., and S. Sitkin. 1990. "Facts, Figures, and Organizational Decisions: Carter Racing and Quantitative Analysis in the Organizational Behavior Classroom." *Journal of Management Education* 14 (1):62–81. doi:10.1177/105256298901400108.

Butterfield, Kenneth D., Linda Klebe Treviño, and Gary R. Weaver. 2000. "Moral Awareness in Business Organizations: Influences of Issue-Related and Social Context Factors." *Human Relations* 53 (7):981–1018. doi:10.1177/0018726700537004.

Campbell, K.A. 2015. "Can Effective Risk Management Signal Virtue-Based Leadership?" *Journal of Business Ethics* 129 (1):115–130. doi:10.1007/s10551-014-2129-4.

Charness, G., and C. Dave. 2017. "Confirmation Bias with Motivated Beliefs." *Games and Economic Behavior* 104 (C):1–23. doi:10.1016/j.geb.2017.02.015.

Chelli, M., and Y. Gendron. 2013. "Sustainability Ratings and the Disciplinary Power of the Ideology of Numbers." *Journal of Business Ethics* 112 (2):187–203. doi:10.1007/s10551-012-1252-3.

Christie, R., and F. Geis. 1970. *Studies in Machiavellianism.* New York, NY: Academic Press.

Committee of Sponsoring Organizations of the Treadway Commission (COSO). 2017. "Enterprise Risk Management – Integrating with Strategy and Performance, Executive Summary." https://www.coso.org/Documents/2017-COSO-ERM-Integrating-with-Strategy-and-Performance-Executive-Summary.pdf

Cranor, C. 2007. "Toward a Non-Consequentialist Approach to Acceptable Risks." In *Risk: Philosophical Perspectives*, edited by T. Lewens, 36–53. New York, NY: Routledge/Taylor and Francis.

Donaldson, T. 2012. "Three Ethical Roots of the Economic Crisis." *Journal of Business Ethics* 106 (1):5–8. doi:10.1007/s10551-011-1054-z.

Erez, A., and A. Grant. 2014. "Separating Data from Intuition: Bringing Evidence into the Management Classroom." *Academy of Management Learning & Education* 13 (1):104–119. doi:10.5465/amle.2013.0098.

Fiske, S. T., and S. E. Taylor. 1991. *Social Cognition*. New York, NY: McGraw-Hill.

Forsyth, D. R. 1992. "Judging the Morality of Business Practices: The Influences of Personal Moral Philosophies." *Journal of Business Ethics* 11 (5–6):461–470. doi:10.1007/BF00870557.

Friedman, M. 2001. "The Social Responsibility of Business is to Increase Its Profits." In *Ethical Theory and Business*, edited by T. Beauchamp and N. Bowie. London, UK: Prentice Hall.

Ghoshal, S. 2005. "Bad Management Theories Are Destroying Good Management Practices." *Academy of Management Learning & Education* 4 (1):75–91. doi:10.5465/amle.2005.16132558.

Gioia, D. A. 1992. "Pinto Fires and Personal Ethics: A Script Analysis of Missed Opportunities." *Journal of Business Ethics* 11 (5–6):379–389. doi:10.1007/BF00870550.

Gioia, D. A. 2017. "Reflections on the Pinto Fires Case." In *Managing Business Ethics: Straight Talk about How to Do It Right*, edited by L. K. Treviño and K. A. Nelson, 99–104. Hoboken, NJ: Wiley.

Haidt, J. 2001. "The Emotional Dog and Its Rational Tail: A Social Intuitionist Approach to Moral Judgment." *Psychological Review* 108 (4):814–834. doi:10.1037/0033-295x.108.4.814.

Hansson, S. O. 2007. "Risk and Ethics: Three Approaches." In *Risk: Philosophical Perspectives*, edited by T. Lewens, 21–35. New York, NY: Routledge/Taylor and Francis.

Hansson, S.O. 2010. "The Harmful Influence of Decision Theory on Ethics." *Ethical Theory and Moral Practice* 13 (5):585–593. doi:10.1007/s10677-010-9232-0.

Harford, T. 2020. "Why We Fail to Prepare for Disasters." *Financial Times*. https://www.ft.com/content/74e5f04a-7df1-11ea-82f6-150830b3b99a

Hayenhjelm, M., and J. Wolff. 2012. "The Moral Problem of Risk Impositions." *European Journal of Philosophy* 20 (S1):E26–E142. doi:10.1111/j.1468-0378.2011.00482.x.

Hill, T. E. Jr., 2012. *Virtue, Rules and Justice: Kantian Aspirations*. Oxford, UK: Oxford University Press.

Jones, T.M. 1991. "Ethical Decision-Making by Individuals in Organizations: An Issue Contingent Model." *Academy of Management Review* 16 (2):366–395. doi:10.5465/amr.1991.4278958.

Kahneman, D. 2002. "Maps of Bounded Rationality: A Perspective on Intuitive Judgment and Choice." *Nobel Prize Lecture*. https://www.semanticscholar.org/paper/Maps-of-Bounded-Rationality%3A-a-Perspective-on-and-Kahneman/1dfcbfc3e6e07c911e2517ef6609b4d4823d4a8f

Kahneman, D. 2011. *Thinking Fast and Slow*. New York, NY: Farrar, Straus and Giroux.

Kahneman, D., and A. Tversky. 1979. "Prospect Theory: Analysis of Decision under Risk." *Econometrica* 47 (2): 263–291. doi:10.2307/1914185.

Kant, I. 2002. *Groundwork for the Metaphysics of Morals*. New Haven, CT: Yale University Press.

Kish-Gephart, J. J., D. A. Harrison, and L. K. Treviño. 2010. "Bad Apples, Bad Cases, and Bad Barrels: Meta-Analytic Evidence about Sources of Unethical Decisions at Work." *The Journal of Applied Psychology* 95 (1): 1–31. doi:10.1037/a0017103.

Klayman, J. 1995. "Varieties of Confirmation Bias." *Psychology of Learning and Motivation* 32:385–418.

Kohlberg, L. 1969. "Stage and Sequence: The Cognitive – Developmental Approach to Socialization." In *Handbook of Socialization Theory and Research*, edited by D. A. Goslin. Chicago, IL: Rand McNally.

Kohlberg, L. 1981. *The Philosophy of Moral Development*. San Francisco, CA: Harper & Row.

Kouchaki, M., K. Smith-Crowe, A. P. Brief, and C. Sousa. 2013. "Seeing Green: Mere Exposure to Money Triggers a Business Decision Frame and Unethical Outcomes." *Organizational Behavior and Human Decision Processes* 121 (1):53–61. doi:10.1016/j.obhdp.2012.12.002.

Lewens, T. 2007. *Risk: Philosophical Perspectives*. New York, NY: Routledge/Taylor and Francis.

Meißner, M., and J. Oll. 2019. "The Promise of Eye-Tracking Methodology in Organizational Research: A Taxonomy, Review, and Future Avenues." *Organizational Research Methods* 22 (2):590–617. doi:10.1177/1094428117744882.

Melé, D., A. Argandoña, and C. Sanchez-Runde. 2011. "Facing the Crisis: Toward a New Humanistic Synthesis for Business." *Journal of Business Ethics* 99 (1):1–4. doi:10.1007/s10551-011-0743-y.

Nelson, G., and D. Gilbertson. 1991. "Machiavellianism Revisited." *Journal of Business Ethics* 10 (8):633–639. doi:10.1007/BF00382884.

Nozick, R. 1974. *Anarchy, State, and Utopia*. New York, NY: Basic Books.

O'Fallon, M. J., and K. D. Butterfield. 2005. "A Review of the Empirical Ethical Decision-Making Literature: 1996–2003." *Journal of Business Ethics* 59 (4):375–413.

Peterson, M. 2007. "On Multi-Attribute Risk Analysis." In *Risk: Philosophical Perspectives*, edited by T. Lewens, 68–83. New York, NY: Routledge/Taylor and Francis.

Petrick, J. A. 2011. "Sustainable Stakeholder Capitalism: A Moral Vision of Responsible Global Financial Risk Management." *Journal of Business Ethics* 99 (S1):93–109. doi:10.1007/s10551-011-1157-6.

Pirson, M. 2017. *Humanistic Management: Protecting Dignity and Promoting Well Being*. Cambridge, UK: Cambridge University Press.

Pirson, M. 2019. "A Humanistic Perspective for Management Theory: Protecting Dignity and Promoting Well-Being." *Journal of Business Ethics* 159 (1):39–57. doi:10.1007/s10551-017-3755-4.
Pirson, M. 2020. "A Humanistic Narrative for Responsible Management Learning An Ontological Perspective." *Journal of Business Ethics* 162 (4):775–793. doi:10.1007/s10551-020-04426-3.
Pirson, M., and P. Lawrence. 2010. "Humanism in Business: Towards a Paradigm Shift?" *Journal of Business Ethics* 93 (4):553–565. doi:10.1007/s10551-009-0239-1.
Rawls, J. 1971. *A Theory of Justice*. Cambridge, MA: Harvard University Press.
Rest, J. 1986. *Moral Development: Advances in Research and Theory*. New York, NY: Praeger.
Robertson, Diana, John Snarey, Opal Ousley, Keith Harenski, F. DuBois Bowman, Rick Gilkey, and Clinton Kilts. 2007. "The Neural Processing of Moral Sensitivity to Issues of Justice and Care." *Neuropsychologia* 45 (4): 755–766. doi:10.1016/j.neuropsychologia.2006.08.014.
Rommel, S., and R. G. Folger. 2009. "Business Ethics and the Brain." *Business Ethics Quarterly* 19 (1):1–31. doi:10.5840/beq20091911.
Rotter, J. B. 1966. "Generalized Expectancies for Internal versus External Control of Reinforcement." *Psychological Monographs: General and Applied* 80 (1):1–28. doi:10.1037/h0092976.
Scanlon, T. M. 1998. *What We Owe to Each Other*. Cambridge, MA: Harvard University Press.
Scharding, T.K. 2015. "Imprudence and Immorality: A Kantian Approach to the Ethics of Financial Risk." *Business Ethics Quarterly* 25 (2):243–265. doi:10.1017/beq.2015.17.
Schoen, E. 2017. "The 2007-2009 Financial Crisis: An Erosion of Ethics: A Case Study." *Journal of Business Ethics* 146 (4):805–830. doi:10.1007/s10551-016-3052-7.
Scordis, N.A. 2011. "The Morality of Risk Modeling." *Journal of Business Ethics* 103 (S1):7–16. doi:10.1007/s10551-012-1220-y.
Sharot, T. 2011a. "The Optimism Bias." *Current Biology: CB* 21 (23):R941–R945. doi:10.1016/j.cub.2011.10.030.
Sharot, T. 2011b. *The Optimism Bias: A Tour of the Irrationally Positive Brain*. New York, NY: Pantheon/Random House.
Shawver, T.J., and W. F. Miller. 2017. "Moral Intensity Revisited: Measuring the Benefit of Accounting Ethics Interventions." *Journal of Business Ethics* 141 (3):587–603. doi:10.1007/s10551-015-2711-4.
Sinclair, M., N. Ashkanasy, and P. Chattopadhyay. 2010. "Affective Antecedents of Intuitive Decision Making." *Journal of Management & Organization* 16 (3):382–398. doi:10.5172/jmo.16.3.382.
Sirois, L.-P., J. Bédard, and P. Bera. 2018. "The Informational Value of Key Audit Matters in the Auditor's Report: Evidence from an Eye-Tracking Study." *Accounting Horizons* 32 (2):141–162. doi:10.2308/acch-52047.
Sitkin, S., and L. Weingart. 1995. "Determinants of Risky Decision-Making Behavior: A Test of the Mediating Role of Risk Perceptions and Propensity." *Academy of Management Journal* 38 (6):1573–1592.
Slovic, P., M. Finucane, E. Peters, and D. G. McGregor. 2002. "The Affect Heuristic." In *Heuristics and Biases: The Psychology of Intuitive Judgement*, edited by T. Gilovich, D. Griffin and D. Kahneman, 397–420. Cambridge, UK: Cambridge University Press.
Smith, N. C., and D. Rönnegard. 2016. "Shareholder Primacy, Corporate Social Responsibility, and the Role of Business Schools." *Journal of Business Ethics* 134 (3):463–478. doi:10.1007/s10551-014-2427-x.
Tenbrunsel, A. E., and K. Smith-Crowe. 2008. "Ethical Decision Making: Where We've Been and Where We're Going." *Academy of Management Annals* 2 (1):545–607. doi:10.5465/19416520802211677.
Treviño, L. K., and K. A. Nelson. 2017. *Managing Business Ethics: Straight Talk about How to Do It Right*. Hoboken, NJ: Wiley.
Vermaelen, T. 2009. "Maximizing Shareholder Value: An Ethical Responsibility?" In *Mainstreaming Corporate Responsibility*, edited by N. C. Smith & G. Lenssen, 206–218. Chichester, UK: Wiley.
Wehinger, G. 2013. "Banking in a Challenging Environment: Business Models, Ethics and Approaches towards Risks." *OECD Journal: Financial Market Trends* 2012 (2):79–88. doi:10.1787/fmt-2012-5k4bwnpkvk6f.
Wolff, J. 2007. "What is the Value of Preventing a Fatality?" In *Risk: Philosophical Perspectives*, edited by T. Lewens, 54–67. New York, NY: Routledge/Taylor and Francis.
Young, G., and D. S. Hasler. 2010. "Managing Reputational Risks: Using Risk Management for Business Ethics and Reputational Capital." *Strategic Finance* 92 (5):37–46.

Decoupling in CSR reports: a linguistic content analysis of the Volkswagen Dieselgate scandal

Dirk Holtbrügge and Marcus Conrad

ABSTRACT
This study examines whether and how Corporate Social Responsibility reports of firms in the automobile industry differ in regards to their linguistic composition and their decoupling tendencies. Based on Basu and Palazzo's process model, the Volkswagen emission scandal ('Dieselgate') is analyzed from a linguistic content perspective by comparing Volkswagen's CSR reports with those of its biggest competitors. By applying the Linguistic Inquiry and Word Count Software, we identify linguistic characteristics that can help to detect deception markers. More specifically, we show how CSR reports of de-couplers and implementors differ in terms of morphology, syntax, semantics and pragmatics by developing and applying a linguistic analysis' framework. The data provided mixed support for our hypotheses. The analysis revealed that de-couplers, among other factors, use more articles, more words per sentences, a more negative emotional tone and fewer words connected to risks and anxiety, while verb tense and informal language only had ambiguous or even no influence. The study contributes to the current understanding of CSR reporting, the debate on CSR decoupling, and the linguistic perspective of CSR research. Moreover, it specifies the linguistic domain of Basu and Palazzo's process model.

Based on Basu and Palazzo's (2008) process model and on a linguistic content analysis, this study aims at contributing to the current understanding of the concept of decoupling in CSR reports by detecting linguistic indicators that explain deviations between CSR reports and CSR actions. By applying the Linguistic Inquiry and Word Count (LIWC) software, we compare the CSR reports of the 15 largest car manufacturers worldwide and analyze whether there are linguistic differences in the use of morphological, syntactic, semantic and pragmatic categories that can be connected to truthful communication (implementors) or fraudulent deviations (de-couplers).

In CSR literature, the gap between communication and realized actions and activities is often referred to as decoupling (Crilly, Hansen, and Zollo 2012; Dans 2015; Jamali, Lund-Thomsen, and Khara 2017; Siano et al. 2017). For example, MacLean, Litzky, and Holderness (2015) emphasize the link between decoupling of ethics program adoption from implementation. In particular, they analyze the crucial role of personal perceptions and behaviors and reveal "potent individual-level consequences of decoupling" (361). Rasche and Gilbert (2015) focus on business schools' tendencies toward decoupling and state that competing institutional pressures increase the probability of decoupling tendencies. Wickert, Scherer, and Spence (2016) analyze the effects of firm size and organizational costs on decoupling and summarize that small firms can more easily realize CSR activities compared to big firms, but small firms have an advantage in regard to an easier and less costly CSR communication. Frostenson, Helin, and Sandström (2012) analyzed decoupling in the code of conducts of two retail companies and argue that decoupling cannot always be considered as managerial hypocrisy. Cetindamar and Ozkazanc-Pan (2017) connected decoupling to the disparity between stated goals and their actual operationalization for venture capital impact investors. Beverland and Luxton (2005) described strategic decoupling for wine producers looking to reach cultural authenticity, meaning that internal operations were not integrated with the communicated outside brand image. Lately, Haberstroh et al. (2017) emphasize the phenomenon of moral decoupling of consumer behavior from immoral business practices, which contradict CSR.

While existing studies primarily emphasize the reasons for and consequences of decoupling from an individual, organizational and institutional perspective, they are not able to fully explain why some companies show a high congruence between CSR reports' communication and actions while other companies with similar characteristics decouple CSR actions from communication. This possible incongruence between communication and action is part of Basu and Palazzo's (2008) process model that explains how managers think, talk, and act drawing on linguistic features. The authors argue that "understanding what a firm thinks, says, and tends to do in relation to others is likely to strengthen CSR analysis" (Basu and Palazzo 2008, 133). Building on this linguistic and conative dimension, Crilly, Hansen, and Zollo (2016) and Newman et al. (2003) point to the predictive power of language and state that the linguistic analysis of official documents can indicate whether there is a congruence of CSR actions and CSR communication or whether these are likely to be decoupled from each other. The authors argue that untruthful and deceptive communication articulates itself in different ways than communication of firms or individuals that intend to walk their talk, and thus, ensure compliance of communication with actions. Hence, our research question states: How do CSR reports from firms that decouple differ linguistically from firms that do not decouple?

We use the case of Volkswagen (VW) (Volkswagen 2014), one of the biggest car manufacturers worldwide, intentionally deceiving its stakeholders and society by installing a defeat device in its diesel vehicles, to illustrate our analysis. VW used this defeat device in more than 11 million vehicles and caused much higher toxic emissions and pollutants in daily traffic compared to the testing grounds where the cars' software recognized when being tested. While the Volkswagen Group has agreed with the US authorities to pay fines amounting to billions of US dollars, it is still unclear which effects the fraudulent behavior might have on VW's trustworthiness and stakeholder reputation (Cavazos, Rutherford, and Berman 2018; Clemente and Gabbioneta 2017; Elson, Ferrere, and Goossen 2015; Raman, Garg, and Thapliyal 2019; Siano et al. 2017).

While several reasons for VW's emission scandal have been mentioned in previous research, such as VW's technology-obsessive corporate culture, ineffective corporate governance, and authoritarian leadership style (Meck 2016; Sattelberger 2016; Schneider 2016; Scholz 2016), only very few studies have analyzed this case from a corporate social responsibility (CSR) perspective (e.g. Siano et al. 2017). Whereas Siano's et al.'s study focuses on the VW's CSR reports only, we compare those with their biggest competitors. We also specify their communication findings by analyzing the morpho-syntactic and semantic-pragmatic dimension of linguistics.

Indeed, VW has always been very active in communicating its CSR activities by, among others, publishing detailed CSR reports including references to their many sustainability awards. For example, VW stated in the 2014 CSR report: "Our pursuit of innovation and perfection and our responsible approach will help to make us the world's leading automaker by 2018—both economically and ecologically." The current emission scandal revealed, however, that VW failed to meet its own stated intentions and policies of acting socially and environmentally responsible and that there is a large gap between VW's CSR communication and its actual CSR activities. This paper aims to shed light on this disparity by analyzing the linguistics used in VW's CSR reporting.

Theory and hypotheses

Theoretical framework

Almost all large companies nowadays issue CSR reports, codes of conducts, speeches about sustainable business practices or similar documents of defining their social and environmental responsibility. While CSR reports have achieved large attention in the management literature, Brine, Brown, and Hacket (2007) and Karaye, Ishak, and Che-Adam (2014) criticize that they only indicate the willingness, but not the real execution in regard to CSR. Having only this minimal CSR compliance can be "deadly to the firm" (Joyner and Payne 2002, 299). Weaver, Treviño, and Cochran (1999) add that some companies introduce CSR strategies, but decouple their intentions and statements from the realized actions. Crilly, Hansen, and Zollo (2016) emphasize the problematic relationship between CSR reports and their execution in practice, also basing their study on a linguistic analysis. The authors define firms that consistently realize their CSR policies as implementors whereas those that do not are called de-couplers.

Meyer and Rowan (1977, 341) define decoupling as "gaps between (organizations') formal structures and their ongoing activities." Haack, Schoeneborn, and Wickert (2012, 819) relate the concept of decoupling to CSR and define it as "the organizational misalignment between surface structures and actual activities." Christensen, Morsing, and Thyssen (2013, 374) emphasize that "corporate talk is cheap and […] CSR communication is shallow, manipulative and insincere, [when] decoupled from the daily practices of the organization." The authors add that it is necessary "to let action follow words and to walk the talk" (373) instead of decoupling one from the other. Similarly, Graafland and Smid (2016, 2) argue that CSR is only "ceremonial if companies decouple policies from implementation […]. Decoupling is […] more likely in loosely coupled organizational fields, characterized by ambiguity, uncertainty, multiple conflicting expectations, high transaction costs, limited regulatory commitment, and the absence of mechanisms to monitor compliance."

Decoupling does not always imply negative consequences (Christensen, Morsing, and Thyssen 2013), but might be also caused by the need for adaptation to fast-changing environments. Moreover, managers do not only decouple intentionally, but also because of not being aware of how to transfer communication into actions. Information asymmetry between managers and stakeholders, and between different local markets can also foster deviations (Christian Aid 2004; Crilly, Hansen, and Zollo 2016; Matten and Moon 2008). Furthermore, the decoupling of policy from practice is often not noticed by stakeholders due to intentional cover-ups (Zajac and Westphal 2004). These take place when firms try to deceive stakeholders and hide their harming activities. This intentional decoupling is harming to stakeholders as well as the firm.

The phenomenon of decoupling can be explained by the process model of organizational sense-making (Basu and Palazzo 2008). The authors argue that managers' communication represents itself in linguistic terms whereas actions are part of the conative domain. "Such a process view of CSR locates the phenomenon as an intrinsic part of an organization's character" and "argues for a deeper examination of organizational character along the tripartite process dimensions" of cognitive (thinking), linguistic (saying) and conative (behavior) aspects (Basu and Palazzo 2008, 124). Hence, decoupling takes place when differences occur between those process dimensions.

The linguistic analysis of the detection of decoupling of CSR activities from CSR reports is based on the assumption that language is not a neutral instrument through which reality is described and reported, but a constitutive process that shapes and generates organizations and

Table 1. Linguistic studies dealing with decoupling tendencies.

Author(s)	Linguistic connection to decoupling
Newman et al. (2003)	Deceptive communication is characterized by the use of fewer first-person singular pronouns, fewer third person pronouns, more negative emotion words ("hate", "anger", "enemy"), fewer exclusive words ("but", "except") and more motion verbs ("walk", "move", "go"). Moreover, compared to truth-tellers, liars showed lower cognitive complexity.
Douglas Clinton (2008)	When comparing specific sections in annual reports, companies with restatements used significantly fewer colons, fewer words per sentence, fewer optimistic words, more words related to downward directions, fewer words describing certainty, fewer of the words "note" and "see", fewer self-references, more past-tense words, and fewer present tense words.
Tausczik and Pennebaker (2010)	Deceptive statements compared with truthful ones are moderately descriptive, distanced from self, and more negative.
Larcker and Zakolyukina (2012)	Both deceptive CEOs as well as CFOs use more references to general knowledge, fewer non-extreme positive emotion words, and fewer shareholder value references. However, CEOs use more extreme positive emotion words and fewer anxiety words. In contrast, CFOs use more negation words and use more extreme negative emotion words and swear words.
Goel and Gangolly (2012)	Six categories of linguistic cues have been associated with fraudulent financial reporting: (a) use of complex sentential structures, (b) difficulty of reading and comprehension as measured by readability index, (c) use of positive tone, (d) use of passive voice, (e) use of uncertainty markers and (f) use of adverbs.
Hauch et al. (2012)	Liars use fewer exclusive words, self- and other-references, fewer time-related, but more space-related, negative and positive emotion words, and more motion verbs or negations than truth-tellers.

their perceptions of reality (Christensen, Morsing, and Thyssen 2013). Based on the *(Neo-) Whorfian* approach (Fabb 2016; Whorf 2012) that language represents our way of thinking and influences our actions, linguistic analysis can help to differentiate between deceptive and truthful communication in regards to previously announced actions (Crilly, Hansen, and Zollo 2016; DePaulo et al. 2003; Hart 2014; Langacker 2008). One can argue that the language used in a CSR report only represents the opinion of the author, but research states that individual and group adaptation to corporate values is the case in an organizational setting (Argyris 1957; Christensen, Morsing, and Thyssen 2013). Therefore, we consider the firms' CSR reports not as individual statements, but as an indicator for corporate values and culture—expressed linguistically through the word and text of each and every employee.

Linguistic analysis of decoupling has recently been applied in the management literature (Table 1). For example, Newman et al. (2003) showed that deceptive communication is characterized by, among others, more negative emotion words, fewer exclusive words and more motion words. Moreover, de-couplers showed lower cognitive complexity. Tausczik and Pennebaker (2010) revealed that deceptive communication is moderately descriptive, distanced from self, and more negative. Crilly, Hansen, and Zollo (2016) found evidence that the use of the future tense, a negative emotional tone and inclusive language correlate with deceptive communication, and thus, indicate decoupling.

The aforementioned articles provide interesting results and can be used as a first indication for developing hypotheses. Nevertheless, those are also characterized by several shortcomings. For example, only one study is explicitly related to CSR. Moreover, the categories included in the linguistic analysis are often not systematically derived but eclectic and incoherent which leads to ambivalent results. Moreover, those results are not based on a full integration into a linguistic framework. Consequently, the results of these studies remain fragmented and, sometimes, contradictory.

In order to conduct a more systematic linguistic analysis of CSR reports, we refer to a commonly used categorization in linguistics as "the scientific study of language" (Crystal 2011, 283) and developed a comprehensive research model (Figure 1). This consists of two dimensions, namely, a morpho-

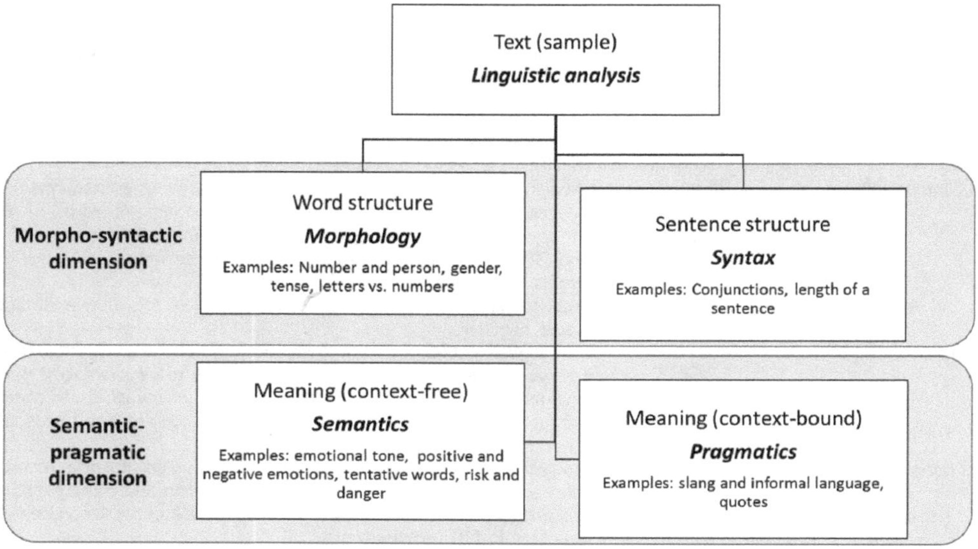

Figure 1. Dimensions of linguistic analysis.

syntactic dimension and a semantic-pragmatic dimension, both containing two different categories. We decided to use this framework to ensure an approach that includes all possible dimensions without any prior or later exclusion. We make the selection of tested categories less eclectic and more coherent.

On the morpho-syntactic dimension, morphology "refers to the study of the internal structure of words, and of the systematic form—meaning correspondences between words" (Booij 2012: 7). Syntax, as the second category of the morpho-syntactic dimension, "deals with the rules governing the combination of words in sentences" (Crystal 2011, 314). Hence, these two dimensions—also called morpho-syntactic categories (Booij 2012)—analyze the smallest units of language: words with their letters, number and person, their gender and tense, numbers, as well as sentences with their conjunctions and length. These "little words can provide a window" into how individuals deal with and respond to a specific situation and thus have large explanatory power (Chung and Pennebaker 2013: 16).

On the semantic-pragmatic dimension, semantics refers to the meaning of signs whereas pragmatics deals with the context, situation and relationship between actors (Crystal 2011). While morphology and syntax relate to the structure of language, semantics and pragmatics include meaning. Semantics is defined as the "the study of literal, decontextualized, grammatical meaning" (Frawley 1992, 1) and includes categories like emotional or tentative words. It contains the lexical stock of words and idioms for fundamental concepts and ideas that each language provides. Pragmatics also considers the context of communication, i.e. "the participants involved, the situation in which the discourse occurs, and the social structures that have an influence on how the participants interpret texts" (Pollach 2003, 281). It takes into account that the same term can have different meanings in various situations. For example, formal language and complex sentences may be appropriate in one certain situation and not be understood in another.

In the following, this categorization of linguistic analysis is systematically used for the derivation of our research hypotheses. While the first half of hypotheses relate to the morpho-syntactic dimension, the second half of hypotheses refer to the semantic-pragmatic dimension.

Research hypotheses

An important category of morphology is the subject of a sentence, often expressed in the first person singular or plural. In personal conversations, the frequent usage of words like "I," "me" and "myself" indicates that a person is primarily focused on his/her own actions and thoughts (Newman et al. 2003). The frequent usage of words like "we," "us," "ourselves," on the contrary, shifts the focus as well as the responsibility from the individual to the group or organizational level. CSR reports are official statements of firms rather than of individual managers. The frequent usage of the I-form is therefore likely to indicate that managers pose their individual interest above those of the firm without considering the benefit for all stakeholders. They underline their own discretionary power and put less emphasis on organizational rules and concerns. Ott et al. (2011) support this argumentation by concluding that the word "I" has the most deceptive explanatory power compared to all other words used, whereas "we" is considered as truthful. Sometimes, using the I-form is referred to as responsible behavior because it avoids the diffusion of responsibility. However, drawing on possible differences between the linguistic and conative perspective on an organizational level, responsibility has to be communicated and acted by everyone and anyone in the corporation. This is achieved through group decisions, which are derived from more active discussions based around a "we"-feeling (Tjosvold, Yu, and Hui 2004). Hence, we propose:

H1a: CSR reports of de-couplers use more words with an individual or I-focus.

H1b: CSR reports of de-couplers use fewer words with a collective or we-focus than those of implementors.

A second morphologic element of language is words that indicate gender. Women tend to be more responsible and care-taking, which might result in a higher intrinsic motivation for CSR compliance (Ruegger and King 1992; Setó-Pamies 2015). Furthermore, it was found that men rather tend to deviate from the truth than women when describing themselves (Hancock, Toma, and Ellison 2007). Dreber and Johannesson (2008: 1) agree that "men are significantly more likely than women to lie." In this context, research on gender-specific communication has discovered that women tend to use fewer articles like "a" or "the" than men do. This is reflected in women's higher orientation on social dimensions, whereas men rather focus on more concrete details which are expressed through articles (Newman et al. 2008). The focus on the social dimension can be considered as a crucial part of CSR reporting. Therefore, we assume:

H2: CSR reports of de-couplers contain more articles than those of implementors.

Another element of morphology is the tense. Crilly, Hansen, and Zollo (2016) found that the use of specific tenses is an indication of decoupling. De-couplers tend to use the future tense and future references in their reports more often instead of the past tense and past references. Implementors like to point out what they have achieved in the past, whereas de-couplers make future promises without being able to refer to past achievements (Bond and DePaulo 2006). Moreover, studies found that individuals that more often refer to past events and incidents are better in forecasting future developments in society and economics (Lachman et al. 2008). Dahl (2000) adds that future references are less binding and obligating compared to past achievements which can be easily monitored and verified. Therefore, it can be assumed that the usage of past references is connected to more experience, more differentiated evaluations and less wishful thinking. All this fosters the avoidance of deceptive communication and ensures the realistic execution of previously made commitments. Thus, we propose:

H3a: CSR reports of de-couplers contain more future references than those of implementors.

H3b: CSR reports of de-couplers contain less past references than those of implementors.

The morphology of a text consists of words that are defined and constructed by a combination of letters, and of numbers that express quantities, values or measurements. As almost all published CSR reports nowadays draw on common reporting standards, they all include numbers and quantitative measures. However, the amount of numbers and quantifiable measures still differs. A high degree of numbers implies a quantitative focus, which can be linked to a strong economic orientation toward turnover, profits, ratios or key performance indicators (Kristof 2003; Strauss 2003). Waters (1991) also states that a strong economic orientation is expressed, among other factors, by numbers and quantities. According to Ählström (2010: 77), "there is a need to decouple talk and action of corporate responsibility due to the pressure from the financial markets to increase profits." A strong focus on CSR would rather result in fewer numbers and quantitative measures and a more frequent use of abstract terms and qualitative statements. In comparison to profit or shareholder value, CSR is a latent construct that is much more difficult to measure (Beelitz and Merkl-Davies 2012). Consequently, truthful communication about CSR would result in the use of fewer numbers and quantitative measures. Thus, we state:

H4: CSR reports of de-couplers use more numbers and quantitative measures than those of implementors.

Conjunctions are an important element of the syntactic structure of language. They connect different thoughts with each other and can be inclusive or exclusive. Inclusive conjunctions are, for example, "and," "as well as," "additionally" and "with," whereas exclusive conjunctions are "or," "but," "nevertheless," "versus" as well as words like "only," "not" or "if" (Pennebaker and King 1999). Crilly, Hansen, and Zollo (2016) and Newman et al. (2003) state that inclusive language is mainly used by de-couplers. Inclusive conjunctions connect different thoughts, aspects and arguments without excluding others. Inclusive language was proven to have a negative correlation to CSR compliance. This might relate to the fact that de-couplers tend to use exaggerations and make big promises (Bond and DePaulo 2006). Defining responsibilities as open-ended is easier than realistically limiting the scope of CSR. Moreover, as Newman et al. (2003) argue, untruthful communication comes to the core by more simple language. On the contrary, exclusive language helps to differentiate between thoughts, aspects and arguments that are included and those that are not. Carefully thinking of where to be active and what to say and what to deny, characterizes implementors. Managers who use exclusive language aim at highlighting necessary tradeoffs and compromises, and then realize these commitments (Crilly, Hansen, and Zollo 2016). Thus, we state:

H5: CSR reports of de-couplers contain more inclusive and less exclusive language than those of implementors.

Another important category of syntax is the length of a sentence. As Douglas Clinton (2008) states, de-couplers use sentences with fewer words per sentence. The intention of realizing CSR commitments expresses itself in more complex formulations which result from careful and detailed thinking and, hence, in more words per sentence. Hauch et al. (2012, 3) state that "truth-tellers are believed to use [...] more complex explanations of what occurred, liars are believed to engage less in such explanations." CSR as a complex phenomenon needs differentiated and detailed explanations. In order to communicate CSR activities properly and in nuanced way, complex, detailed and longer explanations are needed, which results in longer sentences. Thus, we propose:

H6: CSR reports of de-couplers have fewer words per sentence than those of implementors.

In regard to semantics, it can be differentiated whether a text is written in a more "upbeat" or "downbeat" style, as well as by the usage of more positive or negative emotion words (Pennebaker et al. 2015a). The emotional tone of a text helps to detect de-couplers with their deceptive communication. As Vrij (2000) states, intentional de-couplers feel bad and mentally pressured due to the reason that they try to deceive others. The guilt of lying is burdening them, and this can cause inner tension, which correlates with language that consists of more negative emotion words like "hate," "worthless," "sad" or "enemy" (DePaulo et al. 2003). Knapp, Hart, and Dennis (1974) add that de-couplers tend to use more negative remarks about other groups than implementors. Zuckerman et al. (1981) classify these negative emotional statements as markers for deceptive communication. Newman et al. (2003) and Hauch et al. (2012) find support for this correlation between negative emotion words and decoupling as well. In contrast, an emotional attachment to happiness and satisfaction expresses itself in more positive language and, hence, is rather used by implementors. Considering those negative and positive emotions in a text, we assume that the language of de-couplers tends to be more negative and less positive. Moreover, the emotional tone of de-couplers in general is more "downbeat" than "upbeat" (Pennebaker et al. 2015a). Thus, we state:

H7a: CSR reports of de-couplers contain more negative emotion words than those of implementors.

H7b: CSR reports of de-couplers contain less positive emotion words than those of implementors.

H7c: CSR reports of de-couplers have a more negative, downbeat emotional tone than those of implementors.

Moreover, de-couplers tend to use fewer words describing certainty (Douglas Clinton 2008). Burdened by the guilt of lying, de-couplers try to relativize their statements with more vague formulations and more tentative words, like "perhaps" and "maybe," in order to give their statements a more ambiguous character. Goel and Gangolly support this argumentation by stating that fraudulent communication expresses itself by the use of more "uncertainty markers." Ambiguous and vague communication is therefore typical of de-couplers and congruent with their intention to put less pressure on the realization of CSR intentions. Hence, we derive:

H8: CSR reports of de-couplers contain more tentative words than those of implementors.

Companies and their executives that consider CSR as one of their core values tend to reflect actively and explicitly about risks of their actions and initiatives (March and Shapira 1987). Considering possible consequences of one's actions causes anxiety and worries, and can result in different decisions and outcomes (Raghunathan and Pham 1999). Firms that care less about their social impact will use these categories less often. Thus, we conclude:

H9: CSR reports of de-couplers use less words connected to risks and anxiety than those of implementors.

A fourth category of linguistics is pragmatics which considers the use of language in different contexts. Depending on the context, identical terms may have different meanings. For example, formal language is more appropriate in an official context, while informal terms may be better understood in a private conversation. In regards to the official context, Ingenbleek, Binnekamp, and Goddijn (2007, 546) refer to "the core of the formulation [which] is a tradeoff process between ethical norms […] and market opportunities […]." We assume that firms use formal and elaborated language if they regard CSR reports as official documents illustrating their CSR activities trustworthily and reliably—although these reports may not be legally binding. This includes the absence of slang and informal language. As one example, "bragging" should be avoided and CSR communication needs to be factual (Du, Bhattacharya, and Sen 2010). The "key challenge of CSR communication is to overcome stakeholder skepticism and to generate favorable CSR attributions" (Du, Bhattacharya, and Sen 2010, 17) which can be achieved by trustworthy and formal communication toward all stakeholders. At the same time, firms that regard CSR reports as less relevant and less formal and binding documents are more likely to decouple their CSR activities from CSR reporting. Hence, they tend to use more slang and informal language. Therefore, we propose:

H10: CSR reports of de-couplers use more slang and informal language than those of implementors.

The last hypothesis relates to the use of quotes. Previous research found that deceptive communication is characterized by frequent reference to others, e.g. in fraudulent webpages (Grazioli and Jarvenpaa 2000). Liars often use statements of others as pretext. Frequent quotations diffuse responsibility inside and outside the organization and may be used as an excuse for promises that could not be hold. Moreover, group-based decision and statements are less likely to result in negative outcomes than individual responsibility, which can be related to personal quoting of executives (Whyte 1991). Based on these considerations, we propose:

H11: CSR reports of de-couplers include more quotes than those of implementors.

Methodology

This study applies a linguistic content analysis on CSR reports in order to test the hypotheses derived in the previous section. The analysis is based on the methodology of Crilly, Hansen, and Zollo's (2016) CSR reports analysis, Newman et al.'s (2003) linguistic analysis, and the approach of Chung and Pennebaker (2008). In particular, this study executes an analysis of car manufacturers' CSR reports in order to explore their linguistic composition.

Linguistic content analysis is well established in academic research (Bowman and Haire 1976; Crilly, Hansen, and Zollo 2016; Guthrie and Mathews 1985; Milne and Adler 1999; Moir 2001; Patten and Crampton 2004) and is based on counting specific words, phrases or structures within a text or a set of texts. As Lock and Seele (2015: 30) argue: "Communication sciences and business ethics are neighboring disciplines, which allow the transfer of quantitative content analysis from communication sciences to business ethics." Basu and Palazzo's (2008, 132) add that "if specific combinations of cognitive, linguistic, and conative features were found in certain firms but not in others, they would likely provide a reliable indication of these firms' CSR performance." Thus, this approach is reliable and valid with regard to our focus on the linguistic dimensions of morphology, syntax, semantics and pragmatics of a text.

The linguistic content analysis is conducted with the Linguistic Inquiry and Word Count (LIWC) software developed by Pennebaker et al. (2015a; 2015b). The program has been existing for more than a decade and has been continuously improved in order to serve academic purposes of linguistic analysis. Newman et al. (2003, 667) state that the program is "even more accurate at detecting deception than untrained human judges." For this study, the 2015 version is applied. The LIWC analyzes texts by counting defined words and assigning these words to specific categories. Specifically, it uses pre-defined dictionaries in order to analyze the inserted documents for specific text characteristics, like the amount of numbers, use of tenses, keywords, and other morpho-syntactic and semantic-pragmatic categories.

Sample

The sample contains the CSR reports of the 15 largest car manufacturers worldwide (see Table 2). We considered CSR reports on the Group level which for VW, for example, includes the brands of Volkswagen, Audi, Porsche, Seat and Skoda, among others. The Dieselgate was discovered in September 2015 and hence we used the reports of the biggest 15 automotive Groups published in the timeframe 2015/2016.

We regard the restriction to the top 15 companies as appropriate as they comprise more than 80 percent of global car production. Since the sample includes two other large German car manufacturers, BMW (12th) and Daimler (14th), it allows checking for intercultural bias of our results as well. All reports were downloaded from the respective firm homepage. SAIC (13th) was excluded from the analysis because their CSR report was only issued in Mandarin, a language not suitable for analysis by the LIWC.

Table 2. Descriptive data for all documents, ranking derived from OICA 2015.

Rank	Company	Year	Word count
1	Toyota	2016	34,358
2	Volkswagen	2011	52,009
2	Volkswagen	2012a	71,965
2	Volkswagen	2012b	44,347
2	Volkswagen	2013	70,548
2	Volkswagen	2014	72,394
3	Hyundai	2016	61,326
4	General Motors	2015	59,329
5	Ford	2015/2016	74,387
6	Nissan	2016	62,394
7	Fiat	2015	88,788
8	Honda	2015	50,555
9	Suzuki	2015	66,092
10	Renault	2015	246,680
11	PSA	2014	136,224
12	BMW	2015	50,281
13	SAIC	Excluded from analysis: no English document available.	
14	Daimler	2015	49,018
15	Mazda	2015	92,206
Average			76.828

We also conducted an additional test about which reporting standard was used in order to control for possible differences caused by regulatory influences. We found that 13 out of 15 firms rely on the Global Reporting Initiative (GRI) Standard in its fourth version. The only firms that did not use this standard were Toyota and Suzuki. Thus, a systematic bias due to different reporting standards can be excluded.

Statistical analysis

In the beginning, we used the LIWC for the analysis. All CSR reports were loaded into the program and categories that were derived from our hypotheses were selected for analysis. After having analyzed all documents with the LIWC software, we transferred the values into SPSS for further calculations. The procedure was conducted multiple times by two researchers to ensure compliant results for all values. No differences were found in those executions.

Results

Descriptive data

Table 2 gives an overview of the documents that were analyzed with the LIWC. In total, 14 reports (SAIC was excluded) published in 2015/2016 were analyzed. The length of the documents range from 34,358 to 246,680 words with an average length of 76,828 words. All reports were analyzed for the 18 categories that are connected to the hypotheses.

Before testing our hypotheses, two robustness checks were executed. First, we checked whether VW's latest CSR report of 2014 differs from those published in 2011, 2012 and 2013. A t-test revealed no significant differences at a 0.01 level of probability. Therefore, we conclude that the latest five CSR documents from VW (all published before the Dieselgate) do not differ in regard to their linguistic composition.

Second, we tested for potential cultural bias (e.g. Evans and Levinson 2009) and compared VW's latest CSR report with those of the other two German companies BMW and Daimler. A t-test revealed significant differences for most of the analyzed categories. Thus, we conclude that potential differences between VW's CSR reports and the industry average are not biased by cultural differences. Table 3 presents the means and standard deviations for all categories. A two-tailed t-test was conducted in

Table 3. Means, standard deviations and results of *t*-tests for all categories.

Linguistic dimension	Linguistic category	Indicator (from LIWC)	Unit	VW (mean)	VW (SD)	Industry (mean)	Industry (SD)	Two-tailed t-test	Hypo-thesis
Morpho-logy	Number and person	I	%	0.23	0.17	0.06	0.07	0.08*	H1a: ✓
		we	%	0.69	0.39	1.22	1.08	0.15	H1b: X
	Gender	Article usage	%	7.07	0.43	5.94	1.18	0.01***	H2: ✓
	Tense	Focus-future	%	0.55	0.10	0.61	0.19	0.40	H3a: X
		Focus-past	%	1.43	0.08	1.16	0.21	0.00***	H3b: X
	Letters vs. numbers	Number	%	9.68	3.42	8.39	2.38	0.38	H4: (✓)
		Quantitative	%	2.39	0.47	1.93	0.48	0.09*	
Syntax	Conjunctions	Conj (inclusive)	%	4.35	0.61	4.91	0.81	0.19	H5: X
		Differ (exclusive)	%	0.99	0.07	0.97	0.22	0.79	
	Length of a sentence	WPS (words per sentence)	Raw number	27.71	2.06	31.79	5.22	0.03**	H6: ✓
Semantics	Positive and negative emotions	Negemo (negative emotions)	%	0.51	0.08	0.57	0.10	0.32	H7a: X
		Posemo (positive emotions)	%	2.46	0.13	3.11	0.71	0.06*	H7b: ✓
	Emotional tone	Tone	Formula	62.56	3.09	72.22	11.94	0.02**	H7c: ✓
	Tentative words	Tentative	%	0.81	0.07	0.74	0.21	0.35	H8: X
	Risk and anxiety	Risk	%	0.56	0.05	0.86	0.20	0.00***	H9: ✓
		Anxiety	%	0.15	0.04	0.21	0.07	0.09*	
Pragmatics	Slang and informal language	Informal	%	0.61	0.46	0.40	0.30	0.39	H10: X
	Quotes	Quote	%	0.96	0.19	0.47	0.17	0.00***	H11: ✓

Significance levels: $^{*}p<.10$; $^{**}p<.05$, $^{***}p<.01$/Hypothesis results: ✓= confirmed, X = rejected order to check for significant differences between the CSR reports of VW and those of its main competitors (industry). The results for this analysis can be found in Table 3.

Test of hypotheses

In Hypothesis H1a, we proposed that CSR reports of de-couplers use more words with an individual or I-focus, whereas H1b postulated that de-couplers use fewer words with a collective or we-focus than those of implementors. With a mean of 0.23%, VW uses more I-form words than the industry average (0.06%). This difference is significant at a 0.10-level and hence H1a is confirmed. The "We-form" is used more often in the benchmark industry, with an average of 1.22%, than by VW (0.69%), albeit this difference is not significant. Hence, H1b is not supported.

We find support for Hypothesis 2 which proposed that CSR reports of de-couplers contain more articles than those of implementors. The difference between VW (7.07%) and the industry average (5.94%) is statistically significant at a 0.01-level.

Hypothesis 3a und 3 b proposed that CSR reports of de-couplers contain more future and less past references than those of implementors. Contrary to our expectation, the CSR reports of VW are more past-oriented (1.43%) than those of competitors (1.16%). No significant differences were found for future orientation. Thus, H3a and H3b are rejected.

As expected in Hypothesis 4, CSR reports of VW contain more numbers (9.68%) than those of competitors (8.39%). However, this difference is not statistically significant. In line with our argument, VW uses more quantitative measures (2.39%) than in the industrial average (1.93%). This difference is significant at a 0.1-level. Thus, H4 is partially supported.

Contrary to our argument in Hypothesis 5, VW uses less inclusive conjunctions (4.35%) compared to the industry benchmark (4.91%). Exclusive language is almost equally used by VW (0.99%) and the other automobile manufacturers (0.97%). Therefore, H5 is rejected.

Hypothesis 6 proposed that CSR reports of de-couplers have fewer words per sentence than those of implementors. VW's CSR reports' sentences were shorter (27.71 words) than those of its competitors (31.79 words). The difference is statistically significant at a 0.05-level. Thus, H6 is fully supported.

In Hypotheses 7a and 7 b, we assumed that CSR reports of de-couplers contain more negative and less positive emotion words than those of implementors. VW uses more negative emotion words (0.51%) than the industry average (0.10%). However, the differences are not statistically significant and hence H7a is not supported. Positive emotion words were less used by VW (2.46%) than by its competitors (3.11%), being statistically significant at a 0.1-level. Thus, we can support H7b. Moreover, in congruence with our argumentation, CSR reports of de-couplers have a more negative, downbeat emotional tone than those of implementors. The value of this Emotional Tone Indicator is expressed on a spectrum of 0 to 100, with 0 being sad and 100 being happy. 'A number around 50 suggests either a lack of emotionality or different levels of ambivalence' (Pennebaker et al. 2015a, 22). VW has an Emotional Tone Indicator of 62.56 whereas the industry average is almost 10 points higher with 72.2. The difference is significant on a 0.05-level. Hence, H7c is supported.

Hypothesis 8 proposed that CSR reports of de-couplers contain more tentative words than those of implementors. Hypothesis 8 is not supported. No significant differences are revealed between the scores for VW (0.81%) and for its competitors (0.74%).

In Hypothesis 9, we argued that CSR reports of de-couplers use less words connected to risks and anxiety than those of implementors. VW uses fewer words connected to risk (0.56%) and anxiety (0.15%) than the other car producers do (risk: 0.86%; anxiety: 0.21%). The differences are significant at a 0.01-level and 0.1-level respectively. Hence, H9 is fully supported.

Hypothesis 10 proposed that CSR reports of de-couplers use more slang and informal language than implementors. While this score is higher for VW (0.61%) than for its competitors (0.40%), the difference is not statistically significant. Therefore, H10 is not supported.

Our last Hypothesis H11 claimed that CSR reports of de-couplers include more quotes than those of implementors. A highly significant difference on a 0.01-level was revealed between VW (0.96%) and its competitors (0.17%). Thus, the data fully support H11.

Discussion

We employed Basu and Palazzo's (2008) process model that connects linguistics and behavior, and the concept of organizational decoupling and a model of linguistics that includes the four dimensions of morphology, syntax, semantics, and pragmatics, to formulate 11 research hypotheses. We conducted a linguistic content analysis of VW's CSR reports and compared it with a sample of 14 other large car manufacturers by using the LIWC software. We found evidence that VW's CSR reports differ significantly from those of its competitors in all four linguistic dimensions. Thus, we support the view of previous studies that the linguistic content analysis is an appropriate methodology for distinguishing truth tellers from de-couplers (Crilly, Hansen, and Zollo 2016; DePaulo et al. 2003; Newman et al. 2003). Moreover, we are in line with Lock and Seele (2015) who argue that content analysis is a helpful tool for combining communication and linguistic sciences with business ethics. Our study can be considered as a first innovative approach that provides a toolset for further linguistic analysis in this context.

More specifically, we found that the CSR reports of the VW Group—in comparison to its competitors—contain significantly more I-forms, articles and quantitative measures, longer sentences, less positive emotion words and a lower emotional tone, more words related to risks and anxiety, as well as more quotes. Those results are congruent with Kaufman's (2015) analysis which found significant differences between VW's CSR reports and those of its competitors concerning the use of important CSR keywords, such as non-carbon gases. Thus, the results show that differences cannot only be observed for specific keywords but also in regards to linguistic dimensions, such as morphology, syntax, semantics and pragmatics.

However, one reason for the rejection of H3a and H3b (past vs. future tense) may be the long history of VW's CSR reports in comparison to competing companies. VW's first English CSR report was published in 2001, while the first CSR reports of Toyota or PSA Peugeot Citroën, for example, were published in English for the first time in 2011 and 2008 respectively. Thus, VW may use the past tense more often than carmakers with a shorter CSR (reports') history in order to refer to past reports or projects. Future studies may consider this aspect and compare companies that started to report about their CSR activities in similar years. A potential explanation for the rejection of H5 may be that some conjunctions cannot be unambiguously classified as inclusive or exclusive. For example, "or" can have both, an inclusive and exclusive meaning. Pennebaker et al. (2015a; 2015b) mention the problematic psychometrics and poor internal reliabilities of those two categories. Similarly, inclusive conjunctions, such as "and" and "with," become exclusive when they are connected to the term "not." Thus, future studies should apply more specific measures of inclusive and exclusive conjunctions that take into consideration the semantic context in which they are used. Moreover, the non-significant difference in H8 may be explained by the generally low usage of tentative words in the two subsamples. Since external auditors and consultancies (GRI Sustainability Disclosure Database 2017; PricewaterhouseCoopers 2017) increasingly monitor CSR reports, companies tend to avoid tentative statements that could be interpreted as uncertainties or loopholes for future violations. Thus, only marginal differences with regard to this semantic category can be observed. One explanation for the rejection of H10 may be that CSR reports are generally written in a formal language. Thus, while differences between VW and the industry average can be observed, the absolute amount of slang and informal words is very low. Moreover, external auditors and consultancies may generally advise companies to avoid informal language in CSR reports.

Theoretical contribution

As an important theoretical contribution, this study enriches the concept of decoupling by connecting it to linguistics. Language can be a window into the true intentions of the authors of a text. By developing and applying a systematic model of linguistic dimensions, we extend existing research which is often eclectic and incoherent and show that specific linguistic categories can be used as deception markers. However, only parts of our research hypothesis were supported and no systematic differences between the explanatory power of the categories of morphology, syntax, semantics, and pragmatics were found. We consider the use of Basu and Palazzo's (2008) process model in our empirical analysis as another theoretical contribution of our study. Overall, we emulate the authors' idea that CSR has to be viewed from a tripartite process perspective as the analysis of the cognitive (thinking), linguistic (saying) and conative (behavior) dimensions might help to shed light on corporations' CSR compliance and their decoupling tendencies. Our study shows which specific linguistic categories allow for the determination of differences between the linguistic and conative dimensions and, thus, specify Basu and Palazzo's model in a concrete context.

Contribution to practice

As a major practical contribution, this study helps stakeholders to detect CSR decoupling before it becomes obvious in the form of public scandals. For example, NGOs, public relations agencies and firms can run linguistic tests on CSR reports or codes of conducts in order to analyze whether hidden and, yet, unknown decoupling tendencies exist in these documents. Thus, linguistic analyses could prevent potential wrongdoings in the future. Our results can help managers to reflect on their own communication and that of their colleagues in order to recognize intents to mislead. However, our results can also guide companies and managers of how to phrase their statements in a linguistically appropriate way and, thus, disguise intentional decoupling.

Limitations and implications for future research

Despite the contributions to theoretical and practical knowledge, some limitations have to be mentioned. First, the methodology of linguistic content analysis is not yet fully developed. For example, the LIWC categories were originally developed for studies in the clinical and psychological context which consist of a different language and word structures than CSR reports (Newman et al. 2003). Nevertheless, recently, as stated earlier, the LIWC was also be applied regularly in the business and management context. Different contexts use different text corpora, and this cannot be fully captured by linguistic analysis that is rather content-blind. One example is negations that have to be put in context, e.g. "I am not happy" versus "I am sad" (Dönges 2009). Thus, future studies may refine the methodology of linguistic content analysis and, for example, develop measures which reflect the construct of CSR in a more valid way.

Furthermore, it could be worthwhile to use the same methodology for the analysis of CSR reports of companies in other industries where decoupling took place, e.g. Union Carbide, Nike, Exxon or Shell (Banerjee 2008). Also, the financial scandals of Enron in the year 2001 and Wirecard in 2020 could yield valuable insights. It would be interesting to see whether linguistic differences between those firms and implementors in the same industry can be observed too, and how these differences connect to the findings of this study. In this regards, future research also has to consider how new ISO norms or the new EU regulations for CSR reporting, implemented after 2015/2016, might influence the results of our study.

Finally, the linguistic content analysis could be extended with a web of meanings and visual perspective (Kassinis and Panayiotou 2018; Meyer et al. 2013). The inclusion of pictures and visualizations could shed further light on decoupling tendencies in CSR reports. As nonlinguistic elements play an increasing role in corporate communication, future studies in this context should therefore include this aspect.

ORCID

Dirk Holtbrügge http://orcid.org/0000-0002-9004-5274

References

Åhlström, J. 2010. "Corporate Response to CSO Criticism: Decoupling the Corporate Responsibility Discourse from Business Practice." *Corporate Social Responsibility and Environmental Management* 17 (2):70–80. doi: 10.1002/csr.232.

Argyris, C. 1957. *Personality and Organization: The Conflict between System and the Individual.* New Yok: Harper & Row.

Banerjee, S. B. 2008. "Corporate Social Responsibility: The Good, the Bad and the Ugly." *Critical Sociology* 34 (1): 51–79. doi: 10.1177/0896920507084623.

Basu, K., and G. Palazzo. 2008. "Corporate Social Responsibility: A Process Model of Sense-Making." *Academy of Management Review* 33 (1):122–136. doi: 10.5465/amr.2008.27745504.

Beelitz, A., and D. M. Merkl-Davies. 2012. "Using Discourse to Restore Organizational Legitimacy: 'CEO-Speak'after an Incident in a German Nuclear Power Plant." *Journal of Business Ethics* 108 (1):101–120. doi: 10.1007/s10551-011-1065-9.

Beverland, M., and S. Luxton. 2005. "Managing Integrated Marketing Communication (IMC) through Strategic Decoupling: How Luxury Wine Firms Retain Brand Leadership While Appearing to Be Wedded to the Past." *Journal of Advertising* 34 (4):103–116. doi: 10.1080/00913367.2005.10639207.

Bond, C. F., and B. M. DePaulo. 2006. "Accuracy of Deception Judgments." *Personality and Social Psychology Review: An Official Journal of the Society for Personality and Social Psychology, Inc* 10 (3):214–34. doi: 10.1207/s15327957pspr1003_2.

Booij, G. 2012. *The Grammar of Words: An Introduction to Linguistic Morphology*, Oxford, UK: Oxford University Press.

Bowman, E. H., and M. Haire. 1976. "Social Impact Disclosure and Corporate Annual Reports." *Accounting." Organizations and Society* 1 (1):11–21. doi: 10.1016/0361-3682(76)90004-0.

Brine, M., R. Brown, and G. Hackett. 2007. "Corporate Social Responsibility and Financial Performance in the Australian Context." *Economic Round-up* Autumn 2007:47.

Cavazos, D. E., M. Rutherford, and S. L. Berman. 2018. "Assessing the Effect of Government Surveillance on Firm Supererogation: The Case of the US Automobile Industry." *Business Ethics: A European Review* 27 (2):156–63. doi: 10.1111/beer.12179.

Christensen, L. T., M. Morsing, and O. Thyssen. 2013. "CSR as Aspirational Talk." *Organization* 20 (3):372–393. doi: 10.1177/1350508413478310.

Christian Aid. 2004. *Behind the Mask: The Real Face of Corporate Social Responsibility.* London, UK: Christian Aid.

Chung, C. K., and J. W. Pennebaker. 2008. "Revealing Dimensions of Thinking in Open-Ended Self-Descriptions: An Automated Meaning Extraction Method for Natural Language." *Journal of Research in Personality* 42 (1): 96–132. doi: 10.1016/j.jrp.2007.04.006.

Chung, C. K., and J. W. Pennebaker. 2013. *Counting Little Words in Big Data: The Psychology of Communities, Culture, and History.* Austin, TX: The University of Texas at Austin.

Cetindamar, D., B. Ozkazanc-Pan. 2017. "Assessing Mission Drift at Venture Capital Impact Investors." *Business Ethics: A European Review* 26 (3):257–270. doi: 10.1111/beer.12149.

Clemente, M., and C. Gabbioneta. 2017. "How Does the Media Frame Corporate Scandals? The Case of German Newspapers and the Volkswagen Diesel Scandal." *Journal of Management Inquiry* 26 (3):287–302. doi: 10.1177/1056492616689304.

Crilly, D., M. T. Hansen, and M. Zollo. 2012. "Faking It or Muddling through? Understanding Decoupling in Response to Stakeholder Pressures." *Academy of Management Journal* 55 (6):1429–1448. doi: 10.5465/amj.2010.0697.

Crilly, D., M. T. Hansen, and M. Zollo. 2016. "The Grammar of Decoupling: A Cognitive-Linguistic Perspective on Firms' Sustainability Claims and Stakeholders' Interpretation." *Academy of Management Journal* 59 (2):705–729. doi: 10.5465/amj.2015.0171.

Crystal, D. 2011. *Dictionary of Linguistics and Phonetics*. Vol. 30. Berlin, New York: John Wiley & Sons.

Dahl, Ö. (Ed.). 2000. *Tense and Aspect in the Languages of Europe*. Walter de Gruyter.

Dans, E. 2015. "Volkswagen and the Failure of Corporate Social Responsibility." Forbes Online. Accessed March 15, 2019. https://www.forbes.com/sites/enriquedans/2015/09/27/volkswagen-and-the-failure-of-corporate-social-responsibility/#1d0dc84c4405.

DePaulo, B. M., J. J. Lindsay, B. E. Malone, L. Muhlenbruck, K. Charlton, and H. Cooper. 2003. "Cues to Deception." *Psychological Bulletin* 129 (1):74–118. doi: 10.1037/0033-2909.129.1.74.

Douglas Clinton, B. 2008. "Can we Detect Fraud Earlier?" *Strategic Finance* 90 (4):51.

Dreber, A., and M. Johannesson. 2008. "Gender Differences in Deception." *Economics Letters* 99 (1):197–9. doi: 10.1016/j.econlet.2007.06.027.

Dönges, J. 2009. Psychologie. Sprachanalyse. Du bist, was du sprichst. Accessed November 28, 2019. www.spektrum.de/pdf/gug-09-01-s024-pdf/975890?file.

Du, S., C. B. Bhattacharya, and S. Sen. 2010. "Maximizing Business Returns to Corporate Social Responsibility (CSR): The Role of CSR Communication." *International Journal of Management Reviews* 12 (1):8–19. doi: 10.1111/j.1468-2370.2009.00276.x.

Elson, C. M., C. K. Ferrere, and N. J. Goossen. 2015. "The Bug at Volkswagen: Lessons in Co-Determination, Ownership and Board Structure." *Journal of Applied Corporate Finance* 27 (4):36–43. doi: 10.1111/jacf.12144.

Evans, N., and S. C. Levinson. 2009. "The Myth of Language Universals: Language Diversity and Its Importance for Cognitive Science." *The Behavioral and Brain Sciences* 32 (5):429–448. doi: 10.1017/S0140525X0999094X.

Fabb, N. 2016. "Linguistic Theory, Linguistic Diversity and Whorfian Economics." In *The Palgrave Handbook of Economics and Language*, edited by V. Ginsburgh and S. Weber, 17–60. London: Palgrave Macmillan.

Frawley, W. 1992. *Linguistic Semantics*. Hillsdale, New Jersey: Lawrence Erlbaum Associates.

Frostenson, M., S. Helin, and J. Sandström. 2012. "The Internal Significance of Codes of Conduct in Retail Companies." *Business Ethics: A European Review* 21 (3):263–275. doi: 10.1111/j.1467-8608.2012.01657.x.

Graafland, J., and H. Smid. 2019. "Decoupling among CSR Policies, Programs, and Impacts: An Empirical Study." *Business & Society* 58 (2):231–267. doi: 10.1177/0007650316647951.

Grazioli, S., and S. L. Jarvenpaa. 2000. "Perils of Internet Fraud: An Empirical Investigation of Deception and Trust with Experienced Internet Consumers." *IEEE Transactions on Systems, Man, and Cybernetics – Part A: Systems and Humans* 30 (4):395–410. doi: 10.1109/3468.852434.

GRI Sustainability Disclosure Database. 2017. "Benefits of Reporting." https://www.globalreporting.org/information/sustainability-reporting/Pages/reporting-benefits.aspx.

Goel, S., and J. Gangolly. 2012. "Beyond the Numbers: Mining the Annual Reports for Hidden Cues Indicative of Financial Statement Fraud." *Intelligent Systems in Accounting, Finance and Management* 19 (2):75–89. doi: 10.1002/isaf.1326.

Guthrie, J. E., and M. R. Mathews. 1985. "Corporate Social Accounting in Australasia." In *Research in Corporate Social Performance and Policy*, 251–277. JAI Press.

Haack, P., D. Schoeneborn, and C. Wickert. 2012. "Talking the Talk, Moral Entrapment, Creeping Commitment? Exploring Narrative Dynamics in Corporate Responsibility Standardization." *Organization Studies* 33 (5–6):815–845. doi: 10.1177/0170840612443630.

Haberstroh, K., U. R. Orth, S. Hoffmann, and B. Brunk. 2017. "Consumer Response to Unethical Corporate Behavior: A Re-Examination and Extension of the Moral Decoupling Model." *Journal of Business Ethics* 140 (1):161–173. doi: 10.1007/s10551-015-2661-x.

Hancock, J. T., C. Toma, and N. Ellison. 2007. "The Truth About Lying in Online Dating Profiles." Proceedings of the SIGCHI conference on Human factors in computing systems, San Jose, California, USA, April 28–May 03,2007, ACM, New York, NY, 449–452.

Hancock, J. T., L.E. Curry, S. Goorha, and M. Woodworth. 2007. "On Lying and Being Lied to: A Linguistic Analysis of Deception in Computer-Mediated Communication." *Discourse Processes* 45 (1):1–23. doi: 10.1080/01638530701739181.

Hart, C. 2014. *Discourse, Grammar, and Ideology: Functional and Cognitive Perspectives*. London, UK: Bloomsbury.

Hauch, V., J. Masip, I. Blandon-Gitlin, and S. L. Sporer. 2012. "Linguistic Cues to Deception Assessed by Computer Programs: A Meta-Analysis." In *Proceedings of the EACL 2012 Workshop on Computational Approaches to Deception Detection*, 1–4. Avignon, France: Association for Computational Linguistics.

Ingenbleek, P., M. Binnekamp, and S. Goddijn. 2007. "Setting Standards for CSR: A Comparative Case Study on Criteria-Formulating Organizations." *Journal of Business Research* 60 (5):539–548. doi: 10.1016/j.jbusres.2007.01.004.

Jamali, D., P. Lund-Thomsen, and N. Khara. 2017. "CSR Institutionalized Myths in Developing Countries: An Imminent Threat of Selective Decoupling." *Business & Society* 56 (3):454–486. doi: 10.1177/0007650315584303.

Joyner, B. E., and D. Payne. 2002. "Evolution and Implementation: A Study of Values, Business Ethics and Corporate Social Responsibility." *Journal of Business Ethics* 41 (4):297–311. doi: 10.1023/A:1021237420663.

Kassinis, G., and A. Panayiotou. 2018. "Visuality as Greenwashing: The Case of BP and Deepwater Horizon." *Organization & Environment* 31 (1):25–47. doi: 10.1177/1086026616687014.

Kaufman, A. C. 2015, September 25. "People Probably Should Have Been More Suspicious Of Volkswagen." Accessed March 15, 2019. http://www.huffingtonpost.com/entry/people-probably-should-have-been-more-suspicious-of-volkswagen_us_560589a2e4b0af3706dc148f.

Knapp, M. L., R. P. Hart, and H. S. Dennis. 1974. "An Exploration of Deception as a Communication Construct." *Human Communication Research* 1 (1):15–29. doi: 10.1111/j.1468-2958.1974.tb00250.x.

Karaye, Y. I., Z. Ishak, and N. Che-Adam. 2014. "The Mediating Effect of Stakeholder Influence Capacity on the Relationship between Corporate Social Responsibility and Corporate Financial Performance." *Procedia – Social and Behavioral Sciences* 164:528–534. doi: 10.1016/j.sbspro.2014.11.142.

Kristof, K. M. 2003, August 26. "Study Ties Biggest CEO Raises to Largest Layoffs." Accessed March 15, 2019. http://articles.latimes.com/2003/aug/26/business/fi-execpay26.

Lachman, M.E., C. Röcke, C. Rosnick, and C.D. Ryff. 2008. "Realism and Illusion in Americans' Temporal Views of their Life Satisfaction: Age Differences in Reconstructing the Past and Anticipating the Future." *Psychological Science* 19 (9):889–897. doi: 10.1111/j.1467-9280.2008.02173.x.

Langacker, R. W. 2008. *Cognitive Grammar: An Introduction*, Oxford UK: Oxford University Press.

Larcker, D. F., and A. A. Zakolyukina. 2012. "Detecting Deceptive Discussions in Conference Calls." *Journal of Accounting Research* 50 (2):495–540. doi: 10.1111/j.1475-679X.2012.00450.x.

Lock, I., and P. Seele. 2015. "Quantitative Content Analysis as a Method for Business Ethics Research." *Business Ethics: A European Review* 24:S24–S40. doi: 10.1111/beer.12095.

MacLean, T., B. E. Litzky, and D. K. Holderness. 2015. "When Organizations Don't Walk Their Talk: A Cross-Level Examination of How Decoupling Formal Ethics Programs Affects Organizational Members." *Journal of Business Ethics* 128 (2):351–368. doi: 10.1007/s10551-014-2103-1.

March, J. G., and Z. Shapira. 1987. "Managerial Perspectives on Risk and Risk Taking." *Management Science* 33 (11):1404–1418. doi: 10.1287/mnsc.33.11.1404.

Matten, D., and J. Moon. 2008. "Implicit' and 'Explicit' CSR: A Conceptual Framework for a Comparative Understanding of Corporate Social Responsibility." *Academy of Management Review* 33 (2):404–424. doi: 10.5465/amr.2008.31193458.

Meck, G. 2016. *Auto Macht Geld: Die Geschichte der Familie Porsche Piëch*. Rowohlt Berlin Verlag GmbH.

Meyer, J. W., and B. Rowan. 1977. "Institutionalized Organizations: Formal Structure as Myth and Ceremony." *American Journal of Sociology* 83 (2):340–363. doi: 10.1086/226550.

Meyer, R. E., M.A. Höllerer, D. Jancsary, and T. Van Leeuwen. 2013. "The Visual Dimension in Organizing, Organization, and Organization Research: Core Ideas, Current Developments, and Promising Avenues." *Academy of Management Annals* 7 (1):489–555. doi: 10.5465/19416520.2013.781867.

Milne, M.J., and R. W. Adler. 1999. "Exploring the Reliability of Social and Environmental Disclosures Content Analysis." *Accounting, Auditing & Accountability Journal* 12 (2):237–256. doi: 10.1108/09513579910270138.

Moir, L. 2001. "What Do We Mean by Corporate Social Responsibility?" *Corporate Governance: The International Journal of Business in Society* 1 (2):16–22. doi: 10.1108/EUM0000000005486.

Newman, M. L., J. W. Pennebaker, D. S. Berry, and J. M. Richards. 2003. "Lying Words: Predicting Deception from Linguistic Styles." *Personality & Social Psychology Bulletin* 29 (5):665–675. doi: 10.1177/0146167203029005010.

Newman, M. L., C. J. Groom, L. D. Handelman, and J. W. Pennebaker. 2008. "Gender Differences in Language Use: An Analysis of 14,000 Text Samples." *Discourse Processes* 45 (3):211–236. doi: 10.1080/01638530802073712.

OICA. 2015. "World Motor Vehicle Production. OICA correspondents survey, World Ranking Of Manufacturers." Accessed March 15, 2019. http://www.oica.net/wp-content/uploads//ranking2015.pdf.

Ott, M., Y. Choi, C. Cardie, and J. T. Hancock. 2011. "Finding Deceptive Opinion Spam by Any Stretch of the Imagination." Proceedings of the 49th Annual Meeting of the Association for Computational Linguistics: Human Language Technologies-Volume 1, Association for Computational Linguistics, 309–319.

Patten, D. M., and W. Crampton. 2004. "Legitimacy and the Internet: An Examination of Corporate Web Page Environmental Disclosures." *Advances in Environmental Accounting & Management. Journal of Applied Communication Research* 25 (2):31–57.

Pennebaker, J. W., and L. A. King. 1999. "Linguistic Styles: Language Use as an Individual Difference." *Journal of Personality and Social Psychology* 77 (6):1296–1312. doi: 10.1037/0022-3514.77.6.1296.

Pennebaker, J. W., R. J. Booth, R. L. Boyd, and M. E. Francis. 2015a. *Linguistic Inquiry and Word Count: LIWC2015*, Austin, TX: Pennebaker Conglomerates.

Pennebaker, J. W., R. L. Boyd, K. Jordan, and K. Blackburn. 2015b. *The Development and Psychometric Properties of LIWC*. Austin, TX: University of Texas at Austin.

Pollach, I. 2003. "Communicating Corporate Ethics on the World Wide Web: A Discourse Analysis of Selected Company Web Sites." *Business & Society* 42 (2):277–287. doi: 10.1177/0007650303042002006.

PricewaterhouseCoopers. 2017. "17th Annual Global CEO Survey. Business Success Beyond the Short Term: CEO Perspectives on Sustainability." Accessed March 15, 2019. https://www.pwc.com/gx/en/sustainability/ceo-views/assets/pwc-ceo-summary-sustainability.pdf.

Raghunathan, R., and M. T. Pham. 1999. "All Negative Moods Are Not Equal: Motivational Influences of Anxiety and Sadness on Decision Making." *Organizational Behavior and Human Decision Processes* 79 (1):56–77. doi: 10.1006/obhd.1999.2838.

Rasche, A., and D. U. Gilbert. 2015. "Decoupling Responsible Management Education: Why Business Schools May Not Walk Their Talk." *Journal of Management Inquiry* 24 (3):239–252. doi: 10.1177/1056492614567315.

Raman, G. V., S. Garg, and S. Thapliyal. 2019. "Integrative Live Case: A Contemporary Business Ethics Pedagogy." *Journal of Business Ethics* 155 (4):1009–1032. doi: 10.1007/s10551-017-3514-6.

Ruegger, D., and E. W. King. 1992. "A Study of the Effect of Age and Gender upon Student Business Ethics." *Journal of Business Ethics* 11 (3):179–186. doi: 10.1007/BF00871965.

Sattelberger, T. 2016, June 16. "Wir hier oben." Accessed March 15, 2019. http://www.zeit.de/2016/24/manager-fuehrungsstil-selbstherrlichkeit-krise-unternehmen.

Scholz, C. 2016, January 25. "Volkswagen verpatzt den Kulturwandel." Accessed March 15, 2019. http://www.manager-magazin.de/unternehmen/autoindustrie/volkswagen-warum-matthias-mueller-die-falsche-wahl-fuer-vw-war-a-1073722.html.

Schneider, M. C. 2016. *Volkswagen. Eine Deutsche Geschichte*. Berlin/Munich, Germany: Berlin Verlag.

Setó-Pamies, D. 2015. "The Relationship between Women Directors and Corporate Social Responsibility." *Corporate Social Responsibility and Environmental Management* 22 (6):334–345. doi: 10.1002/csr.1349.

Siano, A., A. Vollero, F. Conte, and S. Amabile. 2017. "More than Words': Expanding the Taxonomy of Greenwashing after the Volkswagen Scandal." *Journal of Business Research* 71:27–37. doi: 10.1016/j.jbusres.2016.11.002.

Strauss, G. 2003, 25 August. "CEOs Still Sitting on Piles of Pay." *USA Today* C3:7.

Tausczik, Y. R., and J. W. Pennebaker. 2010. "The Psychological Meaning of Words: LIWC and Computerized Text Analysis Methods." *Journal of Language and Social Psychology* 29 (1):24–54. doi: 10.1177/0261927X09351676.

Tjosvold, D., Z. Y. Yu, and C. Hui. 2004. "Team Learning from Mistakes: The Contribution of Cooperative Goals and Problem-Solving." *Journal of Management Studies* 41 (7):1223–1245. doi: 10.1111/j.1467-6486.2004.00473.x.

Volkswagen, A. G. 2014. "Strategy. Annual Report 2014." Accessed March 25, 2018 http://annualreport2014.volkswagenag.com/strategy.html.

Vrij, A. 2000. *Detecting Lies and Deceit: The Psychology of Lying and the Implications for Professional Practice*. Chichester, UK: Wiley.

Waters, J. A. 1991. "(Corporate) Morality as an Organizational Phenomenon." In *Unternehmensethik*, edited by V. H. Steinmann, 278–300. Stuttgart, Löhr. Betriebswirtschaftlicher Verlag Dr. Th. Gabler GmbH, Wiesbaden 1989.

Weaver, G. R., L. K. Treviño, and P. L. Cochran. 1999. "Integrated and Decoupled Corporate Social Performance: Management Commitments, External Pressures, and Corporate Ethics Practices." *Academy of Management Journal* 42 (5):539–552.

Whorf, B. L. 2012. *Language, Thought, and Reality: Selected Writings of Benjamin Lee Whorf*. Cambridge, Massachusetts: MIT Press.

Whyte, G. 1991. "Diffusion of Responsibility: Effects on the Escalation Tendency." *Journal of Applied Psychology* 76 (3):408–415. doi: 10.1037/0021-9010.76.3.408.

Wickert, C., A. G. Scherer, and L. J. Spence. 2016. "Walking and Talking Corporate Social Responsibility: Implications of Firm Size and Organizational Cost." *Journal of Management Studies* 53 (7):1169–1196. doi: 10.1111/joms.12209.

Zajac, E. J., and J. D. Westphal. 2004. "The Social Construction of Market Value: Institutionalization and Learning Perspectives on Stock Market Reactions." *American Sociological Review* 69 (3):433–457. doi: 10.1177/000312240406900306.

Zuckerman, M., B. M. DePaulo, 1981. and, and R. Rosenthal. "Verbal and Nonverbal Communication of Deception." In *Advances in Experimental Social Psychology*, edited by L. Berkowitz, 1–59. New York: Academic Press.

The ethical challenge of Big Tech's "disruptive philanthropy"

Paul Manning, Nigel Baker and Peter Stokes

ABSTRACT

This article provides a review of research into global philanthropy and the disruptive practices of new technology companies. In this article we detail how "Big Tech" has created a new marketization of philanthropy, based on its sectoral values of innovation, entrepreneurialism and focus on financial and performance metrics. Consequently, we argue for a new ontology of philanthropy that acknowledges marketization as its guiding principle. The study examines and compares different market-focused, philanthropic paradigms, which have evolved through the business values of Big Tech and examines their moral motivations. The topic is viewed through the lens of 'hybrid organizations'; a model for nonprofit entities and social businesses which, in turn, are seeking a market-oriented pathway of balancing the twin demands of managing mission and money. A conceptual framework is then provided to inform practitioners in nonprofit organizations about the issues and risks of engaging with the new types of philanthropy, to which we collectively refer as 'disruptive philanthropy'. The article concludes by recommending further research into the ethics of Big Tech to understand the true motivations behind its philanthropic practices at a time when the sector is under intense governmental and media scrutiny.

Introduction

Being digital is different. We are not waiting on any intervention. It is here. It is now. It is almost genetic in its nature, in that each generation will become more digital than the preceding one (Negroponte 1995, 231).

Nicholas Negroponte, the digital visionary and founding director of MIT's Media Lab, gave a foretaste in the mid-1990s of how the digital age would be one of permanent evolution across all fields. This study analyzes how the rapid growth of Big Tech companies (Reich 2015) since Negroponte's forecast, has disrupted established approaches to philanthropy in three key areas. First, companies have sought to embed societal benefits in their value chains through adopting practices termed "blended value" (Bugg-Levine and Emerson 2011) and "shared value" (Porter and Kramer 2011). Second, the digital economy has given rise to new philanthropic paradigms which implant its business ethics and practices of being data-focused, strategic-minded and results-oriented (Moody 2008; Goldman 2016)). Third, entrepreneurs, such as Microsoft's Bill Gates and Facebook's Mark Zuckerberg, have amassed fortunes and established philanthropic foundations at a much earlier age than their historical predecessors like Carnegie (Carnegie 2006) and Rockefeller. They have, however, been accused of "disruptive philanthropy" (Horvath and Powell 2016; Brakman Reiser 2017); that is, for being anti-democratic in replacing the public sphere with the scale of their giving. This study adopts the term "disruptive philanthropy" on a wider basis to include all the paradigms which have emerged through the digital economy and Big Tech, and examines their moral motivations. Reich (2015) defines Big Tech as the technology companies such as Google, Amazon and Apple who use their great power and resources to make the "free market" function on their behalf, dominating our economy and politics.

The topic is viewed through the lens of "hybrid organizations," a model for nonprofit entities and social businesses which is an entrepreneurial and market-oriented pathway of balancing the twin demands of managing mission and money (Battilana and Dorado 2010). Just like like nonprofits organization hybrid organizations blur the boundaries of the traditional for-profit/nonprofit divide by pursuing social and environmental issues, but, in addtion, also prioritize generating income to accomplish their mission. In this sense they operate in a commercial framework (Haigh and Hoffman 2012). Further, this hybrid form of social entrepreneurship is creating a paradigm shift in the not-for-profit sector, as the trend is for new philanthropic organizations to be designed to embrace this new hybrid form (Dees 2008).

Big Tech has pioneered these new philanthropic models, which are hybrid in nature, as they obscure the boundaries between nonprofit and commercial activities, For example, the founder of eBay, Pierre Omidyar, turned his philanthropic foundation into a limited liability company in 2003 in order to fund social projects with a nonprofit grant or a for-profit investment, whichever was likely to have the greater impact (Omidyar 2011). Reflecting on this approach, Google decided to create Google.org as a for-profit philanthropic wing in 2006, expressing an interest in funding projects that were more entrepreneurial and market-based than traditional charitable ones (Wallace 2006; Lim 2007).

This article provides a guide to nonprofits about the issues and risks they need to consider if they adopt any of the philanthropic paradigms originating from the digital economy to transform into a more market-oriented hybrid organization. While the philanthropic practices inspired by the digital economy may appeal to hybrid organizations, the rapidly-changing perceptions of the ethics of Big Tech provide a global challenge for both theory and practice in evaluating and understanding the evolving risks of accepting its philanthropy and philanthropic paradigms. For the new paradigms to succeed, there is a requirement for an alignment of ethical and strategic interests between the donor and recipient (Letts et al. 1997; Bugg-Levine and Emerson 2011). In this article, interconnecting literature streams on the new paradigms and hybrid organizations are synthesized into a conceptual framework: first to enable nonprofits to understand the characteristics sought by more market-oriented philanthropy and, second, to be cognizant of the ethical and operational risks of becoming a hybrid organization.

The core argument is that Big Tech has created a new marketization of philanthropy, based on its sectoral values of innovation, entrepreneurialism and quantification through use of data. In this break with previous practices, marketization has been elevated to the key organizing principle, with all aspects of philanthropy being framed with reference to market. It follows that the established notions of philanthropy (Carroll 1979, 1991) have been rendered anachronistic for understanding, analyzing and engaging with this new environment, as there has been a paradigm shift toward using market forces to create social change (Dees 2008). The original assumptions underpinning Carroll's "pyramid of corporate social responsibility" (1991) were that businesses followed their economic responsibility of making a profit, worked in accordance with the law and behaved ethically. The fourth layer of the pyramid was philanthropy, which can be thought of as "the icing on the cake," with businesses contributing in cash or kind to communities. Carroll's original intention was that the four characteristics, taken as a whole, defined the responsible business and while his moral principles may endure, it is argued that, contemporaneously, his pyramid is harder to apply when Big Tech blurs the lines between "economic" and "philanthropic" activities.

This study aims to add to the understanding of the "disruptive philanthropy" paradigms for scholars, as well as for practitioners charged with raising funds in a more market-oriented environment (Eikenberry and Drapal Kluver 2004; Omidyar 2011). The study's research questions are as follows:

1. What are the key characteristics of the new forms of philanthropy? and (2) How should practitioners and scholars conceptualize and respond to, and engage with, this new form of philanthropy?

Scope and methodology

The study takes the form of a narrative, conceptual review, to present an elucidation of contemporary corporate philanthropy and CSR research, as well as what is known about the new paradigms of the twenty-first century. This mode of review is chosen as being suitable when attempting to link together studies on different topics, for the purpose of interconnection, as well as being a valuable, theory-building technique (Baumeister and Leary 1997). The aim is to use the review to tackle the emerging topic of new funding paradigms with the hope of developing a conceptual model to inform research and to help nonprofits seeking funding (Webster and Watson 2002). The researchers are aware that a narrative review can be affected by the reviewer's subjectivity (Randolph 2009) but every measure was undertaken to take a constructive and balanced approach to building theory. The review focuses on inter-connected literature streams concerning the new philanthropic paradigms and hybrid organizations, as follows:

- Venture philanthropy: that is, encouraging foundations to use venture capital practices to strengthen the core capacity of beneficiaries (Letts et al. 1997).
- Impact investing: investment strategies with financial returns and express social and environmental aims (Bugg-Levine and Emerson 2011; Omidyar 2011).
- Shared value: policies and operating practices that enhance the competitiveness of a company while advancing economic and social conditions in the communities in which they operate (Porter and Kramer 2011).
- Data philanthropy: private sector holders of 'Big Data' making it available for the public good (Kirkpatrick 2013; Stempeck 2014).
- Hybrid organizations: those which manage the competing logics of "… the pursuit of the dual mission of financial sustainability and social purpose" (Battilana and Dorado 2010).

The range of literature searched presented extremes. For example, at the time of writing, a Boolean search of Google Scholar for "corporate social responsibility" yielded 523,000 results, but for a combination of "data philanthropy" and "management," only 297. Attempts were made to access material from peer-reviewed journals, rated 2*, and above, according to rankings from the Chartered Association of Business Schools Journal Guide. The emerging nature of the topic, however, means some of the literature on the newer paradigms is drawn from practitioner literature, and academic books.

After preliminary searches in Google Scholar, detailed searches were made in the business and management sections of academic databases JSTOR, EBSCO and ProQuest for articles rated 2* and above, using the search terms "corporate social responsibility," "CSR" and "nonprofit," and "non-profit" and "social business". A similar process was repeated in business and management literature for "corporate philanthropy," coupled with "nonprofit," "non-profit" and "social business," and a third search for "hybrid organization" and "hybrid organisation". The process yielded

44 articles for corporate social responsibility, 65 for corporate philanthropy and 38 for "hybrid organization"/"hybrid organisation," after screening for relevance.

Two of the paradigms reviewed—"Venture Philanthropy" and "Impact Investing"—spring from single conceptual articles. A small body of empirical work surrounds each. The venture philanthropy article by Letts et al. (1997) had been cited 460 times, and Bugg-Levine and Emerson, 242—indicating they have possibly prompted more discussion than action. By comparison, a separate search of Google Scholar, demonstrated that Porter and Kramer's 2011 article on "Creating Shared Value" had been cited nearly 9,800 times (as at time of writing on April 2nd, 2020). Articles on "shared value" were included in the review as the authors claim the concept has influenced digital companies like Google and IBM, and because of its dominance in current literature on CSR and corporate philanthropy Further searches were made of references and bibliographies in related works, as well as of Google and academic data bases. Data philanthropy is addressed in the context of examining the literature surrounding the philanthropic and CSR activities stemming from the large, twenty-first century digital corporations.

There was a clear gap in the business and management literature here surrounding contemporary philanthropic activity and related ethical issues—although it is anticipated that this will be a fast-moving area of research with, for example, controversy over Facebook allowing the political consultancy, Cambridge Analytica, to gain access to the data of tens of millions of the platform's users without their permission, according to Rosenberg et al. (2018) in *The New York Times*. To fill this apparent void, literature was also drawn from legal and data science journals and practitioner material. In all, 32 articles were selected on venture philanthropy, 12 on shared value, 13 on impact investing and 39 on digital philanthropy, including data philanthropy. In terms of digital philanthropy, the search centered on the conceptual and ethical issues and excluded new technologies which have impacted on philanthropy, such as crowd-funding. In total, this review is based on 244 articles.

Findings

Theoretical framework

The literature provides compelling arguments for nonprofit entities wishing to consider becoming hybrid organizations, adopting a less-rigid definition of what is nonprofit activity and what is commercial. Austin et al. (2006) argue that the distinction between social and commercial entrepreneurship is not dichotomous, but rather a continuum ranging from purely social to purely economic. They posit that charitable activity must reflect economic realities, while economic activity must generate social value. There are elements of symmetry with Silicon Valley's "disruptive mantra" (Brakman Reiser 2017) and its desire for innovation (Schervish, et al. 2001; Moody 2008). While hybrid organizations are not perceived as disrupters in the nonprofit sector, they have been described as "positive deviants," acting as institutional entrepreneurs, "changing the rules of the game for all organizations" (Haigh and Hoffman 2012).

The definitions of a hybrid organization offered by the literature also echo the aspirations of the digital economy's funding models, including venture philanthropy, impact investing and shared value. Holt and Littlewood (2015) describe hybrids as existing at the interface between for-profit and nonprofit models, adopting a mission-driven business ethos while pursuing social or environmental goals. Battilana et al. (2012) contend that an "integrated hybrid model produces both social value and commercial revenue through a single unified strategy". A shared link, however, is that they all confront the challenge of "competing logics" in "the pursuit of the dual mission of financial sustainability and social purpose" (Battilana and Dorado 2010).

Along the continuum of social versus economic benefits, however, resides a series of challenges for hybrid organizations, ranging from tensions between mission and finances (Santos et al. 2015) which can lead to mission drift (Ebrahim et al. 2014; Cetindamar and Ozkazanc-Pan 2017) or revenue drift with measurement tools needed to evaluate both social and financial performance (Ponte et al. 2017). Equally, the challenges of balancing profit, and nonprofit, logics can lead to concerns over organizational identity, generating confusion among staff and stakeholders. Both Rawhouser et al. (2015) and Thomasson (2009) underscore how ambiguity of identity, borne of stakeholder confusion, can be a factor in mission drift. Jay (2013) says those who establish hybrid organizations have to navigate paradox to achieve an effective organization and be prepared to evolve a new identity.

Microfinance banks are cited as one of the highest-profile examples of hybrid organizations (Battilana and Dorado 2010). The concept was developed by the economics Nobel laureate Muhammad Yunus, who in 1976 founded the Grameen bank to give small loans without collateral to help entrepreneurs lift themselves out of poverty in Bangladesh (Yunus et al. 2010). Stakeholders replace shareholders as the focus of value maximization. The authors note that established multinational companies have shown some CSR interest in the Grameen concept.

There is some skepticism, however, that the companies support the "triple bottom line" of financial, social and environmental benefits (Elkington 1998). Yunus et al. (2010) conclude that "ultimately only one bottom line usually matters: financial profit". Battilana and Dorado (2010) stress that there is no "ready-to-wear" model for dealing with the tensions this can cause. Their research into two microfinance organizations in Bolivia illustrates the disruptive effect of conflict between the competing demands of two logics—banking and social welfare. They recommend that to achieve sustainability, a novel hybrid organization needs to develop a common organizational identity which strikes a balance between the logics and prevents the emergence of subgroups whose different identities emphasize the tensions. Accordingly, the literature on hybrid organizations provides a lens through which to assess the kinds of challenges which nonprofits might encounter when entering a more market-oriented environment, working with donors, or funders, whose backgrounds are in a commercial culture.

From "positive deviance" (Haigh and Hoffman 2012) to navigating paradox (Jay 2013), nonprofits face the management of significant cultural and operational challenges and, depending on the model of philanthropy they embrace, have to discern whether their funder is only really interested in the financial bottom line (Yunus et al. 2010). It is clear from the literature that there is no single definition of "hybrid organization." This article takes a synoptic view of hybrid organizations to incorporate the literature discussed above to provide the following understanding: The risks factors to be assessed by nonprofits organizations that are considering a more market-oriented approach as a hybrid organization through engaging with the new disruptive philanthropic paradigms.

Disruptive philanthropy defined

Technology continues to drive disruptive change rapidly (Bughin and Van Zeebroeck 2017), with the next wave of technological developments encompassing, by way of example, driverless cars and the acceleration of the robotic replacement of jobs (McKinsey Global Institute 2013). As well as enabling new business models for companies like Amazon, Apple iTunes and Dell (Sosna et al. 2010), this literature review posits that the wealth created by high-growth technology companies, such as E-Bay, Microsoft and Google, has had a profound, but less-publicized, effect on the twenty-first century paradigms of philanthropy and corporate social responsibility, creating a more market-oriented approach. It is inspired, in part, by a new genre of "entrepreneurial philanthropists," like E-Bay founder Pierre Omidyar and Microsoft's Bill Gates, who are not simply giving away their money but also want to invest their know-how, connections and reputation to achieve a high rate of social return (Harvey et al. 2011).

The term "disruptive philanthropy" was originally applied to large-scale donors, including Bill Gates, by Horvath and Powell (2016). They argue that the scale of the giving has changed the institutional environment surrounding philanthropy to the point that it risks eroding democracy. Rather than complementing the work of the state, they say "disruptive philanthropy" replaces the public sphere with private initiatives for special public purposes, dubbed by some as philanthro-capitalism (Bishop and Green 2009). Instead of plugging a gap in public spending, Horvath and Powell argue that such initiatives crowd out the public sector, reducing its legitimacy, replacing civic goals with narrower concerns about efficiency and markets. They believe that disruptive philanthropy seeks to shape civic values in the image of funders' interests. This is an easier case to argue in a national setting, but more difficult in a transnational one where, for example, Bill Gates has been able to fund campaigns across borders to tackle diseases such as polio and malaria. Brakman Reiser (2017) says the kinds of "for-profit" philanthropic structures adopted by Omidyar and the Chan-Zuckerberg Initiative offers flexibility, privacy and control for the founders—but fit the "disruptive mantra" which has driven much of Silicon Valley's success. This study adopts a broader definition of "disruptive philanthropy" to include the range of paradigms which have evolved from Big Tech's business practices.

The disruptive paradigms

The disruption of philanthropy by the digital economy can be tracked back to the dot.com boom of the 1990s when entrepreneurs encouraged foundations to use venture capital practices to strengthen the core capacity of their grantees in addition to funding charitable programs. (Letts et al 1997). It coincided with new thinking about how corporates and the nonprofits sectors could work together to achieve greater social value—a concept referred to as a "blended value proposition" (BVP) by Emerson (2003). He stressed the need for a BVP which integrates, and affirms, the greatest maximization of social, environmental and economic value within a single firm, whether for-profit or nonprofit, coupled with the metrics and tracking systems to measure the progress of all three. In one of the most-cited articles on CSR, Porter and Kramer (2011) went a step farther, and put forward the idea of "shared value"—their "big idea" to persuade business to create economic value in a way which also generates value for society by addressing its needs and challenges. The authors contend that most companies remain stuck in a "social responsibility" mind-set in which societal issues are at the periphery, not the core. As the century progresses, the concepts of impact investing (Bugg-Levine and Emerson 2011) emerges where social investors seek to recoup their funds at, or below, market rates. It is followed by data philanthropy, whereby donating, or sharing, data can be a corporate contribution to social programs or make policy-making more effective (Kirkpatrick 2013). Humanitarian response to disasters, urban planning and academic research could all benefit from the sharing of large data sets by private enterprise (Stempeck 2014). As Table 1 illustrates, these concepts originate, and were published, in the United States. This new approach to philanthropy puts market-based solutions at its core; in this conception of philanthropy the metrics of finance were not seen as antithetical to philanthropy, but rather as integral to optimizing its success.

In terms of literature, the new paradigms suffer to a degree from "the liability of newness" in that the ideas spring from conceptual studies with limited empirical data to test and/or justify their theories. Each of the paradigms will be discussed in detail but, as the definitions in Table 1 detail, each brings a market-oriented approach to nonprofits. A focus with the new paradigms—specifically venture philanthropy and impact investing—is on increasing capacity in nonprofits by avoiding "misguided frugality" (Dees 2012), which can undermine problem-solving efforts through opting for sacrifice rather than investment. Boards and staffs need to focus on building the capacity of their entire organizations, and not just implementing projects, if they are to have

Table 1. 21st century paradigms of philanthropic support for mission-driven organizations

Paradigm	Definition	Publication
Venture Philanthropy (Letts et al. 1997)	Encouraging foundations to use venture capital practices to strengthen the core capacity of their grantees as well as funding charitable programs.	Harvard Business Review
Impact Investing (Bugg-Levine and Emerson 2011)	Investment strategies that bring financial returns while intentionally improving social and environmental conditions.	Innovations (MIT Press)
Shared Value (Porter and Kramer 2011)	Re-inventing capitalism by combining value creation with meeting societal needs.	Harvard Business Review
Data Philanthropy (Kirkpatrick 2013; Stempeck 2014)	Private sector holders of "Big Data" make it available for the public good.	Harvard Business Review

Source: Baker, N., author.

social impact (McKinsey & Company for Venture Philanthropy Partners 2003). This is a departure from previous ways of thinking about CSR and philanthropy—particularly the latter.

It could be argued, however, that those two modes of funding enable nonprofits ultimately to strengthen their own organizations and have a significant element of determination of their future direction. That is less the case with shared value and data philanthropy. Porter and Kramer (2011) urged businesses to re-invent capitalism by building societal needs into their value chains, providing a potential opportunity for nonprofits to work with businesses, but with the emphasis on convincing for-profit businesses to change their ways of working. Organizations that wish to turn Big Data to social good, inevitably need to partner with businesses which have the data, technology and human expertise to carry out the analysis (Kirkpatrick 2013).

Venture philanthropy

The "new donors" of philanthropy, who emerged from Silicon Valley during the dot.com boom, were not content to write a cheque and let the money be invested and distributed by others (Frumkin 2003; Wagner 2002). These new technology entrepreneurs felt "mainstream philanthropy"—predominantly from grant-giving foundations—failed to support innovation, build the infrastructure of nonprofits or demand tangible results. The influential article by Letts et al. (1997) stirred the debate on bringing venture capital practices to the nonprofit sector. They identified a "serious problem for the non-profit sector: no-one is investing in non-profit organizational capacity." Instead of just providing grants, the authors outlined the key elements of a venture capital approach, and urged adoption by grant-giving foundations. The comparisons of approaches are laid out in Table 2 below:

The key contrast highlighted in the table is in the financial motivations which frame the venture capitalists' approach toward a more active and directive engagement, in stark contrast to the more cautious and less interventionist approach of the grant-giving foundations.

Letts and Ryan (2003) refined their venture philanthropy (VP) model into one called "high-engagement philanthropy" defining a specific, coherent, longer-term approach where the funder believes that improving the performance of the nonprofit organization is the best means of achieving their social goals. The three key elements are alignment of interests of the grantor and grantee, reliable grant money for seven years or more, and strategy coaching. Frumkin (2003) believes that improving nonprofit strategy through management consulting is critical to lasting success of VP, along with new metrics to measure organization performance, referred to as "social return on investment." Empirical data are limited on the outcomes of venture philanthropy. However, those available do provide indicators to the mind-set of the venture philanthropist,

Table 2. Comparative approaches

Venture capitalist	*Foundation*
Risk Management: Calculate chances of success before investing.	Financial risks far less likely to be of concern, with foundation unlikely to be held account over performance of grantees.
Performance measures: Agreed metrics to gauge performance.	Focus on short-term program success with no support for long-term capacity in grantee organizations.
Closeness of relationship: Board involvement and mentoring of management.	Arm's length involvement with grantee organizations.
Amount of funding: Venture investors help raise funding for next stage of growth.	Nonprofits "undercapitalized" by grantors and "starved" of general operating support.
Length of relationship: Five to seven years, and possibly longer.	Between one and three years.
The Exit: The venture investor exits when it has steered the organization to a viable future.	Nonprofits face time-consuming search for funds when foundation funding runs out.

Adapted from Letts et al. (1997).

which enables nonprofits to understand the factors which might attract investment or the cultural clashes which such a relationship might present.

An early investigation into the phenomenon of VP was carried out by Schervish et al. (2001), who conducted qualitative research with 28 "high-tech wealth holders," and two of their spouses, about their involvement with "high-impact philanthropy," including VP. They defined a high-tech wealth holder as a person who "has made or is making the majority of his or her wealth from direct participation as an owner or a top executive with equity holdings in a high-tech business." The donors were found to be "market conscious" and "knowledge based" applying their own, and others', intellectual capital to meet the philanthropic need. They insisted on research and "due diligence" for the start of any new venture.

Other skills and approaches they employed included strategic thinking, a belief in teamwork and partnering rather than competition, an optimistic view in the ability of the individual to make a difference, the application and development of human capital as the basis of solving society's problems and a conviction that innovation and constant change are crucial to progress. The findings were echoed by Moody (2008) who conducted qualitative research with the practitioners and proponents of VP mainly in the Silicon Valley area of California. He found that many practitioners were seeking to build a new philanthropic culture. Some of the traits found among the "dot.commers and entrepreneurs" were being "data focused," strategic minded, results oriented, comfortable with "charts and graphs and deadlines". Other epithets included "very analytical" and "innovation junkies" who thought traditional grant-making approaches were slow, inefficient and unproductive.

Mair and Hehenberger (2014) studied the interaction in Europe between the advocates of a traditional philanthropy model and those of a VP model. A key difference between traditional philanthropy and venture philanthropy was reciprocity. In the case of VP, the terms of "giving, receiving and returning" are made explicit. Even though VP investing is often solely based on grants, the investors were unapologetic about the fact that "gifts are not free". A principal difference between the models was that VP prescribed "investments" and hands-on involvement in the management of organizations carrying out social projects, whereas traditional philanthropy favored hands-off support of projects in the form of grant-making.

Gordon (2014) conducted case studies of four UK foundations established by venture philanthropists to administer their funds, although their activities were primarily international and focused on Africa. An important element for the philanthropy teams was to know if the potential investee organization had the ambition, desire and capability to strive for the "big win." Business rigor, and openness to change, feature as the key issues which nonprofits need to embrace, based on empirical evidence from both sides of the Atlantic. It is clear from the selection process used by venture philanthropists, outlined by Gordon (2014) that nonprofit management entering this process would face the issues outlined by the analysis of hybrid organizations. The price to pay for building greater internal capacity could be a loss of control. While venture philanthropists potentially offer longer-term support than foundations, success could mean an eventual exit by the VP and a possible "takeover" by government or another body. The aims of both donor and recipient may be greater societal impact, but the cost could be loss of control for the original nonprofit.

Impact investing

Impact investing has emerged in the last 15 years as a way of providing capital for social programs, whereby investors seek to recoup their capital at, or below, market rates (Rangan et al. 2011). Like philanthropists, impact investors aim to achieve social goals (Brest and Born 2013). The term "impact investing" was coined in 2007 by the Monitor Institute in the United States—a social enterprise cum think tank—after the Rockefeller Foundation invited leaders in finance, philanthropy and development to discuss ways of building a global industry striving for investments with a positive social and environmental impact (Höchstädter and Scheck 2015). The architects of the concept say that, in reality, it builds on a tradition going back to Quakers in seventeenth century England who sought to align their investment and purchase decisions with their values (Bugg-Levine and Emerson 2011). Brest and Born (2013) argue that an investment has impact only if it increases the quantity or quality of an enterprise's social outcome beyond what would have otherwise occurred. In other words, if impact investing leads to a better outcome than if the market had provided capital, then impact has been achieved. Brest and Born also state that social investors fall into two categories—"concessionary" or "non-concessionary." Concessionary investors are willing to make some financial sacrifice by taking greater risk or accepting lower returns to achieve their goals. Non-concessionary investors are not willing to make a financial sacrifice, but their investments remain socially-motivated, and are often called mission-related. Impact investing has similarities with "shared value," in as much as Bugg-Levine and Emerson (2011) argue that society can no longer waste capital and talent by organizing itself round the separate poles of financial return and social good. They coin the term "blended value" to indicate that activities are organized to seek both wealth and social justice.

In carrying out an analysis of the meaning of impact investing, Höchstädter and Scheck (2015) acknowledge that there is limited academic literature on the topic, with the discourse mainly driven by practitioners. However, Glänzel and Scheuerle (2016) provide empirical evidence of what they see as impediments to the emerging social impact investment field in Germany from the perspective of investors and social entrepreneurs. While impact investors can also provide supportive management expertise, their research found impact investing was not without conflict. They question where financial return can be achieved when addressing social problems. Both investors and investees saw insecure income models as a risk for taking up investment capital. Measuring social returns—beyond what might have occurred without the investment—was hard to assess. Finally, the approach of investors and investees were shaped by their own logics: investees by the social sector logic, while impact investors mostly followed the logic of commercial finance markets.

Furthermore, Pierre Omidyar, the founder of eBay, defined himself as having been an impact investor as early as 2004 (Omidyar 2011), as he had created a philanthropic foundation after the flotation of eBay in the 1990s. For illustration, in 2004 he established a limited liability company called the Omidyar Network, to invest in businesses, or organizations, with a social purpose. A "hybrid approach" of blending for-profit and nonprofit skills left the Omidyar Network free to make a grant or take an equity stake in a social-purpose company. Omidyar maintained that the market orientation allowed his Network to take greater risks, akin to venture capitalists who might get only two out of 10 investments right, but reap great rewards for the right risks. A similar market-orientation approach was taken by fellow eBay veteran Jeff Skoll, who originally supported, and popularized, social entrepreneurship through his philanthropic Skoll Foundation, established in 1999 (Nee 2012). Skoll said there was a need for a new type of foundation—more flexible, with a long-term horizon and which understood what it was like to be an entrepreneur. That was counter to the traditional foundation which gave short-term funding, demanded a lot of plans and burdened the social entrepreneur with detail. Skoll maintains he can make greater "social good" with a potential for-profit venture than by giving money away to an NGO in the same field.

From the limited literature, impact investing appears to offer flexibility of opportunity for the socially-motivated investors—the ability to pursue their aims through nonprofits or through for-profit businesses—depending on which they consider the most effective route. Nonprofits however, would need to exercise caution as to whether they could meet the expectations of impact investors, particularly if they were non-concessionary. The nonprofit would need to consider, as highlighted by Glänzel and Scheuerle (2016), whether a financial return was realistic while countering a social problem.

Shared value

Dominant voices in the debate over the relationship between philanthropy, grant-giving foundations and business have been those of Porter and Kramer. A series of four articles in the *Harvard Business Review* between 1999 and 2011 has been cited, nearly 28,000 times according to Google Scholar on April 2nd, 2020. Their main agenda is creating value in new ways—using scarce philanthropic resources to their maximum potential. In the series of articles, they cite large corporates as having adopted the practice already. While the authors weaken their case by not going into detailed case studies, they point to large technology companies like Google, IBM, Intel, Cisco and Microsoft, providing a starting point for organizations wishing to identify potential partners in a shared-value proposition.

The authors' initial perspective, in their 1999 article, "Philanthropy's New Agenda: Creating Value," was urging foundations to generate social benefits beyond the purchasing power of their grants, outlining four ways they could achieve it. However, it can be argued that their main message was a re-packaging of themes from Letts et al. (1997). The "four ways" included calling for foundations to select the best grantees, similar to the due diligence process of venture philanthropists. Porter and Kramer (1999) also argued that foundations could create more value if they became a fully-engaged partner of grant recipients, improving the effectiveness of their organizations. Again, there are echoes here of venture philanthropists' desires to improve core capacity in the organizations they support. Porter and Kramer urged foundations to create value by "signaling other funders"—in, other words, attracting other donors to the causes they support. This reflects the key role of the venture capitalist helping a business to find other funders, particularly prior to exit. The fourth entreaty was to advance the state of knowledge and practice by funding research and systematic progression of projects. Additionally, the authors make clear that, as with business, that strategy in "giving," depends on choosing a unique position, and not being all things to all people. Every major activity of a foundation must be tailored to its positioning. It could be argued that this knowledge is as important to a grantee as a grantor, in terms of identifying a donor whose interests are aligned with the recipient.

In their second article, "The Competitive Advantage of Corporate Philanthropy," Porter and Kramer (2002) sought to debunk the "myth" of strategic philanthropy by companies. They maintained that much activity passed off as strategic was, in fact, public relations, advertising or brand promotion. The core of their argument is that in a world of open, knowledge-based competition, companies do not function in isolation from society around them, and for corporate giving to be truly strategic, it has to deliver benefits for both the business and the society, and do so to positive commercial effect. The theme of "shared value" is developed farther in the third article,

"Strategy and Society: The Link between Competitive Advantage and Corporate Social Responsibility" (Porter and Kramer 2006). Again, the authors advocate that the essential test that should guide CSR is not whether a cause is worthy but whether it presents "an opportunity to create shared value, creating a benefit for society while being valuable for the business."

Their articles culminate in "Creating Shared Value. How to reinvent capitalism—and unleash a wave of innovation and growth" (Porter and Kramer 2011) which seeks to redefine value creation from short-term financial performance to creating economic value while also addressing society's needs. The study posits that most companies are stuck in a "social responsibility" mind-set where societal issues are at the periphery, not the core. The authors claim "shared value" is not social responsibility, philanthropy, or even sustainability, but a new way to achieve economic success, by "expanding the total pool of economic and social value." Businesses are urged to find the benefits by reexamining their value chains. An example is cited within energy use and logistics, where the British retailer Marks and Spencer stopped the purchase of supplies from one hemisphere to ship to another, reducing carbon emissions significantly, but also saving the business up to £175 million a year.

While the articles are conceptual, they underscore that from foundations, to corporate philanthropy and CSR, the potential biggest gains are from philanthropic funds used strategically which, in the case of businesses, is giving which enhances their value chains while bringing optimal benefits to society. This has important implications for any nonprofit seeking philanthropic funding in terms of understanding which donors might derive an opportunity for shared value from their cause.

Although Porter and Kramer's shared-value concept is widely cited in the literature, it is also met with skepticism. For example, Dembek et al. (2016) examine in their literature review whether "shared value" is a theoretical concept or just a "management buzzword". They conclude that it is unlikely any social problems will be solved through shared value, but it may be possible to use it to address some unmet needs. They posit that shared value as a theoretical concept is at a nascent stage and needs clearer definition before it can avoid the accusation of being a buzzword. Others are critical of its originality. Crane et al. (2014) accuse Porter and Kramer of being simplistic in their view of the tradeoffs which businesses have to make between economic and social goals. In addition, shared value is seen as ignoring earlier ideas of reconceiving products and markets through creating partnerships or hybrid organizations, like microfinance, or social enterprises. However, Pfitzer et al. (2013) studied more than 30 companies which, they said, had innovated to create social benefits and business value. They were embedding a social mission in a corporate culture—and in many cases co-creating with external stakeholders, including universities, NGOs and governments. The examples cited, however, were big companies like Dow Chemicals, Nestlé, Novartis, Mars and Intel. It is clear the onus is on corporates to create shared value, bringing in other stakeholders as required.

For a nonprofit or charity seeking funding, depending on possible participation in a "shared value" project would be high risk as a mechanism for achieving philanthropic support. The examples cited by Porter and Kramer are from large businesses. Persuading them to adjust their value chains would be a complex process, requiring a great exposure to risk by the company concerned beyond a conventional philanthropic donation. Therefore, it is a mechanism realistically more viable when a company has mapped out a strategic direction which involves embedding a social mission and is seeking other stakeholders. It is a paradigm of which nonprofits need to be aware, in case an appropriate opportunity arises, but realistically not one easily initiated from outside a company.

Data philanthropy (information as philanthropic currency)

Facebook exemplifies both the risks and the benefits of "data philanthropy"—a term coined to describe the use of private sector data for socially-beneficial purposes (Lev-Aretz 2019). The unauthorized use of personal data from the social media platform to target potential voters in the 2016 U.S. presidential election prompted an international legal and ethical debate. The data had originally been obtained for research purposes (Rosenberg et al. 2018). By comparison, in

2017 Facebook launched its "Disaster Maps" initiative, as part of its "Data for Good" program, to share real-time information with response teams dealing with natural disasters. By April, 2020, Facebook's Disaster Maps website said responders had used the data in more than 100 disasters globally to assess whether communities had access to power and cellular networks and which services and supplies they need most.

In the digital age, data have become a powerful currency of both CSR and corporate philanthropy, with companies like Google, Facebook, Apple and eBay amassing more data about people and their behavior, health, markets and networks than many governments (Shkabatur 2019). To deal with the challenges which this presents, a new branch of ethics—data ethics—has emerged (Floridi and Taddeo 2016). They point out that even if donated data are anonymized, individuals could be "re-identified" through data mining, data-linking, data merging and re-use of large data sets. "Group privacy" may also be at stake, where the identification of types of individuals may lead to group discrimination like ageism, ethnicism or sexism. Facebook emphasizes on its Disaster Maps website that it only uses "de-identified" information and takes steps to stop it being "re-identified". However, nonprofits seeking to acquire data will have to navigate the "moral ambiguity" (Taddeo 2017) of whether data philanthropy is more likely to foster morally good outcomes, like societal and individual welfare, scientific progress and good governance, as opposed to negative ones.

Data are also "porous," in that they can be accessed across borders and create security concerns. The case of Google's withdrawal from the mainland Chinese market in 2010 raises the moral question of how data can be compromised. Google withdrew after what it described as a "highly sophisticated and targeted attack" by the Chinese government attempting to access the email accounts of human rights activists (Tan and Tan 2012). Indeed, Google, Yahoo! and Microsoft all stood accused of absolving themselves of moral responsibility by initially agreeing to censorship in order to do business in China (Dann and Haddow 2008). For a nonprofit seeking use of data philanthropy, it also raises the concern of whether large, digital companies will compromise ethics in pursuit of profit, if the commercial gain is deemed big enough. Stempeck (2014) urges that companies need to think about who would be harmed by the release of data before making information available. Of course this puts a potentially rich new resource in the hands of data holders—but has the potential to cause confusion as to what is purely commercial, when it is enlightened self-interest (Smith 2003) and when it is fulfilling a purely philanthropic or CSR role. An ethical issue with data philanthropy for nonprofits and hybrid organizations is whether it creates a dependence on the donor for use of technology and expertise to access it—analogous to how technology companies offer free or discounted software for use by nonprofits.

Amid the legal debate about the efficacy of "data philanthropy," a solution has been proffered over how to ensure ethical management of user data. Shkabatur (2019) challenges current regulatory approaches and calls for a "global data commons" where any private company which operates an online platform collecting and processing its users' data should be encouraged to take part in the data commons regime. The "global data commons" would be responsibly managed in a manner which would contribute to the business models of the platform companies and to large societal objectives. The proposal amplifies a suggestion made earlier when the concept of data philanthropy was first mooted. In 2009, the United Nations' secretary-general set up the Global Pulse initiative to find out whether "Big Data" and real-time analytics could make policy-making more agile and effective (Kirkpatrick 2013). The director of the UN initiative, Robert Kirkpatrick, believed it was an effective way of using data from mobile networks, social media and online forums to safeguard vulnerable populations by the early tracking of the spread of health epidemics, changes in food prices, inflation and employment levels. He envisioned a time when the private sector contributed to a "real-time data common" with the potential to achieve "massive social impact". Nevertheless, there is a highly commercialized digital environment, with a market logic as its organizing principle, which has resulted in Big Tech companies being the most important repositories for large-scale user data,. Legal arguments also endure as to whether private sector organizations have the right to offer customer data for re-use, even if anonymized. For example, Lev-Aretz (2019) acknowledges that socially-beneficially use of data has enormous potential, however she also raises the question whether data collected from the owner for a specific purpose can legally be donated for another purpose? Is the data collector legally the owner? Further, the term "philanthropy" is described as "odd" in the context, as data can be offered for re-use at minimal, or no, cost with no practical limit, compared with other forms of philanthropy comprising money, tangible gifts or services.

Facebook amply illustrates that data can be used as a force for good but provides a salutary lesson of what can happen if security over user privacy is not managed scrupulously. For smaller nonprofits, there are likely to be ethical risks in managing third-party data which would require the support of the data donor. If that were a large technology company, a nonprofit would need to assess whether it was binding itself to the donor indefinitely as a source not only of data but also of the technology and resource to manage it. At the very least, before potentially creating a hybrid organization with the donor, there would need to be a deep understanding of its ethical stand, whether interests were truly aligned, or the donor's interest simply a vehicle for its own strategic advancement.

Disruption of ethics in the digital age

Negroponte's vision of the digital age bringing "irrevocable and unstoppable" change across all fields (Negroponte 1995, 231) seemingly applied at first to philanthropic models emanating from the working practices of Big Tech. A later development was the fast-changing perception of the ethics of Big Tech. At the beginning of the twenty-first century, their moral motivations were favorably regarded, to the extent that they were able to "wear a Teflon mantle that keeps social issues from sticking to them" (Krumsiek 2003). As Krumsiek expressed it: "Microsoft has yet to kill any whales." The limited academic literature on the CSR and philanthropic activities of the large digital companies has since been overshadowed by headlines about wide-scale tax avoidance (Lanis and Richardson 2015), being prepared to accept censorship in China (Dann and Haddow 2008; Tan and Tan 2012) and unsanctioned use of private user data from Facebook during the 2016 U.S. presidential election campaign (Rosenberg, Confessore, and Cadwalladr 2018). Now their own technology is being employed to disrupt their businesses, with companies like Facebook and Twitter struggling to get to grips with their platforms being used extensively by governments and malicious actors for "computational propaganda"—the use of algorithms, automation and human curation to purposely manage and distribute misleading information over social networks (Woolley and Howard 2018).

While Porter and Kramer (2011) advocate companies creating "shared value" to further society's needs, the literature presents a strong case for nonprofits to assess carefully whether they have "shared values" with donors from the digital domain, particularly if they seek to achieve success in creating a hybrid organization. A key test needs to be alignment of ethical, as well as strategic, interests (Bugg-Levine and Emerson 2011; Letts et al. 1997) and trust and transparency, particularly when sharing knowledge in data philanthropy (Floridi and Taddeo, 2016; Taddeo 2017). Ironically, if Big Tech companies adopt a hybrid approach for their own activities, there are indications it can lead to a lack of transparency. Google.org, the search company's charitable wing, is cited as an example of how a hybrid philanthropic structure provides it with the freedoms to use market mechanisms to further its aims, if necessary through political means (Lim 2007) but does not enforce the same legal requirement for accountability and transparency which would normally apply to commercial or political activities by nonprofits (Rana 2008). Under those circumstances, an investee or partner nonprofit might be left wondering where the true division lies between Google.org and the Google commercial entity.

In re-defining philanthropy, the influence of Big Tech would appear to have removed the consensus which saw corporate philanthropy and corporate social responsibility defined through the views of Carroll (1979; 1991) for the last 20 years of the twentieth century. He argued that for a definition of corporate social responsibility to fully address the entire range of obligations to society it must embody economic, legal, ethical and discretionary categories of business performance. The primary responsibility was economic—to make goods which customers wanted and sell them at a profit. He believed that a business needed to act ethically within the laws and regulations which society expected. Only then could it address the "discretionary" social roles like CSR which were "not mandated, not required by law and not even generally expected of business in an ethical sense." In re-visiting his 1979 work, Carroll (2016) acknowledges that philanthropy, or business giving, is now an unremarkable expectation of the public and reflects that while there is sometimes an altruistic motive for the giving, it is conducted mainly to enhance, or augment, the company's reputation; that is not for self-sacrificing reasons. Carroll contends that his "pyramid" remains a sustainable stakeholder framework and should be taken as a unified whole—with the four constituent elements not seen sequentially or as a hierarchy. In this study we argue that his view may hold good for traditional service or manufacturing industries, however it does not address the detailed alignment of interests required between a Big Tech funder and a mission-driven, nonprofit organization, particularly if their operational activities become enmeshed through paradigms, such as shared value or data philanthropy.

Accordingly, nonprofits engaging with philanthropy from Big Tech need to be mindful whether alignment of interest is transitory or illusory, lasting only as long as it brings financial benefit to the Big Tech company. The recent breaches in Big Tech's "Teflon coating" could arguably put pressure on them to increase philanthropic expenditure to improve their reputations, traditionally a tactic of industries like alcohol and tobacco which have to atone for what is seen as socially-irresponsible behavior (Brammer and Millington 2005). Again, the question needs to be asked whether their alignment can be considered long-term. It is noticeable that Microsoft Philanthropies was established in 2015—15 years after the Bill and Melinda Gates Foundation, and after the adverse publicity over tax avoidance. For nonprofits, however, seeking support from a new philanthropic culture inspired by digital wealth, they have to understand the rationale driving such funders, and be assured that the hybrid approach to mission and money leads to a greater increase in social benefit overall, rather than a sacrifice of social benefit to increase commercial profits, as highlighted by Yunus et al. (2010). An assessment needs to be made whether the aim is akin to shared value or more a reversion to the hard-line view expressed by economist Milton Friedman in his 1962 book, "Capitalism and Freedom," that there was "one and only one social responsibility of business - to use its resources and engage in activities designed to increase its profits ... " (Friedman 1962).

In the twenty-first century, the approach of technology companies could be considered in line with a general trend, which points to corporate philanthropy growing more strategic over time as opposed to altruistic (Carroll 2016; Maas and Liket 2011). Companies hope to provide strategic philanthropy by finding synergies between organizational core competencies and resources to achieve both organizational and social benefits (Thorne McAlister and Ferrell 2002). In other words, the philanthropy is not just about donating money—but linking the organization's core skills, and unique ability, in order to benefit society (Bruch and Walter 2005). This, however, emphasizes the need for transparency about a company's ultimate aims, so a mission-driven partner in a hybrid venture has a clear understanding of the funder's strategic intent. Ultimately, if Negroponte's prophecy runs its course, the Big Tech companies will find themselves disrupted—by new business models or government regulation. Nonprofits need to be sure that if Big Tech profits tumble, the specter of Friedman is not the image awaiting them.

Conceptual model: market-orientation for nonprofit organizations

While the empirical evidence of the effects of new paradigms of CSR and philanthropy is limited, it is clear that nonprofit organizations need to have an understanding of how giving inspired by "digital

TABLE 3. Conceptual model for nonprofits seeking hybrid engagement with the digital economy.

Step 1

- ***Decision Factors Faced by Non-Profits***
  - Level of market orientation desired
  - Level of requirement for increased core capacity
  - Level of control to be ceded: "Gifts are not free"
  - Level of ethical alignment: Avoid "moral ambiguity"

Step 2

- ***Qualities "New Donors" Seek in Non-Profits***
  - Alignment of strategic interests and time horizon
  - Data-focused: measurable impact and analytical approach
  - Market-conscious: entrepreneurial and chasing "The Big Win"
  - Innovative: need to satisfy "innovation junkies".

Step 3

- ***Risks Faced in Managing "Competing Logics"***
  - Tensions between mission and finance
  - Avoiding mission drift and/or revenue drift
  - Need for a clear organizational identity
  - Avoiding staff and stakeholder confusion

Source: Baker, N., author.

wealth" is becoming more strategic, market-oriented, and fueling a growth in the number of hybrid organizations. For nonprofits seeking hybrid engagement with the "new donors" created by digital wealth, the challenge is understanding the factors which attract funders, counterbalanced with the risks and challenges involved in managing the relationship. From the literature, a three-step conceptual framework has been devised to guide the process for nonprofits, displayed in Table 3 above.

Step 1 invokes the logic of Austin et al. (2006) that the distinction between social and commercial entrepreneurship is not dichotomous, but on a continuum ranging from purely social to purely economic. While the two characteristics must co-exist, the nonprofit needs to weigh its tolerance to the level of market-orientation it is prepared to accept, with an understanding of how that can affect its level of control and culture. A need for increased core capacity could point to venture philanthropy and impact investing, but with an understanding outlined by Mair and Hehenberger (2014) that "gifts are not free" and that the recipient of funding will be sufficiently entrepreneurial to make the money work hard. While empirical evidence on data philanthropy is not available in the literature, Taddeo (2017) leads to a wider point for all philanthropy recipients: understanding that there is no "moral ambiguity" of purpose between the giver and the receiver.

Step 2 clearly lays out the common factors which the "new donors" of venture philanthropy and impact investing seek in their grantees or investees—inspired by the traits of actors in the digital economy. A key requirement is alignment of interests (Letts and Ryan 2003) with recipients prepared to accept strategy coaching and support over a long-time horizon of seven years, or more. This builds on the thinking of Porter and Kramer (1999) that foundations can create more value with a fully-engaged partner. Being "data focused" and analytical is a recurring theme (Goldman 2016; Letts et al. 1997; Moody 2008). Impact investors, in particular, are looking for entrepeneurialism (Brest and Born 2013) in their search for a social outcome beyond what would have occurred with capital provided purely by the market. The "new donors" are also "innovation junkies" (Moody 2008) and "market conscious" (Schervish et al. 2001). They seek investee organizations prepared to strive for a "big win" (Gordon 2014), which supports the view of Porter and Kramer (1999) that donors need to find a unique position to maximize impact.

Step 3 highlights the risks which have to be managed by nonprofits seeking to advance their mission by creating a hybrid organization—applicable when dealing with the kinds of strategically-focused donors created by the digital economy. It is clear from the literature that tensions can occur with the creation of an entrepreneurial hybrid organization which has a dual mission of financial sustainability and social purpose, known as "competing logics" (Battilana and Dorado 2010). These broadly fall into two categories—the tensions between the two cultures of mission and money when a nonprofit takes a more market-oriented approach, and the issues surrounding clarity over the identity of the organization to internal and external stakeholders. Nonprofits wishing to adopt a more market-oriented approach need to balance carefully the competing tension between mission and finances to avoid mission drift (Ebrahim et al. 2014; Santos et al. 2015) or its counterpart of revenue drift (Ponte et al. 2017). The other main challenge is to ensure that staff and other stakeholders understand the identity of the hybrid organization. As outlined by Jay (2013), those who establish hybrid organizations have to navigate paradox and be prepared to evolve a new organizational identity which embraces both the cultures of mission and money.

Implications for theory and practice

This article has outlined the changing nature of philanthropy in the past quarter of a century, with new paradigms influenced by the commercial values of Big Tech and the digital economy. For scholars of corporate philanthropy it denotes a further progression from the rigid views of Friedman that a firm's only obligation was to increase its profits (Friedman 1962) through the views of Carroll (1979, 1991) that corporate philanthropy could only take place after a company had fulfilled its economic, legal and ethical obligations to society.

A new ontology of philanthropy has been outlined where the boundaries between commercial activity and philanthropic activity are less clear, as demonstrated by Google.org and the Omidyar Network. As Carroll (2016) acknowledges, this coincides with business giving being an everyday expectation of the public. In turn, nonprofits can undertake commercial activities to achieve social impact through hybrid organizations which seek to balance mission and money.

For practitioners, the key to understanding the new philanthropies from the digital economy is that they reward activity which emulates the business values of Big Tech: innovation, entrepreneurialism and a focus on performance data. For nonprofit organizations interested in pursuing funding from Big Tech or the digital economy, the new paradigms are clearly defined, with risks and benefits outlined. The risks of engaging with funding from the digital economy are synthesized into a conceptual framework, along with the risk factors associated with managing a hybrid organization in order to achieve a more market-oriented approach to achieving social impact.

The implications for practitioners are that hybrid organizations, with their commercial values, are not a fleeting development but rather represent a paradigm shift in the practice and understanding of philanthropy in the twenty-first century. Practitioners, therefore, need to understand fully this new paradigm of philanthropy.

Conclusion

This study has answered the research questions by identifying the key characteristics of the new forms of philanthropy, demonstrating how practitioners and scholars might engage with them. By implanting the values of the digital economy, Big Tech has changed the nature of corporate philanthropy and corporate social responsibility to create what we have termed collectively "disruptive philanthropy". As demonstrated in the conceptual model, the primary issue for not-profits considering embracing any of the disruptive philanthropies is understanding whether its values are clearly aligned with those of funders so there is no "moral ambiguity" in the relationship. The paradox which needs to be managed is understanding where the real benefits lie when, within the new ontology, companies blur the boundaries between corporate giving and business benefits, raising concerns that "gifts are not free" (Mair and Hehenberger 2014).

Recommendations derived from this study include further research to understand whether new codes of governance are feasible to ensure transparency between Big Tech's philanthropic and business benefits, particularly when a social mission is claimed to be in its value chain. In addition, more exploration is required into whether there are changing levels of philanthropy by Big Tech companies like Facebook and Google as the sector comes under intense governmental and media scrutiny.

ORCID

Paul Manning http://orcid.org/0000-0003-3231-3653

References

Austin, J., H. Stevenson, and J. Wei-Skillern. 2006. "Social and Commercial Entrepreneurship: Same, Different, or Both?" *Entrepreneurship Theory and Practice* 30 (1):1–22. doi: 10.1111/j.1540-6520.2006.00107.x.

Battilana, J., and S. Dorado. 2010. "Building Sustainable Hybrid Organizations: The Case of Commercial Microfinance Organizations." *Academy of Management Journal* 53 (6):1419–40. doi: 10.5465/amj.2010.57318391.

Battilana, J., M. Lee, J. Walker, and C. Dorsey. 2012. "In Search of the Hybrid Ideal." *Stanford Social Innovation Review* 10 (3):50–5.

Baumeister, R. F., and M. R. Leary. 1997. "Writing Narrative Literature Reviews." *Review of General Psychology* 1 (3):311–20. doi: 10.1037/1089-2680.1.3.311.

Bishop, M., and M. Green. 2009. *Philanthrocapitalism: How Giving Can save the World.* New York: Bloomsbury Press.

Brakman Reiser, D. 2017. "Disruptive Philanthropy: Zuckerberg, the Limited Liability Company, and the Millionaire Next Door." *Brooklyn Law School, Legal Studies Paper No* 536 :1–48. Accessed February 10, 2018. 10.2139/ssrn.3049021.

Brammer, S., and A. Millington. 2005. "Corporate Reputation and Philanthropy: An Empirical Analysis." *Journal of Business Ethics* 61 (1):29–44. doi: 10.1007/s10551-005-7443-4.

Brest, P., and K. Born. 2013. "When Can Impact Investing Create Real Impact." *Stanford Social Innovation Review* 11 (4):33–48.

Bruch, H., and F. Walter. 2005. "The Keys to Rethinking Corporate Philanthropy." *MIT Sloan Management Review* 47 (1):48–55.

Bugg-Levine, A., and J. Emerson. 2011. "Impact Investing: Transforming How We Make Money While Making a Difference." *Innovations* 6 (3):9–18. doi: 10.1162/INOV_a_00077.

Bughin, J., and N. Van Zeebroeck. 2017. "The Best Response to Digital Disruption." *MITSloan Management Review* 58 (4):79–86.

Carnegie, A. 2006. "The Gospel of Wealth." In *The Autobiography of Andrew Carnegie and His Essay the Gospel of Wealth*, edited by M. C. Waldrep and J. B. Kopito, 321–36. New York, NY: Signet Classics.

Carroll, A. B. 1979. "A Three-Dimensional Conceptual Model of Corporate Performance." *Academy of Management Review* 4 (4):497–505. doi: 10.5465/amr.1979.4498296.
Carroll, A. B. 1991. "The Pyramid of Corporate Social Responsibility: Toward the Moral Management of Organizational Stakeholders." *Business Horizons* 34 (4):39–48. doi: 10.1016/0007-6813(91)90005-G.
Carroll, A.B. 2016. "Carroll's Pyramid of CSR: Taking Another Look." *International Journal of Corporate Social Responsibility* 1 (1):1–8. doi: 10.1186/s40991-016-0004-6.
Cetindamar, D., and B. Ozkazanc-Pan. 2017. "Assessing Mission Drift at Venture Capital Impact Investors." *Business Ethics: A European Review* 26 (3):257–70. doi: 10.1111/beer.12149.
Crane, A., G. Palazzo, L.J. Spence, and D. Matten. 2014. "Contesting the Value of "Creating Shared Value."" *California Management Review* 56 (2):130–53. doi: 10.1525/cmr.2014.56.2.130.
Dann, E. G., and N. Haddow. 2008. "Just Doing Business or Doing Just Business: Google, Microsoft, Yahoo! and the Business of Censoring China's Internet." *Journal of Business Ethics* 79 (3):219–34. doi: 10.1007/s10551-007-9373-9.
Dees, G. J. 2008. "Philanthropy and Enterprise: Harnessing the Power of Business and Social Entrepreneurship for Development." *Innovations* 3 (3):119–32. doi: 10.1162/itgg.2008.3.3.119.
Dees, G. J. 2012. "A Tale of Two Cultures: Charity, Problem Solving, and the Future of Social Entrepreneurship." *Journal of Business Ethics* 111 (3):321–34. doi: 10.1007/s10551-012-1412-5.
Dembek, K., P. Singh, and V. Bhakoo. 2016. "Literature Review of Shared Value: A Theoretical Concept or a Management Buzzword?" *Journal of Business Ethics* 137 (2):231–67. doi: 10.1007/s10551-015-2554-z.
Ebrahim, A., J. Battilana, and J. Mair. 2014. "The Governance of Social Enterprises: Mission Drift and Accountability Challenges in Hybrid Organizations." *Research in Organizational Behavior* 34:81–100. doi: 10.1016/j.riob.2014.09.001.
Eikenberry, A.M., and J. Drapal Kluver. 2004. "The Marketization of the Nonprofit Sector: Civil Society at Risk?" *Public Administration Review* 64 (2):132–40. doi: 10.1111/j.1540-6210.2004.00355.x.
Elkington, J. 1998. "Partnerships from Cannibals with Forks: The Triple Bottom Line of 21st Century Business." *Environmental Quality Management* 8 (1):37–51. doi: 10.1002/tqem.3310080106.
Emerson, J. 2003. "The Blended Value Proposition: Integrating Social and Finanancial Returns." *California Management Review* 45 (4):35–51. doi: 10.2307/41166187.
FACEBOOK Data for Good: Disaster Maps. Accessed April 2, 2020. https://dataforgood.fb.com/tools/disaster-maps/
Floridi, L., and M. Taddeo. 2016. "What is Data Ethics?" *Philosophical Transactions Royal Society A* 374 (2083): 1–5. Accessed August 8, 2017. doi: 10.1098/rsta.2016.0360.
Friedman, M. 1962. *Capitalism and Freedom*. Chicago and London: The University of Chicago Press.
Frumkin, P. 2003. "Inside Venture Philanthropy." In *Third Sector in Transition*, 7–15. Boston: Institute for the Study of Economic Culture, Boston University.
Glänzel, G., and T. Scheuerle. 2016. "Social Impact Investing in Germany: Current Impediments from Investors' and Social Entrepreneurs' Perspectives." *VOLUNTAS: International Journal of Voluntary and Nonprofit Organizations* 27 (4):1638–68. doi: 10.1007/s11266-015-9621-z.
Goldman, P. 2016. "How a New Generation of Business Leaders Views Philanthropy." *Harvard Business Review* :1–5. https://hbr.org/2016/02/how-a-new-generation-of-business-leaders-views-philanthropy
Gordon, J. 2014. "A Stage Model of Venture Philanthropy." *Venture Capital* 16 (2):85–107. doi: 10.1080/13691066.2014.897014.
Haigh, N., and A. J. Hoffman. 2012. "Hybrid Organizations: The Next Chapter of Sustainable Business." *Organizational Dynamics* 41 (2):126–34. doi: 10.1016/j.orgdyn.2012.01.006.
Harvey, Charles, Mairi Maclean, Jillian Gordon, and Eleanor Shaw. 2011. "Andrew Carnegie and the Foundations of Contemporary Entrepreneurial Philanthropy." *Business History* 53 (3):425–50. doi: 10.1080/00076791.2011.565516.
Holt, D., and D. Littlewood. 2015. "Identifying, Mapping, and Monitoring the Impact of Hybrid Firms." *California Management Review* 57 (3):107–26. doi: 10.1525/cmr.2015.57.3.107.
Horvath, A., and W. Powell. 2016. "Contributory or Disruptive: Do New Forms of Philanthropy Erode Democracy?" In *Philanthropy in Democratic Societies*, edited by R. Reich, C. Cordelli and L. Bernholz, 87–122. Chicago: The University of Chicago Press.
Hchstädter, A. K., and B. Scheck. 2015. "What's in a Name: An Analysis of Impact Investing Understandings by Academics and Practitioners." *Journal of Business Ethics* 132 (2):449–75.
Jay, J. 2013. "Navigating Paradox as a Mechanism of Change in Hybrid Organizations." *Academy of Management Journal* 56 (1):137–59. doi: 10.5465/amj.2010.0772.
Kirkpatrick, R. 2013. "A New Type of Philanthropy: Donating Data." *Harvard Business Review* :1–3. Accessed March 21. https://hbr.org/2013/03/a-new-type-of-philanthropy-don.
Krumsiek, B. 2003. "Socially Responsible High Tech Companies: Emerging Issues." *Journal of Business Ethics* 43 (3):179–87. doi: 10.1023/A:1022929812030.

Lanis, R., and G. Richardson. 2015. "Is Corporate Social Responsibility Performance Associated with Tax Avoidance?" *Journal of Business Ethics* 127 (2):439–57. doi: 10.1007/s10551-014-2052-8.

Letts, C. W., and William P. Ryan. 2003. "Filling the Performance Gap: High Engagement Philosophy." *Stanford Social Innovation Review* 1 (1):26–33.

Letts, Christine W., W. P. Ryan, and A. S. Grossman. 1997. "Virtuous Capital: What Foundations Can Learn from Venture Capitalists." *Harvard Business Review* 75 (2):36–50.

Lev-Aretz, Y. 2019. "Data Philanhtropy." *Hastings Law Journal* 70 (6):1491–545. https://repository.uchastings.edu/hastings_law_journal/vol70/iss6/3.

Lim, C. 2007. "Google.org, for-Profit Charitable Entity: Another Smart Decision by Google." *Kansas Journal of Law and Public Policy* :29–55.

Maas, K., and K. Liket. 2011. "Talk the Walk: Measuring the Impact of Strategic Philanthropy." *Journal of Business Ethics* 100 (3):445–64. doi: 10.1007/s10551-010-0690-z.

Mair, J., and L. Hehenberger. 2014. "Front-Stage and Backstage Convening: The Transition from Opposition to Mutualistic Coexistence in Organizational Philanthropy." *Academy of Management Journal* 57 (4):1174–200. doi: 10.5465/amj.2012.0305.

McKinsey Global Institute 2013. *Disruptive Technologies: Advances That Will Transform Life, Business, and the Global Economy*. San Francisco, CA: McKinsey & Company.

McKinsey & Company for Venture Philanthropy Partners. 2003. "Effective Capacity Building in Nonprofit Organizations." *New Directions for Philanthropic Fundraising* 40:103–11. doi: 10.1002/pf.36.

Moody, M. 2008. "Building a Culture': The Construction and Evolution of Venture Philanthropy as a New Organizational Field." *Nonprofit and Voluntary Sector Quarterly* 37 (2):324–52. doi: 10.1177/0899764007310419.

Nee, E. 2012. "Ideas Q & A." *Stanford Social Innovation Review* Spring:1–4.

Negroponte, Nicholas. 1995. *Being Digital*. New York: Alfred A. Knopf.

Omidyar, P. 2011. "How I Did It: EBay's Founder on Innovating the Business Model of Social Change." *Harvard Business Review* 1–4. Accessed September 1. https://hbr.org/2011/09/ebays-founder-on-innovating-the-business-model-of-social-change

Pfitzer, M., V. Bockstette, and M. Stamp. 2013. "Innovating for Shared Value." *Harvard Business Review*: 2–9. https://hbr.org/2013/09/innovating-for-shared-value

Ponte, D., C. Pesci, and P.F. Camussone. 2017. "Between Mission and Revenue: Measuring Performance in a Hybrid Organization." *Managerial Auditing Journal* 32 (2):196–214. doi: 10.1108/MAJ-11-2015-1276.

Porter, M. E., and M. R. Kramer. 2011. "Creating Shared Value." *Harvard Business Review* 89:62–77.

Porter, Michael E., and Mark R. Kramer. 1999. "Philanthropy's New Agenda: Creating Value." *Harvard Business Review* 77 (6):121–6.

Porter, Michael E., and Mark R. Kramer. 2002. "The Competitive Advantage of Corporate Philanthropy." *Harvard Business Review* 80 (12):2–15.

Porter, Michael E., and Mark R. Kramer. 2006. "The Link between Competitive Advantage and Corporate Social Responsibility." *Harvard Business Review*: 1–14. https://hbr.org/2006/12/strategy-and-society-the-link-between-competitive-advantage-and-corporate-social-responsibility

Rana, S. 2008. "From Making Money without Doing Evil to Doing Good without Handouts: The Google.org Experiment in Philanthropy." *Journal of Business & Technology Law* 3 (1):87–96.

Randolph, J. J. 2009. "A Guide to Writing the Dissertation Literature Review." *Practical Assessment, Research & Evaluation* 14 (13):1–13. Accessed April 17, 2017. http://pareonline.net/getvn.asp?v=14&n=13.

Rangan, V. K., S. Appleby, and L. Moon. 2011. "The Promise of Impact Investing." *Harvard Business School*, Background Note 512-045, February 2012. (Revised July 2012.)

Rawhouser, H., M. Cummings, and A. Crane. 2015. "Benefit Corporation Legislation and the Emergence of a Social Hybrid Category." *California Management Review* 57 (3):13–35. doi: 10.1525/cmr.2015.57.3.13.

Reich, R. B. 2015. *Saving Capitalism: For the Many, Not the Few*. New York: Alfred A. Knopf.

Rosenberg, M., N. Confessore, and C. Cadwalladr. 2018. "How Trump Consultants Exploited the Facebook Data of Millions." *The New York Times*. New York, 17 March. Accessed January 8, 2019. https://www.nytimes.com/2018/03/17/us/politics/cambridge-analytica-trump-campaign.html.

Santos, F., A.C. Pache, and C. Birkholz. 2015. "Making Hybrids Work: Aligning Business Models and Organizational Design for Social Enterprises." *California Management Review* 57 (3):36–58. doi: 10.1525/cmr.2015.57.3.36.

Schervish, P. G., M. A. O'Herlihy, J. J. Havens, and R. B. Pamplin. Jr. 2001. *Agent-Animated Wealth and Philanthropy: The Dynamics of Accumulation and Allocation among High-Tech Donors*. Boston: Association of Fundraising Professionals.

Shkabatur, J. 2019. "The Global Commons of Data." *Stanford Technology Law Review* 22 (2):354–411.

Smith, N. C. 2003. "Corporate Social Responsibility: WHETHER or HOW?" *California Management Review* 45 (4): 52–76. doi: 10.2307/41166188.

Sosna, M., R. N. Trevinyo-Rodriguez, and S. R. Velamuri. 2010. "Business Model Innovation through Trial-and-Error Learning: The Naturhouse Case." *Long Range Planning* 43 (2–3):383–407. doi: 10.1016/j.lrp.2010.02.003.

Stempeck, M. 2014. "Sharing Data Is a Form of Corporate Philanthropy." *Harvard Business Review* 2-6. Accessed July 24. https://hbr.org/2014/07/sharing-data-is-a-form-of-corporate-philanthropy

Taddeo, M. 2017. "Data Philanthropy and Individual Rights." *Minds and Machines* 27 (1):1–5. doi: 10.1007/s11023-017-9429-2.

Tan, J., and A. Tan. 2012. "Business under Threat, Technology under Attack, Ethics Under Fire: The Experience of Google in China." *Journal of Business Ethics* 110 (4):469–79. doi: 10.1007/s10551-012-1494-0.

Thomasson, A. 2009. "Exploring the Ambiguity of Hybrid Organisations: A Stakeholder Approach." *Financial Accountability & Management* 25 (3):353–66. doi: 10.1111/j.1468-0408.2009.00481.x.

Thorne McAlister, D., and L. Ferrell. 2002. "The Role of Strategic Philanthropy in Marketing Strategy." *European Journal of Marketing* 36 (5/6):689–705. doi: 10.1108/03090560210422952.

Wagner, L. 2002. "The 'New' Donor: Creation or Evolution?" *International Journal of Nonprofit and Voluntary Sector Marketing* 7 (4):343–52. doi: 10.1002/nvsm.191.

Wallace, N. 2006. Blending Business and Charity. 28 September. Accessed May 26, 2017. https://www.philanthropy.com/article/Blending-BusinessCharity/173001.

Webster, J., and R. T. Watson. 2002. 'Analyzing the past to Prepare for the Future: Writing a Literature Review." *MIS Quarterly* 26 (2):13–23.

Woolley, Samuel C, and Philip N. Howard. 2018. "Computational Propaganda Worldwide." In *Computational Propaganda. Political Parties, Politicians, and Political Manipulation on Social Media*, edited by S. C. Woolley and P. N. Howard, 3–15. New York: Oxford University Press.

Yunus, M., B. Moingeon, and L. Lehmann-Ortega. 2010. "Building Social Business Models: Lessons from the Grameen Experience." *Long Range Planning* 43 (2–3):308–25. doi: 10.1016/j.lrp.2009.12.005.

Dynamic capabilities and environmental sustainability for emerging economies' multinational enterprises

Pervaiz Akhtar, Subhan Ullah, Saman Hassanzadeh Amin, Gaurav Kabra and Sarah Shaw

ABSTRACT

The purpose of this study is to enhance our understanding of how macro (country)—level dynamic capabilities (DC), such as government environmental policies, legal and market requirements, and technological advances, and micro (firm)—level DC, such as organizational size, culture, and managerial characteristics, are related to emerging economies multinationals' environmental sustainability policies and practices. Limited studies explore linkages between macro-and micro-level DC and environmental sustainability, which urge emerging economies' multinationals to reconsider their environmental policies and practices in order to compete with enterprises from developed countries. We develop a theoretical framework and offer propositions about the fundamental links between macro and micro DC and emerging economies environmental sustainability efforts. The propositions can be empirically tested in subsequent studies using country-level and firm-level data to examine the interactions between macro-and micro-level capabilities, in relation to sustainable policies and procedures, for multinationals in emerging economies.

Dynamic capabilities (DC) originate from the resource-based view (RBV) of a firm, and these capabilities are linked with "identifiable processes and strategic routines that managers may synthesize to evaluate their resources and integrate them together, generating new applications and value-added strategies" (Eisenhardt and Martin 2000, 1107). As Beske, Land, and Seuring (2014) noted, DC are very difficult to conceptualize and they represent bundles of capabilities, not necessarily a single process. Examples of DC include localized business practices linked with macro- and micro-level characteristics, such as culture, service quality, advanced technology, economic environments, social relationships, communication facilities, infrastructure, and government policies. These factors signify that DC is a source through which emerging economies' multinational companies (MNC) conduct their businesses (Beske, Land, and Seuring 2014; Bhaskaran and Sukumaran 2007; LaBahn and Harich 1997; Teece 2014; Williamson 2015). Empirical research shows that DC help enterprises to improve performance and value creation (Naldi, Wikström, and Von Rimscha 2014).

The fast-paced internationalization of emerging economies MNC and their desire to move into and seek strategic resources in international markets (see Cui, Meyer, and Hu 2014) provide an opportunity for companies to understand the DC of these enterprises, and suggest guidance for other MNC embarking upon this transformational journey. In the process of investing abroad, MNC from emerging economies not only seek resources, but they also share their expertise arising from "location-specific specialties at home" (Luo and Tung 2007). Furthermore, emerging economies demonstrate a unique institutional and legal environment, and theories developed in the Western world may not unanimously be applied to these economies (Chakrabarty and Wang 2012; Xu et al. 2013). Emerging economies MNC differ significantly from their counterparts in developed countries, in terms of size, structures, operations, and managerial characteristics (Kotabe, Jiang, and Murray 2011). However, like developed markets, emerging economies also share some similar characteristics (Meyer and Peng 2016), and therefore it can provide an interesting context to explore the relationship between DC rooted in macro-and micro levels and sustainability practices. Increasingly, academics and practitioners have started focusing on emerging economies MNC. For example, Jormanainen and Koveshnikov (2012) carried out a content analysis of articles on emerging economies MNC in top tier management journals published between 2000 and 2010. They found that emerging economies MNC have substantially increased during this reporting period, highlighting the importance of this research area in the academic literature.

The concepts of sustainability and sustainable operations determined by DC are integral components of corporate strategies. The need to explore the linkages between DC and environmental sustainability is driving organizations to reconsider their operations and strategies (Beske, Land, and Seuring 2014; Chen, Fung, and Yuen 2019; Gruchmann and Seuring 2018; Hall and Howe 2012; Nidumolu, Prahalad, and Rangaswami 2009; Sölvell and Zander 1995; Teece 2014). Further, Atkinson (2000) and Pagell and Wu (2009) argued that sustainable DC are the ones that drive firms to achieve multi-dimensional performance, namely environmental, financial and social sustainability. This means that regulations relating to the outcomes of emerging economies' MNC are partly driven by the sustainable practices of organizations. Thus, sustainability is affected by overall DC (i.e., both macro-and micro-level capabilities). Such capabilities may result in financial and non-financial benefits, such as lower cost, better product outcomes, and enhanced service quality, significant waste reduction, efficient energy consumption, and, most importantly, environmental protection/adaptation (Hall and Howe 2012; Parboteeah, Helena, and Cullen 2012; Williamson 2015).

Employees (e.g., managers) and organizational practices are considered to be micro-level DC (Teece 2007). In other words, these capabilities represent the cognitive abilities of corporate managers who control MNC (Bhaskaran and Sukumaran 2007; Helfat and Peteraf 2015; Zhou and Li 2010). For example: "the capability for sensing opportunities and threats can be developed and improved through both the cognitive and creative capacities of individuals and some organizational processes such as research and development activities" (Molina-Azorín 2014, 110). At a firm-level, it includes human DC (e.g., human resource expertise), physical (e.g., firms' geographical location and specialized equipment) and organizational, strong internal corporate governance and control, which can be utilized by implementing value-enhancing corporate strategies (Eisenhardt and Martin 2000, 1107). The ability for a firm and its employees to be innovative and entrepreneurial can help in sensing and seeking out new opportunities in the wider business ecosystem ahead of the competition, thus, encompassing the elements of both macro-and micro-level capabilities (Teece 2007). In summary, DC are "the strategic routines by which firms achieve new resource configurations as markets emerge, collide, split, evolve, and die" (Eisenhardt and Martin 2000, 1107).

Macro-level DC are represented by external institutional factors, such as government policies and regulations, stakeholders, market requirements and the external economic and business environments in which firms operate. How well a firm performs in a dynamic business environment is dictated by a combination of both macro-and micro DC factors (Porter 1985). For instance, Adner and Kapoor (2010) described the Airbus A380 case study. They noted the challenges faced by Airbus in the pursuit of product innovation, did not reside just within the focal firm itself, but extended into the firm's wider ecosystem, beyond the dyad. Thus, in order to obtain a holistic view of how sustainable DC affects the performance of emerging economies' MNC, there is a need to assess both macro-and micro-level factors that straddle sustainable practices. Furthermore, macro DC may be argued by some simply as factors that influence a firm's DC/performance. Yet, from a system's perspective, a firm exists within a wider business ecosystem and macro DC form part of the overall system of "capabilities," which a firm can possess and leverage to improve sustainable performance. For instance, not all emerging MNC will leverage or take advantage of government policies/incentives/taxes and local markets to drive sustainable improvement, particularly if they are SMEs trading locally compared to a large company trading globally within the same country context (Raţiu and Mortan 2014). Thus, a firm's micro DC may influence how well it leverages the macro DC and vice versa.

Micro-level DC are analyzed here at both the individual and the organization levels, which is an extension of the RBV theory. The issue with looking at micro-level DC in isolation is that it does not offer an explanation as to why certain organizations sustain a competitive advantage in dynamic environments and others do not, even when they possess similar resources (Yassien and Jordan 2015). Thus, there is a need to address both micro- and macro-level DC simultaneously to understand how they interrelate to achieve environmental sustainability. Yet, very little research has investigated the impact of both micro and macro DC. For instance, many studies have explored only micro-level DC, such as individuals and organizations (Argote and Ren 2012; Eisenhardt, Furr, and Bingham 2010; Hodgkinson and Healey 2011; Teece 2007, 2012), however, there is a need to understand both, if emerging multinational enterprises want to succeed in entering new markets.

MNC enterprises have the capacity and resources to effectively respond to environmental factors (Rugman 1985). For instance, by responding to pressures from regulatory bodies (Bengtsson 1993) or they may approach it more symbolically in legitimizing corporate actions (Kuznetsov and Kuznetsova 2012). Despite the increasing awareness about environmental sustainability in the last couple of decades, the subject area is becoming a mainstream focus in the field of business and management (Dooley 2017; EMAS Board 2011; Hall and Howe 2012). For example, more than 223,149 companies from 159 countries had registered with the Environment Management System Certification (i.e., ISO 4001) by 2010 (ISO 2010). Similarly, the number of registered companies' for Eco-Management and Auditing Scheme (EMAS) doubled to 4,659 between 1997 and 2011 (EMAS Board 2011). However, Marcus and Anderson (2006) noted that, while DC does not necessarily result in improved performance of environmental management systems, they can result in improved performance of the overall supply chain. A recent study by Shaw et al. (2016) concluded that ISO 14001 adoption was evident and growing in developing nations, such as Thailand because it was seen as a pre-requisite for trading with developed nations.

Beske, Land, and Seuring (2014) proposed eight distinctive capabilities: (1) knowledge assessment; (2) knowledge acquisition; (3) ability development; (4) search, selection, and integration of partners; (5) supply chain foundations; (6) produce and process development; (7) relationship management; and (8) reflexive controls. They proposed that if a capability, such as knowledge acquisition, helps to integrate new knowledge into the knowledge base of a firm, which results in a change or adaptation to that firm within its wider supply chain, then, it can be considered a DC. However, fundamental questions still need to be addressed. Firstly, much of the extant research requires more in-depth reviews. Secondly, it is acknowledged that companies need to focus on environmental issues under the wider umbrella of corporate social responsibility (CSR). Yet, the literature addressing the key macro-and micro DC that strengthen environmental sustainability has not articulated the missing links between macro-and micro-level capabilities and environmental performance/sustainability (Beske, Land, and Seuring 2014; Chen, Fung, and Yuen 2019; Dooley 2017; Thompson and Cavaleri 2010; Williamson 2015). Thirdly, the literature in this area has focused predominantly on MNC from the Western world and not emerging economies. Thus, this research is timely as it explores the interaction between DC and the sustainable and CSR practices of these emerging economies MNC.

Further, progress in the area of environmental sustainability has been gradual in practice, particularly in the context of developing economies (Pagell and Wu 2009; Williamson 2015; Zhou and Li 2010). Although few studies, with the exception of Park, Russel, and Lee (2007), Beske, Land, and Seuring (2014), and Williamson (2015), have investigated the relationship between DC and sustainability dimensions, the missing links remain between macro- and micro-level DC and environmental sustainability. To cover this gap in the literature, we develop a conceptual framework and research agenda, from the existing literature, that can be used in understanding the relationship between DC and sustainability practices in the context of emerging economies MNC. We explore the interaction between macro- and micro-level DC and their perceived impact on the environmental practices of emerging economies MNC. We propose six propositions that could be tested in subsequent empirical research, and the conclusions arising from this study are presented in the final section of this article.

Theoretical framework and propositions

DC Macro-level DC external factors (e.g., government policy and regulations toward sustainability, the use of modern technology to reduce harmful emissions, market requirements, and economic environments), can directly or indirectly influence micro-level DC and environmental sustainability. Both institutional and stakeholder theories play an influential role in understanding how firms respond to their external business environments. For instance, although many environmental management standards are voluntary, many organizations are coerced or encouraged to adopt them by suppliers, customers, and, in some cases, through government tax incentives (Shaw et al. 2016). In other contexts, organizations may feel that they need to conform or simply mimic the action of competitors (DiMaggio and Powell 1983; Shaw et al. 2016).

Micro-capabilities, such as the organizations' structure/size, environmental policy, management characteristics (board independence, culture, gender diversity, amongst others), and the types of coordination[1] for their environmental effectiveness, also affect environmental sustainability, leading to operational, financial, social and strategic advantages for emerging economies' MNC. The implementation of firm-level (micro) DC may yield many benefits, but also need resources, extra time, financial costs and managerial coordination efforts. RBV theory and its extension provides a useful lens through which the micro DC of emerging economies' MNC can be understood (Barney, Ketchen, and Wright 2011; Hart and Dowell 2011). This is because a firm's resources and capabilities, such as employees, leadership teams and business culture, play an important role in the successful implementation of environmental practices, and ultimately enhance performance through triple-bottom-line (Elkington 2004).

Teece (2007) noted that in fast-moving business environments, dominated by various factors, such as global competition and differing market conditions, understanding the success of a firm cannot be just limited to a macro or micro view of DC, but how firms harness both. Further, the literature on the relationship between DC and environmental sustainability reports has conflicting results. For instance, Teece (2007) argued that DC could be a source of sustainable advantage, while Eisenhardt and Martin (2000) argued that it could be a source of sustainable disadvantage as these [dynamic] capabilities are "itself not stable." Peteraf, Di Stefano, and Verona (2013) suggested that these two contrasting paradigms coexist with some logical assumptions and researchers can use these assumptions from both perspectives in developing an integrated framework of DC. Figure 1 below describes the interrelationship between macro-level (i.e., country-level) and

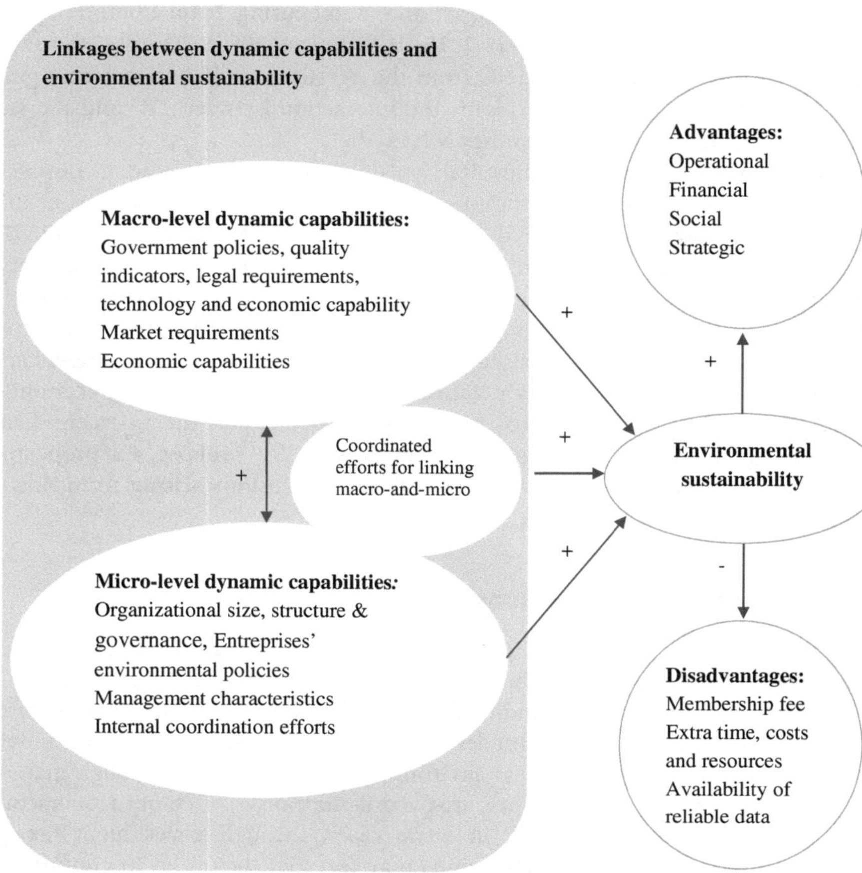

Figure 1. Framework of DC and environmental sustainability for emerging economies' MNC.

micro-level (i.e., firm-level) DC. The interaction between micro and micro-level DC has positive implications for organizational environmental sustainability. These micro-macro level interactions also result in firm-level operational, financial, social, and strategic advantages. Further examples of the interaction between macro-micro level capabilities are presented in the following sections (also shown in Figure 1).

Macro-level DC

Government policies, quality indicators, legal requirements, and technology

Macro-level DC are shaped by government policies, regulations, and practices that support multinational enterprises' efforts to promote their representation. For instance, the Malaysian government has introduced an economic program aimed at strengthening Malays' MNCs representation in the country. Substantial preferences in business, education, housing, and employment have been given to Malays. Preferential contracts have also been given to Malays, and, in turn, political, economic, and social changes have been seen in Malaysian macro-level DC. This new era has created competition for Chinese MNC, which have also made efforts to enter into partnerships with foreign enterprises. This development has challenged the level of DC for Chinese enterprises, competing with local Malaysian MNC (Bhaskaran and Sukumaran 2007).

Government policies direct firms toward environmental leadership and ultimately enable coordination between parties (such as companies, governments, and other regulatory agencies), which put cooperative efforts in place to achieve environmental sustainability. For example, the government of Canada developed a variety of new supporting policies that ultimately have resulted in a joint Commission on Resources and Environment, which helps enterprises to integrate sustainability guidelines into their environmental business strategies. The independent commission crystalized a provincial strategy that focuses on coordination within and between government departments to further develop environmental sustainability. Similar developments are made for emerging economies' multinational enterprises and represent examples of how institutional pressure is shaping these nations' landscapes around environment sustainability (Sarkis, Zhu, and Lai 2011). However, such developments need government-level efforts to strengthen macro-level DC for MNC enterprises and their links with environmental sustainability practices.

Switzerland, Latvia, Norway, Luxembourg, and Costa Rica are leading in terms of being environmentally and friendly, compared to other nations. This is because they have achieved better results on key environmental performance measures (EPI 2012). These results achieved in the context of developed markets suggest that middle-income countries like Latvia (GDP $12,938 per capita) and Costa Rica (GDP $19,238 per capita) can potentially achieve remarkable environmental outcomes which implies that, although generating income and wealth creation is important, good environmental policies and practices are the key determinants of success. Additionally, the policies of leading countries do not only focus on internal-governmental coordination but also working together with industries and environmentalists that play a key role in achieving environmental sustainability (Bachmann 2003; EPI 2012; Graafland and Smid 2017).

The Environmental Performance Index (EPI) report concludes that environmental challenges and issues vary between countries. The results from EPI recommend using a local approach, namely, the identification of local problems and finding solutions accordingly. The EPI report also finds that developing countries' governments fail to implement systematic processes to verify environmental data, such as water quality, waste management, recycling, and toxic exposures (EPI 2012; Graafland and Smid 2017; Liang and Liu 2017). These findings raise concerns about the quality of regulations, governance, and the accuracy of available data in the area of environmental sustainability.

It is thus important, for government departments to introduce stringent environmental laws and regulations that can lead toward environmental certification schemes, which also require enterprises to incorporate environmentally friendly regulations and practices, as an integral part of their corporate strategies. Gabzdylova, Raffensperger, and Castka (2009) and Shaw et al. (2016) found that government regulations are key drivers for adopting sustainable practices and need to be mandatory rather than voluntary in order to improve the environmental practices. The survey conducted by Collins, Roper, and Lawrence (2010) showed that companies are not strongly compelled to adopt sustainable practices, particularly in developing countries (Liang and Liu 2017).

Sustainable and environmental practices are fundamentally embedded in the environmental laws that vary significantly across countries, regions, and even cities. Thus, companies that are governed by better environmental regulations, and comply fully with sustainable practices, may yield considerable financial and non-financial advantages over competing firms (Liang and Liu 2017; Nidumolu, Prahalad, and Rangaswami 2009). Thus, the institutional pressure from the government is key to the successful implementation of environmental sustainability within the wider macro business environment.

Market requirements

It is pivotal for companies to consider new market requirements and expectations from various stakeholders (e.g., customers, consumers, and media), who also impact enterprises' environmental strategies. For example, the media is an important source of sustainability awareness for consumers who can reward/punish compliant/non-compliant firms. Markets are growing with environmentally informed consumers and customers, and these stakeholders demand factual evidence for environmental support from and compliance by multinational enterprises. Customers are also willing to pay a premium for environmental certification programs (Grolleau, Mzoughi, and Thomas 2007).

Modern consumers give significant consideration to environmentally friendly MNC. For instance, enterprises, such as the Carbon Trust in the UK, use carbon labels and other media to create consumer awareness about environmental sustainability, which is one of the reasons that today's green consumers demand greener products and services. Thus, pressure from customers is key drivers, as they raise concerns about product environmental quality and regulations (Gabzdylova, Raffensperger, and Castka 2009).

Considering customers' and consumers' preferences can help to build corporate image and reputation. In turn, this makes trading between the domestic market and foreign markets much easier (Shaw et al. 2016). Ultimately, such considerations provide a greater ability to work with superior partners in the industry (Gabzdylova, Raffensperger, and Castka 2009). Particularly, the policies and focus of leading overseas markets have significantly shifted toward environmental sustainability. For example, some retailers have recently developed "Certification Schemes" such as EurepGAP and GlobalGAP that assure conformity with environmental and labor requirements and product safety for consumers. Further, many large MNC voluntarily reports their environmental performance through schemes, such as the Global Reporting Initiative, as a way to showcase, their environmental credibility. For instance, Tesco PLC, having 30.7 percent market share of the UK's retail sector (and being one of the fourth largest world retailers), has recently developed a certificate scheme, called Nature Choice. This certification not only establishes firm-level environmental standards but also specifies size, taste, shelf life, and a variety of other product-related attributes. In fact, it does not matter whether Tesco's suppliers are from developed countries or emerging economies, they have to comply with the terms and conditions required by the certification (Saunders, Guenther, and Driver 2010).

Market requirements also demand environmental-friendly product policies, such as sustainable packaging, labeling, and product development using recycled content. Such policies also improve the reputation and legitimacy of multinational organizations. These factors, linked with manufacturing, production and reverse supply chains, attract, and retain business partners, which, in turn, help to increase a firm's market share (Sharma et al. 2010). MacRae et al. (2012) argued that sustainable packaging and labeling reduce costs and promote recycling and energy saving. Such practices not only help in protecting the environment, but may also result in enhanced corporate disclosure relating to environmental issues, i.e., use of chemicals, nutrition, and health and safety, and issues concerning animal welfare. However, it is unlikely that manufacturers would voluntarily label their products with information and data about policies that are environmentally harmful. Thus, effective macro-level (country-level) environmental legislations can play a crucial role in coercing firms to comply with health and safety as well as with the environmental standards (MacRae et al. 2012; Tobler, Visschers, and Siegrist 2011).

Product labeling should also include transportation modes and distance traveled, as they heavily affect environmental sustainability. Such information helps consumers to purchase local products and reduce harmful environmental impacts (Tobler, Visschers, and Siegrist 2011). For instance, locally produced vegetables in the Netherlands require 6 MJ per kg. However, the same quantity of vegetables transported from Africa to the Netherlands requires 88 MJ (Tobler, Visschers, and Siegrist 2011). A recent survey shows that environmentally focused consumers consider transportation distances and prefer to buy products local than global (Tobler, Visschers, and Siegrist 2011).

When entering a new market, a firm is able to develop "difficult to replicate" DC, which can be used to continuously harness, create, extend, upgrade, and protect their asset base (Teece 2007, 1319). Teece (2007) disaggregates this into three main components: (1) to sense and shape opportunities and threats; (2) to seize opportunities; and (3) to maintain competitiveness through enhancing, combining, protecting, and when necessary, reconfiguring the business enterprise's intangible and tangible assets. From a theoretical perspective, such ability requires the coordination of not only macro but also micro DCto realize these opportunities/threats and achieve environmental sustainability.

In summary, pressure by stakeholders, such as customers, suppliers and final consumers, are the key parameters that drive to build DC that are linked with sustainable practices. The literature in this area shows that consumers often have insufficient knowledge to assess environmentally friendly products. Additionally, governments' pressure often fails to enforce stringent regulations relating to packaging and labeling. Governments can develop and enforce environmental policies and can create environmental awareness, which can force MNC to build their DC regarding environmentally friendly practices (MacRae et al. 2012; Mikalef and Adamantia 2017; Tobler, Visschers, and Siegrist 2011). However, it is the coordination efforts, both at the macro- and micro-level, which together have a synergistic effect in developing difficult-to-replicate DC.

For instance, at a macro level companies are under immense pressure from shareholders in the stock market, as well in the consumer/product market, to demonstrate their sustainable credentials. Large global companies, like Clariant, a world leader in specialty chemicals, have to demonstrate their green compliance to shareholders by being part of programs such as the Dow Jones Sustainability Index or the FTSE Good Index (Clariant 2007). However, at a firm level, companies may also set-up voluntary disclosure committees, CSR/sustainability committees, or even appoint sustainability directors, to signal their focus on and commitment to business ethics and sustainability. Clariant, who has a dedicated Vice President for Sustainability, has integrated sustainability programs across and within its operations, from the corporate strategy down to processes and product development to become number one on the Dow Jones Sustainability Index. Together, the interaction between such external enforcement and internal commitment may positively affect a firm's contribution to CSR activities.

Economic capability

The key factors that strengthen the economic capability of a country could include high income and better exports, contributing to gross domestic product (GDP) (Van Phan and O'Brien 2019). Consequently, such economic activities result in higher demand for goods and services, resulting in an increased need for imports and exports, which increases the carbon footprint of supply chains (local versus global).

In building economic capabilities, governments may develop different legislations for firms according to their size, structures, and operations. For example, the government often places direct and indirect costs, such as social contributions of employers, taxation and compliance costs, to meet legal requirements. In addition, the requirements are often very stringent for larger firms compared to requirements for smaller firms with limited resources. Enterprises may face challenges to meet such costs, as a one-size-fits-all approach may not be suitable in promoting environmental and sustainability-related practices. Therefore, to avoid the risk of noncompliance and subsequent execution, governments may develop supporting policies and tax incentives that assist enterprises to overcome firm-specific disadvantages in meeting environmental compliance.

The complexity of government procedures and regulations, shortage of labor, unemployment, and competitive hostility also affect enterprises that, in turn, affect DC. The development of economic institutions, such as supporting infrastructures, banks and education systems, is important to the building of macro-level economic capabilities (Smallbone and Welter 2001).

To measure the performance of macro capabilities, Elekdag (2008) recommends three indicators, namely, interest rates, oil prices, and GDP. Among these indicators, GDP is widely used in the academic literature (Elekdag 2008). However, GDP only considers the total market production and it cannot be used to measure the overall welfare of a country, so it can provide misleading signals to policymakers. A recommendation is to consider the real household income, household consumption, and net national income that are closely associated with household living standards that are linked with macro-capabilities. It is also suggested that measures of income, consumption, and wealth should be accompanied by those indicators that imitate their distribution. Additionally, healthy competition in targeted markets also provides opportunities that could significantly influence DC and relative policies (Pisano 2017; Sölvell and Zander 1995).

Based on the above discussion, we present the following propositions that can be tested in subsequent research:

Proposition 1: There is a positive relationship between key macro-level DC and environmental sustainability.

Proposition 2: There is a positive relationship between key macro-level DC and micro-level DC.

Micro-level DC

Organizational size, structure, governance, and relevant policies

Large MNC that have grasped commercial benefits from environmental sustainability include Unilever and Proctor and Gamble. These companies consider the natural environment as a central concern to customers, shareholders, and staff (Redclift 2005). Such big companies can easily afford environmental certification schemes, which could be costly for emerging economies' MNC. For example, an average environmental management program could cost around €150,000. Thus, the probability of registering and implementing an environmental certification scheme is associated with larger firms (Grolleau, Mzoughi, and Thomas 2007).

In fact, there is no such enterprise that negatively impacts social and natural systems (i.e., environmental sustainability). However, some companies and industry sectors may do better than others in achieving environmental sustainability (Pagell and Wu 2009). For example, the damage to the environment [air emissions] in the electricity sector decreased by nearly 50 percent between 1987 and 1994. Similarly, in the agriculture sector, a significant reduction has been observed in PM_{10}; however, CO_2 and SO_2 have gradually increased in the agriculture industry (Atkinson 2000). Simnett, Vanstraelen, and Chua (2009) believed that companies in utilities, finance, and mining are more likely to focus on the assurance of their sustainability reports.[2] Pagell and Wu (2009) also scrutinized ten sustainable enterprises, namely, Snack Food, Food and Beverage, Pizza Restaurants, Cleaning Products, Forest and Wood Products, Electric Scraps, Paper Products, Lighting Products, Building Renovation, and IT Equipment. The findings show that majority of these organizations mainly focused on: (1) employees' training about environmental sustainability; (2) linking their corporate strategy and performance measurement systems to sustainable practices; (3) sustainability issues as part of their daily conversations; (4) developing guidelines for acquiring certifications; (5) transportation and production efficiency; (6) the use of advanced technology; (7) the integration of sustainability into the entire organization; and (8) building micro-level DC by emphasizing internal operations (Pagell and Wu 2009; Redclift 2005).

Gabzdylova, Raffensperger, and Castka (2009) believe that firm size seems to be an important factor in the adoption of environmental practices. In support, Gallo and Christensen (2011) found that large enterprises with sufficient manpower and funds were better off in responding to sustainability-related regulations. This can be explained by the RBV, suggesting that, compared to small organizations, large organizations have access to greater resources such as finance, people, systems, and processes that increase their ability and capability to implement environmental sustainability practices (Nawrocka, Brorson, and Lindhqvist 2009). Research also showed that a firm's ownership structure (public or private) is strongly related to environmentally sustainable practices. It has also been observed that innovative enterprises are more likely to be successful in employing environmental sustainability initiatives (Arora and Hartley 2017; Gallo and Christensen 2011).

Firm-level internal control systems could significantly influence a firm's CSR practices. Almost every country has now implemented a formal corporate governance code. A corporate governance code includes guidelines and best practices, and the board of directors is required to comply with such national-level regulations and guidelines in order to enhance the accountability and transparency of its organizations (Jamali, Safieddine, and Rabbath 2008). If governance regulations are implemented in an effective way, they can contribute to stakeholder activities (e.g., CSR initiatives) to make firms more visible and to preserve corporate legitimacy. We, therefore, expect a positive relationship between a firm's internal governance structure and environmental sustainability.

Management characteristics and coordination efforts

Managers' relevant education, past experience, and environmental support, traditional measures, modern preventive systems can improve the performance of the natural environment that reflects an enterprise's environmental policy (Grolleau, Mzoughi, and Thomas 2007). In particular, top management perceptions and support, such as employees' empowerment, rewards, environmental training and frequent internal, and external coordination efforts, could also affect sustainable practices. Top management especially reflects micro-level policies and corporate culture. It is important therefore to match such factors to encourage the implementation of environmental practices (Akhtar et al. 2018; Bachmann 2003). Moreover, a corporate strategy that encourages employees to work from home may also help in reducing energy usage, travel costs, and time (Nidumolu, Prahalad, and Rangaswami 2009). In support, the study also found that one-tenth of surveyed companies had 21–50% of employees who worked from home using telecommunication and other online tools, and, as a result, these enterprises have saved \$550–700 million dollars, and their production capacity improved by 10–20%. Consequently, employees' job satisfaction levels increased significantly (Nidumolu, Prahalad, and Rangaswami 2009). Gabzdylova, Raffensperger, and Castka (2009) and Collins, Roper, and Lawrence (2010) also believe that corporate values, employees' commitment, satisfaction and the belief of top management to embrace CSR initiatives are the fundamental firm-specific factors that drive environmental sustainability.

Additionally, the efficiency relating to environmental sustainability is derived from working together with business partners to develop eco-friendly raw materials, production, and waste reduction. Coordination efforts are important and help in improving corporate image and legitimacy, reducing associated litigation costs arising from noncompliance with environmental laws. In this way, key business coordinators can play a vital role in promoting awareness and developing collaborations with other organizations to protect the environment. For example, Wal-Mart develops guidelines for its suppliers (including those in emerging markets), and together with their suppliers, they set out targets to increase energy efficiency by 25 percent and reduce packaging costs by 5% in few years (Nidumolu, Prahalad, and Rangaswami 2009). Concisely, the coordinated efforts between participant companies, government and regulation agencies can lead to environmental sustainability. These arguments lead to the following propositions:

Proposition 3: There is a positive relationship between key micro-level DC and environmental sustainability.

Proposition 4: There is a positive relationship between the coordination efforts (i.e., linking macro-and micro-level DC and coordination efforts within departments and with supply chain partners) and environmental sustainability.

Environmental sustainability, advantages, and disadvantages

In 1987, the concept of sustainability was defined as "development that meets the needs of the present without compromising the ability of future generations to meet their own needs" (Redclift 1993, 8). The three dimensions of sustainability (i.e., environmental, economic, and social) can be contradictory, as well as complimentary with each other (Mollenkopf et al. 2010). For example, if a number of developed economies agree on promoting environmental sustainability, it may not necessarily be equally applicable to those emerging economies that seek more natural resources' exploration and wealth (e.g., China, India). Thus, definitions of sustainability are still vague, broad in scope and can mean different things to different countries (Atkinson 2000; Pagell and Wu 2009). Furthermore, cultural and political changes such as globalization, de-globalization (e.g., the UK leaving the EU and the US foreign policies) and ongoing wars in countries such as Afghanistan and Iraq, have increased the number of challenges for the global environmental development and sustainability (Casey 2018; Redclift 2005).

As discussed in the preceding section (Hall and Howe 2012; Parboteeah, Helena, and Cullen 2012), emerging markets MNC' are likely to enjoy the financial and non-financial benefits associated with environmental sustainability. The potential advantages include cost savings related to waste reduction, material, health and safety, and labor. Saving these costs generates additional revenue that enables emerging economies MNC to expand their existing business models into overseas markets. There is obviously no substitute to sustainability, although some CEOs have raised concerns that embedding sustainability in each aspect of the business model would be too costly for their organizations. They also assert that sustainable production demands new technology and processes that increase immediate costs, and consumers may not be willing to pay extra for eco-products, although some researchers may argue against this statement (e.g., Grolleau, Mzoughi, and Thomas 2007). That is why top management often divorce environmental sustainability from their core business policy and strategies (Nidumolu, Prahalad, and Rangaswami 2009).

The key advantages of environmental sustainability include improvement in operational performance (i.e., increasing profit by cost savings on energy usage, waste management, water usage, chemicals and transportation cost reduction, social outcomes (i.e., stakeholder trust and satisfaction), strategic benefits (i.e., better market access, greater understanding of the modern business preferences, brand recognition, joint decision-making, effective regulations, and benchmarking guidelines) (Carter and Rogers 2008; Collins, Roper, and Lawrence 2010; Hall and Howe 2012; Parboteeah, Helena, and Cullen 2012). The disadvantages are; membership fee, extra time to fill in the forms and to follow burdensome bureaucratic procedures, having extra costs related to the adoption of new technology, and the cost relating to the environmental audit and assurance (Collins, Roper, and Lawrence 2010; Grolleau, Mzoughi, and Thomas 2007; Nidumolu, Prahalad, and Rangaswami 2009). We offer the following proposition:

> Proposition 5: Environmental sustainability results in more advantages than disadvantages, when these advantages are supported by macro- and micro-level DC.

Conclusion and future research

Empirical studies have extensively debated the determinants of CSR and its impact on corporate performance and market valuation. Although the concept of environmental sustainability was coined a few decades ago, not enough research has been conducted to investigate the key linkages between DC and environmental sustainability, particularly in the context of emerging economies MNC. Within the framework of DC, the major macro-capabilities that directly and indirectly affect environmental sustainability include government policies, legal and market requirements, technological advances and economic capacities. These factors are also associated with MNC micro-level capabilities, such as management characteristics, environmental strategies, operations, and coordination efforts. We argue that the coordinated efforts by those players involved in promoting environmental sustainability (i.e., government, companies, supply chain partners, and regulatory agencies) could significantly affect firm-level initiatives (voluntary and mandatory) relating to environmental sustainability. We suggest that future studies should explore and test the interaction between country-level and firm-level DC.

The propositions presented in this research can be empirically tested using secondary data on DC and environmental sustainability. It thus provides a conceptual framework for further empirical research and for the testing of the propositions in a case study or industry setting through surveys or using panel data already available on different databases. We also suggest utilizing the interaction between firm-level ESG (environmental, social and governance) data and the country-level indicators of institutional quality (rule of law and judicial efficiency) to test the propositions presented in this article. We also suggest that there is no harm in using a "cherry-picking" or benchmarking approach, whereby emerging economies MNC can benefit from best practices used by their competing firms in developed countries. This might help them to take a proactive approach in order to tackle environmental issues (Akhtar et al. 2012; EPI 2012). We also argue that informal norms distributed through vibrant media (social, print, and electronic media) could also be used as a tool to reward/punish compliant and non-compliant firms in the area of environmental sustainability. We suggest stringent environmental regulations for companies operating in emerging economies, consequently, substantial fines and penalties can be implemented for those companies violating environmental regulations. We also suggest that compliance with environmental programs should be required as a "listing requirement" on all major stock exchanges around the world so that firms can be de-listed from stock markets in the event of noncompliance with environmental regulations.

Notes

1. With the introduction of corporate governance regulations around the world, many companies have now established committees that look after the corporate social responsibility and sustainability related affairs of an organization – namely, the corporate social responsibility committee, sustainability committee – making efforts to link different dynamic capabilities so better environmental results can be obtained.
2. Sustainability assurance is very similar to an audit where the social and environmental policies/activities of an organization are examined by an independent external consulting/auditing firm. The assurance certificates issued by the consulting/auditing firm give some assurance to investors and other stakeholders that the social and environmental activities of an organization are independently verified and hence such disclosure can be trusted. Currently, the Big Four auditing firms frequently issue assurance certificates for large and listed companies.

References

Adner, R., and R. Kapoor. 2010. "Value Creation in Innovation Ecosystems: How the Structure of Technological Interdependence Affects Firm Performance in New Technology Generations." *Strategic Management Journal* 31 (3):306–333. doi:10.1002/smj.821.

Akhtar, P., Z. Khan, J. G. Frynas, Y. K. Tse, and R. Rao-Nicholson. 2018. "Essential Micro-Foundations for Contemporary Business Operations: Top Management Tangible Competencies, Relationship-Based Business Networks and Environmental Sustainability." *British Journal of Management* 29 (1):43–62. doi:10.1111/1467-8551.12233.

Akhtar, P., N. Marr, E. Garnevska, and S. Ahmed. 2012. "Chain Coordinators and Their Role in Selected Agri-Food Supply Chains: Lessons from Pakistan, New Zealand and United Kingdom." *Food Chain* 2 (1):104–116. doi:10.3362/2046-1887.2012.008.

Argote, L., and Y. Ren. 2012. "Transactive Memory Systems: A Micro Foundation of DC." *Journal of Management Studies* 49 (8):1375–1382. doi:10.1111/j.1467-6486.2012.01077.x.

Arora, A. S., and N. Hartley. 2017. "Sustainability, Institutions, and Internationalization in Emerging Markets: Role of Sustainable Innovation for Sustainable World Development." *International Journal of Emerging Markets* 12 (1):920–926.

Atkinson, G. 2000. "Measuring Corporate Sustainability." *Journal of Environmental Planning and Management* 43 (2):235–252. doi:10.1080/09640560010694.

Bachmann, R. 2003. "The Coordination of Relations across Organizational Boundaries." *International Studies of Management and Organization* 33 (2):7–21. doi:10.1080/00208825.2003.11043681.

Barney, J. B., D. J. Ketchen, and M. Wright. 2011. "The Future of Resource-Based Theory: Revitalization or Decline?" *Journal of Management* 37 (5):1299–1315. doi:10.1177/0149206310391805.

Bhaskaran, S., and N. Sukumaran. 2007. "National Culture, Dynamic Capabilities and Management Practices: Consequential Relationships?" *Cross Cultural Management: An International Journal* 14 (1):54–67. doi:10.1108/13527600710718831.

Bengtsson, L. 1993. "Governmental Markets, Regulations, and Hierarchies: Building Trust in the Face." International Studies of Management *and* Organization 23 (1):47–68. doi:10.1080/00208825.1993.11656600.

Beske, P., A. Land, and S. Seuring. 2014. "Sustainable Supply Chain Management Practices and Dynamic Capabilities in the Food Industry: A Critical Analysis of the Literature." *International Journal of Production Economics* 152:131–143. doi:10.1016/j.ijpe.2013.12.026.

Carter, C., and D. Rogers. 2008. "A Framework of Sustainable Supply Chain Management: Moving toward New Theory." *International Journal of Physical Distribution and Logistics Management* 38 (5):360–387. doi:10.1108/09600030810882816.

Casey, C. A. 2018. "De-Globalization and the Disintegration of the European News System 1918–34." *Journal of Contemporary History* 53 (2):267–291. doi:10.1177/0022009416678917.

Chakrabarty, S., and L. Wang. 2012. "The Long-Term Sustenance of Sustainability Practices in MNCs: A Dynamic Capabilities Perspective of the Role of R&D and Internationalization." *Journal of Business Ethics* 110 (2): 205–217. doi:10.1007/s10551-012-1422-3.

Chen, I. S. N., P. K.O. Fung, and S. S. M. Yuen. 2019. "Dynamic Capabilities of Logistics Service Providers: Antecedents and Performance Implications." *Asia Pacific Journal of Marketing and Logistics* 31 (4):1058–1075. doi:10.1108/APJML-12-2017-0308.

Clariant. 2007. "Clariant Achieves Best-in-Class Rankings in 2017 Dow Jones Sustainability Index." Accessed October 22, 2019. https://www.clariant.com/en/Corporate/News/2017/09/Clariant-achieves-bestinclass-rankings-in-2017-Dow-Jones-Sustainability-Index.

Collins, E., J. Roper, and S. Lawrence. 2010. "Sustainability Practices: Trends in New Zealand Businesses." *Business Strategy and the Environment* 19 (8):479–494. doi:10.1002/bse.653.

Cui, L., K. E. Meyer, and H. W. Hu. 2014. "What Drives Firms' Intent to Seek Strategic Assets by Foreign Direct Investment? A Study of Emerging Economy Firms." *Journal of World Business* 49 (4):488–501. doi:10.1016/j.jwb.2013.12.003.

DiMaggio, P. J., and W. W. Powell. 1983. "The Iron Cage Revisited: Collective Rationality and Institutional Isomorphism in Organizational Fields." *American Sociological Review* 48 (2):147–160. doi:10.2307/2095101.

Dooley, K. 2017. "Value Chain Systemicity: "Promoting Organizational Creativity and Environmental Sustainability in Low Velocity Industries." *Journal of Cleaner Production* 140:1903–1913. doi:10 1016/j.jclepro.2016.09.075.

Eisenhardt, K.M., and J. A. Martin. 2000. "Dynamic Capabilities: What Are They?" *Strategic Management Journal* 21 (10–11):1105–1121. doi:10.1002/1097-0266(200010/11)21:10/11<1105::AID-SMJ133>3.0.CO;2-E.

Eisenhardt, K., N. Furr, and C. Bingham. 2010. "Micro-Foundations of Performance: Balancing Efficiency and Flexibility in Dynamic Environments." *Organization Science* 21 (6):1263–1273. doi:10.1287/orsc.1100.0564.

Elekdag, S. 2008. "How Does the Global Economic Environment Influence the Demand for IMF Resources?" *IMF Staff Papers* 55 (4):624–653.

Elkington, J. 2004. *The Triple Bottom Line: Does It All Add Up*. London: Routledge.

EMAS Board. 2011. "Systematic Environmental Management Creating Added Value with EMAS." Accessed October 22, 2019. https://pfm.management/wpcontent/uploads/2014/06/Creating_Added_Value_with_EMAS_EN.pdf.

EPI. 2012. "Environmental Performance Index and Pilot Trend Environmental Performance Index." Accessed October 22, 2019. https://sedac.ciesin.columbia.edu/data/set/epi-environmental-performance-index-pilot-trend-2012.

Gabzdylova, B., J. Raffensperger, and P. Castka. 2009. "Sustainability in the New Zealand Wine Industry: Drivers, Stakeholders and Practices." *Journal of Cleaner Production* 17 (11):992–998. doi:10.1016/j.jclepro.2009.02.015.

Gallo, P., and L. Christensen. 2011. "Firm Size Matters: An Empirical Investigation of Organizational Size and Ownership on Sustainability-Related Behaviours." *Business and Society* 50 (2):315–349. doi:10.1177/0007650311398784.

Graafland, J., and H. Smid. 2017. "Reconsidering the Relevance of Social License Pressure and Government Regulation for Environmental Performance of European SMEs." *Journal of Cleaner Production* 141:967–977. doi:10.1016/j.jclepro.2016.09.171.

Grolleau, G., N. Mzoughi, and A. Thomas. 2007. "What Drives Agrifood Firms to Register for an Environmental Management System." *European Review of Agricultural Economics* 34 (2):233–255. doi:10.1093/erae/jbm012.

Gruchmann, T., and S. Seuring. 2018. "Explaining Logistics Social Responsibility from a Dynamic Capabilities Perspective." *The International Journal of Logistics Management* 29 (4):1255–1278. doi:10.1108/IJLM-08-2017-0200.

Hall, G.M., and J. Howe. 2012. "Energy from Waste and the Food Processing Industry." *Process Safety and Environmental Protection* 90 (3):203–212. doi:10.1016/j.psep.2011.09.005.

Hart, S. L., and G. Dowell. 2011. "A Natural Resource-Based View of a Firm: Fifteen Years After." *Journal of Management* 37 (5):1464–1479. doi:10.1177/0149206310390219.

Helfat, C.E., and M. A. Peteraf. 2015. "Managerial Cognitive Capabilities and the Micro Foundations of Dynamic Capabilities." *Strategic Management Journal* 36 (6):831–850. doi:10.1002/smj.2247.

Hodgkinson, G., and M. Healey. 2011. "Psychological Foundations of Dynamic Capabilities: Reflexion and Reflection in Strategic Management." *Strategic Management Journal* 32 (13):1500–1516. doi:10.1002/smj.964.

ISO. 2010. "ISO 9001 Certifications Top One Million Mark, Food Safety and Information Security Continue Meteoric Increase." Accessed October 15, 2019. https://www.isoceltd.com/iso-9001-certifications-top-one-million-mark-food-safety-and-information-security-continue-meteoric-increase.

Jamali, D., A. M. Safieddine, and M. Rabbath. 2008. "Corporate Governance and Corporate Social Responsibility Synergies and Interrelationships." *Corporate Governance: An International Review* 16 (5):443–459. doi:10.1111/j.1467-8683.2008.00702.x.

Jormanainen, I., and A. Koveshnikov. 2012. "International Activities of Emerging Market Firms." *Management International Review* 52 (5):691–725. doi:10.1007/s11575-011-0115-y.

Kotabe, M., C. X. Jiang, and J. Y. Murray. 2011. "Managerial Ties, Knowledge Acquisition, Realized Absorptive Capacity and New Product Market Performance of Emerging Multinational Companies: A Case of China." *Journal of World Business* 46 (2):166–176. doi:10.1016/j.jwb.2010.05.005.

Kuznetsov, A., and O. Kuznetsova. 2012. "Business Legitimacy and the Margins of Corporate Social Responsibility in the Russian Context." *International Studies of Management & Organization* 42 (3):35–48. doi:10.2753/IMO0020-8825420302.

LaBahn, D. W., and K. R. Harich. 1997. "Sensitivity to National Dynamic Capabilities: Effects on U.S.-Mexican Channel Relationship Performance." *Journal of International Marketing* 5 (4):29–51. doi:10.1177/1069031X9700500404.

Liang, D., and T. Liu. 2017. "Does Environmental Management Capability of Chinese Industrial Firms Improve the Contribution of Corporate Environmental Performance to Economic Performance? Evidence from 2010 to 2015." *Journal of Cleaner Production* 142 (4):2985–2998. doi:10.1016/j.jclepro.2016.10.169.

Luo, Y., and L. Tung. 2007. "International Expansion of Emerging Market Enterprises: A Springboard Perspective." *Journal of International Business Studies* 38 (4):481–498. doi:10.1057/palgrave.jibs.8400275.

MacRae, R., M. Szabo, K. Anderson, F. Louden, and S. Trillo. 2012. "Empowering the Citizen-Consumer: Re-Regulating Consumer Information to Support the Transition to Sustainable and Health Promoting Food Systems in Canada." *Sustainability* 4 (9):2146–2175. doi:10.3390/su4092146.

Marcus, A., and M. Anderson. 2006. "A General Dynamic Capability: Does It Propagate Business and Social Competencies in the Retail Food Industry." *Journal of Management Studies* 43 (1):19–46. doi:10.1111/j.1467-6486.2006.00581.x.

Meyer, K.E., and M. W. Peng. 2016. "Theoretical Foundations of Emerging Economy Business Research." *Journal of International Business Studies* 47 (1):3–22. doi:10.1057/jibs.2015.34.

Mikalef, P., and P. Adamantia. 2017. "Information Technology-Enabled Dynamic Capabilities and Their Indirect Effect on Competitive Performance: Findings from PLS-SEM and fsQCA." *Journal of Business Research* 70:1–16. doi:10.1016/j.jbusres.2016.09.004.

Molina-Azorín, J. F. 2014. "Micro-Foundations of Strategic Management: Toward Micro–Macro Research in the Resource-Based Theory." *BRQ Business Research Quarterly* 17 (2):102–114. doi:10.1016/j.brq.2014.01.001.

Mollenkopf, D., H. Stolze, W. L. Tate, and M. Ueltschy. 2010. "Green, Lean, and Global Supply Chains." *International Journal of Physical Distribution and Logistics Management* 40 (1/2):14–41. doi:10.1108/09600031011018028.

Naldi, L., P. Wikström, and M. B. Von Rimscha. 2014. "Dynamic Capabilities and Performance: An Empirical Study of Audiovisual Producers in Europe." *International Studies of Management and Organization* 44 (4):63–82. doi:10.2753/IMO0020-8825440404.

Nawrocka, D., T. Brorson, and T. Lindhqvist. 2009. "ISO 14001 in Environmental Supply Chain Practices." *Journal of Cleaner Production* 17 (16):1435–1443. doi:10.1016/j.jclepro.2009.05.004.

Nidumolu, R., K. Prahalad, and M. Rangaswami. 2009. "Why Sustainability is Now the Key Driver of Innovation." *Harvard Business Review* 87 (9):56–64.

Pagell, M., and Z. Wu. 2009. "Building a More Complete Theory of Sustainable Supply Chain Management Using Case Studies of 10 Exemplars." *Journal of Supply Chain Management* 45 (2):37–56. doi:10.1111/j.1745-493X.2009.03162.x.

Parboteeah, K., A. Helena, and J. Cullen. 2012. "Propensity to Support Sustainability Initiatives: A Cross-National Model." *Journal of Business Ethics* 105 (3):403–413. doi:10.1007/s10551-011-0979-6.

Park, H., C. Russel, and J. Lee. 2007. "National Culture and Environmental Sustainability: A Cross-National Analysis." *Journal of Economics and Finance* 31 (1):104–121. doi:10.1007/BF02751516.

Peteraf, M., G. Di Stefano, and G. Verona. 2013. "The Elephant in the Room of Dynamic Capabilities: Bringing Two Diverging Conversations Together." *Strategic Management Journal* 34 (12):1389–1410. doi:10.1002/smj.2078.

Pisano, G. P. 2017. "Towards a Prescriptive Theory of Dynamic Capabilities: Connecting Strategic Choice, Learning, and Competition." *Industrial and Corporate Change* 26 (5):747–762. doi:10.1093/icc/dtx026.

Porter, M. E. 1985. *The Competitive Advantage: Creating and Sustaining Superior Performance*. NY: Free Press.

Rațiu, P., and M. Mortan. 2014. "EMAS Implementation in SMEs: Driving Forces and Barriers." *Managerial Challenges of the Contemporary Society* 7 (2):73–79.

Redclift, M. 1993. "Sustainable Development: Needs, Values, Rights." *Environmental Values* 2 (1):3–20. doi:10.3197/096327193776679981.

Redclift, M. 2005. "Sustainable Development (1987–2005): an Oxymoron Comes of Age." *Sustainable Development* 13 (4):212–227. doi:10.1002/sd.281.

Rugman, A. M. 1985. "Multinationals and Global Competitive Strategy." *International Studies of Management & Organization* 15 (2):8–18. doi:10.1080/00208825.1985.11656406.

Sarkis, J., Q. Zhu, and K.-H. Lai. 2011. "An Organizational Theoretic Review of Green Supply Chain Management Literature." *International Journal of Production Economics* 130 (1):1–15. doi:10.1016/j.ijpe.2010.11.010.

Saunders, C. M., M. Guenther, and T. Driver. 2010. "Sustainability Trends in Key Overseas Markets: Market Drivers and Implications to Increase Value for New Zealand Exports." Research Report No. 319, Lincoln University, New Zealand.

Sharma, A., G. Iyer, A. Mehrotra, and R. Krishnan. 2010. "Sustainability and Business-to-Business Marketing: A Framework and Implications." *Industrial Marketing Management* 39 (2):330–341. doi:10.1016/j.indmarman.2008.11.005.

Shaw, S., D. B. Grant, N. Shenin, and S. Chaisurayakarn. 2016. "Using Environmental Reporting Tools in the Supply Chain: Perspectives from UK, Finland and Thailand." Proceedings of the 21st Annual Logistics Research Network (LRN) Conference, University of Hull, UK, September 2016.

Simnett, R., A. Vanstraelen, and W. Chua. 2009. "Assurance on Sustainability Reports: An International Comparison." *The Accounting Review* 84 (3):937–967. doi:10.2308/accr.2009.84.3.937.

Smallbone, D., and F. Welter. 2001. "The Role of Government in SME Development in Transition Economies." *International Small Business Journal: Researching Entrepreneurship* 19 (4):63–77. doi:10.1177/0266242601194004.

Sölvell, Ö., and I. Zander. 1995. "Organization of the Dynamic Multinational Enterprise: The Home-Based and the Heterarchical MNE." *International Studies of Management and Organization* 25 (1–2):17–38. doi:10.1080/00208825.1995.11656650.

Teece, D. J. 2007. "Explicating Dynamic Capabilities: The Nature and Micro-Foundations of (Sustainable) Enterprise Performance." *Strategic Management Journal* 28 (13):1319–1350. doi:10.1002/smj.640.

Teece, D. J. 2012. "Dynamics Capabilities: Routines versus Entrepreneurial Action." *Journal of Management Studies* 49 (8):1395–1401. doi:10.1111/j.1467-6486.2012.01080.x.

Teece, D. J. 2014. "A Dynamic Capabilities-Based Entrepreneurial Theory of the Multinational Enterprise." *Journal of International Business Studies* 45 (1):8–37. doi:10.1057/jibs.2013.54.

Thompson, J. P., and S. Cavaleri. 2010. "Dynamic Knowledge, Organizational Growth, and Sustainability: The Case of Prestwick Memory Devices." *International Studies of Management and Organization* 40 (3):50–60. doi:10.2753/IMO0020-8825400303.

Tobler, C., V. H. M. Visschers, and M. Siegrist. 2011. "Organic Tomatoes versus Canned Beans: How Do Consumers Assess the Environmental Friendliness of Vegetables?" *Environment and Behavior* 43 (5):591–611. doi:10.1177/0013916510372865.

Van Phan, P., and M. O'Brien. 2019. "Multidimensional Wellbeing Inequality in a Developing Country: A Case Study of Vietnam." *Social Indicators Research* 145 (1):157–183. doi:10.1007/s11205-019-02104-0.

Williamson, P. J. 2015. "The Competitive Advantages of Emerging Market Multinationals: A Re-Assessment." *Critical Perspectives on International Business* 11 (3/4):216–235. doi:10.1108/cpoib-02-2014-0008.

Xu, D., and K. E. Meyer. 2013. "Linking Theory and Context: 'Strategy Research in Emerging Economies' after Wright et al. (2005)." *Journal of Management Studies* 50 (7):1322–1346. doi:10.1111/j.1467-6486.2012.01051.x.

Yassien, E., and A. Jordan. 2015. "Big Picture of Dynamic Capabilities." *Journal of Management Research* 7 (5):63–78. doi:10.5296/jmr.v7i5.8007.

Zhou, K. Z., and C. B. Li. 2010. "How Strategic Orientations Influence the Building of Dynamic Capability in Emerging Economies." *Journal of Business Research* 63 (3):224–231. doi:10.1016/j.jbusres.2009.03.003.

Index

Note: **Bold** page numbers refer to tables; *italic* page numbers refer to figures and page numbers followed by "n" denote endnotes.

Kolibri 360 GmbH
Ferdinand-Jühlke-Straße 7
99095 Erfurt, Deutschland
produktsicherheit@kolibri360.de

Optimization Methods for Finite Element Analysis and Design

Optimization Methods for Finite Element Analysis and Design describes recent developments in Finite Element Methods (FEM). It gives a brief introduction of the applications of AI-based nature-inspired metaheuristic algorithms and machine learning (ML) at various stages of FEM. The book covers a range of state-of-the-art application areas including medical equipment, structural analysis and machinery products.

It explores the applications of optimization and ML techniques in mesh smoothing, quality improvement and Laplacian and Taubin smoothing. The book also discusses the optimization of cable nets and steel frames using nature-inspired metaheuristic methods.

Advances in Metaheuristics

Series Editors:

Patrick Siarry, Universite Paris-Est Creteil, France

Anand J. Kulkarni, Institute of Artificial Intelligence, Dr Vishwanath Karad MIT World Peace University

Metaheuristics for Enterprise Data Intelligence
Edited by Dr Kaustubh Sakhare, Dr Vibha Vyas, Dr Apoorva S. Shastri

Handbook of AI-Based Metaheuristics
Edited by Patrick Siarry, Anand J. Kulkarni

Metaheuristic Algorithms in Industry 4.0
Edited by Pritesh Shah, Ravi Sekhar, Anand J. Kulkarni, Patrick Siarry

Constraint Handling in Cohort Intelligence Algorithm
Ishaan R. Kale, Anand J. Kulkarni

Hybrid Genetic Optimization for IC Chip Thermal Control: with MATLAB® Applications
Mathew V. K., Tapano Kumar Hotta

Handbook of Moth-Flame Optimization Algorithm: Variants, Hybrids, Improvements, and Applications
Edited by Seyedali Mirjalili

Combinatorial Optimization under Uncertainty: Real-Life Scenarios in Allocation Problems
Edited by Ritu Arora, Prof. Shalini Arora, Anand J. Kulkarni, Patrick Siarry

AI-Based Metaheuristics for Information Security in Digital Media
Edited by Apoorva S Shastri, Mangal Singh, Anand J. Kulkarni, Patrick Siarry

Graph Coloring
Maurice Clerc

Automatic Generation of Algorithms
Victor Parada

Optimization Methods for Finite Element Analysis and Design
Ishaan R. Kale, Sujin Bureerat, Ravipudi Venkata Rao

For more information about this series please visit: https://www.routledge.com/Advances-in-Metaheuristics/book-series/AIM

Optimization Methods for Finite Element Analysis and Design

Edited by

Ishaan R. Kale, Sujin Bureerat, and Ravipudi Venkata Rao

CRC Press
Taylor & Francis Group
Boca Raton London New York

CRC Press is an imprint of the
Taylor & Francis Group, an **informa** business

Designed cover image: Shutterstock

First edition published 2026
by CRC Press
2385 NW Executive Center Drive, Suite 320, Boca Raton FL 33431

and by CRC Press
4 Park Square, Milton Park, Abingdon, Oxon, OX14 4RN

CRC Press is an imprint of Taylor & Francis Group, LLC

ISBN: 978-1-032-93210-1 (hbk)
ISBN: 978-1-032-93212-5 (pbk)
ISBN: 978-1-003-56491-1 (ebk)

DOI: 10.1201/9781003564911

Typeset in Minion
by KnowledgeWorks Global Ltd.

Contents

Foreword

THE APPLICATION OF FINITE ELEMENT ANALYSIS HAS BECOME ONE OF THE MOST CRITICAL processes before manufacturing any product. This is because it is always better to resolve the failure problems virtually and prevent them from occurring. It is like a non-destructive analysis, preventing/minimizing company losses. Understanding these analyses assumes greater importance when designing equipment and structures so they do not fail while operating in the field by practicing engineers. Finite element analysis (FEA) has multiple applications in aerospace, mechanical and civil design, composite materials, electronics engineering, mobile design, etc. It is very heartening to see that this book is a collection of eight great concepts encompassing the latest research on FEA and related fields like structural and design optimization, fluid dynamics, meshing, etc.

FEA is a numerical method, and a high-quality mesh is essential for accurate results. The first chapter briefly explains the applications of optimization and machine learning (ML) techniques in mesh smoothing and quality improvement. It then explains different types of meshes and reviews various techniques for enhancing mesh quality. Meshing is not only related to structural analysis but also encompasses areas like virtual reality (VR), scientific computing, video game design and medical imaging. Chapter 2 focuses on techniques such as Laplacian and Taubin smoothing, exploring the practicality of these techniques regarding the visual and numerical accuracy of models by considering the limitations, such as mesh shrinkage and over-smoothing. Moreover, current research trends that incorporate the integration of ML integration are also discussed.

After discussing mesh smoothing, the book moves on to structural optimization in Chapter 3. This chapter covers the static deformation of cable nets. The conic programming algorithm is used to analyze cable nets and other highly flexible structures because it simplifies defining the strain energy accumulated in a cable during the deformation process. Chapter 4 analyses different blade profiles and materials that can be used for the turbine rotor blade. The mathematical model is generated for the design, giving outputs for the velocity triangles, forces and other core design values. It is followed by computational fluid dynamics (CFD) analysis. The above design achieved a successful blade selection for the application that not only passed in generating thrust figures but also under working load conditions.

In Chapter 5, the optimal design of frame structures using the fuzzy reinforced Jaya algorithm (FRJ) is considered. The fuzzy module in the FRJ constantly tracks the search process and attempts to adjust the algorithm search behavior based on the governing condition of the desired problem. Two steel frame examples, a one-bay, eight-story frame and a three-bay, fifteen-story frame, were analyzed to test the algorithm's efficacy. The generated behavioral diagrams indicate that the fuzzy module in FRJ significantly enhances the algorithm's search process compared to traditional Jaya. The study carried out in Chapter 6 reviewed the optimization and analysis of structural systems such as truss systems, cable systems, tensegrity structures and plate systems and their solutions with metaheuristic methods. It was found from the literature that the use of metaheuristics with classical approaches of finite element and energy minimization theory can provide a solution that considers all non-linearities without additional modification.

Chapter 7 discusses heat exchanger design using the marathon runner algorithm (MRA), a novel metaheuristic optimization technique. It explains the analytical model that gives rise to the governing equations and then describes the details of economic optimization concerning three case studies. The statistical analysis proves that MRA performs well while solving complex engineering problems. Predicting fracture and damage of single-lap Epoxy-Eglass composite joints under cyclic loading is the agenda of the last chapter. The study analyzes the effects of different stiffness values of epoxy resin, modified with various percentages of graphene oxide nanoparticles (GONPs), on joint performance. The results show a positive influence of stiffness values corresponding to different percentages of GONPs, resulting in improved mechanical parameters of the adhesive for fatigue strength under cyclic loading.

This book aims to connect two important areas of analysis: finite element methods and optimization. The presentation is good, and the language is easy to understand. I am sure it will serve as a good reference for exploring optimization in FEA.

Dr Mandar S. Sapre (Maths Enthusiast),
Research Assistant Professor,
Institute of Artificial Intelligence,
Dr Vishwanath Karad MIT World Peace University, Pune, Maharashtra, India

Editor Biographies

Ishaan R. Kale holds a PhD in Nature-Inspired Optimization Techniques from Symbiosis International University. He received his MEng in Mechanical Design Engineering from Maharashtra Institute of Technology, Pune University and BEng from North Maharashtra University. His research interests include design engineering, constraint handling, metaheuristic optimization algorithms and hybrid metaheuristics.

Sujin Bureerat received the BEng degree in Mechanical Engineering from Khon Kaen University, Thailand, and the PhD degree in Engineering from Manchester University, United Kingdom. He is a professor with the Department of Mechanical Engineering, Khon Kaen University. His research interests include: multidisciplinary design optimization, metaheuristics, aeroelasticity and aircraft design.

Ravipudi Venkata Rao is a renowned mechanical engineering academic specializing in optimization techniques, design and manufacturing. With significant contributions to nature-inspired metaheuristic algorithms, he has authored numerous books and research papers, influencing fields like structural optimization, computational mechanics and intelligent manufacturing systems worldwide.

Contributors

Gebrail Bekdaş
Department of Civil Engineering
Istanbul University – Cerrahpaşa
Istanbul, Türkiye

Y. U. Chavande
Department of Mechanical Engineering
Dr Vishwanath Karad MIT World Peace University
Pune, MH, India

Arushi Dadhich
School of Computer Science Engineering and Technology
Bennett University
Greater Noida, UP, India

Subhranil Das
University of Petroleum and Energy Studies (UPES)
Dehradun, UK, India

Archit Dogra
Symbiosis Institute of Technology
Symbiosis International (Deemed University)
Pune, MH, India

Grzegorz Dzierżanowski
Warsaw University of Technology
Warsaw, Poland

Zong Woo Geem
Department of Smart City
Gachon University
Seongnam, Korea

R. R. Ghadge
Department of Mechanical Engineering
Dr Vishwanath Karad MIT World Peace University
Pune, MH, India

Ishaan R. Kale
Institute of Artificial Intelligence
Dr Vishwanath Karad MIT World Peace University
Pune, MH, India

Suhail Khaliq
Department of Mechanical Engineering
Dr Vishwanath Karad MIT World Peace University
Pune, MH, India

Sanghun Kim
Department of Civil and Environmental Engineering
Temple University
Philadelphia, PA, USA

Anvi Kohli
School of Computer Science Engineering and Technology
Bennett University
Greater Noida, UP, India

Anand J. Kulkarni
Institute of Artificial Intelligence
Dr Vishwanath Karad MIT World Peace University
Pune, MH, India

Rashmi Kumari
School of Computer Science Engineering and Technology
Bennett University
Greater Noida, UP, India

Mahsa Moloodpoor
Mechanical Engineering Department
Ege University
Izmir, Turkey

Ali Mortazavi
Department of Civil Engineering
Izmir Democracy University
Izmir, Turkey

Sinan Melih Nigdeli
Department of Civil Engineering
Istanbul University – Cerrahpaşa
Istanbul, Türkiye

Ayla Ocak
Department of Civil Engineering
Istanbul University – Cerrahpaşa
Istanbul, Türkiye

Akshay M. Pillai
Symbiosis Institute of Technology
Symbiosis International (Deemed University)
Pune, MH, India

Pritee M. Purohit
Army Institute of Technology,
Pune, MH, India

Anand A. Ramgude
Army Institute of Technology
Pune, MH, India

Mandar S. Sapre
Institute of Artificial Intelligence
Dr Vishwanath Karad MIT World Peace University
Pune, MH, India

Raghwendra Kishore Singh
Department of Electronics and Communication Engineering
Bharat Institute of Engineering and Technology
Hyderabad, TS, India

Arya Sunil
School of Computer Science Engineering and Technology
Bennett University
Greater Noida, UP, India

Bryan Thomas
Symbiosis Institute of Technology
Symbiosis International (Deemed University)
Pune, MH, India

Yusuf Cengiz Toklu
Department of Civil Engineering
Beykent University
Istanbul, Türkiye

Atharva Uplenchwar
Northeastern University
Boston, MA, USA

CHAPTER 1

A Brief Review of Different Optimization and Machine Learning Techniques for Mesh Refinement

Anand A. Ramgude, Pritee M. Purohit, Mandar S. Sapre and Anand J. Kulkarni

1.1 INTRODUCTION

Engineering and scientific disciplines rely on finite element analysis (FEA), a numerical technique that can be used to get approximate solutions for partial differential equations (PDEs) [Schneider et al., 2019]. This method involves utilizing a finite-dimensional space of functions to approximate solutions within discrete elements known as finite elements, forming a crucial aspect of FEA. Mesh generation is a vital step in this process, impacting the reliability and precision of FEA results.

Mesh adaptivity emerges as a technique aimed at enhancing the accuracy and efficiency of FEA [Johnen et al., 2017]. This involves adjusting the mesh by refining the regions of poor quality. The objective is to achieve a specified level of accuracy. Various techniques have been employed to improve the quality of finite element models, such as node-movement strategies like Laplacian smoothing to enhance geometry quality [Durand et al. 2019]. However, relying solely on Laplacian smoothing may not always guarantee improved mesh quality and may lead to inverted elements. Adaptive strategies like h-adaptivity and anisotropic h-adaptivity are indispensable in applying FEA to engineering practices. Additional techniques, including hexahedral mesh smoothing, untangling and optimization-based approaches, contribute to refining finite element models' quality.

1.2 DIFFERENT TYPES OF MESHING TECHNIQUES

The different meshing techniques used in FEA are as follows:

a. **Structured meshing:** In structured meshing, the domain is segmented into a systematic grid comprising quadrilateral elements for the two-dimensional (2D) figures

DOI: 10.1201/9781003564911-1

or hexahedral elements for the 3D figures. This methodology provides a straightforward approach to data storage and facilitates efficient numerical computations, particularly suited for geometries with regular shapes. Nevertheless, its applicability encounters challenges when addressing irregular or intricate domains.

b. **Unstructured meshing:** Unstructured mesh generation entails the creation of a mesh featuring elements with irregular shapes, such as triangles in two dimensions or tetrahedra in three dimensions. This approach proves highly advantageous when dealing with intricate geometries and necessitates adaptive mesh refinement (AMR). Bellenger and Coorevits (2005) used AMR using h-adaptive scheme.

c. **Hex-Dominant meshing:** This technique aims to create predominantly hexahedral elements in three-dimensional (3D) domains while allowing some tetrahedral or pyramid elements in regions with complex geometry. This methodology is focused on generating meshes that consist primarily of hexahedral elements within 3D domains. Simultaneously, it permits the inclusion of tetrahedral or pyramid elements in regions characterized by complex geometry. This approach balances the regularity and simplicity of hexahedra and the adaptability required to capture intricate geometric features in specific mesh areas effectively.

d. The other methods include boundary layer meshing, mesh extrusion and real-time adaptive meshing. Tlili et al. (2020) used hybrid meshes for FEA.

1.3 DIFFERENT METHODS TO IMPROVE HEXAHEDRAL TYPES OF MESHES

A rapid and uncomplicated approach to enhance the quality of hexahedral (hex-) grids involves a more straightforward method than current techniques. This method focuses on detangling and improving mesh quality through an angle optimization strategy. During untangling, boundary surfaces can deform to allow for a more viable solution. Subsequently, a non-inverting deformation is employed to revert the deformed volume to its original state. Optimization is concentrated in the local area surrounding inverted or low-quality elements. This technique is effective for various hex-meshes created through different methods. Xu et al. (2018) used edge angle optimization using Jacobian as the mesh metric.

Nguyen and Kim (2019) introduced an inventive shape optimization technique based on the level set approach, employing trimmed hexahedral meshes. These meshes, generated using the marching cubes technique, dynamically adapt to changes in topology and shape during optimization. The zero-iso surface for a level set type of function is utilized to split background hexahedral mesh elements. The marching cubes algorithm introduces face ambiguity, and a proposed method addresses the nonconforming type of the polyhedral elements at the interface of the objects. To determine the movement of the zero-iso surface, the Hamilton-Jacobi, a transport type of equation, is computed with a normal velocity field defined on a hexahedral mesh. Results from numerical experimentation showcase the effectiveness of this approach [Nguyen & Kim, 2019]. Schneider et al. (2019) developed a methodology that offers a natural and efficient solution for addressing shape optimization challenges within the context of explicitly discretized meshes during the optimization process. All tested elliptic PDEs consistently yielded remarkable outcomes. Knupp (2022) developed geometric parameters in the target matrix mesh optimization paradigms.

Another approach is to use open source techniques for mesh refinement. HexaLab is a WebGL application designed for real-time visualization, assessment and exploration of hexahedral meshes. Researchers leverage it to scrutinize mesh structures, identify vulnerabilities and experiment with novel solutions. On the other hand, practitioners can utilize HexaLab to assess mesh quality and its suitability for simulations. The tool offers diverse visualization and volume inspection features and access to a repository of meshes accessible to the public. HexaLab is a valuable instrument for visualizing, assessing and sharing findings due to its easily reproducible and well-organized data and visuals [Bracci et al., 2019]. Utilizing the model's overall structure as a guide, the geometrical optimization of hexahedral meshes was enhanced. The technique involved moving the base complex's location and adjusting the positions of singular lines and mesh vertices based on a parameterization energy function. The extracted basic complex structure was aligned with the input using a topologically compatible frame field. Empirical findings, particularly for models with concave curves, demonstrated that the suggested approach effectively improved the mesh quality [Wang et al., 2021].

1.4 OPTIMIZATION TECHNIQUES FOR THE IMPROVEMENT OF MESH

Mesh quality plays a vital role in obtaining an accurate FEA solution. The Laplacian smoothing method, aimed at enhancing all-hexahedral unstructured meshes, was found ineffective and could potentially lead to inverted components. Knupp (2003) developed mesh metrics, which were used as objective functions to solve optimization problems in mesh refinement. Li and Huang (2009), in their research, demonstrated the use of AMR as a significant method to obtain finite element method (FEM) solutions for approximating PDE with optimal convergence rates.

Yilmaz and Kuzuoglu (2009) used particle swarm optimization (PSO) to improve the shape quality of hexahedral meshes, ensuring untangled elements and optimization as an objective function constructed for each hexahedral component using the condition number for each node. It has demonstrated effectiveness on numerous meshes with complex geometries.

Eisenträger et al. (2020) developed advanced and improved condition number-based objective functions which can be used for mesh refinement using optimization. The authors explained that local mesh refinement has been integral to FEM for addressing challenging issues related to singularities; however, the traditional condition number, $Cond = O(h2\_min)$, where h_min is the minimum length of elements, led to significant values due to h_min approaching infinitesimally close to singular points. To circumvent this challenge, the authors introduced a low effective condition number. The issue associated with *Cond* was overcome by utilizing the maximum element length, $h(1)$, to establish the simplified type of effective condition numbers ($Cond\_EE$) within limits of $O(1), O(h{\wedge}1.5),$ *or* $O(h{\wedge}0.5)$. Notably, $Cond\_EE$ was considerably smaller than Cond. Numerical experiments were conducted for the validation of the stability analysis,

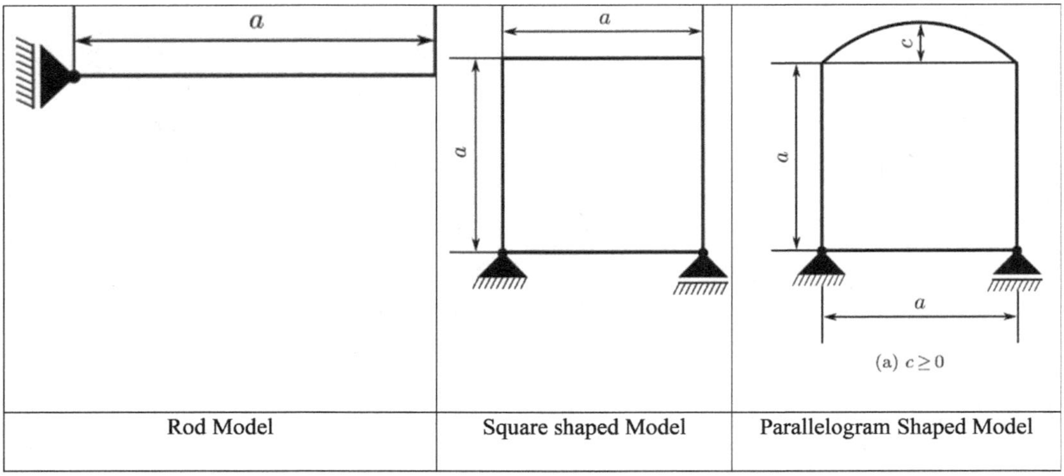

FIGURE 1.1 Various models to study the influence of the shape function [Eisenträger et al., 2020].

confirming reasonable, effective condition values and producing commendable FEM results. This research examined the stiffness matrix condition number for three high-order FEM techniques. The effect of basic types of distortions identified by Lee and Bathe (1993) on the condition number was thoroughly investigated on seven models. The three sample models are shown in Fig. 1.1.

The numerical results were compared with condition number estimates obtained from the literature. The study was carried out using three methods – the p-FEM, spectral element method (SEM) and 2D isogeometric analysis (IGA) demonstrated good agreement though in limited situations, such as single-element geometries or cases involving constant Jacobi matrices of the element maps [Eisenträger et al., 2020].

Wei et al. (2015) developed a novel approach to smoothing hexahedral meshes integrating the geometric transformation based local regularization and global optimization using the volumetric Laplacian operator. The quadratic optimization algorithm was based on node-smoothing method, which can improve mesh quality only based on node movements without altering mesh topology, was applied. The scaled Jacobian metric was used as an objective function to evaluate the mesh quality and the geometric constraints were used on surface meshes. Results shown in Fig. 1.2 demonstrate that the proposed method outperforms other advanced techniques in terms of both overall and minimum mesh quality.

Johnen et al. (2017) developed an innovative approach to enhance hex-meshes, employing an angle-based optimization strategy using recursive subdivision algorithm. Jacobian metric was used as the objective function considering 20 cases. Lagrange shape functions for the linear hexahedron were used for developing this algorithm. The method proved easy to implement, demonstrating its effectiveness on hex-meshes generated through various methods. The new algorithm stood out for its simplicity and efficiency, enabling the analysis of over six million hexahedral elements per second on a personal computer.

Durand et al. (2019) developed a physics-based smoothing method where the mesh is considered as a deformable media. The method is versatile and applicable to 2D and 3D

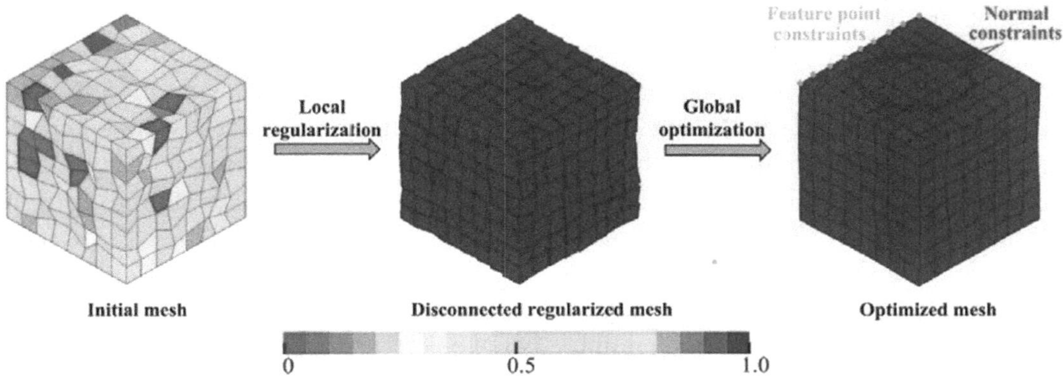

FIGURE 1.2 Local regularization to global optimization [Wei et al., 2015].

finite element meshes composed by virtually any type of element, including less conventional ones such as wedges and pyramid. This technique leverages nodal forces to deform each element toward an optimally positioned reference element, enhancing the overall mesh quality. A comprehensive quality metric is applied to assess different types of elements. The suggested algorithm significantly improves mesh quality with just a few iterations, offering simplicity in computer implementation (Fig. 1.3). This method outperforms traditional Laplacian-based approaches in reducing the proportion of poorly shaped elements.

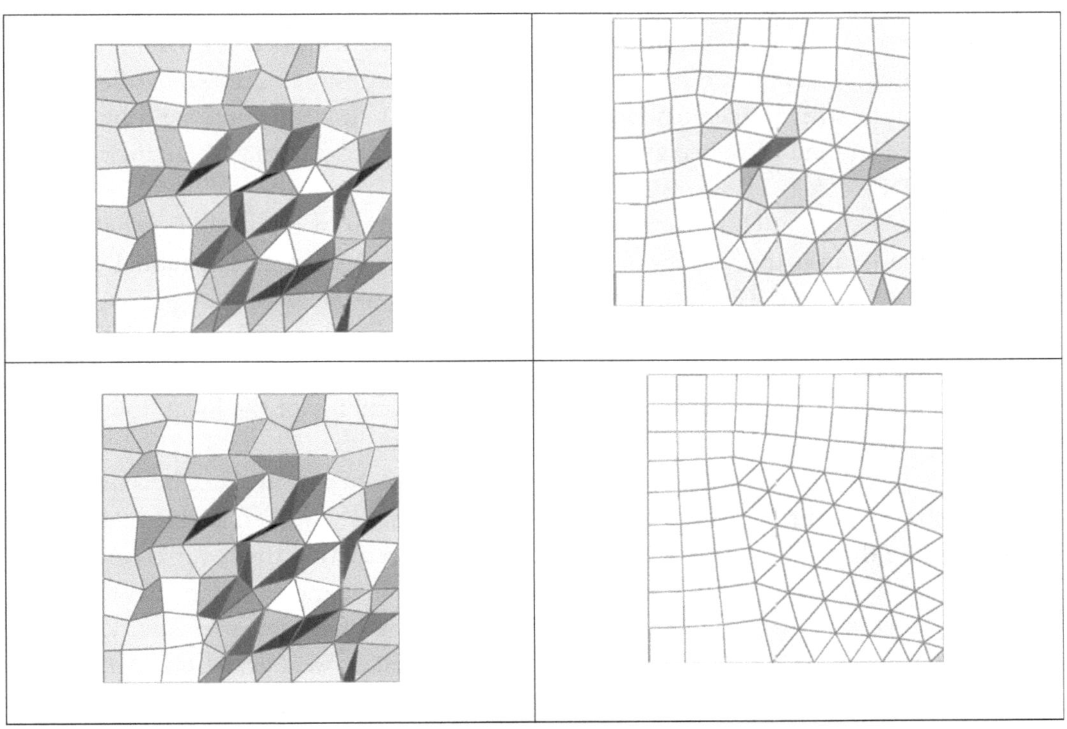

FIGURE 1.3 Mesh smoothing algorithms (iterations I, II, III) [Durand et al., 2019].

Another study investigates using the cohort intelligence (CI) algorithm for mesh smoothing of intricate objects while maintaining element connectivity. The algorithm restricts the movement of external nodes based on the object's geometry, aiming to minimize the condition number of each element. The efficacy of the CI algorithm's follow-best method and roulette wheel variants is meticulously evaluated across six iterations. The process shows significant promise as a precise approach to improving the quality of finite element meshes, offering versatility for applications in diverse engineering disciplines. Sapre et al. (2021) proposed an optimization-driven smoothing technique to improve the quality of hexahedral meshes without introducing reversed elements. The numerical optimization algorithm incorporates a condition number-based objective function and the cohort intelligence algorithm. The technique's effectiveness is demonstrated on a cubical model with various element sizes, although further development is needed to address more intricate geometries. This includes handling prismatic elements with hexahedral meshes and geometries featuring stress concentration zones. Adjustments to applicant behavior could be considered to enhance convergence time [Sapre et al., 2019]. The surface and the wireframe mesh are shown in Fig. 1.4.

1.5 MACHINE LEARNING BASED MESHING TECHNIQUES

Machine learning (ML) techniques can automatically generate a model using data from past experiences. ML algorithms can map a reduced data set from real-time measurements of a structure into a detailed/high-fidelity FEA models of the same system. Brevis et al. (2021) introduced the concept of machine-learning minimal-residual (ML-MRes) finite element discretization of PDEs. These methods are tuned within a ML framework and are tailored for the accurate computation of output quantities of interest, regardless of the underlying mesh size. Elementary one dimensional (1D) and 2D elliptic and hyperbolic problems were studied using weight functions up to 20 parameters with artificial neural network (ANN).

Tingfan, Wu et al. (2022) proposed a mesh optimization method that embeds a ML regression model into the variational mesh adaptation. The regression model captures the mapping between the initial mesh nodes and the flow field so that the variational method can move mesh nodes iteratively by solving the mesh function built from the estimated flow field on the updated mesh via the regression model. Results show that the proposed method significantly improves the accuracy of the local flow features on the adaptive meshes.

Zhang et al. (2020) introduced a novel approach to automatic unstructured mesh generation using ML to predict an optimal mesh for a previously unseen problem. An ANN is used to train the mesh generation software based on predicting the required local mesh density throughout the domain. The performance is tested using two standard test problems, a single elliptic PDE and a system of PDEs associated with linear elasticity. In both cases, high-quality meshes for arbitrary polygonal geometries were generated using a variety of user-selected error norms.

Baiges et al. (2020) presented a reduced-order model based on adaptive finite element meshes and a correction term obtained using an ANN (FAN-ROM). The high-fidelity

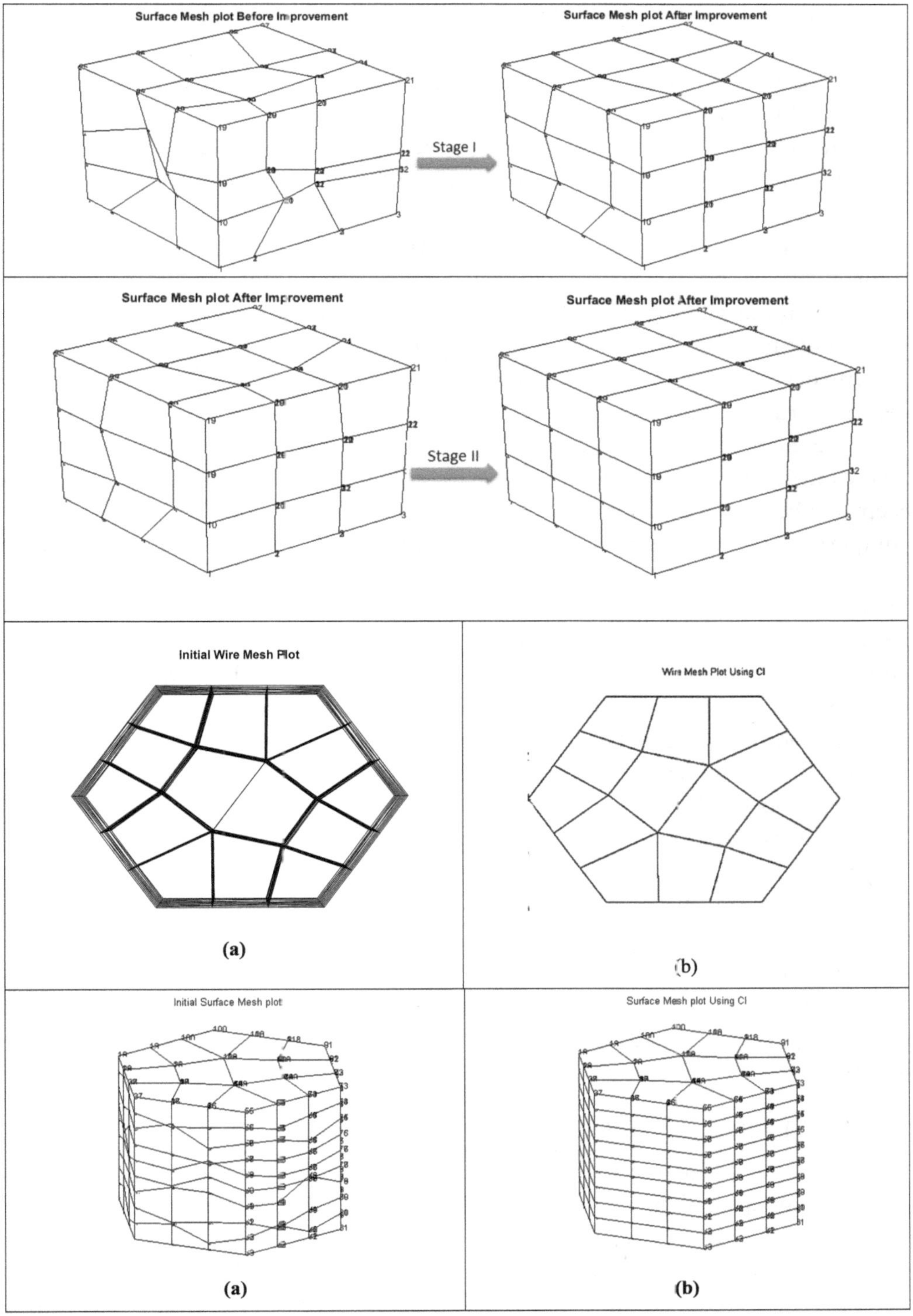

FIGURE 1.4 Initial meshing and after optimization meshing plots [Sapre et al., 2019, 2021].

simulation is run using an adaptively refined mesh, and the results obtained are compared with those of a coarse mesh model. From this comparison, a correction forcing term was computed for each training configuration. A model for the correction term was built using an ANN, and the final reduced order model was obtained by putting together the coarse mesh model plus the ANN model for the correction forcing term. The methodology was applied to non-linear solid mechanics problems and transient quasi-incompressible flows. The results showed the reduced computational costs.

Wattel et al. (2023) focused on a novel refinement technique called "data refinement" (d-refinement) in the context of architected metamaterials for model-free data-driven computational mechanics (DDCM) simulations. This technique automatically turns regular elements into data-driven ones, improving numerical efficiency and accuracy. The d-refinement concept can be used with a neural network trained on microscale data. It uses a predefined rule to match physically admissible states to observed material response data.

The d-refinement technique can outperform traditional incremental solvers such as the Newton-Raphson technique in speed without any loss of accuracy. The d-refinement concept can be used with a neural network trained on microscale data. The d-refinement technique uses a predefined rule to match physically admissible states to observed material response data.

Hawi and Ghanem (2024) developed a novel framework for the global mesh refinement of composite materials using statistical learning. By simultaneously observing low-fidelity (coarse-mesh) and high-fidelity (fine-mesh) solutions of the FEM simulations, the joint probability distribution of the observed quantities is trained. The data-driven representative volume elements (RVEs) were used to collect and combine snapshots of solutions across different mesh resolutions. The approach significantly reduced the number of required function evaluations while maintaining high accuracy, thus enhancing efficiency of FEM simulations.

Freymuth et al. (2024) proposed a novel adaptive swarm Markov decision process in which a mesh is modeled as a system of simple collaborating agents that may split into multiple new agents. This framework allows for a spatial reward formulation that simplifies the credit assignment problem, which we combine with message passing networks to propagate information between neighboring mesh elements. The results were compared with existing heuristics, and it was observed that high-quality mesh was generated with double the speed.

1.6 CONCLUSION AND FUTURE RECOMMENDATIONS

In FEA, hexahedral elements in mesh generation often yield coarse meshes. Strategies for improving a suboptimal mesh include techniques such as flipping and smoothing. Among these, Laplacian smoothing is a basic and widely adopted method for refining polygonal meshes. However, they have an issue of generating inverted elements with negative Jacobian. Optimization techniques offer a promising approach for mesh smoothing and mesh refinement. Several mesh metrics developed in the literature are used as objective functions for mesh smoothing as an optimization problem. The most widely used mesh metrics are condition number, and the Jacobian. The optimization algorithms are coded using C++ and MATLAB programming. The survey shows that the comparable results were obtained using optimization algorithms.

Another approach is by considering the mesh as a huge data which can be analyzed using AI and ML algorithms. The mesh details file can be exported as a csv file which can be used for further analysis. The intricate mathematical adjustments required to transform an inadequate element into a superior one can be easily streamlined by applying these algorithms. Many new techniques like d-refinement are the outcomes of ML-based approach. Leveraging these diverse and well-established AI and ML algorithms holds the potential to achieve higher accuracy in FEA within a more condensed timeframe. The techniques in the literature have been applied to a specific analysis problem and there are many types of FEA where these AI- and ML-based techniques can be applied in future.

REFERENCES

Abdelmalek, Z., Rehman, K.U., Kousar, N., Fatima, N., & Tlili, I. (2020, May 15). Hybrid meshed finite element analysis (HMFEA) of corrugated magnetized ongoing shear thinning/thickening liquid streams. *Journal of Molecular Liquids*, 306, 112915.

Baiges, J., Codina, R., Castanar, I., & Castillo, E. (2020). A finite element reduced-order model based on adaptive mesh refinement and artificial neural networks. *International Journal for Numerical Methods in Engineering*, 121(4), 588–601.

Bellenger, E., & Coorevits, P. (2005). Adaptive mesh refinement for controlling cost and quality in finite element analysis. *Finite Elements in Analysis and Design*, 41(15), 1413–1440.

Bracci, M., Tarini, M., Pietroni, N., Livesu, M., & Cignoni, P. (2019). HexaLab.net: An online viewer for hexahedral meshes. *Computer Aided Design*, 110, 24–36.

Brevis, I., Muga, I., & van der Zee, K. G. (2021). A machine-learning minimal-residual (ML-MRes) framework for goal-oriented finite element discretizations. *Computers & Mathematics with Applications*, 95, 186–199.

Durand, R., Pantoja-Rosero, B. G., & Oliveira, V. (2019). A general mesh smoothing method for finite elements. *Finite Elements in Analysis and Design*, 158, 17–30.

Eisenträger, S., Atroshchenko, E., & Makvandi, R. (2020). On the condition number of high order finite element methods: Influence of p-refinement and mesh distortion. *Computers & Mathematics with Applications*, 80(11), 2289–2339.

Freymuth, N., Dahlinger, P., Würth, T., Reisch, S., Kärger, L., & Neumann, G. (2024). Swarm reinforcement learning for adaptive mesh refinement. *Advances in Neural Information Processing Systems*, 36.

Hawi, P., & Ghanem, R. (2024). Mesh refinement as probabilistic learning. *Journal of Machine Learning for Modeling and Computing*, 5(4), 1–21.

Johnen, A., Weill, J. C., & Remacle, J. F. (2017). Robust and efficient validation of the linear hexahedral element. *Procedia Engineering*, 203, 271–283.

Knupp, P. M. (2003). A method for hexahedral mesh shape optimization. *International Journal for Numerical Methods in Engineering*, 58(2), 319–332.

Knupp, P. M. (2022). Geometric parameters in the target matrix mesh optimization paradigm. *Partial Differential Equations in Applied Mathematics*, 5, 100390.

Lee, N. S., & Bathe, K. J. (1993). Effects of element distortions on the performance of isoparametric elements. *International Journal for Numerical Methods in Engineering*, 36(20), 3553–3576.

Li, Z., & Huang, H. (2009). Effective condition number for the finite element method using local mesh refinements. *Applied Numerical Mathematics*, 59(8), 1779–1795.

Nguyen, S. H., & Kim, H. G. (2019). Level set based shape optimization using trimmed hexahedral meshes. *Computer Methods in Applied Mechanics and Engineering*, 345, 555–583.

Sapre, M., Kulkarni, A. J., Chettiar, L., Deshpande, I., & Piprikar, B. (2021). Mesh smoothing of complex geometry using variations of cohort intelligence algorithm. *Evolutionary Intelligence*, 14(2), 227–242.

Sapre, M. S., Kulkarni, A. J., & Shinde, S. S. (2019). Finite element mesh smoothing using cohort intelligence. In Proceedings of the 2nd International Conference on Data Engineering and Communication Technology: ICDECT 2017 (pp. 469–480). Singapore: Springer.

Schneider, T., Hu, Y., Gao, X., & Panozzo, D. (2019, March 21). *A Large Scale Comparison of Tetrahedral and Hexahedral Elements for Finite Element Analysis*. ResearchGate.

Tingfan, W., Xuejun, L., Wei, A., Huang, Z., & Hongqiang, L. (2022). A mesh optimization method using machine learning technique and variational mesh adaptation. *Chinese Journal of Aeronautics*, 35(3), 27–41.

Wang, R., Zheng, Z., Yu, W., Shao, Y., & Gao, S. (2021). Structure-aware geometric optimization of hexahedral mesh. *Computer Aided Design*, 138, 103050.

Wattel, S., Molinari, J. F., Ortiz, M., & Garcia-Suarez, J. (2023). Mesh d-refinement: A data-based computational framework to account for complex material response. *Mechanics of Materials*, 180, 104630.

Wei, P., Lu, D., Huang, T., & Wang, L. (2015). Hexahedral mesh smoothing via local element regularization and global mesh optimization. *Computer Aided Design*, 59, 85–97.

Xu, K., Gao, X., & Chen, G. (2018). Hexahedral mesh quality improvement via edge-angle optimization. *Computers & Graphics*, 70, 17–27.

Yilmaz, A. E., & Kuzuoglu, M. (2009). A particle swarm optimization approach for hexahedral mesh smoothing. *International Journal for Numerical Methods in Fluids*, 60(1), 55–78.

Zhang, Z., Wang, Y., Jimack, P. K., & Wang, H. (2020, June). MeshingNet: A new mesh generation method based on deep learning. In *International conference on computational science* (pp. 186–198). Cham: Springer International Publishing.

CHAPTER 2

Bridging Theory and Practice in Mesh Smoothing Techniques

Rashmi Kumari, Subhranil Das, Raghwendra Kishore Singh, Anvi Kohli, Arya Sunil and Arushi Dadhich

2.1 INTRODUCTION

For applications in computer-aided design (CAD), mesh smoothing algorithms [1, 2] constitute an important constituent in enhancing of mesh quality [3, 4] and finite element analysis (FEA) [4, 5]. These algorithms are very crucial in refining mesh topology by adjustment of the positions of vertices for getting the smoother surface. For retaining the original topology and volumetric properties, this process could be aimed at increasing the aesthetic and computational attributes of the mesh. Among the different proposed techniques employed, Laplacian smoothing [6, 7] emerged as one of the approaches where in each vertex is relocated to its centroid of the neighboring vertices. For this technique, the simplicity and widespread application, with respect to the volume loss and the over-smoothing of sharp features, the fidelity of the model could be compromised to its original geometry [8, 9].

In response to the abovementioned problems, advanced methodologies such as Taubin smoothing [10, 11] had been developed. In this method, lambda-mu strategy has been incorporated which makes the balance between contraction and dilation phases of the mesh which leads to the inherent volume reduction. The overall dimensions and geometrical integrity of the mesh can be saved. Further refinement is achieved through bilateral mesh smoothing where feature-preserving and non-feature-preserving regions can be easily distinguished. In this algorithm, the geometric and photometric distances can be combined where this algorithm adaptively maintains the sharp edges and corners while uniformly smoothing the remaining surfaces [11, 12].

The introduction of mean curvature flow (MCF) [13, 14] and anisotropic smoothing algorithms [15] offer a sophisticated techniques in manipulating the vertex flow along the mesh surface as in the application of differential geometry. As a result, geometric features are preserved by reducing the noise and irregularity mitigation. Optimization-based smoothing algorithms [16, 17] indicate the smoothing process as an optimization problem which minimizes the energy function which quantify the deviations from optimal mesh quality. By introducing the constraints, these algorithms preserve specific features which resulted in the meshes in the superior quality.

DOI: 10.1201/978100356491[illegible]-2

The selection of the optimized smoothing algorithm is dependent upon the number of factors, such as requisite level of detail, the presence of sharp features and the computational [18, 19]. With the development of new technologies, the evolution of mesh smoothing technology has resulted in the developing enhanced methods that offer control, efficiency and efficacy in the mesh smoothing domain. For elevating the quality of digital models across various applications, computational geometry and computer graphics are required at every stage.

Within the area of creating the digital images, three-dimensional (3D) meshes [20, 21] serve a parallel purpose where the different artists, engineers and scientists are involved in creating different entities as required in 3D. A 3D mesh has been considered as the sophisticated geometric construct which is employed on the diverse disciplines such as computer graphics, computational geometry and numerical simulations. It provides a foundational framework where the surface of the object is restructured in three dimensions [22]. The architecture of a 3D mesh is built upon vertices (the discrete points that delineate the shape of the object), edges (the linear segments connecting these points) and faces (the planar sections bordered by edges) where each component plays a critical role in defining the overall structure. Mesh is actually the connecting of the different points located on the corners of the room where walls connect these corners, then in turn, walls connect these corners for making the intended 3D object [23]. While modeling a sphere, vertices are strategically placed across the surface of the sphere which are interconnected by edges forming the cohesive network of triangular faces that cover the sphere [24, 25].

The performance of numerical simulations is influenced by the quality of the underlying 3D mesh. A mesh of good quality is being characterized by its proportioned elements and a strategic distribution that captures both the geometric and characteristic characteristics of the model. However, the creation of a high-quality mesh is a much complicated challenge which is being motivated by the intricate geometries of various types of models, the need for variable element sizes and the imperative for optimally shaped elements. Creating the superior 3D mesh is very large for solving a sophisticated puzzle where each piece must be precisely positioned to accurately cover the original object. In this process, a delicate balance between artistic expression and scientific precision demands a blend of creative vision and rigorous technical expertise.

2.1.1 The Art and Science of Mesh Smoothing

Mesh smoothing, also known as mesh optimization or mesh refinement, is an indispensable technique which is aimed at enhancing the quality of a 3D mesh. In this process, digital refinement session is required for meshes where the primary objective is to fine tune the vertices which are positioned better for making shapes of the element while preserving the original topology and geometric integrity. This technique is crucial across a broad spectrum of applications. Within the domain of computer graphics, smoother meshes contribute more to the visual renderings. Consider the process of designing a digital avatar for a video game or film, a refined mesh ensures that the character appears more realistic and exhibits more natural movements [26, 27].

In the context of numerical simulations, the quality of the mesh is an important factor which influences the precision and stability. While assessing the airflow dynamics around a wing of the aircraft, a mesh of inferior quality could lead to numerical inaccuracies, higher convergence rates and compromises the simulation that leads to suboptimal aerodynamic designs.

The application of the mesh smoothing is beneficial in adaptive methodologies whereas the meshes behave as the dynamic refinement and coarsening for accurately represent solutions. Such modifications can deteriorate mesh quality which involves the smoothing as an integral step in the adaptation cycle by considering the pruning and shaping of a tree. Additionally, mesh smoothing plays a critical role in generating curved meshes which are essential for high-order and isogeometric analysis methods [28]. These advanced methods rely on the creation of high-quality curved elements achievable through mesh smoothing. Despite its critical role, mesh smoothing presents a significant challenge which requires an equilibrium between enhancing element shapes and conserving original geometry. Efficient algorithms are applied for addressing large-scale and intricate geometric challenges.

In order to understand the critical role of mesh smoothing across diverse domains, application in automotive design and medical imaging can be considered. In the automotive sector, designers employ CAD software for conceptualizing new vehicle models where 3D mesh is constructed which outlines the structure of the car. In this mesh, irregularities compromise the precision of aerodynamic simulations. Mesh smoothing techniques can be enhanced by the mesh quality which leads to more accurate simulations and superior final products. Similarly, in the medical field, 3D meshes are applied for detecting the organs or tissues for surgical planning or disease analysis [29]. The fidelity of these meshes is paramount, as inaccuracies can lead to significant errors in surgical simulation which resulted in complications during actual procedures. Through mesh smoothing, medical professionals can refine these representations to improve the safety and effectiveness in treatments.

This chapter will explore some of the diverse strategies of mesh smoothing by studying the principles, constraints and practical applications. Further, ongoing research and prospective developments in this area have been elaborated which offers a thorough examination of mesh smoothing within the framework of mesh-free analysis.

2.2 MESH SMOOTHING TECHNIQUES

2.2.1 Basic Concepts

Mesh smoothing techniques serve as the precision adjustment mechanisms within the domain of 3D mesh refinement, aiming to ameliorate mesh quality through the meticulous realignment of vertex positions, while steadfastly maintaining the mesh's foundational topology. This process can be analogously likened to the nuanced craftsmanship of a sculptor, who, with each subtle strike and carve, endeavors to unearth the latent masterpiece within a marble block.

The metric for assessing a mesh's quality predominantly hinges upon the geometric fidelity of its constitutive elements. For instance, within a triangular mesh, elements that approximate the shape of equilateral triangles are heralded for their high quality, reminiscent of a meticulously crafted patchwork quilt characterized by its harmonious and aesthetically appealing uniformity. In contrast, elongated and slender triangular elements,

TABLE 2.1 Overview of Mesh Quality with Its Triangular Shape

Mesh Quality	Triangular Shape	Energy Value Function
High	Equilateral	Low
Low	Long Skinny	High

akin to a quilt marred by haphazard and irregular patches, are typically eschewed due to their propensity to engender numerical instabilities within simulations.

Embarking on the mesh smoothing process entails a strategic repositioning of the mesh vertices, orchestrated to elevate the elemental quality across the mesh [30, 31]. This objective is generally pursued through the minimization of an energy function, meticulously designed to quantitatively assess mesh quality. Analogous to a scoring system, this energy function allocates lower scores to meshes of superior quality, mirroring the scoring paradigm in golf where lower scores signify superior performance. The criteria for the energy function's assessment may span a diverse array of geometric and algebraic measures, including but not limited to, the angular disposition of elements, aspect ratios and the Jacobian determinant. This multifaceted evaluation process bears a resemblance to the adjudication of a gymnastics event, where the cumulative score integrates multiple performance metrics. In the context of a mesh delineating a sphere's surface, the quintessence of mesh smoothing is to recalibrate vertex positions to foster faces that are as equilateral as possible, thereby achieving a more faithful and precise representation of the spherical geometry. Table 2.1 shows the difference between high-quality mesh and low-quality mesh.

In Table 2.1, the relationship between mesh quality, triangular shape and energy value function has been explained. Also, the values obtained from the table highlight that equilateral triangles represent high-quality meshes with low energy values, while long, skinny triangles indicate low-quality meshes with high energy values. Equilateral triangles are preferred because they distribute forces and deformations uniformly which provide the geometric fidelity and stability in simulations. In contrast, due to uneven vertex distribution and poor shape, long, skinny triangles lead to numerical instability and errors which resulted in increasing the energy function. The values of the energy value function which quantifies the distortion in a mesh. Lower values correspond to more stable and accurate meshes and higher values indicate the need for significant smoothing or adjustment. Thus, low energy value in the triangles enhances mesh performance in both visual and computational applications.

Mesh smoothing techniques are crucial in the area of the 3D modeling and simulation which are essential instruments in creating and manipulating. These techniques facilitate the refinement of meshes which is one of the critical steps in achieving two fundamental objectives, i.e., precise representation of objects in 3D and the assurance of numerical stability. In the detailed step analysis of 3D modeling, a mesh serves as the skeleton which defines the shape and surface of an object. However, an initial mesh is perfectly captured the required geometry or may contain irregularities that deviates from the accuracy and aesthetic quality. Mesh smoothing techniques are employed for adjusting the positions of vertices, smoothing out rough edges and irregularities to more closely align the mesh [32, 33].

Beyond visual and geometric accuracy, numerical stability in simulations is a much needed concern in the application fields such as engineering, physics and medical research, where 3D models are used to simulate physical processes and phenomena. An uneven or poorly constructed mesh can lead to much inaccuracies in these simulations that affect outcomes and potentially lead to erroneous conclusions. By enhancing the quality of the mesh, smoothing techniques reduce these issues which contribute to a stable simulation results. The role of mesh smoothing techniques has become more prominent in different applications related to 3D modeling.

2.2.2 Laplacian Smoothing

2.2.2.1 Laplacian Smoothing: A Closer Look

Laplacian smoothing [34, 35] is one of the important technique within the domain of mesh analogy where the different methodologies are involved by taking the principles of Laplace operator especially in the disciplines of computer graphics and computational geometry. A polygonal mesh consists of the main framework which composed of vertices (points), edges (line segments) and faces (polygonal surfaces) for representing polyhedral objects within 3D solid modeling landscapes.

The application of the Laplacian smoothing basic lies on the repositioning of each mesh vertex to its centroid of the adjacent vertices. In this procedural step, a "smoothing" effect can be introduced by adding the vertices which are close to the neighborhood. The rationale behind this technique is predicated on the notion that averaging the locational attributes of neighboring vertices facilitates the attenuation of irregularities and perturbations inherent within the mesh structure. Through this mechanism, Laplacian smoothing harmonizes the spatial distribution of vertices where the overall geometric and aesthetic quality is improved in the mesh.

2.2.2.2 Methodology

A simple two dimensional (2D) mesh has been considered for 3×3 grid of vertices. After applying Laplacian smoothing, the position of the center vertex has been calculated as the average of its four neighboring vertices. If the original positions of the vertices are evenly distributed, the center vertex is close to the center of the grid.

In the context of image processing, we have been considered as the grayscale image that represents a 2D array of pixel intensities. Each pixel in the image has been considered as the vertex in a graph with edges connecting it to its neighboring pixels. The following are the steps:

1. **Initialization:** Start with the original image.
2. **For each pixel in the image:** Apply the Laplacian smoothing operation where the new intensity of the pixel is calculated as the average of the intensities of its neighboring pixels.
3. **Repeat until convergence:** Repeat the above step for a certain number of iterations where it attains the certain threshold.

After applying Laplacian smoothing, the image will appear smoother with sharp edges, and noise is reduced accordingly. This method is applied to the computer vision where high-frequency noise is reduced which makes the subsequent processing steps like edge detection or object recognition more accurate. The pseudocode for Laplacian smoothing has been shown in Fig. 2.1.

For a more mathematical expression of Laplacian smoothing, let's consider the mesh as a graph where vertices represent points in space, and edges represent connections between these points. The Laplacian smoothing operation for a vertex V_i can be represented using

```
# Initialize the mesh with vertices
vert = get_vertices(mesh)
# Define the number of smoothing iterations num_iterations = N
for iteration in range(num_iterations):
        new_positions = {}
        # Loop through each vertex in the mesh
        for vertex in vertices:
                # Retrieve the neighboring vertices of the current vertex
                neighbors = get_neighbors (mesh, vertex)
                # Calculate the average position of the neighboring vertices
                 average_position = calculate_average_position(neighbors)
                # Store the new position of the current vertex
                        new_positions[vertex] = average_position
        # Update the positions of all vertices in the mesh
        for vertex in vertices:
        set_position(mesh, vertex, new_positions[vertex])
# Function to calculate the average position of neighboring vertices
def calculate_average_position(neighbors):
        sum_position = [0, 0, 0] for neighbor in neighbors:
        sum_position[0] += neighbor.position[0]
        sum_position[1] += neighbor.position[1]
        sum_position[2] += neighbor.position[2]
average_position = [sum_position[0] / len(neighbors), sum_position[1] / len(neighbors),
sum_position[2] / len(neighbors)]
        return average_position
```

FIGURE 2.1 Pseudocode for Laplacian smoothing.

the Laplace- Beltrami operator, which, in the discrete setting of a mesh, approximates the MCF.

The discrete Laplacian operator L for a vertex V_i can be defined as:

$$L(V_i) = \Delta V_i = \frac{1}{|N_i|} \sum_{j \in N(i)} (V_j - V_i) \tag{2.1}$$

where N_i denotes the set of indices of vertices adjacent to V_i, $\frac{1}{|N_i|}$ represents cardinality of N(i), representing the number of neighbors, V_j are the positions of the neighboring vertices and V_i is the position of the current vertex.

2.2.2.2.1 Position Update The new position $V'$of the vertex after applying one iteration of Laplacian smoothing is then given by Eqn. 2.2.

$$V_i' = V_i + \mu \, \Delta V_i \tag{2.2}$$

where μ is a smoothing factor (usually a small positive number) that controls the extent of the smoothing. A larger μ results in a more significant movement of the vertex position per iteration, potentially leading to a smoother but also more distorted mesh if overapplied.

2.2.2.2.2 Vectorial Form for 3D Meshes In a 3D mesh, each vertex position V_i and its neighbors V_j are represented as vectors in making the Laplacian operator and the position update formula applicable in three dimensions which is given in Eqn. 2.3.

$$\Delta V_i = \frac{1}{|N_i|} \sum_{j \in N(i)} \left(V_{ix} - V_{iy,}, V_{jy} - V_{iy,} V_{jz} - V_{iz} \right) \tag{2.3}$$

$$V_i' = V_i + \mu \left(\frac{1}{|N_i|} \sum_{j \in N(i)} \left(V_{ix} - V_{iy,}, V_{jy} - V_{iy,} V_{jz} - V_{iz} \right) \right) \tag{2.4}$$

where, $V_{ix} - V_{iy}$, $V_{jy} - V_{iy}$ and $V_{jz} - V_{iz}$ denote the x, y and z coordinates of vertex, respectively.

While Laplacian smoothing effectively reduces geometric irregularities, it can also lead to mesh shrinkage and detail loss, especially for higher values of μ or after multiple iterations. Advanced variations of Laplacian smoothing, such as weighted Laplacian smoothing or the incorporation of constraints to preserve mesh volume and feature details, are often employed to mitigate these issues.

Figure 2.2 represents a conceptual diagram for a mesh smoothing algorithm using a neural network. On the left, we see a geometric representation with vertices V_1 to V_5, where V' is the predicted position of the free node after smoothing. In this process, neural network approach has been mentioned for application in mesh smoothing where the input layer consists of the coordinates of the ring nodes and the output is calculated as the predicted coordinates of the free node after smoothing. In this neural network, on the right hand side of Fig. 2.2 it consists of an input layer, two hidden layers and an output layer. The coordinates of the ring node serve as the input, the hidden layers process these inputs and

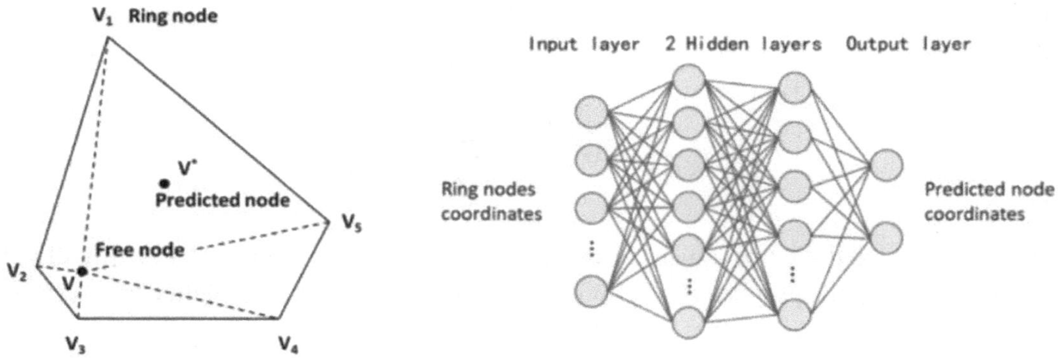

FIGURE 2.2 Neural-based Laplacian smoothing [29].

the output layer generates the new position for the predicted node. In this type of structure, the neural network is trained to predict the optimal position of a vertex based on the positions of its neighboring vertices.

Table 2.2 compares three mesh smoothing methodologies, i.e., OptSmooth, NN-Smoothing and GMSNet which focuses on their rate of convergence, impact on mesh quality and degree of change. OptSmooth has a slower convergence rate which requires more iterations for smoothing the mesh by not affecting the mesh quality. NN-Smoothing converges faster and improves mesh quality by applying learned patterns from trained models which makes it effective in optimizing meshes based on prior training. Finally, GMSNet also achieves faster convergence which has no significant impact and have faster convergence of NN-Smoothing and GMSNet.

2.2.2.3 System Software Implementation

The implementation of the proposed safe route algorithm is made possible through a combination of machine learning (ML) models and real-time data integration using modern software platforms. Data collection is managed using application programming interfaces (APIs) like Google Maps API for traffic information, and public crime data APIs for accessing real-time crime statistics. Web scraping techniques using BeautifulSoup or Scrapy are applied for collecting the data from various social media platforms.

Reinforcement learning (RL) approach has been applied for the proposed method for finding optimal path by employing different libraries installed in OpenAI Gym and Stable-Baselines. Kernel density estimation (KDE) has been implemented by using scikit-learn for identifying high-crime areas. The backend system has been implemented by Django (or Flask) while real-time data processing has been handled by

TABLE 2.2 Comparison of Optimization Techniques Based on the Smoothing Technique

Methodology	Rate of Convergence	Mesh Quality	Degree
OptSmooth [5]	Slower	NA	Not Affected
NN-Smoothing [36]	Faster	Acquired	Trained models
GMSNet [37]	Faster	NA	Not affected

using Apache Kafka to ensure that the system remains responsive to changes in crime reports. Finally, the user-facing application has been integrated with Google Maps API for visualization.

2.2.2.4 System Software Architecture and Cloud Infrastructure

The architecture of the system is utilized by applying the modern web and cloud technologies for ensuring the high performance, scalability, and real-time results. The frontend of the system has been designed by using ReactJS (for web) and Flutter (for mobile) which provides the user-friendly interface where users can enter their starting point and destination and receive optimized route suggestions.

On the backend, Django is used for handling the API logic which allows the communication between the frontend and ML models. The system continuously processes new data from various sources by including the traffic updates and crime statistics. The risk scores are calculated for different routes. The entire system is implemented on the Amazon Web Services (AWS) platform which runs the models using SageMaker that ensures the efficient deployment and real-time inference for users.

2.2.2.5 Applications

Some of the important applications for the abovementioned techniques are as follows:

Simplicity and Speed: Laplacian smoothing is characterized by its rapid execution which makes it a preferred method in various contexts. For easy implementation, data quality has been enhanced which is critical in time-sensitive applications.

Mesh Optimization in Computer Graphics: In computer graphics, 3D models are constructed by using polygonal meshes. These meshes contain irregularities that adversely affect the rendering quality. During the mesh optimization process, Laplacian smoothing is employed for eliminating these irregularities which ensures that the models are more accurately rendered and easier to work.

Image and Signal Processing: The technique is applied in image and signal processing to reduce noise. By considering the values of the pixel or signal values that are mapped to the vertices on a graph, Laplacian smoothing reduces the high-frequency noise.

Machine Learning: In the context of ML, Laplacian smoothing serves as a preprocessing step. It smooths out the feature space by reducing noise and irregularities which makes algorithms more effective in identifying different patterns and making predictions.

Geometric Modeling: Laplacian smoothing is utilized in geometric modeling for smoothing the surfaces of 3D models. The application is particularly relevant in medical imaging and other fields where smooth and accurate representations of surfaces are necessary. By smoothing out imperfections on the surface of models, Laplacian smoothing helps in creating more precise and visually appealing representations.

2.2.2.6 *Limitations and Challenges*

Laplacian smoothing has certain limitations. The first limitation is the tendency for the mesh to shrink which happens because vertices are repositioned to the average location of their neighbors that leads to a reduction in the overall dimensions. This shrinkage can be problematic in scenarios where preserving the original mesh size is essential. Laplacian smoothing does not uniformly enhance mesh quality, i.e., deteriorate the mesh which produces the poorer quality in the elements than those in the original mesh.

Another drawback is the absence of a control mechanism for the smoothing intensity. Without this, oversmoothing occurs that can erase vital features and details which compromise the integrity of the mesh. Laplacian smoothing does not account for the physical characteristics of the modeled object that resulted in unrealistic representations in applications where physical accuracy is crucial.

2.2.3 Advanced Techniques

In the pursuit of refining mesh smoothing methodologies, the academic community has introduced several sophisticated techniques to surmount the constraints inherent in elementary Laplacian smoothing. The Taubin method is widely used which is conceptualized by Gabriel Taubin [38]. In this method, mesh shrinkage phenomenon has been commonly observed in traditional Laplacian smoothing. For this method, vertex movements have been rigorously studied which allows the enhancement in mesh smoothness by compromising the original volume of the mesh.

2.2.3.1 *The Taubin Method: 2 Phase Approach*

Taubin method has been widely used in its biphasic procedure which has been described as a movement of vertices. In this procedure, an initial Laplacian smoothing phase has been covered which is as follows:

1. **Laplacian Smoothing Phase:** In the initial phase, conventional Laplacian smoothing has been formulated where each vertex generates toward the centroid of its adjacent vertices.

2. **Inverse Laplacian Phase:** These vertices have an additional movement phase where the time is receded from the centroid of their neighboring vertices that leads to the initial convergence. In the Taubin method, a customizable framework has been designed which allows for adjustments in order to a more specific smoothing and volume preservation requirements. By manipulating two critical parameters:

   λ (Lambda): This parameter measures the intensity of the initial smoothing phase. The increased value of λ amplifies the smoothing effect.

   μ (Mu): This parameter regulates the intensity of the inverse smoothing phase. More value of μ diminishes the potential shrinkage.

By measuring the precise calibration of λ and μ, the vertex movements can be optimized for achieving the optimal equilibrium between mesh smoothness and volume retention which equals to the vertices with the desired mesh characteristics.

Within the domain of mesh smoothing, a number of methodologies exist where each is explained by its advantages and limitations. These methodologies address the difficulties faced by the various mesh types or specific application. For example, certain specific approaches are inclined to some of the applications such as refining surface meshes, volume meshes and either structured or unstructured meshes. A segment of these methods has been concentrated on enhancement of the elements of poorest quality within the mesh whereas other methods are mainly aimed toward elevating the mesh quality. In addition to that, some strategies incorporate some of the extra information, such as the physical characteristics of the object. There are certain issues in the techniques when physical and geometric approaches are employed. In these approaches, the intrinsic features of the object are preserved which yields more outcomes. In addition to that, optimization-based methods exist which calculate the optimal positioning of each vertex by weighing both the local and global mesh architecture.

2.3 THE ART AND IMPACT OF MESH SMOOTHING

Mesh smoothing methodologies play an important role in the diverse sectors ranging from enhancement of 3D model quality to the precision of numerical simulations and facilitating the generation of visual effects. In this discussion, several principal applications of mesh smoothing are explained by highlighting its impact.

2.3.1 Computer-Aided Design (CAD)

Within the CAD domain, the application of mesh smoothing for generating premium 3D models [39]. The application of the CAD software finds its use in various sectors, such as automotive, aerospace, architecture and product design. In these applications, the precise 3D models are found in designing and testing of products prior to their fabrication. The initial 3D models are framed as within CAD environments which exhibit irregularities and noise. This is common output observed while deriving models from real-world inputs such as 3D scans. Such imperfections can indicate measurement inaccuracies within the larger context. By integrating the mesh smoothing techniques, researchers are able to refine these models which enhance design precision and efficiency.

For an automotive sector, engineers leverage CAD tools for crafting the contours of a vehicle's body by representing the 3D mesh models. The application of mesh smoothing techniques is extremely important for ensuring the mesh faithfully which captures the vehicle body sleek curves. In this refinement, accurate aerodynamic assessments and crash simulations are assessed where the certain factors are critical to the safety of the vehicle.

2.3.2 Virtual Reality

Virtual reality (VR) [40] represents another domain where mesh smoothing techniques have extensive application. VR applies to the immersive 3D environments where the users can interact in real time that employs the 3D meshes for representing these spaces. The development of realistic VR environments poses some of the significant challenges. One of the challenges faced is the utilization of the 3D meshes within VR frameworks that necessitate the high levels of detail for increasing the sense of realism while the efficiency is to facilitate real-time interaction. Mesh smoothing techniques are required in order to fulfill these applications.

Through the refining 3D mesh quality, mesh smoothing techniques contribute to the visual authenticity of VR environments. By minimizing the presence of geometrically sub-optimal elements within the mesh, these techniques enhance the efficiency of the mesh. The outcome is a more fluid and immersive VR experience which plays the critical role of mesh smoothing in the advancement of VR technologies.

2.3.3 Scientific Computing

Within the domain of the scientific computing [41], mesh smoothing techniques play an important role in increasing the precision of numerical simulations. These simulations are integral for modeling and forecasting the dynamics of intricate systems which cover mainly meteorological patterns, fluid dynamics and various physical phenomena. The framework for these simulations measures the resolution of PDEs across a 3D mesh. The integrity of this mesh is very crucial as it directly influences the accuracy and stability. Inferior mesh quality gives rise to the numerical inaccuracies which can lower the rate of convergence.

Applying the mesh smoothing techniques can increase the quality of the mesh which increases the simulations at a precise level. For example, the application of mesh smoothing is instrumental in heightening simulation fidelity which resulted in various geometrical configurations in fluid dynamics in computational fluid dynamics (CFD).

2.3.4 Video Game Design

In the domain of the video game [11], mesh smoothing techniques play an important role which are characterized by their 3D environments and characters. The creation of these 3D assets is a complicated process that maintains the balance of artistic creativity and technical proficiency. The detailed analysis in the mesh can be optimized for efficient real-time rendering.

By applying the mesh smoothing techniques, developers can meet these dual objectives. The quality of 3D meshes can be enhanced by smoothing process which significantly increases the visual representation of the game. In addition to that, optimization of the meshes is efficient rendering which can contribute to the performance of the game which ensures the fluid gameplay across various hardware specifications.

2.3.5 Medical Imaging

In the field of medical imaging [42, 43], mesh smoothing techniques are applied for improving the quality and accuracy of 3D medical images. These images are used for various purposes, such as diagnosing diseases, planning surgeries and studying the human body. Most of the medical images are represented as 3D meshes. However, these meshes can have certain irregularities and noise especially when they are generated from CT or MRI scans. These irregularities can lead to inaccuracies while interpreting the images.

By applying mesh smoothing techniques, doctors as well as researchers can improve the quality of the medical images that leads to more accurate diagnoses. For example, a smooth and accurate 3D model of the anatomy of the patient can help the surgeon in more effective manner that reduces the risk of complications in surgical planning.

2.4 OPTIMIZING NUMERICAL SIMULATION PERFORMANCE

Numerical simulation is one of the powerful tool that can be used in various fields such as engineering, physics and computer science for predicting the behavior of complex systems. However, the accuracy and eficiency of numerical simulations heavily depend on the quality of the underlying mesh. Mesh smoothing techniques can enhance the performance of numerical simulations by improving the quality of the mesh.

2.4.1 Enhancing Accuracy with Mesh Smoothing

The accuracy of a numerical simulation is directly related to the quality of the mesh. The high-quality mesh can accurately represent the geometry of the problem which leads to a more accurate results. On the other hand, a poor-quality mesh leads to the numerical errors.

Mesh smoothing techniques can improve the quality of the mesh by optimizing the position of the vertices. The better-shaped elements can be accurately determined which represents the geometry of the problem. As a result, the accuracy of the numerical simulation is enhanced.

Consider a numerical simulation of fluid flow around an aircraft wing which can demonstrate the working of mesh smoothing technique. The accuracy of the simulation is dependent on the quality of the mesh that represents the geometry of the wing. If the quality of the mesh is poor, the long and skinny elements may not accurately capture the flow patterns around the wing. By applying the Deep Q-Network (DQN) (refer to Fig. 2.3) mesh smoothing techniques, the quality of the mesh can be improved which leads to more accurate predictions.

The pseudocode for DQN mesh smoothing has been shown in Fig. 2.4.

To evaluate the performance of various mesh smoothing techniques, we applied Laplacian smoothing, Taubin smoothing and neural-network-based smoothing on several 3D models. Key performance metrics, including processing time, average vertex displacement and error reduction, were measured to statistically validate the effectiveness of each technique as shown in Table 2.3.

The mean processing time shows that Laplacian smoothing is the fastest, while the neural network-based method is the slowest. However, the neural network approach yields the highest error reduction (35%) with the lowest vertex displacement, indicating better smoothing without distorting the original mesh significantly.

To determine if the differences in error reduction across the three methods are statistically significant, we performed a one-way ANOVA test.

- Null Hypothesis (H0): Significant difference is not observed while reducing the error between the techniques.
- Alternative Hypothesis (H1): Significant difference in error reduction between the techniques is observed as shown in Table 2.4.

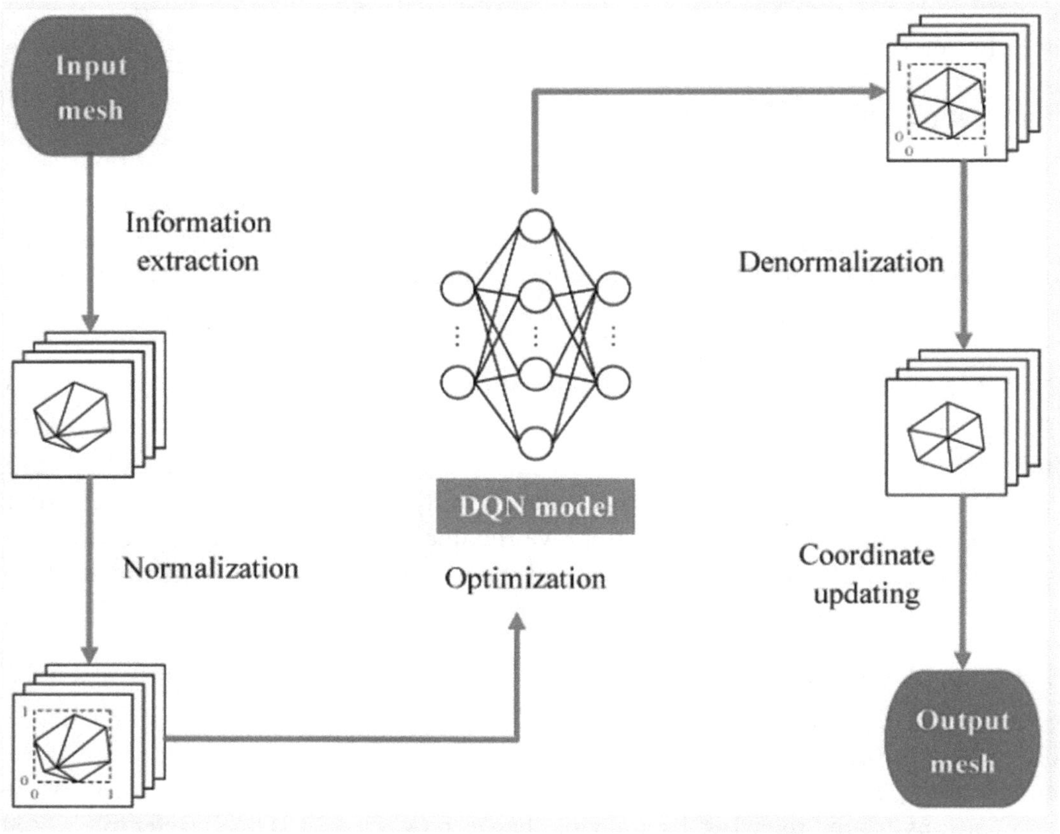

FIGURE 2.3 Flowchart for DQN mesh smoothing technique.

With a p-value of 0.002, the null hypothesis has rejected which concludes that the differences in error reduction between the three methods are statistically significant.

2.4.2 Case Studies

In this section, some of the case studies have been considered for illustrating the impact of mesh smoothing on the performance of numerical simulations.

2.4.2.1 Case Study 1: Computational Fluid Dynamics (CFD)

In CFD [44, 45], numerical simulations are used to predict fluid flow patterns which are based on the Navier-Stokes equations. These equations are a set of nonlinear partial differential equations.

In a CFD simulation, the fluid domain is represented as a 3D mesh. The quality of this mesh can affect the accuracy of the simulation. For example, flow patterns may not be captured if the mesh is coarse, especially in regions of high gradient such as boundary layers or vortices. By applying mesh smoothing techniques, the quality of the mesh can be improved which leads to more accurate simulations. In a study conducted by researchers at

```
Initialize replay memory to capacity D
Initialize action-value function Q with random weights θ
Initialize target action-value function Q̂ with weights θ⁻ = θ
Define reward function R that measures the quality of the mesh
for episode = 1, M do
  Initialize mesh M with initial vertex positions
  Preprocess M to extract relevant features for each vertex
  for t = 1, T do
    for each vertex v in M do
      With probability ϵ select a random smoothing action a_t,
      otherwise a_t = max_a Q feature(v), a; θ)
      Apply action a_t to vertex v to adjust its position
    end for
    Observe new state (updated mesh)
    Calculate reward r_t = R(s_(t+1))
    Store transition (s_t, a_t, r_t, s_(t+1)) in replay memory
    Sample random minibatch of transitions (s_j, a_j, r_j, s_(j+1)) from replay memory
    Set y_j:
      If s_(j+1) is terminal, then y_j = r_j
      Otherwise, y_j = r_j + γ max_a Q̂ feature(v), á; θ́)
    Perform a gradient descent step on y_j - Q(s_j, a_j; θ)^2 with respect to the network parameters θ
    All C steps reset \(θ^- = θ\)
  endfor
end for
```

FIGURE 2.4 Pseudocode for DQN smoothing technique.

TABLE 2.3 Statistical Results for Comparing the Different Mesh Algorithms

Technique	Processing Time (s)	Avg. Vertex Displacement (units)	Error Reduction (%)
Laplacian Smoothing	1.5 ± 0.2	0.025 ± 0.005	15 ± 3
Taubin Smoothing	2.8 ± 0.4	0.015 ± 0.002	25 ± 4
Neural Network	5.2 ± 0.6	0.010 ± 0.001	35 ± 2

TABLE 2.4 ANOVA Results of Measuring the Performance of Three Algorithms

Source of Variation	SS	df	MS	F	p-value
Between groups	526.4	2	263.2	15.78	0.002
Within groups	33.4	12	2.78		
Total	559.8	14			

the University of Michigan, it was found that mesh smoothing techniques could improve the accuracy of CFD simulations of blood flow in the human cardiovascular system.

2.4.2.2 Case Study 2: Finite Element Analysis (FEA)

FEA [46] is another field of study where mesh smoothing techniques can enhance the performance of numerical simulations. Basically, FEA is a numerical technique which is used to solve problems in structural mechanics, heat transfer and electromagnetics.

In FEA, the problem is formulated as a mesh of elements where the quality of this mesh can affect the accuracy and efficiency. If the mesh has poorly shaped elements, it can lead to the numerical instability or slow convergence of the solution.

Mesh smoothing techniques improve the quality of the mesh which leads to more stable and efficient simulations. In a study conducted by researchers at the University of California, it was studied that mesh smoothing techniques could improve the performance of FEA simulations of seismic wave propagation.

2.5 CURRENT RESEARCH AND FUTURE DIRECTIONS

Mesh smoothing techniques have undergone the different variations over several decades where the efficiency and robustness are noted down at each stage. In this domain, several challenges are present which can present as a new opportunity with the rapid progress of technology. In this section, the prevailing research trends and the promising future directions are presented in a more elaborate manner.

2.5.1 Efficient Algorithms for Complex Meshes

The complexity in the meshes is characterized by large element counts that could lead to high levels of detail that remains a challenge in mesh smoothing. A primary focus of current research is on the development of the algorithms that could lead to more complexities with efficiency. Parallel computing techniques have been applied to accelerate the smoothing process. Dividing the mesh into smaller segments and processing them accordingly lead to the significant reductions in computation time. Figure 2.5 shows the working process of 3D Laplacian smoothing.

Additionally, the adaptive smoothing algorithms are applied to different application areas. These algorithms are poorly shaped elements which cover the entire mesh as these algorithms apply concentrate smoothing efforts on those areas. In this approach, the computational resources are effectively utilized for overall mesh quality.

2.5.2 Machine Learning (ML) Approaches to Mesh Smoothing

The recent developments in ML lead to offer a fresh perspective on refining mesh smoothing techniques. ML, with its ability to glean insights from data and make informed decisions independently, presents a promising avenue for addressing the intricate task of optimizing vertex positions in meshes where the ideal configuration isn't always apparent from the outset. One exciting avenue of exploration involves delving into deep learning, a subset of ML characterized by intricate neural networks with numerous layers. Researchers are delving into the realm of deep learning models to uplift mesh quality. They aim to train

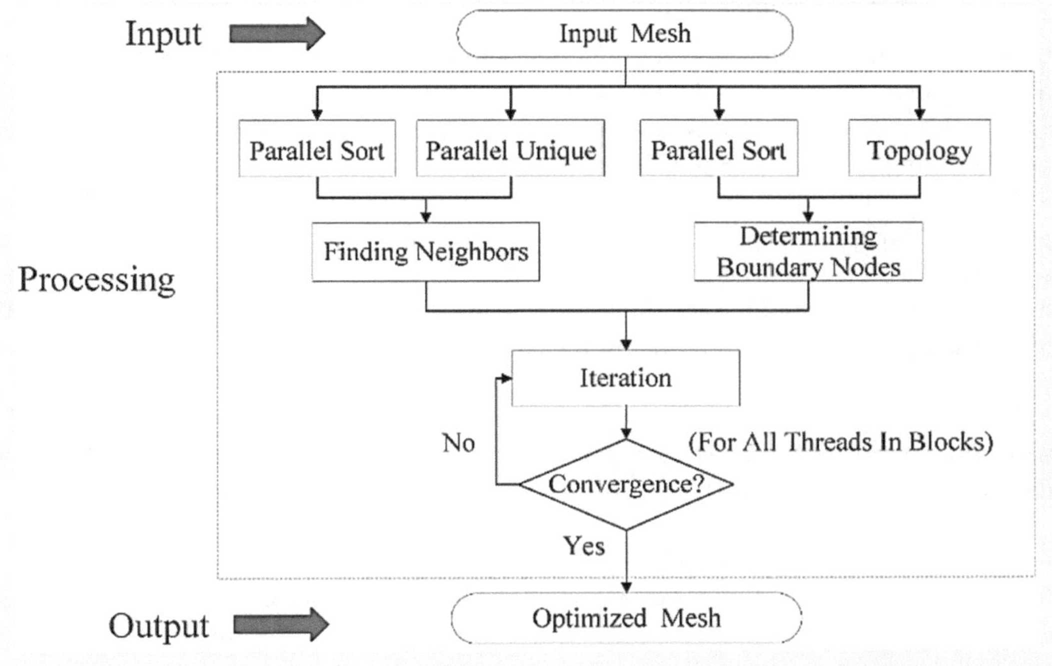

FIGURE 2.5 The whole working process of 3D Laplacian smoothing.

these models using datasets packed with high-quality meshes, with the ultimate goal of developing algorithms adept at autonomously enhancing the quality of new meshes. The schematic graph of deep RL has been shown in Fig. 2.6.

Another captivating approach lies in the realm of RL, a ML paradigm where an agent learns to navigate its environment by trial and error. In the context of mesh smoothing, envision vertices within the mesh take on the role of these agents, while the surrounding elements serve as the environment. Through iterative interactions, these agents adapt and refine vertex positions, leading to an overall enhancement in mesh quality. These ML strategies offer a refreshing take on addressing the challenges inherent in mesh smoothing, heralding a new era of research and innovation in the field [47].

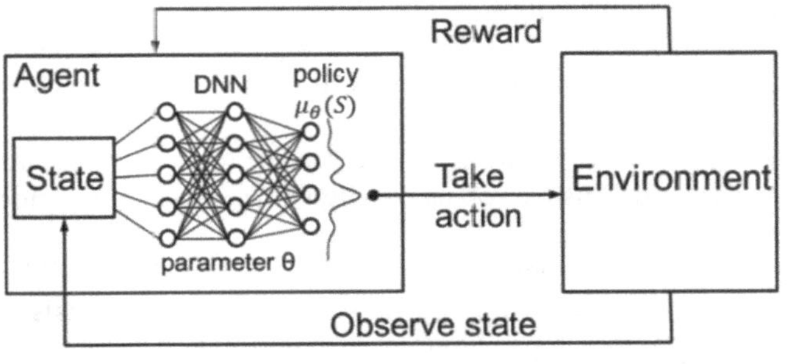

FIGURE 2.6 Schematic graph of deep reinforcement learning.

2.5.3 Potential Innovations and Challenges

Looking forward, mesh smoothing is poised for exciting advancements, especially given the rising demand fueled by 3D printing's popularity. Tailored algorithms are needed to address its unique challenges, such as accommodating the layer-by-layer nature of printing and rectifying errors common in 3D scans [48].

Moreover, integrating mesh smoothing within the mesh generation process itself shows promise. This approach could optimize algorithms, resulting in superior mesh quality and efficiency. Yet, these innovations present hurdles. For example, developing ML models for mesh smoothing demands vast amounts of high-quality training data, a challenge that researchers grapple with. Additionally, the computational intensity of these models might counteract their benefits.

In essence, while mesh smoothing has seen significant strides, the road ahead is rife with both opportunities and challenges. By delving deeper into this realm, researchers can unravel the current state-of-the-art and illuminate potential future trajectories.

2.6 CONCLUSION AND FUTURE SCOPE

In conclusion, mesh smoothing plays an essential role in optimizing 3D models across various domains, ensuring both visual refinement and numerical precision. Techniques like Laplacian and Taubin smoothing, despite their limitations, continue to be fundamental. Recent advancements, particularly with ML, promise enhanced performance, offering new ways to address complex geometries and improve model accuracy. As applications like 3D printing and virtual simulations evolve, the demand for more sophisticated smoothing algorithms will rise, pushing the boundaries of computational geometry and its real-world applications.

Integrating mesh smoothing into the mesh production process itself is an interesting direction to pursue. This could result in algorithms that are more fluid, effective and have higher mesh quality overall. With developments in this area, a vast new avenue for enhancing mesh smoothing methods is becoming available. Mesh smoothing may drastically change as a result of ML algorithms' ability to learn from data and make judgments without the need for explicit programming.

REFERENCES

1. Neic, Aurel, Matthias A. F. Gsell, Elias Karabelas, Anton J. Prassl, and Gernot Plank. "Automating image-based mesh generation and manipulation tasks in cardiac modeling workflows using meshtool." *SoftwareX* 11 (2020): 100454.
2. Wang, Jian, Yibao Li, Yongho Choi, Chaeyoung Lee, and Junseok Kim. "Fast and accurate smoothing method using a modified Allen–Cahn equation." *Computer-Aided Design* 120 (2020): 102804.
3. Reberol, Maxence, Christos Georgiadis, and Jean-François Remacle. "Quasi-structured quadrilateral meshing in Gmsh–a robust pipeline for complex CAD models." *arXiv preprint arXiv:2103.04652* (2021).
4. Solís Pinargote, Nestor Washington, Oleg Yanushevich, Natella Krikheli, Anton Smirnov, Sergey Savilkin, Sergey N. Grigoriev, and Pavel Peretyagin. "Materials and methods for all-ceramic dental restorations using computer-aided design (CAD) and computer-aided manufacturing (CAM) technologies—a brief review." *Dentistry Journal* 12, no. 3 (2024): 47.

5. Huo, S. H., G. R. Liu, J. Q. Zhang, and C. M. Song. "A smoothed finite element method for octree-based polyhedral meshes with large number of hanging nodes and irregular elements." *Computer Methods in Applied Mechanics and Engineering* 359 (2020): 112646.
6. Nath, Dipjyoti, Ankit, Debanga Raj Neog, and Sachin Singh Gautam. "Application of machine learning and deep learning in finite element analysis: a comprehensive review." *Archives of Computational Methods in Engineering* (2024): 1–40.
7. Wang, Bao, Difan Zou, Quanquan Gu, and Stanley J. Osher. "Laplacian smoothing stochastic gradient Markov chain Monte Carlo." *SIAM Journal on Scientific Computing* 43, no. 1 (2021): A26–A53.
8. Krishnan, Vishaal, Abed, Al Makdah Fabio, and AlRahman Pasqualetti. "Lipschitz bounds and provably robust training by Laplacian smoothing." *Advances in Neural Information Processing Systems* 33 (2020): 10924–10935.
9. Kumari, Rashmi, Shivani Goel, and Subhranil Das. "Mathematical modelling of dendritic complexity mechanism in Alzheimer's disease." In *AIP Conference Proceedings*, 2872, no. 1. AIP Publishing, 2023.
10. Das, Subhranil, P. Arvind, Sourav Chakraborty, Rashmi Kumari, and S. Deepak Kumar. "IoT-based solar smart tackle free AGVs for industry 4.0." In *International Conference on Internet of Things and Connected Technologies*, pp. 1–7. Cham: Springer International Publishing, 2020.
11. Agathos, Alexander, Philip Azariadis, and Sofia Kyratzi. "Elliptic Gabriel Taubin smoothing of point clouds." *Computers & Graphics* 106 (2022): 20–32.
12. Su, Ling-Jie, Wen-Long Li, Yu-Qi Cheng, Dong-Fang Wang, Cheng Jiang, Wen-Tao Yang, Hai-Wen Zhang, and Wei Xu. "An adaptive anisotropic bilateral filtering method for mesh data in scale space." *Measurement Science and Technology* 35, no. 6 (2024): 065019.
13. Afify, Mohammed, Davy M. Belk, Bian Linkan, Younes Moubachir, Jamila Hassar, and Zouhair Guennoun. "Investigation on Taubin smoothing performance of additively manufactured structures: case study of the MBB beam using laser powder bed fusion." *International Journal on Interactive Design and Manufacturing (IJIDeM)* 18, no. 1 (2024): 11–31.
14. Guimarães, Felippe, João Batista Marques dos Santos, and João Paulo dos Santos. "Isoparametric hypersurfaces of Riemannian manifolds as initial data for the mean curvature flow." *Results in Mathematics* 79, no. 2 (2024): 96.
15. Guizilini, Vitor, Jie Li, Rares Ambrus, Sudeep Pillai, and Adrien Gaidon. "Robust semi-supervised monocular depth estimation with reprojected distances." In *Conference on Robot Learning*, pp. 503–512. PMLR, 2020.
16. Gimeno, Vicent, and Vicente Palmer. "Parabolicity, Brownian exit time and properness of solitons of the direct and inverse mean curvature flow." *The Journal of Geometric Analysis* 31, no. 1 (2021): 579–618.
17. Zhang, Lvmin, Chengze Li, Yi Ji, Chunping Liu, and Tien-tsin Wong. "Erasing appearance preservation in optimization-based smoothing." In *Computer Vision–ECCV 2020: 16th European Conference, Glasgow, UK, August 23—8, 2020, Proceedings, Part VI 16*, pp. 55–70. Springer International Publishing, 2020.
18. Sapnken, Flavian Emmanuel, Ali Khalili Tazehkandgheshlagh, Benjamin Salomon Diboma, Mohammed Hamaidi, Prosper Gopdjim Noumo, Yong Wang, and Jean Gaston Tamba. "A whale optimization algorithm-based multivariate exponential smoothing grey-holt model for electricity price forecasting." *Expert Systems with Applications* 255 (2024): 124663.
19. Haghtalab, Nika, Tim Roughgarden, and Abhishek Shetty. "Smoothed analysis with adaptive adversaries." *Journal of the ACM* 71, no. 3 (2024): 1–34.
20. Meng, Hao, and Shuming Chen. "Particle swarm optimization based novel adaptive step-size FxLMS algorithm with reference signal smoothing processor for feedforward active noise control systems." *Applied Acoustics* 174 (2021): 107796.

21. Juhász, Ákos György, Monika Nanys, Balázs Pinke, Alexandre Fadel, Marcin Godzierz, Krisztina Juriga-Tóth, Kolos Molnár, Dávid Juriga, and Angéla Jedlovszky-Hajdú. "Formation of three-dimensional polysuccinimide electrospun fiber meshes induced by the Combination of $CaCl_2$ and humidity." *Macromolecular Rapid Communications* 45, no. 7 (2024): 2300625.
22. Zhang, Chang-Bin, Peng-Tao Jiang, Qibin Hou, Yunchao Wei, Qi Han, Zhen Li, and Ming-Ming Cheng. "Delving deep into label smoothing." *IEEE Transactions on Image Processing* 30 (2021): 5984–5996.
23. Yang, Greg, Tony Duan, J. Edward Hu, Hadi Salman, Ilya Razenshteyn, and Jerry Li. "Randomized smoothing of all shapes and sizes." In *International Conference on Machine Learning*, pp. 10693–10705. PMLR, 2020.
24. Battulwar, Rushikesh, Masoud Zare-Naghadehi, Ebrahim Emami, and Javad Sattarvand. "A state-of-the-art review of automated extraction of rock mass discontinuity characteristics using three-dimensional surface models." *Journal of Rock Mechanics and Geotechnical Engineering* 13, no. 4 (2021): 920–936.
25. Huang, Xinhai, Junjie Ding, Jin Ben, Jianbin Zhou, and Qishuang Liang. "Unified multi-structural element modeling methods using icosahedral discrete global grid systems." *Mathematical Geosciences* 56, no. 2 (2024): 361–386.
26. Wickramasinghe, U., E. Remelli, G. Knott, and P. Fua (2020). Voxel2mesh: 3d mesh model generation from volumetric data. In *Medical Image Computing and Computer Assisted Intervention–MICCAI 2020: 23rd International Conference, Lima, Peru, October 4–8, 2020, Proceedings, Part IV 23* (pp. 299–308). Springer International Publishing.
27. Keshavarzi, M. *Contextual Spatial Computing: A Generative Approach.* University of California, Berkeley, 2022.
28. Chafiq, Maryam, Abdelkarim Chaouiki, and Young Gun Ko. "Recent advances in multifunctional reticular framework nanoparticles: A paradigm shift in materials science road to a structured future." *Nano-Micro Letters* 15, no. 1 (2023): 213.
29. Morelli, Myles, Tommaso Bellosta, and Alberto Guardone. "Efficient radial basis function mesh deformation methods for aircraft icing." *Journal of Computational and Applied Mathematics* 392 (2021): 113492.
30. Ammendolea, Domenico, Fabrizo Greco, Paolo Lonetti, Raimondo Luciano, and Arturo Pascuzzo. "Crack propagation modeling in functionally graded materials using Moving Mesh technique and interaction integral approach." *Composite Structures* 269 (2021): 114005.
31. Behnoudfar, Pouria, Gabriele Loli, Alessandro Reali, Giancarlo Sangalli, and Victor M. Calo. "Explicit high-order generalized-α methods for isogeometric analysis of structural dynamics." *Computer Methods in Applied Mechanics and Engineering* 389 (2022): 114344.
32. Tejo-Otero, Aitor, Irene Buj-Corral, and F. Fenollosa-Artés. "3D printing in medicine for preoperative surgical planning: a review." *Annals of biomedical engineering* 48, no. 2 (2020): 536–555.
33. Wang, Ye, You Yang, and Qiong Liu. "Feature-aware trilateral filter with energy minimization for 3D mesh denoising." *IEEE Access* 8 (2020): 52232–52244.
34. Yamada, Hiroshi. "Spatial smoothing using graph Laplacian penalized filter." *Spatial Statistics* 60 (2024): 100799.
35. Jund, Asaad A.; Abdolrahman Dadvand; Imad A. Aziz; and Kawa MA Manmi. "An extended Laplacian smoothing for boundary element analysis of 3D bubble dynamics." *Engineering Analysis with Boundary Elements* 160 (2024): 76–88.
36. Chen, YingXian, HongXia Yang, YongChao Ye, and JiaYing Li. "Generation of 3D finite element mesh of layered geological bodies in intersecting fault zones." *Plos one* 19, no. 1 (2024): e0293193.
37. Yu, Qianqian, and Guangzhou Zhu. "Digital Restoration and 3D Virtual Space Display of Hakka Cardigan Based on Optimization of Numerical Algorithm." *Electronics* 12, no. 20 (2023): 4190.

38. Wang, Nianhua, Laiping Zhang, and Xiaogang Deng. "Unstructured surface mesh smoothing method based on deep reinforcement learning." *Computational Mechanics* (2023): 1–24.
39. Bullins, Brian. "Highly smooth minimization of non-smooth problems." In *Conference on Learning Theory*, pp. 988–1030. PMLR, 2020.
40. Guo, Yufei, Chuanrui Wang, Zhe Ma, Xuhui Huang, Kewu Sun, and Rongli Zhao. "A new mesh smoothing method based on a neural network." *Computational Mechanics* 69 (2022): 425–438.
41. Yechuri, Sivaramakrishna, and Sunnydayal Vanambathina. "A U-net with Gated Recurrent Unit and Efficient Channel Attention Mechanism for Real-time Speech Enhancement." In *2022 IEEE International Conference on Advanced Networks and Telecommunications Systems (ANTS)*, pp. 363–368. IEEE, 2022.
42. Vlah, Daria, Vanja Čok, and Uroš Urbas. "VR as a 3D modeling tool in engineering design applications." *Applied Sciences* 11, no. 16 (2021): 7570.
43. Wohlgenannt, Isabell, Alexander Simons, and Stefan Stieglitz. "Virtual reality." *Business & Information Systems Engineering* 62 (2020): 455–461.
44. Haghighat, Ehsan, and Ruben Juanes. "SciANN: A Keras/TensorFlow wrapper for scientific computations and physics-informed deep learning using artificial neural networks." *Computer Methods in Applied Mechanics and Engineering* 373 (2021): 113552.
45. Chover, Miguel, Carlos Marín, Cristina Rebollo, and Inmaculada Remolar. "A game engine designed to simplify 2D video game development." *Multimedia Tools and Applications* 79 (2020): 12307–12328.
46. Venu, D. N. "Classification analysis for local mesh patterns using medical image segmentation." *IJFANS International Journal of Food and Nutritional Sciences* 11, no. 12 (2022): 5232–5241.
47. Shen, Ruiqing, Zeren Jiao, Trent Parker, Yue Sun, and Qingsheng Wang. "Recent application of computational fluid dynamics (CFD) in process safety and loss prevention: A review." *Journal of Loss Prevention in the Process Industries* 67 (2020): 104252.
48. Szabó, Barna, and Ivo Babuška. *Finite Element Analysis: Method, Verification and Validation*. Wiley, 2021.

CHAPTER 3

Static Deformation of Cable Nets

The Conic Programming Approach

Grzegorz Dzierżanowski

3.1 INTRODUCTION

The main challenge in the mechanics of cables derives from their extreme slenderness. To visualize this, consider a simple, two-segment cable system, with each segment spanning the distance, L, see Fig. 3.1. When the span changes due to the action of external force, P, both segments behave dissymmetrically regarding that change. Namely, the segment sags if the span decreases to $L-d$, and it stretches elastically if the span increases to $L+d$.

Mechanically speaking, cable elements are utterly flexible when subjected to the slightest compression but withstand the tension of considerable intensity while remaining in the elastic deformation range. In other words, cables accumulate elastic energy only when they are stretched. Mathematical aspects of this phenomenon are discussed in Sec. 3.2.

Formation of any construction with similar mechanical properties, e.g., guyed masts, suspension bridges, fabric membranes, etc., begins with initial tensioning intended to

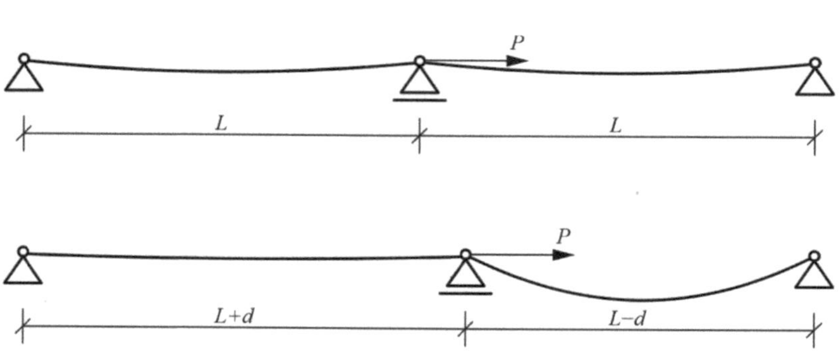

FIGURE 3.1 Two-segment cable loaded antisymmetrically at the middle roller support: reference configuration (top), deformed configuration (bottom).

DOI: 10.1201/9781003564911-3

achieve a structural form of sufficient kinematical stability. This explains the term *tension structure* coined in [15]. The elastic deformation theory identifies tension structures with *reference configurations* capable of carrying external loads. In this way, the cable system takes three different configurations: *complete rest* (before pre-tensioning), *reference* or *undeformed* (after pre-tensioning, but before applying the service load), and *actual* or *deformed* (after applying the service load).

The spatial form of reference configuration depends on the intensities of pre-tensioning forces. They may be chosen so that the self-weight of the reference configuration is the lowest possible, see [11], or otherwise optimal, as in, e.g., [3, 22]. The optimal initial tensioning of a naturally flexible structural form is independent of any external load applied during the cable system's life cycle.

In engineering practice, the intensities of pre-tensioning forces are large enough to reduce the cable sagging due to their self-weight. Therefore, the mechanical effect of the self-weight is not considered in this study, which justifies the assumption that the reference net is built of segments with straight axes. This, in turn, allows for identifying the reference cable lengths with their spans. Such an approach is long established in the literature; see [1, 6, 14, 21]. For more detailed considerations, particularly involving the sagging effect of hanging cables, the reader is referred to [2, 8, 13, 20].

Cable systems are typically analyzed for their mechanical response, both static and dynamic, as well as for the optimal structural shape; the latter is usually referred to as *form-finding*. Numerical strategies to achieve both goals are frequently based on the Force Density Method, see [11, 12, 22] or the Finite Element Method, see [2, 3, 19]. In both instances, the equilibrium of a structure is implicitly assumed. Put differently, equilibrium equations are built into the governing equations of the problem.

The present research starts from the general mechanical principle, stating that the equilibrium of the structure corresponds to the minimum of its potential energy. From a mathematical standpoint, equilibrium equations express the necessary conditions of the minimum. The question is to find the minimum value of a convex objective functional whose argument belongs to a convex set. Identifying the objective function with its epigraph (also a convex set) allows recasting the original problem in the *epigraph form*, see Sec. 3.3 and [5, 16] for more details. After further reformulation, the problem under study involves minimization with constraints that can be expressed in the conic form. Therefore, *conic programming* is appropriate for the computational part of the study; see Sec. 3.4 for essential facts about this technique.

In the scope of cable systems, the energy minimization approach has been discussed in, e.g., [6, 21]. The authors applied various (chiefly gradient-based) nonlinear programming methods to directly minimize convex functionals. The results provided in the above-referenced papers are compared in Sec. 3.5 to those obtained in the present research.

Conic programming also proved to be an appropriate framework for a broader spectrum of problems in the mechanics of highly flexible structures. The authors of [14] used it to establish the minimum complementary energy principle for geometrically nonlinear cable nets in terms of stress resultants only, and the study in [4] regarded advanced optimum design problems for plane membranes.

Mechanical problems related to tension-only structures can be easily recast to embrace constructions entirely in compression; see, for instance, [9, 10] for the discussion concerning archgrids subjected to transmissible loads.

3.2 MECHANICS OF A CABLE NET

3.2.1 Geometry

For the definiteness and clarity of the exposition, assume the three-dimensional physical space parameterized by the Cartesian coordinates (x_1, x_2, x_3). Next, consider a net made of m cable segments interconnecting n nodes. The spatial pattern of segments is arbitrary; in particular, they may form loops with both ends attached to the same node. However, such elements are impractical for engineering purposes and, therefore, omitted in the modeling.

Introduce $\boldsymbol{a}_1, \boldsymbol{a}_2, \boldsymbol{a}_3 \in \mathbb{R}^n$ for the vectors of node coordinates in the reference configuration of the net. Also, write $\boldsymbol{H} \in \mathbb{R}^{m \times n}$ for the incidence matrix of the net understood as the directed graph with m edges (net segments) and n vertices (net nodes). Without loss of generality, it can be assumed that segments are directed from nodes having lower ordinal numbers (preceding nodes) to nodes having larger ones (succeeding nodes). For each $e = 1, \ldots, m$, the e-th row in $\boldsymbol{H}$ uniquely indicates the link between the nodes at the ends of e-th cable segment. The link is coded by putting "-1" in the column corresponding to the preceding node, "1" in the column corresponding to the succeeding one, and "0" otherwise. Suppose that $({}^*n_e, n_e^*)$ are the ordinal numbers of the preceding and succeeding node for the e-th segment, and ${}^*n_e < n_e^*$. Then $\boldsymbol{H}(e, {}^*n_e) = -1$, $\boldsymbol{H}(e, n_e^*) = 1$, and the remaining entries, $\boldsymbol{H}(e, \cdot) = 0$.

Let $\boldsymbol{h}_e \in \mathbb{R}^n$ denote the vector identified with the e-th row of matrix $\boldsymbol{H}$. With this, the length of the e-th cable segment, $e = 1, \ldots, m$, in the reference configuration,

$$L_e = \sqrt{(\boldsymbol{h}_e|\boldsymbol{a}_1)^2 + (\boldsymbol{h}_e|\boldsymbol{a}_2)^2 + (\boldsymbol{h}_e|\boldsymbol{a}_3)^2}. \tag{3.1}$$

Here, we adopt the notation $(\boldsymbol{f}|\boldsymbol{g}) \equiv \boldsymbol{f}^\top \boldsymbol{g}$, where "$\top$" stands for the transposition operation.

3.2.2 Deformation

Suppose that the nodes are supported sufficiently to prevent a rigid body motion of the net. This means that displacements of nodes are *kinematically admissible* only if they result in the change of length for at least one cable element. To introduce the notion of kinematically admissible displacement vectors, we write $\boldsymbol{v} \in \mathcal{K}$, where $\boldsymbol{v} \equiv (\boldsymbol{v}_1, \boldsymbol{v}_2, \boldsymbol{v}_3)$ and $\boldsymbol{v}_1, \boldsymbol{v}_2, \boldsymbol{v}_3 \in \mathbb{R}^n$ stand for the vectors of node displacement components in the corresponding spatial directions. For example, if the i-th node is pinned, then the kinematically admissible $\boldsymbol{v}$ is such that $\boldsymbol{v}_1(i) = \boldsymbol{v}_2(i) = \boldsymbol{v}_3(i) = 0$. If node translation is constrained only in the x_1-direction and arbitrary otherwise, then $\boldsymbol{v}_1(i) = 0$, while $\boldsymbol{v}_2(i)$ and $\boldsymbol{v}_3(i)$ remain unconstrained, etc. More general support conditions (including imposed settlements) can also be modeled.

Let L_e denote the reference length of the e-th cable, $e = 1, \ldots, m$, and write $d_e(\boldsymbol{v})$ for its change due to the deformation of the reference system caused by $\boldsymbol{v} \in \mathcal{K}$. Similarly to (3.1), set

$$L_e + d_e(\boldsymbol{v}) = \sqrt{(\boldsymbol{h}_e|\boldsymbol{a}_1 + \boldsymbol{v}_1)^2 + (\boldsymbol{h}_e|\boldsymbol{a}_2 + \boldsymbol{v}_2)^2 + (\boldsymbol{h}_e|\boldsymbol{a}_3 + \boldsymbol{v}_3)^2}, \tag{3.2}$$

with the constraint, $L_e + d_e \geq 0$. Next, define,

$$\Delta_e(\boldsymbol{v}) = d_e(\boldsymbol{v}) + \frac{T_e}{k_e} L_e, \tag{3.3}$$

where $T_e \geq 0$ stands for the intensity of the pre-tensioning force applied to the e-th segment.

Remark 3.1:

If $T_e > 0$, then the reference length of the cable, L_e, is different from its length at complete rest; the latter is given by $L_e(1 - T_e/k_e)$. If $T_e = 0$, then the length at complete rest coincides with the reference length.

Remark 3.2:

By (3.3), Δ_e denotes the total elongation of the cable, measured from the configuration of complete rest to the deformed configuration. If $\Delta_e > 0$, then

$$\varepsilon_e(\boldsymbol{v}) = \frac{\Delta_e(\boldsymbol{v})}{L_e}, \tag{3.4}$$

has the physical meaning of axial strain due to initial tensioning, T_e, and elastic elongation, d_e, combined.

3.2.3 Potential Energy

Let $k_e = E_e A_e$ denote the axial stiffness of the e-th cable. Here, E_e stands for Young's modulus of cable's material, and A_e is the cross-section area. The strain energy accumulated in the e-th segment during its deformation is given by

$$U(\Delta_e(\boldsymbol{v})) = \frac{k_e L_e}{2}\left(\frac{\Delta_e(\boldsymbol{v})}{L_e}\right)^2 = \frac{k_e}{2L_e}(\Delta_e(\boldsymbol{v}))^2, \tag{3.5}$$

and we require that $U = 0$ for $\Delta_e \leq 0$. Therefore, we reformulate (3.5) to be

$$U(\Delta_e(\boldsymbol{v})) = \frac{k_e}{2L_e} \min_{q_e \geq 0} (\Delta_e(\boldsymbol{v}) + q_e)^2. \tag{3.6}$$

Notice that the function $\Delta_e \to U(\Delta_e)$ is convex for each $e = 1, \ldots, m$. Hence, the epigraph, epi U, is a convex set, see Fig. 3.2.

Let $\boldsymbol{P} \equiv (\boldsymbol{P}_1, \boldsymbol{P}_2, \boldsymbol{P}_3)$ denote the vector of loads concentrated at nodes and suppose that $\boldsymbol{P}_i \in \mathbb{R}^n$, $i = 1, 2, 3$, represent load components (including reactions) in the directions of Cartesian coordinate system. Then, the potential energy of the cable net,

$$\Phi(\boldsymbol{v}) = \sum_{e=1}^{m} U(\Delta_e(\boldsymbol{v})) - (\boldsymbol{P}|\boldsymbol{v}). \tag{3.7}$$

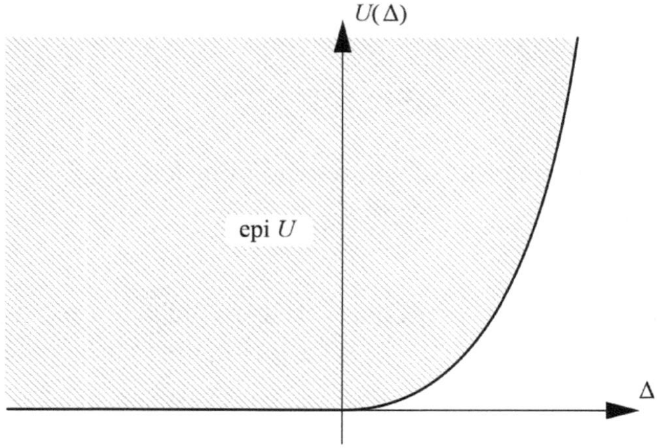

FIGURE 3.2 Strain energy, U, (thick line), and its epigraph, epi U, (dashed region).

3.3 THE MINIMIZATION PROBLEM

Equilibrium of the cable net loaded by $\boldsymbol{P}$ is achieved when the potential energy, Φ, is minimal. The minimum potential energy problem reads:

$$\begin{array}{lll} \text{Minimize} & \Phi(\boldsymbol{v}) & \text{as in } (3.7), \\ \text{subject to} & \boldsymbol{v} \in \mathscr{K}, & \\ & U(\Delta_e(\boldsymbol{v})) & \text{as in } (3.6) \text{ for each } e = 1, \ldots, m, \\ & \Delta_e(\boldsymbol{v}) & \text{as in } (3.3) \text{ for each } e = 1, \ldots, m. \end{array} \quad (P_0)$$

To make (P_0) numerically tractable by conic programming, we consider $\boldsymbol{v}_1, \boldsymbol{v}_2, \boldsymbol{v}_3 \in \mathbb{R}^n$ and $\Delta, \boldsymbol{q} \in \mathbb{R}^m$ independent on one another. Then, to recast (P_0) in the epigraph form, we introduce an auxiliary variable $s \in \mathbb{R}$. With this, the vector of unknowns, $\boldsymbol{x} \in \mathbb{R}^{3n+2m+1}$,

$$\boldsymbol{x} = \begin{bmatrix} \boldsymbol{v}_1 \\ \boldsymbol{v}_2 \\ \boldsymbol{v}_3 \\ \Delta \\ \boldsymbol{q} \\ s \end{bmatrix}. \quad (3.8)$$

Components of $\boldsymbol{x}$ are subject to inequality constraints. From (3.2) and (3.3), it follows that

$$L_e\left(1 - \frac{T_e}{k_e}\right) + \Delta_e \geq \sqrt{(\boldsymbol{h}_e|\boldsymbol{a}_1 + \boldsymbol{v}_1)^2 + (\boldsymbol{h}_e|\boldsymbol{a}_2 + \boldsymbol{v}_2)^2 + (\boldsymbol{h}_e|\boldsymbol{a}_3 + \boldsymbol{v}_3)^2}, \quad (3.9)$$

for $e = 1, \ldots, m$.

We also rewrite (3.7) as

$$s \geq \sum_{e=1}^{m} U(\Delta_e(\boldsymbol{v})) = \sum_{e=1}^{m} \frac{k_e}{2L_e}(\Delta_e + q_e)^2. \tag{3.10}$$

With this, the objective function, Φ, in (P_0) is now replaced by $j(\boldsymbol{x}) = (\boldsymbol{c}|\boldsymbol{x})$, where

$$\boldsymbol{c} = \begin{bmatrix} -\boldsymbol{P}_1 \\ -\boldsymbol{P}_2 \\ -\boldsymbol{P}_3 \\ \boldsymbol{0} \\ \boldsymbol{0} \\ 1 \end{bmatrix}, \tag{3.11}$$

and $\boldsymbol{0} \in \mathbb{R}^m$ denotes the all-zeros vector. Consequently, the epigraph form of (P_0) reads:

$$\begin{array}{lll} \text{Minimize} & j(\boldsymbol{x}) & \\ \text{subject to} & \boldsymbol{v}_1, \boldsymbol{v}_2, \boldsymbol{v}_3, \text{and } \Delta_e & \text{as in (3.9) for each } e = 1, \ldots, m, \\ & \Delta, \boldsymbol{q}, \text{and } s & \text{as in (3.10)}, \\ & \boldsymbol{q} \geq \boldsymbol{0}. & \end{array} \tag{P}$$

3.4 CONIC REFORMULATION OF THE PROBLEM (*P*)

The constraints (3.9) and (3.10) can be reformulated using the concept of *quadratic cones.* In this section, we explain only the idea's essential features that lead to the conic reformulation of (*P*). The reader is referred to [17] for more information.

Following [5], recall that a set $\mathscr{C} \in \mathbb{R}^d$ is called a *d-dimensional convex cone,* if for every $\boldsymbol{x}_1, \boldsymbol{x}_2 \in \mathscr{C}$ we have $\boldsymbol{x}_1 + \boldsymbol{x}_2 \in \mathscr{C}$, and for every $\boldsymbol{x} \in \mathscr{C}$ and $\alpha \geq 0$ we have $\alpha\boldsymbol{x} \in \mathscr{C}$. Sets

$$\mathscr{C}^d = \left\{ \boldsymbol{x} \in \mathbb{R}^d \text{ such that } x_1 \geq \sqrt{(x_2)^2 + \cdots + (x_d)^2} \right\}, \tag{3.12}$$

called *the d-dimensional quadratic cone,* and

$$\mathscr{C}_r^d = \left\{ \boldsymbol{x} \in \mathbb{R}^d \text{ such that } x_1 \geq 0, x_2 \geq 0, \text{and } 2x_1x_2 \geq (x_3)^2 + \cdots + (x_d)^2 \right\}, \tag{3.13}$$

said to be *the d-dimensional rotated quadratic cone,* are of principal interest in our research.

The constraint (3.9) regards the components $\boldsymbol{v}_1, \boldsymbol{v}_2, \boldsymbol{v}_3$, and Δ_e of vector $\boldsymbol{x}$. Taking

$$\boldsymbol{x}_e = \begin{bmatrix} L_e\left(1 - \dfrac{T_e}{k_e}\right) + \Delta_e \\ (\boldsymbol{h}_e|\boldsymbol{a}_1 + \boldsymbol{v}_1) \\ (\boldsymbol{h}_e|\boldsymbol{a}_2 + \boldsymbol{v}_2) \\ (\boldsymbol{h}_e|\boldsymbol{a}_3 + \boldsymbol{v}_3) \end{bmatrix} \in \mathbb{R}^4, \tag{3.14}$$

we recast (3.9) as

$$\boldsymbol{x}_e \in \mathscr{C}^4, \text{ where } e = 1, \dots, m. \tag{3.15}$$

Considering (3.10), we see that it involves the components $\Delta, \boldsymbol{q},$ and s of vector $\boldsymbol{x}$. Assuming,

$$\boldsymbol{x}_0 = \begin{bmatrix} 1 \\ s \\ \sqrt{\dfrac{k_1}{L_1}}(\Delta_1 + q_1) \\ \vdots \\ \sqrt{\dfrac{k_1}{L_1}}(\Delta_m + q_m) \end{bmatrix} \in \mathbb{R}^{2+m}, \tag{3.16}$$

we redefine (3.10) to be

$$\boldsymbol{x}_0 \in \mathscr{C}_r^{2+m}. \tag{3.17}$$

Consequently, the optimization problem (P) takes the form:

$$\begin{aligned} &\text{Minimize} && j(\boldsymbol{x}) && \\ &\text{subject to} && q_e \geq 0 && \text{for each } e = 1, \dots, m, \\ & && \boldsymbol{x}_e \in \mathscr{C}^4 && \text{for each } e = 1, \dots, m, \\ & && \boldsymbol{x}_0 \in \mathscr{C}_r^{2+m}. && \end{aligned} \qquad (P_{\text{conic}})$$

3.5 VERIFICATION OF THE NUMERICAL SCHEME

Example 3.1: First, we discuss the example from [6, p. 89]. To this end, we consider a seven-segment cable net sketched in Fig. 3.3. Cables have constant axial stiffness, $k = 220000$ [N], and they are pre-tensioned by $T = 500$ [N]. The intensity of load, $P = 200$ [N]. In Table 3.1, the results reported in [6] are compared with those obtained by methods of the present study.

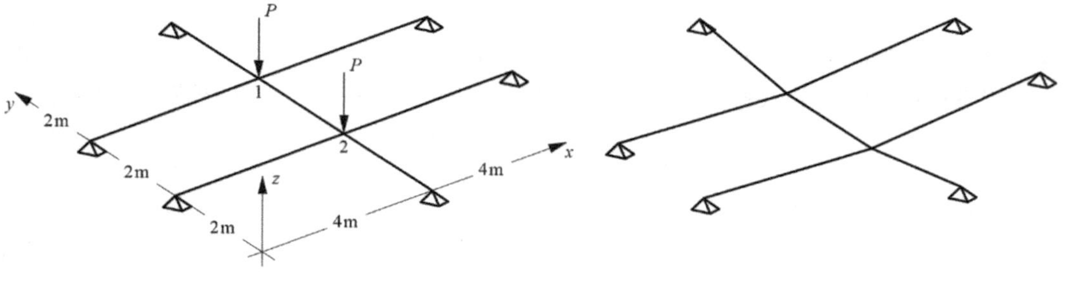

FIGURE 3.3 Seven-segment cable structure considered in Example 3.1: reference configuration (left), deformed configuration (right). Remark: The direction of the z-axis has been reversed.

TABLE 3.1 Comparison of Results for Example 3.1

Node Number	Direction	Displacement Reported in [6] [mm]	Displacement Obtained in This Study [mm]	Difference [%]
1	x	0.00000	0.00000	0.00
	y	3.28947	3.29976	0.30
	z	−199.43100	−199.74936	0.15
2	x	0.00000	0.00000	0.00
	y	−3.28947	−3.29976	0.30
	z	−199.43100	−199.74936	0.15

The computational procedure for (P_{conic}) was coded in MATLAB R2024a with MOSEK 10.2.5 package containing conic programming libraries, see [18].

Example 3.2: Second, we formulate the (P_{conic}) problem for the net analyzed in [21]. Cable segments of the net shown in Fig. 3.4 have constant axial stiffness, $k = 6500000$ [N], they are pre-tensioned by $T = 25000$ [N], and the intensity of applied load, $P = 5000$ [N]. In Table 3.2, the results reported in [21] are compared with those obtained by methods of the present study.

Example 3.3: Third, we discuss analytically the two-segment cable tackled in the Introduction, see Fig. 3.1. To this end, we assume that the pre-tensioning force is equal in both segments, $T_1 = T_2 = T$ (segments are numbered from left to right). Next, we notice that kinematically admissible displacements of nodes are such that only the horizontal translation of the loaded node is allowed; let us denote its value by v and suppose that $v > 0$ if the node translates in the direction of the force, P. Then, $|L+v|$ and $|L-v|$ represent lengths of segments 1 and 2, respectively. By (3.14) and (3.15), we get

$$L\left(1-\frac{T}{k}\right)+\Delta_1 \geq |L+v| \quad \text{and} \quad L\left(1-\frac{T}{k}\right)+\Delta_2 \geq |L-v|, \tag{3.18}$$

while (3.16) and (3.17) give

$$2s \geq \frac{k}{L}\left(\Delta_1+q_1\right)^2+\frac{k}{L}\left(\Delta_2+q_2\right)^2. \tag{3.19}$$

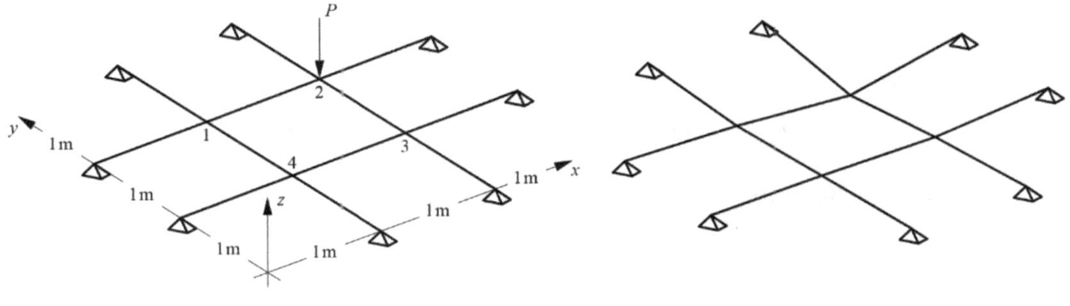

FIGURE 3.4 Twelve-segment cable structure considered in Example 3.2: reference configuration (left), deformed configuration (right). Remark: The direction of the z-axis has been reversed.

TABLE 3.2 Comparison of Results for Example 3.2

Node Number	Direction	Displacement Reported in [21] [mm]	Displacement Obtained in This Study [mm]	Difference [%]
1	x	0.54	0.54	0.00
	y	0.06	0.06	0.00
	z	−15.14	−15.24	0.66
2	x	0.58	0.59	1.72
	y	0.58	0.59	1.72
	z	−49.99	−50.25	0.52
3	x	0.06	0.06	0.00
	y	0.54	0.54	0.00
	z	−15.14	−15.24	0.66
4	x	0.03	0.03	0.00
	y	0.03	0.03	0.00
	z	7.53	7.62	1.20

With $\boldsymbol{x} = [v\ \Delta_1\ \Delta_2\ q_1\ q_2\ s]^\top$ and $\boldsymbol{c} = [-P\ 0\ 0\ 0\ 0\ 1]^\top$, the objective function,

$$j(\boldsymbol{x}) = s - Pv, \tag{3.20}$$

hence, minimum j is attained at minimum s and maximum Pv. The latter means that $v \geq 0$.

The range for translation of the loaded node is $0 \leq v \leq L$. Then, the absolute value sign in right-hand sides of both inequalities in (3.18) can be dropped. With this,

$$\Delta_1 \geq v + \frac{T}{k}L \quad \text{and} \quad \Delta_2 \geq -v + \frac{T}{k}L. \tag{3.21}$$

Consequently,

$$\begin{aligned} &\Delta_1 > 0, \Delta_2 > 0, \quad q_1 = q_2 = 0 && \text{and} \quad s \geq \frac{k}{2L}\left((\Delta_1)^2 + (\Delta_2)^2\right) && \text{for} \quad v < \frac{T}{k}L, \\ &\Delta_1 > 0, \Delta_2 \leq 0, \quad q_1 = 0, q_2 = \Delta_2 && \text{and} \quad s \geq \frac{k}{2L}(\Delta_1)^2 && \text{for} \quad v \geq \frac{T}{k}L. \end{aligned} \tag{3.22}$$

Minimizing in Δ_1, Δ_2 and s gives

$$s = \begin{cases} \dfrac{k}{L}\left(v^2 + \dfrac{T^2}{k^2}L^2\right) & \text{for} \quad v < \dfrac{T}{k}L, \\ \dfrac{k}{2L}\left(v + \dfrac{T}{k}L\right)^2 & \text{for} \quad v \geq \dfrac{T}{k}L, \end{cases} \tag{3.23}$$

and combining (3.20) with (3.23) finally forces, see Fig. 3.5,

$$v = \begin{cases} \dfrac{P}{2k}L & \text{if} \quad P < 2T, \\ \dfrac{P - T}{k}L & \text{if} \quad P \geq 2T. \end{cases} \tag{3.24}$$

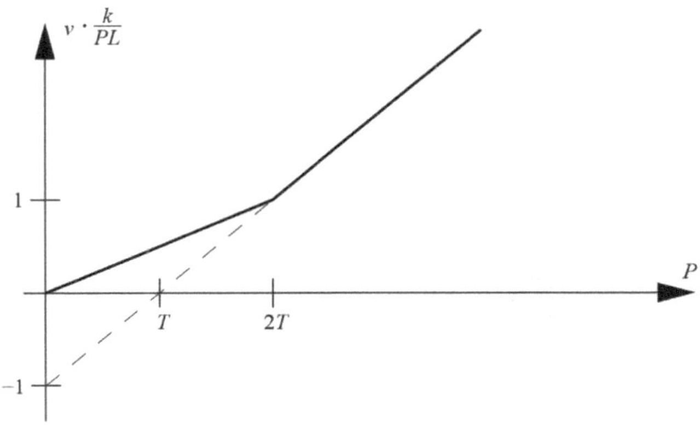

FIGURE 3.5 Two-segment cable problem: illustration of the solution (3.24).

3.6 CONCLUSIONS

Cables are parts of long-span constructions, e.g., guyed masts, sailboat masts, or suspension bridges. Hence, the significance of cable-stayed structures in engineering can hardly be overestimated. This fact fuels a constant demand for reliable and robust computing methods of the static and dynamic response of such constructions. However, the nonlinear mechanical behavior of cables makes the numerical simulation of their deformation challenging. Hence, discussing suitable computational strategies is open to new ideas and algorithms.

This paper proposes a numerical method that may be a reliable alternative to the well-established techniques based on finite element discretization. The proposed approach involves direct minimization of the potential energy of the pre-tensioned cable system; hence, it is correctly set on the grounds of structural mechanics. Moreover, it provides accurate analytical solutions to benchmark problems and passes the verification test against the results reported in the literature; thus, it proves to be mathematically straightforward and numerically efficient.

The energy minimization problem initially regards a convex, albeit nonlinear, functional subject to inequality constraints. Using the techniques of conic programming makes it possible to recast the optimization task in a form that involves the linear objective function whose argument belongs to the intersection of several convex sets.

The main advantage of applying conic programming in analyzing cable nets and other highly flexible structures lies in the simplicity of defining the strain energy accumulated in a cable during the deformation process. This energy is strictly positive only when the cable is stretched and equals zero otherwise. Overcoming this difficulty involves considering the epigraph of strain energy function instead of the function itself.

Conic programming is suitable for analyzing a larger class of problems posed in the mechanics of civil engineering constructions. For example, it may be used for the optimal design of thin membranes that also fall into the category of highly flexible tension structures. However, a slight change in the assumptions regarding the action of the external loads carries the discussion over to the case of structures that are entirely in compression, e.g., archgrids subjected to transmissible forces or masonry structures.

REFERENCES

1. Atai A. A., Steigmann D. J.: On the nonlinear mechanics of discrete networks, *Arch. Appl. Mech*, 67, 1997.
2. Bertrand C., Acary V., Lamarque C.-H., Savadkoohi A. T.: A robust and efficient numerical finite element method for cables, *Int. J. Num. Meth. Engng*, 121, 2020.
3. Bletzinger K.-U., Ramm E.: Structural optimization and form-finding of light weight structures, *Comp. Struct*, 79, 2001.
4. Bołbotowski K.: Optimal design of plane elastic membranes using the convexified Föppl's model, *Appl. Math. Optimiz*, 90, 2024.
5. Boyd S., Vandenberghe L.: *Convex Optimization*, Cambridge University Press, 2004.
6. Buchholdt H. A.: *An Introduction to Cable Roof Structures* (Second Edition), Thomas Telford Ltd, 1999.
7. Cannarozzi M.: Stationary and extremum variational formulations for the elastostatics of cable networks, *Meccanica*, 20, 1985.
8. Coyette J. P., Guisset P.: Cable network analysis by a nonlinear programming technique, *Engng. Struct*, 10, 1988.
9. Dzierżanowski G., Czubacki R.: Optimal archgrids spanning rectangular domains, *Comp. Struct*, 242, 2021.
10. Dzierżanowski G., Hetmański K.: Optimal design of archgrids: The second-order cone programming perspective, *Arch. Civil Engng*, 67, 2021.
11. Dzierżanowski G., Wójcik-Grząba I.: Optimal form-finding of cable systems, *Arch. Civil Engng*, 66, 2020.
12. Dzierżanowski G., Wójcik-Grząba I.: Optimal design of trusses: The force density perspective, [In:] Kale I. R., Sadollah A. (Eds.): *Optimization Methods for Structural Engineering*, pp. 21–40, Springer, 2023.
13. Greco L., Impollonia N., Cuomo M.: A procedure for the static analysis of cable structures following elastic catenary theory, *Int. J. Solids Struct*, 51, 2014.
14. Kanno Y., Ohsaki M.: Minimum principle of complementary energy of cable networks by using second-order cone programming, *Int. J. Solids Struct*, 40, 2003.
15. Lewis W. J.: *Tension Structures: Form and Behaviour*, Thomas Telford, 2003.
16. Luenberger D. G.: *Optimization by Vector Space Methods*, John Wiley and Sons, 1974.
17. *MOSEK Modelling Cookbook*, https://docs.mosek.com/modeling-cookbook/index.html
18. *MOSEK Optimization Toolbox for MATLAB 10.2.5*, https://docs.mosek.com/latest/toolbox/index.html
19. Ozdemir H.: A finite element approach for cable problems, *Int. J. Solids Struct*, 15, 1979.
20. Peyrot A. H., Goulois A. P.: Analysis of cable structures, *Comp. Struct*, 10, 1979.
21. Pietrzak J.: Matrix formulation of static analysis of cable structures, *Comp. Struct*, 9, 1978.
22. Schek H.-J.: The force density method for form finding and computation of general networks, *Comp. Meth. Appl. Mech. Engng*, 3, 1974.

CHAPTER 4

Design and Analysis of Gas Turbine Rotor Blade with Film Cooling for Aeronautical Applications

Akshay M. Pillai, Archit Dogra, Atharva Uplenchwar, Bryan Thomas and Ishaan R. Kale

4.1 INTRODUCTION

Turbines are used in several industries to generate power from different power generation sources such as hydroelectric, nuclear, gas, etc. The most recent turbines have been developed in a way such that they burn less fuel simultaneously at a higher temperature to achieve high power output from the turbine. Running a lean working fluid condition leads to higher thermal stresses on the turbine and its blades and crude cooling designs found on older turbine designs fails when subjected to these thermal cycles over and over again (Tian et al., 2021). Hence, this led to the advent of advanced cooling systems for the turbine and its blades in order to withhold in these high temperature and stressed situations. Simultaneously, there has been advancement in material technology and newer alloys have been introduced that have lower thermal coefficients of expansion in order to assist to withstand in high temperature working conditions.

Typically, a gas turbomachine has three main components. These consist of a compressor, combustion chamber and turbine. In compressor, the air is first compressed leading to an increase its pressure. This high-pressure air then enters the combustion chamber where the fuel and air are mixed in the desired ratio and then ignited. This is the primary process which is responsible for the production of the necessary power. Next, the exhaust gases enter the turbine, and when the turbine expands, these gases are released into the atmosphere (Htwe et al., 2015). When designing a turbine blade, it is crucial to study its flow characteristics using velocity triangles to see how the gas/working fluid interacts with the blade. Once the gas/fluid enters the stator, it is usually accelerated to some extent with respect to the absolute frame of reference. The flow when entering the rotor experiences

DOI: 10.1201/9781003564911-4

acceleration to a certain degree in relation to the relative frame of reference (Anton and Wiberg, 2013).

In a typical aircraft turbine, higher temperature leads to increase the thrust. However, these higher temperatures have jeopardized the integrity of the high-pressure turbine components and specifically the turbine blades (Mishra et al., 2017). In the current market, the materials that are being used in the turbines have melting points comparatively lower than the combustion temperatures of the turbine (1300–1400K), thus making it necessary to come up with a suitable method for cooling (Chen et al., 2019; Han, 2018). It can be observed that along with development of cooling technologies for the rotor, higher inlet rotor temperature could be achieved allowing for better efficiency (Jabbar et al., 2014). Along with the working of a turbine, understanding the nomenclature of aerofoils is an important part of designing the working conditions for the turbine. Aerofoils are the shapes that allow for an unobstructed flow of air, i.e., they allow for a smoother flow of air around them. Various aerofoil forms are available and the optimum one must be selected for a particular working condition and application. Aerofoils vastly differ in a turbine depending on the stage, i.e., from the compressor stage that imparts work, to the turbine stage that extracts work from the fluid. Most of the blades have a base design inspired from aerofoils. This is because aerofoils reduce turbulence while cutting through air and have a low drag coefficient. It should also have adequate thickness. Suitable angle of attack is determined in order to reduce drag and avoid obstructing the flow of air to pervert choking. A channel is designed in a serpentine manner while also incorporating a plenum in order to ensure that a steady flow of coolant is maintained. Film diffusion holes are designed to ensure even distribution of coolant along the surface of the blade (Anton and Wiberg, 2013). In film cooling, cool air is bled from the compressor stage, ducted to the internal chambers of the turbine blades and discharged through small holes in the blade walls. This air provides a thin, cool insulating blanket along the external surface of the turbine blade (Bogard and Thole, 2006). An impingement cooling system is an array of jets of high velocity fluid which is made to strike a target surface. This heat transfer cooling system plays a significant role in many industrial applications. This is due to the fact that the impinged jet provides higher rate of heat and mass transfer (Metzger et al., 1972).

There are a wide range of materials that can be used for the construction for a turbine blade. The working temperature has a considerable effect on the turbine rotor blade. Titanium is one of the materials that have a higher temperature cap of 2018.6K when compared to other materials of copper and nickel composition (Htwe et al., 2015). There are certain alloys available specifically used for these applications such as Alloy 713 C which is a nickel-chromium base cast alloy and can withstand great physical stresses up to 1800°F. This alloy is known for its exceptional properties such as good castability, resistance to oxidation, thermal fatigue and outstanding structural stability. A jet engine, if broadly classified, can be divided into five sections. The intake, compression chamber, combustion chamber, turbine and exhaust (Rolls-Royce, 1996). In order to produce thrust a huge amount air is brought into the engine by the inlet via a fan. The air is then fed into a number of compressor stages which compresses the air and raises its temperature to a more suitable temperature for combustion. This is followed by the thorough mixing of the air and fuel which is combusted and then moves to the turbine and then it exits via the exhaust nozzle. In this paper, the design of rotor blades of turbines for aeronautical applications from the calculation stage all the way to the simulation stage is worked upon. This is initiated by selecting an aerofoil profile followed by its computer-aided design (CAD) design and subsequent structural and computational fluid dynamics (CFD) simulations to determine whether the calculations and parameters selected for the blade profile were suitable (Zhou et al., 2017).

The paper is organized as follows: Section 4.2 discusses the base methodology along with the selection of the primary design parameters that includes the engine selection. Section 4.3 consists of the first iteration design calculations which gives the initial values for the design parameters. Section 4.4 explains the mathematical model generated for the design which gives outputs for the velocity triangles, forces and other such core design values. Section 4.5 discusses steps followed for the first iteration of the blade design, which results in the generation of first 3D CAD model including the CFD and structural simulations. Section 4.6 improves on the first iteration design by introducing varying angle of twist in the blade profile. Section 4.7 consists of the concluding remarks and future recommendations.

4.2 METHODOLOGY AND BASE DESIGN

For the design of the rotors blade several parameters needs to be calculated. As such along with the turbine blade, the compressor must be designed with its exterior shroud and various other components. For the design purpose, a single stage turbine is considered to power the engine. Although a single stage would be able to meet the power requirements for an engine which actually has multiple stages, it is still possible to design. A few aircraft engines were considered for this, among the top contenders are the General Electric GE 90, GE9X and GE F110. A GE F110 is selected due to two reasons. It is a more compact engine having smaller blade and being a turbofan engine, the thrust and the required power are being equated. GE F110 is a military grade engine used in fighter jets, such as the Boeing F15 Eagle, and the Lockheed Martin F-16C/D and F-16E/F Fighting Falcons. The GE F110-132 model is considered between the GE F110-129 and the F110-132. The general specifications of the engine GE F110 are presented in Table 4.1. All the data provided below is adopted from the F110-GE Turbofan catalogue.

TABLE 4.1 GE F110 Specifications

Specifications	**F110-129**	**F110-132**
Thrust Class	129 KN	142 KN
Length	4.6 m	4.7 m
Airflow	122.4 kg/s	124.7 Kg/s
Max Diameter	1.2 m	1.2 *m*
Bypass Ratio	0.76	0.68
CPR	33.3	33.3
Peak Core rpm	13314	13314
EGT	1620 °C	1620 °C

TABLE 4.2 Air Properties at 25000 Feet

Property	Value
Density	0.54 kg/m^3
Temperature	−34.47 °C/ 238.677 K
Pressure	0.29 atm/ 29841.61 Pa

The initial idea was to design the blade ground static, i.e., in a scenario where the plane is on the runway at full throttle ready for takeoff. However, that poses different issues as in a ground static case the engine wouldn't be at its highest temperature load. Hence a dynamic setting may be required. The design point is chosen at 25000 feet above sea level, based on that the ambient pressure (P_a) and temperature (T_a) for the mathematical model is presented in Table 4.2. An iterative design approach was taken as it involved constant improvement in the design. This iterative design process is meant to stop only when the design can be improved no more. A general outline of the design methodology followed is given below (refer Fig. 4.1). It showcases the various steps taken in order to achieve a satisfactory design using an iterative step method, where based on the simulations any design changes are incorporated so as to constantly improve and generate an optimal design.

4.3 INITIAL CALCULATIONS FOR ENGINE PARAMETERS

The design is always initiated at mean diameter (D_{mean}) of the annular space to get preliminary values for the design of the turbine. The parameters selected for calculation at selected design point are exhaust gas temperature (T_g), ambient pressure (P_a), ambient temperature (T_a), mass flow rate ($\dot{m}$) of exhaust gas, pressure of exhaust gas and the turbine pressure ratio (TPR). To start the initial design, it is imperative to create an initial design point. Keeping this in mind, an initial value of the efficiency of turbine stage (η_t) is assumed, generally for one stage the efficiency between 0.88 and 0.90 is considered. As mentioned in the design theory, compressor-turbine matching is an important step to decide the TPR. The steps to calculate the parameters associated with the design are as follows:

U_{mean} mean blade speed

D_{mean} mean diameter

D_{tip} tip diameter

$\bar{d}$ root to tip diameter ratio

M at the exit of the stator or total temperature-based λ

Step 1: The critical speed ratio (λ) is given by:

$$\lambda = \frac{V}{a_{cr}} \tag{4.1}$$

Critical speed (a_{cr}) is based on the total temperature, and is given by:

$$a_{\text{cr}} = \sqrt{\gamma_g R T_{0i}} \tag{4.2}$$

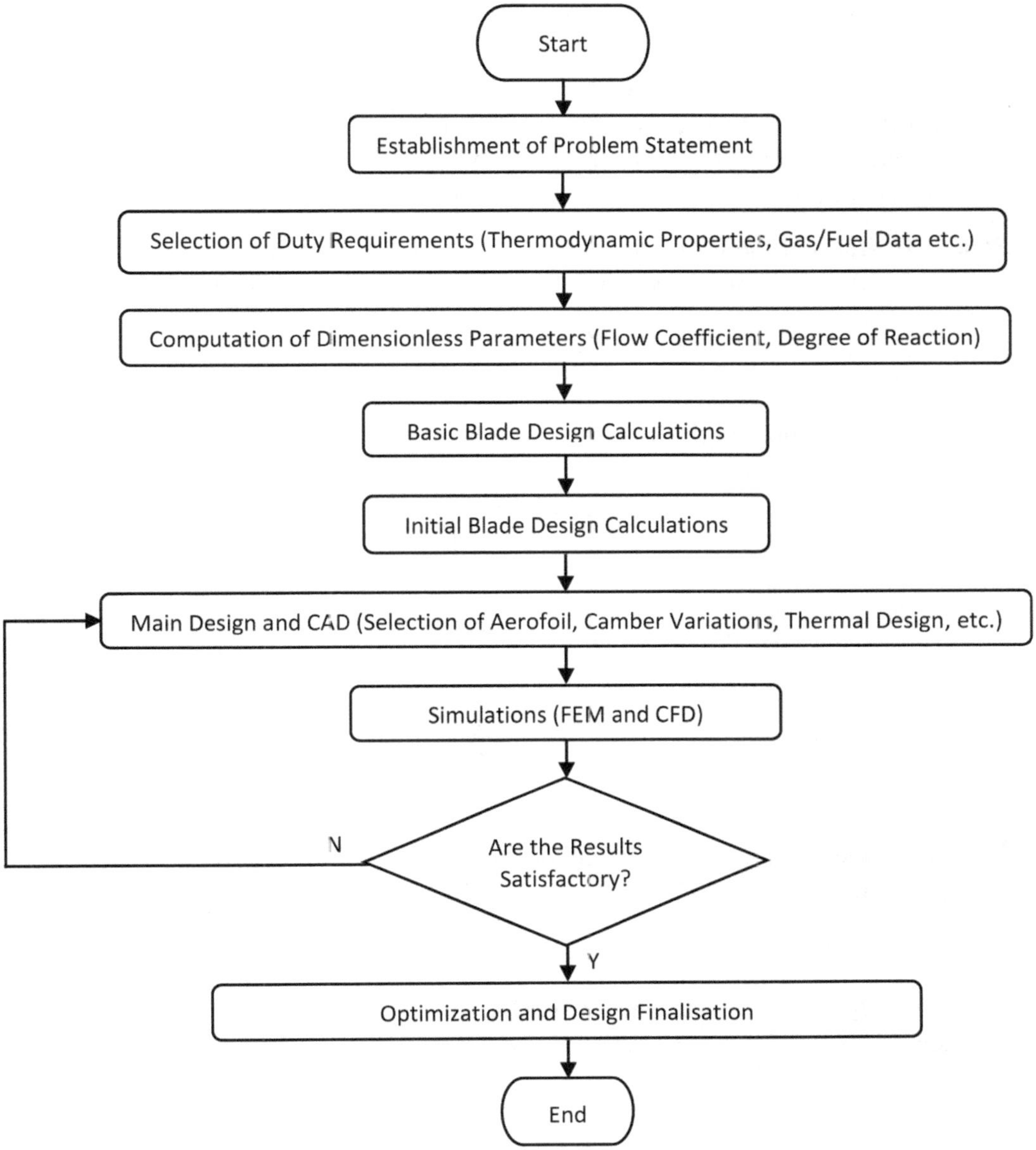

FIGURE 4.1 Overview of Design Methodology.

For the basis of the calculation of λ it is important to know the inlet velocity to the turbine, this is done by varying the dimensions of the annular space in which the turbine blade resides. The outlet velocity from the first set of stator nozzles could be supersonic; however, the inlet velocity for the rotor is brought down to the sonic speed, given by Eq. 4.2.

Step 2: Blade passage wall temperature (T_{wt}) is determined by the following formula:

$$T_{wt} = T_{0t} - \frac{C_2^2 - V_2^2}{2C_p} = T_{0t} - \frac{\gamma_g - 1}{2\gamma_g R}\left(V_2^2 - V_{r2}^2\right) \tag{4.3}$$

The values for the absolute and relative velocities are obtained by making velocity triangles for the turbine rotor blade. This can be done in one of two ways, either assuming the camber value of the aerofoil and its associated α and β values or selecting a preliminary symmetric aerofoil on the basis of which by varying its camber for α and β. The second method is an iterative method and requires multiple iterations with different aerofoils to obtain a feasible result.

Step 3: The ratio of the wall temperature to the total temperature of the turbine at the throat of the stator nozzle is then calculated by the following formula:

$$\frac{T_{\text{wt}}}{T_{0t}} = 1 - \frac{\gamma_g - 1}{\gamma_g + 1}\left(2\lambda_u\lambda_2 \sin\alpha_2 - \lambda_u^2\right) \tag{4.4}$$

where, the values of the $\lambda_{2\text{abs}}$ to the $\lambda_{2\text{rel}}$ is calculated as follows:

$$\frac{\lambda_{2\text{abs}}}{\lambda_{2\text{rel}}} = \frac{\cos\beta_2}{\cos\alpha_2}\sqrt{\frac{T_{\text{wt}}}{T_{0t}}} \tag{4.5}$$

$$\lambda_{2\text{abs}} = \frac{C_2}{a_{cr}} \tag{4.6}$$

$$\lambda_{2\text{rel}} = \frac{V}{a_{cr}} \tag{4.7}$$

$$\lambda_u = \frac{U}{a_{\text{cr}}} \tag{4.8}$$

Step 4: To select the velocity triangle of the rotor inlet it is necessary to identify the Mach Number (M), which can be obtained by the relation:

$$M_{2\text{rel}} = J_1\left(M_2 - M_{2u}\right) \tag{4.9}$$

where J_1 can be set between 1.2 and 1.4. This process needs to be repeated for the stage exit and J_2 is set between 2.5 and 4.5.

$$M_3 = J_2\left(M_{3\text{rel}} - M_{3u}\right) \tag{4.10}$$

$$M_{3u} = M_{2u}\sqrt{\frac{T_2}{T_3}} \tag{4.11}$$

Here the subscript '3' denotes the values at the exit stage. And the values with the subscript '2' at the rotor inlet. It is noted that for moderate pressure drops the flow of the rotor may be entirely subsonic, that is for $p < 2$. For values of the pressure ratio above 2.5 the flow has a good chance of becoming transonic at the end of the stator. This is because this region is restricted by a throat. Due to this constriction, the flow might push toward becoming supersonic. This, depending on the design so far may be allowed or it may have to be controlled so as to revert the flow into a subsonic condition.

Step 5: Using the continuity equation to establish a relation between the mass flow from the inlet of the turbine, i.e., at the stator to the exit of the rotor to establish the s.

$$\rho_t V_t s_t = s\rho_3 V_3 \sin\beta_{3\text{eff}} \tag{4.12}$$

From here it is important to consider the fact that due to the throat constriction there might be some diffusion. Although this is mild but causes a resultant change in density and hence a drop in velocity as well. Therefore,

$$\rho_t V_t > \rho_3 V_3 \tag{4.13}$$

Hence, the $\beta_{3\text{eff}}$ is given by the throat area ratio.

$$\sin\beta_{3\text{eff}} = \frac{s_t}{s} \tag{4.14}$$

4.4 MATHEMATICAL MODEL FOR ROTOR BLADE

As such a mathematical model (refer Fig. 4.2) was made for the design calculations of the rotor. The software used for this endeavor is Scilab and Scilab XCOS. For most of the calculations a CSV file containing the parameters to be varied in the design is generated. This is then imported into the Scilab workspace from where a visual mathematical model is generated in XCOS.

The model consists of multiple 'Super_F blocks'. Each of which contains the modeled formulae for a specific purpose. The TPR block finds out the turbine pressure ratio and also outputs the T_g as an input for the Thermals block. The velocity triangles block finds out and outputs the stage work done and V_r. It also finds the various angles associated with velocity triangles (i.e., β, θ and φ). The other two blocks (Thermals, Forces and stresses) are

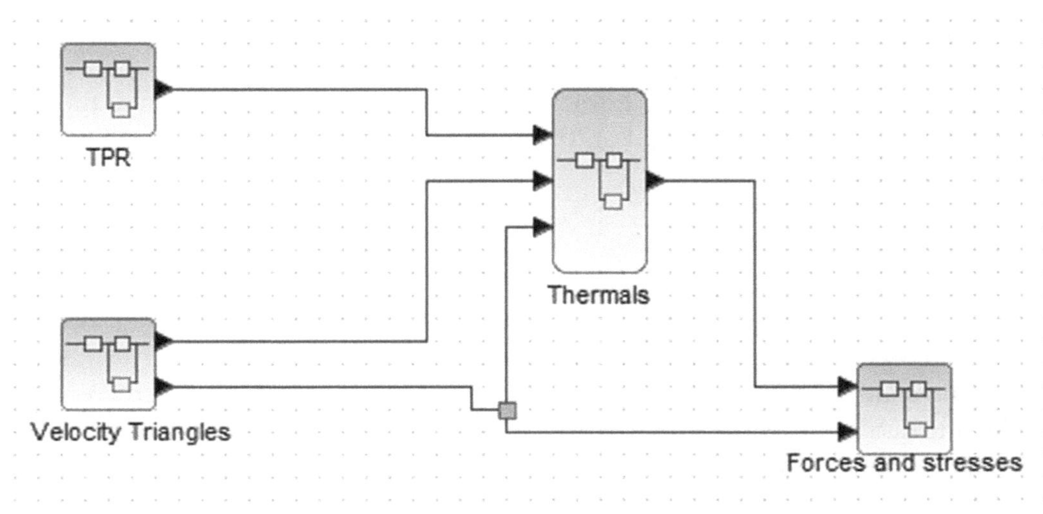

FIGURE 4.2 Mathematical Model Overview.

supportive blocks that give an idea so as to input boundary conditions into the simulation or as a mathematical validation of existing simulation results.

4.4.1 TPR Block and Compressor – Turbine Matching

For the design of a turbine for a jet engine it is important to take into account the compressor's effect on the turbine. Hence, before starting design we need to look into a comprehensive matching of the turbine and compressor to obtain the *TPR*. The compressor and turbine are mounted on the same shaft meaning that ideally, W_t and W_c are equal, i.e., W_c on the fluid is equal to the work imparted on the turbine by the fluid.

The compressor work is given by the equation:

$$W_c = \frac{c_p T_{ci}}{\eta_c}\left(\text{CPR}^{\left(\frac{\gamma_g - 1}{\gamma_g}\right)} - 1\right) \tag{4.15}$$

Similarly, the work done by the turbine is given by:

$$W_t = \eta_t c_p T_{ti}\left(1 - \text{TPR}^{\left(\frac{\gamma_g - 1}{\gamma_g}\right)}\right) \tag{4.16}$$

These equations are rearranged to obtain the TPR required for the design.

$$\text{TPR}^{\left(\frac{\gamma_g - 1}{\gamma_g}\right)} = 1 - \frac{c_p T_{ci}}{\eta_c \eta_t T_{ti}}\left(\text{CPR}^{\left(\frac{\gamma_g - 1}{\gamma_g}\right)} - 1\right) \tag{4.17}$$

Using this equation now the pressure drop across the compressor can be specified and accordingly the pressure loss across the turbine or the TPR can be found out. Hence, the TPR cannot be arrived at alone, it must be found out in tandem with the CPR at the design point. The TPR Block models (refer Eq. 4.3) to find out the TPR and also outputs the EGT out of the Super_F block (refer Fig. 4.3). The result calculated is found in the 'AFFICH_m' block and was found out to be 0.02.

4.4.2 Velocity Triangles

The inlet and outlet angles for a turbine blade matter a lot as they define the net power generated by the turbine. In case of a gas turbine used in aviation the main purpose is to drive the turbofan to achieve the appropriate rpm which in turn propels the air through the engine and bypass channels. The turbofan and the exit nozzle combined create the required thrust figures for the aircraft. The main considerations taken to create velocity triangles are the blade speed derived from the blade rpm, the inlet velocity of the fluid and the static inlet and exit angles α and β, respectively.

The model uses the following set of equations (4.18) to (4.25) to analyze the various velocities associated with a turbine rotor blade. As a data set is required to execute the

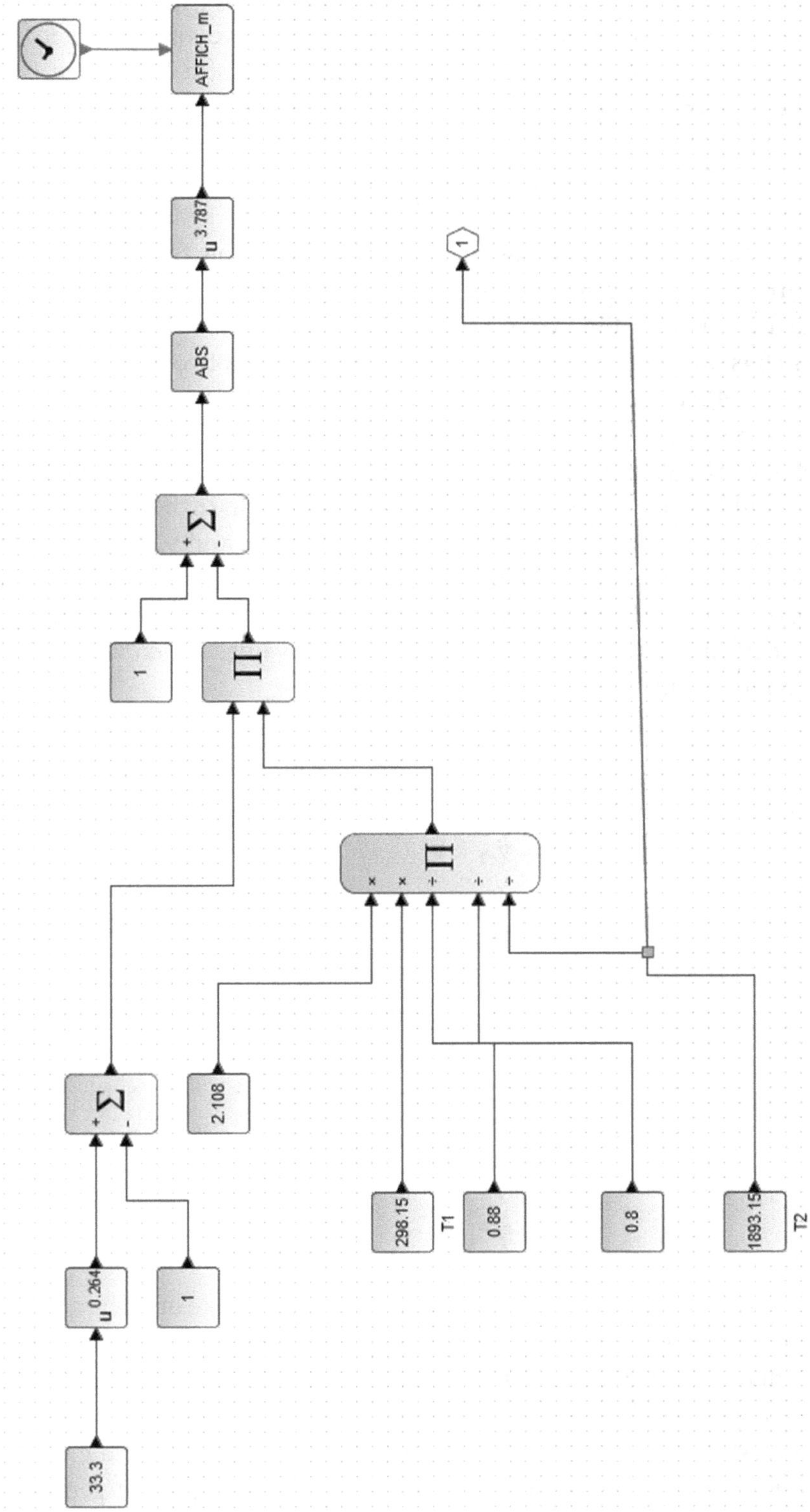

FIGURE 4.3 TPR Super_F Block.

model, as such the variable parameters as mentioned above were put into an excel sheet. Alpha and beta (α and β) were varied to get the remaining two angles namely, theta and phi (θ and φ). The α and β values are used to identify V_{w1} and V_{f1}. Given the various parameters, the max rpm for the GE F110-132, from a loading experiment was found to be 13314 rpm, using the D_{mean} of the annular space, the liner velocity at the D_{mean}, U, came to be 239.1119 m/s. U and V_{w2} are used to get V_{r2}. From here we interpret the value of θ using the inverse sine function. For the sake of simplicity, it is always assumed that V_r at inlet and at exit are the same and as such $V_{r2} = V_{r3}$. We know to calculate the value of V_{w3} which in turn is used to calculate V_3 and V_{f3} subsequently. This enables us to get the value of φ. The final and most important detail obtained from this block is the theoretical stage work which is only obtained from the whirl component of velocities of the inlet and outlets (refer Fig. 4.4). The data obtained from the model is in the form of graphs shown in Fig. 4.6. The value of θ increases from iteration 0 to somewhere close to iteration 2400. This is as expected. The abrupt cut in the graph at around 80° is due to the fact that, whilst most α values would return an equivalent θ value, at a certain α the value of sine inverse θ is nonsensical to the model, as such no values are returned, and as such θ never reduces in value. φ, on the other hand, does have an absolute sense as it depends on β which increases from 0 to 90 and then returns to the initial state, as such for each value of β there exists a value of φ. The gap in the graph again indicates values which do not make sense to the model (refer Fig. 4.5–4.8).

$$V_{f2} = V_2 \text{Sin } \alpha \tag{4.18}$$

$$V_{w2} = V_2 \text{Sin } \beta \tag{4.19}$$

$$V_{r2} = V_{w2} - U \tag{4.20}$$

$$V_{w3} = V_{r3} - U \tag{4.21}$$

$$V_3 = \frac{V_{w3}}{\cos\beta} \tag{4.22}$$

$$V_{f3} = V_3 \sin\beta \tag{4.23}$$

$$\theta = \sin^{-1}\frac{V_{f2}}{V_{r2}} \tag{4.24}$$

$$\varphi = \sin^{-1}\frac{V_{f3}}{V_{r3}} \tag{4.25}$$

Although the GE F110-132 engine being used is just for the sake of reference, it is imperative to interpret the data we obtain in comparison to the data given by the manufacturer. The engine produces 142 KN of thrust over multiple stages, here the stage work done by a singular stage appears to be close to that value at the 0th iteration. However, this value cannot be taken. At 0° of α, the air is hitting the blade head on, converting its full kinetic energy into work as it hits the blade, and considering the air speed it generates a huge amount of force. However, in a gas turbine engine it is impossible to create such an angle

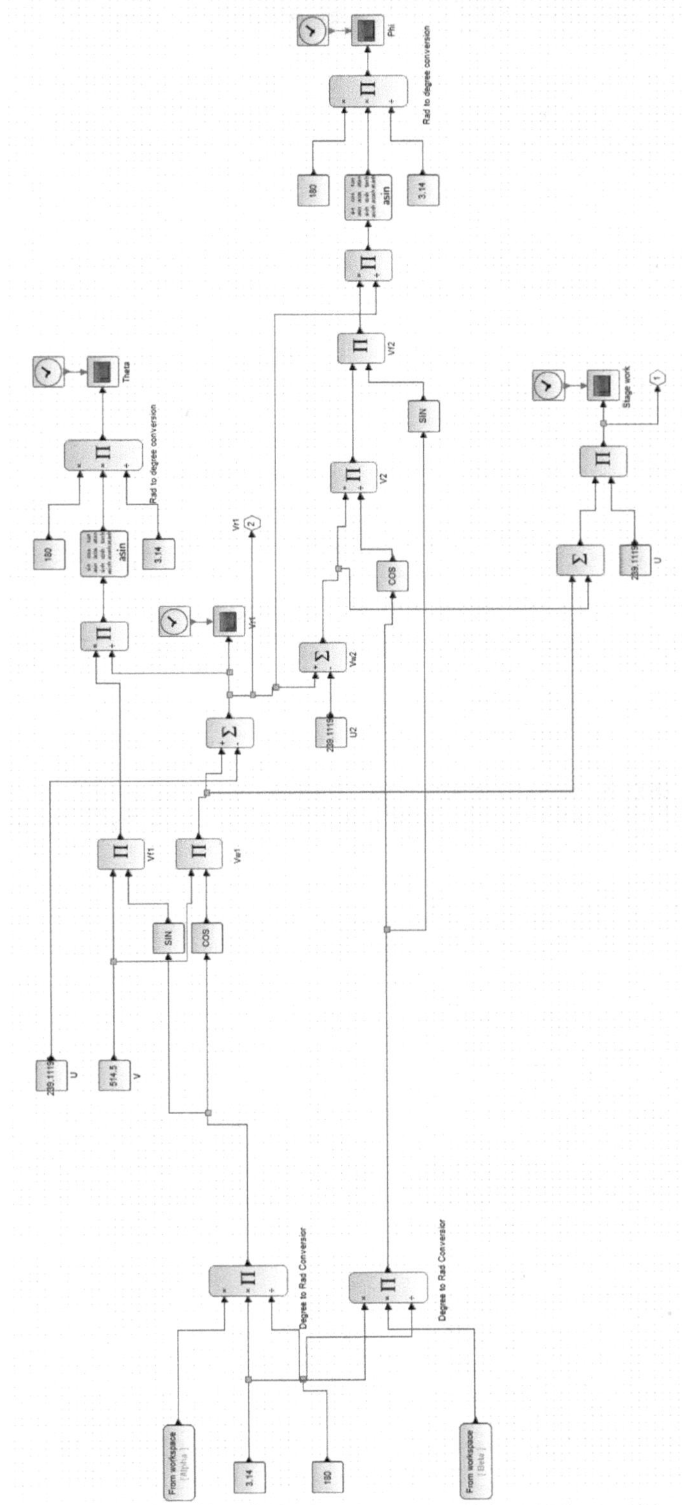

FIGURE 4.4 Velocity Triangle Super_F Block.

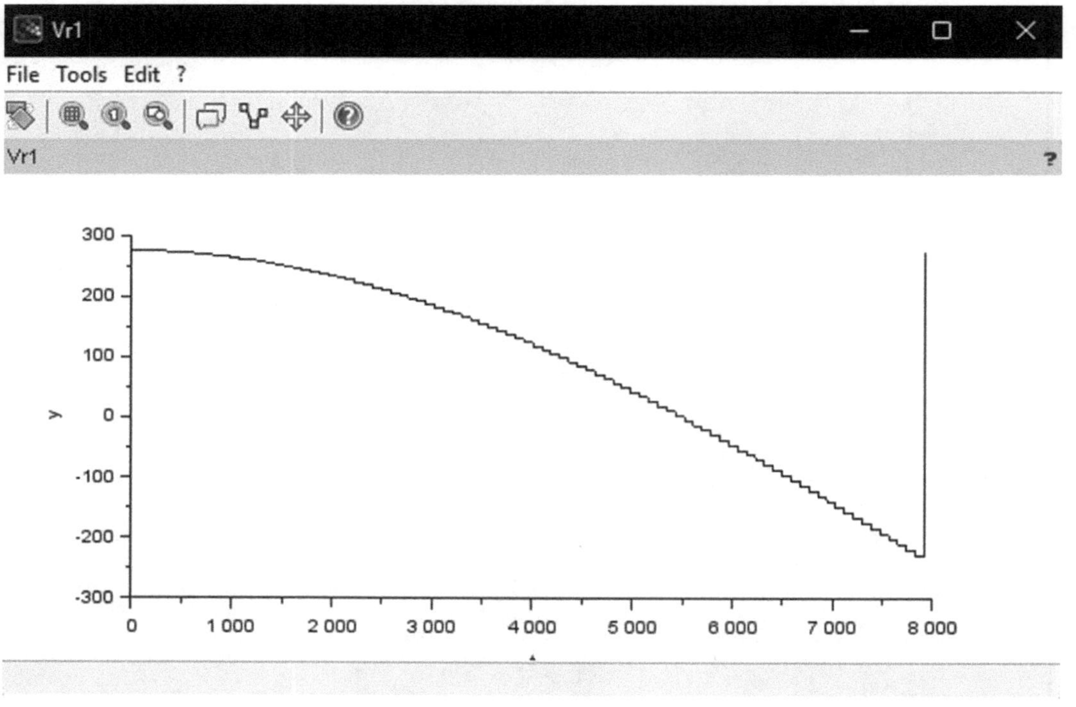

FIGURE 4.5 V_{r1} vs No. of Iterations.

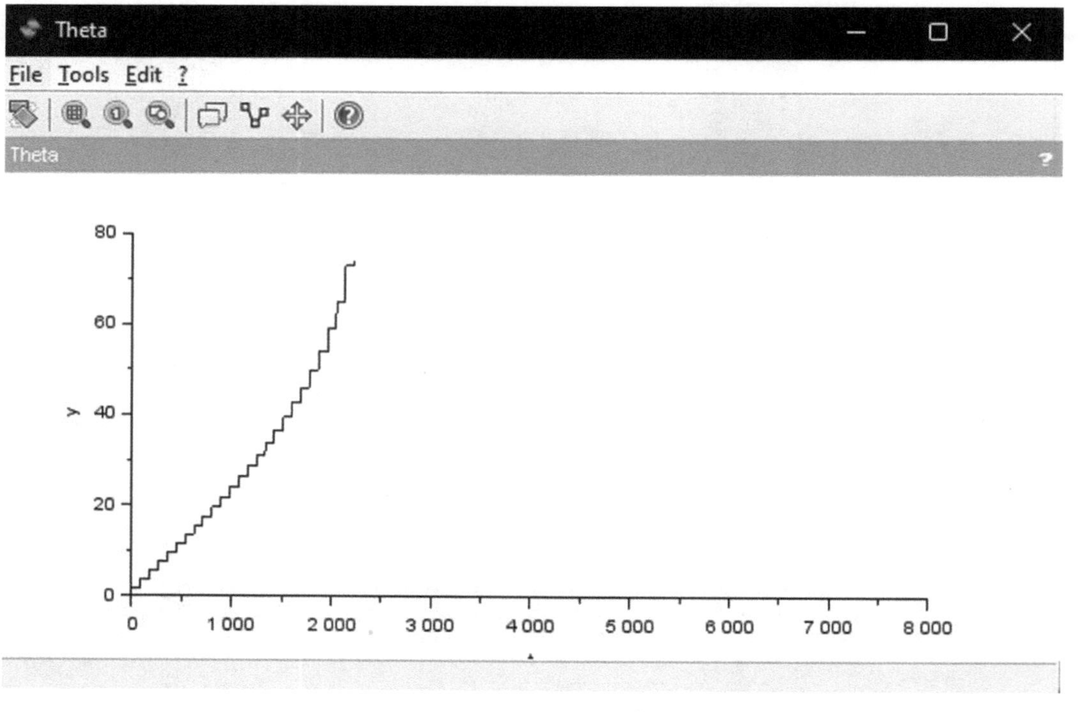

FIGURE 4.6 θ vs No. of Iterations.

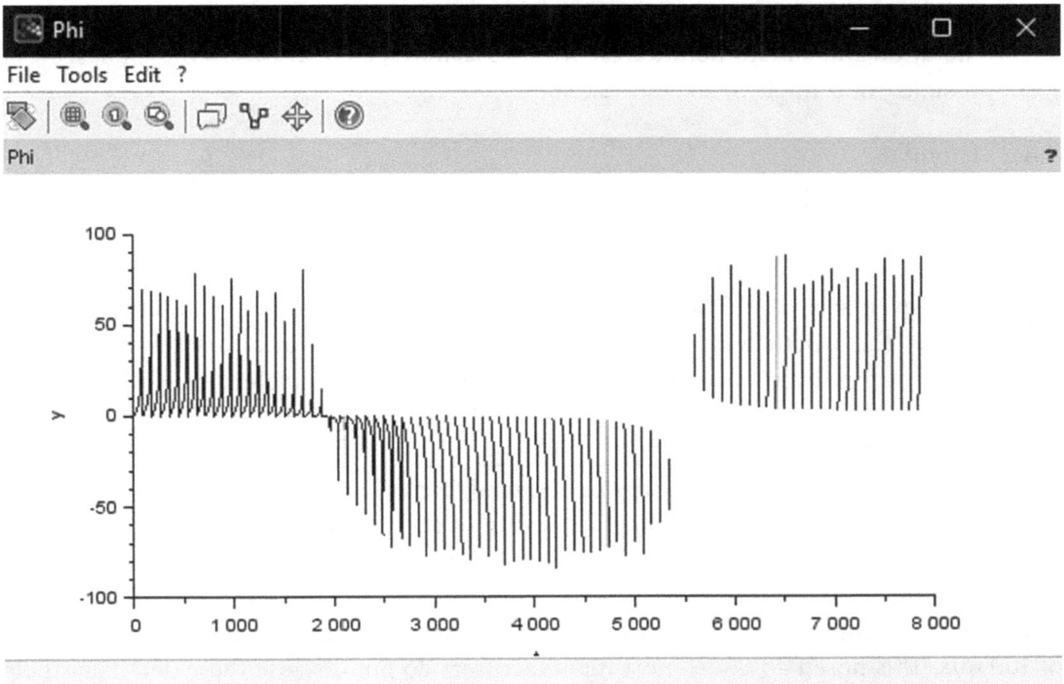

FIGURE 4.7 φ vs No. of Iterations.

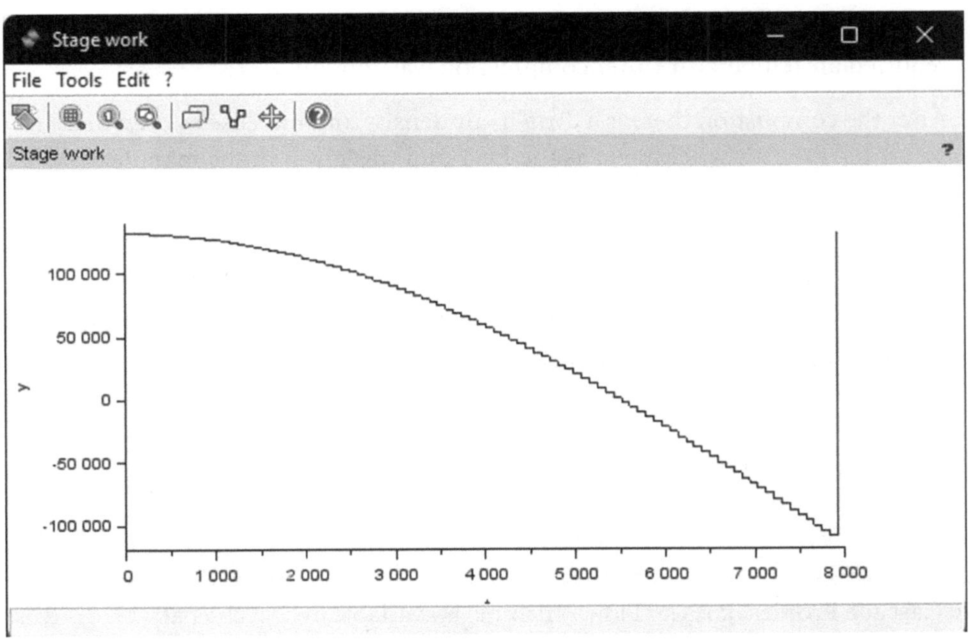

FIGURE 4.8 Stage Work vs No. of Iterations.

of attack for the blade as such this value must be ignored. Hence, the values between the 1500th iteration and 2000th iteration is favorable as it has, comparatively, the highest stage work possible. An α angle of 20° was taken.

4.4.3 Thermals

The Thermals Super_F block (refer to Fig. 4.9) is the last block which needs to be run before the rest of the design can start. As it gives the required temperature inputs for the simulations. Due to the work imparted on the blade there will be a loss in the kinetic and thermal energy; however, as it would be an impossible task to calculate both simultaneously it is assumed that the kinetic loss doesn't occur. Hence, the stage work causes a drop in the temperature of the air, as such the rotor exit air temp can be calculated.

4.5 FIRST ITERATION DESIGN

With the values for the velocity triangles obtained from the mathematical model, the first iteration design could begin. Although majority of the prerequisites for the design were already determined at this point, one important aspect still remained. The air velocity at the turbine inlet was selected to be Mach 1.5; however, the pressure and air density at this point remained uncertain. This is because air is treated as a compressible fluid above a V of 100 m/s. This posed an issue, most manufacturers do not disclose these details in their data sheets, as it is not required to be known by a customer, and especially for a military aircraft engine such as the one selected obtaining this data would have been impossible. Considering we were using this particular power unit only as a reference, some assumptions regarding the required data, were made.

1. The air density after compression could be calculated, as we had the CPR, and the required air temperature after compression was roughly 700 K.
2. After the combustion there is a drop in air density and increase in pressure. The temperature of the air was known as the EGT and was given in the manufacturer's datasheet. This meant that as long as the pressure, density and temperature obeyed the Ideal Gas Law, any pressure and density for the given temperature were valid, whilst maintaining an air density lower than that obtained after the compressor.
3. The annular area could be adjusted so as to obtain an air velocity of Mach 1.5, which meant determining the required blade span.

4.5.1 Aerofoil Selection

Aerofoils for a gas turbine rotor blade were especially hard to discover. Conventional NACA, Eppler or Seilig series blades are not used for these purposes, as mentioned in the literature review each and every aerofoil is purpose built for a distinctive purpose. For the purposes of this work, after strenuous research, a Soviet declassified document titled 'Atlas of the Cascade Profiles of Axial Flows Turbine' is available by Deych et al. (1976). This provided with profiles required for the design. An example of this is Aerofoil C-7025A (refer Fig. 4.10) which is used as a stator.

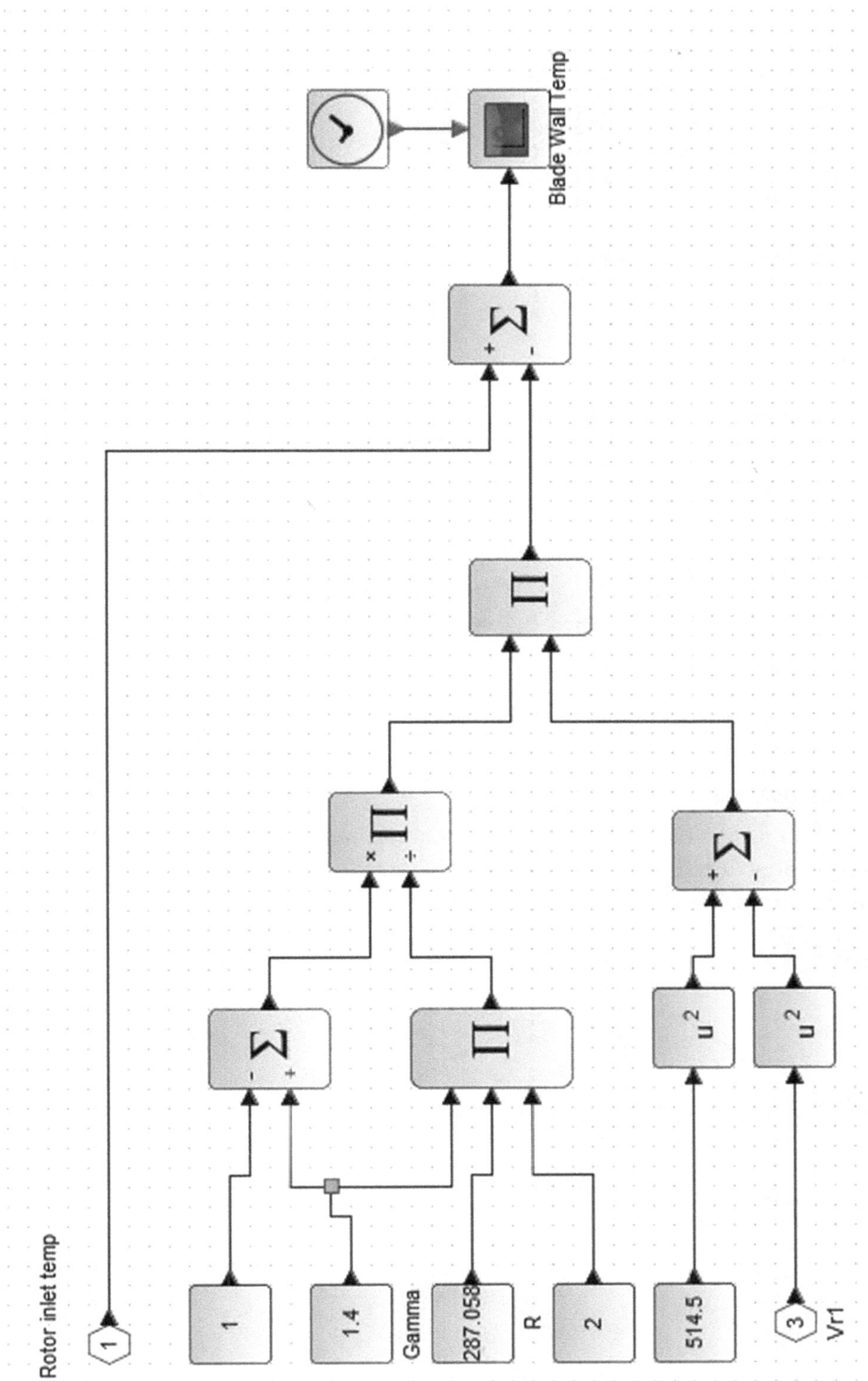

FIGURE 4.9 Thermals Super_F Block.

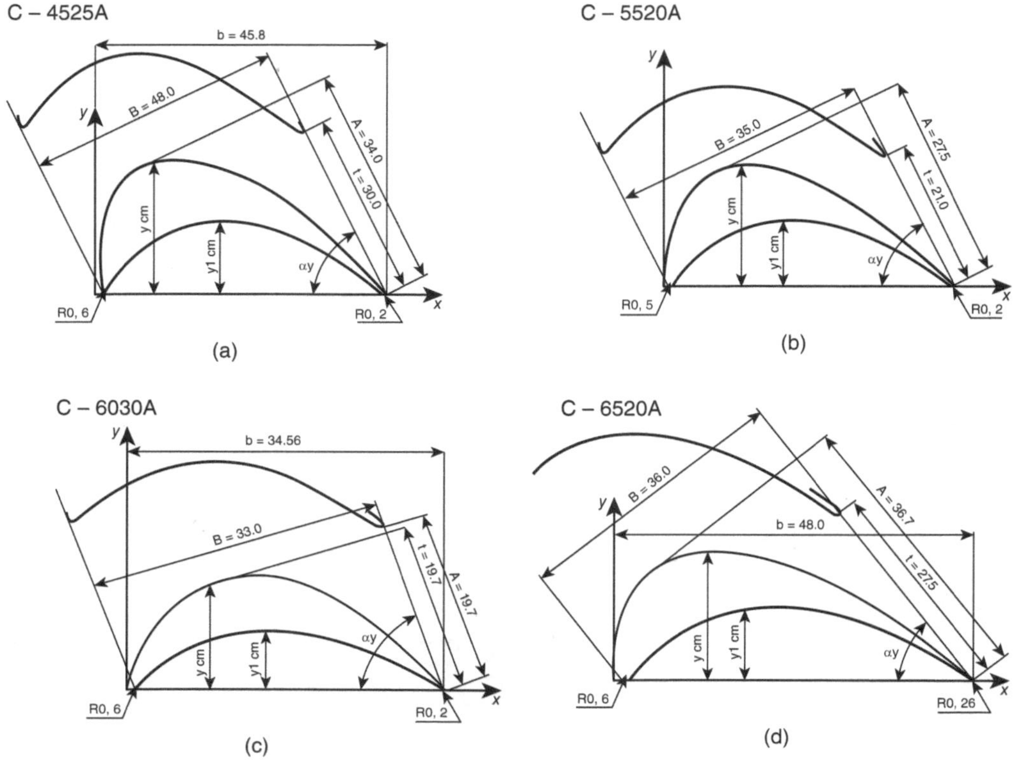

FIGURE 4.10 Aerofoils: (a) C-4245A, (b) C-5520A, (c) C-6030A, (d) C-6520A (Deych et al., 1976).

4.5.2 2D Simulations

To analyze the most suitable aerofoils, 2D simulation were conducted based on lift force. The aerofoils shortlisted for the blade were C-4245A, C-5520A, C-6030A, C-6520A (refer Fig. 4.10) and C-7025A (refer Fig. 4.11). All these blades were selected due to their

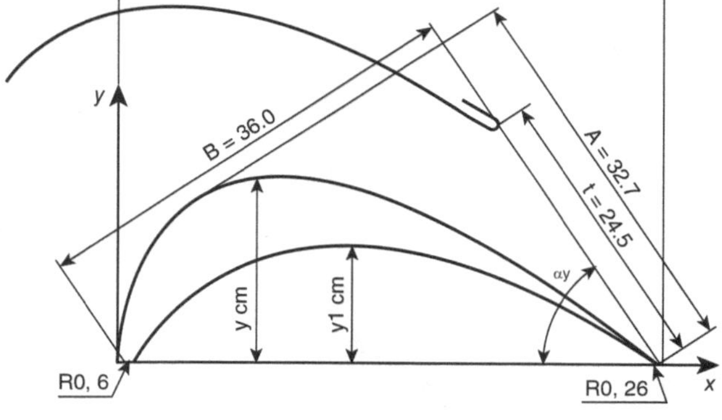

FIGURE 4.11 C-7025A Aerofoil (Deych et al., 1976).

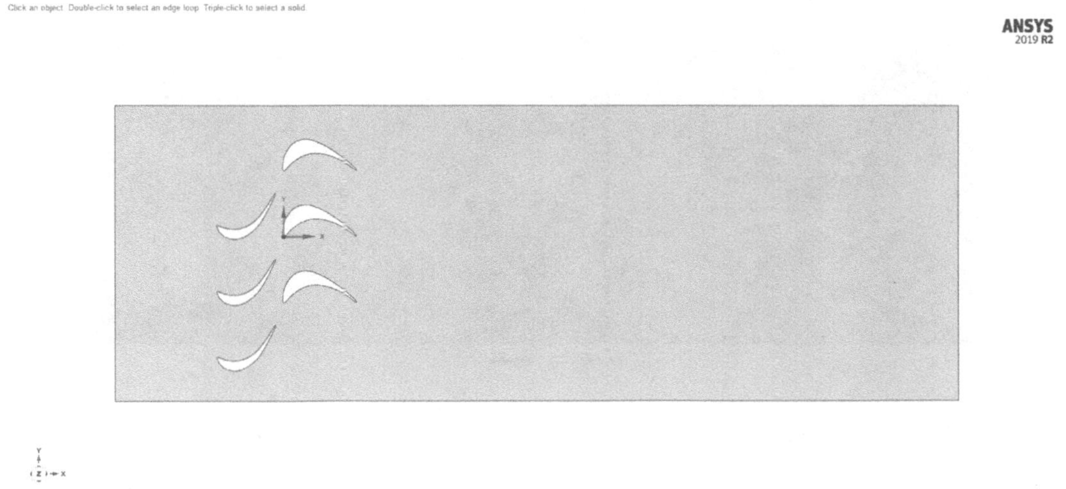

FIGURE 4.12 2D Geometry for C-5520A.

nonsymmetric cambered profile, along with a secondary factor of thickness which was considered so as to incorporate the cooling channels required. C-7025A was selected to act as the stator for the simulations as its thin profile meant that it would be troublesome to incorporate the cooling system whilst maintaining structural integrity, especially around the trailing edge of the blade. The simulation parameters were kept the same for all the blades. As for the geometry a 2D rectangular enclosure with three sets of stator and rotor blades (refer Fig. 4.12). This is done to ensure that the middle blade experiences flow as it would in actuality between two blades on either side. The stator blade is positioned such that the airflow is channeled to the rotor blade at an angle of 20°.

The spacing between the blades was kept at 40 mm, this was the ideal spacing possible which allowed for minimum effect of the air striking the two peripheral blades. The mesh was kept as fine as possible for the simulation to allow for minimum deviation in the accuracy of the results. The mesh settings were as follows:

1. All triangular meshing method
2. Mesh sizing for domain – 1mm
3. Region refinement level at blade – 3

For the given mesh the mesh metrics came out to be (refer Fig. 4.13 and Fig. 4.14):

1. Max element skewness: between 0.00 and 0.10
2. Max Element aspect ratio: between 1.00 and 1.20
3. Max Element quality: 0.90 and 1.00

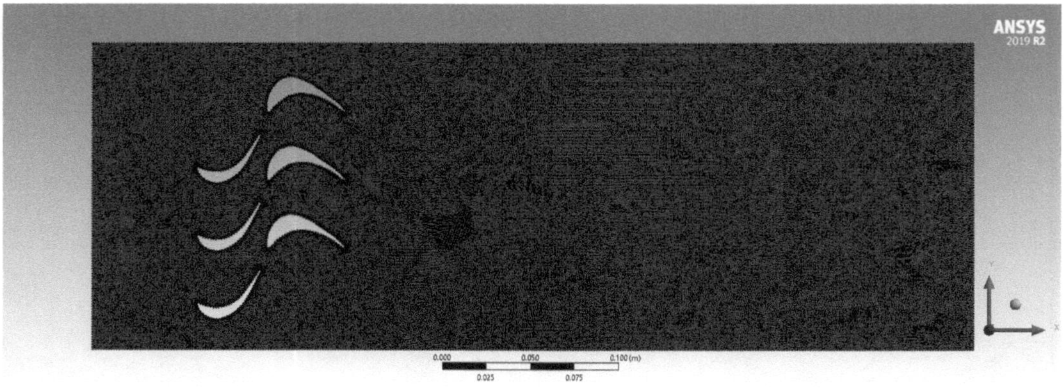

FIGURE 4.13 Meshed Geometry C-5520A.

The given mesh was satisfactory and met the criterion for a good mesh, hence it could be simulated (refer Fig. 4.15). The simulation parameters set in ANSYS Fluent are as given below:

1. SST-K omega equation was used
2. Air density – 1.82 Kg/m^3
3. Wall boundary conditions given at top and bottom
4. Inlet boundary condition with velocity 514.5 m/s
5. A pressure outlet is provided
6. Hybrid initialization
7. Run set for 5000 iterations

With these settings the main results from the simulations that were extracted were the velocity contour, pressure contour and the lift force plot for the blade profile.

The velocity profile gives us an idea where and how the flow separation occurs of the blade (refer Fig. 4.16). As observed, flow separation occurs well after the leading edge of the

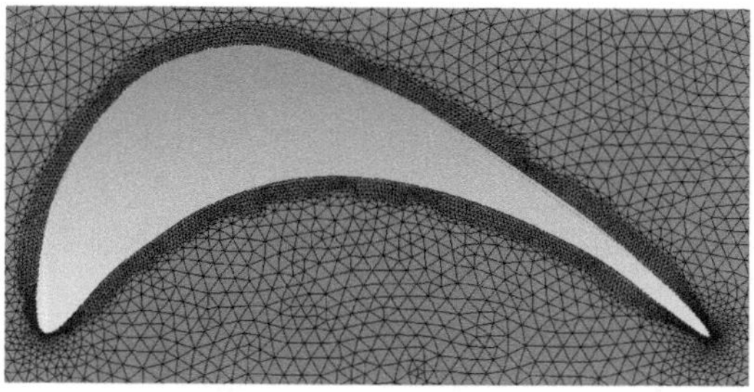

FIGURE 4.14 Close up of Rotor Blade Refinement.

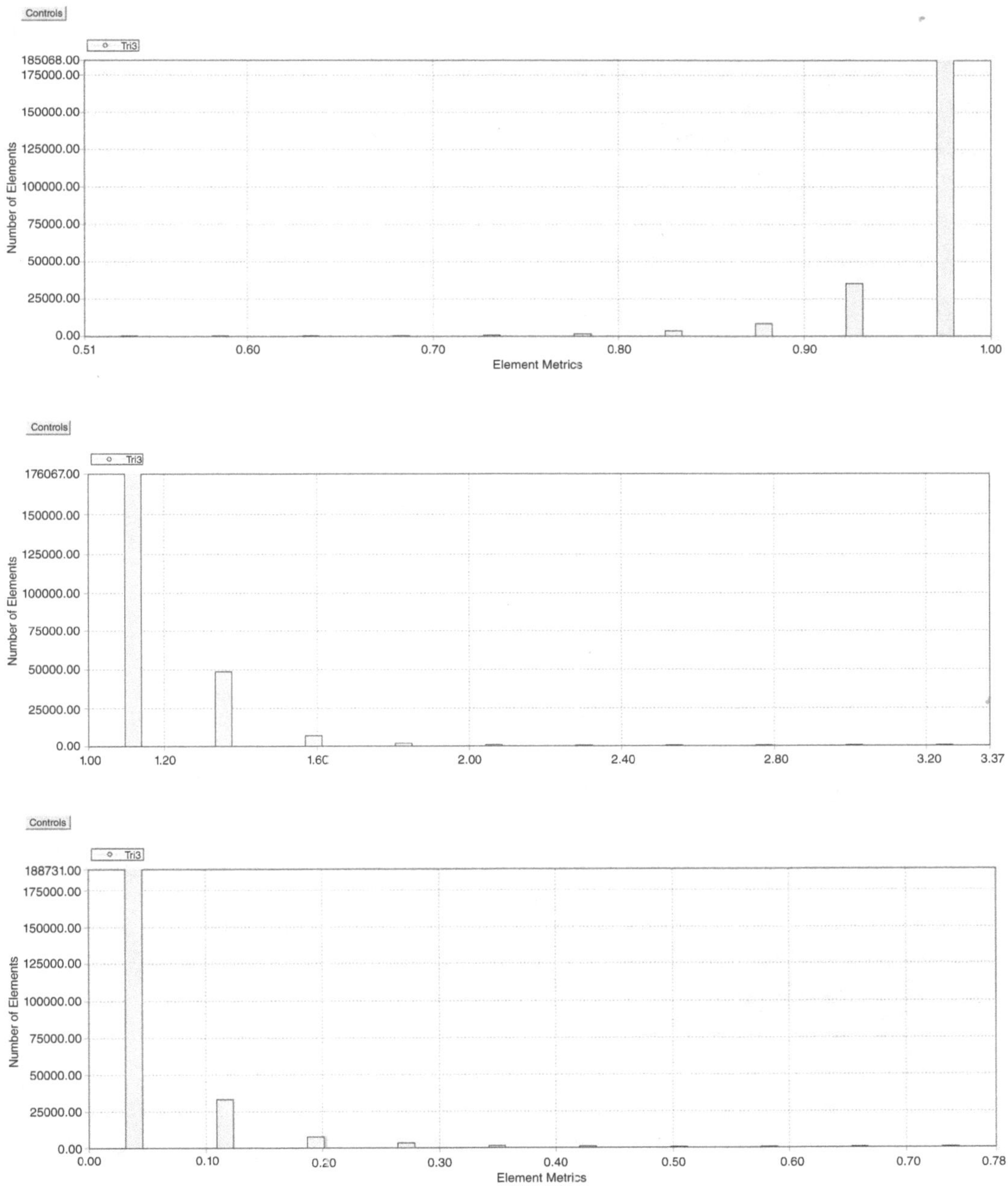

FIGURE 4.15 Mesh Metrics.

blade, meaning the blade angle chosen is working efficiently. If there was flow separation toward the leading edge of the blade, the angle would have had to be reduced. The lift being generated on an aerofoil is due to the pressure differential on the top and bottom of the aerofoil. The pressure contour shows a good pressure differential forming on the central wing surface (refer Fig. 4.17).

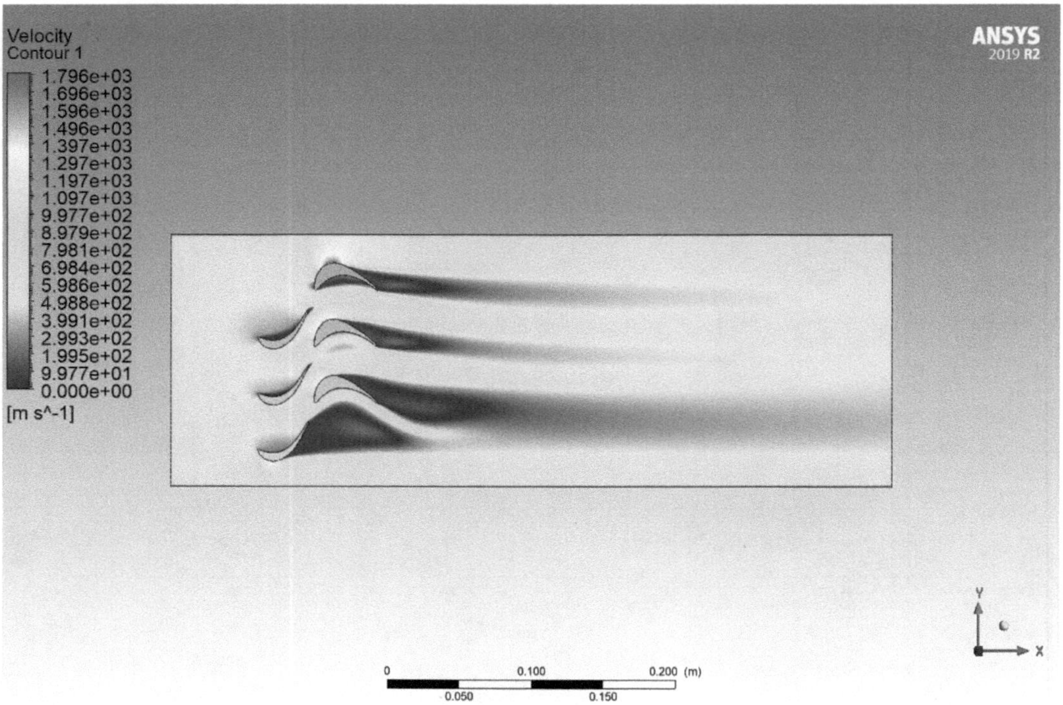

FIGURE 4.16 Velocity Contour C-5520A.

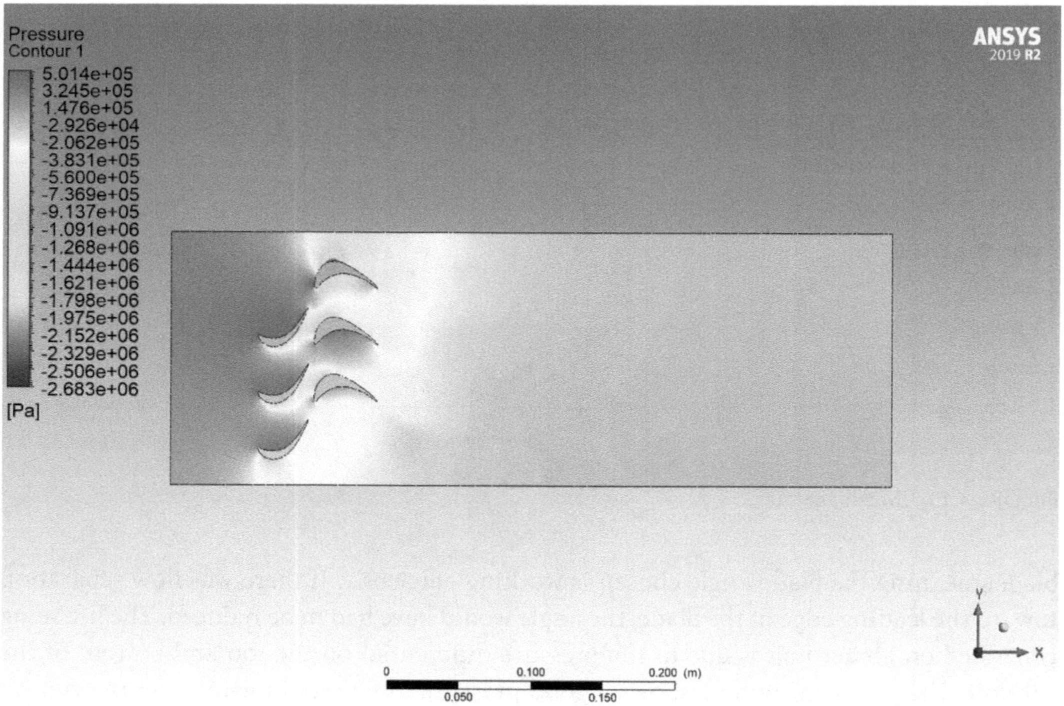

FIGURE 4.17 Pressure Contour C-5520A.

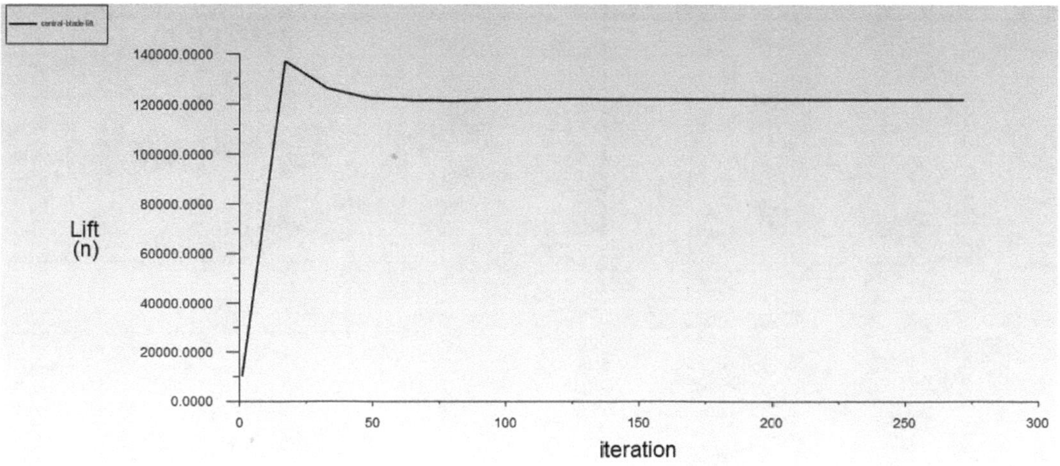

FIGURE 4.18 Lift Force vs Iterations Plot C-5520A.

The lift force generated on the central aerofoil blade is about 45000 N (refer Fig. 4.18). The lift force is high due to the extreme fluid velocity and the nonexistent area of the aerofoil in a 2D cross section. It should also be noted that the drag force is negligible at such high velocities. It must be noted that the drag force is negligible at such high velocities due to the extremely small frontal area of contact.

Similarly, the other three blades were simulated under the same parameters and the same mesh settings. Their results are presented in Fig. 4.19 and Fig. 4.20.

Hence, the lift force generated by each of these elements was found out. This is tabulated in Table 4.3.

It is evident that C-5520A gives the highest lift force; hence, it was selected for further design.

4.5.3 Determination of Annular Area and Blade Span

After the selection of a 2D blade profile, the next logical step is the generation of a 3D CAD of the blade. However, this poses an issue as the annular area and the span of the blade itself is unknown. As this information is not provided by the manufacturer. To find the annular area we have a few things which are known; firstly, the air speed required on the blade is known, now if the air density is known then the required flow rate can be calculated and the annular area found out. However, the density and pressure after combustion is unknown, only the temperature is given by the manufacturer. As long as pressure, density and temperature variations are in accordance with the ideal gas equations, we can select an apt pressure and density for a given temperature, to find out the annular area. The ideal gas equation (Kurz and Brun, 2016) is presented as follows:

$$PV = mR_{\text{specific}}T \tag{4.26}$$

$$P = \frac{m}{V}R_{\text{specific}}T = \rho R_{\text{specific}}T \tag{4.27}$$

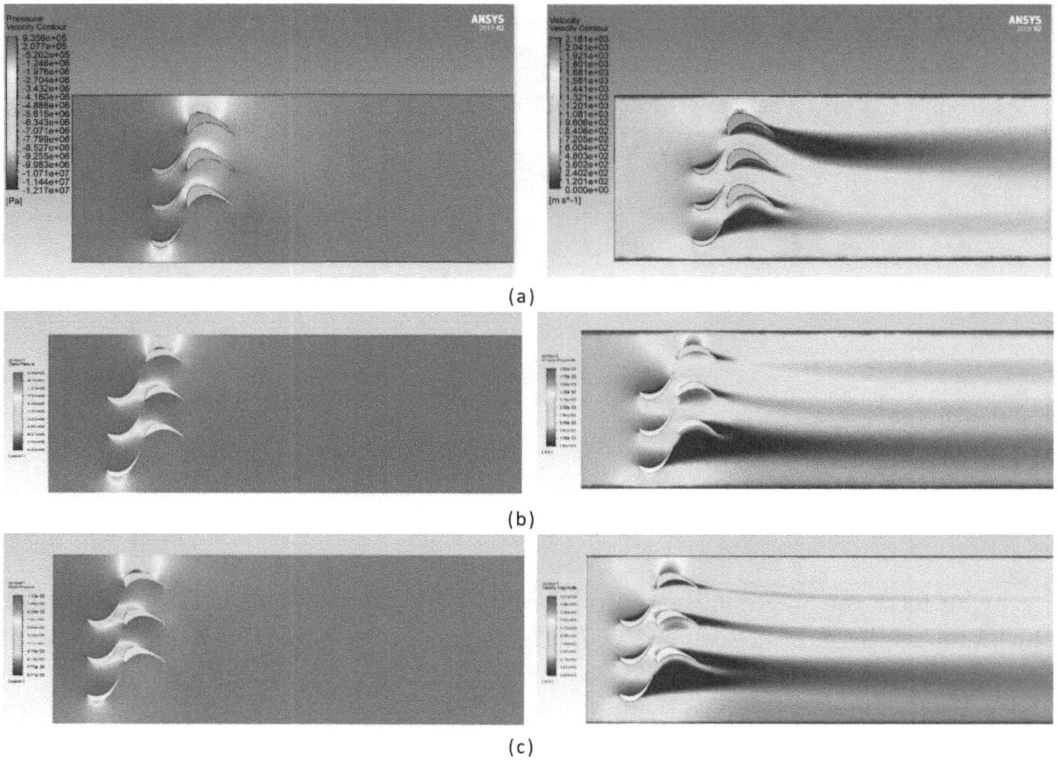

FIGURE 4.19 Pressure and Velocity Contour: (a) C-4525A, (b) C-6030A, (c) C-6520A.

Hence, density can be varied from 0.01 to the maximum possible density, which is after compression to select an appropriate fluid density. This was done with increments of 0.01 and terminated at fluid density 5 kg/m³. The relation between the two is shown in Fig. 4.21.

A density of 3.57 was chosen. This was acceptable as it was below the density after compression, keeping in line with loss of density post combustion, but also because it allowed us to increase the blade span. As for the annular area, it is assumed that the rated $\dot{m}$ of the engine flows through the core, i.e., 124.7 kg/s. $\dot{m}$ is given as

$$\dot{m} = \rho * A_{\text{annular}} * v \tag{4.28}$$

As the air velocity on the blade was pre-determined to be somewhere between Mach 0.8 and Mach 1.5. Using the above formulae, we can determine annular area and required blade span. The density of the air was taken the same as after compressor as it would be the density at which the maximum force would be experienced. Hence, any alterations in air density, as long as below this level remains valid. A blade span of 63 mm was selected as it was sufficient in length, and ideal for the conditions it works under. The blades for the low-pressure turbine are generally small and are driven by the high velocity air, requiring a small blade span for any annular area (refer Table 4.4).

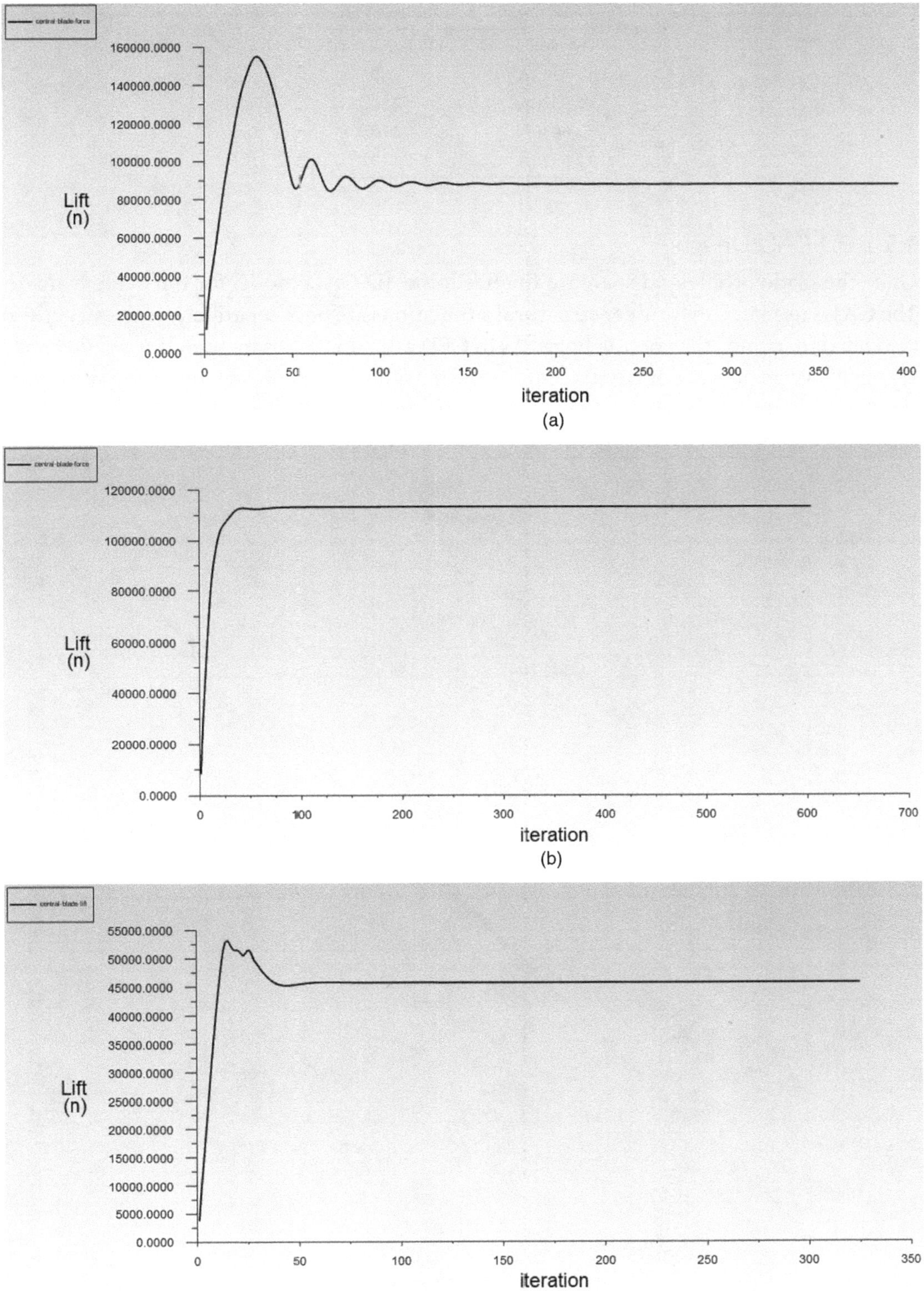

FIGURE 4.20 Lift Plot: (a) C-4245A, (b) C-6030A, (c) C-6520A.

TABLE 4.3 Aerofoil Lift Force

Aerofoil	Lift Force (KN)
C-4245A	87
C-5520A	130
C-6030A	110
C-6520A	120

4.5.4 3D CAD Design

Once the blade profile and span are finalized, the 3D CAD model for the blade is made. The CADs used in CFD and for structural simulations are built separately, as the structural CAD had to include the cooling holes. As in CFD a 3D domain is meshed this would create extremely large number of circular edges which would cause many errors to pop up across the domain. End plates were added to the base and top of the blade to create a virtual air seal. This can be seen in the CAD for the rotor blade (refer Fig. 4.22).

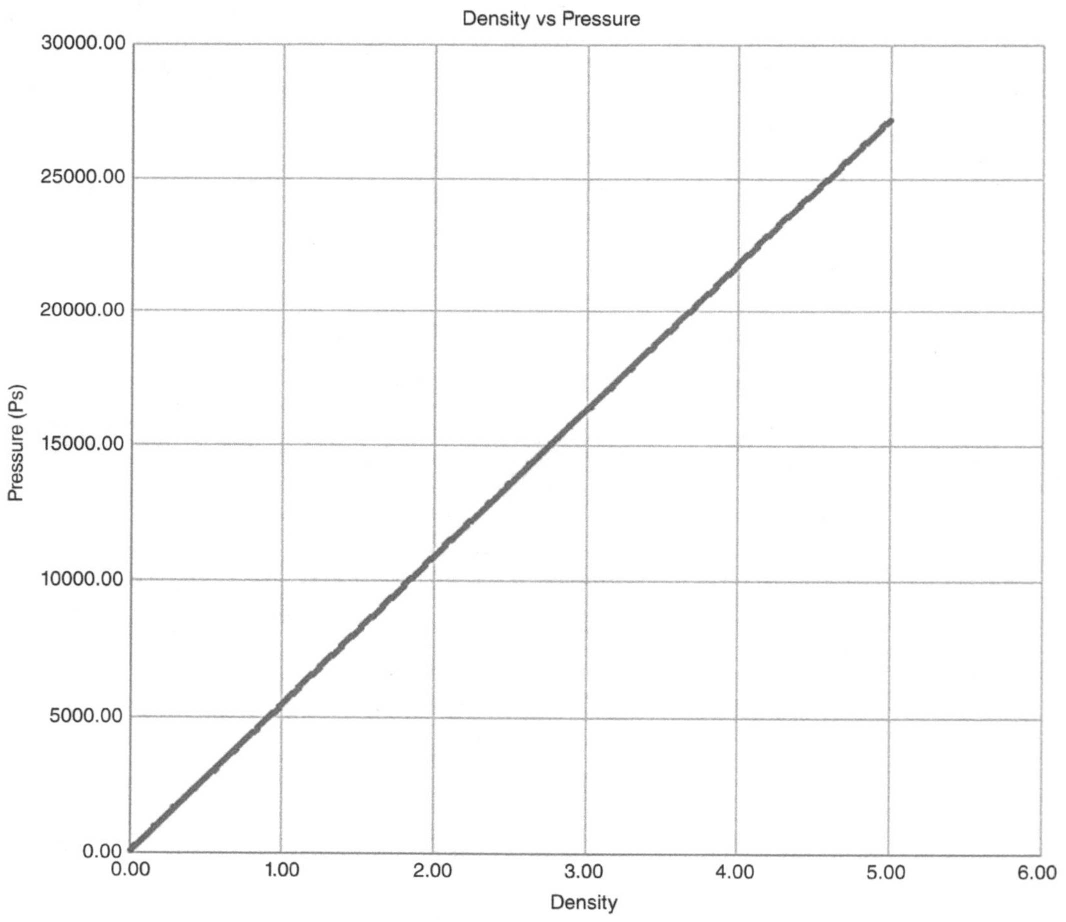

FIGURE 4.21 Density vs Pressure Plot.

TABLE 4.4 Blade Span Calculations

Mach Number	Annular Area	R1 (Root Radius)	R2 (Tip Radius)	Blade Span
0.8	0.091	0.050	0.175	0.125
		0.100	0.195	0.095
		0.150	0.225	0.075
		0.200	0.261	0.061
		0.25	0.300832	0.050832
		0.300	0.344	0.044
		0.350	0.388	0.038
		0.400	0.434	0.034
		0.450	0.480	0.030
		0.500	0.527	0.027
0.9	0.081	0.050	0.166	0.116
		0.100	0.187	0.087
		0.150	0.218	0.068
		0.200	0.255	0.055
		0.250	0.296	0.046
		0.300	0.339	0.039
		0.350	0.384	0.034
		0.400	0.430	0.030
		0.450	0.477	0.027
		0.500	0.524	0.024
0.95	0.077	0.050	0.163	0.113
		0.100	0.184	0.084
		0.150	0.216	0.066
		0.200	0.253	0.053
		0.250	0.294	0.044
		0.300	0.338	0.038
		0.350	0.383	0.033
		0.400	0.429	0.029
		0.450	0.476	0.026
		0.500	0.523	0.023
1	0.073	0.050	0.160	0.000
		0.100	0.182	0.082
		0.150	0.213	0.063
		0.200	0.251	0.051
		0.250	0.292	0.042
		0.300	0.336	0.036
		0.350	0.381	0.031
		0.400	0.428	0.028
		0.450	0.475	0.025
		0.500	0.522	0.022
1.1	0.066	0.050	0.153	0.103
		0.100	0.176	0.076
		0.150	0.209	0.059
		0.200	0.247	0.047
		0.250	0.289	0.039

(Continued)

TABLE 4.4 Blade Span Calculations *(Continued)*

Mach Number	Annular Area	R1 (Root Radius)	R2 (Tip Radius)	Blade Span
		0.300	0.333	0.033
		0.350	0.379	0.029
		0.400	0.425	0.025
		0.450	0.473	0.023
		0.500	0.521	0.021
1.25	0.058	0.050	0.143	0.093
		0.100	0.167	0.067
		0.150	0.201	0.051
		0.200	0.241	0.041
		0.250	0.284	0.034
		0.300	0.329	0.029
		0.350	0.375	0.025
		0.400	0.422	0.022
		0.450	0.470	0.020
		0.500	0.518	0.018
1.5	0.049	0.050	0.211	0.161
		0.100	0.228	0.128
		0.15	0.253969	0.103969
		0.200	0.286	0.086
		0.250	0.323	0.073
		0.300	0.363	0.063
		0.350	0.406	0.056
		0.400	0.449	0.049
		0.450	0.494	0.044
		0.500	0.540	0.040

The stator was kept the same span as the rotor for simplicity. Just like the 2D simulations, the first iteration 3D CAD was created with three stator rotor pairs to better simulate the effect of adjacent blades on a central blade. The blade spacing also remained consistent with the 2D simulation done before. The first iteration of this was the blades in a straight

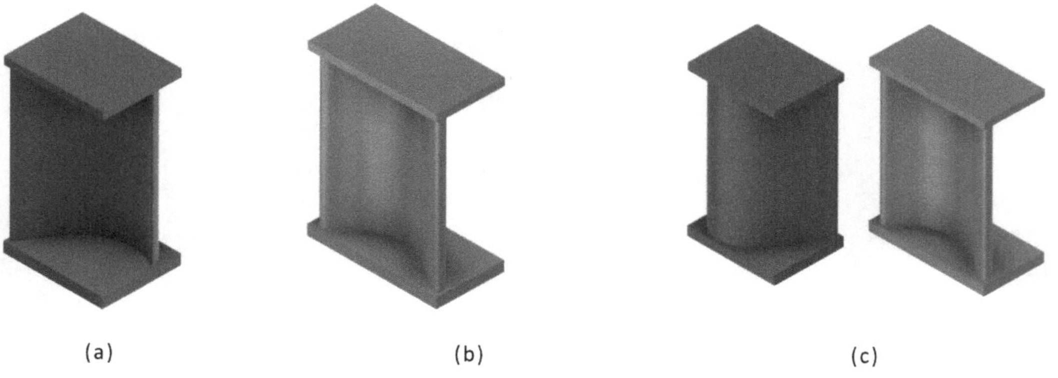

FIGURE 4.22 3D CAD: (a) Stator, (b) Rotor, (c) Stator Rotor Pair.

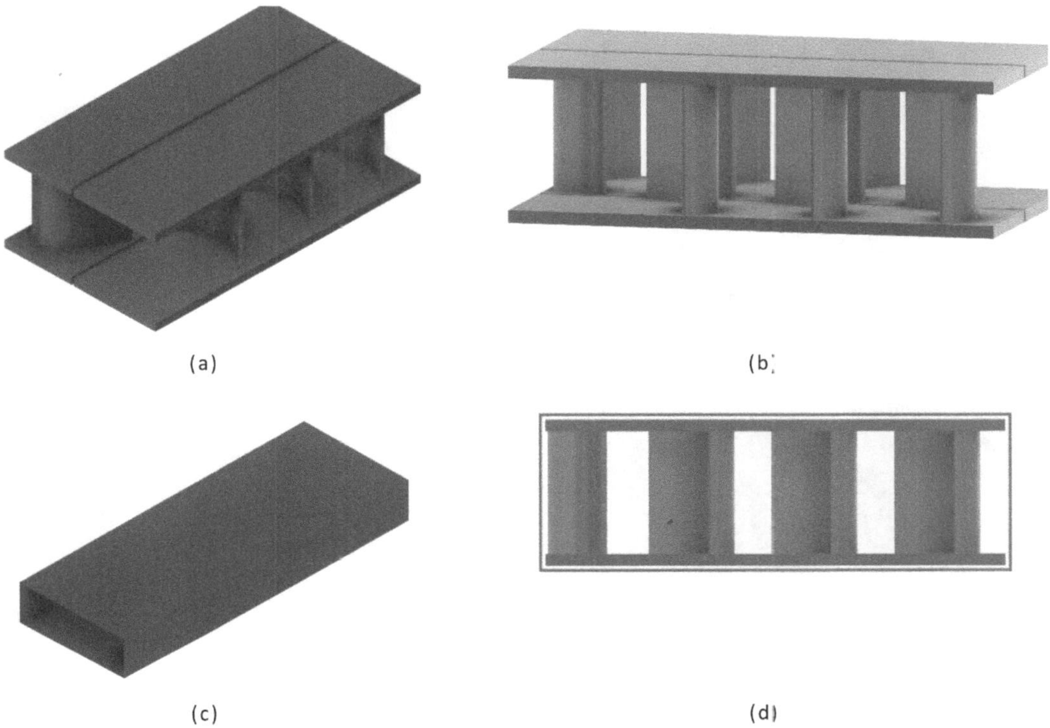

FIGURE 4.23 C-5520A in Line CAD: (a) Iso, (b) Skewed Front View, (c) Enclosure Iso, (d) Front View with Enclosure.

line. The spacing between the stator and rotor blade was kept 5 mm. A rectangle enclosure was made for the rotor blades (refer Fig. 4.23).

As one can imagine, the blades of an actual turbine engine are not in a straight line, they are placed in a circular fashion around the core. As such, the second CAD generated was for more accurate results. The three pairs of stator and rotor blades were placed around a central point 0.150 m from the central root of the rotor blade.

The stator and rotor blades were also offset so as to achieve an inlet angle of 20°. An unforeseen consequence of having the blades along a circular path is that the inlet angle is now a 3D angle, meaning there is an additional component which neither can be avoided nor changed. It should be kept in mind that as the blades move, the inlet angle will vary in a range between 0° and 20°. 20° is the set optimal inlet angle for the design (refer Fig. 4.24).

The final CAD to be prepared for the first iteration design was the one for the structural simulations. This would have to be a detailed CAD with the cooling holes to be preplaced, as they would be points for stress concentration in the simulations (refer Fig. 4.25).

4.5.5 CFD Simulations

Due to the geometry being complex, the meshing process would be intricate. 3D geometry, the ANSYS Mesher failed to mesh the bodies repeatedly due to insufficient

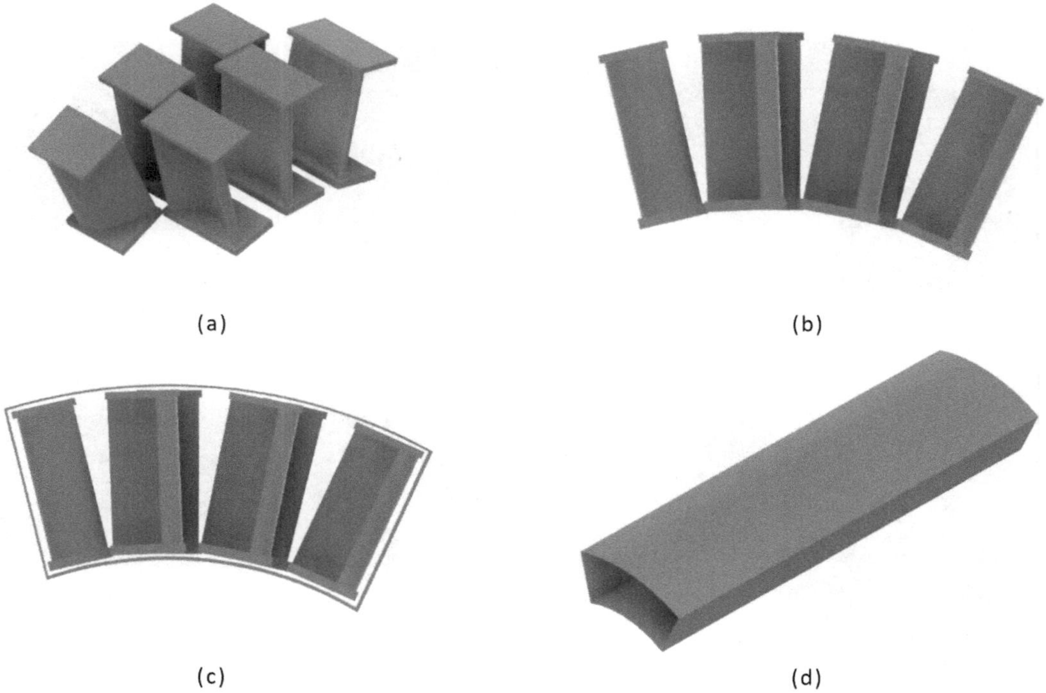

FIGURE 4.24 C-5520A Blades about Axis: (a) Isometric View of Blades, (b) Front View Blades, (c) Front View with Enclosure, (d) Isometric View with Enclosure.

processing power. As such, an alternative to do 3D simulation software was required. SIMSCALE, a cloud-based simulation software, was chosen. As the processing of the simulation was outsourced, this meant that multiple simulations could be handled simultaneously, which would come in handy considering the time frame of the work. As the enclosure was built before hand as it was not always a Cuboidal enclosure,

FIGURE 4.25 C-5520A Structural CAD: (a) Front View (b) Isometric View.

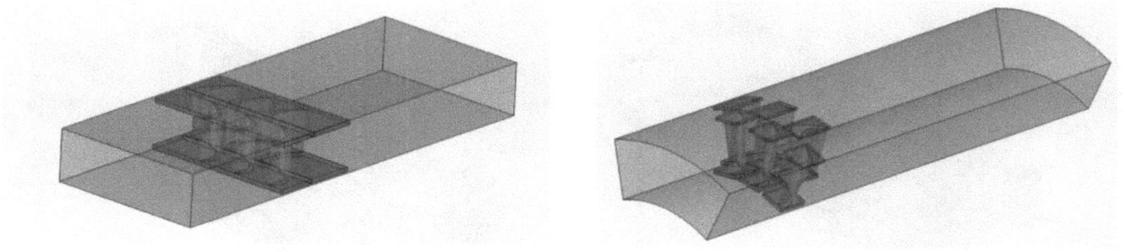

FIGURE 4.26 Inline Blade Configuration Enclosure and Circular Blade Configuration Enclosure.

volume extraction was done on both the inline and circular simulation setups (refer Fig. 4.25 and Fig. 4.26).

The simulation parameters for all the simulations were kept constant. The mesh settings also for the most part was kept constant; however, if there is any change in the settings it is mentioned wherever required (refer Fig. 4.27 and Fig. 4.28).

Mesh settings:

1. Hex dominant meshing algorithm used
2. Fine mesh applied
3. Surface refinement on central stator and rotor blade: 2–5 mm applied.

Obtained mesh statistics:

1. For the inline configuration:
2. For circular configuration:
    a. Cell count: 12.4 million cells
    b. Node count: 14.7 million nodes

The mesh was of acceptable standard as the average skewness was about 0.075, average non-orthogonality was 6.07 and average volume ratio for the mesh was 1.88. Meaning the mesh was good enough to proceed to the next stage.

For both configurations, a K-omega shear stress transport (SST) model was used. This model switches between the K-epsilon and K-omega models based on a proximity system. K-omega is better for flows near obstructions, while as K-epsilon is better to simulate flows away from a surface. Hence, the K-omega model would yield better results in a far field setup to observe the flow as was the case with the current simulations.

The air properties were kept as discussed with a density of 3.57 kg/m^3, and kinematic viscosity of 2.922e-4 m^2/s. The expected boundary conditions were assigned to the domain, i.e., velocity inlet, pressure outlet and walls with no slip conditions on the top and bottom walls of the enclosure. The lift force was calculated on the body as it

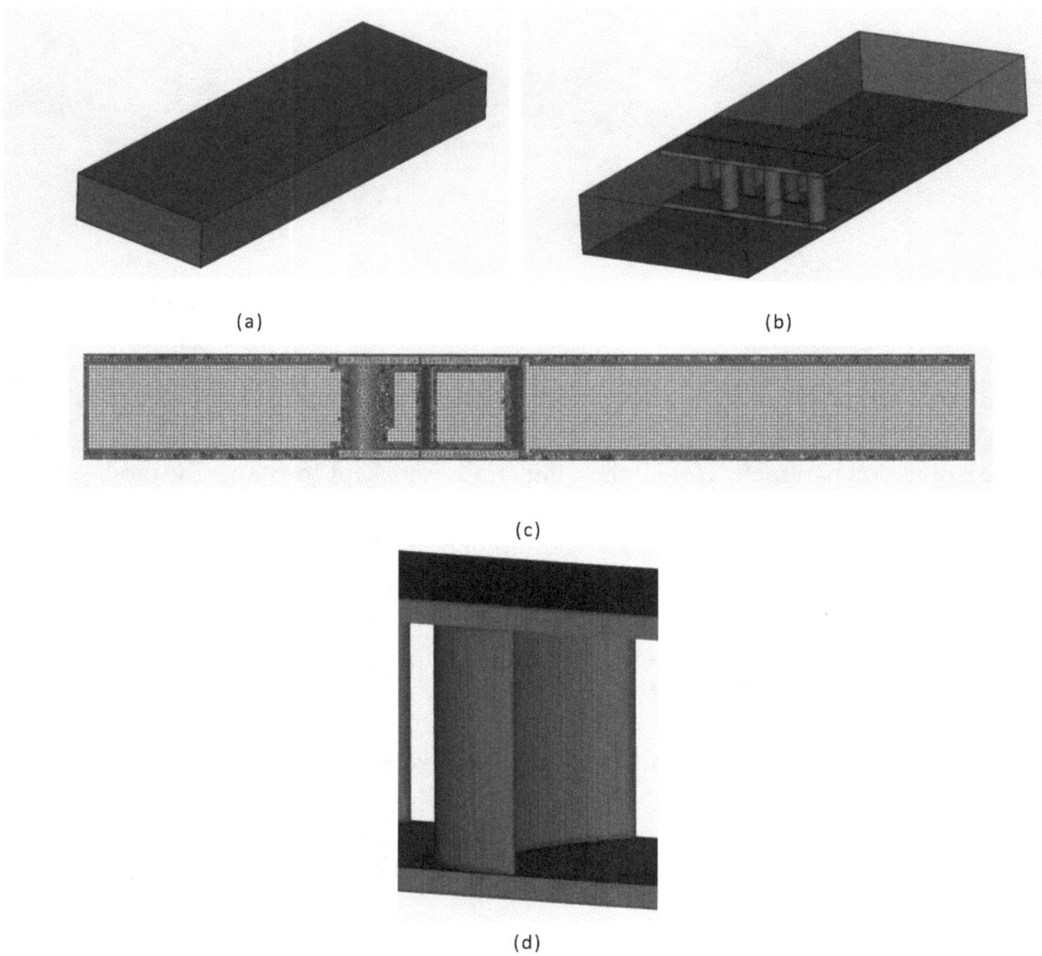

FIGURE 4.27 Inline Configuration Mesh: (a) Iso, (b) Iso Internal, (c) Mesh Clip of Domain, (d) Close Up of Blade.

was the most important result required. Both simulations were set to run for a thousand iterations.

For the results, firstly the inline configuration is shown in Fig. 4.29.

At the end of the 1000 iterations the lift force came to be 9778.59 N and drag came out to be 786.122 N respectively. However, it must be kept in mind that this is in an inline configuration, meaning the inlet angle is actually 20°. In actuality, in a circular setup this force would drop due to angle actually being a 3D angle approximation of 20°.

The pressure and velocity contour provided below give us a better idea so as to how and in which direction the force is being applied. It is clear that the fluid is generating the pressure differential in the correct direction. Where the fluid velocity is more the pressure drops, which is in accordance with Bernoulli's principle. The drag force is mainly coming into picture due to the high-pressure zone evident on the leading edge of the central blade

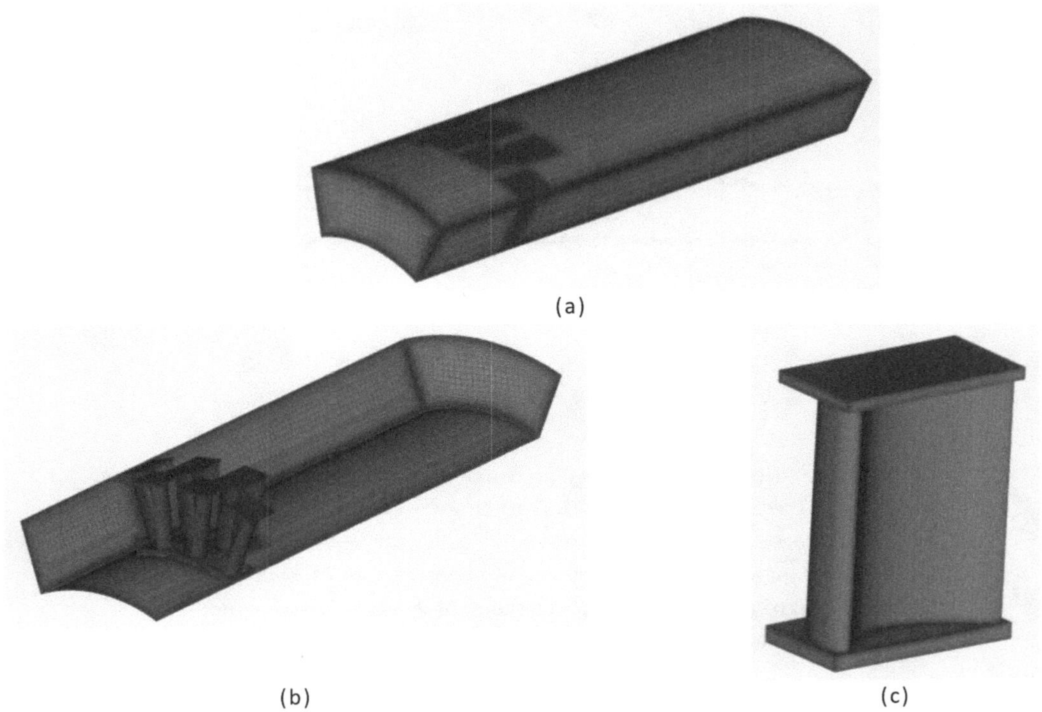

FIGURE 4.28 Circular Configuration Mesh: (a) Iso, (b) Iso Internal, (c) Close Up of Blade.

in the pressure contour; however, that cannot be avoided as such and the drag force itself is negligible, hence it is but a minor inconvenience (refer Fig. 4.30).

As mentioned before for a more accurate representation of the actual turbine a circular configuration was prepared. The simulation is done under identical conditions as the inline configuration. The results of the circular configuration are presented in Fig. 4.31 and Fig. 4.32.

The lift force for the circular configuration is reduced as expected. It came to be 8507.719 N with a drag component of 1605.062 N. As expected, the circular offset has resulted a reduction in lift force whilst a marginal increase in drag. However, a force of approximately 8500 N on 60 mm blade is very high, causing thermal and rotational stresses to be felt at high level. This is to be kept in mind whilst developing the next iteration design.

Just as before, the high-pressure region below the central blade can be observed. The pressure contour also shows a bit of flow interference on the leading edge, as the 3D angle is not exactly 20° but a close approximation, this is to be expected.

4.5.5.1 Structural Simulation

Structural simulations were carried out in ANSYS static structural system. The geometry was modeled in solid works and imported to the SpaceClaim Platform (refer Fig. 4.33).

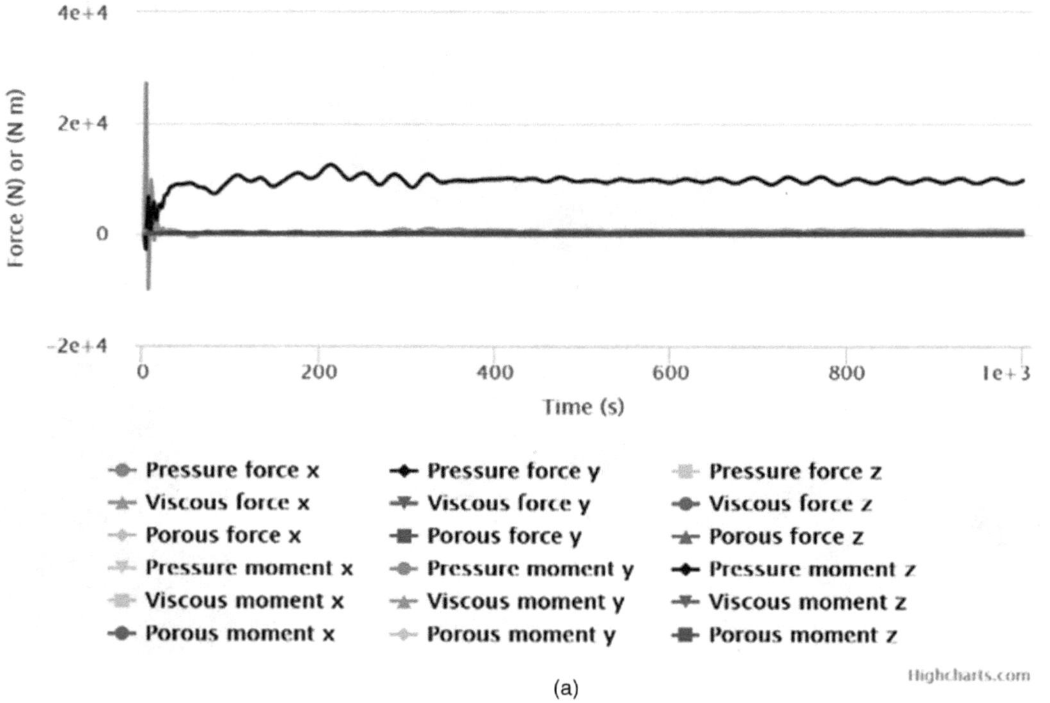

(a)

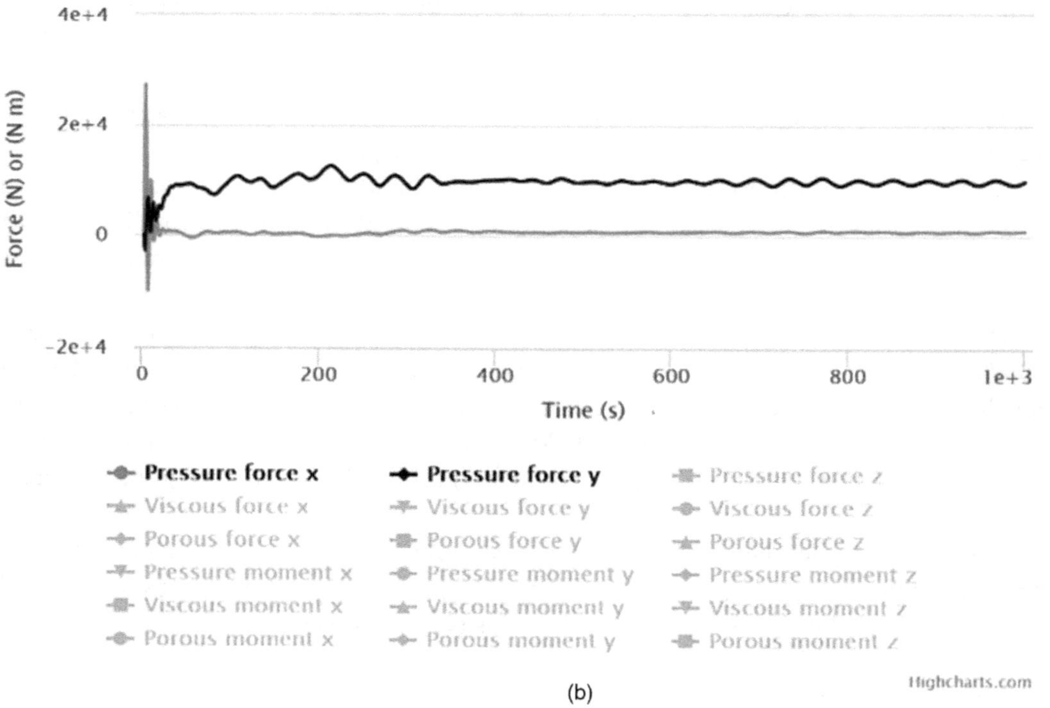

(b)

FIGURE 4.29 Inline Configuration Forces: (a) All Forces, (b) Lift [y] and Drag [x] Isolated.

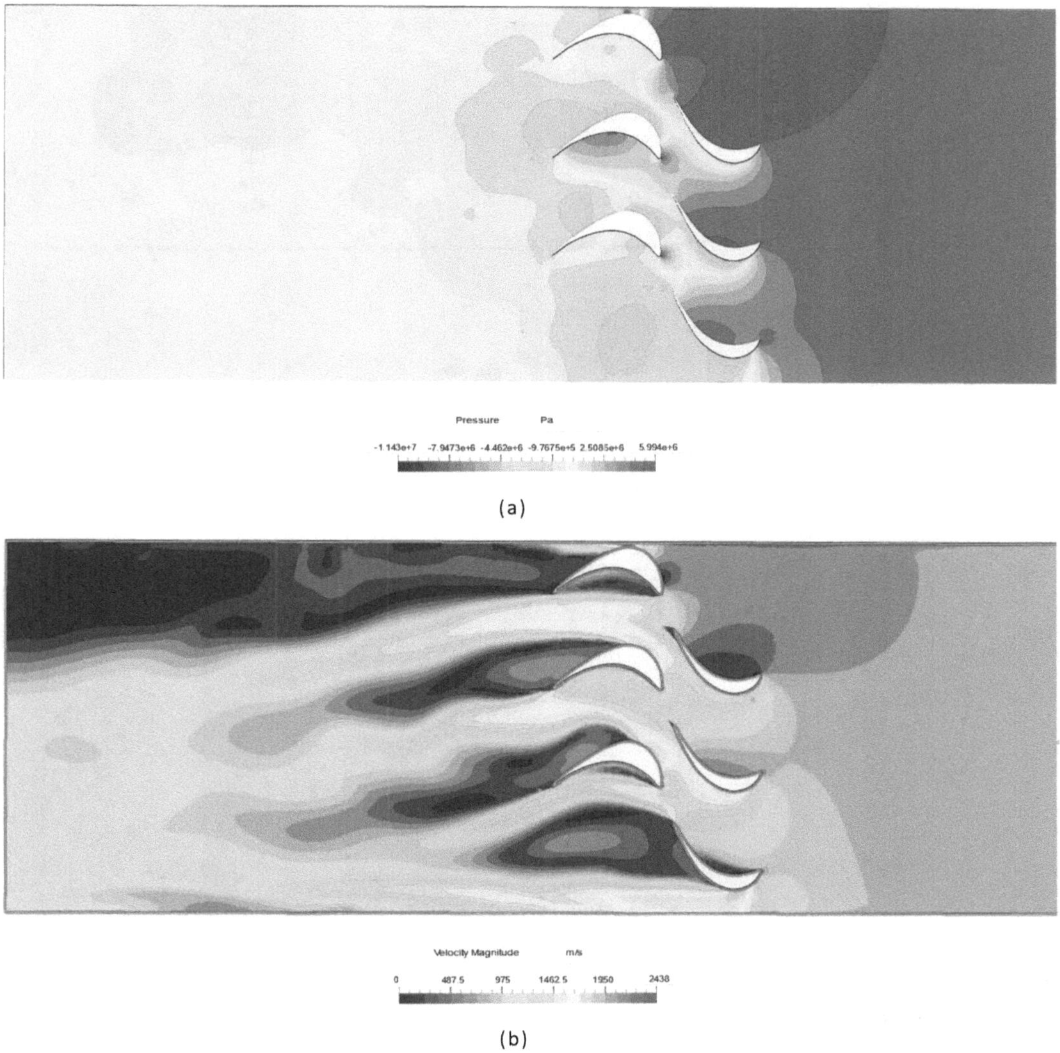

FIGURE 4.30 Inline Configuration Contours: (a) Velocity, (b) Pressure.

The body contained the required cooling holes, as well as the parallel cooling channels. Which can be seen in the cross section provided. Meshing (refer to Fig. 4.34) was done using the ANSYS Mesher with the following settings:

1. Mesh element size: 0.5 mm
2. Face meshing applied of flat surfaces
3. Refinement level 2 applied on blade surface
4. Mesh defeaturing on

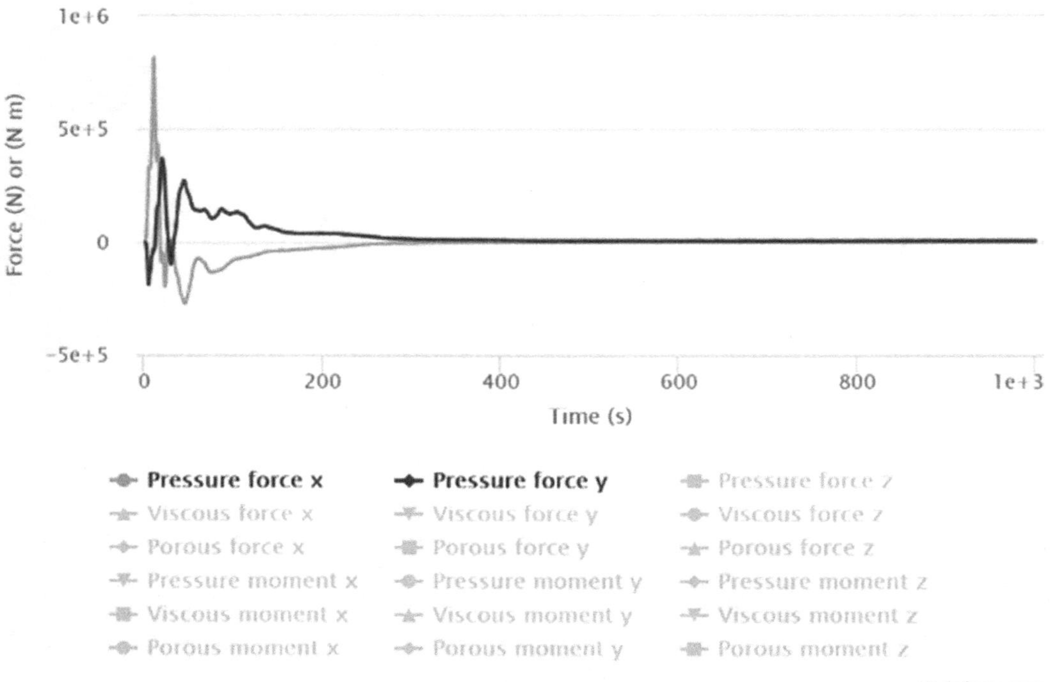

(a)

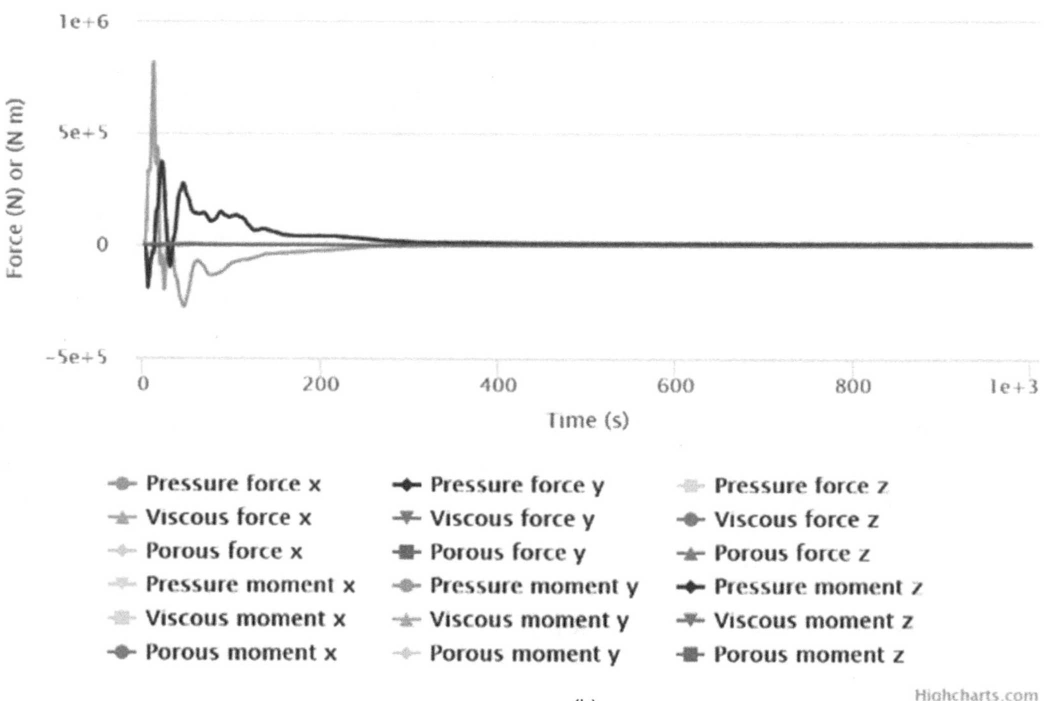

(b)

FIGURE 4.31 Circular Configuration Forces: (a) All Forces, (b) Lift [y] and Drag [x] Isolated.

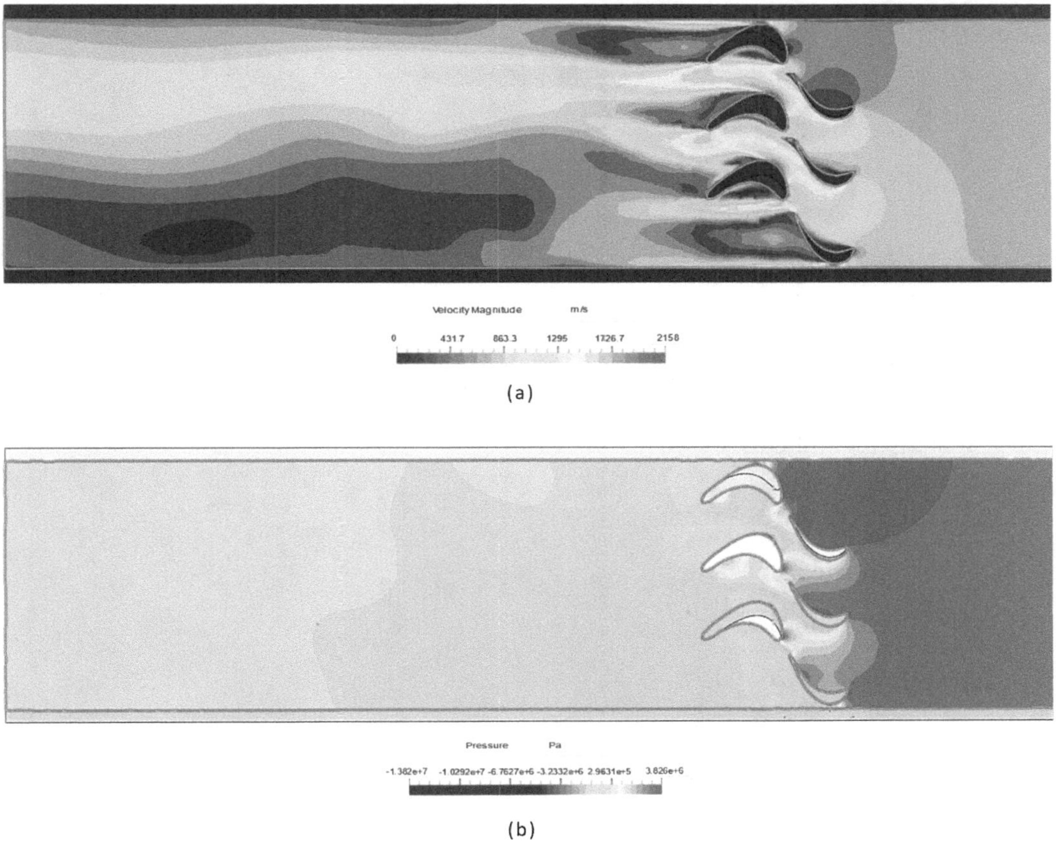

FIGURE 4.32 Circular Configuration Contours: (a) Velocity, (b) Pressure.

FIGURE 4.33 Structural Simulation Geometry: (a) Iso, (b) Cross Section.

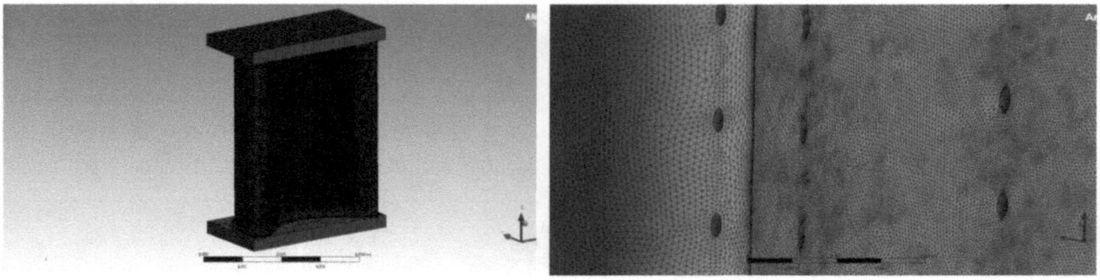

(a) (b)

FIGURE 4.34 Structural Blade Mesh: (a) Iso, (b) Close-up.

Mesh Statistics and Quality

1. Cell count: 3082810 elements
2. Node count: 4585362 nodes
3. Max aspect ratio: 5.72
4. Max skewness: 0.25
5. Max element quality: 0.85

It was meshed really fine so as to ensure better accuracy.

4.5.5.2 Material Selection

With the advancement of the technology in the aerospace industry, more powerful gas turbines have been developed, which in turn led to the need of high temperature resistant materials, for high load applications (Mouritz, 2012). Unfortunately, higher thrust figures also meant higher exhaust gas temperatures. Nickel-based superalloys have been used in the aerospace industry for a long time now, because of its high strength and long fatigue life combined with good resistance to oxidation and corrosion at high temperature. This superalloy is the material of choice for the hottest engine components that are required to operate above 800°C. Without doubt, one of the most remarkable properties of nickel superalloys that is utilized in jet engines is their outstanding resistance against creep and stress rupture at high temperature. Most materials experience rapid creep at temperatures of 30–40% of their melting temperature. For example, aluminium and titanium alloys, which are used in the cooler regions of jet engines, creep rapidly above 150 and 350°C, respectively. Nickel superalloys resist creep so well that they can be used at 850°C, which is over 70% of their melting temperature. Compared with the materials used in aircraft structures, aluminium, titanium and magnesium alloys, the stress rupture strength of nickel-based alloys is outstanding.

For the engine selected in our thesis dependent on its application, the exhaust gas temperature ranges between 1200°C and 1700°C/1800°C. For this particular application, according to the research conducted, Inconel 718 proved to be a more than sufficient material.

The following boundary conditions were assigned to the body.

1. Fixed support on lower base.
2. Force of 1.15×10^5 N applied on the top face to simulate centrifugal load.
3. Hydrostatic force applied to the blade surface with a resultant 514.5 m/s^2 of acceleration at an incident angle of 20° to the blade.

After simulation, it was observed that the blade yielded a maximum deformation of 1 mm on the end plate corner, with a few stress points around the joining of the blade. This yielded a factor of safety below 1, meaning the body was failing. As expected, this is not acceptable and rectifications needed to be made, which are covered in a later section. The holes were another aspect of concern; however, after simulation it was clear that the stress generated on the holes was not causing any failure (Zhang et al., 2021). The results of the simulation are presented in Fig. 4.35 and Fig. 4.36.

4.5.5.3 Corrective Measures

As a result of the failure in structural simulations, corrective measures had to be taken. As such the blade thickness was increased from 1.5 mm to 2 mm, and some changes were also made in the simulation parameters to better express the conditions the blade experienced. A rough mount was also created to assign as fixed support during the simulation. The internal cooling channels were left as is, as simulating a solid blade would obviously yield wrong results. The hole diameter was also left unchanged at 0.7 mm. The following mesh settings were used:

1. Default element size – 2 mm
2. Face meshing applied to flat faces.
3. Face sizing of 1 mm applied to the end plates.
4. Face sizing of 0.2 mm applied to the blade faces.

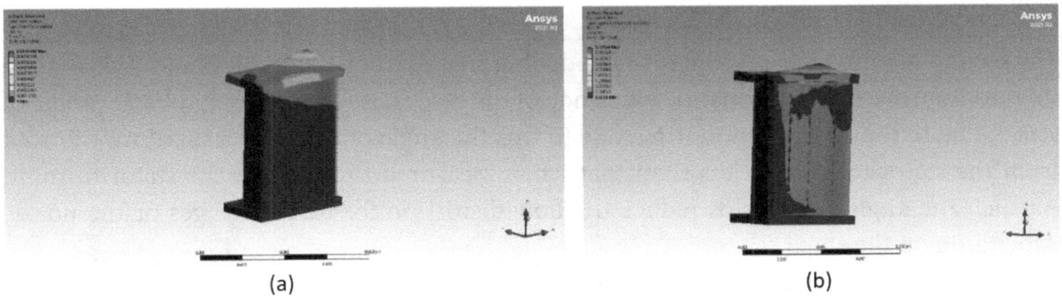

FIGURE 4.35 Simulation Results: (a) Total Deformation, (b) Equivalent Stress.

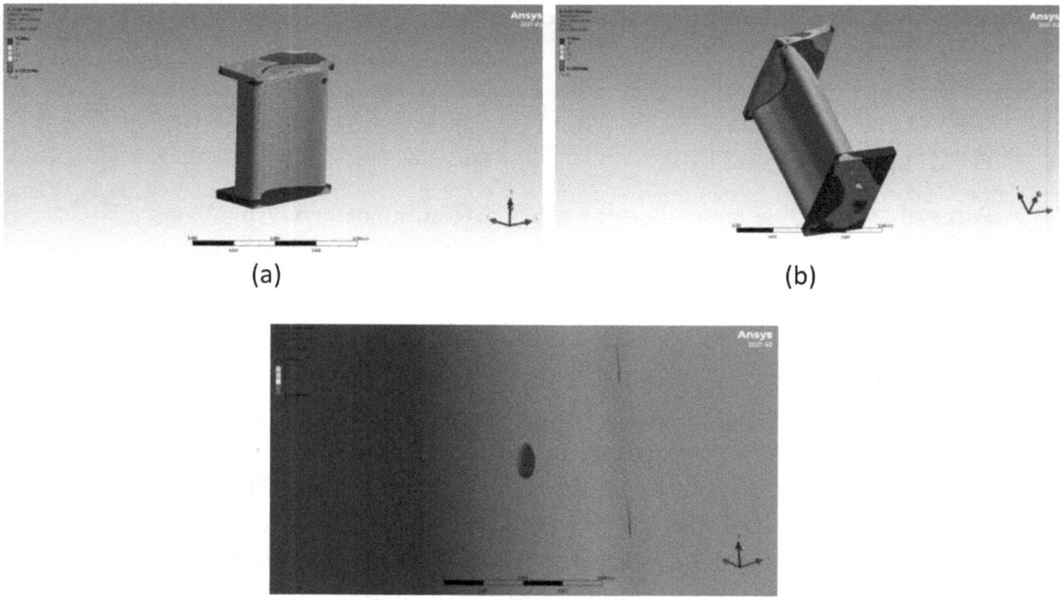

(a) (b) (c)

FIGURE 4.36 Factor of Safety: (a) Iso, (b) Edge Failure, (c) Close Up of Cooling Hole.

As mentioned before to better simulate the blade condition, changes were made to the simulation parameters. Mainly, the force applied on the top face was removed. Instead, rotational velocity boundary condition was assigned to the body, and the peak rpm of the turbine was taken for the value of rotational velocity. The fixed support was given on the mount faces instead of being placed directly on the endplate. This resulted in better accuracy of any endplate deformation (refer Fig. 4.37 and Fig. 4.38).

As can be observed by the images above, the maximum deformation 0.12 mm, with a factor of safety above 1 on the blade, the design was hence passing the structural simulation. With this the first iteration design was considered to be concluded. The design was satisfactory with the given parameters and a base design to build upon was set.

4.6 SECOND ITERATION DESIGN

The second iteration design consists introducing an angle of twist to the blade. This is done so as to improve the aerodynamic efficiency of the blades. As the blades have a 3D angle of attack due to the circular mounting, due to this the angle of attack measured root to root from the stator to rotor is less than that when measured tip to tip of the stator to rotor. As such the angle twist helps reduce the flow distortion for further stages or the nozzle depending on the stage.

Determining the angle of twist and the point of twist is almost an impossible task. The number of parameters require an almost unexpected data collected over a period of years. Hit and trial method hence is the best way to proceed.

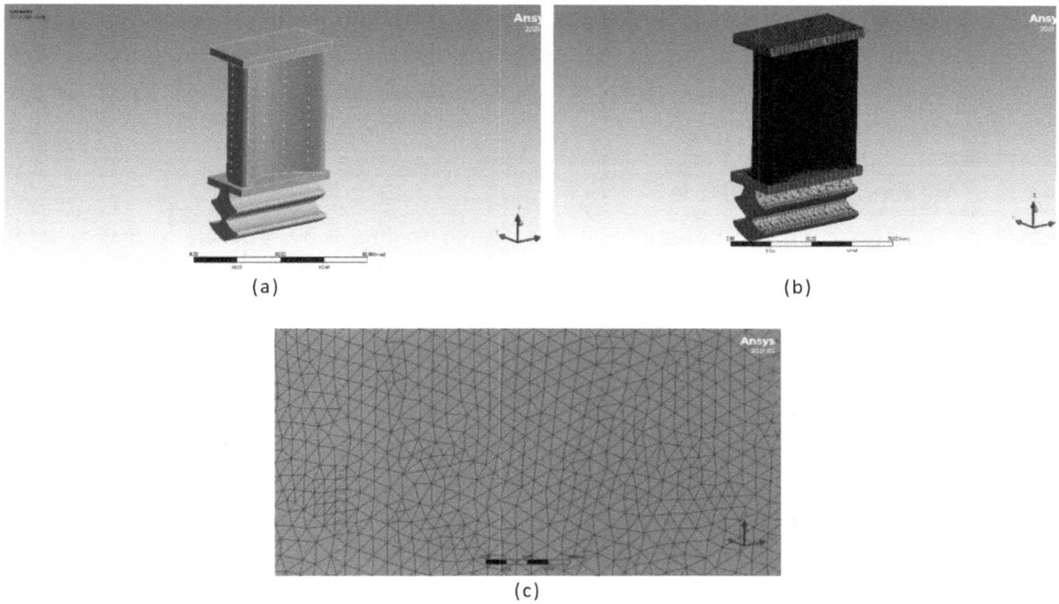

FIGURE 4.37 (a) Blade Geometry, (b) Mesh, (c) Close-Up of Mesh.

FIGURE 4.38 Corrective Simulation Results: (a) Total Deformation, (b) Equivalent Stress, (c) Factor of Safety.

The blade twist was chosen in increments of 5°. A max angle of twist was taken to be 25° either side. Positive twist was considered when the top element was rotationally offset downwards in top view, negative twist was considered when the top element was rotationally offset upwards.

4.6.1 CAD Design of the Blade

CAD designs for each individual twist are shown in Fig. 4.39. The blade was twisted about a point 3/4th the chord length of the blade projected on the cambered spline for the blade.

For the simulation the blades were again paired with the stators. The stators were the same as in the first iteration design. All of the CADs were simulated in the circular setup as mentioned in Section 5.4.

All the blades have identical enclosure and blade stator rotor offset to ensure that there is no other factor than the twist of the blade which can cause any increase or decrease in blade force (refer Fig. 4.40).

4.6.2 CFD and Selection of Twist Angle

As was done in Section 5.5, simulations were done under the same mesh conditions for all the blades to avoid any disparity in result. All aspects of the simulation were kept the same including the number of iterations so as to not cause any unwanted alterations to the results (refer Fig. 4.41).

Mesh settings:

1. Hex dominant meshing algorithm used
2. Fine mesh applied
3. Surface refinement on central stator and rotor blade: 2–5 mm applied.

The fluid property and other parameters were kept the same as the ones used for the straight blade. The K-Omega SST model was used. The final criterion for blade selection was the higher force obtained due to the blade twist. The next few pages contain the velocity, pressure contours along with force plots (refer Fig. 4.42–Fig. 4.51).

It can be seen from the results of the blades shown above, each blade was behaving as expected. The final selection of the blade was dependent on the lowest force reduction. The result of all the force plots is provided in Table 4.5.

The blade twist was taken to be –25°, as it resulted in minimal loss in mechanical effort on the blade. In reality, this would've been a base result, on which multiple parameters would've been varied to determine the perfect angle of twist; however, due to the time constraints this is not possible.

4.6.3 Second Iteration Structural Simulation

The structural CAD was also created with –25° twist. The holes on the blade were maintained at 30° from the vertical tangential line for each of the cooling channels.

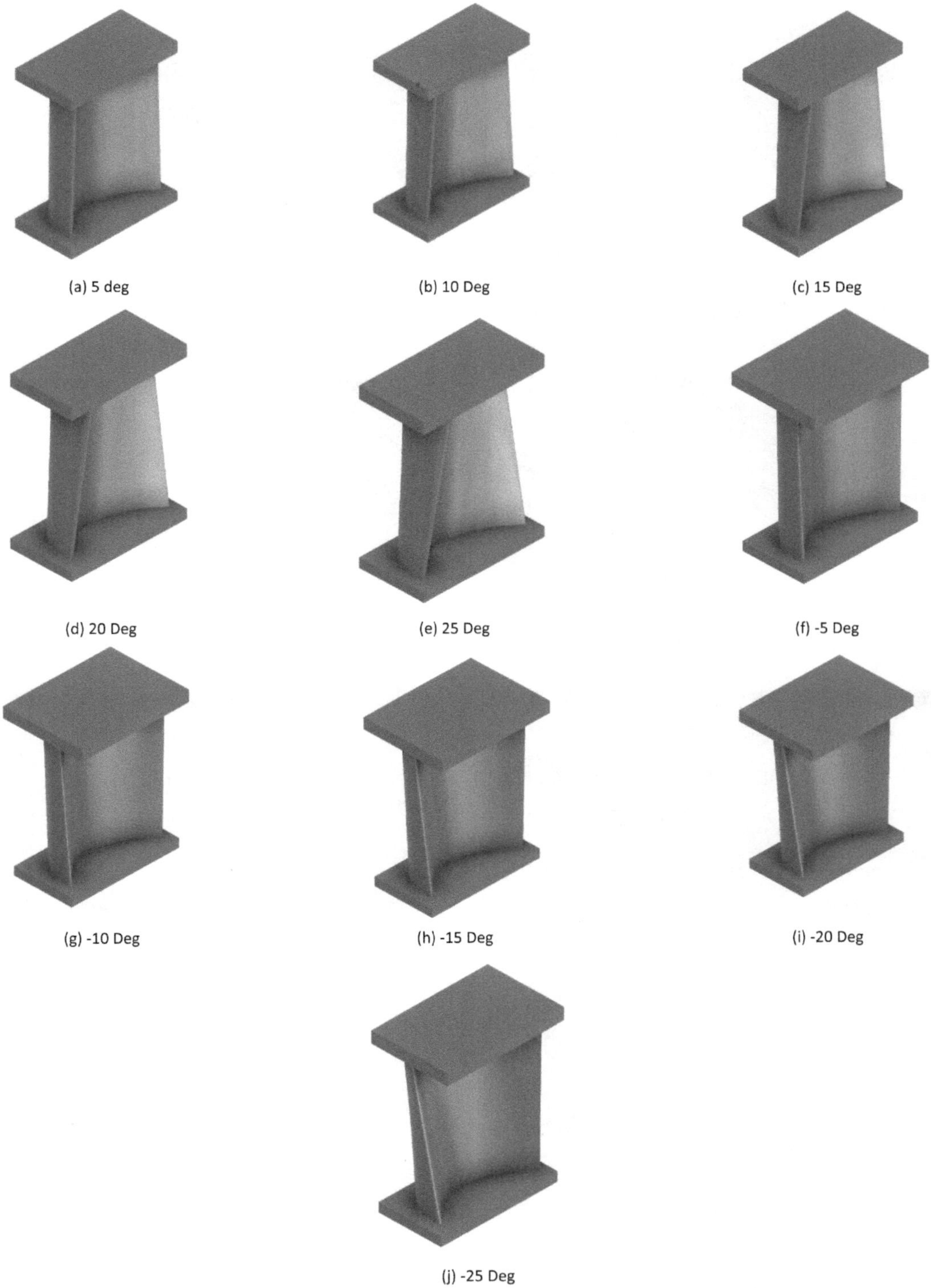

FIGURE 4.39 Twisted Blade CADs.

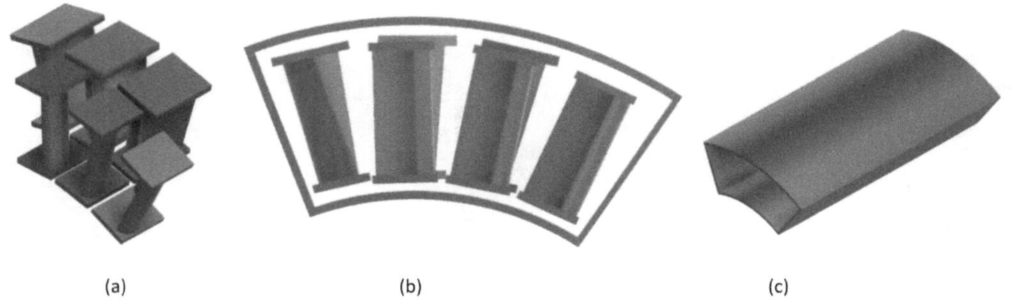

FIGURE 4.40 –15° Twist Blade CAD (a) Stator Rotor Pair Iso, (b) Enclosure FV, (c) Enclosure ISO.

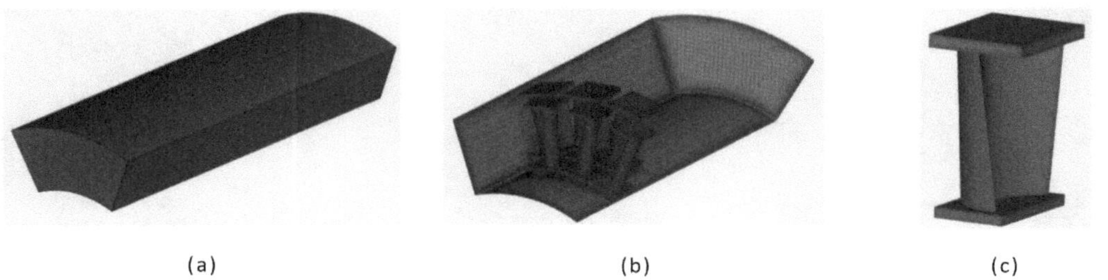

FIGURE 4.41 –25° Twist Mesh: (a) Enclosure Iso, (b) Internal Iso, (c) Blade.

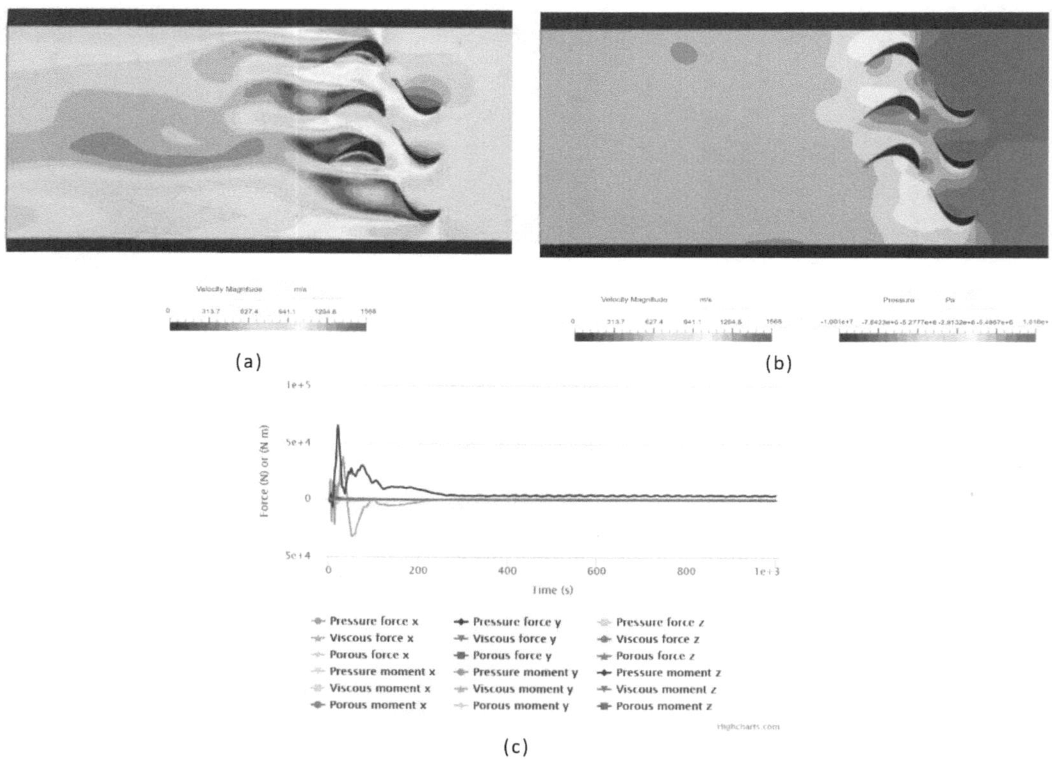

FIGURE 4.42 5° Twist: (a) Velocity Contour, (b) Pressure Contour, (c) Force Plot.

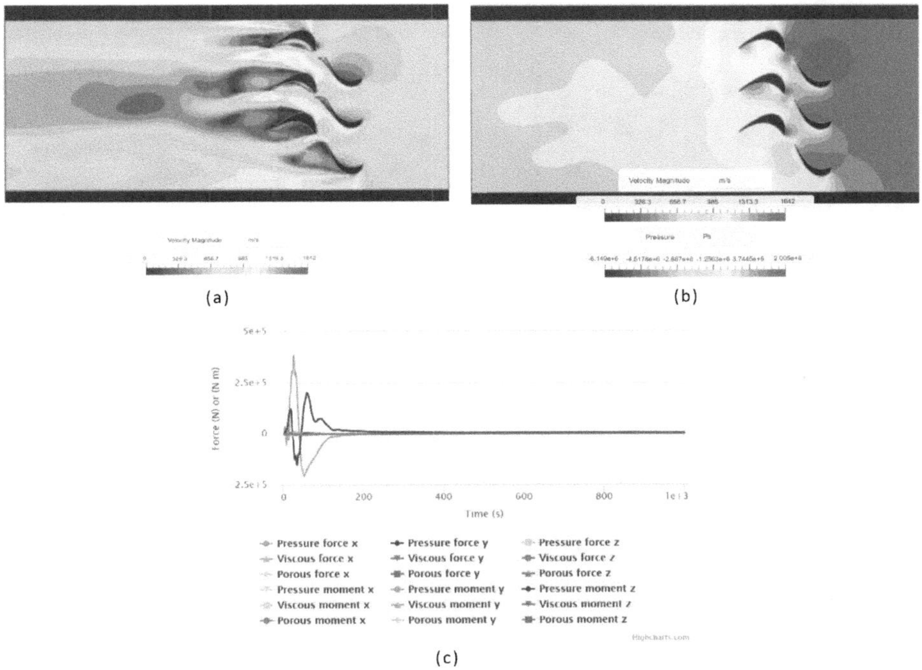

FIGURE 4.43 10° Twist: (a) Velocity Contour, (b) Pressure Contour, (c) Force Plot.

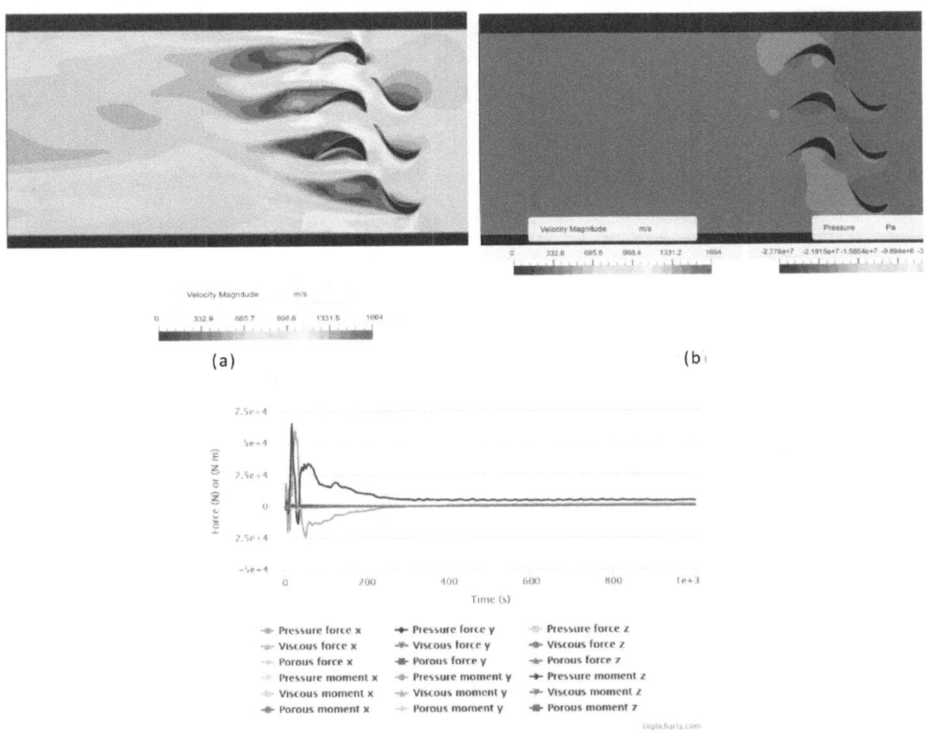

FIGURE 4.44 15° Twist: (a) Velocity Contour, (b) Pressure Contour, (c) Force Plot.

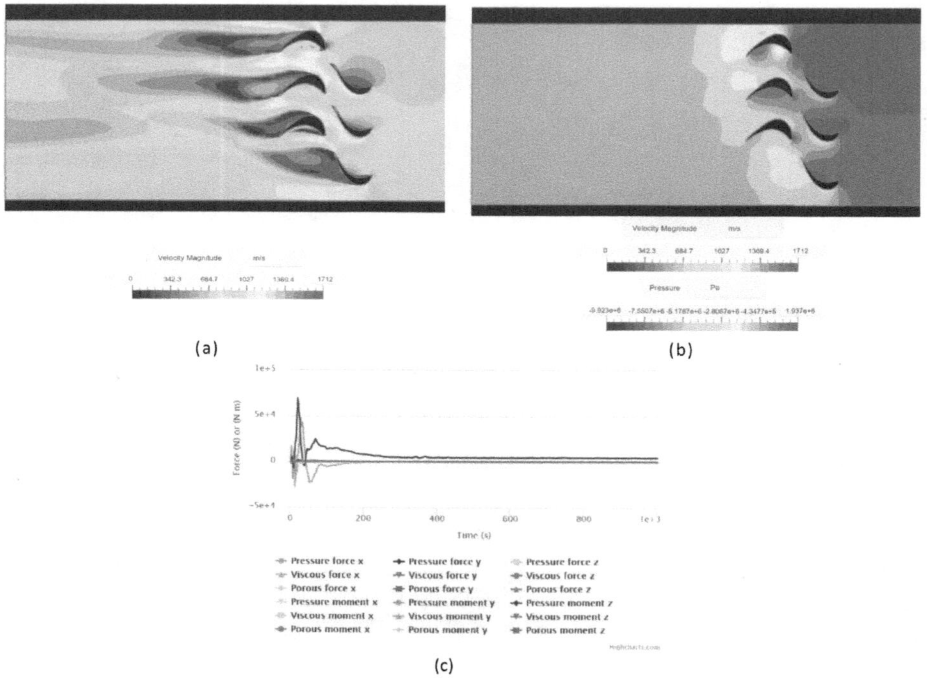

FIGURE 4.45 20° Twist: (a) Velocity Contour, (b) Pressure Contour, (c) Force Plot.

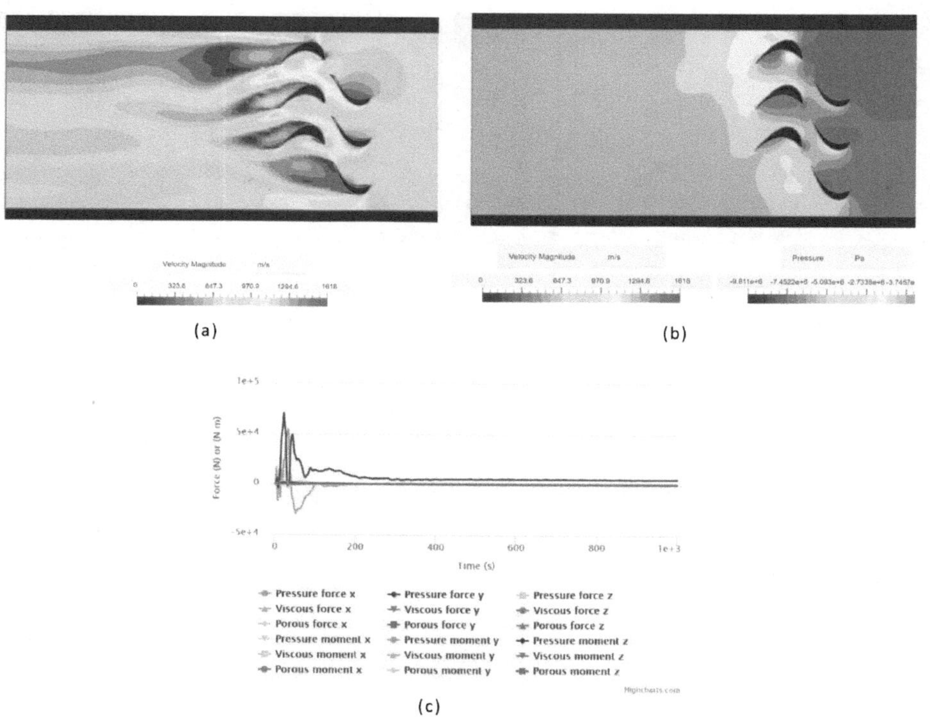

FIGURE 4.46 25° Twist: (a) Velocity Contour, (b) Pressure Contour, (c) Force Plot.

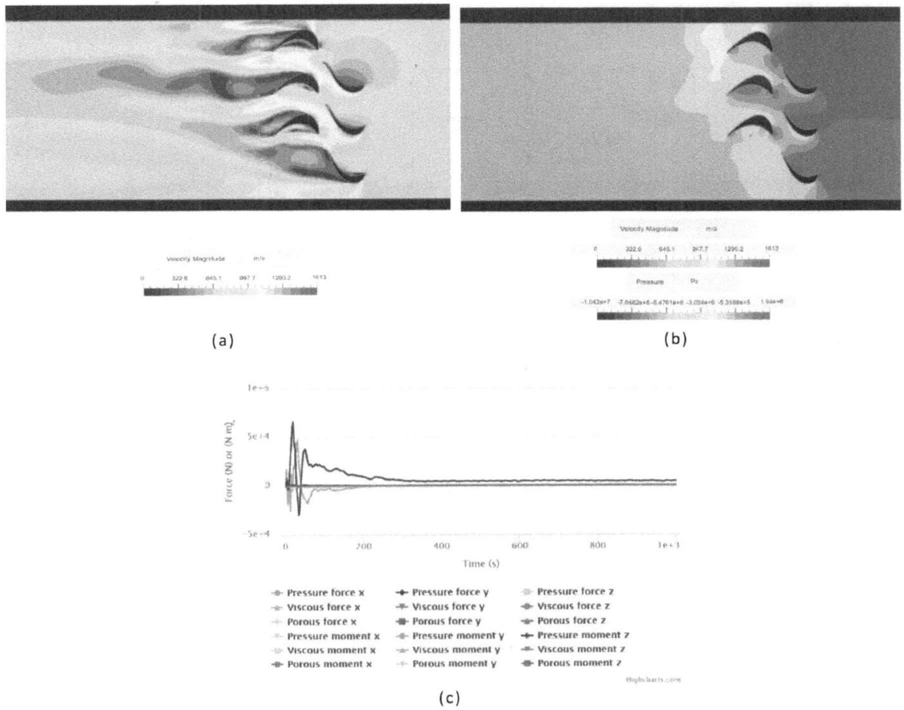

FIGURE 4.47 −5° Twist: (a) Velocity Contour, (b) Pressure Contour, (c) Force Plot.

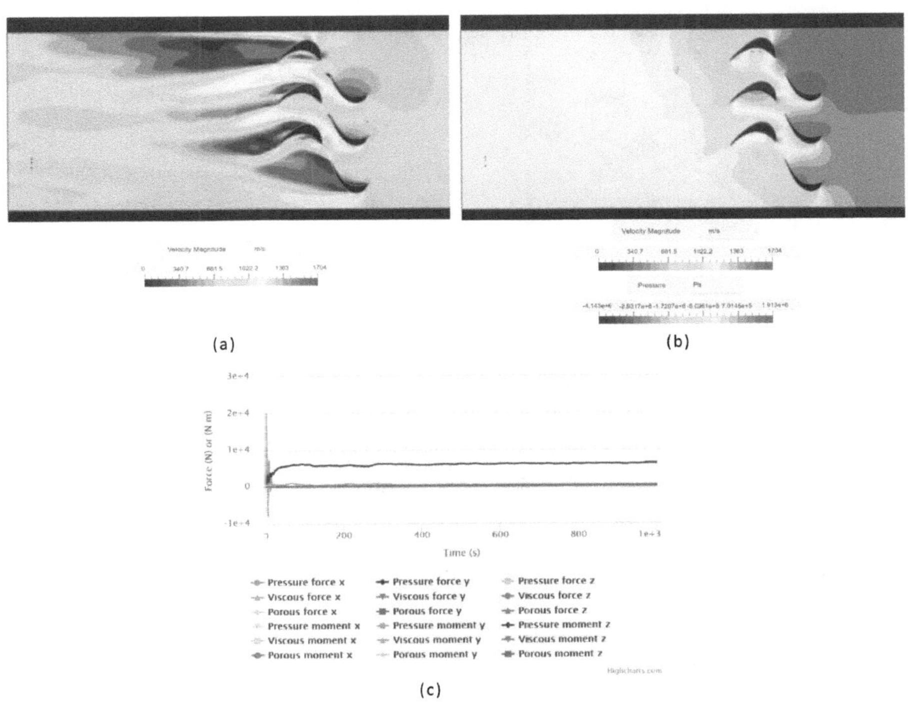

FIGURE 4.48 −10° Twist: (a) Velocity Contour, (b) Pressure Contour, (c) Force Plot.

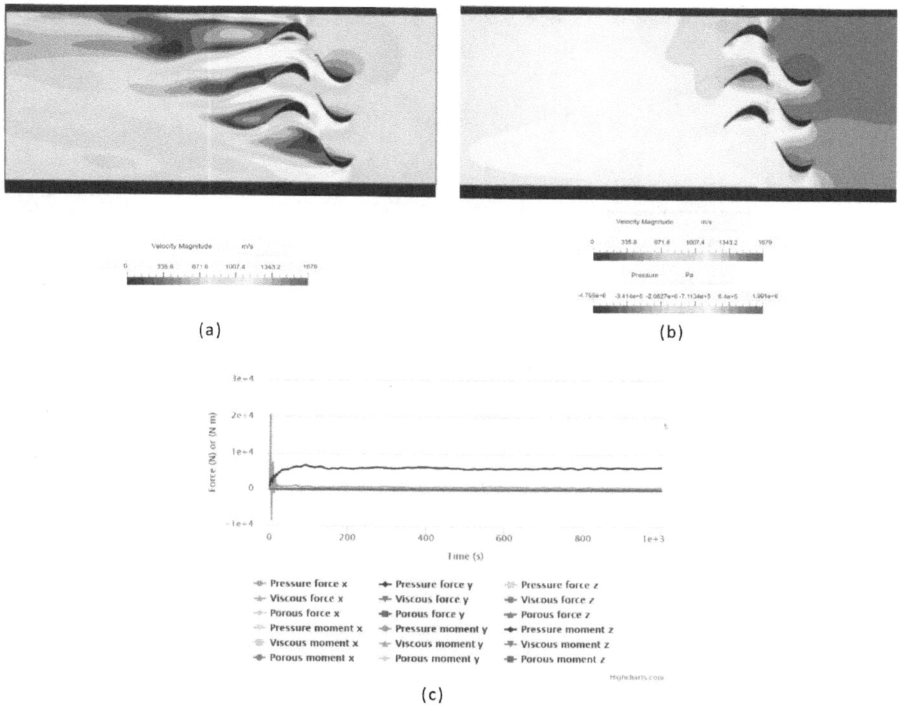

FIGURE 4.49 −15° Twist: (a) Velocity Contour, (b) Pressure Contour, (c) Force Plot.

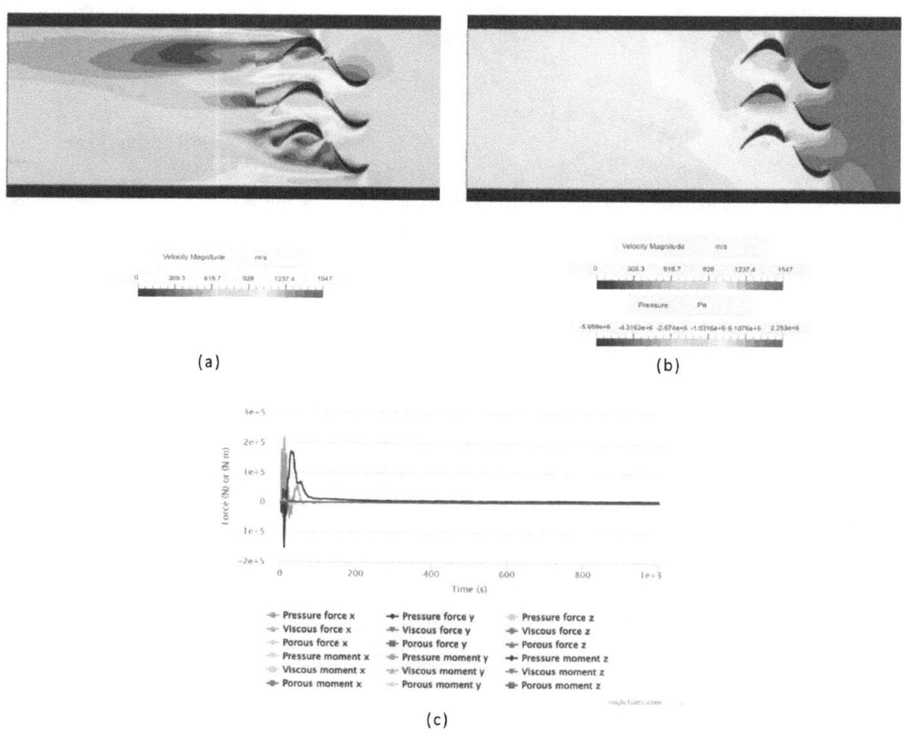

FIGURE 4.50 −20° Twist: (a) Velocity Contour, (b) Pressure Contour, (c) Force Plot.

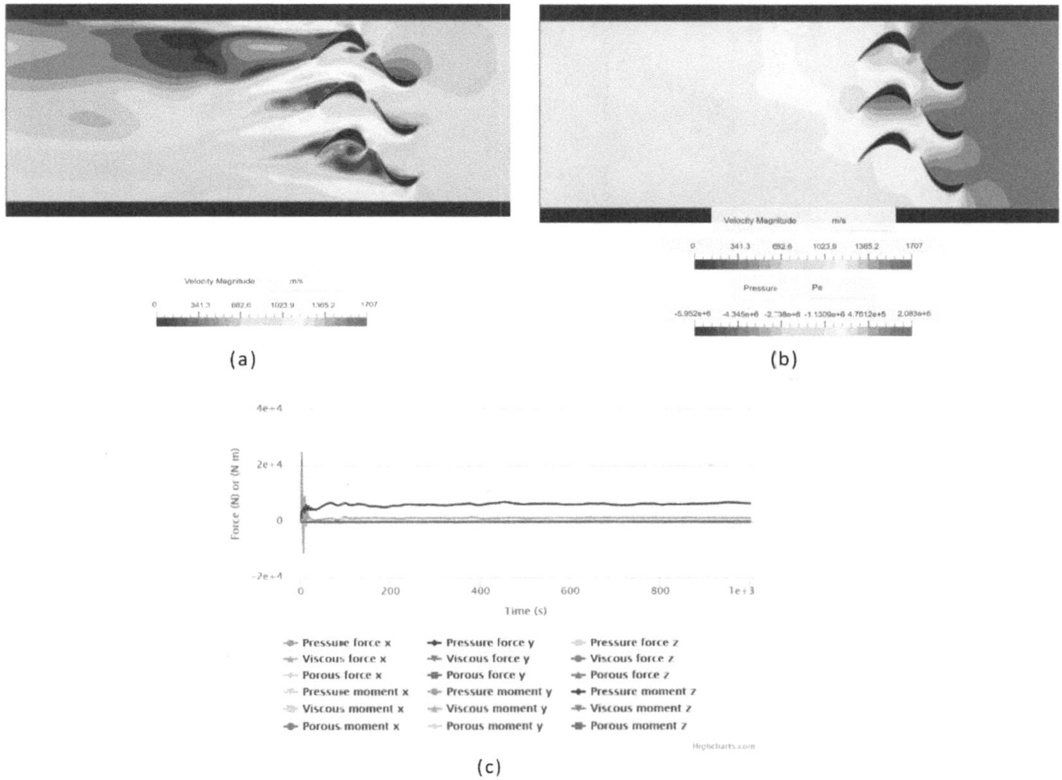

FIGURE 4.51 –25° Twist: (a) Velocity Contour, (b) Pressure Contour, (c) Force Plot.

The simulation parameters were identical to that of the straight blade simulation, along with the mesh parameters (refer Fig. 4.52–Fig. 4.54).

As a refresher, the following mesh settings were used:

1. Default element size – 2 *mm*
2. Face meshing applied to flat faces.
3. Face sizing of 1 mm applied to the end plates.
4. Face sizing of 0.2 mm applied to the blade faces.

TABLE 4.5 Twisted Blade Forces Tabulated

Blade Angle	**Force**	**Blade Angle**	**Force**
5	4345	–5	4766
10	4709	–10	6163
15	4063	–15	6260
20	4612	–20	5556
25	5258	–25	6511

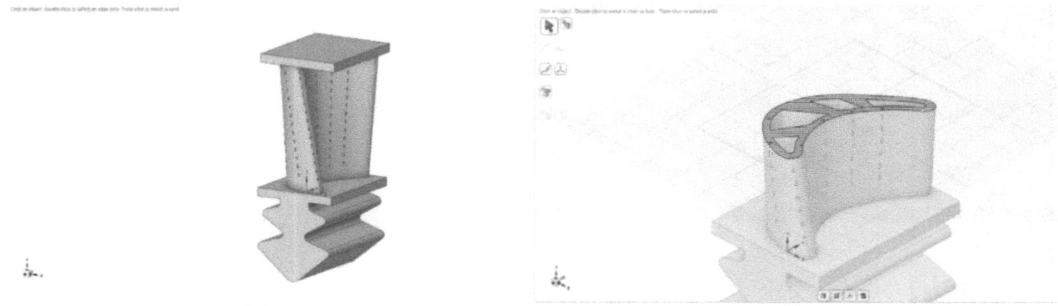

(a) (b)

FIGURE 4.52 Twisted Blade Structural CAD: (a) Iso, (b) Cross-Sectional View.

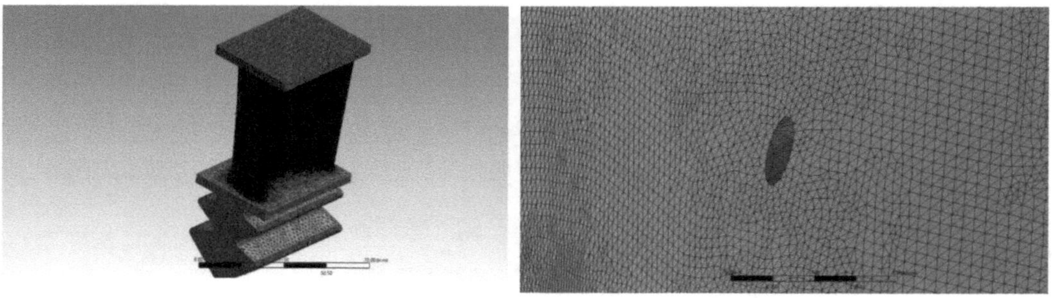

(a) (b)

FIGURE 4.53 Twisted Blade Structural Mesh: (a) Iso View, (b) Close-up.

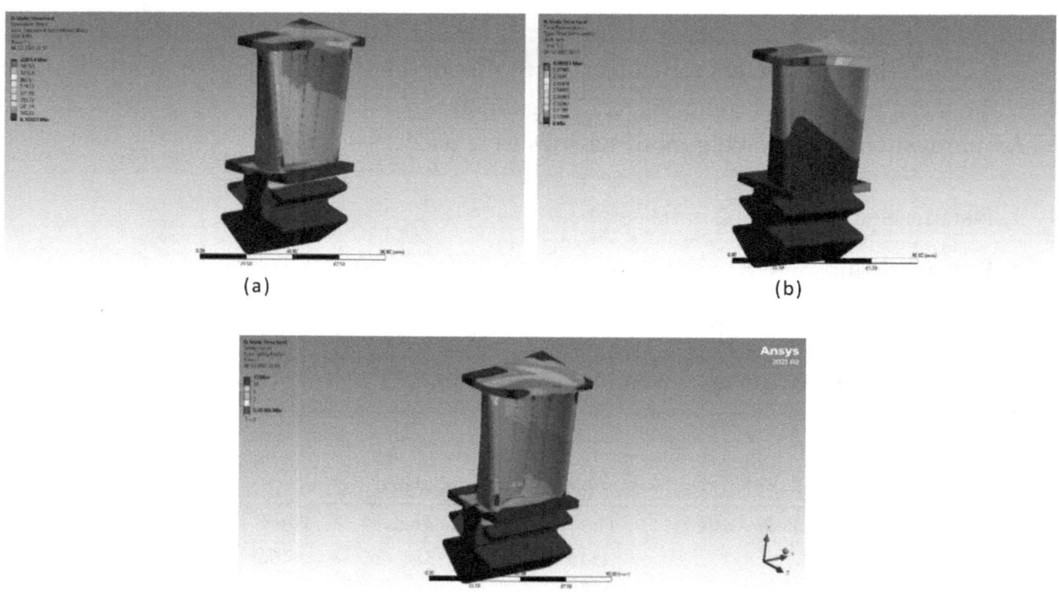

(a) (b) (c)

FIGURE 4.54 (a) Total Deformation, (b) Equivalent Stress, (c) FOS.

The analysis was based on the boundary conditions such as fixed support on the mount faces, rotational velocity boundary condition and hydrostatic pressure on the blade surfaces.

Maximum deformation of the blade was under 1 mm at 0.93 mm. The factor of safety of the body was above 1, and at maximum was 15 on the mounts due to the fixed support boundary condition. The result was satisfactory as the blade was passing the structural simulations without failure.

4.7 CONCLUSION

The aim of the work was to plan and design a rotor blade that is utilized in first stage of a gas turbine used in the aviation industry. The engine selected for this design criteria is the General Electric F110 which is a military grade engine, which proved to be a more than sufficient for a design standpoint. The profile selected for blade and the stator was C-5520A and C-7025A, respectively. In order to validate the design of the blade for selected problem statement, mathematical models were produced on SCILAB, which consisted of four major components; turbine pressure ratio, thermal values, velocity triangle components and forces and stresses experienced by the blade. This design would be quite primitive and would require multiple design iterations in order to be optimal for use.

For CFD simulations, three pairs of rotor and stator blades were set apart at a distance of 0.150 m from the central root. Simulations for the same would-be time- and work-intensive, hence a cloud based computational software SIMSCALE was selected. It was simulated for pressure and velocity using 1000 iterations, the lift force came out to be 9778.59 N and drag at 786.122 N. These pressure and velocity contours would provide variation of pressure across the blade profile. However, in a circular setup this force would drop due to the angle being a 3D approximation of 20°. The structural simulations were carried out on the ANSYS static structural module and once receiving a suitable mesh for the geometry, was tested for load failure, structural integrity and deformation. Maximum deformation seen on the body was 0.93 mm and all areas passed a minimum factor of safety of 1.

For the second iteration design, a twist was introduced into the blade in order to increase aerodynamic efficiency with values ranging from –25° to 25° at an increment of 5°. Once again, these blades were subjected to simulations for pressure and velocity, from which it was observed that a twist of –25° was optimal. The –25° blade profile is then subjected to a structural simulation for which satisfactory results were achieved. From the above design, it was able to achieve a successful blade selection for the application that not only passed in generating thrust figures but also under working load conditions.

NOMENCLATURE

λ	Critical speed ratio
λ_2	Critical speed ratio at rotor entry
λ_{2abs}	Absolute critical speed ratio at rotor entry
λ_{2rel}	Relative critical speed ratio at rotor entry
λ_u	Critical blade speed
V	Flow velocity at the entry of the first stage rotor

a_{cr}	Critical speed
T_g	Exhaust gas temperature
P_a	Ambient pressure
T_a	Ambient temperature
U_{mean}	Mean blade velocity
D_{mean}	Mean diameter
D_{tip}	Tip diameter
$\overline{d}$	Root to tip diameter ratio
γ_g	Specific heat capacity of the gas
$R_{specific}$	Specific gas constant
T_{0i}	Turbine inlet temperature
T_{0t}	Turbine total temperature
T_{wt}	Blade passage wall temperature
V_2	Absolute velocity at rotor inlet
V_r	Relative velocity of the rotor at rotor inlet
C_p	Specific heat capacity at constant pressure
g	Ratio of specific heat capacity
α	Guide vane angle—inlet
β	Guide vane angles—outlet
θ	Blade angle at Inlet
φ	Blade angle at outlet
M	Mach number
M_2	Mach number at rotor entry
M_3	Mach number at rotor exit
M_u	Mach number of blade speed
M_{2u}	Mach number of blade speed at rotor inlet
M_{3u}	Mach number of blade speed at rotor outlet
M_{2rel}	Relative Mach number for rotor entry
M_{3rel}	Relative Mach number for rotor exit
J_1	Flow coefficient—preliminary stage
J_2	Flow coefficient—stage exit
T_2	Temperature at rotor inlet
T_3	Temperature at rotor exit
s	Blade spacing/pitch
s_t	Throat width
V_t	Velocity at throat
ρ_t	Density at throat
β_{3eff}	Mass averaged effective flow exit angle
W_c	Work done by the compressor
T_{ti}	Temperature at turbine inlet
W_t	Work done by the turbine
η_c	Compressor efficiency
c_p	Specific heat

η_t	Turbine efficiency
CPR	Compressor pressure ratio
T_{ci}	Temperature at compressor inlet
TPR	Turbine pressure ratio
U	Mean linear velocity
V_3	Velocity at rotor exit
V_t	Velocity at throat
V_{r2}	Relative velocity at inlet
V_{r3}	Relative velocity at outlet
V_f	Flow velocity
V_{f2}	Flow velocity at inlet
V_{f3}	Flow velocity at outlet
V_w	Whirl velocity
V_{w2}	Whirl velocity at inlet
V_{w3}	Whirl velocity at outlet
P	Pressure
V	Volume
m	Mass
T	Temperature
ρ	Density
ρ_t	Density at throat
$\dot{m}$	Mass flow rate
$A_{annular}$	Annular area
v	Velocity

REFERENCES

Anton, N. and Wiberg, W., 2013. Aerodynamic design of a gas turbine rotor blade for the KTH test turbine. ISRN LUTMDN/TMHP-13/5284-SE.

Bogard, D.G. and Thole, K.A., 2006. Gas turbine film cooling. Journal of Propulsion and Power, 22(2), pp.249–270.

Chen, Z., Zhang, Z., Li, Y., Su, X. and Yuan, X., 2019. Vortex dynamics-based analysis of internal crossflow effect on film cooling performance. International Journal of Heat and Mass Transfer, 145, p.118757.

Deych, M.Y., Philipp, G.A. and Lazarev, L.Y., 1976. Atlas of the Cascade Profiles of Axial Flow Turbine, Defence Technical Information Centre.

Han, J.C., 2018. Advanced cooling in gas turbines 2016 Max Jakob Memorial Award paper. Journal of Heat Transfer, 140(11).

Htwe, W.L., Win, H.H. and San, N.A., 2015. Design and thermal analysis of gas turbine blade. International Journal of Mechanical and Production Engineering, 3(7), pp.62–66.

Jabbar, A.A., Rai, A.K., Reedy, P.R. and Dakhil, M.H., 2014. Design and analysis of gas turbine rotor blade using finite element method. International Journal of Mechanical and Production Engineering Research and Development, ISSN (P), pp.2249–6890.

Kurz, R. and Brun, K., 2016. Gas turbine performance. In Asia Turbomachinery & Pump Symposium. 2016 Proceedings. Turbomachinery Laboratories, Texas A&M Engineering Experiment Station.

Metzger, D.E., Baltzer, R.T. and Jenkins, C.W., 1972. Impingement cooling performance in gas turbine airfoils including effects of leading edge sharpness. Journal of Engineering for Gas Turbines and Power, 94(3), 219–225.

Mishra, R.K., Thomas, J., Srinivasan, K., Nandi, V. and Bhatt, R.R., 2017. Failure analysis of an un-cooled turbine blade in an aero gas turbine engine. Engineering Failure Analysis, 79, pp.836–844.

Mouritz, A.P., 2012. Introduction to Aerospace Materials. Elsevier.

Rolls-Royce (1996). The Jet Engine. Rolls Royce technical Publications; 5th ed. Edition

Tian, K., Tang, Z., Wang, J., Vujanović, M., Zeng, M. and Wang, Q., 2021. Numerical investigations of film cooling and particle impact on the blade leading edge. Energies, 14(4), p.1102.

Zhang, C., Bai, L., Fu, J., Khalatov, A. and Yang, Y., 2021. Discharge coefficients and aerodynamic losses for cylindrical and cratered film-cooling holes with various coolant crossflow orientations. Journal of the Brazilian Society of Mechanical Sciences and Engineering, 43(3), pp.1–15.

Zhou, J., Wang, X., Li, J. and Lu, H., 2017. CFD analysis of mist/air film cooling on a flat plate with different hole types. Numerical Heat Transfer, Part A: Applications, 71(11), pp.1123–1140.

CHAPTER 5

Optimal Design of Frame Structures Based on the Finite Elements Analysis Using Fuzzy Jaya Algorithm

Ali Mortazavi

5.1 INTRODUCTION

Optimization algorithms can be broadly classified into two main categories: gradient-based and metaheuristic. Gradient-based methods, while effective for simpler problems, often struggle with complex optimization landscapes due to their reliance on gradient calculations. To address the increasing complexity of modern optimization challenges, researchers have turned to metaheuristic algorithms. Inspired by natural phenomena and physical principles, metaheuristic methods offer a more flexible and efficient approach. Unlike gradient-based methods, they do not require explicit gradient calculations, making them suitable for a wider range of problems. Two key components underpin metaheuristic algorithms: exploration and exploitation. Exploration involves searching the solution space broadly to discover new and potentially better solutions, while exploitation focuses on refining existing solutions by exploring their local neighborhoods. The balance between exploration and exploitation is crucial for effective optimization, ensuring a combination of global and local search [1].

Different algorithms are developed to solve the optimization problems. Each of them is inspired from different phenomenon like physics rules, social behaviors, and survival behavior of the different species. For instance, particle swarm optimization (PSO) [2] and ant colony optimization (ACO) [3] are inspired from natural behavior of the colonies on finding food sources or avoid from enemies. Teaching and learning based optimization (TLBO) [4] is inspired from knowledge-based interaction between teacher and students in a classroom. Genetic algorithm (GA) [5] is an evolutionary algorithm that is inspired from the evolution concept among the different species in the nature. Gravitational search algorithm (GSA) [6] imitates the Newtonian rule between masses in the nature.

These methods are global optimization techniques and can be applied to a variety of problem types. However, the reported results indicate that their performance may vary depending

DOI: 10.1201/9781003564911-5

on the specific optimization problem. To improve their performance, they can be integrated with some auxiliary modules like Bayesian probabilistic modules. The studies show that adding some extra logical regulation modules can improve the search capability of these algorithms especially in solving more complex engineering problems [7, 8]. For instance, adding a Bayesian forecasting module to interactive search algorithm (ISA) can highly improve its search performance in solving mechanical optimization problems [9, 10]; adding fuzzy logical module to this algorithm could considerably improve its search performance for solving mathematical, mechanical, and structural optimization problems [11–13]. Butterfly optimization algorithm (BOA) and differential evolution (DE) algorithms are also combined with fuzzy modules and both reinforced methods demonstrated higher quality search performance on solving distinct optimization problems [14, 15]. It should be noted that in some cases hybridization of two or more algorithms also lead to putting forward a new more capable algorithm. For instance, the ISA algorithm combined the affirmative search patterns of PSO and TLBO algorithms [16]; in [17], the GA algorithm is combined with PSO to solve the stability of the laminates. In [18], the harmony search (HS) [19] algorithm is combined with DE [20].

Frames and trusses are some of the most prevalent structures in civil engineering, making their cost-effective and safe design critically important. These structures are optimized considering different aspect like size, layout and topology of the system. For instance, in [21] the topology of the frame structures with flexible joints is considered. In [22], optimum design of planar steel frames under load and resistance factor design-American Institute of Steel Construction (LRFD-AISC) specifications are considered. In [23–25], respectively the frame and truss structures are optimized for topology of seismic isolations systems, size and layout and size and topology of the system. In the current chapter, a reinforced metaheuristic method called fuzzy reinforced Jaya (FRJ) algorithm is applied to size optimization of the planar frames considering AISC-LRFD specifications. The effectiveness of the proposed algorithm is assessed using two benchmark optimization problems involving steel frames, each with specific strength and displacement constraints.

5.2 PROBLEM FORMULATION

The objective function and related constraints for the weight minimization of the frame structure can be generally formulated as follows:

$$\begin{aligned}
&\text{Minimize} \quad f(X)=W(A_i)=\sum_{i=1}^{N_e}\rho_i A_i L_i \\
&\text{Subjected to} \\
&g_{Dj}=\frac{\Delta_j(A_i)}{\Delta_u}-1\le 0 \quad j=1,2,\ldots,N \\
&g_{Si}=\begin{cases}\left(\dfrac{P}{\phi P_n}+\dfrac{8}{9}\left(\dfrac{M_{ux}}{\phi M_{nx}}+\dfrac{M_{wx}}{\phi M_{wx}}\right)\right)-1, \text{ for } \dfrac{P_u}{\phi P_n}\ge 0.2 \\[2ex] \left(\dfrac{P_u}{24\phi P_n}+\dfrac{M_{ux}}{\phi M_{nx}}+\dfrac{M_{wx}}{\phi M_{wx}}\right)-1, \text{ for } \dfrac{P_u}{\phi P_n}< 0.2\end{cases} \qquad i=1,2,\ldots,N_e
\end{aligned} \tag{5.1}$$

where, W represents the total weight of the structural members. For each member i, its cross-sectional area, material density and length are denoted by ρi, Ai and Li, respectively. The constraint conditions g_{Dj} and g_{Sj} ensure that the steel frame adheres to design requirements. g_{Dj} represents displacement violations, while g_{Sj} checks for stress violations based on AISC-LRFD specifications. Δj is the displacement of the jth floor, and Δu is the maximum allowable displacement, typically set at 1/300 of the floor height. Pu and Mu are the required axial force and bending moment, respectively, while P_n and M_n are the nominal axial and bending capacities.

The finite element method (FEM) is applied to solve the structural systems. FEM is a powerful numerical technique widely used in structural engineering to analyze frame systems. By dividing a complex structure into smaller, simpler elements, FEM can accurately model the behavior of frames under various loads and boundary conditions. This approach allows for the precise calculation of displacements, stresses and strains within the frame, enabling engineers to assess its structural integrity and performance. FEM's versatility and accuracy make it an indispensable tool for designing safe, efficient and cost-effective frame structures. To provide more detail about this technique, the related formulation for a frame structure that involves beam elements is given in following:

$$f = \boldsymbol{K}\,U$$

where,

$$\boldsymbol{K} = \boldsymbol{T}^T \boldsymbol{K}_g \boldsymbol{T}$$

$$\boldsymbol{K}_g = \sum_{i=1}^{n} \boldsymbol{k}_i^g$$

$$\boldsymbol{T} = \begin{bmatrix} \cos(\gamma) & \sin(\gamma) & 0 & 0 \\ -\sin(\gamma) & \cos(\gamma) & 0 & 0 \\ 0 & 0 & \cos(\gamma) & \sin(\gamma) \\ 0 & 0 & -\sin(\gamma) & \cos(\gamma) \end{bmatrix}, \tag{5.2}$$

$$f = \begin{bmatrix} V_1 \\ M_1 \\ V_2 \\ M_2 \end{bmatrix}, U = \begin{bmatrix} u_1 \\ \theta_1 \\ u_2 \\ \theta_2 \end{bmatrix},$$

$$\boldsymbol{k}^g = \frac{EI}{L^3} \begin{bmatrix} 12 & 6L & -12 & -6L \\ 6L & -4L^2 & -6L & 4L^2 \\ -12 & -6L & 12 & 6L \\ 6L & 2L^2 & -6L & -2L^2 \end{bmatrix}$$

in which, for a beam element, f shows the force vector in which V and M are nodal shear force and bending moment, respectively; γ is the angle of the element with respect to the horizontal axis. Also, U shows the displacement vector of beam element in which u_i *and* θ_i are nodal displacement and rotation, receptively. The stiffness matrix for beam element based on the Euler-Bernoulli formulation in which L, E and I show the length, elasticity module of the material and moment of inertia, respectively. By assembling this matrix into a global matrix and solving corresponding linear system of equation, the nodal displacements are found.

5.3 FUZZY JAYA ALGORITHM

The FRJ algorithm applied the main search pattern of Jaya algorithm but uses a fuzzy parameter (τ) to adjust the search behavior algorithm. This method is mathematically formulated as follows:

$$
\begin{aligned}
&{}^{t+1}\boldsymbol{X}_i = {}^{t}\boldsymbol{X}_i + \tau_i \odot \left(\boldsymbol{X}^{\text{Gbest}} - \left|{}^{t}\boldsymbol{X}_i\right|\right) + \overline{\tau}_i \odot \left(\left|{}^{t}\boldsymbol{X}_i\right| - \boldsymbol{X}^{\text{Worst}}\right) \\
&\text{where,} \\
&\tau_i = \mu_i r_i\,, \\
&\overline{\tau}_i = 1 - \tau_i
\end{aligned}
\tag{5.3}
$$

where, τ_i is the fuzzy tendency factor for the ith agent, designates the inclination of the agent to either move toward the best agent ($\boldsymbol{X}^{\text{Gbest}}$) or distance oneself from the underperforming agent ($\boldsymbol{X}^{\text{Worst}}$); the term of $\overline{\tau}_i$ is the complement of τ_i; while μ_i denotes the fuzzy decision factor.

A dimensionless metric known as the normalized objective function (NOF) is utilized to enable the fuzzy mechanism to fairly evaluate agents. The NOF for the ith agent is mathematically defined as follows:

$$
NOF_i = \frac{f(\boldsymbol{X}_i) - f\left(\boldsymbol{X}^{\text{Best}}\right)}{f\left(\boldsymbol{X}^{\text{Worst}}\right) - f\left(\boldsymbol{X}^{\text{Best}}\right) + \varepsilon}, \quad i = 1, 2, \ldots, \text{ps} \tag{5.4}
$$

in which, NOF_i is the normalized value of problem's objective function for desired agent, in this condition the lower NOF indicates a better condition for a minimization problem; $\text{f}(\boldsymbol{X}_i)$ shows the objective function for the current agent, $\text{f}(\boldsymbol{X}^{\text{Best}})$ and $\text{f}(\boldsymbol{X}^{\text{Worst}})$ are designated the best and the worst agents, respectively; to prevent division by zero condition, a small positive scalar (i.e., ε=1E-6) is applied; *ps* demonstrates the population size. The given fuzzy module continuously traces the optimization procedure, and according to the former quantity of the fuzzy decision factor (${}^{\text{old}}\mu_i$) and NOF_i value provides the updated fuzzy decision factor (μ_i) as below for ith agent [26].

$$
\mu_i = {}^{\text{old}}\mu_i + \Delta\mu_i \tag{5.5}
$$

For generating $\Delta\mu_i$, the fuzzy mechanism employs the logical guidelines outlined in the Table 5.1. In this table, the linguistic terms 'L', 'M' and 'S' represent 'Large', 'Medium' and 'Small' for the input membership functions. For the output membership functions, the abbreviations 'LNV', 'SNV', 'LPV', 'SPV' and 'ZV' correspond to 'Large Negative Value', 'Small Negative Value', 'Large Positive Value', 'Small Positive Value' and 'Zero Value'. Table 5.1 provides the membership functions used for the fuzzification and defuzzification

TABLE 5.1 Fuzzy Rules Used to Tune μ Parameter

	Input		Output
Rule No.	**NOF$_i$**	$^{old}\mu_i$	$\Delta\mu_i$
1	S	S	SNV
2	S	M	ZV
3	S	L	SPV
4	M	S	MNV
5	M	M	ZV
6	M	L	MPV
7	L	S	LPV
8	L	M	ZV
9	L	L	LNV

TABLE 5.2 Pseudo Code of the FRJ Technique

```
Initiate random population
while (none of the stopping conditions are satisfied)
    for (each agent X_i)
        Calculate the Normalized Objective Function (NOF_i) using Eq. (5.4)
        Calculate the fuzzy decision factor (μ_i) using the fuzzy rules given in Table 5.1 and Fig. 5.1
        Update current agent's location using Eq. (5.3)
        if new location is amended, f(^(t+1) X_I) < f(^t X_I)
            hold the new agent and replace the old one
        else
            hold the old agent and reject the updated agent
        end
    end
end
```

of fuzzy variables, while Table 5.2 outlines the operating mechanism of the defined fuzzy decision-making system.

For more illustration the pseudocode for this algorithm is given as follows:

5.4 NUMERIC EXAMPLES

The current section devoted to assessing the effect of the adding fuzzy module is tested on the performance of Jaya algorithm. For this aim, both of the standard and reinforced methods are applied to solve two frame structures and results are compared. All restrictions are made according to the AISC requirements [27]. Also, in all examples, the members were selected from the 267 available W-shaped (after eliminating the profiles with same specifications) rolled steel sections listed in AISC-ASD (allowable stress design) database [28].

5.4.1 A Single-Bay Eight Story Frame System

A single-bay, eight-story steel frame was analyzed in the initial example. This frame was subjected to lateral forces as depicted in Fig. 5.2. The steel used has a modulus of elasticity of 200 GPa and a specific weight of 76.8 kN/m^3. The frame's members were categorized into eight groups, as illustrated in Fig. 5.3. The only design constraint was to limit the roof

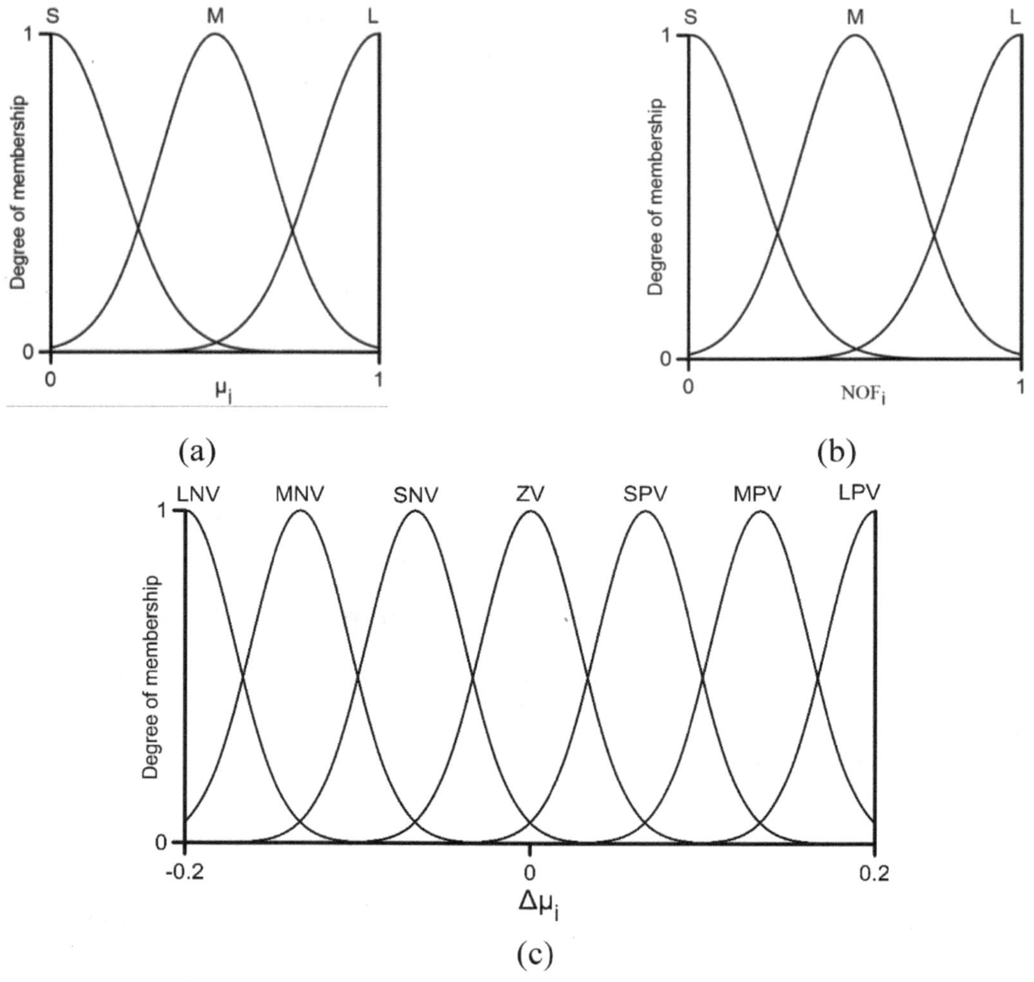

FIGURE 5.1 The Membership Functions Associated with (a) μ_i, (b) NOF_i and for output (c) $\Delta\mu_i$.

floor's displacement to 5.08 cm. Attained results are tabulated in Table 5.3. Based on the given results the fuzzy part of the FRJ technique functions effectively in regulating the algorithm's search behavior that causes the FRJ to find a more accurate solution (a lighter system). Also, considering the standard deviation (Std.) the FRJ exhibits greater stability in its optimization procedure. Also, the required objective function evaluations (OFEs) indicate that the FRJ required lower computational cost.

5.4.2 A Three-Bay Fifteen-Story Frame System

The steel frame in question is a three-bay, 15-story structure with 105 members with 64 joints. The system's columns are divided into ten separate groups, while beams are put single group. The outer columns are grouped separately for every three consecutive stories, beginning from the foundation, while the inner columns form a separate group. This categorization results in eleven distinct design variables. illustrates the member groupings.

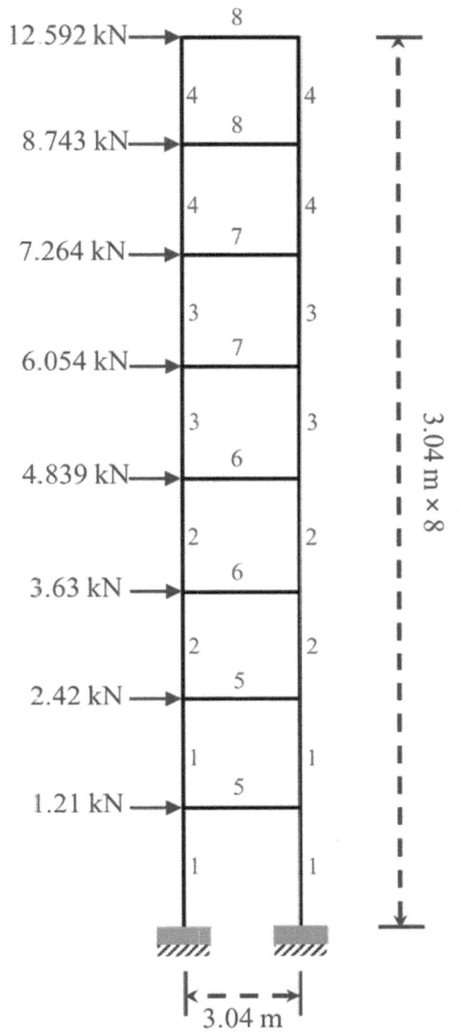

FIGURE 5.2 A Single-Bay Eight Story Frame System.

The steel's modulus of elasticity is E = 200 GPa, and its yield stress is Fy = 248.2 MPa. Each beam's unbraced length is assumed to be one-fifth of its span, and the columns are considered unbraced throughout their length. The design constraints for this frame adhere to the American Institute of Steel Construction Load and Resistance Factor Design (AISC-LRFD) guidelines. The maximum displacement of the top floor is limited to 23.5 cm.

The results obtained from the FRJ method are summarized in Table 5.4. The fuzzy module within the FRJ effectively modifies the algorithm's search process, leading to more precise solutions and a lighter system. Additionally, the FRJ exhibits greater stability during the optimization process, as evidenced by its lower standard deviation (Std.). Also, the required objective function evaluations (OFEs) indicate that the FRJ required lower computational cost.

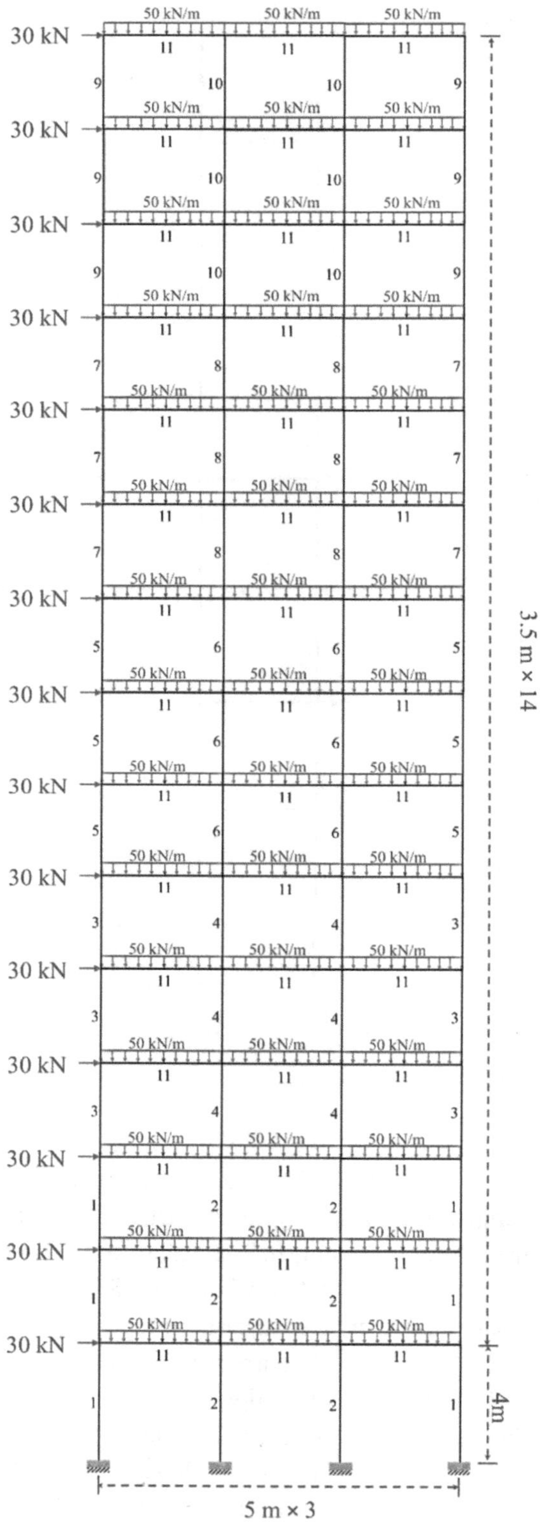

FIGURE 5.3 A Three-Bay 15-Story Frame System.

TABLE 5.3 Assessment of Single-Bay Eight Story Frame Three-Bay

	Methods	
Element Group	**Jaya**	**FRJ**
1	W18×35	W18×35
2	W14×26	W16×31
3	W16×26	W16×31
4	W14×26	W12×14
5	W24×62	W18×35
6	W18×35	W18×35
7	W16×31	W18×35
8	W12×30	W16×31
Best Weight	34.21	31.86
Mean Weight	36.99	33.21
OFEs	2010	1550
Std.	4.24	2.56

TABLE 5.4 Assessment of Three-Bay, 15-Story Frame Performance

	Methods	
Element Group	**Jaya**	**FRJ**
1	W12×96	W14×99
2	W27×161	W27×161
3	W27×84	W27×84
4	W24×104	W24×104
5	W10×68	W16×67
6	W30×90	W18×86
7	W8×48	W8×48
8	W24×68	W12×65
9	W8×28	W8×31
10	W10×39	W10×39
11	W21×50	W21×44
Best Weight	391.42	389.24
Mean Weight	422.01	393.3
OFEs	3750	2985
Std.	11.346	4.01

5.5 DISCUSSION ABOUT THE SEARCH BEHAVIOR OF THE ALGORITHMS

In this section, the impact of the additional fuzzy module on the search behavior of the desired algorithm is evaluated by generating behavioral diagrams. To achieve this, the population diversity index is first defined as follows:

$$ {}^{t}\text{Div} = \frac{1}{N|L|} \sum_{i=1}^{N} \sqrt{\sum_{j=1}^{D} \left(x_i^j - \overline{x}^j \right)^2} \tag{5.6} $$

where ${}^{t}\text{Div}$ indicates the population diversity, N designates the number of agents, D indicates the dimension of the problem, L designates the lengthiest diagonal span of the search space. Additionally, x_i^j is the ith agent's jth component, and $\overline{x}^j$ is the mean value of the jth dimension. A decrease in population diversity indicates that agents have clustered closely together, focusing their search on a domain's specific region. Smaller diversity, therefore, highlights the algorithm's local search (exploitation) behavior. Conversely, exploration behavior of the search process is increased via a higher level of diversity.

To track the algorithm's search behavior, the normalized diversity index ($N\text{Div}$) and its conjugate ($\overline{N\text{Div}}$) are mathematically described as follows:

$$\begin{aligned} N\text{Div} &= \frac{{}^{t}\text{Div}}{\text{Div}_{\max}} \times 100 \\ \overline{N\text{Div}} &= \frac{\text{Div}_{\max} - {}^{t}\text{Div}}{\text{Div}_{\max}} \times 100 \end{aligned} \tag{5.7}$$

in which, ${}^{t}\text{Div}$ displays the current diversity, and $\text{Div}_{\max}$ indicates the maximum diversity. According to given argument, a greater ${}^{t}N\text{Div}$ indicates the higher exploitation search behavior, while a larger ${}^{t}\overline{N\text{Div}}$ illustrates the greater global search (exploration) behavior. The corresponding behavioral diagrams for the three-bay 15-story frame system are given in Fig. 5.4. These diagrams demonstrate that the fuzzy module of FRJ effectively regulates the algorithm's search behavior in comparison with regular Jaya. Such that, after approximately 200 iterations, the search behavior undergoes a complete shift, becoming smoother, more stable, and experiencing only minor adjustments.

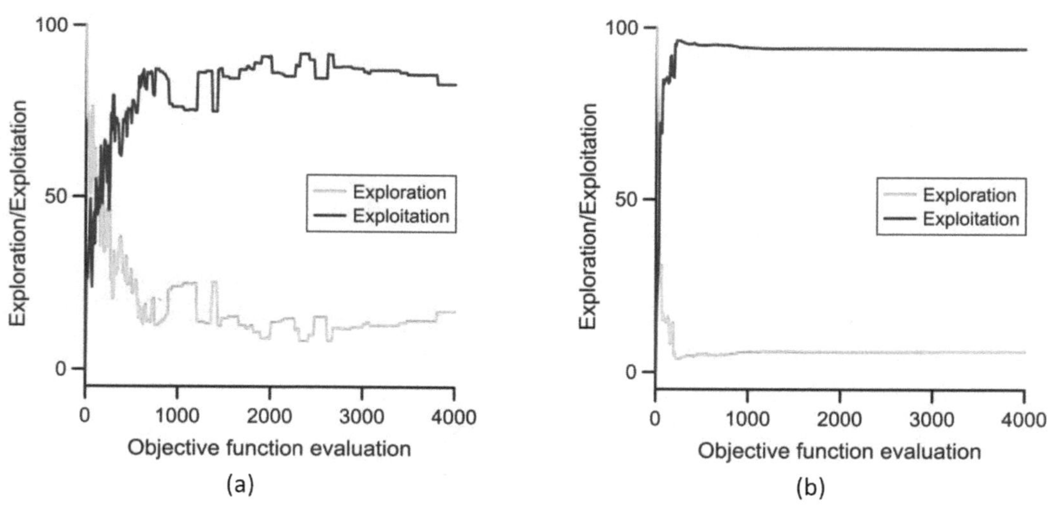

FIGURE 5.4 Behavioral Diagrams for (a) Jaya and (b) FRJ Methods.

5.6 CONCLUSION

In this section the performance of a Fuzzy Reinforced Jaya algorithm so-called FRJ is compared with its standard version (i.e., Jaya) on solving sizing optimization of planar frame systems. The fuzzy module in the FRJ constantly tracks the search process and attempts to adjust the algorithm search behavior based on the governing condition of the desired problem. To assess the FRJ algorithm's effectiveness in structural optimization, it is used for analyzing two steel frame examples: a one-bay, eight-story frame, and a three-bay, 15-story frame. The optimal designs produced by the FRJ algorithm demonstrate its potential as a powerful tool for steel frame optimization.

An analysis of the member drift and allowable stress ratios highlights the algorithm's optimization effectiveness, as the story drift values consistently approach the maximum allowable limits, and most members' stress ratios are close to 1. This indicates that the FRJ algorithm efficiently pushes the boundaries of the search domain to find optimal solutions. Comparing the FRJ results to its standard counterpart, it is observed its superior ability to minimize the weight of selected steel frames. The FRJ algorithm's stability is evident in its low standard deviation (Std) values, calculated from ten independent design runs. Furthermore, the FRJ in comparison with standard Jaya, can improve the required computational cost (nearly 20%). This makes it a reliable choice compared to other algorithms especially in comparison with standard Jaya. Also, the generated behavioral diagrams indicate that the fuzzy module in FRJ significantly enhances the algorithm's search process compared to traditional Jaya. After initial iterations (nearly 200 iterations), the search becomes more refined and consistent, with minimal fluctuations. Its versatility and ease of use make the FRJ algorithm applicable to various complex structural optimization problems.

REFERENCES

1. Mortazavi A, Şeker S. Enhanced quadratic approximation integrated with butterfly optimization: A new search algorithm tested on structural and mathematical problems. Revista de la construcci6n. 2021;20:215–35.
2. Kennedy J, Eberhart R. Particle swarm optimization. Neural Networks, 1995 Proceedings, IEEE International Conference in 1995. p. 1942–8 vol. 4.
3. Dorigo M, Blum C. Ant colony optimization theory: A survey. Theoretical Computer Science. 2005;344:243–78.
4. Rao RV, Savsani VJ, Vakharia DP. Teaching–learning-based optimization: A novel method for constrained mechanical design optimization problems. Computer-Aided Design. 2011;43: 303–15.
5. Holland JH. Genetic algorithms and adaptation. In: Selfridge OG, Rissland EL, Arbib MA, editors. Adaptive Control of Ill-Defined Systems Boston, MA: Springer US; 1984. p. 317–33.
6. Rashedi E, Nezamabadi-pour H, Saryazdi S. GSA: A gravitational search algorithm. Information Sciences. 2009;179:2232–48.
7. Mortazavi A. Improved drosophila food-search algorithm for structural and mechanical optimization problems. In: Kale IR, Sadollah A, editors. Optimization Methods for Structural Engineering Singapore: Springer Nature Singapore; 2023. p. 53–65.
8. Mortazavi A. A novel type-2 decision mechanism for dynamic parameter adaptation: Theory and application in mathematical and structural problems. Neural Computing and Applications. 2024;36(31):19729–57.

9. Mortazavi A. Bayesian interactive search algorithm: A new probabilistic swarm intelligence tested on mathematical and structural optimization problems. Advances in Engineering Software. 2021;155:102994.
10. Ali Mortazavi. Solving structural optimization problems with discrete variables using interactive fuzzy search algorithm. Structural Engineering and Mechanics. 2021;79:247–65.
11. Mortazavi A. Interactive fuzzy Bayesian search algorithm: A new reinforced swarm intelligence tested on engineering and mathematical optimization problems. Expert Systems with Applications. 2022;187:115954.
12. Mortazavi A. Large-scale structural optimization using a fuzzy reinforced swarm intelligence algorithm. Advances in Engineering Software. 2020;142:102790.
13. Mortazavi A. Interactive fuzzy search algorithm: A new self-adaptive hybrid optimization algorithm. Engineering Applications of Artificial Intelligence. 2019;81:270–82.
14. Mortazavi A, Moloodpoor M. Enhanced butterfly optimization algorithm with a new fuzzy regulator strategy and virtual butterfly concept. Knowledge-Based Systems. 2021;228:107291.
15. Mortazavi A, Moloodpoor M. Differential evolution method integrated with a fuzzy decision-making mechanism and virtual mutant agent: Theory and application. Applied Soft Computing. 2021;112:107808.
16. Mortazavi A, Toğan V, Nuhoğlu A. Interactive search algorithm: A new hybrid metaheuristic optimization algorithm. Engineering Applications of Artificial Intelligence. 2018;71:275–92.
17. Barroso ES, Parente E, Cartaxo de Melo AM. A hybrid PSO-GA algorithm for optimization of laminated composites. Structural and Multidisciplinary Optimization. 2017;55:2111–30.
18. Xia HG, Wang QZ. Hybrid differential evolution harmony search algorithm for power economic dispatch problems. Applied Mechanics and Materials. 2013;415:345–8.
19. Lee KS, Geem ZW. A new meta-heuristic algorithm for continuous engineering optimization: Harmony search theory and practice. Computer Methods in Applied Mechanics and Engineering. 2005;194:3902–33.
20. Storn R, Price K. Differential evolution – A simple and efficient heuristic for global optimization over continuous spaces. Journal of Global Optimization. 1997;11:341–59.
21. Fredricson H, Johansen T, Klarbring A, Petersson J. Topology optimization of frame structures with flexible joints. Structural and Multidisciplinary Optimization. 2003;25:199–214.
22. Sellami M. Optimum design of planar steel frames under LRFD-AISC specifications using a step-by-step descent algorithm. Structural and Multidisciplinary Optimization. 2022;65:176.
23. Mortazavi A. A novel binomial strategy for simultaneous topology and size optimization of truss structures. Engineering Optimization. 2024:1–35.
24. Kandemir EC, Mortazavi A. Optimization of seismic base isolation system using a fuzzy reinforced swarm intelligence. Advances in Engineering Software. 2022;174:103323.
25. Mortazavi A. Size and layout optimization of truss structures with dynamic constraints using the interactive fuzzy search algorithm. Engineering Optimization. 2020;53(3):369–91.
26. Mortazavi A. A fuzzy reinforced Jaya algorithm for solving mathematical and structural optimization problems. Soft Computing. 2024;28:2181–206.
27. AISC. American Institute of Steel Construction (AISC). Manual of steel construction allowable stress design. 9th ed. Chicago, IL. 1989:1–360.
28. https://www.aisc.org/globalassets/aisc/manual/v15.0-shapes-database/aisc-shapes-database-v15.0.xlsx.

CHAPTER 6

Total Potential Optimization Using Metaheuristic Algorithms for Analysis of Structural Systems

Gebrail Bekdaş, Ayla Ocak, Sinan Melih Nigdeli, Yusuf Cengiz Toklu, Sanghun Kim and Zong Woo Geem

6.1 INTRODUCTION

Structural systems are systems that are generally named by considering the material or order of the skeleton that holds the system up. It can accommodate more than one load-bearing elements together. In the design of many structures such as bridges, stadiums, cultural centers and similar structures, cable and bar elements are preferred together or separately, and the elements in the system can form a planar or three-dimensional truss arrangement. Examples of these structures are tensegrity structures where cable and bar elements work together, plate systems consisting of plate elements, truss systems using bar elements and cable systems using cables. Each system has its reasons and advantages for being preferred for use in its field. The most important of these are the prevailing wind effect in the region where it will be applied, the accessibility of construction resources, and the need for material and workmanship. The following can be given as examples of why structural systems are preferred: In plate systems, steel plate shear walls can be preferred for reasons such as assembly speed, material savings, resistance to lateral forces and energy dissipation ability, while tensegrity systems are used in field, library, arena and similar suspended roof systems and are recommended for space structures due to reasons such as material lightness, ease of transportation and assembly [1–3]. When looking at tension structures, cable systems are preferred due to their advantages in terms of durability, flexibility, material weight and cost, and these systems are preferred in structures such as bridges, wide-span roof structures and power supply lines [4–6]. Truss structures, on the other hand, provide economical and practical application

DOI: 10.1201/9781003564911-6

solutions similar to cable systems, and offer advantages for construction in terms of durability, safety, construction speed and workmanship.

The basic design focus of structural systems is the need for lightweight designs where work and labor are less and the economy is more. In the design of such systems, optimization methods are used to minimize the volume of material in the structure and to reduce costs, and designs are generally considered topology optimization problems that target the most appropriate material distribution for the conditions. When research on plate systems is examined, it is seen that methods such as reducing the volume of material, minimizing dynamic reactions, minimizing the maximum strain energy for the volume, maximizing stiffness based on strain energy and minimizing weight and static displacement are used for design [7–13]. In the design of truss structures, optimization objective functions such as minimizing the volume and weight of the material and minimizing the work done by the applied load are used similarly to plate systems [14–18]. In cable systems, it is known that these systems support the design with cable tension. When the studies on cable structural systems are examined, it is seen that among the optimization purposes for optimum designs, topics such as cost, deflection and stress minimization, cable force adjustment, bending energy and counterweight sum are investigated [19–23]. Thanks to the tensegrity structures created by using cable systems together with bar elements, they are frequently preferred in roof and similar designs and are recommended among the most suitable designs for space structures. In the production process of tensegrity structures, which are examples of future structural design, the optimization process is especially important in terms of cost. Thanks to the optimum design of tensegrity structures, the reduction of work and labor as much as possible, the low weight and volume of materials in terms of ease of transportation, etc. make these systems an ideal option for structures to be built in space. In the studies conducted on the optimization of tensegrity structures, the subjects such as maximization of the total tension and pressure difference in the structure, minimization of the number of cables and the mass of the structure, adjustment of member internal forces and pre-stressing have been preferred according to the design requirements [24–28]. In general, it is understood that the optimization purposes of the mentioned systems are similar in the optimum design of structural systems. In tensegrity structures, the presence of cables and bar elements together makes the system analysis quite difficult regarding the tension that will occur in the cables and the compression effect in the bar elements. The main purpose of such systems is to obtain designs that aim to keep the displacements of tensegrity elements, which require difficult analyses, at the minimum level as much as possible. In other words, to limit the amount of work that tensegrity structural elements will do under external loads. The work done and the energy of the system are directly related. In tensegrity structural designs, another method used for the optimum design process is the minimization of the total potential energy of the system. The potential energy existing in a stationary structure decreases as the structure moves due to the law of conservation of energy and gives way to kinetic energy. Therefore, to keep the displacement of the structure under external loads at a minimum level, the total potential energy in the structure must be minimized. In this way, the nonlinear behavior of the tensegrity structural elements is significantly limited by optimization.

Various algorithms and parametric methods are adopted and included in studies for the optimization of structural systems. The fact that the method used as an optimization tool is easy to apply and provides an effective solution is an important element in terms of design efficiency. In recent years, metaheuristic algorithms have been frequently used in studies on structural system designs due to their speed in reaching the optimum solution and their simple and understandable structure. These algorithms are inspired by the instinctive behaviors of living beings, various natural events and situations that occur in a spontaneous order in the universe. Various metaheuristic algorithms have been developed based on many events and behaviors such as bats finding their way with echolocation, the pollination process of flowers, the law of gravity and mass interaction, learning and teaching behavior and the path that bees follow to search for food [29–33]. The harmony search (HS) algorithm is a metaheuristic algorithm developed by Geem et al. [34], which is obtained by converting the process of searching for the most suitable harmony into a mathematical expression. In structural system designs, the HS algorithm and its derivatives are among the heuristic methods that are successfully applied as a good optimization tool in obtaining optimum designs. There are many studies in the literature on the design optimization of structural system elements using the HS algorithm [35–39].

Within the scope of this review study, in the second section, research was conducted on the analysis of cable, truss, plate and tensegrity structural systems with metaheuristic algorithms and total potential energy optimization, and some summary information about the optimization studies of these systems was presented. Total potential energy optimization with metaheuristics is an alternative method to classical analysis methods and it can be adapted to all types of analysis and nonlinearities without making complicated modifications. In the third section, a tensegric structural system example was taken and total potential energy optimization was performed. In the optimization, the energy minimization process was performed on the MATLAB program [40] using the adaptive harmony search (AHS) algorithm, which was developed by adapting the parameters of the HS algorithm, and the obtained results were presented.

6.2 DESIGN OPTIMIZATION OF STRUCTURAL SYSTEMS WITH METAHEURISTIC METHODS

Structural systems are systems that are recommended to be optimized to obtain designs that are more economical, safer and suitable for the boundary conditions of the load-bearing system elements. Various algorithms and parametric methods can be used in the optimization process of these systems. Metaheuristic algorithms are a preferred optimization tool due to reasons such as ease of application, fast solution generation and simple and understandable structure. It stands out as a frequently used method in structural system optimization studies. It is frequently preferred in the optimum design of plate systems, truss systems, cable, and tensegric structural system types. Within the scope of the study, research was conducted on the design of the four structural systems mentioned with metaheuristic algorithms. The information obtained on the optimum design of these systems is presented below.

6.2.1 Plate Systems

Plate systems are systems where plates are used in structural elements such as shear walls, girders, laminated composites and roof covers. Plate elements can be used as linear or folded plates. In designs, the optimum selection of plate section dimensions, aspect ratio and plate thickness is important in terms of ease of production and buckling load effect. The areas of use of plate systems vary according to the need. The increase in the transportation and transportation sector and the adverse traffic conditions experienced each passing day increase in the need for bridges and therefore the number of plate girder examples that can be used in bridges. Steel plate girders used in plate systems in bridge designs are frequently preferred in today's designs for different construction purposes such as reducing vehicle traffic and providing pedestrian passage and railway lines. They provide advantages such as increasing construction speed, heavy load-carrying capacity and ease of maintenance. A steel plate girder example is shown in Fig. 6.1.

In the optimization of plate system designs using plate girders, it is quite common to use metaheuristic methods. Since they are prone to bending under load, the plate girder cross-sectional area is generally minimized by using stiffener spacing, web plate and flange thinness boundary conditions for optimization processes. In studies on plate girder elements, Çakıroğlu et al. used the HS algorithm in cross-sectional area minimization; Erdal et al. used hunting search and firefly algorithms in weight minimization; Negrin et al. used the biogeography-based optimization algorithm in minimizing weight, material and production costs; Pavlovic et al. used the sine cosine algorithm, whale optimization algorithm and hybrid in cross-sectional area minimization [41–44].

In recent years, multistory high-rise building designs have become quite widespread. This situation has led to a search for a solution by challenging the stability of structures exposed to lateral forces such as wind and earthquakes. At this point, steel plate shear

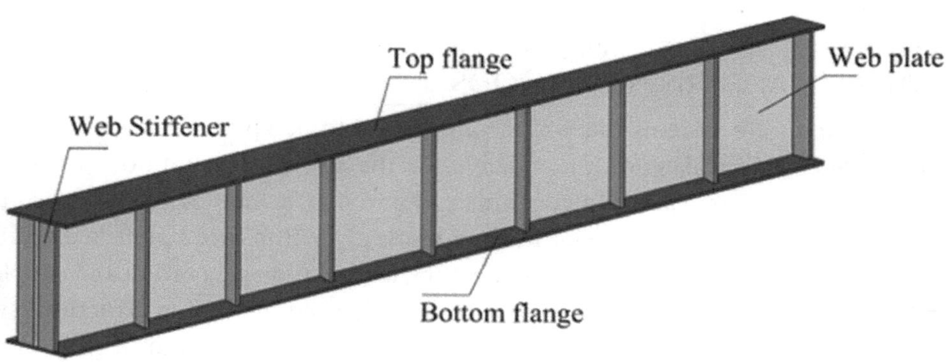

FIGURE 6.1 Steel plate girder example.

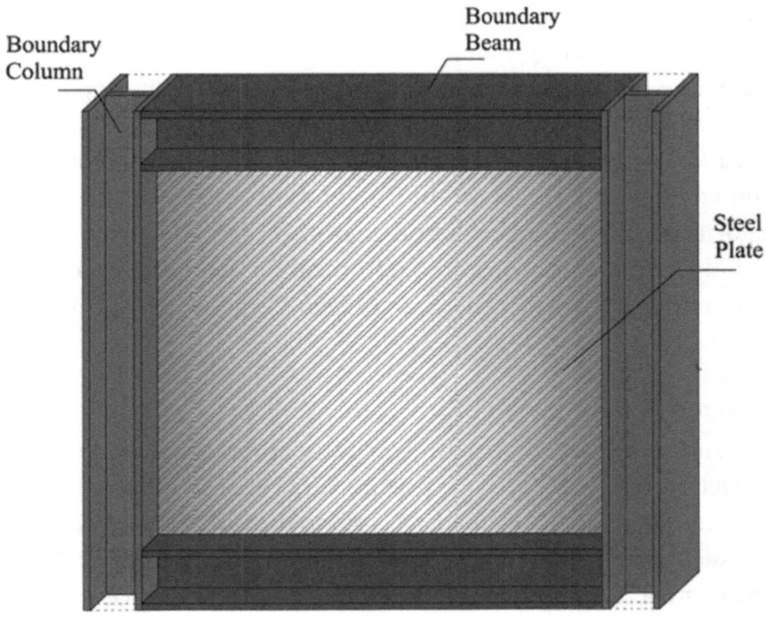

FIGURE 6.2 Steel plate shear wall example.

walls have emerged as an alternative that facilitates the stability of tall structures by providing the resistance of the system against lateral forces. It is considered advantageous due to its construction speed, remarkable ductility, high initial stiffness value and its effect on reducing seismic mass [45, 46]. An example of a steel plate shear wall is shown in Fig. 6.2.

In plate wall system designs, the web plate thickness limit is generally determined for optimization, and the optimization process is completed under behavioral constraints. There are studies on design with metaheuristic methods. Gholizadeh and Shahrezaei used a bat algorithm considering web plate boundaries and constraints for size optimization and optimum steel plate shear wall placement of steel frames to minimize the weight of the structure [47]. Kaveh and Farhadmanesh used a colliding bodies optimization algorithm for size optimization of steel plate shear wall structure under constraints such as shear strength, inter-story displacement, vertical and horizontal element stiffness and boundary element strength, aiming to minimize the standard deviation of story drift and weight of the structure in a two-dimensional frame [48]. He et al. applied optimization under strength, stiffness, inter-story drift, plate wall shear bearing, boundary element inertia and construction constraints with the algorithm they derived from a genetic algorithm for weight minimization for layout optimization of steel plate shear walls in steel frames [49]. Daryan et al., in the example of steel plate shear wall, minimized the weight under various constraints with modified dolphin echolocation algorithm and bat algorithms for plate wall layout and size optimization [50].

Composite materials are frequently preferred materials in many engineering fields due to their high durability. Composite plates are produced from these materials in plate system designs and are used in various areas of construction. In optimization studies in composite structures, applications are generally made to increase the buckling load capacity of composite plates due to their tendency to buckle under excessive load. In optimization studies carried out with heuristic methods with composite plates, the buckling load and fundamental natural frequency of the plates, thermal buckling temperature maximization and elastic strain energy and weight minimization were targeted, and heuristic algorithms such as HS algorithm, differential evolution algorithm, partial swarm optimization algorithm, cultural algorithm, optics-inspired optimization algorithm, league championship algorithm, nondominated sorting genetic algorithm II and whale optimization were used [38, 51–59].

6.2.2 Truss Systems

In structural designs, large-span structures require attention in terms of material quantity and construction safety. Instead of covering large spans with a solid body, providing transitions with hollow structure elements has led to the use of truss systems as an alternative system for such structures. Today, truss systems are used to cover large spans safely for many types of structures such as exhibition and event areas, bridges, roofs, stadiums, sports complexes and large-scale structures. Figure 6.3 shows an example of a planar truss used in a bridge.

In the optimum design of truss systems, studies are generally carried out to reduce the volume of the material. In this way, lighter and more economical designs can be obtained. Metaheuristic algorithms are frequently used in optimization tools in truss system designs. In their research in 2021, Renkavieski and Parpinelli [60] examined 71 metaheuristic algorithms used for the optimization of truss systems and ranked ten popular metaheuristic algorithms used in more than three studies from the most frequently preferred to the least as follows: particle swarm optimization, genetic algorithm, differential evolution algorithm, teaching-learning based optimization, HS algorithm,

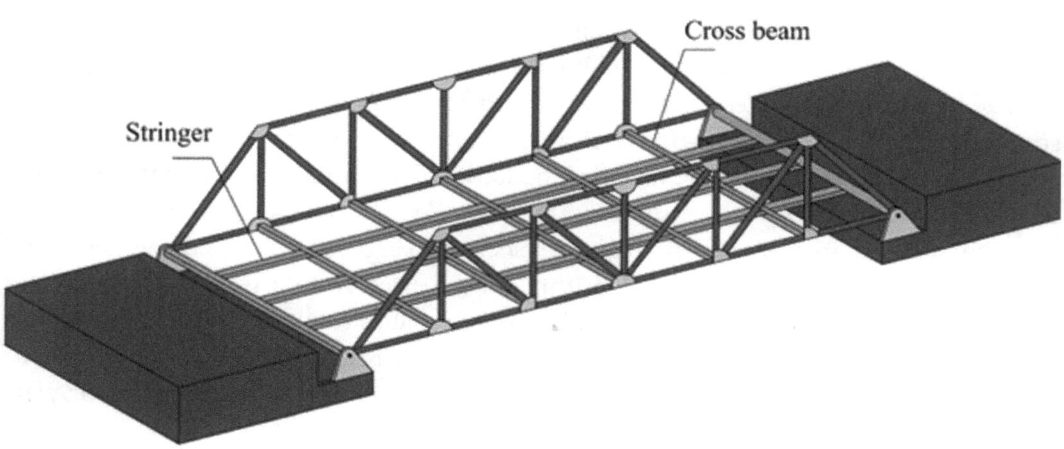

FIGURE 6.3 Truss bridge example.

firefly algorithm, colliding bodies optimization, symbiotic organisms search algorithm, big bang big-crunch optimization and evolution strategy algorithm [32, 34, 61–68]. When we look at the optimization studies conducted for truss systems, there are many examples of sizing optimization applications that aim to minimize weight or volume. In the last decade, optimum truss studies conducted with metaheuristic algorithms have generally used sizing optimization [69–75], shape and size optimization [76–80], topology optimization [81–83] and combined topology, shape and sizing optimization [84–87] applications.

6.2.3 Cabled Structures

Cabled systems are systems that aim to provide stability by utilizing the tension of the cables used in the structure. The most common examples are seen in bridge designs. In addition, cables can be used to provide tension for partial roof coverings in certain areas such as shades in architecture. Cables support the structure in bridge designs alone or together with truss systems. It is an effective system for crossing long spans. These systems, which are advantageous in terms of material savings, can provide more economical designs compared to other bridge types. A visual example of a cable-stayed bridge is shown in Fig. 6.4.

In the optimization of cable structures, the first constraint to be considered is the initial stress constraint of the cable. In the design, optimizing the pre-stress based on strength is one of the preferred optimization targets. Optimization requirements are shaped according to other structural system elements where cable systems are used alone or together. Cable systems are frequently used in the designs of shell structures. In the literature, the number of studies using metaheuristic methods in shell structure design optimization where cables are used is increasing day by day. In the optimization applications made, joint optimization, shape and section optimization have been the subject of studies [88–90].

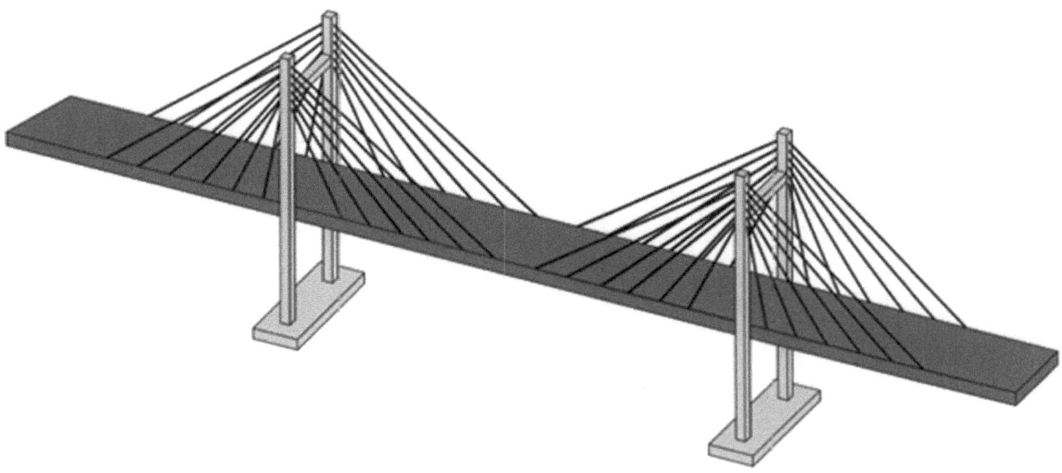

FIGURE 6.4 Cable-stayed bridge example.

In bridge designs where cables are used, many elements need to be considered such as cable forces, number of cables, cable diameter, and main span distance. Design optimization studies with metaheuristic algorithms are quite common in optimizing structures with many bridge design variables such as cable-supported bridges, cabled stayed bridges, and suspension bridges in cable systems. In the studies, the objective functions of cable-stayed bridges are to minimize the material cost, deck mass, pylon top displacement and weighted bending energy total and to maximize the live load, and design constraints such as strength, stiffness and stability are applied [91–95].

6.2.4 Tensegrity Structures

Tensegrity systems are structural systems that use struts and cables together, enabling lighter designs compared to truss systems. Tensegrity structures consist of elements such as metal, wood, cable, wire and flexible tape, which act as compression and tension [3]. It is among the recommended structural systems due to having alternative options in terms of material, providing an aesthetic appearance, ease of transportation, requiring lower costs and allowing a lightweight design. It is recommended for space structures, especially in structural designs to be used in space engineering, thanks to its advantages in terms of weight, assembly and transportation [96–101]. Figure 6.5 shows a visual example of a tensegrity structure.

In the optimum design of tensegrity structures, minimizing element stress and maximizing structural stiffness are important for design. The form-finding process of tensegrity elements is also a subject of optimization studies. In design optimization, there are optimization studies targeting one or more objectives [102–105].

Metaheuristic methods are frequently preferred as an optimization tool in the optimum design of tensegrity structures. There are many sample applications of metaheuristic optimization studies in the literature. Some of the studies can be summarized as follows: Do et al. proposed a modified differential evolution algorithm that aims to minimize a

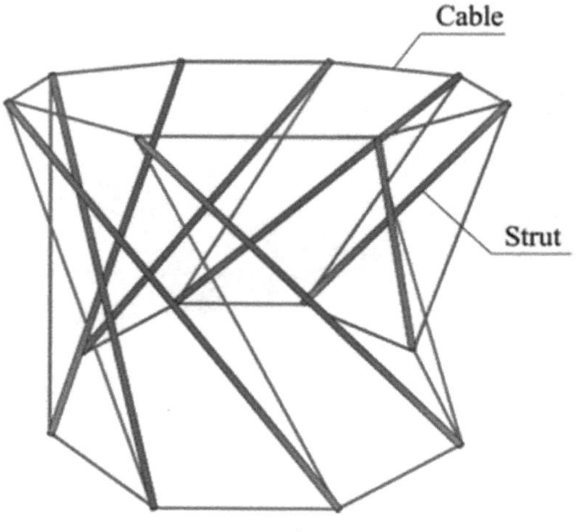

FIGURE 6.5 Tensegric structure example.

function consisting of eigenvalues and force density for form-finding optimization in tensegrity structure design [106]. Toklu and Uzun performed total potential optimization (TPO) aiming to minimize potential energy by using genetic algorithms on two- and three-dimensional tensegrity samples [107]. Do and Lee presented a modified symbiotic organisms search algorithm for optimization for form-finding targets of tensegrity systems with pin-jointed structures [108]. Ma et al. applied topology optimization for tensegrity tori ring stiffness based on a genetic algorithm [109]. Yıldız and Lesioutre performed dimensioning and pre-stress optimization for tensegrity space boom structures by using a particle swarm optimization algorithm to minimize mass and increase stiffness [110]. Bekdaş et al. minimized the total potential energy of a tensegrity system by using an AHS algorithm for the stability of elements [3]. Feng et al. applied mass optimization with a quantum beetle search algorithm to minimize structure mass in tensegrity grid, plate, and shell structure examples [111].

6.3 TOTAL POTENTIAL OPTIMIZATION WITH METAHEURISTIC ALGORITHMS FOR ANALYSIS OF A TENSEGRIC STRUCTURE

Tensegrity structures are systems consisting of cables and struts. Due to its geometry, it is prone to nonlinear displacements. In the design optimization of these systems, reducing the energy of the system is a recommended method for the stability of tensegrity structural elements. The aim here is to reduce the energy generated as a result of the work to be done by displacing the tension and compression elements and to ensure that the structure remains stable. This method is called total potential optimization.

In this study, a TPO process is applied for the analysis of a tensegrity structure example. In the optimization, the AHS algorithm developed by Geem et al. is used by adapting the algorithm parameters to make them most suitable. The algorithm used for the optimization application was selected among the ten metaheuristic algorithms that Toklu et al. tried for TPO [112]. Energy minimization was applied to the tensegrity structure model used in the study under various loadings. In the optimization, it was aimed to find displacement results of the tensegrity structure elements under loading were presented.

6.3.1 Methodology

In this section, details and equations of the TPO method and information about the AHS algorithm method and equations as the metaheuristic algorithm used in the study are given.

6.3.1.1 Total Potential Energy for Tensegrity Structures

Tensegric structural elements consist of tension and compression elements. These elements can exhibit nonlinear behavior under external loads. The general design of tensegrity structures causes many uncertain situations in terms of statics and kinematics [112, 113]. The nonlinear behavior of tension and compression elements difficulties in the stiffness of the structure. Taking these into account, controlling the displacements of tensegrity structural elements is necessary for structural stiffness. The process of reducing the potential energy of the structural system makes the structure more stiffness. Minimizing the total potential energy provides a faster analysis compared to the finite element and Eulerian-Lagrangian solution methods preferred in stiffness structural designs [114]. In the analysis of a tensegrity structure, the lengths of tensegrity elements are calculated at the beginning and after loading. The calculation equation for the initial lengths of the tensegrity structural elements is shown in Equation 6.1, the calculation equation for the lengths of the deformed state is shown in Equation 6.2, and the vector of displacements at the nodes of the tensegrity element deformed after loading is shown in Equation 6.3.

$$L_0 = \sqrt{(x_j - x_i)^2 + (y_j - y_i)^2 + (z_j - z_i)^2} \tag{6.1}$$

$$L_D = \sqrt{(x_j - x_i + u_j - u_i)^2 + (y_j - y_i + v_j - v_i)^2 + (z_j - z_i + w_j - w_i)^2} \tag{6.2}$$

$$D = \begin{bmatrix} u_1 & v_1 & w_1 & \cdots & u_{Nj} & v_{Nj} & w_{Nj} \end{bmatrix} \tag{6.3}$$

In the equations, the coordinates of the starting point of the tensegric elements are shown with x_i, y_i and z_i. The ending coordinates are x_j, y_j and z_j. The initial length of the element is expressed as L_0, and the changed length after loading is expressed as L_D. The representation of the representative coordinates of the tensegrity structural elements is given in Fig. 6.6. The lengths of the deformed shape of the elements are shown with the symbols u, v and w, and the joint number of the element is shown with Nj in Equation 6.3. The stress calculation of the deformed element in the structure is given in Equation 6.4.

$$\varepsilon = \frac{L_D - L_0}{L_0} \tag{6.4}$$

By determining the displacements of the tensegrity elements, the stress (σ) value, which is a function of strain, is calculated as in Equation 6.5. If there is a previously formed stress

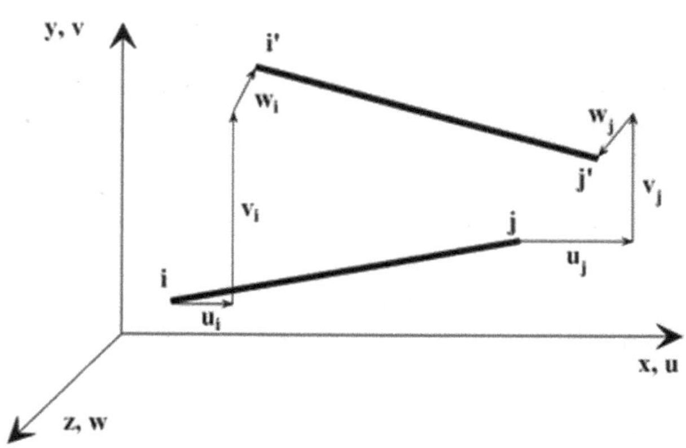

FIGURE 6.6 A structural element with dimensions.

(σ_0) in the structure, this value is considered, and the stress is calculated as in Equation 6.6. The initial stress of the structure is expressed as σ_0.

$$\sigma = \sigma(\varepsilon) \tag{6.5}$$

$$\sigma = \sigma(\varepsilon) + \sigma_0 \tag{6.6}$$

The amount of stress per unit volume in a tensegrity structure is expressed as the strain energy density and is shown with the symbol "*e*". The strain energy density is equal to the area under the stress-strain graph. In a tensegrity structure without pre-stressing, the strain energy is calculated as in Equation 6.7. In the case of pre-stressing, the strain energy density is calculated as in Equation 6.8.

$$e(\varepsilon) = \int_0^{\varepsilon} \sigma(\varepsilon) d\varepsilon \tag{6.7}$$

$$e(\varepsilon) = \int_0^{\varepsilon} \sigma(\varepsilon) d\varepsilon + \sigma_0 \varepsilon \tag{6.8}$$

In the calculation of strain energy for the bar element of the Tensegric structure, the strain energy density is calculated by multiplying the cross-sectional area (A) and the deformed length (L_D) of the compression element. The strain energy of the cable elements is calculated only when they are under tension. The strain energy (S) calculation is given in Equation 6.9.

$$S = AL_D e \tag{6.9}$$

The total potential energy (U) in a Tensegric structure is calculated by taking into account the displacement and work done by the system under external loads as shown in Equation 6.10 [115].

$$U(\varepsilon) = \sum_{j=1}^{N_m} e_j A_j L_j - \sum_{i=1}^{N_P} P_i u_i \tag{6.10}$$

In Equation 6.10, the number of elements is N_m, the cross-sectional area of the bar elements is A_j, the bar element length is L_j, the external loads are P_i, the degree of freedom of the external loads is N_P and the displacements under the external loads are shown as u_i. In the case of a pre-stress in the Tensegric structure, the work to be done by this tension force is added to Equation 6.10.

6.3.1.2 Optimization with Adaptive Harmony Search Algorithm

HS algorithm is a metaheuristic method developed by Geem et al. [34] inspired by the process of searching for the best harmony. When a musician improvises, they can be inspired by a piece that has listened to before and found pleasing, can produce a new harmony from scratch, or can replay a melody that likes in memory. The HS algorithm also produces harmony vectors improvisationally, just like a musician's HS process, and updates each new harmony it produces with the old one according to its better. Harmony vectors are produced and stored within the given limit values as in Equation 6.11.

$$X_{\text{new}} = X_{\min} + rand\ (X_{\max} - X_{\min})\ if\ \ HMCR \leq rand \tag{6.11}$$

In Equation 6.11, the new harmony vector X_{new}, the harmony lower and upper limit values are shown as $X_{\min}$ and $X_{\max}$, respectively. The harmony memory consideration ratio value from the harmonic search algorithm factors is expressed as HMCR.

Another harmony production equation for harmony vectors is given in Equation 6.12. The HMCR value is taken into account in determining which of these two production equations will be used. If the HMCR value is smaller or equal to a number randomly selected between 0 and 1, Equation 6.11 is used to produce new harmony vectors, and if the HMCR value is larger than the random number, Equation 6.12 is used to produce new harmony vectors.

$$X_{\text{new}} = X_n + rand\ \text{FW}\ (X_{\max} - X_{\min})\ if\ \ HMCR > rand \tag{6.12}$$

The FW given in Equation 6.12 is the fret width value among the HS algorithm factors. X_n is the nth harmony.

After the harmony vectors are produced, they are compared according to the objective function. The better result according to the objective function is replaced with the old one in each production and the aim is to find the best harmony. The algorithm has two design factors, HMCR and FW values. These are assigned by giving a number at the beginning. However, it is not possible to know that the given value is the optimum value for the problem. Choosing these values as optimum increases the success of the algorithm. By assigning an initial value in the optimization for HMCR and FW values, it is possible to adapt the most suitable parameter for the problem in the given range. In this way, the algorithm is adapted to show its best performance. The algorithm obtained by adapting the parameters is called the AHS algorithm. The calculation equations containing the adaptation of HMCR and FW values are given in Equation 6.13 and Equation 6.14, respectively.

$$HMCR = HMCR_{\text{in}}\left(1 + \frac{t}{mt}\right) \tag{6.13}$$

$$\text{FW} = \text{FW}_{\text{in}}\left(1 - \frac{t}{mt}\right) \tag{6.14}$$

$HMCR_{\text{in}}$ given in the equations indicates the initial value of HMCR, FW_{in} indicates the initial value of FW, mt indicates the maximum iteration, t indicates the iteration number.

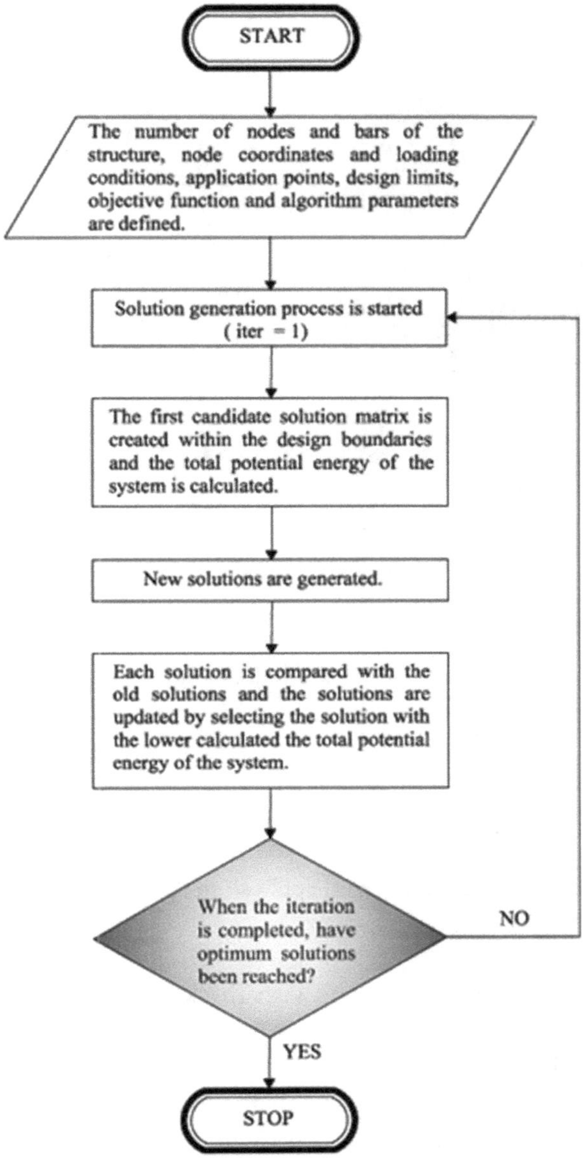

FIGURE 6.7 A flowchart of the analysis process.

The purpose of the tensegrity structure optimization to be used in the study is to minimize the total potential energy of the system. The deviations at the nodal points of the structure are taken as the design variables of the optimization. The flow diagram summarizing the tensegrity structure optimization process is shown in Fig. 6.7.

6.3.2 Numerical Example

In this study, a tensegrity system, which is shown in Fig. 6.8 and taken from the work of Nuhoğlu and Korkmaz [116], is considered a numerical implementation for TPO. In

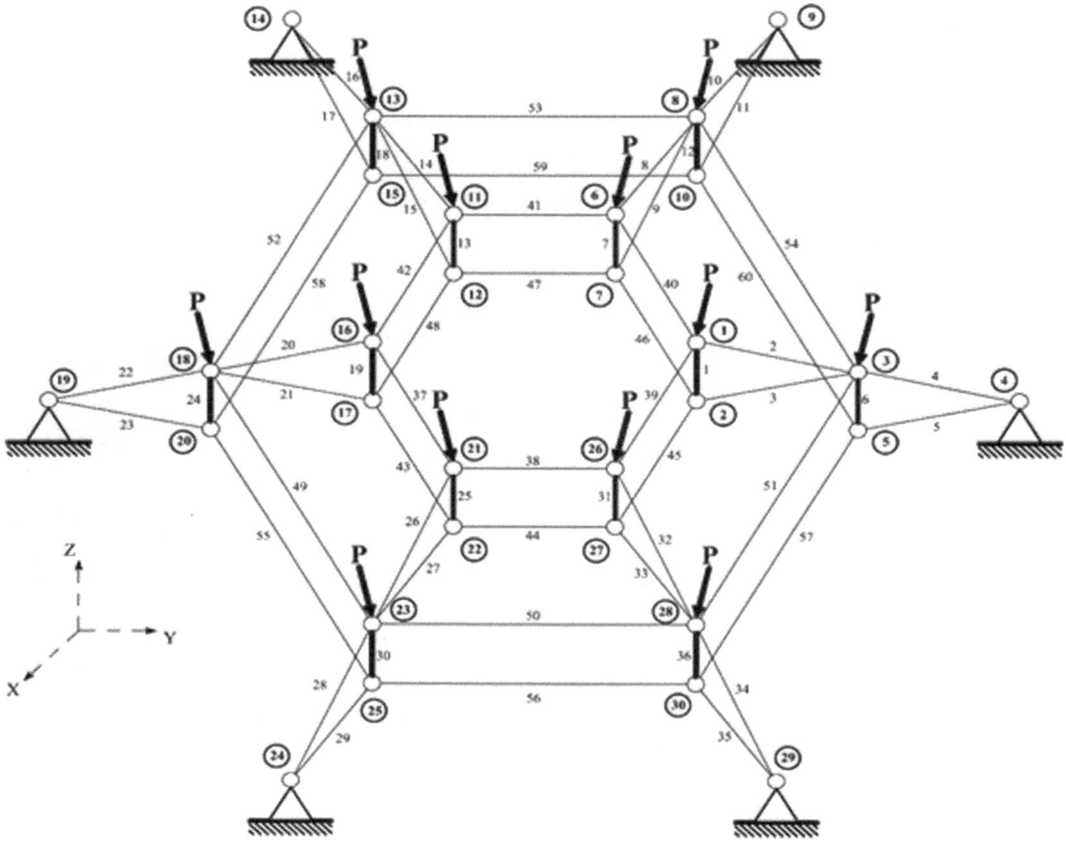

FIGURE 6.8 3-D tensegrity system numerical application example.

this tensegrity system, struts are shown with thick lines, and cables are shown with thin lines. The axial stiffnesses of the strut and cable elements are EA = 1,253,490 kN and EA = 148,460 kN, respectively. A P load of 10 kN is applied to the nodes 1, 3, 6, 8, 11, 13, 16, 18, 21, 23, 26 and 28 shown in Fig. 6.8. The system is pre-stressed and the stability of the tensegrity structure is provided by a pre-stressing force of 300 kN applied to the cables.

There are 30 nodes in the Tensegric structure and a total of 60 elements consisting of strut cables. The top view of the Tensegric structure with its dimensions is given in Fig. 6.9. The height view of the system, taking into account the area between nodes 4 and 19, is shown in Fig. 6.10 with its dimensions.

The coordinates of the undeformed nodes of the tensegrity structure before loading are given in Table 6.1.

In the system, node number 19 is accepted as the zero point of the x, y and z planes. Total potential energy minimization is applied to the Tensegric system with an AHS algorithm under P load and pre-stress. The constant values and algorithm factor used for TPO are given in Table 6.2.

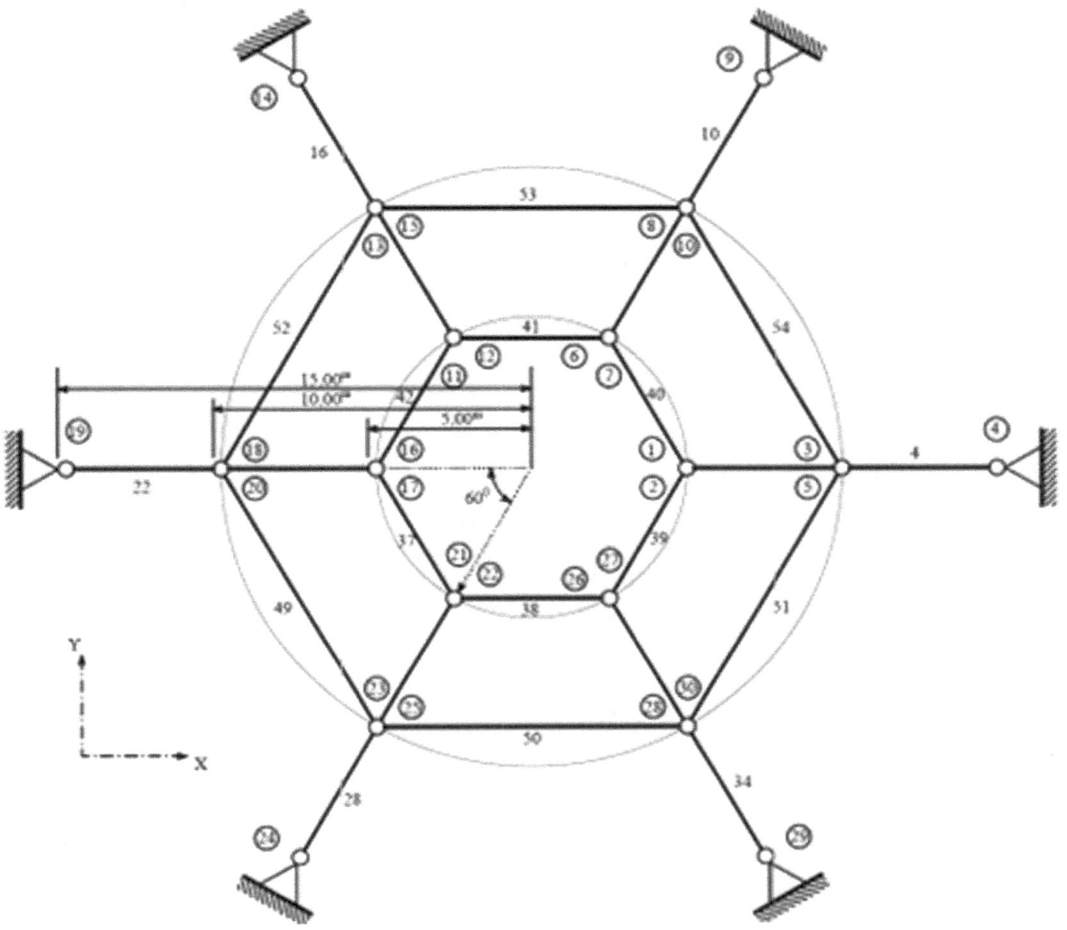

FIGURE 6.9 Lay-out of tensegrity system.

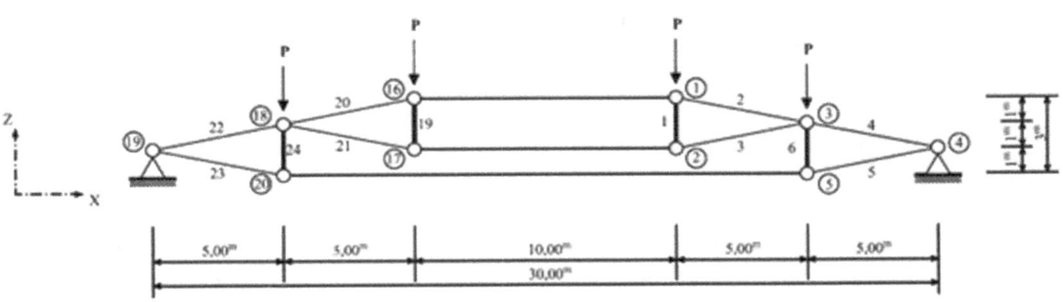

FIGURE 6.10 Elevation view.

TABLE 6.1 Undeformed Joint Coordinates for Tensegrity System

	Coordinates (mm)		
Node No	x	Y	Z
1	0.00	20000.00	2000.00
2	0.00	20000.00	0.00
3	0.00	25000.00	1000.00
4	0.00	30000.00	0.00
5	0.00	25000.00	−1000.00
6	4330.13	17500.00	2000.00
7	4330.13	17500.00	0.00
8	8660.25	20000.00	1000.00
9	12990.38	22500.00	0.00
10	8660.25	20000.00	−1000.00
11	4330.13	12500.00	2000.00
12	4330.13	12500.00	0.00
13	8660.25	10000.00	1000.00
14	12990.38	7500.00	0.00
15	8660.25	10000.00	−1000.00
16	0.00	10000.00	2000.00
17	0.00	10000.00	0.00
18	0.00	5000.00	1000.00
19	0.00	0.00	0.00
20	0.00	5000.00	−1000.00
21	−4330.13	12500.00	2000.00
22	−4330.13	12500.00	0.00
23	−8660.25	10000.00	1000.00
24	−12990.38	7500.00	0.00
25	−8660.25	10000.00	−1000.00
26	−4330.13	17500.00	2000.00
27	−4330.13	17500.00	0.00
28	−8660.25	20000.00	1000.00
29	−12990.38	22500.00	0.00
30	−8660.25	20000.00	−1000.00

TABLE 6.2 The Design Parameters for the Tensegrity System

Symbol	Definition	Value
HMCR	Harmony memory considering rate	0.5–1
$HMCR_{in}$	Initial harmony memory considering rate	0.5
FW	Fret width	0–0.05
FW_{in}	Initial fret width	0.05
mt	Maximum iteration number	100000
t	Iteration number	1–1000000
pn	Population number	30
s	Number of struts	12
c	Number of cables	48
EA_s	Axial stiffness for strut (kN)	1.253.490
EA_c	Axial stiffness for cable (kN)	148.460

TABLE 6.3 Analyses of Results for the Tensegrity System

	Displacement (mm)		
Node No	u	V	w
1	2.6921	−5.9278	−57.9468
2	−4.4307	−5.0331	−57.8904
3	−2.5550	−11.8390	−51.3511
4	0.0000	0.0000	0.0000
5	3.8197	6.4651	−51.1203
6	−4.2306	−3.9350	−56.3315
7	−7.7700	−0.1092	−56.2817
8	−12.3447	−3.6998	−54.8049
9	0.0000	0.0000	0.0000
10	8.3410	−0.0319	−54.5581
11	−7.0098	3.0353	−66.3702
12	−4.4863	5.2697	−66.3206
13	−10.3629	8.8418	−59.3525
14	0.0000	0.0000	0.0000
15	5.2680	−7.1953	−59.0886
16	−1.8628	8.0848	−68.4635
17	1.7461	5.2063	−68.4128
18	1.6751	12.9769	−56.9624
19	0.0000	0.0000	0.0000
20	−2.7373	−7.6524	−56.7047
21	5.2895	6.5266	−67.4600
22	4.8311	−0.1499	−67.3980
23	11.4337	4.8628	−53.8050
24	0.0000	0.0000	0.0000
25	−7.3140	−1.2728	−53.5671
26	7.6124	−0.4811	−62.1885
27	2.0647	−5.5176	−62.1279
28	9.4982	−7.6089	−52.1820
29	0.0000	0.0000	0.0000
30	−4.20	5.93	−51.95
Energy (N-mm)		65559584.66	

The analysis results obtained from the TPO applied to the pre-stressed tensegrim system example are shown in Table 6.3. The iteration-dependent plot of the energy result obtained is shown in Fig. 6.11. As seen in Figure 11, the algorithm is effective in finding a nearly exact solution after 10,000 iterations.

6.4 CONCLUSIONS

In this study, the optimum design and analysis of plate systems, truss systems, cabled structures and tensegrity structures with metaheuristic algorithms have been reviewed, and the design constraints used in the optimization of these structural systems, optimization objectives and current studies have been included. As a result of the research, the preferred shape, dimensioning, topology and similar optimization studies and the preferred metaheuristic algorithms have been mentioned. In light of the observations obtained, it

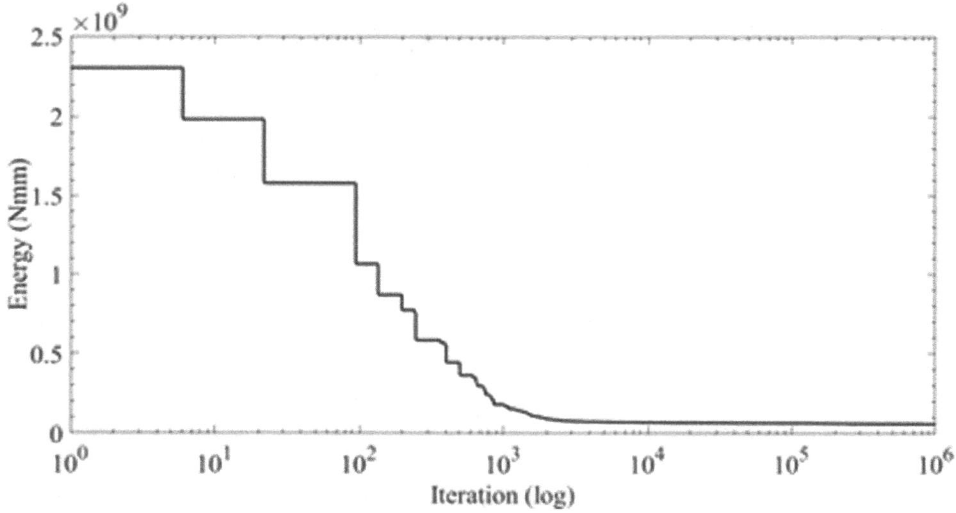

FIGURE 6.11 Optimized total potential energy vs. number of iterations graph.

is seen that in plate systems, the aim is often to reduce the weight of the structure and increase the buckling load, and the optimization of the dimensioning and layout is studied. In truss systems, section optimization studies on weight, volume and cost reduction are quite common. Based on the research on cabled structures, it is understood that joint, shape and section optimizations of these systems are preferred, and cable forces, tension and strength restrictions are generally taken. Similar situations are the case in tensegrity structures where cables can be used as tension elements. In addition, studies on the potential energy minimization of the system, which leaves behind complex analyses called TPO, are increasing and are suggested. Within the scope of the study, the TPO method was explained and applied in a tensegrity system. In the application, a metaheuristic algorithm, an AHS algorithm, was used to analyze the tensegrity structure system. As a result of the research, it was seen that the TPO process is an effective method and has potential in the design of tensegrity systems, which are seen as the space structures of the future.

As shown in the tensegrity structure example in this review chapter, TPO using AHS is an effective method for systems that are hard to solve via conventional methods without modification. The usage of metaheuristics with classical approaches of finite element and energy minimization theory can provide a solution considering all nonlinearities without additional modification.

REFERENCES

1. Rao, B. V., Sunanda, K., Alapati, M., & Viswanadh, G. K. (2022). Structural optimization of steel plate shear wall with different perforation configurations and locations. *Materials Today: Proceedings*, *62*, 6561–6567.
2. Verma, A., & Sahoo, D. R. (2019). Seismic design procedure for staggered steel plate shear wall. In *Proceedings of the International Conference on Earthquake Engineering and Structural Dynamics* (pp. 81–94). Springer International Publishing.

3. Bekdaş, G., Ocak, A., Nigdeli, S. M., & Toklu, Y. C. (2024). A metaheuristic-based method for analysis of tensegrity structures. *The Structural Design of Tall and Special Buildings*, *33*(7), e2091.
4. Mai, D. D., Bao, T. D., Lam, T. D., & Mai, H. T. (2024). Physics-informed neural network for nonlinear analysis of cable net structures. *Advances in Engineering Software*, *196*, 103717.
5. Abad, M. S. A., Shooshtari, A., Esmaeili, V., & Riabi, A. N. (2013). Nonlinear analysis of cable structures under general loadings. *Finite elements in analysis and design*, *73*, 11–19.
6. Kim, N. I., Thai, S., & Lee, J. (2016). Nonlinear elastoplastic analysis of slack and taut cable structures. *Engineering with Computers*, *32*, 615–627.
7. Balogh, B., & Lógó, J. (2014). Optimal design of curved folded plates. *Periodica Polytechnica Civil Engineering*, *58*(4), 423–430.
8. Kropiowska, D., Mikulski, L., & Szeptyński, P. (2019). Optimal design of a Kirchhoff-Love plate of variable thickness by application of the minimum principle. *Structural and Multidisciplinary Optimization*, *59*, 1581–1598.
9. Fares, M. E., Elmarghany, M. K., & Atta, D. (2015). The influence of the normal strain effect on the control and design optimization of functionally graded plates. *Composites Part B: Engineering*, *77*, 440–453.
10. Lógó, J., Balogh, B., & Pintér, E. (2018). Topology optimization considering multiple loading. *Computers & Structures*, *207*, 233–244.
11. Bagherinejad, M. H., & Haghollahi, A. (2020). Study on topology optimization of perforated steel plate shear walls in moment frame based on strain energy. *International Journal of Steel Structures*, *20*(4), 1420–1438.
12. Deepika, M. M., & Onkar, A. K. (2021). Multicriteria optimization of variable thickness plates using adaptive weighted sum method. *Sādhanā*, *46*(2), 82.
13. Amir, O., & Majdouba, A. (2024). Mesh-based topology, shape, and sizing optimization of ribbed plates. *Structural and Multidisciplinary Optimization*, *67*(6), 103.
14. Chun, J., Song, J., & Paulino, G. H. (2019). System-reliability-based design and topology optimization of structures under constraints on first-passage probability. *Structural Safety*, *76*, 81–94.
15. Da Silva, L. A. R., Torii, A. J., & Beck, A. T. (2023). Hyperstatic and redundancy thresholds in truss topology optimization considering progressive collapse due to aleatory and epistemic uncertainties. *Probabilistic Engineering Mechanics*, *71*, 103384.
16. Palizzolo, L., & Tabbuso, P. (2019). Reliability-based design optimization of trusses under dynamic shakedown constraints. *Structural and Multidisciplinary Optimization*, *60*, 1097–1108.
17. Sotiropoulos, S., & Lagaros, N. D. (2022). A two-stage structural optimization-based design procedure of structural systems. *The Structural Design of Tall and Special Buildings*, *31*(3), e1909.
18. Jootoo, A., & Lattanzi, D. (2018). Extraction of structural system designs from topologies via morphological analysis and artificial intelligence. *Designs*, *2*(1), 8.
19. Martins, A. M., Simões, L. M., & Negrão, J. H. (2016). Optimum design of concrete cable-stayed bridges. *Engineering Optimization*, *48*(5), 772–791.
20. Wang, D., Wang, L., Li, Z., & Xiang, S. (2024). Optimization and control of cable forces in a hybrid beam cable-stayed bridge based on a distributed algorithm. *Engineering Optimization*, *56*(5), 720–739.
21. Song, C., Xiao, R., & Sun, B. (2018). Optimization of cable pre-tension forces in long-span cable-stayed bridges considering the counterweight. *Engineering Structures*, *172*, 919–928.
22. Ding, Y., Xiang, Z., Li, Y., Zhang, X. S., & Zhou, Y. (2020). A practical and safe optimization method for temporary cable layout on the upper beam of beam-arch composite rigid frame bridge. *International Journal of Safety and Security Engineering*, *10*(1), 89–95.
23. Wang, Z., Zhang, N., & Cheng, Q. (2023, May). Multi-objective optimization-based reasonable finished state in long-span cable-stayed bridge considering counterweights. In *Structures* (Vol. 51, pp. 1497–1506). Elsevier.

24. Liu, K., & Paulino, G. H. (2019). Tensegrity topology optimization by force maximization on arbitrary ground structures. *Structural and Multidisciplinary Optimization*, *59*, 2041–2062.
25. Wang, Y., Xu, X., & Luo, Y. (2020). Topology-finding of tensegrity structures considering global stability condition. *Journal of Structural Engineering*, *146*(12), 04020260.
26. Wang, Y., Xu, X., & Luo, Y. (2021). Minimal mass design of active tensegrity structures. *Engineering Structures*, *234*, 111965.
27. Xu, X., Huang, S., Wang, Y., & Luo, Y. (2023). A generalized objective function based on weight coefficient for topology-finding of tensegrity structures. *Applied Mathematical Modelling*, *115*, 541–567.
28. Lu, J., Xu, Z., & Pan, J. (2023). Design of tensegrity torus based on bilevel optimization model. *Mechanics Research Communications*, *134*, 104222.
29. Yang, X. S. (2010). A new metaheuristic bat-inspired algorithm. In Nature-inspired cooperative strategies for optimization (NICSO 2010) (pp. 65–74). Springer, Berlin, Heidelberg.
30. Yang, X. S. (2012). Flower pollination algorithm for global optimization. Lecture Notes in Computer Science. In Durand-Lose, J., Jonoska, N., 27, Springer, London, 7445, 240–249.
31. Rashedi, E., Nezamabadi-Pour, H., & Saryazdi, S. (2009). GSA: a gravitational search algorithm. *Information sciences*, *179*(13), 2232–2248.
32. Rao, R. V., Savsani, V. J., Vakharia, D. P. (2011). Teaching-learning-based optimization: a novel method for constrained mechanical design optimization problems. Computer-Aided Design, 43, 303–15.
33. Karaboğa, D. (2005). An idea based on honeybee swarm for numerical optimization (Vol. 200, pp. 1–10). Technical report-tr06. Erciyes University, engineering faculty, computer engineering department.
34. Geem, Z. W., Kim, J. H., & Loganathan, G. V. (2001). A new heuristic optimization algorithm: harmony search. *simulation*, *76*(2), 60–68.
35. Ocak, A., Bekdaş, G., & Nigdeli, S. M. (2022, September). Comparison of classical and adaptive parameter setting for harmony search on a structural optimization problem. In *Proceedings of 7th International Conference on Harmony Search, Soft Computing and Applications: ICHSA 2022* (pp. 363–368). Singapore: Springer Nature Singapore.
36. Cheng, M. Y., Prayogo, D., Wu, Y. W., & Lukito, M. M. (2016). A Hybrid Harmony Search algorithm for discrete sizing optimization of truss structure. *Automation in Construction*, *69*, 21–33.
37. Degertekin, S. O. (2012). Improved harmony search algorithms for sizing optimization of truss structures. *Computers & Structures*, *92*, 229–241.
38. Cakiroglu, C., Bekdaş, G., & Geem, Z. W. (2020). Harmony search optimization of dispersed laminated composite plates. *Materials*, *13*(12), 2862.
39. De Almeida, F. S. (2016). Stacking sequence optimization for maximum buckling load of composite plates using a harmony search algorithm. *Composite Structures*, *143*, 287–299.
40. The MathWorks, Matlab R2018a. Natick, MA 2018.
41. Cakiroglu, C., Bekdaş, G., Kim, S., & Geem, Z. W. (2020). Optimization of Shear and lateral-torsional buckling of Steel Plate Girders Using Meta-Heuristic Algorithms. *Applied Sciences*, *10*(10), 3639.
42. Erdal, F., Tunca, O., Taylan, H., Ozcelik, R., & Sogut, H. (2022). Influence of trapezoidal and sinusoidal corrugation on the flexural capacity of optimally designed thin-walled beams. *Structural Engineering and Mechanics, An Int'l Journal*, *84*(1), 63–76.
43. Negrin, I., Kripka, M., & Yepes, V. (2023). Design optimization of welded steel plate girders configured as a hybrid structure. *Journal of Constructional Steel Research*, *211*, 108131.
44. Pavlović, G. V., Zdravković, N. B., Marković, G. Đ., Savković, M. M., & Bulatović, R. R. (2024). Optimization of welded I-girder of the single-beam bridge cranes. *International Journal of Steel Structures*, *24*(4), 969–985.

45. Ghosh, S., Adam, F., & Das, A. (2009). Design of steel plate shear walls considering inelastic drift demand. *Journal of Constructional Steel Research*, *65*(7), 1431–1437.
46. Astaneh-Asl, A. (2001). *Seismic behavior and design of steel shear walls*. Moraga, CA: Structural Steel Educational Council.
47. Gholizadeh, S., & Shahrezaei, A. M. (2015). Optimal placement of steel plate shear walls for steel frames by bat algorithm. *The Structural Design of Tall and Special Buildings*, *24*(1), 1–18.
48. Kaveh, A., & Farhadmanesh, M. (2019). Optimal seismic design of steel plate shear walls using metaheuristic algorithms. *Periodica Polytechnica Civil Engineering*, *63*(1), 1–17.
49. He, J., Lin, S., Li, Y., Dong, X., & Chen, S. (2022). Genetic algorithm for optimal placement of steel plate shear walls for steel frames. *Buildings*, *12*(6), 835.
50. Daryan, A. S., Salari, M., Palizi, S., & Farhoudi, N. (2023, February). Size and layout optimum design of frames with steel plate shear walls by metaheuristic optimization algorithms. In *Structures* (Vol. 48, pp. 657–668). Elsevier. https://www.sciencedirect.com/science/article/abs/pii/S2352012422011572
51. Lakshmi, K., & Rao, A. R. M. (2015). Optimal design of laminate composite plates using a dynamic hybrid adaptive harmony search algorithm. *Journal of Reinforced Plastics and Composites*, *34*(6), 493–518.
52. Ho-Huu, V., Do-Thi, T. D., Dang-Trung, H., Vo-Duy, T., & Nguyen-Thoi, T. (2016). Optimization of laminated composite plates for maximizing buckling load using improved differential evolution and smoothed finite element method. *Composite Structures*, *146*, 132–147.
53. Kaveh, A., Dadras, A., & Malek, N. G. (2018). Buckling load of laminated composite plates using three variants of the biogeography-based optimization algorithm. *Acta Mechanica*, *229*, 1551–1566.
54. Keshtegar, B., Nguyen-Thoi, T., Truong, T. T., & Zhu, S. P. (2021). Optimization of buckling load for laminated composite plates using adaptive Kriging-improved PSO: a novel hybrid intelligent method. *Defence Technology*, *17*(1), 85–99.
55. Jalili, S., Khani, R., Maheri, A., & Hosseinzadeh, Y. (2022). Performance assessment of meta-heuristics for composite layup optimization. *Neural Computing and Applications*, *34*, 2031–2054.
56. Le-Anh, L., Nguyen-Thoi, T., Ho-Huu, V., Dang-Trung, H., & Bui-Xuan, T. (2015). Static and frequency optimization of folded laminated composite plates using an adjusted differential evolution algorithm and a smoothed triangular plate element. *Composite Structures*, *127*, 382–394.
57. Vosoughi, A. R., & Nikoo, M. R. (2015). Maximum fundamental frequency and thermal buckling temperature of laminated composite plates by a new hybrid multi-objective optimization technique. *Thin-Walled Structures*, *95*, 408–415.
58. Wang, W., Wang, Q., Zhong, R., Chen, L., & Shi, X. (2023). Stacking sequence optimization of arbitrary quadrilateral laminated plates for maximum fundamental frequency by hybrid whale optimization algorithm. *Composite Structures*, *310*, 116764.
59. Vo-Duy, T., Ho-Huu, V., Do-Thi, T. D., Dang-Trung, H., & Nguyen-Thoi, T. (2017). A global numerical approach for lightweight design optimization of laminated composite plates subjected to frequency constraints. *Composite Structures*, *159*, 646–655.
60. Renkavieski, C., & Parpinelli, R. S. (2021). Meta-heuristic algorithms to truss optimization: literature mapping and application. *Expert Systems with Applications*, *182*, 115197.
61. Kennedy, J., & Eberhart, R. (1995, November). Particle swarm optimization. In *Proceedings of ICNN'95-International Conference on Neural Networks* (Vol. 4, pp. 1942–1948). IEEE.
62. Holland, J. H. (1984). Genetic algorithms and adaptation. Adaptive *Control* of *Ill-Defined Sys*tems, *16*, 317–333.
63. Storn, R., & Price, K. (1997). Differential evolution—a simple and efficient heuristic for global optimization over continuous spaces. *Journal of Global Optimization*, *11*, 341–359.

64. Yang, X. S. (2009, October). Firefly algorithms for multimodal optimization. In *International Symposium on Stochastic Algorithms* (pp. 169–178). Berlin, Heidelberg: Springer Berlin Heidelberg.
65. Kaveh, A., & Mahdavi, V. R. (2014). Colliding bodies optimization: a novel meta-heuristic method. *Computers & Structures, 139*, 18–27.
66. Cheng, M. Y., & Prayogo, D. (2014). Symbiotic organisms search: a new metaheuristic optimization algorithm. *Computers & Structures, 139*, 98–112.Ç
67. Erol, O. K., & Eksin, I. (2006). A new optimization method: big bang–big crunch. *Advances in Engineering Software, 37*(2), 106–111.
68. Huning, A. (1976). Evolutionsstrategie. *Optimierung technischer Systeme nach Prinzipien der biologischen evolution. JSTOR, 62*(2), 298–300.
69. Azad, S. K., Hasançebi, O., & Saka, M. P. (2014). Guided stochastic search technique for discrete sizing optimization of steel trusses: a design-driven heuristic approach. *Computers & Structures, 134*, 62–74.
70. Dizangian, B., & Ghasemi, M. R. (2019). Border-search and jump reduction method for size optimization of spatial truss structures. *Frontiers of Structural and Civil Engineering, 13*, 123–134.
71. Kooshkbaghi, M., & Kaveh, A. (2020). Sizing optimization of truss structures with continuous variables by artificial coronary circulation system algorithm. *Iranian Journal of Science and Technology, Transactions of Civil Engineering, 44*, 1–20.
72. Adil, B., & Cengiz, B. (2020). Optimal design of truss structures using weighted superposition attraction algorithm. *Engineering with Computers, 36*(3), 965–979.
73. Jawad, F. K., Ozturk, C., Dansheng, W., Mahmood, M., Al-Azzawi, O., & Al-Jemely, A. (2021, April). Sizing and layout optimization of truss structures with artificial bee colony algorithm. *Structures*, 30, 546–559. https://www.sciencedirect.com/science/article/abs/pii/S2352012421000199
74. Barakat, S., Alhalabi, M., Mostafa, O., & Fattouh, I. H. (2022). Size optimization of truss structures using calibrated shuffled complex evolution algorithm. *Jordan Journal of Civil Engineering, 16*(4), 540–548.
75. Moosavian, H., Mesbahi, P., Moosavian, N., & Daliri, H. (2023). Optimal design of truss structures with frequency constraints: a comparative study of DE, IDE, LSHADE, and CMAES algorithms. *Engineering with Computers, 39*(2), 1499–1517.
76. Dede, T., & Ayvaz, Y. (2015). Combined size and shape optimization of structures with a new meta-heuristic algorithm. *Applied Soft Computing, 28*, 250–258.
77. Ho-Huu, V., Nguyen-Thoi, T., Truong-Khac, T., Le-Anh, L., & Vo-Duy, T. (2018). An improved differential evolution based on roulette wheel selection for shape and size optimization of truss structures with frequency constraints. *Neural Computing and Applications, 29*, 167–185.
78. Nguyen-Van, S., Nguyen, K. T., Luong, V. H., Lee, S., & Lieu, Q. X. (2021). A novel hybrid differential evolution and symbiotic organisms search algorithm for size and shape optimization of truss structures under multiple frequency constraints. *Expert Systems with Applications, 184*, 115534.
79. Azizi, M., Aickelin, U., Khorshidi, H. A., & Shishehgarkhaneh, M. B. (2022). Shape and size optimization of truss structures by Chaos game optimization considering frequency constraints. *Journal of Advanced Research, 41*, 89–100.
80. Van, T. H., Tangaramvong, S., & Gao, W. (2023). Chaotic heterogeneous comprehensive learning PSO method for size and shape optimization of structures. *Engineering Applications of Artificial Intelligence, 126*, 107014.
81. Tejani, G. G., Savsani, V. J., Bureerat, S., Patel, V. K., & Savsani, P. (2019). Topology optimization of truss subjected to static and dynamic constraints by integrating simulated annealing into passing vehicle search algorithms. *Engineering with Computers, 35*, 499–517.

82. Wang, J., Li, Y., Hu, G., & Yang, M. (2022). An enhanced artificial hummingbird algorithm and its application in truss topology engineering optimization. *Advanced Engineering Informatics*, *54*, 101761.
83. Niño-Álvarez, L. H., & Begambre-Carrillo, O. J. (2023). Multiobjective topology optimization of planar trusses using stress trajectories and metaheuristic algorithms. *Revista Facultad de Ingeniería Universidad de Antioquia*, (107), 9–25.
84. Fiore, A., Marano, G. C., Greco, R., & Mastromarino, E. (2016). Structural optimization of hollow-section steel trusses by differential evolution algorithm. *International Journal of Steel Structures*, *16*, 411–423.
85. Serpik, I. N., Alekseytsev, A. V., & Balabin, P. Y. (2017). Mixed approaches to handle limitations and execute mutation in the genetic algorithm for truss size, shape, and topology optimization. *Periodica polytechnica civil engineering*, *61*(3), 471–482.
86. Mortazavi, A., & Togan, V. (2017). Triangular units-based method for simultaneous optimizations of planar trusses. *Advances in Computational Design*, *2*(3), 195–210.
87. Dang, K. D., Nguyen-Van, S., Thai, S., Lee, S., Luong, V. H., & Lieu, Q. X. (2022). A single-step optimization method for topology, size, and shape of trusses using hybrid differential evolution and symbiotic organisms search. *Computers & Structures*, *270*, 106846.
88. Shan, Y. L., Wu, H., & Gao, B. Q. (2014). Topology configuration and prestress optimization of cable-supported shell with robustness evaluation index. *International Journal of Space Structures*, *29*(3), 113–120.
89. Liu, X., Zhang, A., Zhang, X., & Tian, C. (2016). Particle swarm optimization algorithm for suspendome structure under multiple loading cases. *Engineering Computations*, *33*(3), 767–788.
90. Mottahedin, A., & Keyvani, J. (2023). Optimum design of cable domes using enhanced colliding bodies optimization algorithm with the substructuring method. *Iranian Journal of Science and Technology, Transactions of Civil Engineering*, *47*(5), 2571–2580.
91. Lute, V., Upadhyay, A., & Singh, K. K. (2009). Computationally efficient analysis of cable-stayed bridge for GA-based optimization. *Engineering Applications of Artificial Intelligence*, *22*(4-5), 750–758.
92. Hassan, M. M., El Damatty, A. A., & Nassef, A. O. (2015). Database for the optimum design of semi-fan composite cable-stayed bridges based on genetic algorithms. *Structure and Infrastructure Engineering*, *11*(8), 1054–1068.
93. Arellano, H., Tolentino, D., & Gómez, R. (2019). Optimum criss crossing cables in multi-span cable-stayed bridges using genetic algorithms. *KSCE Journal of Civil Engineering*, *23*, 719–728.
94. Santos, C. A., El Damatty, A. A., Pfeil, M. S., & Battista, R. C. (2020). Structural optimization of two-girder composite cable-stayed bridges under dead and live loads. *Canadian Journal of Civil Engineering*, *47*(8), 939–953.
95. Song, C., Xiao, R., Sun, B., Wang, Z., & Zhang, C. (2023). Cable force optimization of cable-stayed bridges: a surrogate model-assisted differential evolution method combined with B-spline interpolation curves. *Engineering Structures*, *283*, 115856.
96. Furuya, H. (1992). Concept of deployable tensegrity structures in space application. *International Journal of Space Structures*, *7*(2), 143–151.
97. Benaroya, H. (1993). Tensile-integrity structures for the moon. *Applied Mechanics of a Lunar Base, Applied Mechanics Reviews*, *46*(6), 326–335.
98. Sultan, C. (1999). *Modeling, design, and control of tensegrity structures with applications.* Lafayette, IN: Purdue University. https://www.proquest.com/openview/091c9c855bcd156ad0adf7d96d98eee4/1?cbl=18750&diss=y&pq-origsite=gscholar
99. Sultan, C., Corless, M., & Skelton, R. T. (1999, June). Peak-to-peak control of an adaptive tensegrity space telescope. In *Smart Structures and Materials 1999: Mathematics and Control in Smart Structures* (Vol. 3667, pp. 190–201). SPIE.

100. Tibert, G. (2002). *Deployable tensegrity structures for space applications* (Doctoral dissertation, KTH).
101. (2008). *A practical guide to tensegrity design*. Available online: http://www.angelfire.com/ma4/bob_wb/tenseg.pdf (March 20, 2025).
102. Adam, B., & Smith, I. F. (2007). Tensegrity active control: multiobjective approach. *Journal of Computing in Civil Engineering, 21*(1), 3–10.
103. Cai, J., & Feng, J. (2015). Form-finding of tensegrity structures using an optimization method. *Engineering Structures, 104*, 126–132.
104. Xu, X., Wang, Y., & Luo, Y. (2018). An improved multi-objective topology optimization approach for tensegrity structures. *Advances in Structural Engineering, 21*(1), 59–70.
105. Zhao, L., Liu, K., Li, C., Jin, L., & Sun, Z. (2021, July). Form-finding of tensegrity structures utilizing a nonlinear fletcher-reeves conjugate gradient method. In *2021 IEEE International Conference on Real-time Computing and Robotics (RCAR)* (pp. 732–737). IEEE.
106. Do, D. T., Lee, S., & Lee, J. (2016). A modified differential evolution algorithm for tensegrity structures. *Composite Structures, 158*, 11–19.
107. Toklu, Y. C., & Uzun, F. (2016). Analysis of tensegrity structures by total potential optimization using metaheuristic algorithms. *Journal of Aerospace Engineering, 29*(5), 04016023.
108. Do, D. T., & Lee, J. (2017). A modified symbiotic organisms search (mSOS) algorithm for optimization of pin-jointed structures. *Applied soft computing, 61*, 683–699.
109. Ma, S., Yuan, X. F., & Xie, S. D. (2019). A new genetic algorithm-based topology optimization method of tensegrity tori. *KSCE Journal of Civil Engineering, 23*, 2136–2147.
110. Yildiz, K., & Lesieutre, G. A. (2022). Sizing and prestress optimization of Class-2 tensegrity structures for space boom applications. *Engineering with Computers, 38*(2), 1451–1464.
111. Feng, X., Lou, X., Lv, H., & Su, Y. (2024, July). Study on lightweight design of tensegrity structures with multi-self-stress modes. In *Structures* (Vol. 65, p. 106750). Elsevier.
112. Toklu, Y. C., Bekdaş, G., Yücel, M., Nigdeli, S. M., Kayabekir, A. E., Kim, S., & Geem, Z. W. (2021). Total potential optimization using metaheuristic algorithms for solving nonlinear plane strain systems. *Applied Sciences, 11*(7), 3220.
113. Tran, H. C., & Lee, J. (2011). Geometric and material nonlinear analysis of tensegrity structures. *Acta Mechanica Sinica, 27*, 938–949.
114. Istianto, D. T., Tjong, W. F., Prayogo, D. (2022). Analısıs non-linear struktur tensegrity menggunakan total potential energy optimization with metaheuristic methods (TPO/MA). *Dimensi Utama Teknik Sipil, 9*(2), 97–115.
115. Toklu, Y. C. (2004). Nonlinear analysis of trusses through energy minimization. *Computers & structures, 82*(20-21), 1581–1589.
116. Nuhoglu, A., & Korkmaz, K. A. (2011). A practical approach for nonlinear analysis of tensegrity systems. *Engineering with Computers, 27*, 337–345.

CHAPTER 7

Optimal Design of Heat Exchanger Systems Using Marathon Runner Algorithm

Mahsa Moloodpoor and Ali Mortazavi

7.1 INTRODUCTION

Heat exchangers play a vital role in a wide range of industrial and residential applications, including power generation, chemical processing and HVAC systems. The efficient design of these systems is crucial for optimizing energy consumption, reducing costs and minimizing environmental impact. However, the complexity of heat exchanger design lies in balancing multiple conflicting objectives such as heat transfer efficiency, pressure drop and material costs, while adhering to various operational and safety constraints. This multi-objective nature makes the design process a challenging optimization problem, which has led to the increasing use of advanced optimization techniques.

In recent years, metaheuristic algorithms have gained significant attention for their ability to provide near-optimal solutions for complex engineering problems [1]. These algorithms, inspired by natural processes or phenomena, offer flexibility and robustness in exploring vast search spaces, making them suitable for solving highly non-linear and multi-modal optimization problems [2, 3]. Among the numerous metaheuristic algorithms available, conventional techniques like genetic algorithm (GA) [4], particle swarm optimization (PSO) [5] and differential evolution (DE) [6] have been widely applied in distinct fields [7–12]. Despite their success, there is a continuous demand for novel and more efficient optimization methods to improve solution quality and reduce computational time.

Optimization algorithms are generally classified into two main categories: gradient-based and non-gradient-based methods [13, 14]. Non-gradient-based algorithms are often preferred due to several advantages over their gradient-based counterparts. Notably, they do not require gradient information of the objective function, making them suitable for problems with non-differentiable, discontinuous or highly complex functions [15, 16]. Additionally, they can initiate the search process from any arbitrary point within the

DOI: 10.1201/9781003564911-7

search domain, without being constrained to a specific starting point, offering greater flexibility in exploring the solution space [17]. Non-gradient-based optimization algorithms could be categorized in four different groups based on their inspiration. These groups are swarm-based, evolutionary-based, physics-based and social-based [18, 19]. Marathon runner algorithm (MRA) is a novel global optimization technique belonging to the social-based group [20]. Which emulates the endurance and strategic behavior of marathon runners in competitive races. The MRA incorporates mechanisms that simulate energy management, decision-making under fatigue and adaptive strategies used by runners to optimize their performance. These characteristics are particularly advantageous for handling the non-linearities and complexities inherent in heat exchanger design problems.

Additionally, the MRA, inspired by the endurance and pacing strategy of marathon runners, introduces a novel optimization approach that excels in exploring complex search spaces. Unlike traditional methods such as genetic algorithms or particle swarm optimization, which may struggle with premature convergence or local optima, MRA offers a more balanced exploitation-exploration trade-off. This ensures improved global search capabilities and solution diversity. The efficiency and robustness of MRA in solving challenging engineering optimization problems are demonstrated through its superior convergence speed and accuracy, making it a valuable alternative to conventional algorithms.

Despite the extensive development of optimization algorithms in recent years, the search for methods that can reliably solve complex engineering optimization problems remains ongoing. The MRA is a newly proposed metaheuristic method, and while it has shown promise in initial studies, its performance in solving specific engineering benchmark problems, such as the optimization of shell-and-tube heat exchangers (STHEs), has not yet been fully explored. There is a need to evaluate how well MRA handles these types of optimization problems in comparison to more established techniques. By testing its performance on optimal design of STHEs as benchmarks, this study aims to provide valuable insights into the efficacy of MRA and its potential to become a competitive alternative for solving practical optimization challenges in engineering. This evaluation will be beneficial to researchers and practitioners alike, contributing to the ongoing development and refinement of optimization methods in this field.

Cost-efficient design of heat exchangers is at the focal point of researchers of the field. For example, Selbaş et al. (2006) and Caputo et al. (2008) applied the genetic algorithm (GA) to the design optimization of STHEs [21, 22]. Fesanghary et al. (2009) employed the harmony search algorithm (HSA) for optimizing STHE designs, and conducted a global sensitivity analysis to determine how geometric parameters affect cost efficiency. [23]. Ponce-Ortega et al. (2009) proposed an algorithm based on the logic of GA utilized for optimal design of STHEs according to Bell-Delaware heat transfer correlations [24]. Patel and Rao (2010) introduced the PSO technique for STHE design with a focus on economic efficiency [25]. Şencan Şahin et al. (2011) optimized STHE design economically using the artificial bee colony (ABC) algorithm [26]. Mariani et al. (2012) presented quantum particle swarm optimization (QPSO) and employed it to two STHE optimization case studies [27]. Hadidi and Nazari (2013) utilized the biogeography-based optimization (BBO) algorithm to address economic optimization of STHEs [28]. Asadi et al. (2014) employed the cuckoo search algorithm (CSA) to minimize total costs in STHE design [29]. Khosravi et al. (2015) assessed the performance of CSA, firefly algorithm (FFA) and GA in optimal design of STHEs comparatively [30]. Sadeghzadeh et al. (2015) conducted a techno-economic optimization of STHEs employing both PSO and GA [31]. Mohanty (2016) utilized the FFA and gravitational search algorithm (GSA) for cost minimization of STHEs [32, 33]. Vasconcelos Segundo et al. (2017) optimized STHE designs using both standard DE and its variant, trigonometric differential evolution (TDE) [34]. Söylemez et al. (2004) identified the optimum pipe size for double-pipe heat exchangers (DPHEs) by minimizing operation and installation costs for waste heat recovery [35]. Swamee et al. (2008) optimized the inner and outer pipe diameters and utility flow rate to minimize costs related to heat load, pumping power and fluids, using geometric programming [36]. Petrik et al. (2018) explored the optimal design of DPHEs in a book chapter, optimizing inner and outer diameters, mass flow rate, outlet temperature and pipe length to reduce material and operational costs [37]. Peccini et al. (2019) focused on the geometric design of DPHEs, minimizing the heat transfer area through mathematical programming techniques [37, 38]. Moloodpoor et al. (2021) employed an interactive search algorithm combined with an improved fly-back technique for the thermo-economic optimization of DPHEs [39].

The primary aim of this chapter is to apply the MRA to the optimal design of heat exchanger systems and evaluate its performance against four other well-known metaheuristic optimization methods. By addressing both thermo-economic and operational factors, this research seeks to assess the search performance of MRA as an effective tool for solving complex engineering design problems. The results presented in this work highlight the potential of the MRA in providing high-quality solutions with improved computational efficiency, making it a promising approach for optimizing heat exchanger systems.

The rest of the current chapter is arranged as follows: The details of the utilized optimization technique is given in Section 7.2. In Section 7.3, the optimization problem – focused on the design of a shell-and-tube heat exchanger – is thoroughly described. The numerical results are given in Section 7.4. Section 7.5 summarizes the key findings and conclusions drawn from the chapter.

7.2 OPTIMIZATION TECHNIQUE: MARATHON RUNNER ALGORITHM (MRA)

The MRA is an optimization technique inspired from competitive behavior of runners in a real competition. The MRA is a population-based optimization algorithm where each individual in the population represents a potential solution to a given problem. The algorithm begins with a population of n agents, each solving a D-dimensional problem. These agents are initially distributed across the search space. In the case of a D-dimensional problem, the MRA begins by generating an initial population of n agents, as depicted below [20]:

$$\text{Pop} = \begin{bmatrix} \mathbf{X}_1 \\ \cdot \\ \cdot \\ \mathbf{X}_i \\ \cdot \\ \cdot \\ \mathbf{X}_n \end{bmatrix} = \begin{bmatrix} x_{11}, x_{12}, \ldots, x_{1d}, \ldots x_{1D} \\ \cdot \\ \cdot \\ x_{i1}, x_{i2}, \ldots, x_{id}, \ldots, x_{iD} \\ \cdot \\ \cdot \\ x_{n1}, x_{n2}, \ldots x_{nd}, \ldots, x_{nD} \end{bmatrix}, \quad 1 \le i \le n, \text{ and } 1 \le d \le D \tag{7.1}$$

where, n is the number of agents; i is the current agent; D is the dimension of the problem.

In MRA, agents are sorted based on their objective function values. The agent with the lowest objective function value is considered the best and is assigned the highest rank, while the agent with the highest objective function value is considered the worst and is assigned the lowest rank. It means that, for any ith agent, $f(\mathbf{X}_{i+1}) < f(\mathbf{X}_i) < f(\mathbf{X}_{i-1})$. It is evident that the front and rear agents are unavailable for the best and worst performers, respectively. The MRA introduces a concept similar to a "vision point" in a real race. The weighted agent is a mathematical equivalent, calculated as the weighted average of all available agents in the population. This weighted agent represents a collective direction for improvement, guiding the population toward better solutions. The weighted agent ($\mathbf{X}^w$) is calculated as the weighted average of all agents in the population, and is mathematically expressed as follows [20]:

$$\begin{aligned} &\mathbf{X}^w = \sum_{i=1}^{n} \bar{c}_i^w \mathbf{X}_i \\ &\bar{c}_i^w = \left(\hat{c}_i^w \Big/ \sum_{i=1}^{n} \hat{c}_i^w \right) \\ &\text{in which} \\ &\hat{c}_i^w = \frac{\max\limits_{1 \le k \le n}\left(f(\mathbf{X}_k)\right) - f(\mathbf{X}_i)}{\max\limits_{1 \le k \le n}\left(f(\mathbf{X}_k)\right) - \min\limits_{1 \le k \le n}\left(f(\mathbf{X}_k)\right) + \varepsilon}, \quad i = 1, 2, \ldots, n \end{aligned} \tag{7.2}$$

in which, n is the total number of agents (i.e., population size); f (.) is the corresponding value of the objective function; $\min\limits_{1 \le k \le n}(f(\mathbf{X}_k))$ and $\max\limits_{1 \le k \le n}(f(\mathbf{X}_k))$ are the objective function values for the best and the worst agents, respectively; ε is a positive small digit (e.g., 0.0001) to prevent any potential division by 0.

Agents are updated based on their relative ranking, with the aim of improving their positions. This process mimics the behavior of runners who adjust their pace and strategy

TABLE 7.1 The Pseudo Code for the MRA

```
Generating N agents randomly
Sorting generated agents in ascending order (according to objective function values)
while (termination criteria is not met)
    Calculation of the weighted agent (Eq (7.2))
    for (each agent)
        if f(X^w) < f(^t X_i)
            α = +1   [moving toward the X^w] *
        else
            α = −1   [moving away from the X^w] *
        end
        Updating agent's position (Eq. (7.5))
        if the updated agent is better than the current agent
            replacing the current agent with the updated one
        else
            Continuing with the current agent
        end
    end
end
```

depending on their position in the race. According to the provided information, the search pattern of MRA is mathematically defined as below [20].

$$
\begin{aligned}
&{}^{t+1}\mathbf{X}_i = {}^{t}\mathbf{X}_i + r_1 \odot \left({}^{t}\mathbf{X}_{i-1} - {}^{t}\mathbf{X}_i\right) + r_2 \odot \left({}^{t}\mathbf{X}_i - {}^{t}\mathbf{X}_{i+1}\right) + 2.\alpha.r_3 \odot \left(\mathbf{X}^w - {}^{t}\mathbf{X}_i\right) \\
&\textit{where,} \\
&\alpha = sgn\left(f\left({}^{t}\mathbf{X}_i\right) - f\left(\mathbf{X}^w\right)\right)
\end{aligned}
\tag{7.3}
$$

In this equation, $\mathbf{X}_i$ represents the ith agent, t designates the current state and the superscript t+1 denotes the updated state of the related variable. The function $f(.)$ calculates the corresponding value of the objective function for the considered agent. The sign function $sgn(.)$ is –1 if $\mathbf{X}^w$ is in a worse position than the current agent ($\mathbf{X}_i$) and 1 otherwise. α is the factor of decision, that determines if the current agent should move closer to or farther away from $\mathbf{X}^w$. In other words, the weighted agent draws in agents with higher objective function values (worse positions) and repels those with lower objective function values (better positions). r_1, r_2 and r_3 represent three random vectors whose components are uniformly picked from the interval [0, 1]. The $\odot$ operator represents the Hadamard (element-wise) product. For instance, if $\mathbf{q} = [q_1, q_2, \ldots, q_n]$ and $\mathbf{Q} = [Q_1, Q_2, \ldots, Q_n]$ are two arbitrary vectors, $\mathbf{q} \odot \mathbf{Q} = [q_1Q_1, q_2Q_2, \ldots, q_nQ_n]$ [20]. For giving more clarity about the optimization algorithm, the pseudo code of the MRA is given in Table 7.1.

7.3 OPTIMIZATION PROBLEM: SHELL AND TUBE HEAT EXCHANGER (STHE)

The STHEs, illustrated in Fig. 7.1, consist of cylindrical shell housing circular tubes. Heat transfer appears between two fluids: one of the fluids flows inside the tubes, while the other fluid circulates around the tubes within the shell. Additionally, baffles are installed inside

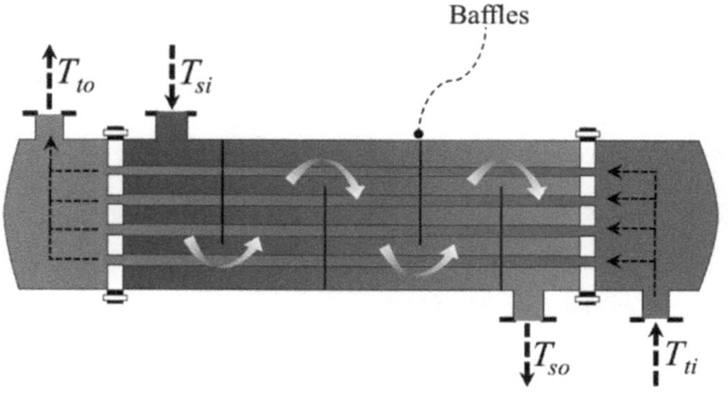

FIGURE 7.1 Schematic view of STHE [41].

the shell to support the tubes for structural stability, prevent tube vibrations and redirect the fluid flow across the tube bundle to enhance the heat transfer coefficient [40]. In the current study, three cases of STHE are assessed. In the current section firstly, the analytical model that gives rise to the governing equations is explained. Then the details of the optimization problem are given with its components as objective function, design variables and constraints. Finally, the details of the case studies are described.

7.3.1 Analytical Model of STHE

Design of these systems starts via calculating the heat load, overall heat transfer coefficient, the logarithmic mean temperature value and its correction factor as below:

$$Q = \dot{m}_s C_{ps}(T_{is} - T_{os}) = \dot{m}_t C_{pt}(T_{ot} - T_{it}) \tag{7.4}$$

$$U = \frac{1}{\frac{1}{h_s} + R_{fs} + \frac{d_o}{d_i}\left(R_{ft} + \frac{1}{h_t}\right)}, \quad d_i = 0.8d_o \tag{7.5}$$

$$\Delta T_{LM} = \frac{(T_{is} - T_{ot}) - (T_{os} - T_{it})}{\ln\left(\frac{(T_{is} - T_{ot})}{(T_{os} - T_{it})}\right)} \tag{7.6}$$

$$F = \frac{\sqrt{R^2+1}}{R-1} \frac{\ln\left(\frac{1-P}{1-PR}\right)}{\ln\left(\frac{2-P\left(R+1-\sqrt{R^2+1}\right)}{2-P\left(R+1+\sqrt{R^2+1}\right)}\right)}, \quad R = \frac{T_{is} - T_{os}}{T_{ot} - T_{it}} \quad and \quad P = \frac{T_{ot} - T_{it}}{T_{is} - T_{it}} \tag{7.7}$$

Then the heat transfer area of the STHE is calculated as follows:

$$A = \frac{Q}{U \Delta T_{LM} F} \tag{7.8}$$

In the following, the heat transfer analysis in both shell and tube sides for calculating the heat transfer coefficients is mathematically presented as below:

Tube side

$$v_t = \frac{\dot{m}_t}{\frac{\pi d_o}{4}\rho_t}\frac{n}{N_t}$$

$$Re_t = \frac{\rho_t v_t d_i}{\mu_t}, \quad Pr_t = \frac{\mu_t C_{pt}}{k_t}$$

$$h_t = \begin{cases} \frac{k_t}{d_i}\left[3.657 + \frac{0.0677\left\{Re_t Pr_t\left(\frac{d_i}{L}\right)\right\}^{1.33}}{1+0.1Pr_t\left\{Re_t\left(\frac{d_i}{L}\right)\right\}^{0.3}}\right] & Re_t \leq 2100 \\ \frac{k_t}{d_i}\left[\frac{\left(\frac{f_t}{2}\right)(Re_t - 1000)Pr_t}{1+12.7\left(\frac{f_t}{2}\right)^{\frac{1}{2}}\left(Pr_t^{0.66}-1\right)}\right] & 2100 < Re_t < 10000 \\ 0.027\frac{k_t}{d_i}Re_t^{0.8}Pr_t^{0.33}\left(\frac{\mu_t}{\mu_{tw}}\right)^{0.14} & Re_t \geq 10000 \end{cases}$$

$$f_t = \begin{cases} \left(1.82\log_{10} Re_t - 1.64\right)^{-2} & Re_t \leq 2100 \\ 0.0054 + 0.00000023\left(Re_t^{\frac{3}{2}}\right) & 2100 < Re_t < 4000 \\ 0.00128 + 0.1143\left(Re_t^{-\frac{1}{3.214}}\right) & Re_t \geq 4000 \end{cases}$$

$$\Delta P_t = \Delta P_{t_{length}} + \Delta P_{t_{elbow}} = \frac{\rho_t v_t^2}{2}\left[\frac{L}{d_i}f_t + 4\right]n$$

Shell side

$$v_s = \frac{\dot{m}_s}{A_s \rho_s}$$

$$Pr_s = \frac{\mu_s C_{ps}}{k_s}$$

$$Re_s = \frac{\rho_s v_s D_e}{\mu_s}$$

$$h_s = 0.36\frac{k}{D_e}Re_s^{0.55}Pr_s^{0.33}\left(\frac{\mu_s}{\mu_{sw}}\right)^{0.14}$$

$$\Delta P_s = f_s\left(\frac{\rho_s v_s^2}{2}\right)\left(\frac{L}{B}\right)\left(\frac{D_s}{d_e}\right)$$

$$f_s = 2b_o Re_s^{-0.15}, \quad for\ b_o = 0.72\ (if\ Re < 40000$$

$$\Delta P_s = f_s\left(\frac{\rho_s v_s^2}{2}\right)\left(\frac{L}{B}\right)\left(\frac{D_s}{d_e}\right)$$

For square and triangular tube pitch arrangements, as shown in Fig. 7.2, the hydraulic diameter of the shell (D_e), is calculated as below [42, 43]:

$$D_e = \begin{cases} \frac{4\left(P_t^2 - \left(0.25\pi d_o^2\right)\right)}{\pi d_o} & \text{for square pitches} \\ \frac{0.4\left(0.43P_t^2 - \left(\frac{0.5\pi d_o^2}{4}\right)\right)}{\pi d_o} & \text{for triangular pitches} \end{cases} \tag{7.9}$$

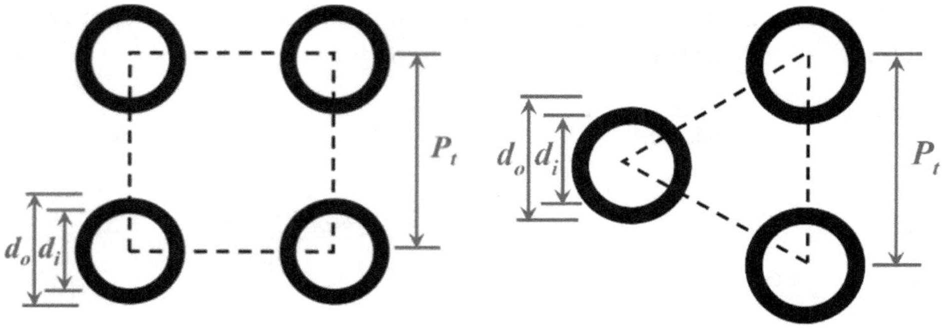

FIGURE 7.2 Square and triangular tube pitch arrangements [41].

The clearance between the adjacent tube, the bundle cross flow area at the center of the shell side, the length of the tubes, the total pumping power and the number of tubes are respectively given as below [40]:

$$Cl = P_t - d_o \tag{7.10}$$

$$A_s = \frac{D_s\ B\ Cl}{P_t} \tag{7.11}$$

$$L = \frac{A}{\pi d_o N_t} \tag{7.12}$$

$$P = \frac{1}{\eta}\left(\frac{\dot{m}_t}{\rho_t}\Delta P_t + \frac{\dot{m}_s}{\rho_s}\Delta P_s\right) \tag{7.13}$$

$$N_t = K_1\left(\frac{D_s}{d_o}\right)^{N_1} \tag{7.14}$$

where, K_1 and N_1 constants are defined according to the number of tube in two different pitch arrangements and tube passes in Table 7.2 [43].

7.3.2 Optimization Problem

In this section, the objective function, design variables and considered constraints of the optimal design problem of a STHE are explained.

TABLE 7.2 K_1 and N_1 Coefficients for Distinct Tube Pitch Arrangements ($P_t = 1.25\ d_o$)

Number of Tube Passes (n)	Triangular Tube Pitch		Square Tube Pitch	
	K_1	N_1	K_1	N_1
1	0.319	2.142	0.215	2.207
2	0.249	2.207	0.156	2.291
4	0.175	2.285	0.158	2.263
6	0.0743	2.499	0.0402	2.617
8	0.0365	2.675	0.0331	2.643

7.3.2.1 Objective Function

The total cost (C_{tot}) of the system is desired as the objective function, which is mathematically given in below:

$$f(\mathbf{X}) = \text{minimize}\left(C_{tot}\right) \tag{7.15}$$

The total cost is calculated considering the capital investment cost (C_i) and total discounted operating cost (C_{oD}) of the heat exchanger as below [22].

$$C_{tot} = C_i + C_{oD} \tag{7.16}$$

where, the investment cost and total discounted operating cost related to pumping power is calculated as below [44]:

$$C_i = 8000 + 259.2\ A^{0.91} \tag{7.17}$$

$$C_o = P\ C_e\ H$$

$$C_{oD} = \sum_{k=1}^{ny} \frac{C_o}{(1+i)^k} \tag{7.18}$$

where, n_y presents the lifetime of the heat exchanger and it is assumed as ten years; i designates the inflation rate it is considered as 10%; energy cost (C_e) is 0.12 €/kWh; H as the work hours in a year is 7000 h/year.

7.3.2.2 Design Variables

Four design variables are considered for optimal design of the STHE. These variables are the diameter of tubes (d_o), length of the tubes (L), diameter of the shell side (D_s) and the baffle space (B). The lower and upper bound of the design variables are given in Table 7.3.

7.3.2.3 Constraints

For optimal design of a STHE via solving an optimization problem, proper constraints should be defined for attaining feasible solutions in the search space. There are six constraints for this problem and they are mathematically defined as below:

$$g_1 = \Delta P_t - \Delta P_{allowable} < 0 \tag{7.19}$$

$$g_2 = \Delta P_t - \Delta P_{allowable} < 0 \tag{7.20}$$

$$g_3 = v_t - 2 < 0 \tag{7.21}$$

TABLE 7.3 Limitations of Design Variables for Optimal Design of STHE

Design Variables	Lower Limit	Upper Limit	Type of Variable
D_s (m)	0.100	1.500	continuous
d_o (m)	0.010	0.051	continuous
L (m)	1.000	5.000	continuous
B (m)	0.050	0.500	continuous

TABLE 7.4 Flow Properties in STHE for Case I, Case II and Case III

	Case I		Case II		Case III	
Process Parameters	**Shell Side: Methanol**	**Tube Side: Brackish Water**	**Shell Side: Kerosene**	**Tube Side: Crude Oil**	**Shell Side: Distilled Water**	**Tube Side: Raw Water**
Mass flow rate (kg/s)	27.80	68.90	5.52	18.80	22.07	35.31
T_i (°C)	95.0	25.0	199.0	37.8	33.9	23.9
T_o (°C)	40.0	40.0	93.3	76.7	29.4	26.7
ρ (kg/m³)	750.0	995.0	850.0	995.0	995	999
C_p (kJ/kg K)	2.84	4.2	2.47	2.05	4.18	4.18
μ (Pa s)	0.00034	0.0008	0.0004	0.00358	0.00080	0.00092
μ_w (Pa s)	0.00038	0.00052	0.00036	0.00213	-	-
k (W/m K)	0.19	0.59	0.13	0.13	0.62	0.62
R_f (m² K/W)	0.00033	0.0002	0.00061	0.00061	0.00017	0.00017
$\Delta P_{allowable}$ (Pa)	68,947	68,947	80,000	80,000	68,947	68,947

$$g_4 = 0.3 - v_s < 0 \tag{7.22}$$

$$g_5 = v_s - 1 < 0 \tag{7.23}$$

$$g_6 = \frac{L}{D_s} - 15 < 0 \tag{7.24}$$

7.3.3 Case Studies

Three case studies for optimal design of the STHE using MRA and selected optimization techniques are considered as follow:

- Case I: a STHE with combination of methanol and sea water and a 4.34 MW heat duty [43]
- Case II: a STHE with combination of Kerosene and Crude oil and a 1.44 MW heat duty [43]
- Case III: a STHE with combination of Distilled water and Raw water and a 0.46 MW heat duty [42]

For Case I triangular pitch pattern and for Case II and Case III square pitch pattern are considered. The flow properties of the considered cases are given in Table 7.4.

7.4 NUMERICAL RESULTS

In this chapter, the effectiveness of a newly developed MRA is evaluated for the optimal design of STHEs. To assess the performance of MRA, four other recently developed and well stablished optimization techniques are selected. The properties and internal parameters of the selected algorithms are given in Table 7.5.

The obtained optimal results using four well-known optimization methods (PSO, JAYA, BOA, ISA) and MRA are presented comparatively in Table 7.6, Table 7.7 and Table 7.8. The

TABLE 7.5 Parameter Setting for the Applied Algorithms

Algorithm	Year	Parameter*	Description
iPSO [45]	2017	$\alpha = 0.4, C_3 = C_4 = 1, C_2 = 2$	Acceleration factors (C_1, C_2, C_3, C_4)
JAYA [46]	2016	-	Parameter free
BOA [47]	2019	$c = 0.01$, $p = 0.8$, a = lineraly decreases from 0.1 to 0.3	Modality (c), power exponent (a), search criteria (p)
ISA [48]	2018	$\tau = 0.3$	Tendency factor(τ)
MRA [20]	2024	-	Parameter free

TABLE 7.6 Optimal Outcomes of STHE Optimization, Case I

Design Parameters	JAYA	iPSO	BOA	ISA	MRA
d_o (m)	0.0100	0.0100	0.0100	0.0100	0.0100
D_s (m)	0.6595	1.0585	1.0581	1.0415	1.0245
L (m)	2.5733	1.0000	1.2315	1.0000	1.0005
B (m)	0.5000	0.4961	0.5000	0.4554	0.4139
n	2	2	2	2	2
N_t	2578	7323	7317	7066	6846
P_t (m)	0.0125	0.0125	0.0125	0.0125	0.0125
v_t (m/s)	1.0687	0.3762	0.3766	0.3899	0.4070
Re_t	10633.9949	3743.6077	3746.6774	3879.8521	3999.7391
Pr_t	5.6949	5.6949	5.6949	5.6949	5.6119
f_t	0.0077	0.0581	0.0581	0.0610	0.0679
h_t (W/m^2 K)	6251.5236	5914.4873	5924.9915	6388.3315	6819.2006
ΔP_t (Pa)	5643.4733	1374.7358	1615.5216	1531.3993	1679.8076
d_e (m)	0.0071	0.0071	0.0071	0.0071	0.0071
v_s (m/s)	0.5620	0.3529	0.3503	0.3908	0.4389
Re_s	8813.9208	5534.6971	5493.6025	6127.7586	6879.7960
Pr_s	5.0821	5.0821	5.0821	5.0821	5.0821
f_s	0.3686	0.3953	0.3957	0.3893	0.3829
h_s (W/m^2 K)	2408.0544	1864.3390	1856.7128	1971.6924	2101.2100
ΔP_s (Pa)	20848.4129	5541.4082	6675.7777	7170.4955	9698.4932
U (W/m^2 K)	836.6631	753.1659	752.1302	779.5149	806.9581
A (m^2)	207.5701	230.5817	230.8992	222.7876	215.2236
C_i (€)	41285.4987	44627.3569	44673.2544	43499.9799	42398.6791
C_o (€/yr)	1221.7489	315.6266	377.2835	390.4215	499.6170
C_{od} (€)	7507.1184	1939.3891	2318.2437	2398.9711	3069.9209
C_{tot} (€) Best value	48792.6172	46566.7460	46991.4981	45897.9509	45468.6000
C_{tot} (€) Mean value	50002.4212	47692.5416	48902.3178	46911.6317	45986.3109
Std. value (€)	0.4519	0.2305	0.6611	0.2495	0.1077

TABLE 7.7 Optimal Outcomes of STHE Optimization, Case II

Design Parameters	JAYA	iPSO	BOA	ISA	MRA
d_o (m)	0.0149	0.0201	0.0102	0.0214	0.0149
D_s (m)	0.6111	0.6640	0.5372	0.6771	0.5769
L (m)	1.8999	2.2997	1.5586	2.1010	1.4038
B (m)	0.1258	0.1154	0.1604	0.1102	0.1140
n	4	4	4	4	4
N_t	706	433	1243	392	613
P_t (m)	0.0186	0.0251	0.0127	0.0267	0.0189
v_t (m/s)	0.9593	0.8595	1.1627	0.8375	1.0938
Re_t	3178.0738	3841.2360	2636.8392	3985.2457	3647.7276
Pr_t	56.4538	56.4538	56.4538	56.4538	56.4538
f_t	0.0466	0.0602	0.0365	0.0633	0.0560
h_t (W/m^2 K)	1164.5445	1285.1029	1126.5735	1301.6301	1547.4855
ΔP_t (Pa)	18181.8168	16322.8512	25501.0965	14328.1042	21566.3901
d_e (m)	0.0147	0.0199	0.0101	0.0212	0.0143
v_s (m/s)	0.4224	0.4237	0.3768	0.4352	0.4999
Re_s	13232.1522	17908.5042	8081.5925	19580.1723	15756.6420
Pr_s	7.6	7.6	7.6	7.6	7.6
f_s	0.3468	0.3314	0.3734	0.3270	0.3376
h_s (W/m^2 K)	1171.0596	1025.3094	1304.3421	1011.4716	1281.1161
ΔP_s (Pa)	16462.2569	16829.6237	11657.4763	16046.7056	17380.0096
U (W/m^2 K)	303.0478	301.1594	307.8127	301.0694	337.722
A (m^2)	63.0962	63.4918	62.1195	63.5108	56.6215
C_i (€)	19262.5809	19326.8285	19103.8206	19329.9098	18205.9120
C_o (€/yr)	472.9658	438.5905	585.4115	393.6777	546.3446
C_{od} (€)	2906.1704	2694.9486	3597.1004	2418.9792	3357.1749
C_{tot} (€) Best value	22168.1486	22021.7772	22700.9210	21748.8890	21563.0869
C_{tot} (€) Mean value	23601.6177	22969.9154	24137.4372	22341.7927	21992.7120
Std. value (€)	0.3920	0.3030	0.5089	0.2988	0.2003

results indicate that the proposed MRA demonstrates promising performance in terms of accuracy and stability across all study cases when compared to other techniques. This indicates that proposed MRA adopted with governing condition of the corresponding problem. Its superior stability relative to other methods highlights its capability to balance local and global search behaviors.

Additionally, the attained optimal costs for all cases are comparatively illustrated in Fig. 7.3, Fig. 7.4 and Fig. 7.5. The portion of the investment cost (C_i) is larger than operating cost (C_{od}) in total cost of the system. Also, the attained optimal cost of the system using MRA is less than the total cost achieved employing other utilized algorithms. This designates the superior performance of the MRA from accuracy aspect.

Figure 7.6 presents the Std. value of the algorithms. It is apparent that the MRA has a lower Std. value than other algorithms. This shows that the MRA due to its successful balance between the exploration and exploitation search behaviors, puts forward a stable search process than other algorithms.

TABLE 7.8 Optimal Outcomes of STHE Optimization, Case III

Design Parameters	JAYA	iPSO	BOA	ISA	MRA
d_o (m)	0.0100	0.0104	0.0227	0.0137	0.0101
D_s (m)	0.6592	0.4653	0.5554	0.5535	0.5375
L (m)	1.0090	1.7583	3.9201	1.9442	1.3412
B (m)	0.5000	0.5000	0.4719	0.5000	0.5000
n	2	2	2	2	2
N_t	2293	944	237	747	1421
P_t (m)	0.0125	0.0130	0.0284	0.0171	0.0120
v_t (m/s)	0.6133	1.3774	1.1516	1.0031	0.9927
Re_t	5327.8987	12443.8476	22708.3623	11937.6502	8628.0596
Pr_t	6.2026	6.2026	6.2026	6.2026	6.2026
f_t	0.0092	0.0074	0.0063	0.0074	0.0080
h_t (W/m^2 K)	3177.3802	6936.5699	5142.0602	5093.6474	5141.2306
ΔP_t (Pa)	1939.0601	10529.3068	7107.3614	5347.0759	5271.4096
d_e (m)	0.0099	0.0103	0.0225	0.0135	0.0099
v_s (m/s)	0.3365	0.4767	0.4231	0.4007	0.4155
Re_s	4140.7899	6100.9952	11820.6241	6756.2131	5111.2345
Pr_s	5.3935	5.3935	5.3935	5.3935	5.3935
f_s	0.4128	0.3895	0.3527	0.3836	0.3996
h_s (W/m^2 K)	3860.6469	4594.1098	3028.2428	3688.7617	4334.8309
ΔP_s (Pa)	3126.5653	7002.8126	6454.8396	4866.3492	4942.7890
U (W/m^2 K)	966.2491	1281.4362	1046.2246	1112.3503	1167.88027
A (m^2)	72.0568	54.3334	66.5486	62.5925	60.0020
C_i (€)	20709.2311	17829.8318	19822.0199	19180.7398	18696.8288
C_o (€/yr)	144.7811	553.8652	414.1056	311.7809	310.7490
C_{od} (€)	889.6174	3403.2621	2544.4999	1915.7592	1909.4155
C_{tot} (€) Best value	21598.8485	21233.0939	22366.5199	21096.4990	20606.2443
C_{tot} (€) Mean value	22400.3462	21951.7817	24118.6888	21852.2217	21096.7311
Std. value (€)	0.4418	0.2856	0.4955	0.2051	0.1411

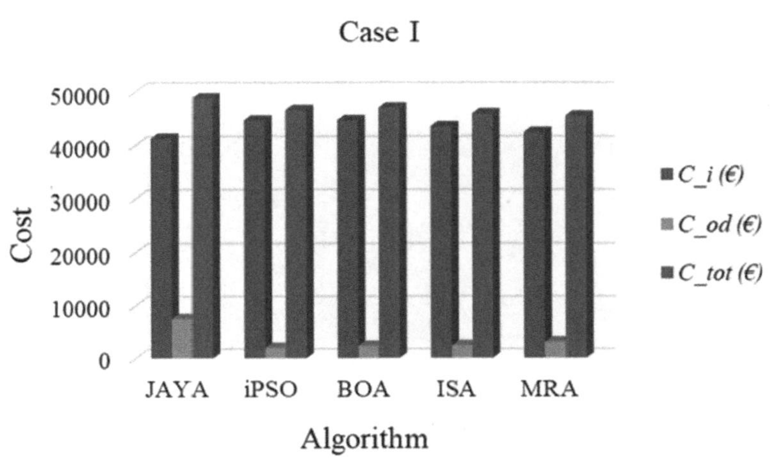

FIGURE 7.3 Optimal costs for STHE, Case I.

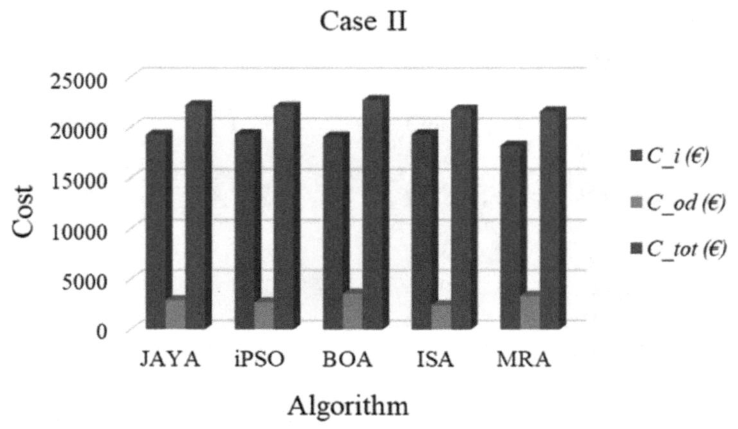

FIGURE 7.4 Optimal costs for STHE, Case II.

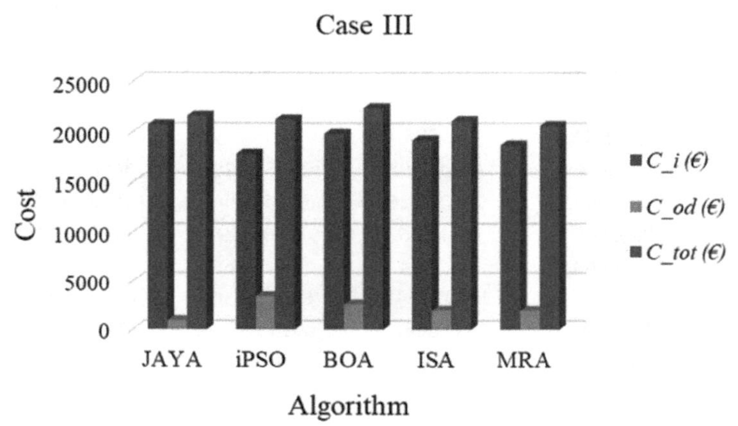

FIGURE 7.5 Optimal costs for STHE, Case III.

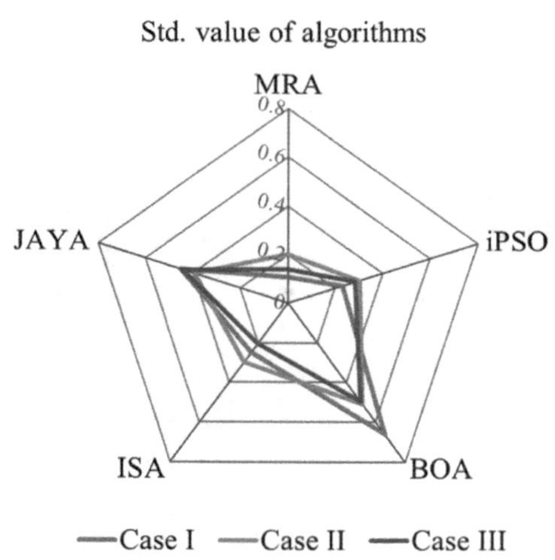

FIGURE 7.6 Std. value of the algorithms.

7.5 CONCLUSION

In this chapter, the recently developed MRA is employed for the optimal design of shell-and-tube heat exchanger systems. The MRA is applied to three distinct heat exchanger optimization case studies. To comprehensively assess the MRA's performance, four other well-established optimization algorithms are used for comparison.

The results underscore several key advantages of using the MRA.

- First, the MRA effectively handles all cases, providing robust solutions independent of initial conditions or step sizes, which are commonly required by gradient-based methods. This feature makes the MRA especially valuable when prior knowledge about the problem is limited.
- Second, the numerical results show that the MRA consistently outperforms the other methods tested, delivering more accurate solutions.
- Third, statistical analysis, including metrics such as mean and standard deviation, reveals that the MRA significantly enhances the stability of the optimization process across all problems. Overall, the MRA demonstrates strong potential for solving complex engineering optimization challenges.

REFERENCES

1. A. Mortazavi, A novel binomial strategy for simultaneous topology and size optimization of truss structures, Engineering Optimization. (2024) 1–35. 10.1080/0305215X.2024.2349100
2. A. Mortazavi, A fuzzy reinforced Jaya algorithm for solving mathematical and structural optimization problems, Soft Computing. 28 (2024) 2181–206. 10.1007/s00500-023-09206-5
3. A. Mortazavi, Interactive fuzzy Bayesian search algorithm: A new reinforced swarm intelligence tested on engineering and mathematical optimization problems, Expert Systems with Applications. 187 (2022) 115954. https://doi.org/10.1016/j.eswa.2021.115954
4. J. Holland, Genetic algorithms and adaptation. In: Selfridge O., Rissland E., Arbib M., editors. Adaptive Control of Ill-Defined Systems. Boston, MA: Springer US; 1984. p. 317–33.
5. J. Kennedy, R. Eberhart, Particle swarm optimization. In: Proceedings of ICNN'95-International Conference on Neural Networks, 1995 Proceedings, IEEE International Conference on 1995. 4 (1995, November) 1942–8.
6. R. Storn, K. Price, Differential evolution – A simple and efficient heuristic for global optimization over continuous spaces, Journal of Global Optimization. 11 (1997) 341–59. 10.1023/A:1008202821328
7. M. Moloodpoor, A. Mortazavi, N. Ozbalta, Thermal analysis of parabolic trough collectors via a swarm intelligence optimizer, Solar Energy. 181 (2019) 264–75. https://doi.org/10.1016/j.solener.2019.02.008
8. G. Zhou, Y. Zhou, W. Deng, S. Yin, Y. Zhang, Advances in teaching–learning-based optimization algorithm: A comprehensive survey (ICIC2022), Neurocomputing. 561 (2023) 126898. https://doi.org/10.1016/j.neucom.2023.126898
9. J. Divasón, J.F. Ceniceros, A. Sanz-Garcia, A. Pernia-Espinoza, F.J. Martinez-de-Pison, PSO-PARSIMONY: A method for finding parsimonious and accurate machine learning models with particle swarm optimization. Application for predicting force–displacement curves in T-stub steel connections, Neurocomputing. 548 (2023) 126414. https://doi.org/10.1016/j.neucom.2023.126414

10. Y. Zhang, Backtracking search algorithm with specular reflection learning for global optimization, Knowledge-Based Systems. 212 (2021) 106546. https://doi.org/10.1016/j.knosys.2020.106546
11. Y. Zhang, Z. Jin, Group teaching optimization algorithm: A novel metaheuristic method for solving global optimization problems, Expert Systems with Applications. 148 (2020) 113246. https://doi.org/10.1016/j.eswa.2020.113246
12. Z. Wang, Q. Luo, Y. Zhou, Hybrid metaheuristic algorithm using butterfly and flower pollination base on mutualism mechanism for global optimization problems, Engineering with Computers. 37 (2021) 3665–98. 10.1007/s00366-020-01025-8
13. M. Moloodpoor, A. Mortazavi, Thermo-economic optimization for saving energy in residential buildings using population-based optimization techniques, Journal of Construction Engineering, Management & Innovation. 5 (2022) 45–63. 10.31462/jcemi.2022.01045063
14. A. Mortazavi, Solving structural optimization problems with discrete variables using interactive fuzzy search algorithm, Structural Engineering and Mechanics. 79 (2021) 247–65. https://doi.org/10.12989/sem.2021.79.2.247
15. M. Moloodpoor, A. Mortazavi, Simultaneous optimization of fuel type and exterior walls insulation attributes for residential buildings using a swarm intelligence, International Journal of Environmental Science and Technology. 19(4) (2022) 2809–22. 10.1007/s13762-021-03323-0
16. V. Toğan, A. Mortazavi, Sizing optimization of skeletal structures using teaching-learning based optimization, An International Journal of Optimization and Control: Theories & Applications (IJOCTA). 7 (2017) 130–41. https://doi.org/10.11121/ijocta.01.2017.00309
17. A. Mortazavi, The performance comparison of three metaheuristic algorithms on the size, layout and topology optimization of truss structures, Mugla Journal of Science and Technology. 5 (2) (2019) 28–41. 10.1615/HeatTransRes.2023048911
18. A. Mortazavi, V. Toğan. Metaheuristic algorithms for optimal design of truss structures. In: Nigdeli S.M. Bekdaş G., Kayabekir A.E., Yucel M., editors. Advances in Structural Engineering – Optimization: Emerging Trends in Structural Optimization. Cham: Springer International Publishing; 2021. p. 199–220.
19. A. Mortazavi, The performance comparison of three metaheuristic algorithms on the size, layout and topology optimization of truss structures, Mugla Journal of Science and Technology. 5 (2019) 28–41. 10.22531/muglajsci.593482
20. A. Mortazavi, Marathon runner algorithm: Theory and application in mathematical, mechanical and structural optimization problems, Materials Testing. 66 (8) (2024) 1267–91. doi:10.1515/mt-2023-0091
21. R. Selbaş, Ö. Kızılkan, M. Reppich, A new design approach for shell-and-tube heat exchangers using genetic algorithms from economic point of view, Chemical Engineering and Processing: Process Intensification. 45 (2006) 268–75. https://doi.org/10.1016/j.cep.2005.07.004
22. A.C. Caputo, P.M. Pelagagge, P. Salini, Heat exchanger design based on economic optimisation, Applied Thermal Engineering. 28 (2008) 1151–9. https://doi.org/10.1016/j.applthermaleng.2007.08.010
23. M. Fesanghary, E. Damangir, I. Soleimani, Design optimization of shell and tube heat exchangers using global sensitivity analysis and harmony search algorithm, Applied Thermal Engineering. 29 (2009) 1026–31. https://doi.org/10.1016/j.applthermaleng.2008.05.018
24. J.M. Ponce-Ortega, M. Serna-González, A. Jiménez-Gutiérrez, Use of genetic algorithms for the optimal design of shell-and-tube heat exchangers, Applied Thermal Engineering. 29 (2009) 203–9. https://doi.org/10.1016/j.applthermaleng.2007.06.040
25. V.K. Patel, R.V. Rao, Design optimization of shell-and-tube heat exchanger using particle swarm optimization technique, Applied Thermal Engineering. 30 (2010) 1417–25. https://doi.org/10.1016/j.applthermaleng.2010.03.001

26. A. Şencan Şahin, B. Kılıç, U. Kılıç, Design and economic optimization of shell and tube heat exchangers using Artificial Bee Colony (ABC) algorithm. Energy Conversion and Management. 52 (2011) 3356–62. https://doi.org/10.1016/j.enconman.2011.07.003
27. V.C. Mariani, A.R.K. Duck, F.A. Guerra, L.d.S. Coelho, R.V. Rao, A chaotic quantum-behaved particle swarm approach applied to optimization of heat exchangers, Applied Thermal Engineering. 42 (2012) 119–28. https://doi.org/10.1016/j.applthermaleng.2012.03.022
28. A. Hadidi, A. Nazari, Design and economic optimization of shell-and-tube heat exchangers using biogeography-based (BBO) algorithm, Applied Thermal Engineering. 51 (2013) 1263–72. https://doi.org/10.1016/j.applthermaleng.2012.12.002
29. M. Asadi, Y. Song, B. Sunden, G. Xie, Economic optimization design of shell-and-tube heat exchangers by a cuckoo-search-algorithm, Applied Thermal Engineering. 73 (2014) 1032–40. https://doi.org/10.1016/j.applthermaleng.2014.08.061
30. R. Khosravi, A. Khosravi, S. Nahavandi, H. Hajabdollahi, Effectiveness of evolutionary algorithms for optimization of heat exchangers, Energy Conversion and Management. 89 (2015) 281–8. https://doi.org/10.1016/j.enconman.2014.09.039
31. H. Sadeghzadeh, M.A. Ehyaei, M.A. Rosen, Techno-economic optimization of a shell and tube heat exchanger by genetic and particle swarm algorithms, Energy Conversion and Management. 93 (2015) 84–91. https://doi.org/10.1016/j.enconman.2015.01.007
32. D.K. Mohanty, Gravitational search algorithm for economic optimization design of a shell and tube heat exchanger, Applied Thermal Engineering. 107 (2016) 184–93. https://doi.org/10.1016/j.applthermaleng.2016.06.133
33. D.K. Mohanty, Application of firefly algorithm for design optimization of a shell and tube heat exchanger from economic point of view, International Journal of Thermal Sciences. 102 (2016) 228–38. https://doi.org/10.1016/j.ijthermalsci.2015.12.002
34. E.H.d. Vasconcelos Segundo, A.L. Amoroso, V.C. Mariani, L.d.S. Coelho, Economic optimization design for shell-and-tube heat exchangers by a Tsallis differential evolution, Applied Thermal Engineering. 111 (2017) 143–51. https://doi.org/10.1016/j.applthermaleng.2016.09.032
35. M. Söylemez, Thermoeconomical Optimization of Double-Pipe Heat Exchanger For Waste Heat Recovery, Journal of Thermophysics and Heat Transfer. 18 (2004) 559–63. 10.2514/1.6149
36. P.K. Swamee, N. Aggarwal, V. Aggarwal, Optimum design of double pipe heat exchanger, International Journal of Heat and Mass Transfer. 51 (2008) 2260–6. 10.1016/j.ijheatmasstransfer.2007.10.028
37. A. Peccini, J.C. Lemos, A.L.H. Costa, M.J. Bagajewicz, Optimal design of double pipe heat exchanger structures, Industrial & Engineering Chemistry Research. 58 (2019) 12080–96. 10.1021/acs.iecr.9b01536
38. A. Peccini, A. Costa, M. Bagajewicz. Globally optimal design of double pipe heat exchangers using local properties and discretized models. Computer Aided Chemical Engineering. 46 (2019) 187–92.
39. M. Moloodpoor, A. Mortazavi, N. Ozbalta, Thermo-economic optimization of double-pipe heat exchanger using a compound swarm intelligence, Heat Transfer Research. 52 (6) (2021) 1–20.
40. S. Kakaç, H. Liu, Heat exchangers: selection, rating, and thermal design 2nd ed, USA: CRC Press LLC; 2002.
41. M. Moloodpoor, A. Mortazavi, M.E. Kartal, Optimization of heat exchanger systems using a fuzzy reinforced swarm intelligence, Heat Transfer Research. 53 (10) (2022) 15–50.
42. D.Q. Kern, Process Heat Transfer, McGraw-Hill, New York; 1950.
43. R.K. Sinnot, Coulson and Richardson's Chemical Engineering. In: Chemical Engineering Design, 4th ed, Butterworth-Heinemann; 2005.
44. M. Taal, I. Bulatov, J. Klemeš, P. Stehlík, Cost estimation and energy price forecasts for economic evaluation of retrofit projects, Applied Thermal Engineering. 23 (2003) 1819–35. https://doi.org/10.1016/S1359-4311(03)00136-4

45. A. Mortazavi, V. Toğan, A. Nuhoğlu, An integrated particle swarm optimizer for optimization of truss structures with discrete variables, Structural Engineering and Mechanics: An International Journal. 61 (3) (2017) 359–70. https://doi.org/10.12989/sem.2017.61.3.359
46. R.V. Rao, Jaya: A simple and new optimization algorithm for solving constrained and unconstrained optimization problems, International Journal of Industrial Engineering Computations. 7 (2016) 19–34.
47. S. Arora, S. Singh, Butterfly optimization algorithm: a novel approach for global optimization, Soft Computing. 23 (2019) 715–34. 10.1007/s00500-018-3102-4
48. A. Mortazavi, V. Toğan, A. Nuhoğlu, Interactive search algorithm: A new hybrid metaheuristic optimization algorithm, Engineering Applications of Artificial Intelligence. 71 (2018) 275–92. https://doi.org/10.1016/j.engappai.2018.03.003

CHAPTER 8

Cohesive Zone Modeling of Epoxy Bonded Composite Lap Joints under Cyclic Loading

Suhail Khaliq, Y. U. Chavande and R. R. Ghadge

8.1 INTRODUCTION

8.1.1 Composites and Nano-Composites

A composite material is a structural system made of two or more materials, or phases, designed to enhance mechanical properties beyond those of the individual components. The stiffer, stronger and discontinuous phase is called the reinforcement, while the less stiff and continuous phase is known as the matrix. Composites are present in nature; for example, timber is a composite made of cellulose fibers held together by lignin, which provides greater strength than cotton fibers alone. A well-known man-made composite is concrete, which combines small pebbles or gravel held together by cement. Concrete is strong under compression, and its tensile properties can be enhanced by adding reinforcements like metal rods or mesh, creating reinforced concrete. The roles of composite material phases vary based on the application and environmental exposure. Low to medium performance composites typically use short fibers or particles as reinforcement, offering limited stiffness and strength. In contrast, high-performance composites utilize continuous fiber reinforcement, significantly enhancing strength and stiffness in the fiber direction. The matrix serves to protect the fibers, bond them together, and facilitate stress transfer between fibers. The area between the phases, i.e., between the matrix and reinforcement, known as the interphase, can play an important role in defining the parameters and characteristics such as fracture toughness, failure mechanisms and the overall elastic behavior to failure of the structural material [1].

8.1.2 Nano-Composites

Nanocomposites are materials composed of two or more elements with distinct physical and chemical properties that remain separate at the microscopic level, forming a single material with phase dimensions between 10 and 100 nanometers. The process of creating a nanocomposite involves integrating one or more nanoscale discontinuous phases

DOI: 10.1201/9781003564911-8

into a continuous matrix to impart enhanced properties. The collective material exhibit attributes that are typically superior to those of the individual components. In the context of nanocomposites, one of the combined material's constituting elements is generally kept at a much higher concentration and forms a continuous matrix completely surrounding the other constituents. These constituents then assume the role of a reinforcements or nano-fillers [2]. Adding nanoparticles significantly improves composite properties, such as fracture toughness, mechanical strength and electrical or thermal conductivity. Typically, the concentration of nanoparticles ranges from 0.25% to 5% by weight to achieve optimal results. Nano-clays such as montmorillonite are the most widely used nanoparticles for reinforcing composite materials. Some of the other nanoparticles used are graphene nanoparticles (GNPs), multi-walled carbon nanotubes (MWCNTs) and silicon-carbide nanoparticles (SiC). Compared to conventional composites, nanocomposites offer better mechanical properties, enhanced structural and thermal stability, improved electrical conductivity, chemical resistance and reduced fluid permeability. However, non-uniform distribution of nanoparticles can lead to agglomeration, degrading the composite's properties. Nanocomposites are increasingly used in engineering, biomedical applications and food packaging. Nanocomposites may be manufactured and processed using the well-known techniques which are used to manufacture general polymers. These processes include thermoforming, extrusion, blow molding, injection molding, and compression or transfer molding. These methods are efficient at allowing a higher throughput which is critical for economically viable production, e.g., glass or polymer fiber reinforced parts used in the automobile industry must be manufactured and at production rate of more than one part per minute if they are to be kept competitive with prevalent traditional technologies and existing materials. Ease of processing gives overall lesser costs which in turn helps to compensate the relatively high material costs that may be incurred because of using nano sized reinforcements [3].

8.1.3 Adhesively Bonded Joints

Adhesive bonding is a technique that joins materials using an adhesive applied between the surfaces of adherent materials, forming an adhesive bond upon solidification. This relatively novel type of joint is rapidly developing as a substitute for conventional fastened and welded mechanical joints in many technologically driven critical applications because they have many potential advantages over the conventionally used mechanical fasteners. Some benefits which these type of joints offer include a considerably reduced structural weight, decreased fabrication cost and an improved tolerance and resistance to damage. The use of adhesively bonded joints in fiber-reinforced composites for structural elements has significantly increased recently. Conventional fasteners usually cause cutting and tearing of fibers, which leads to development of stress concentrations, both of these phenomena decrease the structural strength of the component. In comparison, adhesively bonded joints are significantly continuous and offer the desired advantages of strength-to-weight ratio, flexibility of design and are easier to manufacture. Adhesive bonding is finding applications across various advanced industries, including aerospace, automotive and electronics, as well as in conventional sectors like sports equipment, packaging and construction. These applications can be in the form of single or sandwiched configurations. The structures may be made using various types of fibers, fiber weaves, architectures and resins. Adhesively bonded joints effectively resist static and cyclic loads over extended periods without significant loss of load-bearing capacity. Some of the adhesives used for bonding in structural applications include epoxy resins (good temperature resistance and mechanical strength), cyanoacrylates (fast bonding ability with rubber and plastic, but poor moisture and temperature resistance), acrylics (fast curing ability and tolerance to dirty and less prepared surfaces), polyurethanes (good fatigue resistance and low temperature flexibility), silicones (good sealing properties for low stress applications, high flexibility and highly temperature resistant) and high temperature application adhesives such as bismaleimides, phenolics and polyimides [4].

8.1.3.1 Modes of Failure

Failure modes are a function of bond quality at each interface of the composite structural component, specimen geometry and the type of loading. Their characterization is a must for an enhanced and a better understanding of their properties and those of the resulting joint. In fiber reinforced polymer (FRP) composite adhesive joints, according to the ASTM D5573 standard, modes of failure are typically classified into seven types: Cohesive failure, adhesive failure, thin-layer cohesive failure, light-fiber-tear failure, fiber-tear failure stock-break failure or mixed failure [4]. These modes can be visualized in Fig. 8.1.

8.1.4 Finite Element Analysis of Adhesive Joints

The finite element analysis provides the added benefit of analyzing the stresses developed in a body of almost any material with varied geometrical shapes under a certain given loading condition. Different types of adhesive joints have been subjected to both

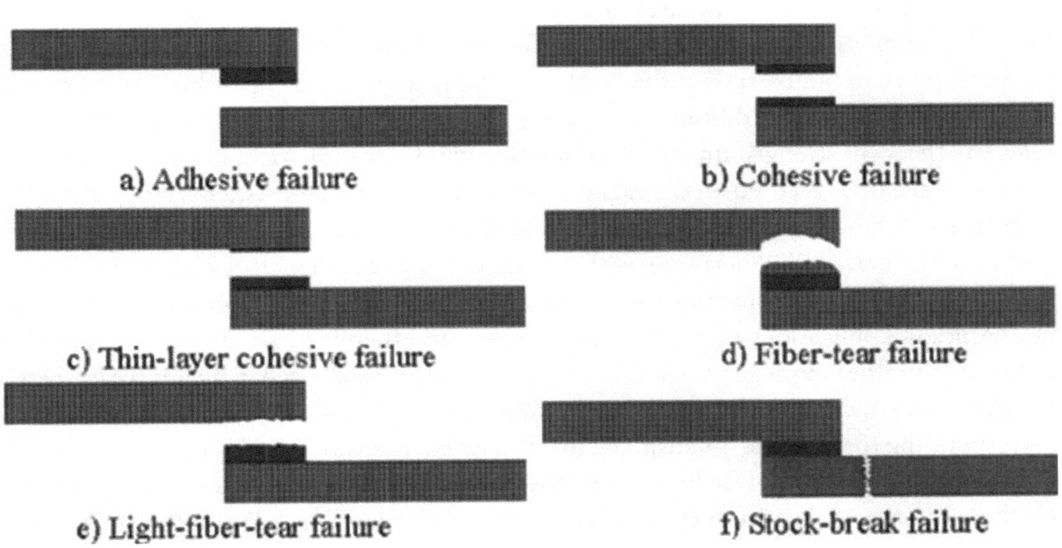

FIGURE 8.1 Failure Modes for Adhesively Bonded Joints. [4].

linear and non-linear analysis and the resulting stresses and strains developed in the adhesive and the adhesively bonded joint have been studied. Since the layer of adhesive is considerably thin compared to the adherends, a finer mesh is required in this area so as to maintain the joint's freedom degrees relatively high. It is necessary that a full finite element analysis includes the effects of various conditions such as shear undergone by the adherend, bending, end effects and non-linear characteristics of the adherends and adhesive. For improved joint strength predictions, numerous research studies have been done in order to analyze adhesively bonded joints having composite materials as adherends with most of them attempting to define an appropriate criterion for failure. Adhesively bonded joints suffer from inherent defects due to their fabrication and manufacturing processes. The crack initiation and subsequent propagation is usually initiated from these already existing defects and further leads to consequent failure of the entire component. The fracture resistance or strength of adhesive joints is dependent on various factors and their combined interactions, e.g., the type of adhesive, curing cycle, composite adherend type, thickness of the adhesive layer, and so on. However, suitable failure prediction criteria are still not available, which poses hurdles toward a more diversified utilization of adhesively bonded joints in structural and other allied engineering applications. An accurate prediction of the strength of adhesively bonded joints is necessary to reduce the need for costly experimentation and testing at the design stage. This makes finite element analysis even more important in the current scenario.

8.1.4.1 Fracture Mechanics Approach

In this approach, toughness, categorized as an energy-based parameter, is used as the primary criterion for predicting failure. In general, it is not possible to accurately predict toughness as a function of normal and shear deformation acting at the crack tip in the adhesive. This deformation acts lengthwise across the interface or through the entire adherend. It is also difficult to utilize the concepts of mixed-mode fracture mechanics, which postulates the occurrence of failure only if the local rate of mixed-mode energy release rate exceeds a certain critical value. Additionally, it is very cumbersome to predict the crack path to calculate the joint strength under varied loading conditions [5]. Most of our linear elastic fracture mechanics is based on the existence of a crack and linear elasticity. However, if the joints are well fabricated, they may not have defects which are large enough to be considered as initial cracks. Furthermore, with respect to laminated structures, plasticity may be induced in the adherend substrate. All these factors limit the usage of linear elastic fracture mechanics in applications of practical importance and therefore, an alternative approach is needed. Another main approach is the stress singularity approach, which is basically the fracture mechanics approach assuming an initial crack. The use of a stress-intensity factor, corresponding to the stress-intensity factor in classical fracture mechanics, which helps in predicting the initiation of fracture for bonded joints, has been investigated [6]. A criterion for the initiation of fracture at the interface for bonded structures has also been suggested. An assumption is made that the fracture initiation occurs when the stress intensity factor reaches its limiting value.

8.1.5 Cohesive Zone Model

Cohesive zone modeling (CZM) is a numerical model that describes the relationship between the relative displacement of two points associated with each other. It relates these points through a force. This force is the traction force, which is an important cohesive parameter. In cohesive elements, this relative displacement is usually defined as the change occurring in the surface normal, and the traction is represented as a function of the displacement with respect to a stiffness tensor. Cohesive elements may not provide an absolute representation of any real physical material, yet they define the forces of cohesion that exists when the elements, adherend and adhesive, are separated from each other. It is also possible to model the cohesive zone elements as a surface with zero initial dimension. This follows that they can be used as individual elements or as interface elements [7]. A simple representation of the cohesive elements and forces is shown in Fig. 8.2 [8]. In a cohesive zone model, all damage mechanisms are proposed in and around a crack tip, leading to the development of a fundamental relation, or a cohesive zone law.

8.1.5.1 Traction Laws

A traction-separation law, or cohesive law, describes the relationship between relative displacement and traction (force) between two points, often represented graphically. Variations of this law can be linear or non-linear and continuous or discontinuous. A

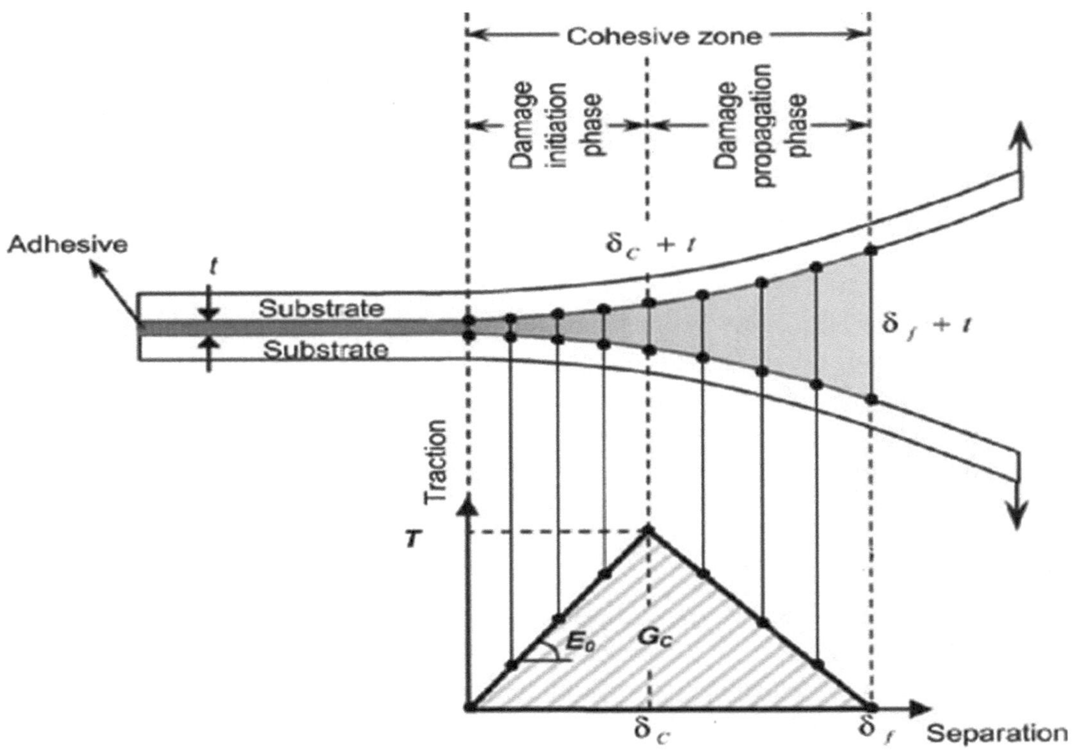

FIGURE 8.2 Traction-Separation Law [8].

traction law may be considered to be made up of two intervals or parts. The first part is the interval between the periods when the displacement and traction force is zone till the damage initiation criterion is satisfied. The fracture or damage initiation criterion corresponds to a point where maximum traction for a certain displacement occurs. This interval is assumed to be the initial stiffness the structural element possesses. The damage initiation criterion is expressed as the maximum traction force or the displacement at this higher limiting value of traction, based on material properties that are known. Once this criterion for damage initiation has been achieved and displacement starts to gradually increase, damage is initiated and the starting elastic behavior no longer exists. The second part can be visualized as the interval between when the damage initiates and when the damage starts to propagate under a set criterion. The damage propagation criterion is explained as the rate of critical energy release. This energy release rate, which is also called the cohesive energy, is actually the product of traction and displacement, i.e., the area under the traction-separation graph. The critical energy release rate is usually assumed to be under tension or shear modes, i.e., under pure modes and mixed modes are ignored. When this critical energy release rate reaches its limiting value, it corresponds to very low or zero traction, indicating full damage. At this point where we say that full damage has occurred, the cohesive zone completely ceased to exist and crack growth initiation happens, eventually the traction reduces to zero as there are no cohesive forces remaining to hold the material in a bonded or joined state and as a result the joints breaks [7].

The exponential, bilinear and the trapezoidal law are the most commonly used traction laws in research and numerical validation of experiments. A suitable traction law is selected depending on the type of material, geometrical shape and experimentation. A bilinear model is most preferable for materials showing a brittle behavior and for modeling delamination, as it offers a good balance between numerical performance, accuracy of results and computational cost. The trapezoidal law is preferred for ductile adhesives. The exponential law gives the best results but is computationally costly.

8.1.5.2 Bilinear Law

The triangular or bilinear law is often chosen for its analytical simplicity. The bilinear law was reframed from a simple rigid linear softening relationship for including an initial stiffness. Since a number of parameters are mostly unknown, the initial stiffness is often chosen to have a very high value. This allows for the assumption of a stiff connection between an opposing point or node pair before damage occurs. This is called the penalty stiffness K. The bilinear law is represented in Fig. 8.3 [7].

8.2 RELATED WORK

Zhemin Jia et al. (2018) [9]: The authors of this paper have evaluated the effect of reinforced GNPs on the fracture toughness of adhesively bonded joints. The experimental investigations have been compared with numerical simulations. Double cantilever beam (DCB) specimens were used for the investigations. Experimental studies showed that, in comparison to neat epoxy adhesive, the fracture toughness showed an increase with the addition of GNPs. The max increase was observed at a concentration of 0.25% by weight,

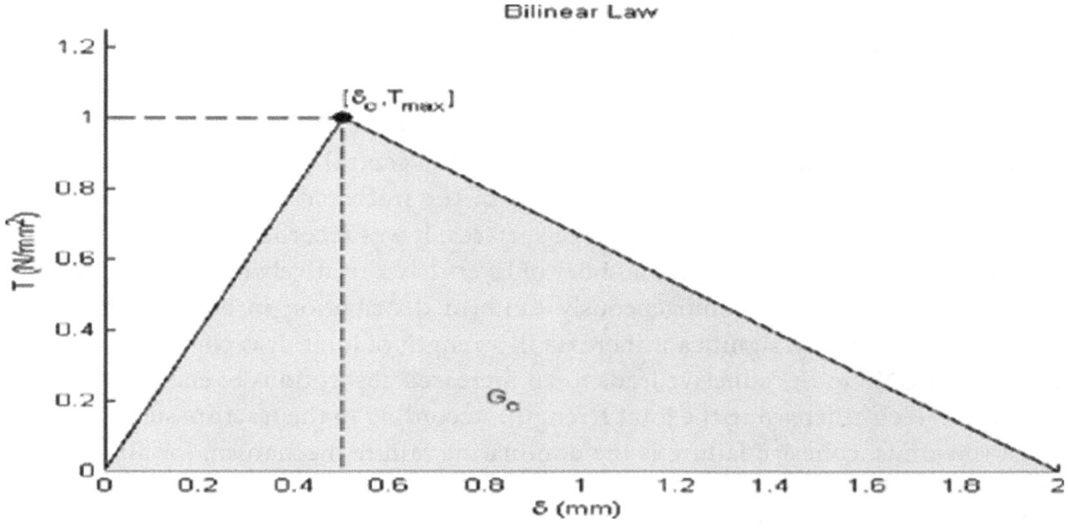

FIGURE 8.3 Bilinear Law [7].

followed by 0.75% and 0.5%, respectively. The results obtained were in agreement with the numerical simulations that followed. The fracture toughness was found to have increased almost fivefold for a concentration of 0.25%. with the increase in concentration the increase in fracture toughness showed a decreased trend. This decrease has been attributed to the aggregation of GNPs at higher concentration.

H. Khoramishad et al. (2017) [10]: In this paper, the authors have examined the effect of graphene oxide nanoparticles (GONPs) on the fracture damage behavior of adhesively bonded epoxy composite joints. The study was conducted with experimentation and numerical simulations. DCB specimens were tested and fracture energy parameters have been determined for the adhesives with and without the nano reinforcements. Different percentages by weight of GONPs were dispersed in the epoxy adhesives and the effect of these nanoparticles on the fracture energy was studied. A cohesive zone model was used to evaluate the effect of these reinforcements on the damage characteristics of epoxy adhesives. The damage behavior was simulated according to a standard traction-separation law. In this study, a bilinear or a triangular traction separation law was utilized for modeling the fracture damage. Three parameters, the cohesive strength, the fracture energy and the initial stiffness, have been defined. The effect of adding 0.3% GONPs has led to an increase of 69% in the fracture energy of the adhesive. However, at a 0.5% concentration, it was observed that due to the agglomeration of the nanoparticles the fracture energy decreased. The numerical results indicated that adding of GONPs leads to a change in the fracture zone length. For optimal results, adding 0.3 wt.% of GONPs increased the cohesive strength and the failure separation by 33% and 27%, respectively.

Hamid Reza Borghei et al. [11]: In this paper, the effects of GNP addition on the strength of simple and rivet-bolted hybrid single-lap joints are studied experimentally. Tensile tests were conducted on specimens of adhesives with different nanoparticle additives. Three samples were tested for each configuration. It is observed that addition of 0.5 wt.% of graphene to the neat epoxy adhesive causes an increase of 24% in the ultimate tensile strength of the used specimens. Also, experimental testing indicated that the most number of stress concentrations are toward the end of the overlap zones. Cracks were initiated at these areas of high stress concentrations. Increase in loading has caused the damage to propagate toward the central portion of the joint area. Scanning electron microscopy (SEM) results of the fractured surfaces indicated that GNP adhesive increased the roughness of surfaces. It was recorded that graphene with a relatively low thickness and less number of layers has a relatively better effect on joint strength. GNPs make a homogeneously uniform distribution in adhesive-graphene composite and cause a significant increase in strength of joint. It is concluded that the addition of GNP to the adhesive leads to an increased absorptions of energy than neat adhesive thereby increasing the joint strength. According to the fracture surface analysis of the joints, cohesive failure is the dominating failure mechanism for all methods of hybrid and bonded joints.

Mohammad Sadigh et al. (2018) [12]: In this paper, the authors studied the effect of reduced graphene oxide (RGO) on the behavior of adhesively bonded lap joints under fatigue loading. Two groups of specimens bonded with neat adhesive and RGO-reinforced adhesive were tested with applied loads varying from 40% to 70% of the static strength of the adhesively bonded joints. Two-dimensional finite element models (FEMs) were used to simulate the fracture in the adhesive joint. Because high stress singularity and stress concentration effects, the mesh was made finer in the overlap regions. Experimentally, lap joints were subjected to sinusoidally varying cyclic loading with a 0.1 load ratio at a frequency of 12 Hz. Comparison of the fatigue life of the joints showed that dispersion of RGO particles led to an increase in fatigue life. It showed an increase in low cycle fatigue range and up to 130% increase in high cycle fatigue range. The results indicate that the joints that were reinforced with RGO showed improved fatigue properties in comparison to the joints without reinforcements. In this study, the maximum values of the attained von-Mises stress were used for estimation of the fatigue life.

G. Scarselli et al. (2017) [13]: Single lap joints (SLJs) of unidirectional composite laminates were experimentally tested and then numerically modeled. Joints bonded with conventional epoxy resin and resin with nano-graphite particles were compared. Finite element (FE)-based simulations were conducted using the CZM. The maximum shear stress and the critical fracture energy for adhesives were obtained. The experimental results showed a considerable enhancement in the mechanical parameters of the adhesive. shear strength showed an 18% increase while the strain energy at break point increased by 53% after adding nano-fillers to the epoxy resin. The load-displacement diagrams are similar for adhesives, i.e., linear behavior can be observed at the starting of the test with a significantly small non-linear region just before failure. The same is observed in the numerical simulations as well. The results obtained from the numerical modeling successfully matched the experimental Load-Displacement curves. The bond contact region was simulated using the cohesive zone model in order to obtain the maximum shear stress and critical fracture energy for the two adhesives. The two parameters in discussion were found to be comparatively higher for the adhesive filled with nanomaterials.

R. Campilho et al. (2012) [14]: This work is based on determining the effects of the cohesive law parameters of a triangular law used to predict the behavior bonded joints with a thin layer of adhesive. It also makes an attempt to evaluate the effect these parameters have on the strength of bonded structures using cohesive zone models. SLJs bonded with a structural adhesive have been analyzed for different lengths of overlap zone from short overlaps with uniform shear stress distribution, to long overlap areas which lead to a considerable development of shear stress variations along the entire overlap length. The numerical analysis was conducted in the FEM package ABAQUS to test the feasibility of a triangular cohesive zone model formulation and to predict the mechanical strength of adhesively bonded joints and to study the impact of cohesive parameters on the joint strength. Two-dimensional simulations were considered for simulation of the joints with four node plane-strain elements (CPE4) and with COH2D4 four-node cohesive elements, compatible with the CPE4 elements. All the joints were reported to have undergone a cohesive failure of the adhesive layer.

C. Salom et al (2018) [15]: The authors, in this work, have evaluated the influence of the GNPs or platelets content by weight percentages on the mechanical and adhesive characteristics graphene reinforced epoxy- GNPs. GNPs percentages of 2%, 4%, 6%, 8%, 10% and 12% by weight were employed for preparing the nanocomposite along with the neat (0%) composite. Tensile tests showed that the strength of 2–4% nanocomposite was similar to neat epoxy setting. This has been attributed to poor dispersion of nanoparticles. The specimen with 6% of GNPs showed an increase in the stiffness values. This increase in the stiffness is about 40% compared to the neat epoxy. Similar trend was observed for the nanocomposite with 12% GNPs. For all the cases, the strain at break and the toughness decreased as the GNP content increased. That is, they were more prone to fracture (fragile) than the neat epoxy. The adhesive was observed to have failed in cohesive mode but very close to the interface. It was found that for low GNP content (0.5%) joint strength increased considerably but an increase in the GNP led to a gradual decrease in the strength of the joints. This phenomenon can be explained by the formation of agglomerates at higher concentrations.

Swetha Chandrasekaran et al. (2014) [16]: This paper investigates the effect of graphene nano-fillers on the fracture toughness and failure mechanism of the epoxy-based polymer composites. This study makes an attempt to understand the relationship between the fracture behavior of epoxy composites having a microstructure of the dispersed nanoparticles in identifying the mechanism which results in the enhancement of toughness parameter. An addition of 0.5% GNPs showed an increase of 24% in the fracture toughness compared to the neat epoxy. This, however, shows a decrease at a 2% concentration due to particle agglomeration. As the filler loading is increased, it is observed the graphene layers separate at various places resulting in a deformed fractured surface due to the combined effect of layers separating and low distance between the successive nanoparticles. Based on these findings the authors conclude that unreinforced epoxy shows a more or less flat fracture surface and the deformed zone formed in GNP-based composite is higher which results in an increased fracture toughness of graphene-reinforced epoxies.

Daniel F. O. Braga et al. (2016) [17]: In this work, the authors have taken up a set of experimental procedures to characterize a structural adhesive and numerically model the behavior of a single-lap joint using epoxy-based adhesive. After the experimentation, two numerical models were developed on ABAQUS which used a combination of 2D plain stress elements and 2D cohesive zone elements. FEM results presented a slightly higher stiffness values, which were justified by the way the displacements were measured in the experimental setup. The experimental and numerical results were in agreement with a variation of about 10%. CZM in this case has been demonstrated to model failure in adhesive joints, but the authors suggest to duly care for the substrate part along with the adhesive part when using high strength, high fracture toughness adhesives as the substrate regions may considerably weaken during the failure of adhesive. The authors observed that in such cases, for numerical modeling, the plastic behavior of the materials should be given due consideration for obtaining better results.

M. Johar et al. (2014) [18]: In this paper, the cohesive modeling for epoxy joints has been carried out. Evolution of damage in the adhesive joint has been expressed as a function of cyclic degradation of interface strength and stiffness. A bilinear traction-separation law was used along with power law variation to simulate the behavior. Mixed-mode fracture has been formulated considering the relative displacement and strain energy release rate. A cyclic displacement of 0.1 mm and an R-ration of 0 were used. Results showed that the cyclic interface damage was initiated and propagated in a similar manner from both the overlap edges and degradation of interface strength and stiffness started to accumulate after only 0.5 cycle of displacement elapsed. The authors conclude that the fatigue damage starts from both ends of the adhesive interface and propagates inwards. The normal stress component is dominant in the cyclic damage initiation process of the adhesive interface.

M. M. Shokrieh et al. (2014) [19]: In this study, the authors have studied the effect of weight fractions of graphene nanoplatelets (GPL) on the fatigue behavior of epoxy polymer. The stiffness of GPL/epoxy nanocomposites at 0.1%, 0.25% and 0.5% wt.% was considered as an effective parameter on fatigue was considered. The fatigue properties have been evaluated by using the modified cantilever beam test. The amplitude of the imposed displacement has been kept as a controllable parameter during experimentation. The number of cycles to failure was counted directly for each test specimen. In the experiments, test setup frequency of 5 Hz has been employed. The results showed that the effect 0.25 wt.% of GPL on fatigue life was more effective in comparison with 0.1 and 0.5 wt.% epoxy. Accordingly corresponding to the addition of GPL, a remarkable increase in fatigue life of epoxy was observed. The improvement to the tune of 22.4, 27.4 and 17 times for these percentages of graphene was seen in the fatigue life.

Chow-Shing Shin et al. (2024) [20]: The paper investigated a novel approach for monitoring the integrity of adhesive joints in composite materials. The study successfully utilized conductivity changes to monitor fatigue damage in single-lap-joint composite specimens. This was achieved by measuring the percentage voltage change when a constant current was applied to the specimen, which reflects the extent of damage. The research found that the percentage voltage change increased monotonically from 0% to 49% as the number of fatigue loading cycles increased. Notably, the voltage changes measured at a load of 500 N were consistently higher than those at 0 N, indicating a significant correlation between applied load and damage progression. The findings have significant implications for the practical use of resistance change as a method for structural health monitoring, highlighting the potential for this technique to enhance the assessment of adhesive joint integrity.

Xiao Han et al. (2024) [21]: The paper presents several significant results regarding the mechanical performance and failure mechanisms of carbon-fiber-reinforced plastic (CFRP) stepped-lap repairs under tensile loading. The results indicated that the tensile strength of the stepped-lap repairs increased with the number of steps. Specifically, the three-step configuration with a slope combination of 1/20-1/20-1/20 exhibited the highest tensile strength and load-bearing capacity among the configurations tested. The study noted a maximum difference of 23.09% and a minimum difference of 7.48% in average peak loads obtained from experiments, highlighting the significance of slope combinations in repair design. The study observed that damage in the adhesive layer initiated and propagated rapidly, while damage within the CFRP laminate developed more slowly. The damage propagation was noted to start from the inner end of the step and extend toward the center of the laminate, indicating a specific failure progression pattern. The fracture morphology varied significantly between single-lap and stepped-lap repairs. Single-lap repairs primarily exhibited cohesive failure, while stepped-lap repairs showed delamination at the bonding interface, along with matrix cracking and interlaminar debonding.

C. M. Jackson et al. (2023) [22]: The study explored various experimental and numerical techniques to characterize the mechanical properties of the PR-2930 adhesive bonded to 2024-T3 Al adherends. The digital imaging correlation (DIC) method was effectively utilized to track crack propagation in high-resolution images, allowing for precise measurement of crack tip locations. The calibration of the DIC system showed a measurement accuracy within 1% when compared to machined reference notches, confirming the reliability of the DIC data. The study identified that the shape of the traction separation laws (TSL) for the tough adhesive PR-2930 transitions to a trapezoidal form as mode II contributions increase. A bilinear TSL with a fracture energy of approximately 3.2 kJ/m^2 was found to fit the DCB data well, while a trapezoidal TSL with a fracture energy of about 14 kJ/m^2 accurately predicted the end-notched flexure (ENF) load-displacement response. The implementation of CZMs in FEA provided a good match to both the crosshead displacement and DIC data, indicating that the models can effectively simulate the adhesive fracture behavior under mixed-mode loading conditions.

T. Nagoshi et al. (2022) [23]: The paper presents significant findings regarding the cohesive failure of epoxy adhesives in CFRP composites. The study identified that cohesive failure occurs predominantly due to micrometer-scale defects within the adhesive layers. The cohesive failure was observed at two main locations: near the interface and within the adhesive itself. This failure initiates 0.1–1 μm away from the interface, indicating that the adhesive's molecular structure plays a critical role in its performance. This finding challenges the assumption that the adhesive interface, which has minimal covalent bonds, would be the weakest point. The FEM analysis indicated that stress profiles peak near the adhesion interface, supporting the observed cohesive failure. The analysis showed that the physical bonding at the DGEBA/TGDDM interface has a tensile strength of approximately 120 MPa, which is higher than the bulk strengths of the individual components. To enhance the reliability of epoxy/epoxy adhesion joints, the authors propose focusing on strengthening physical bonding rather than merely increasing chemical bonds. This approach emphasizes the importance of intermolecular forces in adhesion.

8.2.1 Research Gaps

After conducting a thorough examination of the literature, certain gaps have been identified. Specifically, the cyclic load behavior of the epoxy joints with different percentages of nano-fillers like graphene, and graphene oxide hasn't been explored extensively. Very few works exist that have undertaken numerical simulations for the same. It is important to assess the impact of different parameters in CZM, such as the penalty stiffness and fracture energy. Additionally, it is necessary to establish a correlation between the experimental parameters and the numerical parameters of the cohesive zone model in order to gain a better understanding of the fracture behavior of epoxy joints with different concentrations of GONPs.

8.2.2 Problem Statement

Increased use of composite materials has led to an upsurge in research in the domain of adhesive joints. Joining of composite laminates presents a major challenge. There is a vast scope to identify the methods that can be utilized to join these materials as regards to structural integrity. Bonded joints are the most preferred joints, since they facilitate the use of adhesive to replace mechanical fasteners which cumulatively lead to reduction in the overall weight of the component. Numerical modeling and simulations can help us better understand the effects of various mechanical and cohesive parameters of adhesives to enhance the strength of these joints. Additionally, correlations can be developed between the experimental and numerical parameters to develop an understanding of the damage behavior of adhesive joints. This, in turn, will help in developing joints, which have enhanced mechanical, thermal and electrical properties for use in varied fields of technology.

8.3 MATERIAL PROPERTIES

8.3.1 E-Glass/Epoxy Laminate

The properties of the E-glass/epoxy composite laminate plate are obtained from the AUTODESK HELIUS COMPOSITE software. The thickness of the plies and the orientation of the fiber in the plies are the inputs provided to the AUTODESK HELIUS COMPOSITE. The E-glass/Epoxy material is selected from the template (Fig. 8.4, Fig. 8.5).

Table 8.1 shows the engineering constants of E-Glass/Epoxy laminate. These values are obtained from the AUTODESK HELIUS COMPOSITE software.

8.3.2 Epoxy Resin

The epoxy resin used is EPOXY RESIN EPOFINE 740-1. The properties of this polymer resin are as given in Table 8.2.

The values obtained are in compliance with ASTM standards as mentioned in Table 8.2. This epoxy resin is the adhesive to join the composite substrate. Since it is readily available and less costly, it is used for many applications. It possesses excellent bonding characteristics which makes it the better option for moderate loading conditions.

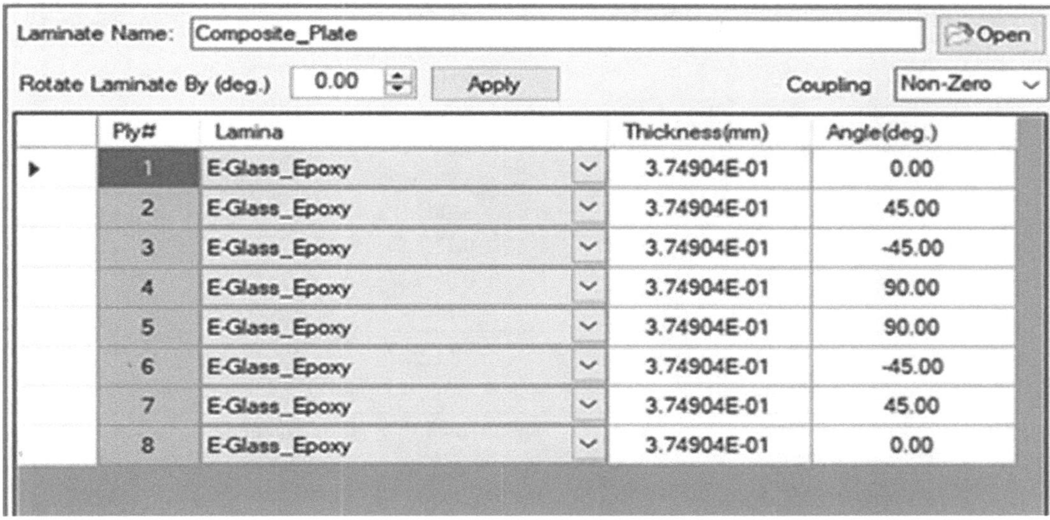

Laminate Name: Composite_Plate   Open

Rotate Laminate By (deg.) 0.00   Apply   Coupling Non-Zero

Ply#	Lamina	Thickness(mm)	Angle(deg.)
1	E-Glass_Epoxy	3.74904E-01	0.00
2	E-Glass_Epoxy	3.74904E-01	45.00
3	E-Glass_Epoxy	3.74904E-01	-45.00
4	E-Glass_Epoxy	3.74904E-01	90.00
5	E-Glass_Epoxy	3.74904E-01	90.00
6	E-Glass_Epoxy	3.74904E-01	-45.00
7	E-Glass_Epoxy	3.74904E-01	45.00
8	E-Glass_Epoxy	3.74904E-01	0.00

FIGURE 8.4 Composite Laminate Properties.

Here in this case the epoxy is also used as matrix wherein the joining of the composite laminate would become easier. This is because of the material continuity in the specimen.

8.3.2.1 Hardener

The hardener used is FINEHARD – 951. Hardener properties are given in Table 8.3.

A hardener is used to cure the epoxy to become hard and helps to form joint. The hardener is mixed in the epoxy resin in the ratio of 0.16:1, i.e., for 100 mL of epoxy resin, 16 mL of hardener is required.

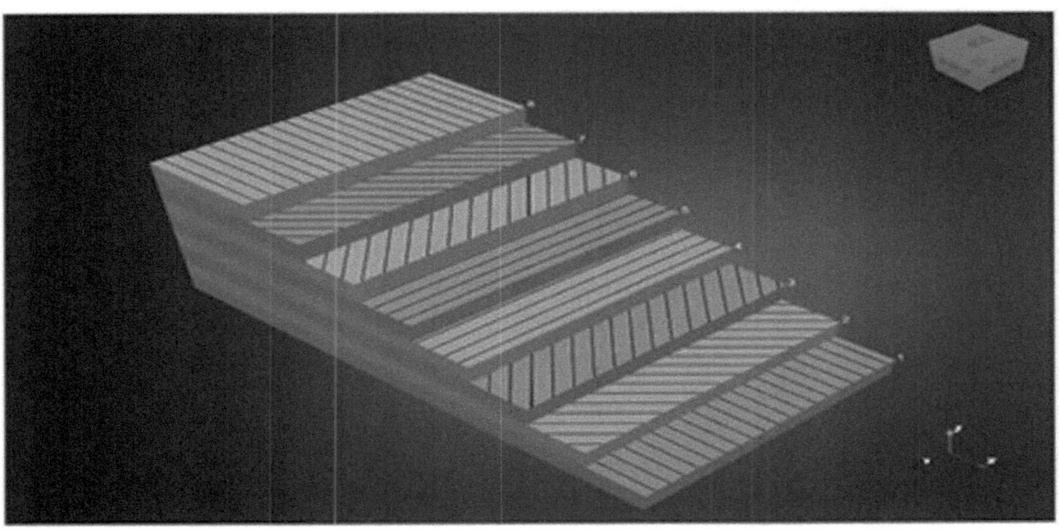

FIGURE 8.5 Ply Orientation in Laminate.

TABLE 8.1 Laminate Properties

E11	44800 MPa
E22	12400 MPa
E33	12400 MPa
G12	5520 MPa
G13	5520 MPa
G23	3600 MPa
ν12	0.28
ν13	0.28
ν23	0.36

TABLE 8.2 Epoxy Resin Properties

Sr. No.	Characteristics	Units	Specification	Measured value	Test Method
1.	Color	-	Colorless	Colorless	Visual
2.	Viscosity @ 25°C, MPa	MPa	9000–11000	9856	ASTM D
3.	Specific Gravity @ 25°C	-	1.15–1.17	1.1585	IS 9162-1979
4.	Epoxy Value	Eq/Kg	5.25–5.55	5.47	ASTM D 1652-11

TABLE 8.3 Hardener Properties

Sr. No.	Characteristics	Units	Measured Value	Test Method
1.	Color	-	Colorless	Visual
2.	Viscosity @ 25°C	MPa	21.7	ASTM D 2196-2010
3.	Specific Gravity @ 25°C	-	0.972	IS 9162-1979

8.4 FINITE ELEMENT ANALYSIS

As discussed in Section 1.5, the cohesive zone model using bilinear traction-separation law is the basis for numerical simulations using FEA. The software package used is ABAQUS 6.14-2 version due to its advanced capabilities in simulating the complex behaviors of anisotropic materials. ABAQUS is widely recognized for its robust material modeling features, making it well-suited for analyzing composite structures under various loading conditions. Since the composite material is anisotropic in nature, its various directional properties have been obtained from HELIUS software. This software specializes in the analysis of composite materials and provides accurate directional properties necessary for our simulations. The anisotropic nature of the composite was characterized using input data from HELIUS, ensuring that our analysis reflected the true mechanical behavior of the laminate. These properties have already been presented in Table 8.1. A non-linear numerical analysis is performed on this software. The specimen has been modeled as per ASTM D-5868. The schematic is given in Fig. 8.6.

8.4.1 Cohesive Zone Model

CZM simulates the development of stress and eventual softening to complete failure, corresponding to material degeneration. ABAQUS offers a collection of cohesive elements that depict adhesive joints, composite materials and other interface integrity and resistance requirements that may be of concern. Related items are used for simulating adhesives, gluing surfaces, gaskets and rock breaking. The solution of these elements relies on the

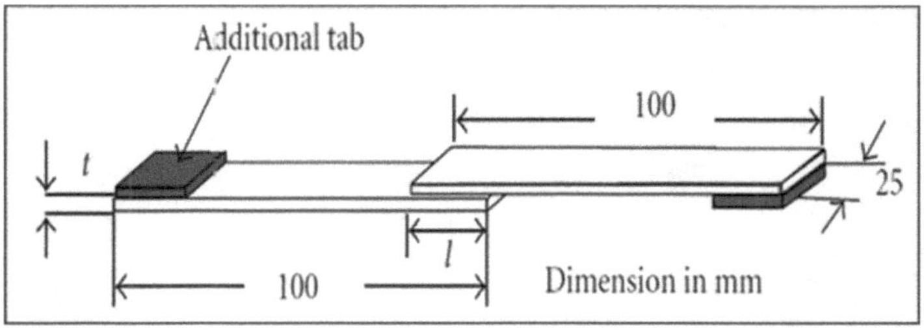

FIGURE 8.6 Specimen Dimensions [34].

particular implementation and is based on certain assumptions that apply to each application's deformation and stress state.

8.4.1.1 *Inverse Method*

The inverse technique involves a procedure for iterative curve fitting between experimental measurement data and corresponding FE prediction. It requires an accurate description of the experimental geometry and an approximate cohesion rule developed on the basis of the material's typical conduct to be modeled. To account for slight differences in geometry between samples, the inverse characterization of adhesive bonds should be implemented separately for each specimen tested.

8.4.2 Modeling of Specimen

The model of the composite single-lap joint is created in ABAQUS. A solid model is created as represented in Fig. 8.7. Material properties of the laminate are assigned to the solid model. The laminate model representation is shown in Fig. 8.8. The properties are extracted using Autodesk Helius software, as specified in Table 8.1, as an input to it. An adhesive thickness of 0.25 mm is taken as its average thickness measured from the samples.

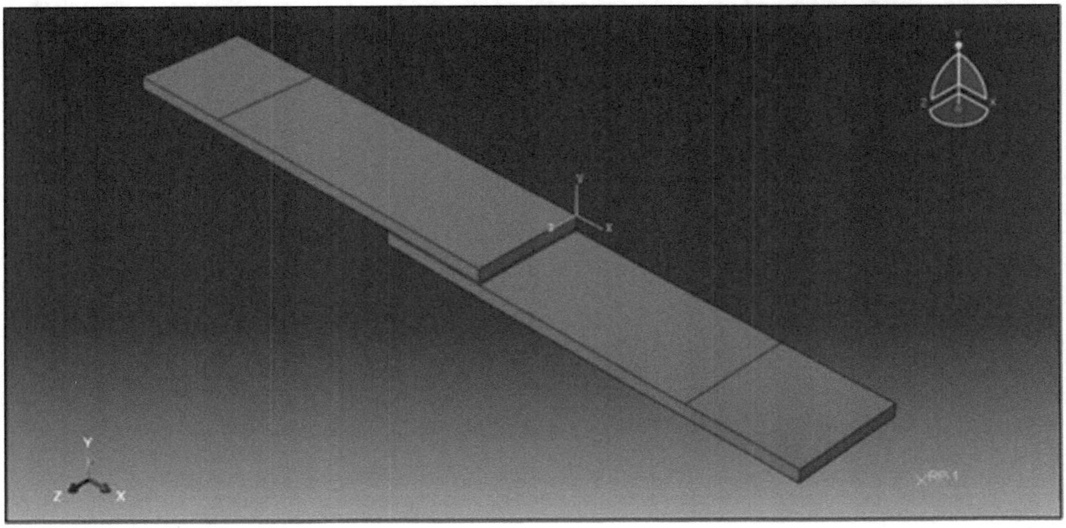

FIGURE 8.7 Specimen Model

FIGURE 8.8 Laminate Model in ABAQUS.

The specimen is modeled as per the dimensions given in ASTM D-5868. The schematic is shown in Fig. 8.6.

8.4.2.1 Adhesive Properties

The adhesive is defined using cohesive zone elements. For this, the material behavior is selected as "Traction". In this study, bilinear cohesive law is selected considering experimental data (Fig. 8.9). The properties selected for cohesive zone model of neat epoxy by using inverse method are shown in Table 8.4.

FIGURE 8.9 ABAQUS Model of Adhesive.

TABLE 8.4 Cohesive Properties

Enn	800 (N/mm)
Ess	600 (N/mm)
Ett	600 (N/mm)

8.4.2.2 Assembly of the Components

The lap joint and the adhesive part are assembled in ABAQUS using the assembly and interaction segments. A Tie constraint is used between the substrate and adhesive surfaces to emulate the actual adhesive behavior of the joint. The substrate surfaces are chosen as master surfaces, while the adhesive surfaces are selected as slave surfaces. Finally, the instances of the substrate and adhesive are aligned together for assembly. The representation is shown in Fig. 8.10.

Since there are total three parts in the assembly, these parts have to be constrained together to avoid free body motion. The adhesive's top layer is constrained to the top adhesive's bottom layer and the bottom layer of the adhesive is connected to the bottom adhesive's top layer. In both the instances the master surface selected is the adherend surface and the slave surface selected is the adhesive surface. The discretization method is kept as surface-to-surface in both the instances.

8.4.2.3 Boundary Conditions

The model is fixed at one end and displacement is given at the other end to simulate the real testing conditions. One end is constrained for all degrees of freedom (DOFs) and the other is given input cyclic displacement of 2.3 mm, varying between an amplitude of 0.1 and a frequency 3 Hz. "ENCASTRE" command for constraining all the six DOFs, i.e., translational and rotational on one end. This fixes one end of the specimen. A reference point (RP) is created at an offset of 10 mm from the moving end. All elemental nodes at the other end are coupled to this RP by constraining all DOFs, shown in Fig. 8.10. The RP is used

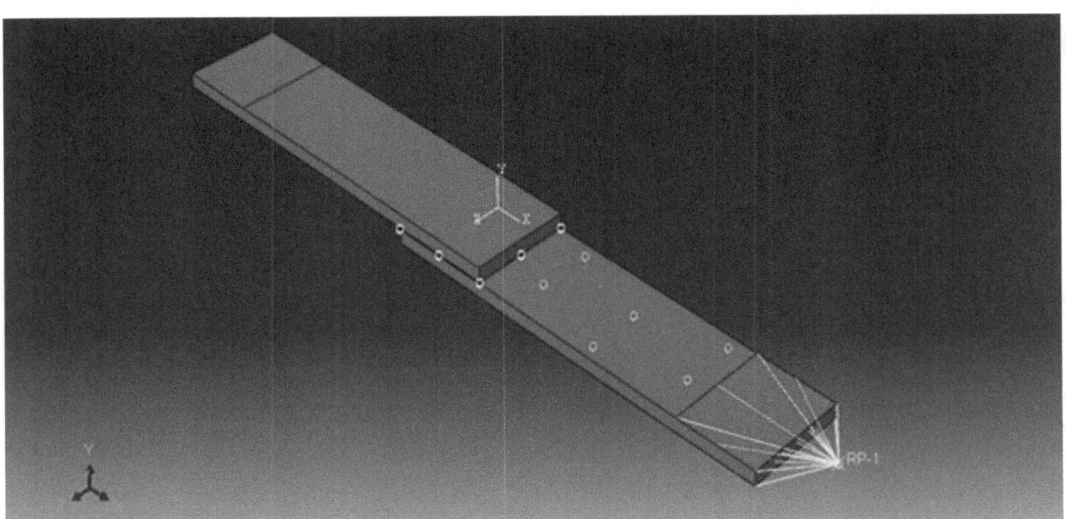

FIGURE 8.10 Assembly and Coupling of Surfaces.

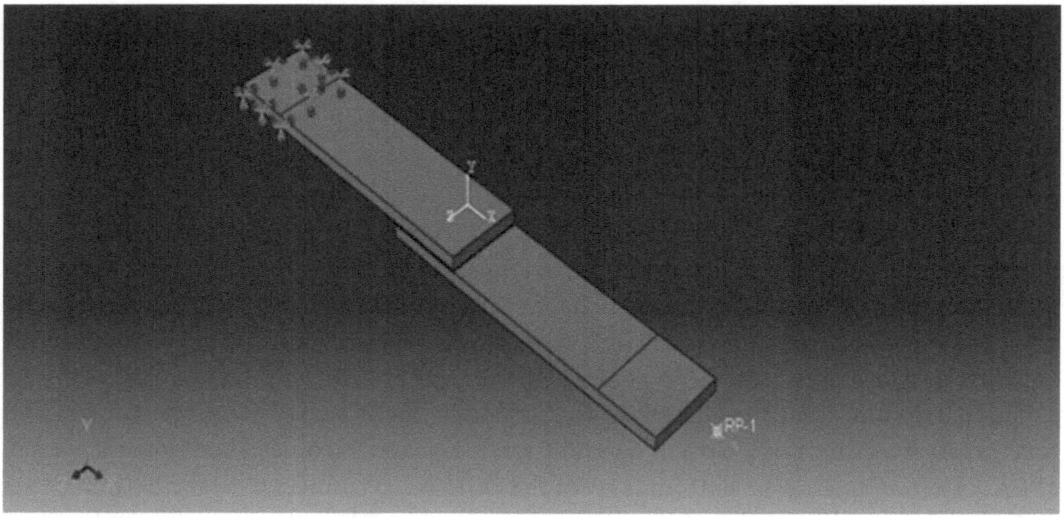

FIGURE 8.11 Boundary Conditions.

for coupling the surfaces for displacement. Displacement is applied at this RP. All surfaces coupled move relative to this RP. The boundary conditions are depicted in Fig. 8.11.

8.4.3 Meshing of Model

For meshing the composite specimen, eight-node solid hex elements (C3D8R) from the 3D stress elements family are used as "reduced integration and hourglass control" option in the solver. Cohesive elements are available in the ABAQUS software to model and simulate the adhesive behavior joints and for modeling of composites and instances where the strength parameters are of concern. For meshing of cohesive zone, eight-node three-dimensional cohesive element (COH3D8) type are used. Figure 8.12 shows the adhesive region after meshing.

FIGURE 8.12 Adhesive Mesh.

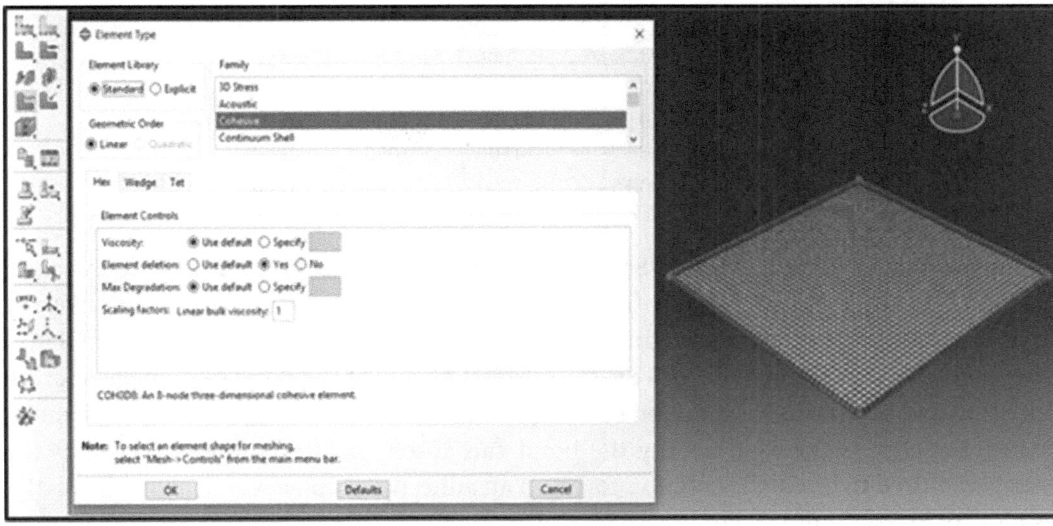

FIGURE 8.13 Cohesive Elements for Adhesive.

Here element deletion is kept on to visualize damage in cohesive region. The element size is kept constant throughout for both the adherend part and adhesive part. These are shown in Fig. 8.13. The complete meshed model is shown in Fig. 8.14.

8.5 RESULTS AND DISCUSSION

The joints were evaluated for three different initial tensile and shear stiffnesses corresponding to 0.25%, 0.5% and 0.75% GONPs respectively, apart from considering neat epoxy (0% GO). The combinations are tabulated in Table 8.5.

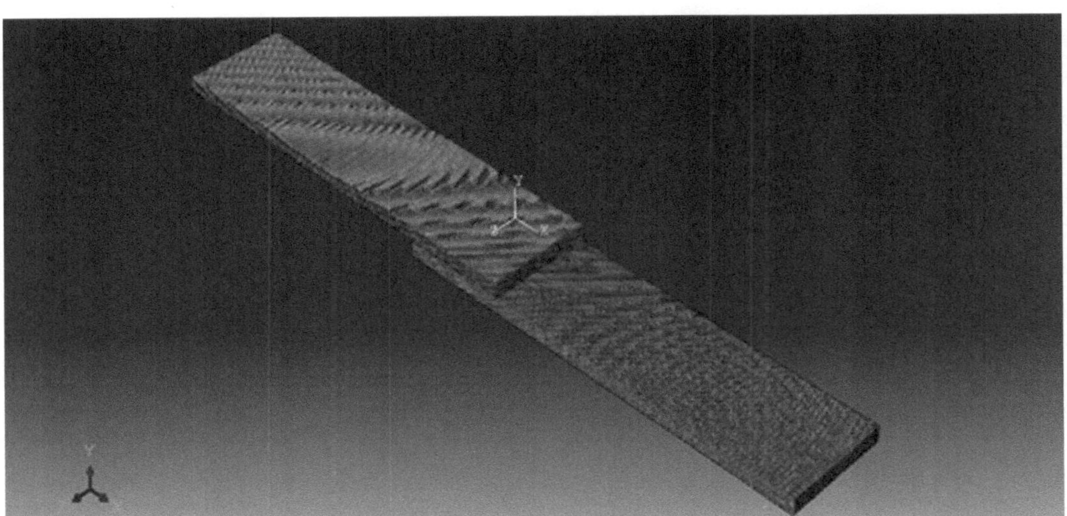

FIGURE 8.14 Meshed Model of SLJ.

TABLE 8.5 Initial Stiffness Values

Case no.	GO %age	Enn	Ess	Ett
I	0	800	600	600
II	0.25	1200	1000	1000
III	0.5	1500	1000	1000
IV	0.75	2000	1200	1200

The primary variable in ABAQUS that quantifies the damage is the stiffness degradation (SDEG). The range of this factor is from 0 to 1. A value of 0 indicates that a cohesive element has undergone no damage while a factor of 1 indicates that the element is completely damaged. The maximum value of Von-Mises stress occurs at the point of damage of crack initiation and progressively keeps on reducing till complete failure of the cohesive element. Fracture energy is the total energy the bond can absorb before failing. It indicates the energy required to break the cohesive forces in an adhesive or cohesive element. The analysis plots of Stress Contour, Force-Displacement, Damage Initiation, Damage Propagation, Debonding and Complete Debonding for all the four cases are presented in Figs. 8.15 to 8.34. The numerical results are presented in Table 8.6.

8.5.1 Analysis for Case I (Neat Epoxy)

8.5.1.1 Stress Contour

The maximum Von-Mises stress is 40.05 MPa. This is stress developed at the crack initiation. The crack propagation starts at this points and beyond this point the stress keeps on reducing till a complete failure or debonding occurs. This can be correlated with the load displacement diagram as shown in Fig. 8.15.

From the Load-Displacement (Fig. 8.16) we observe that the maximum load at failure is 600 KN and the displacement at failure is 1.3 mm. The crack initiates at an

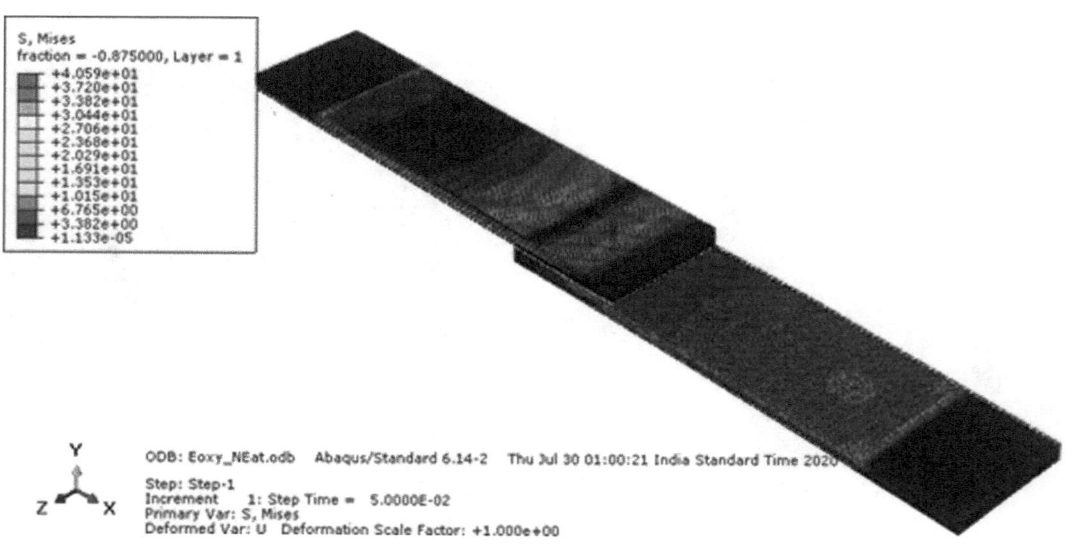

FIGURE 8.15 Stress Contour Case I.

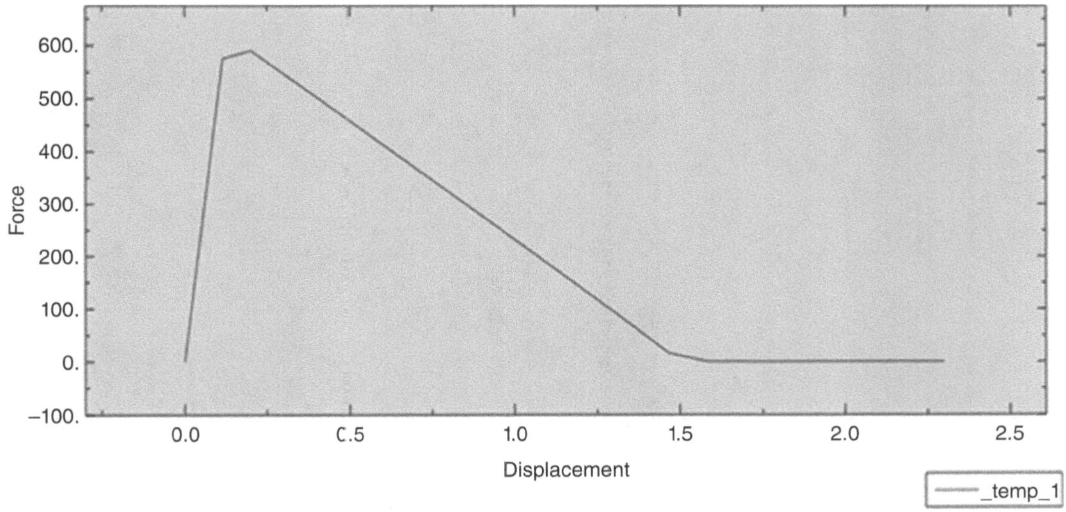

FIGURE 8.16 Force-Displacement Curve Case I.

applied load of 600 KN, then there is propagation of the failure and finally debonding occurs at a displacement of 1.3 mm. The stress value at the crack initiation point is 40.05 MPa.

8.5.1.2 Damage of Cohesive Elements

It can be clearly observed that the damage initiates at the edges of the adhesive or cohesive region. High stresses are developed in this region and the damage propagates further. This is in accordance to the behavior predicted in Section 1.5.1.

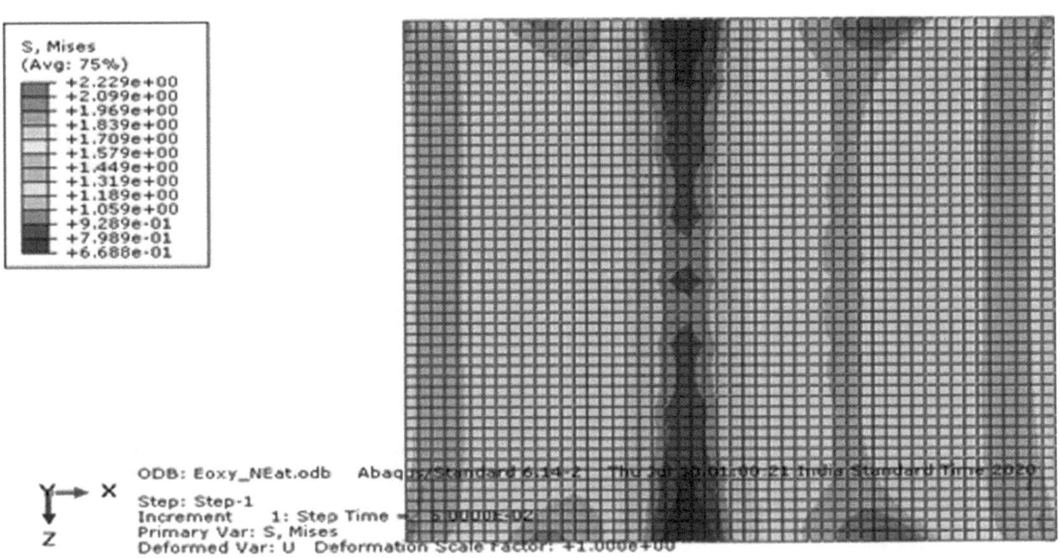

FIGURE 8.17 Damage Initiation Case I.

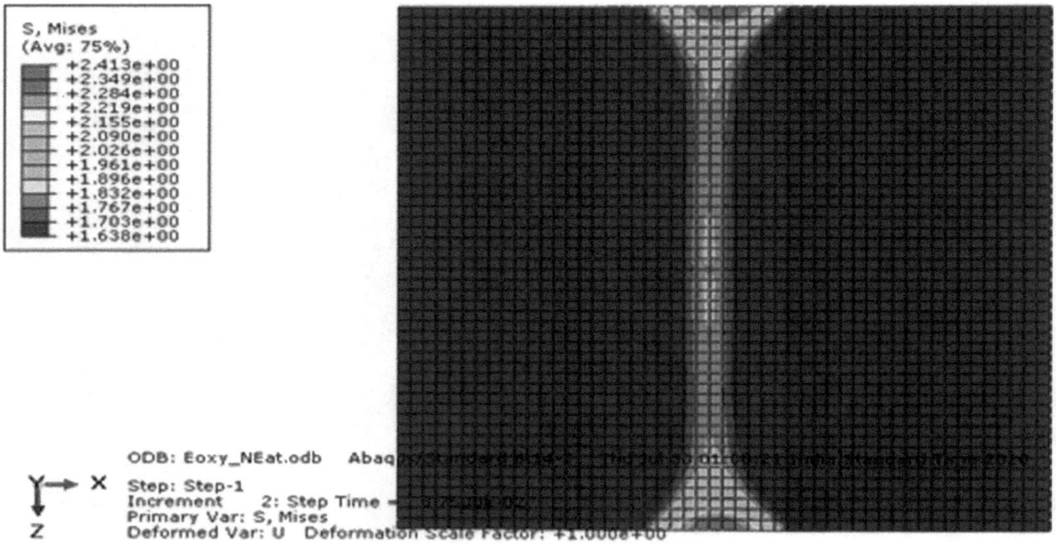

FIGURE 8.18 Damage Propagation Case I.

8.5.2 Analysis for Case II (0.25% GO)

8.5.2.1 Stress Contour:

From the curve it can be observed that the load at failure is 1.8 KN and maximum displacement at failure is 1.6 mm. The crack initiates at an applied load of 1.8 KN, then there is propagation of the failure and finally debonding occurs at a displacement of 1.6 mm. The stress value at the crack initiation point is 100.4 MPa as shown in Fig. 8.21.

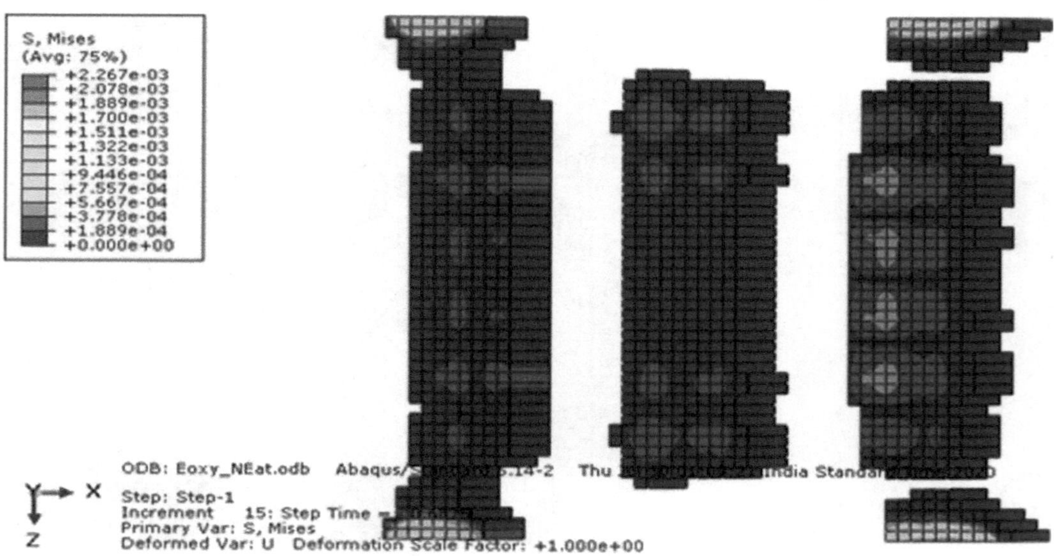

FIGURE 8.19 Debonding in Case I.

FIGURE 8.20 Complete Debonding Case I.

For the stiffness value of 1200 MPa the maximum Von-Mises stress is 104 MPa. This is stress developed at the crack initiation. The crack propagation starts at these points and beyond this point the stress keeps on reducing till a complete failure or debonding occurs. This can be correlated with the load displacement diagram as shown in Fig. 8.22.

8.5.2.2 Damage of Cohesive Elements

The progressive damage of the cohesive elements is represented in Fig. 8.23.

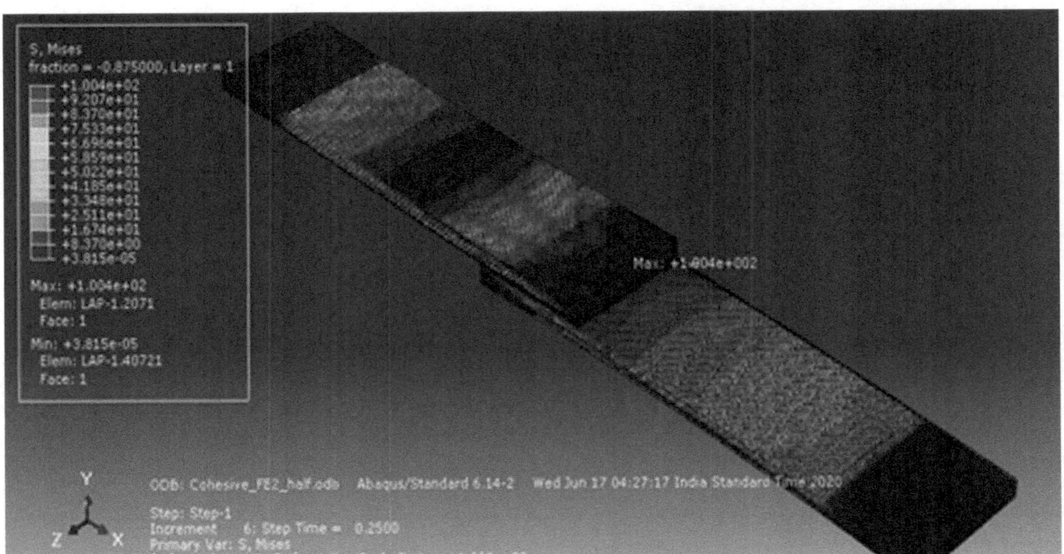

FIGURE 8.21 Stress Contour for Case II.

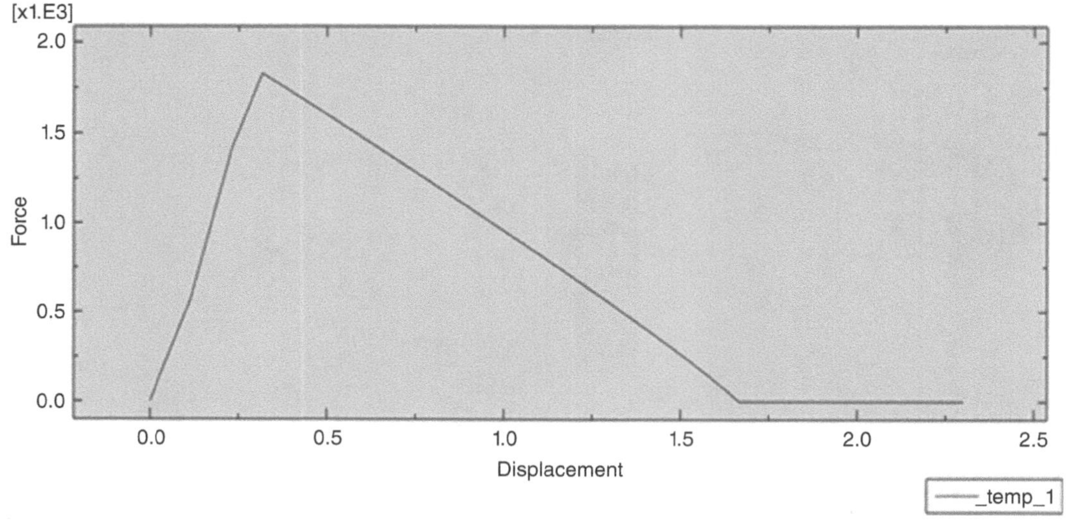

FIGURE 8.22 Load-Displacement Curve Case II.

As in previous case it can be clearly observed that the damage initiates at the edges of the adhesive or cohesive region. High stresses are developed in these regions and the damage propagates further.

In Fig. 8.24 the cohesive elements have failed completely or debonded. The SDEG value of all such elements is 1.

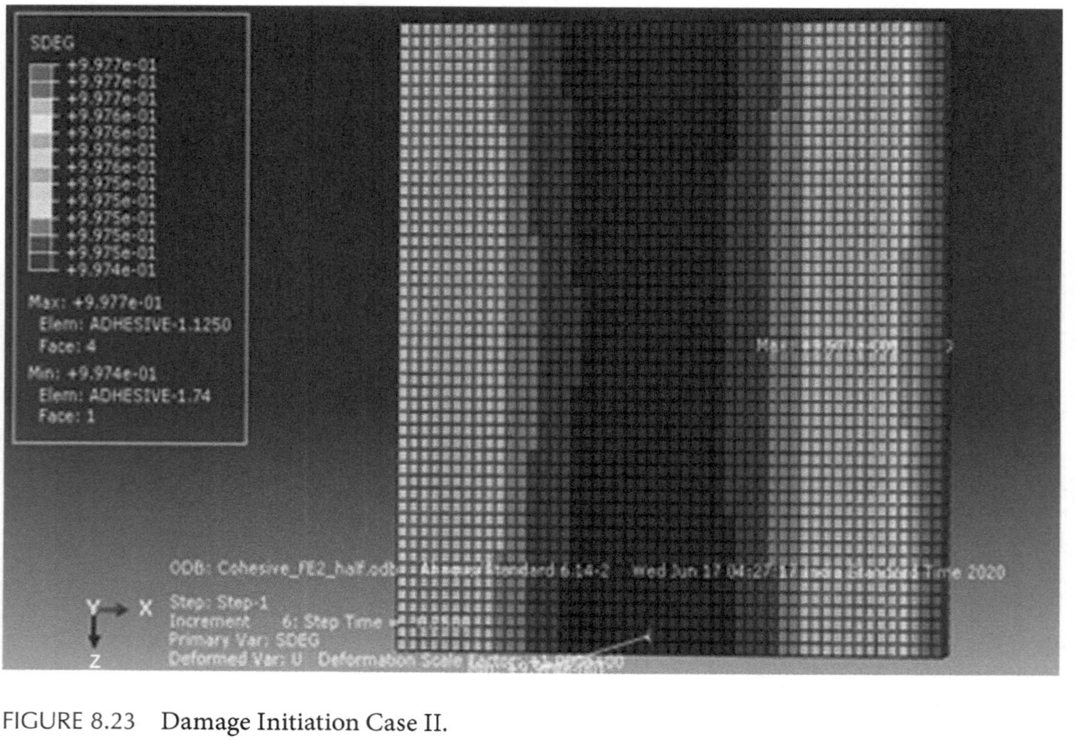

FIGURE 8.23 Damage Initiation Case II.

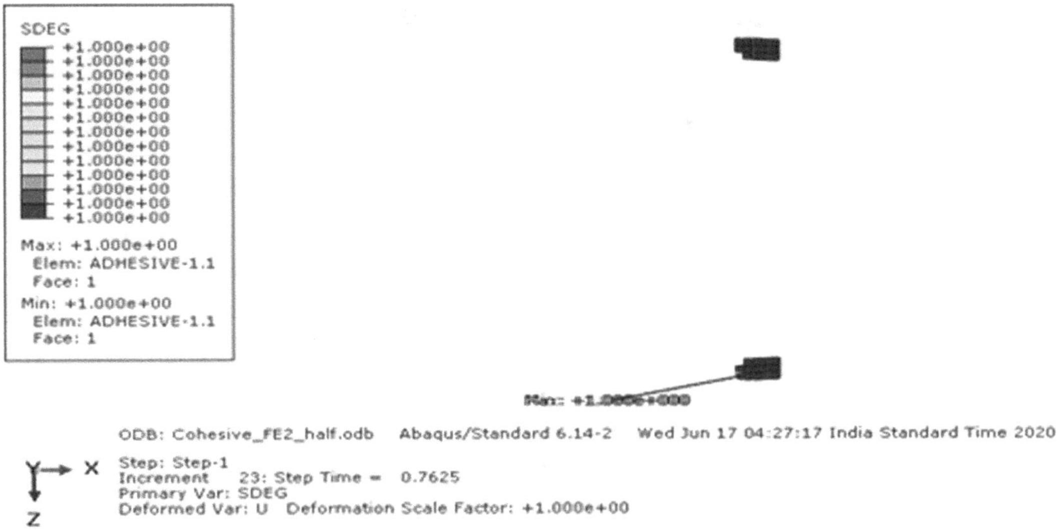

FIGURE 8.24 Debonding in Case II.

8.5.3 Analysis for Case III (0 5% GO)

8.5.3.1 Stress Contour:

The maximum Von-Mises stress is 123.1 MPa. The same trend is followed as in the previous case. Maximum stress concentrations are near the overlap regions (refer Fig. 8.25).

The Load-Displacement or Traction-Separation curve for this case indicates that the damage initiation occurs at an applied load of 2.5 KN and the displacement at failure is 1.9 mm. This shows a considerable improvement in all cohesive parameters compared to the previous case (refer Fig. 8.26).

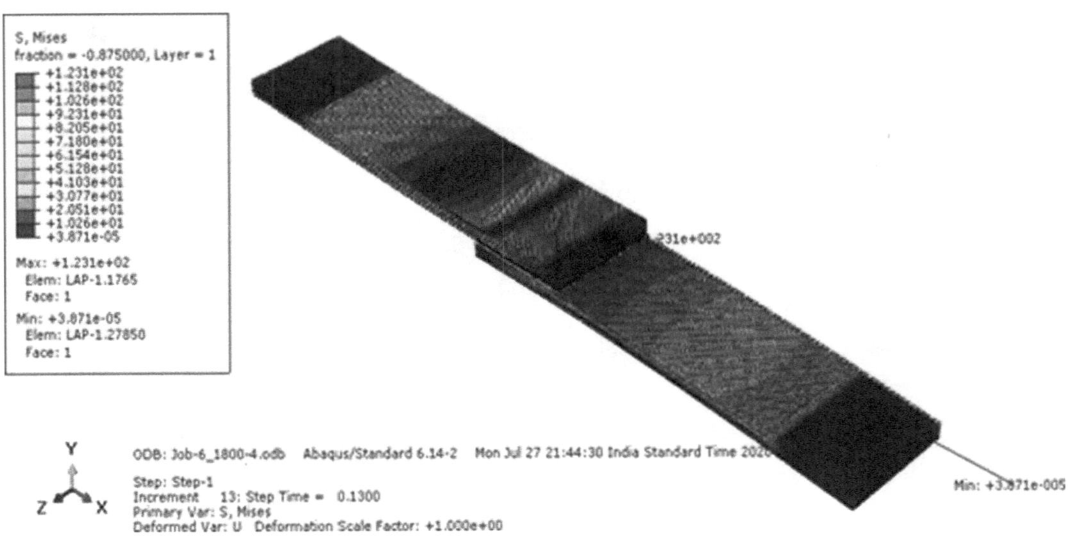

FIGURE 8.25 Stress Contour for Case III.

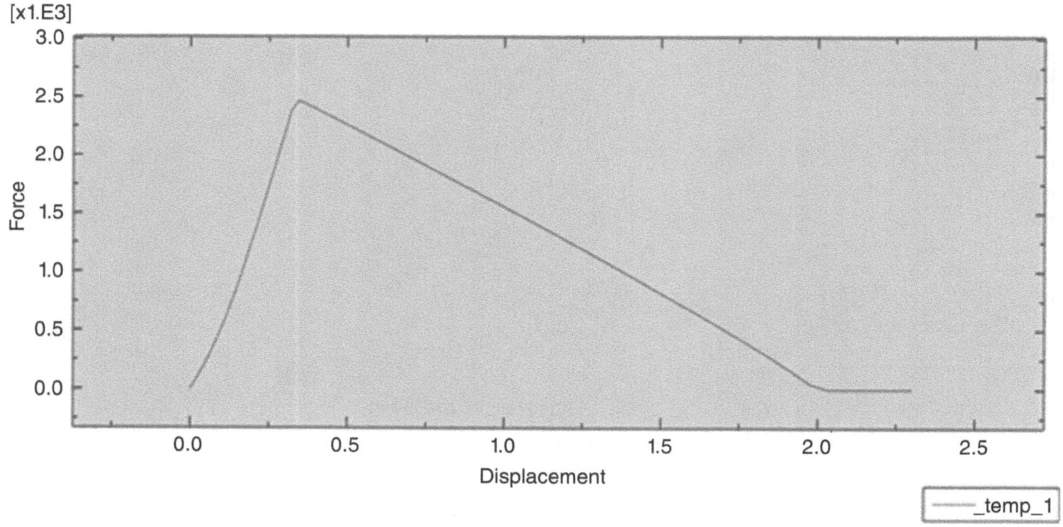

FIGURE 8.26 Load-Displacement Curve for Case III.

From the previous figures (Fig. 8.27, Fig. 8.28, Fig. 8.29, Fig. 8.30), the following observations are made:

1. The damage initiation begins at the edge of the cohesive elements and progress toward the inner part.
2. Compared to the previous case, the maximum load and displacement at failure have increased. This indicates a better fracture resistance.
3. At the debonding stage, the cohesive elements have an SDEG value of 1.

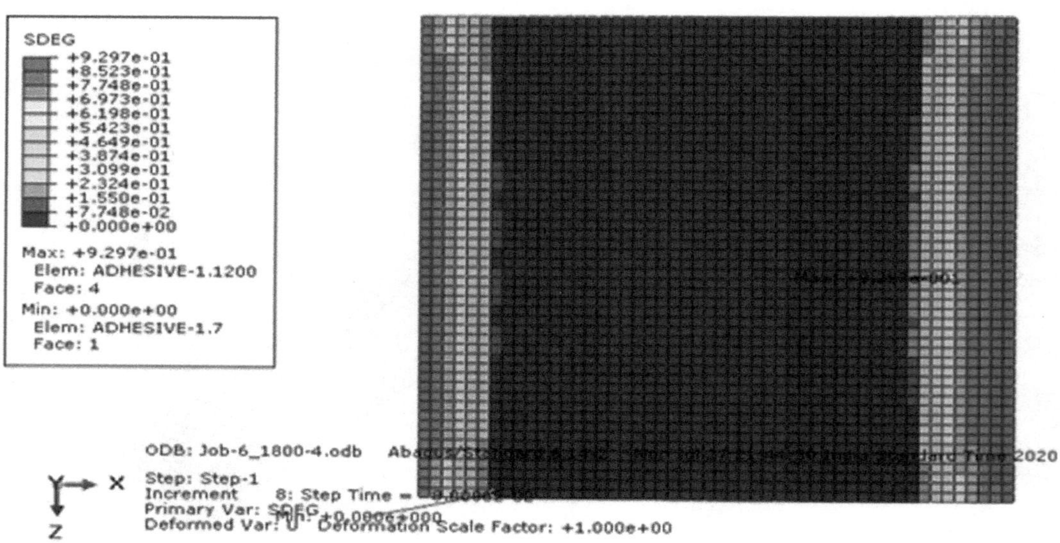

FIGURE 8.27 Damage Initiation Case III.

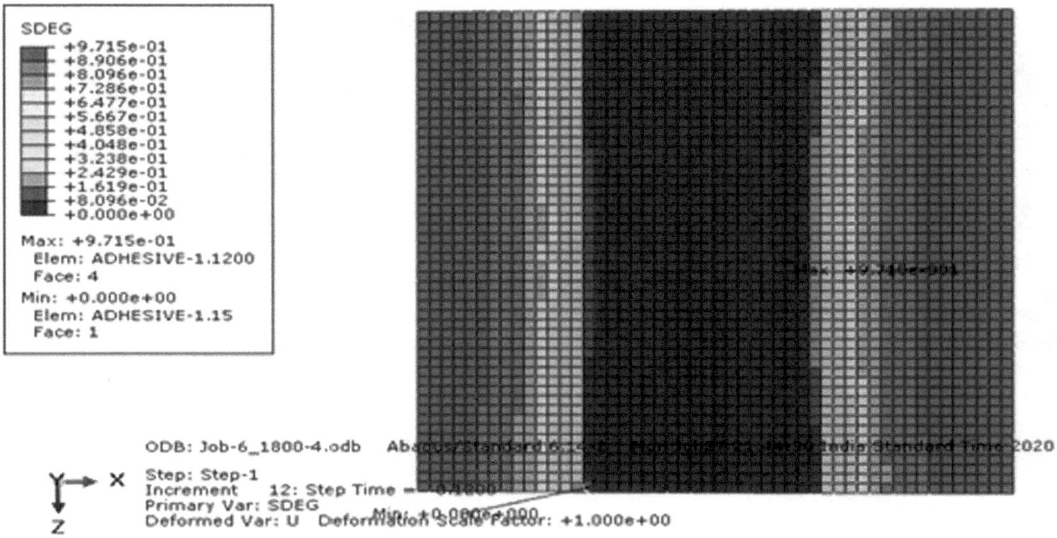

FIGURE 8.28 Damage Propagation Case III.

8.5.4 Analysis for Case IV (0.75% GO)

8.5.4.1 Stress Contours:

From Fig. 8.31, the maximum Von-Mises stress is 138.7 MPa.

8.5.4.2 Load-Displacement Curve

From Fig. 8.32, it can be seen that the failure load is 2600 KN and the displacement at failure is 2.44 mm.

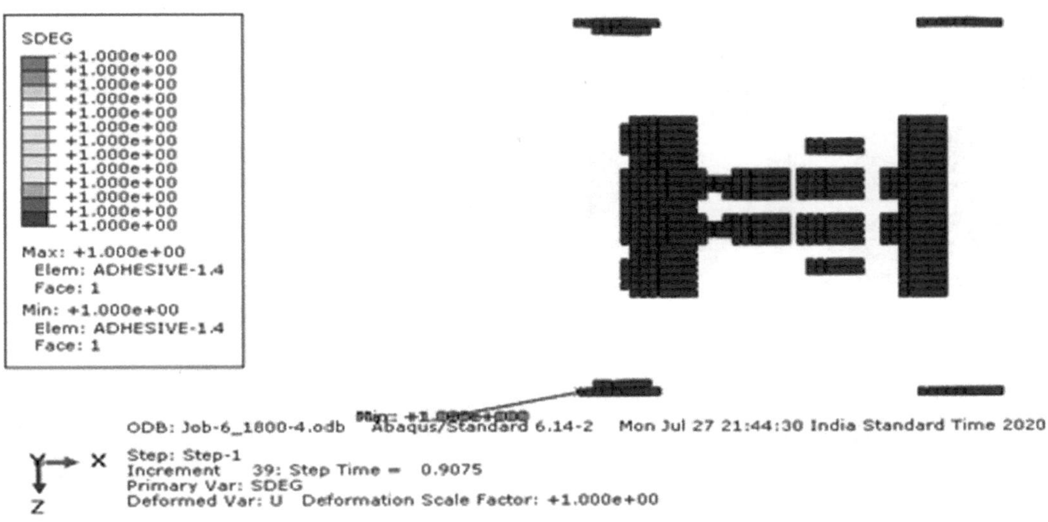

FIGURE 8.29 Complete damage Case III.

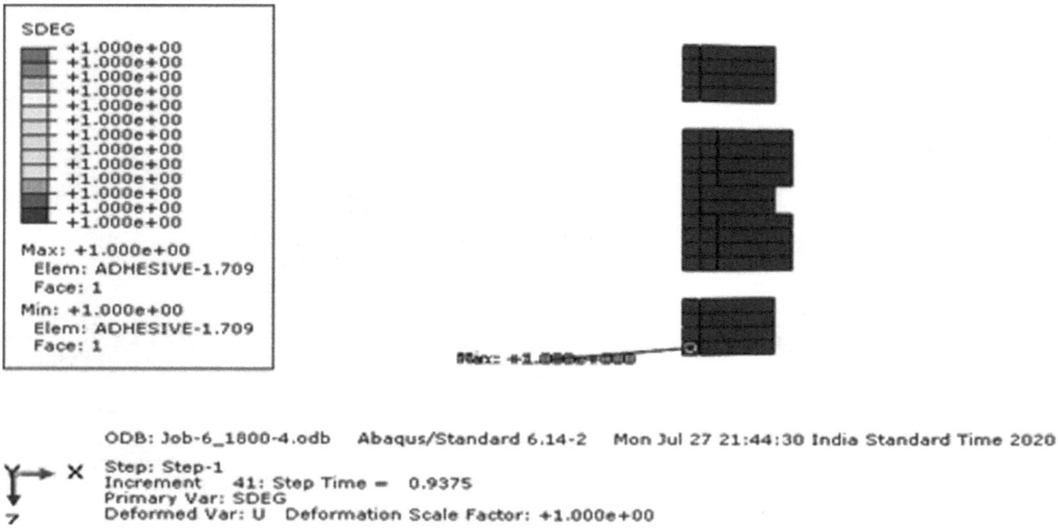

FIGURE 8.30 Complete Debonding Case III.

8.5.4.3 Damage Evolution for Case IV

8.6 CONCLUSIONS

It can be concluded that the fracture behavior of the cohesive element is significantly affected by its initial stiffness. For an initial stiffness of 800 (N/mm), the maximum stress developed at the point of damage is the lowest. This indicates that the damage initiates at a lower stress value compared to cases where the initial stiffnesses are 1200 (N/mm), 1800 (N/mm), and 2000 (N/mm) respectively. For Case II, Case III and Case IV, the maximum

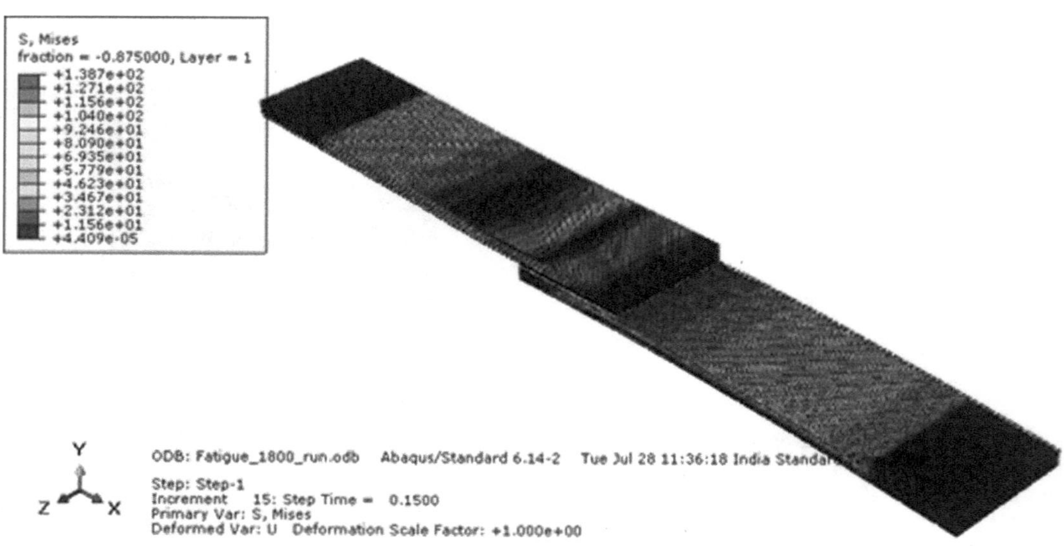

FIGURE 8.31 Maximum Stress Case IV.

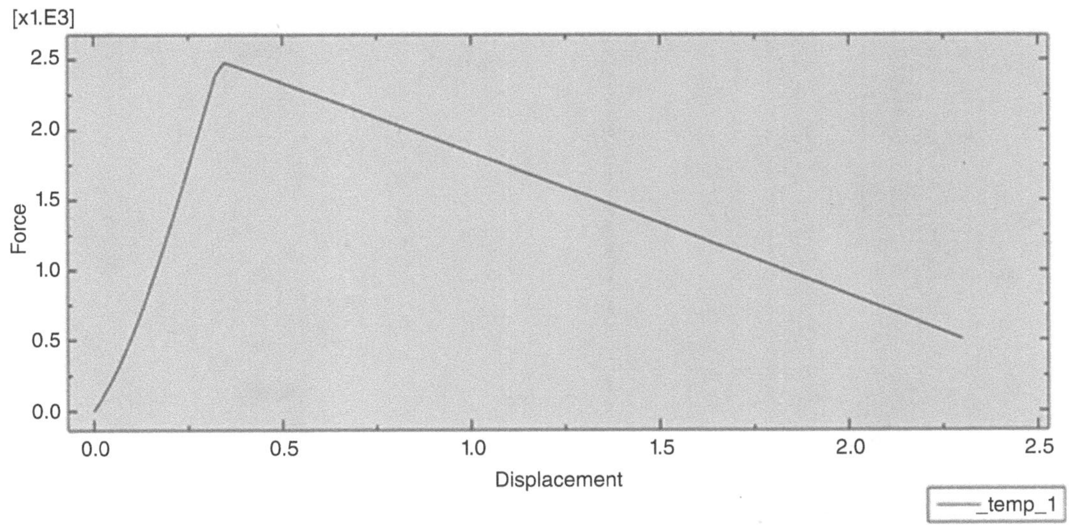

FIGURE 8.32 Load-Displacement Curve for Case IV.

stresses developed are 100.4 MPa, 123.1 MPa and 138.7 MPa respectively. This demonstrates that the initiation of damage begins at a much higher stress value for the adhesive reinforced with nanoparticles. Therefore, it can be concluded that higher stiffness leads to an increased fracture resistance. The load bearing capacity increases with an increase in stiffness. Case II, Case III and Case IV exhibit an approximate three and four times increase respectively compared to Case I. The displacement at failure increases with an increase in stiffness. Case II, Case III and Case IV exhibit an approximate increase of 23%, 25% and 36%, respectively, compared to Case I. In general, the fracture resistance improves with an

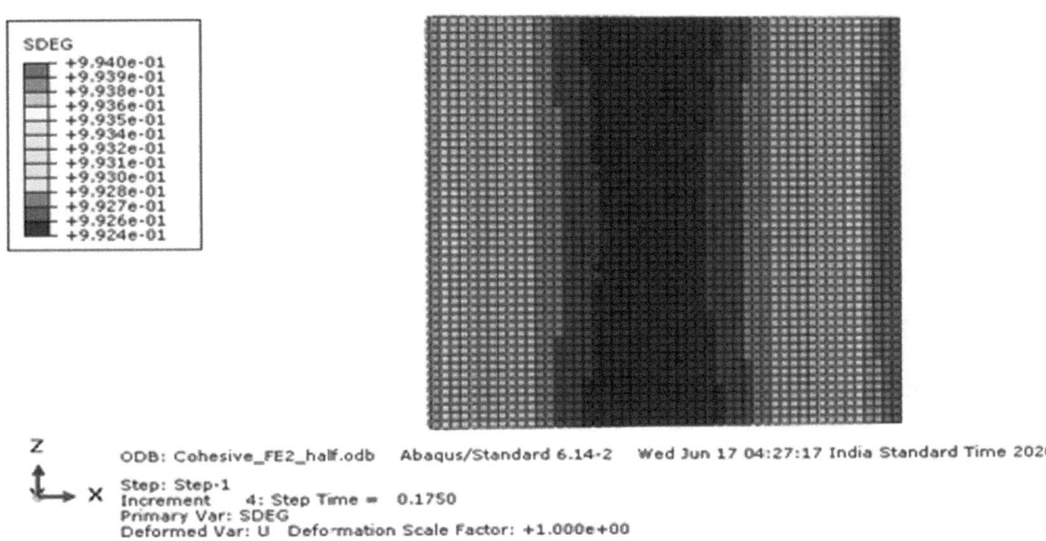

FIGURE 8.33 Damage Initiation Case IV.

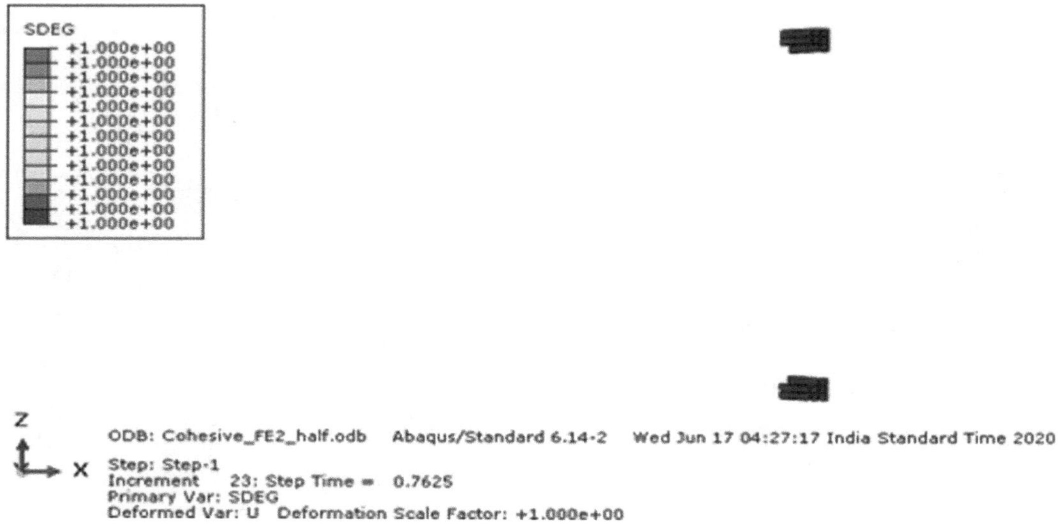

FIGURE 8.34 Debonding Case IV.

TABLE 8.6 Result Summary

Case No.	Initial Stiffness (N/mm)	Max. Stress (MPa)	Max Load (KN)	Displacement (mm)
I	800	40.1	0.6	1.3
II	1200	100.4	1.8	1.6
III	1500	123.1	2.4	2.1
IV	2000	138.7	2.6	2.5

increase in stiffness. This improvement is achieved through the dispersion of nanoparticles in the adhesive. However, these properties may exhibit a decreasing trend at certain concentrations due to a phenomenon known as agglomeration. The software package cannot predict this behavior, and there is no numerical model available to predict the same.

8.7 FUTURE SCOPE

This study may further be extended to evaluate the effect of fracture energy and nominal stresses on the fracture behavior. Additionally, a "number of cycles of failure" approach can be utilized to simulate the behavior of joints under fatigue loads. Furthermore, the response of joints under various cyclic loads, such as sinusoidal, tabular and triangular variations, can be explored through experiments and numerical simulations using different nanomaterials, like MWCNT, to assess their bond strengths for fatigue loading. Moreover, the response to thermal fatigue can be evaluated both experimentally and numerically.

REFERENCES

1. I. M. Daniel, Engineering Mechanics of Composite Materials, New Delhi: Oxford University Press, 2007.
2. Z. Guo, Multifunctional Nano Composites for Energy and Environmental Applications, John Wiley & Sons, 2018.

3. G. Armstrong, "An introduction to polymer nanocomposites," European Journal of Physics, vol. 36, no. 6, pp. 1–34, 2015.
4. d. Silva, "Adhesively bonded joints in composite materials: An overview," in Proceedings of the IMechE, Vol. 223 Part L: Journal of Materials: Design and Applications, 2009.
5. Z. Hutchinson, "Mixed-mode cracking in layered materials," Advances in Applied Mechanics, vol. 29, pp. 63–191, 1992.
6. G. Xu, "Numerical methods for the determination of multiple stress singularities and related stress intensity coefficients," Engineering Fracture Mechanics, vol. 63, no. 6, pp. 775–790, 1999.
7. D. C. Noorman, "Cohesive Zone Modelling in Adhesively Bonded Joints," Delft University of Technology[online].[cit. 2017-08-12]. Dostupné z: http://repository. tudelft. nl., 2014.
8. H. Khoramishad, "Predicting fatigue damage in adhesively bonded joints using a cohesive zone model," International Journal of Fatigue, vol. 32, p. 1146, 2010.
9. Zhemin Jia, "Graphene reinforced epoxy adhesive for fracture resistance," Composites Part B, vol. 155, pp. 457–462, 2018.
10. H. Khoramishad, "The effect of graphene oxide nano-platelets on fracture behavior of adhesively bonded joints," Fatigue & Fracture Engineering Materials & Structures, vol. 00, pp. 1–12, 2017.
11. H. Reza Borghei, B. Behjat, M. Yazdani, "The impact of graphene nanoparticle additives on the strength of simple and hybrid adhesively bonded joints," Journal of Composite Materials, vol. 53(23), pp. 3335–3346, 2019.
12. M. A. S. Sadigh, G. Marami, "Enhancing fatigue life in adhesively bonded joints using reduced graphene oxide additive: Experimental and numerical evaluation," International Journal of Adhesion and Adhesives, vol. 84, pp. 283–290, 2018.
13. G. Scarselli, "Adhesive joints with improved mechanical properties for aerospace applications," International Journal of Adhesion and Adhesives, vol. 75, pp. 174–180, 2017.
14. G. Campilho, "Modelling of single-lap joints using cohesive zone models: Effect of the cohesive parameters on the output of the simulations," The Journal of Adhesion and Adhesives, vol. 88, pp. 513–533, 2012.
15. C. Saloma, "Mechanical properties and adhesive behavior of epoxy-graphene," International Journal of Adhesion and Adhesives, vol. 84, pp. 119–125, 2018.
16. S. Swetha Chandrasekaran, "Fracture toughness and failure mechanism of graphene based epoxy composites," Composites Science and Technology, vol. 97, pp. 90–99, 2014.
17. Daniel F. O. Braga, "Single lap joints numerical modelling and comparison with experimental testing," U. Porto Journal of Engineering, vol. 2, no. 1, pp. 11–20, 2016.
18. M. Johar, "Cyclic cohesive zone model for simulation of fatigue failure process in adhesive joints," Applied Mechanics and Materials, vol. 60, no. 6, pp. 217–221, 2014.
19. M. M. Shokrieh, "Mechanical properties of graphene/epoxy nanocomposites under static and flexural fatigue loadings," Mechanics of Advanced Composite Structures, vol. 1, pp. 1–7, 2014.
20. C. Shin & Shun-Hsuan Huang, "Evaluation of fatigue damage monitoring of single-lap composite adhesive joint using conductivity," Polymers, 16, 2374, 2024. 10.3390/polym16162374.
21. Xiao Han, Mengting Hu, Yangyang Wang, Bo Liu, Lucas Silva, & Xu Guo, "Experiments and modelling of competitive failure behaviour of CFRP stepped-lap repairs with different design parameters," Thin-Walled Structures, 199, 111836, 2024. 10.1016/j.tws.2024.111836.
22. Christopher Jackson, Jeffrey McGuire, Martin Losada, Ian Maskery, Ian Ashcroft, Raffaella De Vita, & David Dillard, "Using cohesive zone models with digital image correlation to obtain a mixed mode I/II fracture envelope of a tough epoxy," Engineering Fracture Mechanics, 295, 109732, 2023. 10.1016/j.engfracmech.2023.109732.
23. Takashi Nagoshi, Y. Harada, S. Nakasumi, N. Yamazaki, K. Hasegawa, K. Takagi, W. Peng, G. Fujii, & Masataka Ohkubo, "Inherent cohesive failure of epoxy adhesive in carbon-fiber-reinforced plastic composites revealed by micro-tensile testing and finite element analysis," Composites Part B: Engineering, 242, 110059, 2022. 10.1016/j.compositesb.2022.110059.

FSC
www.fsc.org
MIX
Papier | Fördert
gute Waldnutzung
FSC® C083411

Kolibri 360 GmbH
Ferdinand-Jühlke-Straße 7
99095 Erfurt, Deutschland
produktsicherheit@kolibri360.de